THE ECLIPSE OF CLASSICAL THOUGHT IN CHINA AND THE WEST

For centuries, the starting points for serious thought about ethics, justice, and government were traditions founded, in China by Confucius, and in the West by his near contemporary Socrates. In both classical traditions, norms were based on human nature; to contravene these norms was to deny part of one's humanity. The Chinese and Western philosophical traditions have often been regarded as mutually unintelligible. This book shows that the differences can only be understood by examining where they converge. It describes the role of these traditions in two political achievements: the formation of the constitutions of Song dynasty China and the American Republic. Both traditions went into eclipse for similar reasons but with quite different consequences: in China, the growth of absolutism, and in the West, the inability of modern political and ethical thought to defend the most fundamental values.

James Gordley is W.R. Irby Distinguished University Professor at Tulane Law School, and Shannon Cecil Turner Professor of Jurisprudence Emeritus at the Berkeley Law School. He is a Fellow of The American Academy of Arts and Sciences, a Corresponding Fellow of The British Academy and a membre titulaire of the Académie internationale du droit comparé. He has been a Guggenheim Fellow and a Fulbright Fellow. He is the author of numerous books and articles including The Jurists: A Critical History (2013), Foundations of Private Law (2006), and The Philosophical Origins of Modern Contract Doctrine (1991).

The Eclipse of Classical Thought in China and the West

JAMES GORDLEY

Tulane University

CAMBRIDGE
UNIVERSITY PRESS

CAMBRIDGE
UNIVERSITY PRESS

University Printing House, Cambridge CB2 8BS, United Kingdom

One Liberty Plaza, 20th Floor, New York, NY 10006, USA

477 Williamstown Road, Port Melbourne, VIC 3207, Australia

314–321, 3rd Floor, Plot 3, Splendor Forum, Jasola District Centre,
New Delhi – 110025, India

103 Penang Road, #05–06/07, Visioncrest Commercial, Singapore 238467

Cambridge University Press is part of the University of Cambridge.

It furthers the University's mission by disseminating knowledge in the pursuit of
education, learning, and research at the highest international levels of excellence.

www.cambridge.org
Information on this title: www.cambridge.org/9781108845151
DOI: 10.1017/9781108954709

First published 2022

A catalogue record for this publication is available from the British Library.

ISBN 978-1-108-84515-1 Hardback

To James Robert Gordley

My father, who was born on an eighty-acre pig farm in 1906, educated in a one room country schoolhouse, and never went to college, became a major executive of a Fortune 500 company. He was a smart man. One day I showed off the knowledge of moral philosophy I had acquired at the elite high school to which he was able to send me. "Dad," I asked, "why is it wrong to rob a bank?" "Don't you know that it is wrong to rob a bank?" "Of course, I do. But how do we know that it is wrong? How could you prove it?" "Don't you know that it is wrong to rob a bank?" The conversation continued in this vein.

The next night he took me outdoors and pointed to the moon. "Is that beautiful?" "Yes, Dad, very beautiful?" "Why?" he asked me. I admitted that I did not know. "You see," he said, "some things just are." Fifty years later I understood why he was right.

Contents

1 **The Dilemma**   1

PART I   TWO ANCIENT TRADITIONS   19

2 **The Beginnings of Ethical Philosophy**   21

   I   Confucius   22
       i   The Wisdom of the Past   22
       ii   His Task   23
       iii His Teaching   24
   II Socrates   27
       i   His Task   27
       ii   His Teaching   28

3 **The Challenge to Virtue and the Discovery of Human Nature**   30

   I   Mencius and his Opponents   31
   II   The Confucian Tradition   31
        i   The Challenge: Yang Zhu and Mozi   31
        ii   The Response of Mencius   36
   III Socrates and the Sophists   38
   IV   Human Nature as a Source of Normative Standards   42

4 **A Normative Psychology**   45

   I   Nourishing Inner Goodness: Mencius   46
   II   Mastering Inner Conflict: Socrates and Plato   49
   III Achieving Harmony   51
        i   Xunzi   51
        ii   Dai Zhen's Reconstruction of Mencius   54
        iii The Aristotelian Tradition   58

5 **The Universality of Normative Standards**   62

   I   Mencius   62

II   Dai Zhen   66
III The Aristotelian Tradition   68

6   **Justice, Propriety, and the Common Good**   80
    I   *Ren* (仁) and the Common Good   80
    II   *Yi* (義) and Distributive Justice   85
    III *Yi* (義) and Commutative Justice   89
    IV   Propriety (*li* 禮)   99
    V   Crime and Punishment   104
    VI   Formal Rules   112

7   **Government**   116
    I   The Origin of Government   116
         i   The Confucian Tradition   116
         ii   The Aristotelian Tradition   117
    II   The Architecture of Government   120
         i   The Monarch   120
         ii   The Worthiest   125
         iii The People   129
    III The Consequences of Misrule   131
         i   The Confucian Tradition   132
         ii   The Aristotelian Tradition   133

    PART II   THE FORMATION OF TWO CONSTITUTIONS   137

8   **A Confucian Empire: Song Dynasty China**   139
    I   The Architecture of Government   140
         i   The Creation of a Governing Elite   140
         ii   The Role of the Scholar-Officials   142
         iii Selection by Examination   144
    II   The Emergence of a Confucian Society   146
    III Principles Compromised   149
         i   The Examination System   149
         ii   The Political System   150

9   **A Democratic Republic: The United States of America** 155
    I   The Right of Resistance   156
         i   The English Whigs   156
         ii   The Founders   157
         iii The Myth of the Influence of John Locke   158
    II   Private Rights and the Common Good   167
    III The Architecture of Government   172
         i   A Mixed Form of Government   172
         ii   The Constitution of the United States of America 175

    iii   Jeffersonian Democracy   181

  IV The Emergence of a Democratic Society   190

   V Principles Compromised   195

     i   Violations of Principle: Slavery and Conquest   195

     ii The Party System   197

PART III   THE ECLIPSE OF CLASSICAL THOUGHT   203

10 Neo-Confucianism   207

   I Beyond Human Nature: The School of Principle   207

  II The Response: The School of Universal Mind   222

11 The Path to Orthodoxy   228

   I The Late Song Dynasty   230

  II The Mongols   234

 III The Ming Dynasty   236

     i   Orthodoxy and Absolutism   236

     ii The Dong Lin Academy   242

     iii Waiting for Dawn   248

12 The Rise and Fall of Western Rationalism   252

   I The Rise of Rationalism   252

     i   Reality   253

     ii Ethics   257

  II Rationalism Discredited: The Critique of David Hume   264

13 The Search for Alternatives   273

   I Positivism   273

     i   Nineteenth-Century Legal Positivism   274

     ii Its Rejection by Jurists   280

     iii Its Revival by Contemporary Philosophers   284

  II Philosophical Liberalism   290

     i   Utilitarianism   292

     ii Kantianism   301

     iii Self-Expression   319

14 Conclusion   331

Appendix   *The Encounter with the Abrahamic Religions*   337

Index   353

Acknowledgments

My greatest debt is to Tong Xu. My previous work has taught me the dangers of writing about a legal system or an intellectual tradition without knowing the language in which the basic texts are written. Tong Xu painstakingly walked me through the original text of every passage I consulted in the works of Confucius, Mencius, Xunzi, Zhu Xi, Wang Yangming, and Dai Zhen, often character by character. I am also grateful for her many useful suggestions, criticisms, and insights.

I am grateful to Adeno Addis, Christopher Boom, Eric Enlow, Scott FitzGibbon, Charles Flanders, Barbara Gordley, James W. Gordley, Hao Jiang, Felipe Jiménez, Brian McCall, James Murphy, Richard Rose, Fr. Augustine Thompson, O.P., and Guiguo Wang for reading all or part of the manuscript and contributing their thoughts.

I would like to thank Randy Asprodites for the cover design.

1

The Dilemma

Modern ethical, political, and legal thought finds itself navigating between two unacceptable alternatives. One is to regard moral standards as absolute, eternal, and invariable. The truth of such standards, however, is impossible to demonstrate. Those who claim a privileged knowledge of them are dangerous since they may try to force their views upon others. The other alternative is to regard moral standards as individual and subjective, and so imperil any real distinction between right and wrong, and just and unjust institutions. The two classical traditions that we will study were viable and enduring because they were not caught in such a dilemma. One was founded in China by Confucius and the other in Greece by his near contemporary Socrates. For centuries, they were the starting points for serious thought about ethics, politics, and law.

Both traditions had a common feature: the conviction that the source of normative standards is human nature. If we live by these standards we flourish as human beings; if we do not, we deny or destroy our humanity and consequently ourselves. In China and the West, this conviction arose in a similar way: it was a response to skeptics who explained moral standards by authority, convention, desire or power. It raised similar questions: What is the source of human desires that conflict with these normative standards? How does a person know what they are? What sort of society best enables each person to live such a life? Although answers differed, the classical thinkers in China and the West were all concerned with how the elements of human nature could be in harmony despite apparent discord; with how human beings are able to know the difference between good and evil despite their fallibility and the diversity of their experience; and how each member of society, by living the life best for himself, can thereby contribute to the good of all. They believed in a constitutional form of government and the roles to be played by a single leader, an elite, and the people. Those concerns contributed to two great political achievements: the constitution of Song dynasty China and that of the American Republic.

Classical thought was eclipsed in China and the West with the rise of philosophies that ground normative standards, not in human nature, but in eternal and immutable principles. That was the approach of the School of Principle that emerged at the end of the Song dynasty and was recognized as the orthodox interpretation of Confucianism in the Ming and Qing. It was the approach of seventeenth- and eighteenth-century rationalist philosophers in the West, whose work was discredited, notably, by David Hume.

Critics in China and in the West were correct in claiming that there were no such principles, or if there were, they had little relationship to human beings as they are or to the world of contingency in which they live. The result, however, was a polarization of political and ethical thought: either moral standards were eternal and immutable, or, it seemed, they must be subjective and individual. The first alternative, which prevailed in China, helped to undermine constitutional rule. The emperor claimed ultimate authority as to what the eternal standards prescribed. The second alternative threatens constitutional rule in the West. If all moral values are subjective and individual, one cannot defend the moral value of human liberty, and the pursuit of happiness ultimately means the pursuit of self-interest.

Two civilizations were thus led astray by the mistakes of intelligent and often well-intentioned people. Chinese leaders are currently seeking guidance from the past to find a version of socialism with Chinese characteristics. They would do well to look to the Confucian tradition as it was before the distortions that became accepted as orthodoxy. Westerners cherish their democratic institutions. They would do well to rediscover the ideas of human happiness, liberty, and the common good on which these institutions were built. These ideas were the last fruit of the classical tradition. They owe nothing to Enlightenment thinkers, including John Locke, and have been distorted by modern liberal philosophers who seek to defend them. Chinese and Westerners can not only learn from their classical traditions but can learn what these traditions at a deeper level have in common. Even forms of government as different as those of Song China and the American Republic can depend upon common principles. They need not reflect alien and mutually hostile world views.

TWO CLASSICAL TRADITIONS

In both traditions, normative standards are grounded on human nature. Every human being has an inborn capacity to recognize that certain ways of living are valuable, and to value living in these ways. To live by these standards is to flourish as a human being.

Nevertheless, neither tradition had a characteristic concept of human nature. Their common belief that normative standards are grounded in human nature raised a variety of questions which they answered in different ways and so led to different conceptions within each tradition.

One such question is why every human being has impulses that are obstacles to living as he should. If these impulses do not have their source in human nature, why are all human beings subject to them? If they do belong to human nature, why do human beings often fear what is good for them and seek what is evil? Is human nature at war with itself?

Another question is why a person would want to act in accordance with normative standards, supposing that he knew what they require. Normative standards govern what a person ought to do, but why should that be what he wants?

A further question is how knowledge of normative standards can be innate. Human nature is universal. Normative standards are not. They vary according to the circumstances and with time and place.

In both traditions, the purpose of government is to enable each person to flourish as a human being. As a matter of justice, each person should have sufficient resources to do so, and be protected in his use of these resources against wrong done by others. Both traditions had a similar conception of justice although the Confucian tradition did not use the term "rights." Writers in the Western classical tradition eventually did speak of rights, but not in the same sense as modern liberals for whom rights are autonomous spheres of action which belong to individuals independently of their roles in community.

There were differences, however, in the role that justice played in each tradition. The Confucians accepted and absorbed a tradition that predated Confucius in which much of human relations depended on *li* (禮), often translated as propriety. *Li* governs how to behave in five relationships: a minister to his ruler, a son to his father, a wife to her husband, a younger brother to an elder brother, and a friend to a friend. These relationships are based on obligations of mutual respect but not on justice. An emperor should listen to his ministers; an elder brother should look out for his younger sibling, but if they fail to do so it is not same as if one person stole another's money. Western writers recognized similar situations in which a person owes a duty but not as a matter of justice or legal obligation. The difference was in the extent to which human relations in China were governed by such duties.

Another difference concerned the aspect of justice to which writers in the two traditions paid the most attention. Confucian writers said much more about how the government should act to ensure that each person had sufficient resources. Western writers said much more about what constituted wrong done by others. One reason was that the Confucians were addressing those responsible for government policies. Another was that writers in the Western classical tradition were heirs not only to Greek philosophy but to Roman law. Western writers integrated the two, using Aristotelian principles to explain the vast corpus of Roman private law which governed such matters as property, contract, and delict or tort.

A third difference concerned what mattered most in the administration of justice. In traditional Chinese law, the most important concern was that the punishments be proportionate to the gravity of the crime that the perpetrator had committed. Much intellectual effort went into comparing punishments to be meted out in different situations. As we will see, although later attempts were made to integrate this approach with Confucian thought, it was not Confucian in origin. It originated in the anti-Confucian state of Qin that reunified China in 221 BC. In contrast, in the West, the most important concern was to define the elements of the offense that constituted a crime. Although Roman criminal law was not well developed, Western jurists constructed a criminal law which attempted to define them.

Although both traditions agreed that the purpose of government is to enable each member of the society to flourish by living a distinctively human life, they had different conceptions of the ideal form of government. In the Confucian tradition, an emperor should govern with the help of an elite of wise and good officials for the benefit of the people. Writers in the Western classical tradition, following Aristotle, said that there are three good forms of government: the rule of one (monarchy); the rule of an elite of the wise and good (aristocracy); and rule by the people (the good kind of democracy). Nevertheless, writers in both traditions discussed the proper role in government of a single ruler, of an elite, and of the people. They all believed that these roles were shaped by the purpose that government should serve.

The classical traditions were the *sine qua non* for two great political accomplishments: the constitution of the Song dynasty in China (960–1279), which has been called the most Confucian of dynasties, and that of the American Republic. In the Song dynasty, the power of the emperor was limited by Confucian principles, by institutions tasked with evaluating his policies, and by the prerogatives of an elite recruited by competitive examinations in the Confucian classics. The ideas that inspired the founders of the American Republic have often been misunderstood. The conventional view is that they were the liberal principles of the Enlightenment to be found par excellence in the works of John Locke. They were not. The conventional view was developed by nineteenth-century liberals in search of an intellectual pedigree. We will see that the founders were inspired neither by Locke nor by modern liberalism but by the ideas of the classical Western tradition.

THE ECLIPSE

In China, the classical tradition was eclipsed by the rise of the School of Principle founded by Cheng Yi (1033–1107) and Zhu Xi (1130–1200); in the West, by the rise of rationalism, which was introduced by Francesco Suárez (1548–1617) and reached its fullest expression with Gottfried Wilhelm Leibniz (1646–1716) and Christian Wolff (1679–1754). The School of Principle was recognized as the orthodox interpretation of Confucianism from the end of the Song dynasty to the fall of the Empire. Rationalism, in its day, seemed unchallengeable, at least in much of continental Europe.

The founders of the School of Principle presented their teachings as the correct interpretation of Confucianism. Suárez presented his work as a refinement of Aristotelian philosophy. Yet they broke with these traditions by rejecting one of their central tenets: that normative standards are grounded in human nature. The School of Principle and the rationalists claimed that normative standards are grounded in eternal and invariable principles. In both cases, the break that they made with classical thought was not appreciated for centuries. In China, the deviation from the teachings of Confucius and Mencius concerning human nature was recognized in the late Ming and the Qing dynasties by Wang Fuzhi (1619–92), Yan Yuan (1635–1704), and Dai Zhen (1724–77). The teachings of the School of Principle were so entrenched by then that their work was ignored. The extent to which Suárez broke with the Western classical tradition has been underscored by Etienne Gilson,[1] John Finnis,[2] and Alasdair MacIntyre.[3] All three observed that Catholic moral theologians who purported to be teaching the moral philosophy of Thomas Aquinas had in fact been teaching that of Suárez.

---

[1]　Etienne Gilson, *Being and Some Philosophers* (Toronto, 1952), 118.
[2]　John Finnis, *Natural Law and Natural Rights* (Oxford, 1980), 45–48.
[3]　Alasdair MacIntyre, *Three Rival Versions of Mora Enquiry, Encyclopaedia, Genealogy, and Tradition* (Notre Dame, Ind., 1990), 73–74.

Because the break with classical thought was not appreciated, scholars who looked backward at moral and political thought before the rise of liberalism often looked no further than rationalism. John Rawls contrasted modern liberalism with what he called "rational intuitionalism." It had four characteristic features, which he distilled from the work of two eighteenth-century Englishmen. These four features are characteristics both of Western rationalism and, with an important qualification, of the School of Principle. Indeed, Rawls' list of four features is a good summary of the similarities between Western rationalism and the School of Principle, on the one hand, and, on the other, of the differences between them and the classical traditions that they supplanted.

To quote Rawls,

> Rational intuitionalism may be characterized by four basic features. . . .
>
> The first . . . says that moral first principles and judgments, when correct, are true statements about an independent order of moral values; moreover, this order does not depend on, nor is it to be explained by, the activity of any actual (human) minds, including the activity of reason.[4]

The meaning of this first feature is clarified in what Rawls regarded as a fourth feature: "[R]ational intuitionalism conceives of truth in a traditional way by viewing moral judgments as true when they are both about and accurate to the independent order of moral values. Otherwise they are false."[5]

These features characterized Western rationalism. The rationalists grounded normative standards on eternal and invariable principles whose existence was independent of any actual human minds. They thought that these principles were like the definitions of mathematical concepts in geometry. One could begin with them and derive conclusions as to what conduct was right and wrong. The members of the School of Principle believed that normative standards were grounded on what they called *li* (理) or principles: hence the name of the school. They were not familiar with Western geometry. Nevertheless, like the definitions of the Western rationalists, *li* were eternal and invariable.

For the Western rationalists and for the School of Principle, these principles have a mode of being of their own that is independent of the world around us. Considered in themselves, they exist eternally. Considered in another way, a principle only exists in things in which it is instantiated or embodied. For the Western rationalists, it exists in this second way when it is actualized. Otherwise, it exists as a possible being. For the School of Principle, a principle exists in this second sense when it is embodied in *qi* (氣), material.

In contrast, in both classical traditions, normative standards are grounded in human nature. For philosophers in these traditions, with the possible exception of Plato, one could no more imagine that justice existing if there were no human beings than one could imagine that a bird's nesting instinct would exist if there were no birds. Plato described justice as a harmony among the elements of human nature. Wang Fuzhi, Yan Yuan, and Dai Zhen said that before the School of Principle, the Confucian tradition had recognized

---

[4] John Rawls, *Political Liberalism* (New York, 1996), 91.
[5] Ibid. 92.

only the principles of concrete things. The innovation of Suárez, according to Gilson, was to think that there are "such things as fully determined essences prior to their existential actualization." He objected that "[t]he Mattheus Passion was not an essence hovering in a limbo of possible essences where Johann Sebastian Bach caught it, so to speak, on the wing."[6]

According to Rawls,

> The second feature [of "rational intuitionism"] says that moral first principles are known by theoretical reason. This feature is suggested by the idea that moral knowledge is gained in part by a kind of perception and intuition, as well as organized by first principles found acceptable on due reflection. It is strengthened by the comparison intuitionalists make between moral knowledge and knowledge of mathematics in arithmetic and geometry. The order of moral values is said to lie in God's reason and to direct the divine will.[7]

Western rationalism did have this feature. Drawing on Western geometry, the rationalists claimed that the normative principles were like the concepts of mathematics. Conclusions about morals and politics could be deduced from them in the same way. The School of Principle held a different view. Western geometry was unknown in China until Euclid was translated by the missionary Matteo Ricci. The School of Principle, influenced by Buddhism, thought that *li* could be known by meditation. If one investigated things, "[a]fter long thought, insight comes spontaneously" (Cheng Yi);[8] "penetration will come as a sudden realization" (Zhu Xi).[9]

In either case, knowledge of the moral principles was esoteric, not in the sense that it is mysterious, but in the sense that few have the requisite mental capacity to understand them. The dream of Leibniz was to be able to say, whenever a moral question arose, "Sir, let us calculate the answer." Thus conceived, knowledge of morality, like mathematics, is a matter for experts. According to the School of Principle, *li* are fully grasped only by those who have reached an exalted state of consciousness. The founders of the school claimed to have done so.

In contrast, from their very beginning, the classical traditions presupposed that each person possesses a knowledge of right and wrong innately, and that the purpose of moral instruction is to enable him to build on that knowledge. Although Confucius and Socrates taught in different ways, neither did so by inculcating moral principles. Their aim was to enable a student to recognize what in some sense he already knew.

Believing, as they did, that their own methods gave them a unique ability to understand moral principles, the Western rationalists and the founders of the School of Principle regarded their innovation as a turning point in history. For the first time, according to the Western rationalists, moral and political thought was truly a science. According to the founders of the School of Principle, *li* had previously been understood only by the legendary sage emperors of China and by Confucius and Mencius. Afterward there was

---

6 Gilson, *Being and Some Philosophers* 211.
7 Rawls, *Political Liberalism* 91–92.
8 *Ho-nan Ch'êng-shi yi-shu.* BSS. 207/12f, from A. C. Graham, *Two Chinese Philosophers: The Metaphysics of the Brothers Ch'êng* (La Salle, Ill., 1992), 78.
9 Zhu Xi, *Complete Works* 44:13a–b (http://ctext.org/wiki.pl?if=gb&res=315560).

an intellectual and moral dark age that ended with the advent of their School. In the late Sung dynasty, members of the School formed hierarchically organized cult-like societies centered around leaders who claimed to have attained such a level of understanding.

Rawls ended his discussion of this second feature by saying that "[t]he order of moral values is said to lie in God's reason and to direct the divine will." For the Western rationalists, the eternal principles did indeed direct the divine will. Their truth was eternal and invariable. God could no more make a human being who need not conform to these principles that he could make a triangle with angles adding up to more than 180°. For the philosophers of the School of Principle, Rawls' statement needs qualification. The *li* of all things were believed to belong ultimately to one *li*. That *li* was God (天 *tian*). As Graham notes, "the great innovation" was to identify *"tian,* 'heaven,' which had previously been conceived as a very vaguely personal power" with *tian li* (天理), an impersonal principle.[10]

According to Rawls,

> The third feature concerns the sparce conception of the person. Although not explicitly stated, this feature may be gathered from the fact that rational intuitionalism does not require a fuller conception of the person and needs little more than the conception of the self and a knower. This is because the content of the first principles is given by the order of moral values available to perception and intuition as organized and expressed by principles acceptable on due reflection. The main requirement, then, is that we be able to know the first principles expressing those values and to be moved by that knowledge. Here a basic assumption is that recognizing first principles as true gives rise, in a being capable of knowing them, to a desire to act from them for their own sake.[11]

As we have already seen, this feature was not a characteristic of either the Chinese or the Western classical traditions. Philosophers in both traditions discussed why a person would want to act in accord with normative standards and, as noted earlier, they answered this question in different ways. Mencius described the capacities belonging to all human beings as both cognitive and volitional. Dai Zhen and Aristotle distinguished cognitive faculties of "wisdom" and "practical reason" the sources of human motivation. But all of them found a place for human motivation. In none of their accounts of human nature is a person simply a "knower." None of them thought that "recognizing first principles as true gives rise ... to a desire to act from them for their own sake."

The Western rationalists did. Once a conclusion about right and wrong had been demonstrated, a person was supposed to act on it simply because it was correct. David Hume saw the gap they had left between moral concepts and motivation. Hume said, "reason alone can never ... give rise to volition."[12] Reasoning about the relationship of concepts could not give rise to desire. Hume concluded that because moral convictions do motivate, they must be feelings or passions. "To have a sense of virtue, is nothing but to *feel* a satisfaction of a particular kind."[13]

---

[10] Graham, *Two Chinese Philosophers* 11, 23.
[11] Rawls, *Political Liberalism* 92.
[12] David Hume, *Treatise of Human Nature* (Oxford, 1888), 2.3.3.4.
[13] Ibid. 3.1.2.3.

In China, this gap was also seen by two philosophers, Lu Hsiang-Shan (1139–93) and Wang Yangming (1472–1529), who opposed the School of Principle. Though separated by centuries, their approaches have enough in common that historians have spoken of a Lu-Wang School or School of Universal Mind (心 *xin*). They objected that knowledge of principle is not sufficient to motivate action. It was wrong to think that one first knows a principle and then acts on it. They concluded that knowledge and action are one. They denied that *li* or principles of moral action exist outside the human mind.

In the West, Hume's critique gave rise to what Roberto Unger called the "subjective point of view." There is no standard of right and wrong beyond what leads an individual to feel a satisfaction of a certain kind. In China, some of the followers of Lu and Wang drew a similar conclusion. An extreme position was taken by Li Zhi (1527–1602): "Yesterday's right is today's wrong. Today's wrong is right again tomorrow. Even if Confucius reappeared today, there is no means of knowing how he would judge right and wrong, so how can we arbitrarily judge everything as if there were a fixed standard?"[14]

In his classic defense of liberalism, Rawls described premodern philosophy in order to discredit it. As we have seen, he was describing the rationalism discredited by David Hume. In his classic attack on liberalism, *Knowledge and Politics*, Roberto Unger described the premises of premodern thought for the same purpose: to show that we can no longer believe in them. In his view, our inability to do so gave rise to modern liberalism. Modern liberalism has failed because it cannot find a substitute for the belief in objective values that was characteristic of premodern thought. Nevertheless, his description of premodern thought is like that of Rawls.

> The metaphysical systems of ancient and medieval Europe accepted the view that all things in nature have intelligible essences. Hence they taught that the mind could understand what the world is really like. . . . [T]he supporters of the doctrine of intelligible essences have gone on to hold that the standards of right and wrong also have essences which thought can comprehend. Plato's ethics and Aquinas' theory of natural law exemplify this last line of argument.[15]

The result of "the abandonment of the doctrine of intelligible essences" is "the subjective conception of value."[16] According to Unger, modern liberalism presupposes a subjective conception of value and then, unsuccessfully, tries to attach a normative value on liberty and democracy and the rule of law.

Rawls spoke of "an independent order of moral values." Unger spoke of the "intelligible essences" of "standards of right and wrong." Do these "essences," as Unger envisioned them, belong to an "order of moral values" that exists "independently of the activity of any actual (human) minds"? Apparently so. When Unger referred to the metaphysical systems of ancient and medieval Europe, he footnoted: "For the development of this view see

---

[14]   Li Chih, "Ch'ien lun," Ts'angshu, p. 7, in Willard Peterson, "Confucian Learning in Late Ming Thought," in Denis C. Twitchett and Frederick W. Mote, eds., *The Cambridge History of China* Volume 8: *The Ming Dynasty, Part 2: 1368–1644* (Cambridge, 1998), 708 at 749.

[15]   Roberto Mangabiera Unger, *Knowledge and Politics* (New York, 1975), 30–31.

[16]   Ibid. 80.

Christian Wolff, *Philosophia Prima sive Ontologia* § 143."[17] The view he described, like that of Rawls, was that of rationalists such as Wolff. Like Rawls, when he looked backward, he did not see the break with the classical tradition.

In China, the School of Principle became recognized as the orthodox interpretation of Confucianism. The examinations by which the ruling elite was chosen were based on the commentaries of Zhu Xi until the examinations were abolished shortly before the end of the Empire. As mentioned earlier, the founders of the School of Principle laid claim to a knowledge of *li* and therefore of moral truth that had been inaccessible to others for centuries. Subsequent history showed how dangerous this claim can be. In the last two Chinese dynasties, the Ming and Xing, the emperors claimed this knowledge for themselves. They therefore had the mind of the legendary sages and their opinion on right and wrong was unchallengeable. No Chinese emperors had made this claim in earlier dynasties, and Confucian scholars would not have accepted it. Although the teachings of the School of Principle were not the cause of the absolutism of the Ming and Ching Emperors, they were its official ideology.

In the West, rationalism was discredited by David Hume. As a result, there seemed to be no middle ground between believing in the objective truth of moral standards, as the rationalists understood it, and taking what Unger called the "subjective point of view."

Nineteenth-century jurists turned to legal positivism. Whether or not ideas about justice were objectively true, laws could be enacted by those in authority and interpreted by courts. Cases must be decided according to these laws alone. If a judge allowed his own, quite possibly subjective, ideas about justice to influence his decision, he would be making the law rather than interpreting it. Therefore, his conclusions must be derived from the laws by logic alone, much as the rationalists believed they could derive conclusions from moral principles. Although this approach is not discredited among jurists, it has been revived by liberal philosophers such as Ronald Dworkin and John Rawls.

Defenders of liberalism also found ways of defending the value of liberty while clinging to at least some of the premises of Hume. When Jeremy Bentham read the work of Hume, "[I] felt as if scales had fallen from my eyes."[18] Immanuel Kant said that reading the work of Hume roused him from his dogmatic slumber.[19] It was Christian Wolff who lulled him to sleep. They defended the value of liberty in quite different ways. Yet the problem for them and other proponents of liberal theories was to navigate between two unacceptable alternatives: that moral standards are objective in the sense of the rationalists, and that they are subjective in the sense that, as Hume said, they are feelings that cannot be genuinely right or wrong.

We will see that Unger was correct about liberalism. There is no navigable route between these alternatives. If one begins with Hume's premises, there is no way to defend any normative values including the value of liberty and of democratic institutions.

---

[17] Ibid. 31, n. 1.

[18] Jeremy Bentham, *A Comment on the Commentaries and a Fragment on Government* (J. H. Burns & H. L. A. Hart, eds., Oxford, 1977), 440.

[19] Immanuel Kant, *Prolegomena zu einer jeden künftigen Metaphysik die als Wissenschaft wird auftreten können* (Riga, 1783), preface.

In China and the West, the dilemma was the same. The outcomes were different but, in both cases, dangerous. It was dangerous in China to accept the School of Principle as orthodox. If its teachings were correct, right and wrong depend on independent and objective moral principles that only a few can understand. Those who said that they did claimed absolute authority. It was dangerous in the West to entertain a "subjective point of view" which permits no one to say what is right or wrong. If nothing is truly right or wrong, one cannot defend the value of freedom or democracy. Moreover, the very terms "freedom" and "democracy" are likely to be misunderstood.

In China and the West, this dilemma appeared only when classical thought was obscured. Many Chinese are now looking to the past to frame institutions with Chinese characteristics. Many Westerners see the snarl in modern Western thought. They would do well to reconsider the value of their own classical traditions.

In doing so, they may find that they can learn from each other. Thinkers in both traditions held a similar view of the foundations of moral and political thought. They addressed similar problems. Their work shaped quite different societies, but its greatness lies in the light it can shed on the value of being human and on what human beings in all societies should value.

METHOD

The methodological problems of comparative philosophy are like those of comparative law and comparative legal history, the fields in which I have done most of my past work. There are two leading approaches to studying the laws of a different country or a past era, both of which are viable, in my view, but they tell you different things. One approach is contextual. One learns about a legal or philosophical idea by examining the context in which it occurred. The way to learn about a rule adopted by a nineteenth-century English judge or one proposed by a sixteenth-century continental jurist or a normative standard formulated by a philosopher in Song China or in medieval Europe is to look closely at his other concerns and those of his contemporaries. Every event is unique and could not have occurred just the way it did in any context but its own.

Scholars in comparative law and legal history have developed another approach which they refer to as "functional." One looks at similar problems that have arisen in different times and places and sees how they have been resolved. The solutions may be alike although they seem to be different because of the language in which they are expressed. Or they may be different because the problem admits of different solutions or because different thinkers approached it with different intellectual tools. This method is both descriptive and critical. Learning how people have tried to solve the problem may shed light on how the problem can be solved. It may show why no viable solution has ever been found.

The functionalist approach only works when people working in different cultural and historical contexts actually did confront similar problems. When they were working on different problems, to compare their solutions is like comparing the design of a battleship to the composition of the Dow Jones Industrial Average. It will not work even if the cultural or historical context is the same.

A functionalist cannot neglect the historical and cultural context if he wishes to understand the problem a historical figure was actually addressing. Conversely, a historian who is studying the context in which that figure worked would do well to recognize that the same problem can arise in other contexts as well. To see a problem purely as a result of its historical context is to contextualize it out of existence.

Because this book uses a functionalist method, it has an unusual structure. It concerns the foundations of ethics, justice, and politics. Yet it does not begin with a set of propositions or basic concepts and use them to build a comprehensive theory. We have become accustomed to such works, particularly since the Enlightenment. Examples are Jeremy Bentham's *An Introduction to the Principles of Morals and Legislation*, Immanuel Kant's *Grundlegung zur Metaphysik der Sitten*, and, more recently, John Rawls' *Theory of Justice* and Ronald Dworkin's *Justice for. Hedgehogs*. We will discuss these works. Like their authors, we will be concerned with the ideas that support normative judgments. Our concern, however, will be with the consequences when philosophers used certain ideas rather than others to address a problem. What happened when they grounded normative standards in human nature? In eternal and immutable principles?

Although this book concerns the history of ideas, it is not a history of the development of Confucian thought nor of the Song dynasty. It is not a history of Western philosophy nor of the formation of the American constitution. Rather it is concerned with how thinkers in different times and places, sometimes building on each other's work and sometimes working independently, faced and resolved a similar range of ethical and political problems. Therefore, we will move between thinkers and eras, not chronologically, but from one problem to the next. We will sometimes compare an approach to a problem in China with a parallel approach in the West. We will sometimes follow the thread of an argument from Mencius to Dai Zhen, who wrote in the eighteenth century, and from Aristotle to Aquinas to early Protestant thought.

Some scholars who take a contextual approach are suspicious of comparative studies of any kind because, necessarily, they must step outside the context in which an idea is embedded in order to make a comparison. Is that even possible? One of the most suspicious is Pierre Legrand whose critique draws heavily on the work of Jacques Derrida. He believes truth in comparative studies is unattainable because of the uniqueness of each culture.[20] Alasdair MacIntyre made the more limited claim that comparison is impossible when traditions or systems of thought are "incommensurable." For that reason, he said that a comparison of the Confucian and Aristotelian traditions is impossible.[21]

[20] Pierre Legrand, "Jameses at Play: A Tractation on the Comparison of Laws," *American Journal of Comparative Law* 65 (2017), 1 (one James is me; the other James is James Whitman, a professor of comparative law and legal history at Yale Law School). For a response, see James Gordley, "Comparison, Law and Culture: A Response to Pierre Legrand," 65 *American Journal of Comparative Law* (2017), 133.

[21] Alasdair MacIntyre, "Incommensurability, Truth, and the Conversation between Confucians and Aristotelians about the Virtues," in Eliot Deutsch, ed., *Culture and Modernity: East-West Philosophic Perspectives* (Honolulu, 1991), 104.

Legrand accurately described the implications of Derrida's work for the comparative study of law, and his objections apply to comparative studies in general. His starting point, like that of Derrida, is that every event is unique and unrepeatable. Therefore, every event can be described in an infinite number of ways. There is no one right description. "[N]o single answer is possible, only singular ones: the foreign law-texts can be read this way, but they can also be read that way. In Derrida's words, '[a] thousand possibilities will always remain open even as one understands something of that sentence which makes sense.'"[22]

Therefore, the choice is up to the describer or the interpreter. "[H]e elects to emphasize certain traces rather than others (while all traces are existent, he will not deem all of them to be equally pertinent) as he proceeds to an assemblage of the traces that he wishes to treat."[23] Legrand concluded that "it is the comparativist-at-law himself who brings the traces into interpretive existence, who makes the traces actively signify, who ascribes dynamic meaning to them, who acts as a facilitator of resonant sense."[24] He quoted Derrida: "Everything given to me under the light appears as given to myself by myself."[25]

Legrand concluded that "ideas like . . . objectivity and truth" should be "relegated to the waste chute."[26] A claim that one's own description is true will not "allow for the recognition and respect of . . . radical singularity." He said, quoting Derrida, that to make such a claim is to exercise "a sovereignty always essentially colonial, which tends, repressibly and irrepressibly, to reduce languages to the One, that is, to the hegemony of the homogeneous."[27]

Legrand and Derrida are at the opposite pole from the Western rationalists. The rationalists lost sight of the singularity of each event. For them, everything is the actualization of a timeless concept or principle that had existed before its actualization. Legrand seems to think that to believe in truth and objectivity, one must understand those terms in the same way as a rationalist. One must accept "Cartesianism"[28] and a "(discredited) Platonic commitment of some sort to grounded, static, essentialist configurations."[29] Descartes, indeed, inspired the rationalist method, and Leibniz was called "the German Plato." When Legrand criticized the "dubious metaphysics"[30] of those like myself who seek objectivity in comparative studies, I think he had in mind a rationalist metaphysics that he and I both reject. Legrand and Derrida have tried to escape rationalism but by following a path that leads them to deny the possibility of objectivity and truth.

An event is not the same from one moment to the next, and so if each moment were utterly unique, one could not speak of "an event." Legrand and Derrida seem to welcome that conclusion. According to Legrand, no description of a culture can "legitimately claim to be correct." "By definition, so to speak, the cultural exists as

---

[22] Legrand, "Jameses at Play" 59, citing Jacques Derrida, *Limited Inc.* 253 (Paris, 1990), 122.
[23] Ibid. 45.
[24] Ibid.
[25] Jacques Derrida, *L'Ecriture et la différence* (Paris, 1967), 136.
[26] Legrand, "Jameses at Play" 115.
[27] Jacques Derrida, *Le Monolinguisme de l'autre* (Paris, 1996), 69.
[28] Legrand, "Jameses at Play" 66.
[29] Ibid. 69.
[30] Ibid.

flux and indeterminacy. It manifests itself as movement. It features a state of becoming."[31] As Derrida said, "[e]quivocity is the congenital mark of any culture."[32] "How," Legrand asked, "could any cultural reading legitimately claim to be *correct?*"

Are all characteristics of everything in flux? Or are some sufficiently stable that I can say, for example, that the world is round, that I have sat all morning in my chair, or that I am writing a book? If everything is in flux, how can Legrand and Derrida even say that they are defending the same position as to the particularity of all things that they defended yesterday? If truth and objectivity belong in the waste chute, how can they even claim that the position they are defending today is true? Legrand, with commendable honesty, concedes that he cannot.

> One's interpretive slate is never clean, one's page is never white. (Evidently, my interpretive slate is not clean either so that, as I sit in the *Café du Progrès* to claim that [one] cannot objectively address "what the law is," I am not making an objective statement. And my page is not white either so that when I argue that [one] cannot enunciate "what the law is" as a matter of truth, I am not making a true statement.)[33]

Aristotle said that one cannot prove the law of non contradiction. But if anyone who denies that law were to affirm anything, he would then be forced to concede that the proposition he affirmed could equally well be denied. Aristotle assumed that would stop him in his tracks. It did not stop Legrand. But if Legrand believes that nothing is true nor false including what he says, why does he want us to believe him?

Legrand and Derrida are correct that every event is unique and could not have occurred just the way it did in any context but its own. It does not follow that true and objective statements are impossible. Statements may be true even though an infinite number of true statements about an event can be made. A person describing the event will indeed select the ones that are of interest to him. For one who is taking a functional approach, the characteristics of a society that are of interest to him are the purposes that its members pursue or that its institutions are structured to achieve. He can describe those characteristics without claiming to give a full description of any particular person or institution. His descriptions may be true even though they are not exhaustive. If true, they describe the purposes that people actually have and that institutions actually serve. People and institutions would have these purposes even if the person making the description had failed to describe them accurately.

This method allows a "recognition and respect" for other cultures that would be impossible if they were so "radically singular" that no objectively true statement could be made about them. If a culture were utterly unique, not only would it have no essence that a concept could capture; it would have no features that a concept could describe. Any word one could apply to any of its features would be like a proper noun that designates but does not describe. If one society valued a purpose or end that was utterly foreign to another society, that end would be unintelligible to members of the other society. We may regard

---

[31] Ibid. 95.
[32] Jacques Derrida, *L'Autre Cap* (Paris, 1991), 16, cited ibid.
[33] Legrand, "Jameses at Play" 80–81.

Babylonian liver divination as superstitious and torture as impermissibly cruel, but we can understand the motivations of those who practiced them. Otherwise, we could only regard those who did so as insane, or perhaps, nonhuman. If all the motivations of another society were utterly foreign, we could no more understand it than we could understand what it would be like to be an octopus. Indeed, we could better understand the motivations of an octopus, at least if it gets hungry as we do.

Alasdair MacIntyre took a less radical position. He claimed that one cannot compare the Confucian and the Aristotelian traditions because they are "incommensurable." He noted that concepts in one tradition have no equivalent in the other. That is so, but it does not make comparison impossible. As MacIntyre noted, there is no Chinese equivalent for *psyche*, the soul. Nevertheless, the Greeks who spoke of *psyche* were addressing the same question as Chinese philosophers: What is human nature like? There is no Greek equivalent for *li* (禮), or propriety. Yet writers in the Aristotelian tradition recognized similar situations in which one person owes a duty to another but not as a matter of justice or legal obligation. The difference was in the extent to which human relations in China were governed by such duties. MacIntyre is correct that there is no Chinese equivalent for *polis*, the Greek city state. The Greek philosophers never imagined that a human being could live best in an empire embracing all civilized peoples, nor the Chinese that he could do so in a *polis*. Yet philosophers in both traditions believed that the purpose of government was to enable each citizen to live a life which would realize his potential as a human being. They considered how government should be structured to serve this purpose, and, in particular, the roles to be assigned to a single ruler, an elite of the wise and good, and the people.

Nevertheless, MacIntyre's argument that the two traditions are "incommensurable" does not turn on the force of these examples. He regarded traditions are incommensurable when each "has its own standard and measures of interpretation, explanation, and justification internal to itself," and there are "no shared standards and measures, external to both systems and neutral between them, to which appeal might be made to adjudicate between" them.[34] "[W]e have no neutral, independent standpoint from which to do so." Consequently, "we may compare Confucianism and Aristotelianism from a Confucian standpoint, or from an Aristotelian."[35] What is true from the one standpoint may be false from the other.

This argument is a key part of MacIntyre's own response to the dilemma that we have just described: either normative standards are "objective" in the way the rationalists believed, or they are "subjective" in the sense that they have no truth value. According to MacIntyre, "[t]he thinkers of the Enlightenment insisted upon a particular type of view of truth and rationality, one in which truth is guaranteed by rational method and rational method appeals to principles undeniable by any fully reflective rational person." "[P]rotagonists of post-Enlightenment relativism and perspectivism claim that if the Enlightenment standards of truth cannot be obtained, theirs is the only possible alternative."[36] He proposed another alternative.

[34]   MacIntyre, "Incommensurability" 109.
[35]   Ibid. 121.
[36]   Alasdair MacIntyre, *Whose Justice? Which Rationality?* (Notre Dame, 1988), 353.

In *Whose Justice? Which Rationality?* he began his argument by describing how two traditions may be incommensurable.

> It may therefore seem to be the case that we are confronted with the rival and competing claims of a number of traditions to our allegiance in respect to our understanding of practical rationality and justice, among which we can have no good reason to decide in favor of any one rather than of the others. Each has its own standards of reasoning; each provides its own background beliefs.[37]

The "relativist challenge" is the claim that "this rather than that can be rational relative to the standards of some particular tradition but not rational as such."[38]

He responded that a claim that a statement is true or false can only be made from within a tradition. It does not make sense to ask about which statements are true or false from a standpoint outside any tradition. There is no such standpoint. If two or more traditions are incommensurable, "[w]ho is in a position to issue a challenge" to the truth of either of them?

> For the person who is do so must ... either be him or herself an inhabitant of one of the two or more rival traditions, owing allegiance to its standards of enquiry and justification ..., or be someone outside all of the traditions, him or herself traditionless. The former alternative precludes the possibility of relativism. Such a person, in the absence of serious epistemological crisis going on within his or her tradition, could have no good reason for putting his or her allegiance to it in question and every reason for continuing that tradition. What of the latter alternative? ... It is an illusion to suppose that there is some neutral standing ground ... independent of all traditions. ... The person outside all traditions lacks sufficient rational resource for enquiry and *a fortiori* for enquiry into what tradition is to be rationally preferred.[39]

Within a tradition there can be progress. Those within the tradition can see that what they once believed to be true was false. But that claim can be made only within a tradition. Progress is made when people ask questions that have arisen within a tradition about the correct interpretation of "authoritative texts" or "[i]ncoherences in the established system of beliefs." The outcome is a set of "reformulations, reevaluations, and new formulations and evaluations."[40] At times, there may be an "epistemological crisis" when "conflicts over rival answers to key questions can no more be settled rationally," when its accustomed "methods of inquiry and ... forms of argument ... [are] disclosing new inadequacies, hitherto unrecognized incoherences." "The solution ... requires the invention or discovery of new concepts and the framing of some new type ... of theory" which "solves the problems that had previously proved intractable in a systematic and coherent way" and does so "in fundamental continuity ... with the shared beliefs in terms of which the tradition had been defined up to this point."[41]

[37] Ibid. 351.
[38] Ibid. 352.
[39] Ibid. 366–67.
[40] Ibid. 354–55.
[41] Ibid. 361–62.

We saw earlier that Legrand's claim that a comparison between the ideas of two societies is impossible was based on Derrida's response to a dilemma: one must either accept an objective view of truth like that of the rationalists, or a subjective view in which truth and objectivity is impossible. Legrand and Derrida did the latter. We can now see that MacIntyre's claim that one cannot compare the Confucian and Aristotelian traditions because they are "incommensurable" is rooted in his response to the same dilemma.

MacIntyre gives a good account of how a tradition can progress, as one might expect from so accomplished an intellectual historian. But the very word "progress" implies that the tradition is better off when it responds to problems arising within that tradition with "new formulations and evaluations" or "requires the invention or discovery of new concepts and the framing of some new type . . . of theory." In what way is the tradition better off? If the reason is that it has come closer to the truth than it was before, we cannot say that the truth has a meaning only in the context of a tradition. If the reason is that people are then more satisfied and less filled with doubt, they would be just as well off if they had never raised questions about their tradition.

Moreover, if MacIntyre were correct about what it means for a statement to be true, then the truth can change. A statement is true when those working within a tradition discover that a new formulation or concept or theory resolves a problem better than some previously held view. But the earth circled the sun when the Ptolemaic account of the universe was the best available. There was a time, as MacIntyre said, when Enlightenment philosophers believed that "truth is guaranteed by rational method and rational method appeals to principles undeniable by any fully reflective rational person." Suppose that their account of truth was the best that their tradition could give at the time that they were writing. Are we to suppose that, at one time, the truth could be found by such a method and that now it no longer can be?

Then there is MacIntyre's own position that one can only regard as true the best explanation that one's own tradition can give. Suppose his position is the best account possible of the meaning of truth within the Western philosophical tradition in which he is working. How can he claim that this account is correct as to all traditions? Those who belong to some other traditions have regarded what they said as true for all time. Were they right about the meaning of truth from the standpoint of their own tradition and wrong only from MacIntyre's?

According to MacIntyre, there is no standpoint outside any tradition by which one can evaluate the truth or falsity of claims made by people within it. By the functional method described earlier, there does not need to be. Those working within different traditions may have been addressing similar problems. If they were, then one can identify these problems and compare the ways in which they were addressed. When the problems are similar, the solutions may be similar despite these differences in context and formulation. When the solutions are not, it may be that each has its advantages and disadvantages, and their importance was evaluated differently. It may be that a solution that works well in the circumstances of one society does not work well in another. It may be that the intellectual tools which were used to resolve the problem in one society were not available in the other. Comparison is all the more useful, both because it illuminates the difficulties faced by people within each tradition and because it sharpens one's understanding of the problem itself.

Such an approach is both descriptive and normative. It describes problems that were actually confronted and answers that were actually proposed, even by people who may have lived in different centuries and who may not have known of each other's work. It is normative because it clarifies what those problems are, and how they might best be solved. There may be many possible solutions. Or there may be none: any attempt to resolve the problem leads to contradictions. In that event, we should consider how the problem arose.

We will see that the classical traditions, which grounded normative standards on human nature, did raise questions, but not the sort that defy any attempt to answer them. The questions concerned which way human nature is constituted and what form of government would best allow each member of society to live a distinctively human life. In contrast, the attempt to ground normative standards on supposedly eternal and invariable principles raised questions which no one could answer. For those in China and in the West who recognized that these questions were unanswerable, a new problem arose: How can normative standards have any truth value if they are not based on such principles? It would seem that they are purely subjective. Liberal theorists since the nineteenth century as well as Legrand, Derrida, and MacIntyre have proposed different answers. Our thesis is that all of them lead to contradictions. One good reason for returning to the path taken by the classical traditions is that it does not lead off that particular cliff.

PART I

TWO ANCIENT TRADITIONS

2

The Beginnings of Ethical Philosophy

The classical traditions that we will study began in China with Confucius, and, in the West, with Socrates, who was born less than thirty years after Confucius died..

Both had a sense of divine mission although neither said a great deal about the divine. Both regarded political life as one of the noblest of vocations yet neither of them held political office. They were teachers. The task they set for themselves was to help others acquire the moral qualities they needed to live a worthwhile life. Both believed that there was no better qualification for political life than the possession of these qualities.

They lived at a time when a class of teachers had emerged who were educating young men in the skills necessary for political life. That task set them apart from the others. In China, other teachers were instructing their pupils in the skills in demand by the kings of independent states who were consolidating their power at the expense of a feudal nobility. They were skills needed for technical and administrative positions. The sophists, Socrates' adversaries, were training their pupils in rhetoric – the art of persuading others – the skill most needed for political success in a Greek city state. The word "sophist" can be translated as "teacher." Confucius and Socrates disparaged these skills.

Nevertheless, they taught in very different ways. Confucius claimed to be transmitting the wisdom of the past. Socrates did not. Confucius taught respect for ancient classics. Socrates was tried and condemned for his disrespect for the one ancient and sacred tradition of the Greeks: the cult of the gods of Homer. Socrates did not look to the Homeric poems for wisdom, unlike the poets of his time who reworked the old stories and deepened their meaning. The Socrates of the *Republic* thought that the works of Homer were morally subversive on account of the conduct they attributed to the gods.

Their methods of teaching were strikingly different. Although Confucius would state maxims in general terms, these maxims often concerned only the aspect of the truth that he wished to explain. Different students might be taught different parts of the truth according to their needs. The students were expected to look within themselves to complete and apply what they had been taught. In contrast, Socrates asked his students to define virtues such as courage, friendship, and temperance. He worked with them to find a definition that was adequate. Often, the search failed, but the students were set on a path that would lead them to truth and virtue.

Nevertheless, both Confucius and Socrates aimed at imparting knowledge that a student in some way already possessed. The possession of that knowledge enabled him to complete the part of the truth that he had been taught by Confucius or to respond to a question about the nature of a virtue put to him by Socrates. To their successors, it seemed to be implicit in their ways of teaching that every human being, by nature, knows, albeit imperfectly, what sort of life he should live.

I CONFUCIUS

i *The Wisdom of the Past*

Confucius (孔子 Kong Zi) called himself "[a] transmitter and not an innovator. I trust and love the ancients."[1] "[I am] not one who was born with knowledge but one who is fond of antiquity, and seeks it diligently."[2] Much of what Confucius learned about the ancients is regarded as myth by modern scholars. Confucius believed it was history, and that belief shaped much of his work.

This history was the source of his conviction that the form of political organization that he saw emerging in his own lifetime as separate states consolidated their power was an aberration. The right form of political organization was an empire ruled by a virtuous monarch. According to this history, Tian (天) conferred a mandate to govern the empire on those who were worthy. When their successors became unworthy, Tian gave the mandate to others. The word Tian is hard to translate. Tian presided over the affairs of the world, but the extent to which he was regarded as a personal God is unclear.

The mandate had once been conferred on Yao (堯). According to Confucius, "Great indeed was Yao as a sovereign! How lofty! Only Tian is great, and Yao modeled himself upon that."[3] Yao chose Shun (舜), a simple but virtuous farmer, to succeed him. Shun was succeeded by his minister Yu (禹). Confucius said, "How sublime was the manner in which Shun and Yu possessed the empire, and yet effortlessly!"[4]

Shun passed the throne to Yu whence it passed to his own son, and so began the first dynasty, the Xia (夏). When its kings fell away from the principles of its founder, the mandate of Tian fell on Tang (湯) who overthrew the last Xia emperor Jie (桀) and founded the Shang (商) dynasty. According to the *Odes* (詩經 *Shi Jing*), "his wisdom and virtue increased each day. He ceaselessly prayed to the emperor in heaven, and the emperor above charged him to govern the nine regions. ... The founder king carried his banner and majestically hefted his axe. His forces were like a blazing fire which no one can check."[5]

---

[1] *Analects* 7.1. Again, I thank Tong Xu, with whom I discussed the original text (http://ctext.org/analects/zh). Throughout, translations are based on her suggestions and on *Confucian Analects, the Great Learning, and the Doctrine of the Mean*, trans. James Legge (2nd ed., Oxford, 1893), and *The Analects*, trans. D. C. Lau (London, 1979).

[2] Ibid. 7.20.

[3] Ibid. 8.19.1.

[4] Ibid. 8.18.

[5] *Odes*, The Sacrificial Odes of Shang, Ode 5, The Yin Wu, p. 310.

The descendants of Tang became unworthy. The *Odes* said of the last Shang emperor: "Alas! that you should have such violent and oppressive ministers, that you should use them in the conduct of affairs! . . . It is not that Tian is unmerciful but that you do not follow the ancient ways. . . . And so your mandate is passing away."[6] Then "Tian surveyed what is below and his mandate passed to Wen (文)."[7]

Wen left the overthrow of the Shang dynasty to his son Wu (武).

> The troops of Shang were many. Their flags were like a forest marshaled in the wilderness of Mu. [Grand-Master Shang-fu said:] "Tian is with you. Have no doubts in your heart."
>
> The wilderness of Mu was vast. The chariots of sandal-wood were bright. The red white-bellied chariot horses were strong. Grand-Master Shang-fu rose like an eagle, aiding king Wu, who attacked and conquered the great Shang. When the next day dawned, everything was still.[8]

Wu founded the Zhou (周) dynasty. But his descendants became unrighteous, like those of Tang. So once again the Way, as Confucius called it, was forsaken.

ii *His Task*

This history shaped Confucius' understanding of his own role. He believed that Tian had given him the task of restoring the Way (道).[9] When the people of Kwang threatened his life, he said: "With King Wen dead, is not culture (文) lodged here in me? If Tian had wanted culture to be destroyed, it would not have come to me. If Tian does not want culture to be destroyed, what can the people of Kuang do to me?"[10] In the past, when Tian had restored the Way, prodigies had occurred: a phoenix had been seen and a strange beast had crawled out of the river with markings on its back. When these prodigies did not accompany his own appearance, Confucius lamented: "The phoenix does not come; the river sends forth no chart: It is finished for me."[11]

Once again, Tian was restoring the Way, but this time in a different manner. In the past, Tian had conferred a mandate to rule on virtuous men. Yet Confucius did not claim that he had a mandate to rule a state. His disciple Zi Gong (子貢) described how things might have been otherwise: "Were our Master to become the head of a state or a noble family, he would be like the man described in the saying: he helps them stand and they stand; he guides them and they follow; he is gentle and they turn to him; he urges them and they work in harmony."[12] In

---

[6] *Odes*, The Third Decade or that of Tang, Ode 1, The Tang, pp. 412–13 (written in the Zhao dynasty, attributed to duke Mu of Shao). It has Wan address these words to Kao-hsin, the last king of the Shang dynasty, perhaps intended as a warning to King Li.

[7] *Odes*, The First Decade or that of Wan Wang, Ode 2, The Taming, pp. 380–81.

[8] Ibid.

[9] It is not clear what Confucius thought about Heaven, but, as Angus Graham noted, "he tends to personify when pondering with awe and humility whether Heaven is on the side of his mission." A. C. Graham, *Disputers of the Tao Philosophical Argument in Ancient China* (La Salle, 1989), 17.

[10] *Analects* 9.5.2–3.

[11] Ibid. 9.9.

[12] Ibid. 19.25.3–4.

the past when the Way was restored, virtuous men were appointed ministers. Confucius was not appointed. "If anyone employed me," he said, "a year would suffice, but in three years everything would be done."[13] Yet he spent most of his life out of office. In contrast to the times of the virtuous emperors, truth was now separated from power.

Confucius concluded that the problem was with the times. In good times, a worthy person rules and chooses worthy people to assist him. In bad times, a worthy person has a different role. He should not be distressed about the lack of office. "The empire has long been without the Way." Tian would use him "as a bell with its wooden tongue,"[14] or as we might say, as a herald's trumpet. He would be a teacher.

His pupils might hold high office though he did not. Yet Confucius said that he would not be distressed even if no one listened to his teachings. A worthy man, a *junzi* (君子) "is not disturbed when people do not recognize him."[15] He acknowledged, however, that although "the *junzi* ... is not troubled by lack of recognition,"[16] he "hates not being mentioned after his death."[17]

Confucius' hope was not disappointed even though his works were proscribed and his followers persecuted during the Qin (秦) dynasty which reunited China. The King of Qin, it is said, ordered all past records burned except those of the state of Qin, as well as "the Odes, Documents, and sayings of the Hundred Schools" and all other books except for writings on "medicine, divination, and planting and sowing." He ordered the execution of the entire family of the Confucians or anyone else who "appealed to the past to condemn the present."[18] Nevertheless, Confucius' teachings were formally accepted by the Han (漢) dynasty that overthrew the Qin. Confucius became the most revered teacher of the longest continuous civilization in human history.

For seven centuries after the end of the Han, though dynasties rose and fell, power usually lay with hereditary nobles and regional warlords. Although Confucius' teachings were not neglected, the institutions of government were systematically reshaped in accordance with them only with the founding of the Song (宋) dynasty in AD 960.

iii *His Teaching*

Confucius lived at a time when the rulers of a few small states were consolidating their power at the expense of a feudal nobility that had dominated China since the fall of the Zhou dynasty. In that respect, it was like the early modern period of Western history. To administer their states, rulers were appointing not only members of noble families but capable people of humble origin.[19] The terms *junzi* (君子) or *shi* (士), which once had referred to only those of noble birth, were now applied to either those who had entered the

---

[13] Ibid. 13.10.
[14] Ibid. 3.24.
[15] Ibid. 1.1.
[16] Ibid. 15.19.
[17] Ibid. 15.20.
[18] Graham, *Disputers of the Tao* 371–72.
[19] Donald J. Munro, *The Concept of Man in Early China* (Stanford, 1989), 4–5.

upper class through their own ability, or those who had obtained virtue through their own effort. These terms are hard to translate but "noble man," or "worthy man" may come closest. Confucius was one of many teachers who trained their pupils to be *junzi*. Other teachers charged money for doing so. Confucius said of himself, "From the man bringing his bundle of dried flesh for my teaching upwards, I have never refused instruction to anyone."[20]

Other teachers taught the technical administrative and military skills in demand among rulers. Confucius believed that a worthy man does not need these skills.[21] He said, "a virtuous man is not an instrument,"[22] or, as we would say, he is not a specialist or a technocrat. Instead, he has qualities that enable him to rule by moral example.

> If a worthy man who is in charge loves propriety, the people will not dare to be disrespectful. If he loves righteousness, the people will not dare to disobey. If he loves trust, the people will not dare to be insincere. If he governs in this way, people from everywhere will come flocking to his kingdom, carrying their children on their backs. [23]

In perfecting his own virtue, he perfects that of others. "The benevolent man, wishing to be established himself, seeks also to establish others; wishing to be successful himself, seeks also the success of others."[24]

High rank is desirable, but the worthy man can do without it. Confucius commended Tai Bo (泰伯), a prime minister of the state of Wu renowned for his integrity. He "was appointed three times and never showed any sign of pleasure; he was dismissed three times and never showed any sign of distress."[25] Although wealth came with high rank, the worthy man can do without it. "Admirable indeed was the virtue of Hui! With a single bamboo dish of rice, a single gourd cup of drink, and living in his mean narrow lane, while others could not have endured the distress, he did not allow his joy to be affected by it."[26] The worthy man should not accept an official position unless he is allowed to govern rightly. "The term 'great minister' refers to one who serves his lord according to the Way and who resigns when this is no longer possible."[27] Even if he does not achieve rank or wealth, "the worthy man is at ease; the inferior man is always anxious."[28]

The goal of Confucius' teaching was to enable his students to become worthy men. To do so required learning, and, indeed, the word *junzi* is often translated as "scholar." Knowledge was not simply a matter of knowing the truth. It was also a matter of moral commitment. "Knowing something is not as good as loving it, and loving is not as good as

[20] *Analects* 7.7.
[21] See H. G. Creel, *Chinese Thought from Confucius to Mao Tsê-tung* (Chicago, 1953), 28–29.
[22] *Analects* 2.12.
[23] Ibid. 13.4.1–3.
[24] Ibid. 6.30.
[25] Ibid. 5.19. See ibid. 8.1.
[26] Ibid. 6.11. Similarly: "A man whose mind is set on truth but who is ashamed of bad clothes and bad food is not fit to be consulted." Ibid. 4.9. "The man who cherishes the love of comfort is not fit to be deemed a virtuous man." Ibid. 14.2. "The virtuous man seeks neither a full belly nor a comfortable home." Ibid. 1.14.
[27] Ibid. 11.24.
[28] Ibid. 7.37.

delighting in it."[29] If a student were not himself inclined toward that path, Confucius could do nothing with him.[30]

He resisted teaching a principle or concept by stating it clearly and consistently, often to the surprise of his students. He preferred to point a student to the truth rather than stating it.

"When I have pointed out one corner of a square to anyone, and he does not come back with the other three, I will not point it out to him a second time."[31] He also believed that one learned moral principles by paying attention to different aspects of them. He did not try to fit all of these aspects into a single definition. When he was asked what filial piety or knowledge or benevolence means, he gave different answers. He explained what filial piety is in four different ways to four students.[32] He gave a student two different explanations of what knowledge is,[33] and a third explanation to another.[34]

Confucius also recognized that the principle that was right for one person might be wrong for another. When Zi Lu (子路) asked whether he should immediately act on what he had heard, Confucius told him "your father and brother are to be consulted." When Ran You (冉有) asked the same question, Confucius said, "immediately put to practice what you hear." Gong Xihua (公西華) pointed out that Confucius had given opposite answers to the same question, and asked him why. Confucius explained that Ran You is "easily discouraged; therefore I urged him forward." Zi Lu "tends to act recklessly; therefore I held him back."[35]

Nevertheless, Confucius did not believe that that the meaning of terms such as filial piety depended upon each student's perspective. Terms had their proper meaning. When Zi Lu told him, "The ruler of Wei has been waiting for your assistance to govern his state. What will you consider as the priority?" Confucius answered, "What is necessary is to rectify names."[36] He seems to have meant, as he said elsewhere, "[t]here is government, when the ruler is ruler, and the minister is minister; when the father is father, and the son is son."[37]

The truth, however, was to be grasped through reflection. Disputation did not play the same role in the Confucian tradition that it has done in Western philosophy since the time of Socrates. For that reason, Western philosophers have tended to undervalue Confucian thought. They have neglected the extent to which their own conclusions have depended less on the force of logic, than on a similar process of thinking things through.

---

[29] Ibid. 6.20.
[30] Ibid. 9.24.
[31] Ibid. 7.8.
[32] Ibid. 2.5–8.
[33] Ibid. 12.22.
[34] Ibid. 2.17.
[35] Ibid. 11.20.
[36] Ibid. 13.3.
[37] Ibid. 12.11. It does not follow, as May Sim suggested, that "the Confucian practice of rightly ordering names profitably be understood as a quest for true definitions" like those sought by Aristotle, and, indeed, Confucius does not seek them. May Sim, *Remastering Morals with Aristotle and Confucius* (Cambridge, 2007), 10.

II SOCRATES

i *His Task*

Like Confucius, Socrates thought he had been given a mission, and, indeed, a divine mission. He described it in the *Apology*, a work that nearly all scholars agree presents his own views, rather than those of Plato. His description is paradoxical. Socrates described himself as a person who has "no wisdom" yet whose mission is to teach people to care for "wisdom and truth and the greatest improvement of the soul."

In the *Apology*, he told his judges:

> I will refer you to a witness who is worthy of credit: that witness shall be the God of Delphi ... You must have known Chaerophon; he was an early friend of mine, and also a friend of yours. ... Chaerophon, as you know, was very impetuous in all his doings, and he went to Delphi and boldly asked the oracle to tell him whether – as I was saying, I must beg you not to interrupt – he asked the oracle to tell him whether anyone was wiser than I was, and the Pythian prophetess answered that there was no man wiser. Chaerophon is dead himself, but his brother, who is in court, will confirm the truth of what I am saying.[38]

Socrates then asked himself "what can the god mean" since "I know I have no wisdom small or great." To solve the puzzle, he inquired of those who had a reputation for wisdom: statesmen, poets, and craftsmen. He found that the statesmen were not wise. Poets said "many fine things" but it could not be "by wisdom" but "by a sort of genius and inspiration" since they were unable to explain the meaning of what they said. Craftsmen, indeed, "did know many things of which I was ignorant, and in this ... certainly were wiser than I," but they were foolish to think that they understood anything beyond their craft. The meaning of the oracle, he decided, is that "God only is wise," and that Socrates is the wisest of men only because he "knows that his wisdom is, in truth, worth nothing."

He concluded that he had been given a mission:

> And so I go about the world, obedient to the god, and search and make enquiry into the wisdom of anyone ... who appears to be wise; and if he is not wise, then in vindication of the oracle I show him that he is not wise; and my occupation quite absorbs me, and I have no time to give either to any public matter of interest or to any concern of my own, but I am in utter poverty by reason of my devotion to the god.

He explained:

> Men of Athens, I honour and love you; but I shall obey God rather than you, and while I have life and strength I shall never cease from the practice and teaching of philosophy, exhorting any one whom I meet and saying to him after my manner: You, my friend, – a citizen of the great and mighty and wise city of Athens, – are you not ashamed of heaping up the greatest amount of money and honour and reputation, and caring so little about wisdom and truth and the greatest improvement of the soul, which you never regard or heed at all? And if the person with whom I am arguing, says: Yes, but I do care; then I do not

---

[38] *Apology* 20–21.

leave him or let him go at once; but I proceed to interrogate and examine and cross-examine him, and if, as I think, he has no virtue in him, but only says that he has, I reproach him. For I know that this is the command of God; and I believe that no greater good has ever happened to the state than my service to God.

Socrates said that his mission had been confirmed and directed by a *daimonion*, a divine sign or spiritual guide, referred to in several dialogues. Because of the promptings of this *daimonion*, Socrates pursued his mission in private life rather than by becoming a statesman:

Someone may wonder why I go about in private giving advice and busying myself with the concerns of others, but do not venture to come forward in public and advise the state. I will tell you why. You have heard me speak at sundry times and in diverse places of an oracle or sign which comes to me . . . This sign, which is a kind of voice, first began to come to me when I was a child; it always forbids but never commands me to do anything which I am going to do. This is what deters me from being a politician. And rightly so, I think. For I am certain, O men of Athens, that if I had engaged in politics, I should have perished long ago, and done no good either to you or to myself.

ii *His Teaching*

Socrates' teaching, like that of Confucius, was meant to lead students to virtue. His method of doing so was strikingly different. As we have seen, Confucius would give a student a fragment of the truth and leave him to work out the rest. He would give conflicting answers to questions about the meaning of filial piety, knowledge, or benevolence on which his students should reflect.

In contrast, Socrates sought the correct definitions of virtues. The *Euthyphro*, the *Laches*, the *Lysis*, and the *Charmides* concern, respectively, the nature of piety, courage, *philia*, sometimes translated as friendship, and *sophrosynē*, sometimes translated as temperance. These early dialogues are believed to reflect Socrates' own views rather than those later ascribed to him by Plato. The method is one that Aristotle called "dialectical." Participants in the dialogue do not try to infer the correct definition of a virtue from a higher-level principle whose truth they accept. They propose a definition and test it by seeing if it leads to unacceptable consequences.

It might seem that Socrates believed that to be virtuous one must know how a virtue should be defined, and that the point of the exercise is to find the correct definition. The early dialogues show the opposite. Participants are portrayed as possessing the virtues of piety, courage, friendship, or temperance. Yet neither they nor Socrates succeed in finding a correct definition. Each definition they propose explains certain instances of such a virtue. Yet it does not explain others. In the end, Socrates expresses his regret that they did not find the answer that they were seeking.

The lesson was not that such questions are unanswerable. That view was held by his adversaries the sophists. They were experts in rhetoric. Socrates attacked them for trying to persuade without caring about the truth. Indeed, the sophists seemed doubtful that one could distinguish between true and false beliefs. In that respect, they were skeptics. Socrates and the other participants in the earlier dialogues were seeking knowledge that they did not yet possess. As William Guthrie observed:

> [The sophists] held that knowledge (as opposed to shifting opinion) was impossible, for there were no stable and indisputable objects to be known. [Socrates] demonstrated to everybody that what they called their knowledge was not knowledge at all. Superficially alike, these two statements were fundamentally different, for that of Socrates was based on an unshakeable conviction that knowledge *was* in principle obtainable, but that, if there was to be any hope of attaining it, the debris of confused and misleading ideas which filled most men's minds must first be cleared away. ... To be a Socratic was not to follow any system of philosophical doctrine. It implies first and foremost an attitude of mind, an intellectual humility easily mistaken for arrogance, since the true Socratic is convinced of the ignorance not only of himself but of all of mankind.[39]

Moreover, in each of these dialogues, although the participants never find a correct definition, they better understand the virtue in question. Its nature has been probed though not fathomed. The very fact that some answers are wrong suggest that the definition of a virtue is not arbitrary. There must be a definition that is right.

Socrates' method presupposes that those who are seeking knowledge in some way already possess it. Otherwise they would be unable to tell that the consequences that follow from a proposed definition are unacceptable. In that respect, his method was like that of Confucius, whose students were expected to learn by reflecting on what they already knew. Both philosophers believed that there are moral qualities that enable one to live rightly, and that the acquisition of these qualities goes hand-in-hand with knowledge. These beliefs are the bedrock of the traditions that they founded.

---

[39] W. C. Guthrie, *Socrates* (Cambridge, 1971), 129.

3

The Challenge to Virtue and the Discovery of Human Nature

Another core idea in both traditions is that human nature is the source of the moral qualities necessary for a good life. To live rightly is to live a distinctively human life. A person is drawn to such a life and is able to recognize its goodness because he is a human being. If he lives wrongly he destroys his humanity and consequently himself. Confucius rarely mentioned human nature (性 *xing*),[1] and Socrates did not do so in his early dialogues. This core idea was a response to those who criticized their teachings.

In China, the chief critics, Yang Zhu (楊朱) and Mozi (墨子), lived after the death of Confucius. They not only attacked Confucian moral teachings but presented three alternative ideas about the basis of morality which we will encounter again. According to one, morality is based on the gratification of desires – on pleasure and pain – although, as we will see, Yang Zhu and Mozi had different ideas of why the gratification of desires mattered. A second idea, introduced by Mozi, was that morality could be based on the principle that no one's desires matter more than anyone else's. Everyone should be treated the same. A third idea, also introduced by Mozi, was that a society cannot live in peace when different people subscribe to different moral standards. The solution is for the emperor to impose the same standards on everyone.

In response, Mencius (孟子 Meng Zi) gave an account of human nature in which human beings have an innate tendency to seek what is good. To live by the teachings of Yang Zhu and Mozi is to throw one's life away.

In Greece, doubts about the basis of morality had been raised in Socrates' lifetime by his adversaries, the sophists. Some of them claimed that morality was based on the gratification of desire. Some of them said it was based on the expression of one's own will. Some denied that it had any basis at all.

In the *Gorgias*, which is one of the last dialogues that is believed to contain his own thoughts rather than those of Plato, Socrates responded to his adversaries in the same way as Mencius. He gave an account of human nature. There is an "order and regularity" in the human soul, as there is in the human body, or in a house, or a ship. Where order and regularity prevail, there is good, and where disorder prevails, there is evil. Disorder in the soul is like sickness in the body, or disrepair or ruin in the house or ship.

---

[1] A. C. Graham, *Studies in Chinese Philosophy and Philosophical Literature* (Albany, 1990), 18.

I MENCIUS AND HIS OPPONENTS

Confucius' disciple Zi Gong noted that there were two topics on which "the Master" said little: "human nature and the Way of Tian."[2] All he said about human nature in the *Analects* is that "by nature, people are nearly alike; by practice, they get to be wide apart."[3]

His grandson Zisi 子思 (c. 481–402 BC) said a bit more. He is generally recognized as the author of the *Doctrine of the Mean* (中庸), later considered to be a classic of the Confucian tradition. According to the *Doctrine of the Mean*: "What Tian has conferred is called nature; accordance with this nature is called the path of duty."[4] He did not question that human beings have a nature and that this path was to be followed.

It is not surprising that they said so little about human nature. Confucius was concerned with how human beings should act, not with what made them human. Those he admonished were neglecting the Way by pursuing rank or wealth, not questioning whether there was such a thing.

During Zisi's lifetime, Mozi and Yang Zhu challenged the teachings of Confucius and Zisi about how a human being should live. Although Zisi had not responded to them, Mencius did.

II THE CONFUCIAN TRADITION

i *The Challenge: Yang Zhu and Mozi*

Mencius believed that the Way taught by Confucius was in danger of perishing because of the teachings of Yang Zhu and Mozi. He was therefore forced to dispute with them, which he disliked.

> The words of Yang Zhu and Mozi fill the country. If you listen to people's discourses everywhere, you will find that they have adopted the views either of Yang or of Mo. . . . I also wish to rectify men's hearts, and to put an end to those perverse doctrines, to oppose their one-sided actions and banish away their licentious expressions, and thus to carry on the work of the three sages. Do I do so because I am fond of disputing? I am compelled to do it. Whoever is able to oppose Yang and Mo is a disciple of the sages.[5]

He disputed their teachings by undertaking a task which Confucius had not found necessary: giving an account of human nature.[6]

---

[2] *Analects* 5.13.

[3] Ibid. 17.2.

[4] *Doctrine of the Mean* 1.1, *Confucian Analects, the Great Learning, and the Doctrine of the Mean*, trans. James Legge (2nd ed., Oxford, 1893).

[5] *Mencius* 3B9.1–2, 9, 13–14. Again, I thank Tong Xu, with whom I discussed the original text (http://ctext.org /mengzi/zh). Throughout, translations are based on her suggestions and on *The Works of Mencius*, trans. James Legge (2nd ed., Oxford, 1895), and *Mencius*, trans. D. C. Lau (London, 1970).

[6] Graham, *Studies* 18; A. C. Graham, *Disputers of the Tao Philosophical Argument in Ancient China* (La Salle, 1989), 109 (speaking of the "Yangist challenge").

Yang Zhu

Yang Zhu (楊朱) claimed Confucian morality is artificial. One finds one's "authentic self" by "gratifying one's wishes and cherishing one's days."

Nothing that Yang Zhu wrote has survived. Those lines appear in an imaginary debate between Confucius and the notorious robber Zhi, a Chinese counterpart of Mack the Knife. Zhi defended the position of Yang Zhu. He told Confucius, "You dare to create rights and wrongs. ... You blindly fabricate filial piety and brotherly love ... " "This way of yours is a crazy, fraudulent, vain, empty and artificial business. It is no way to fulfill your true self." Zhi then explained what he took to be the true self:

> The eyes want to see colors. The ears want to hear sounds. The mouth wants to taste flavors. And the emotions want to be fulfilled. ... If you are not gratifying your wishes and cherishing your days, then you do not understand the Way.

> Before there was government, people did understand the Way.

> In Shen Nong's time they lay down tired and arose wide awake. They knew their mothers but not their fathers and lived together with the deer. They farmed their own food, wove their own clothes, and had no idea of hurting each other. This was the high point that virtue achieved.

Their idyll was spoiled by the so-called sage rulers of antiquity. The first emperor waged war "until the blood flowed a hundred leagues." "Tang exiled his lord [the last ruler of the Xia dynasty], Wu killed Tyrant Zhou [the last ruler of the Shang dynasty], and ever since the strong oppress the weak and the many tyrannize the few."[7] All this happened because people like Confucius "forcefully went against their essence and nature because profit confused them about their true self." Ironically, Yang Zhu and his followers were among the first Chinese philosophers to speak of one's "nature."

Yang Zhu concluded a person by nature should be concerned with what gives pleasure and pain to himself, not others. In another imaginary dialogue, a follower of Mozi, Qin Giuli, attacked that claim. Yang Zhu replied, assisted by his follower Meng Sunyang (孟孫陽).

> Qin Guli asked Yang Zhu, "If you could help the whole world by the loss of a hair off your body, would you do it?"
> Yang Zhu replied, "The world would surely not be helped by a single hair."
> "Suppose that it did help, would you not do it?"
> Yang Zhu did not answer him.
> Meng Sunyang said, "You have not fathomed what is in my master's heart. Let me say it.
> Suppose for a bit of your skin you could get a thousand in gold, would you give it?"
> "I would."
> "Suppose that by cutting off a limb at the joint, you could win a state, would you do it?"
> Qin Guli was silent for a while.

---

7 From Graham, *Disputers of the Tao* 108.

Meng Sunyang continued, "That one hair matters less than skin and skin less than a limb is plain enough. However, many hairs add up to skin, and much skin amounts to limb. A single hair is certainly one thing among the myriad parts of the body, how can one treat it lightly?"[8]

The argument is that although the loss of a hair might seem a trivial sacrifice, there is no logical stopping point between that and the sacrifice of a limb. If one ought to care for others, there is no stopping point short of the total altruism of Mozi which, as we will see, requires a person to care for others as much as for himself.

Mozi

Mozi (墨子), like Yang Zhu, described what is good for a person in terms of what pleases or displeases him. According to the *Mozi*, a canonical compilation of his teachings, "the business of the benevolent man must be to seek diligently to promote what benefits the world and to eliminate what harms it."[9] According to one of his disciples, "Benefit is what one is pleased to get."[10] "Harm is what one is displeased to get."[11]

Yang Zhu regarded people as better off when they experience pleasure or "gratify their wishes." For Mozi, people are better off when they have fewer ungratified wishes and desires. Therefore, their desires should be reduced to the biological minimum. A person cannot be content unless he gratifies his physical desires for food, shelter, and clothing. Once these desires are gratified, he should be content, and therefore at peace. According to the disciple just quoted: "To be at peace is to know no desire or aversion."[12]

Consequently, "those who are benevolent, in making their plans for the world, do not make what is beautiful to their eyes, or pleasing to their ears, or sweet to their mouths, or of comfort to their bodies."[13] A person does not need to desire such things. Instead, the expense of making them should be used to gratify the desires that he has necessarily. The expense harms the poor by "depriving the people of materials for food and clothing."[14] "[W]hen we evaluate them in terms of the low, they do not accord with the benefit of the ten thousand people [that is, of all the world]."[15]

Clothes are "useful . . . to keep out the cold of winter and withstand the heat of summer." Houses are useful "to keep out the wind and cold of winter and withstand the heat of

---

[8] Liezi, "Yang Zhu" (trans. modified from Angus C. Graham, *Disputers of the Tao*, [Chicago, 1989], 60–61).

[9] *Mozi* 32.1; see 15.1 (trans. from Ian Johnston, *The Mozi: A Complete Translation* [New York, 2010]).

[10] Ibid. 40 and 42 A 26. Scholars are agreed that chapters 40–45 of the *Mozi* were written by members of his school but at a considerably later date.

[11] Ibid. 40 and 42 A 27.

[12] Ibid. 40 and 42 A 25. This explanation is more plausible than that of Creel who thought that "to remedy specific evils" Mozi was willing "to sacrifice everything, including human happiness," "not because he wanted men to be unhappy but because he was unable to see beyond a condition in which prevent evils might be removed." H. G. Creel, *Chinese Thought from Confucius to Mao Tsê-tung* (Chicago, 1953), 66. That concern does explain Mozi's unwillingness to divert resources so as to deprive the poor of food, clothing, and shelter. It does not explain his blanket condemnation of any activity that does not serve these purposes.

[13] *Mozi* 32.1.

[14] Ibid.

[15] Ibid. 32.2.

summer, and to provide protection against thieves and robbers." Whatever is "ornamental" serves no purpose and should be eliminated.[16] So should music which serves no purpose at all. Ask a Confucian "Why make music?" and he will reply, "Music is for the purpose of music." "This is like saying, when I ask, 'Why make a house?' that 'A house is for the purpose of a house.'"[17]

Angus Graham criticized Mozi for taking "[v]aluation by utility ... to the extreme of refusal to recognize anything as valuable in itself; this is a utilitarianism which never raises the question 'Useful for what?'"[18] But Mozi was not thinking like a modern utilitarian. For him, the pleasure that comes with gratifying one's desires is not good. What is good is peace, and to be at peace, one must have no ungratified desires.

One might expect Mozi to conclude, as Yang Zhu did, that one should not care whether the desires of others are gratified or not. Instead, he introduced a second principle: one should be equally concerned with the benefit and harm of everyone. He called this principle "universal love (兼爱 jian ai)," although the word "love" 爱 is misleading because he was not describing affection toward others but a principle of equal and impartial concern.[19]

This principle not only seems to be independent of the first but to conflict with it. If a person did care about others, then it would seem that he could not be at peace unless others were at peace as well. Moreover, if each person is motivated by his own desires, why would be equally concerned about the desires of others?

Mozi argued that one should be equally concerned with another's desires because from the point of view of Tian, no one's desires matter more than anyone else's. Tian cares for each person equally. His disciples explained:

> "Master Mozi established and set up Tian's intention to act as a principle and standard just as the wheelwright has his compasses and the carpenter his square."[20] "What do I say constitutes compliance with Tian's intention?" he asked. "I say it is universal love for the people of the world. How do I know that Tian is universal in its love for the people of the world? Because Tian is universal in providing food for them."[21]

Mozi did not argue that each person desires to please Tian or, at least, not to offend him. Rather, to look at matters from Tian's point of view is to look at them objectively. From that perspective, no one's desires are more important than anyone else's.

---

[16] Ibid. 20.1.

[17] Ibid. 48.13. The passage is a tricky one to translate since the same character that means "music" also means "joy." If one translates the Confucian's response, however, as "Music is for the purpose of joy," then Mozi's criticism misses its point. See Ian Johnston, trans., *The Mozi: A Complete Translation* (New York, 2010), p. 687 n. xiv to *Mozi* 49.13 (who suggests a "Confucian play on words" was "deliberately overlooked by the Mohist writer of the present passage"); Graham, *Disputers of the Tao* 40–41 (who translates the Confucian as responding "music is joy" and Mozi as criticizing him for having said, in effect, that "entertainment" is "entertaining").

[18] Graham, *Disputers of the Tao* 40.

[19] Kwong-loi Shun, *Mencius and Early Chinese Thought* (Stanford, 1997), 31.

[20] *Mozi* 28.9.

[21] Ibid. 28.5.

As David Nivison observed, he expected people to observe the principle of impartial concern because it is rational to do so, not because they desire to do so. Objectively, no one's desires do matter more than anyone else's. He observed that in this respect Mozi's account differed from that of Mencius. Mencius said that the principles that should guide a person's behavior are those he is naturally inclined to follow.[22] In Mozi's account, there is a gap between what is rational in the abstract from what motivates a person to act.

Mozi may have been trying to bridge this gap when he argued that everyone would be better off if each person cared for others as much as for himself. "If people were to regard others' states as they regard their own states" or "others' houses as they regard their own house," then no one would cause war or discord.[23] Someone who was about to risk his life in a battle would prefer "to entrust the protection of his house and family" to someone who had the same concern for everyone than one who did not."[24] Yet this argument is not an appeal to self-interest. A person might be better off if others were as concerned with his interests as with their own, but it does not follow that he would be better off if he showed a similar concern for their interests. Granted, he will then be following a different standard that the one he wishes everyone else would follow. He may be acting arbitrarily or irrationally, according to Mozi, but what motivation would he have to act otherwise?

Mozi realized that rationality might be insufficient to induce people to act with impartial concern. To achieve this goal, one therefore needed rewards and punishments.

> If there were a ruler who delighted in these things, and encouraged people with rewards and praise, and intimidated them with penalties and punishments, I think the people would take to universal mutual love and interchange of mutual benefits just like fire goes up and water goes down; they cannot be stopped in the world.[25]
>
> Formerly, King Ling of Jing loved slender waists. During the time of King Ling, the officers of Jing did not eat more than one meal a day. As a result, they had to rely on a stick to get up, and to use the support of the walls when walking. Now restricting one's food is a difficult thing to do, but they did it because it pleased King Ling. So it doesn't take more than a single generation for people to be able to change if they seek to fall in line with the wishes of their superior.[26]

The idea seems to be not only that people would obey, but they would "take to" the "principle of universal love" so that it would become as natural for them to act in accordance with it as for fire to burn upward and water to flow downward.

According to Mozi, people's excessive desires and partiality to their own interests is not the only source of strife. Another is people's partiality to their own opinions or principles. He introduced a third principle to end that partiality: the government should wipe out diversity.

---

[22] David S. Nivison, "Weakness of the Will in Ancient Chinese Philosophy," in David S. Nivison, *The Ways of Confucianism Investigations in Chinese Philosophy* (Chicago, 1996), 79 at 87.

[23] *Mozi* 16.2.

[24] Ibid. 16.6.

[25] Ibid. 16.14.

[26] Ibid.

The ancient times, when people first came into being, were times when there were yet no laws or government, so it was said that people had differing principles. ... People affirmed their own principles and condemned those of other people. ... Throughout the world, people all used water and fire, and poisons and potions to injure and harm one another. As a result, those with strength to spare did not use it to help each other in their work, surplus goods rotted and decayed and were not used for mutual distribution, and good doctrines were obscured and not used for mutual teaching. ...

It is quite clear that what is taken as disorder in the world arises from lack of effective rule. Therefore, the one who was the most worth and able in the world was selected as being the Son of Tian.[27]

The Son of Tian was the emperor. "[W]hat it is that brings order to the world? It is only that the Son of Tian is able to make uniform the principles of the world?"[28] "What the Son of Tian takes to be wrong, all must take to be wrong."[29]

According to some modern scholars, Mozi thought that a common principle or rule was needed because people are self-serving.[30] The evil that arises from self-serving desires, however, arises either when desires go beyond one's biological needs or when people neglect the principle of universal and impartial love. As Kwong-loi Shun noted, for Mozi, the source of disorder is partiality to his one's own principles, not only to one's own interests.[31]

ii *The Response of Mencius*

Rather than criticizing their arguments, Mencius answered Mozi and Yang Zhu by describing human nature.

According to Mencius, a good person possesses four attributes: benevolence (仁), righteousness (義), propriety (禮), and wisdom (智). They develop from four feelings: compassion (惻隱之心), shame (羞惡之心), respect (恭敬之心), and a "sense of right and wrong" (是非之心), respectively.[32] "Right and wrong" (是非) is difficult to translate. The characters literally mean "yes-no." One might describe this feeling as "the sense that some things are so and others are not."

Everyone is born with the capacity for these four feelings. Why a person should have these, rather than others, is a question we will discuss later. The important point for now is that, according to Mencius, "men have these four capacities just as they have their four limbs."[33] Everyone, for example, is born with the capacity to feel sympathy, that is, with "a mind which cannot bear the sufferings of others."

---

[27]   Ibid. 11.1–11.2

[28]   Ibid. 11.3.

[29]   Ibid. 11.4.

[30]   Benjamin Schwartz, *The World of Thought in Ancient China* (Cambridge, 1985), 142, 262.

[31]   Shun, *Mencius* 33.

[32]   *Mencius* 6A6.7.

[33]   Ibid.

If men suddenly see a child about to fall into a well they will without exception experience a feeling of alarm and distress . . . not as a ground on which they may gain the favor of the child's parents, nor as a ground on which they may seek the praise of their neighbors and friends, nor from a dislike of the reputation of having been unmoved by such a thing.[34]

Mencius reassured a king that he had the capacity to be benevolent by pointing out that he had once refused to sacrifice an ox since he could not "bear its frightened appearance, as if it were an innocent person going to the place of death."[35]

A human being lives as he should when these four innate capacities develop without hindrance.

Since all men have these four principles in themselves, let them know to give them all their development and completion, and the issue will be like that of fire which has begun to burn, or that of a spring which has begun to find vent. Let them have their complete development, and they will suffice to love and protect all within the four seas. Let them be denied that development, and they will not suffice for a man to serve his parents.[36]

It is like the growth of barley: "Let it be sown and covered up; the ground being the same, and the time of sowing likewise the same, it grows rapidly up, and, when the full time is come, it is all found to be ripe."[37]

Accordingly, what benefits a person as a human being is not necessarily "what he is pleased to get," as Mozi's disciple put it, nor whether he "gratifies his wishes," as Yang Zhu believed. The principles that develop into benevolence, righteousness, propriety, and wisdom belong to a person's nature. Without them, a person would not be human. He would be "not much different from the irrational animals." According to Mencius, if he gives them up, he destroys himself:

With those who do violence to themselves, it is impossible to speak. With those who throw themselves away, it is impossible to do anything. To disown in his conversation propriety and righteousness, is what we mean by doing violence to one's self. To say, "I am not able to

---

[34] Ibid. 2A6.3–4.

[35] Ibid. 1A7.4. Mencius was not arguing, as some modern scholars have thought, that a person distressed at a child falling into a well or an ox being led to slaughter is required as matter of logical consistency to feel distress at other misfortunes. Liu Shu-hsien, "Some Reflections on Mencius' Views of Heart-Mind and Human Nature," *Philosophy East and West* 46 (1996), 143 at 152; David S. Nivison, "Mencius and Motivation," *Journal of the Academy of Religion* 47(3) (Thematic Issue) (1979), 417. The point of Mencius' argument, as he says himself, is that the feeling of sympathy belongs to human nature because every human being has it. See Irene Bloom, "Mencian Arguments of Human Nature (Jen-Hsing)," *Philosophy East and West* 44 (1994), 19 at 31. Similarly, David Wong observed that Mencius was not trying to convince the king by logical argument but trying to change the king by beginning with a feeling that was "already there" and channeling "into practical deliberation." David B. Wong, "Is There a Distinction Between Reason and Emotion in Mencius?," *Philosophy East and West* 41 (1991), 31 at 39.

[36] *Mencius* 2A6.7. In view of these quotations and those that follow it is hard to see how Roger Ames can be right that these principles "are profoundly more delicate and tentative than one's physical identity" or that human nature is "a cultural product." For criticism of that view, see Bloom, "Mencian Arguments" 19; Liu, "Some Reflections" 148.

[37] *Mencius* 6A7.2.

dwell in benevolence or pursue the path of righteousness," is what we mean by throwing one's self away.[38]

Because right conduct realizes one's nature, Mencius concluded that the standard for right conduct must come from within. Suppose there were some other independent source of moral standards, and these standards conflicted with one's nature. Obedience to them would be self-destructive. His contemporary, Gao 告子, claimed that human nature is neither good nor bad. According to Gao:

> Human nature is like the Qi-willow (杞柳 *qi liu*), and righteousness is like cups and bowls that are carved out from the willow. Cultivating benevolence and righteousness out of human nature is like carving cups and bowls from the Qi-willow.[39]

Mencius answered:

> Can you, leaving the nature of the willow untouched, make with it cups and bowls? You must do violence and injury to the willow, before you can make cups and bowls with it. If you must do violence and injury to the willow in order to make cups and bowls with it, on your principles you must in the same way do violence and injury to humanity in order to cultivate benevolence and righteousness from it! Your words, alas! would certainly lead all men to reckon benevolence and righteousness to be calamities.[40]

If a standard were imposed on a human being, however good and noble, that is alien to his nature, or if he could be transformed into a being that is good and noble but no longer human, he would not be perfected. His humanity would be compromised or destroyed.

III SOCRATES AND THE SOPHISTS

As we have seen, when Mencius discussed human nature, he was responding to Mozi and Yang Zhu who opposed Confucius' teaching concerning how a human being should live. As these adversaries lived after the death of Confucius, he himself did not oppose them. Socrates' adversaries were his contemporaries. In response, like Mencius, he developed an account of human nature. He did so briefly. His account was then developed and revised by his student Plato, and by Plato's student Aristotle.

Socrates' adversaries, the sophists, doubted that one could distinguish between qualities that are virtuous or vicious. They were teachers of rhetoric, and some have attributed their skepticism to their practice of making the wrong case appear to be the right.[41] Some have attributed it to the influence of the earlier philosophers (the pre-Socratics) who were concerned not with ethics, but with the natural world.

---

[38]　Ibid. 4A.10.1.

[39]　Ibid. 6A1.1.

[40]　Ibid. 6A1.2. Whalen Lai believed that Mencius had not shown a conflict because the bowl is still useful, but that is to miss Mencius' point. However useful, the shape of the bowl conflicts with the nature of the willow. Whalen Lai, "Kao Tzu and Mencius on Mind: Analyzing a Paradigm Shift in Classical China," *Philosophy East and West* 34 (1984), 147 at 149.

[41]　W. K. C. Guthrie, *The Sophists* (Cambridge, 1971), 180–81.

Some sophists believed that there was a chasm between *physis* or nature, on the one hand, and *nomos* or law, on the other. Nature was a given. Law was established by convention. According to the fifth-century sophist Antiphon:

> Justice consists in not transgressing the laws and usages (*nomima*) of one's state. Therefore the most profitable means of manipulating justice is to respect the laws when witnesses are present, but otherwise to follow the precepts of nature. Laws are artificial compacts; they lack the inevitability of natural growth. Hence to break the laws without detection does one no harm, whereas any attempt to violate the inborn dictates of nature is harmful irrespective of discovery by others, for the hurt is not merely, as with the lawbreaker, a matter of appearance or reputation but of reality.[42]

As described earlier, in his early dialogues, Socrates challenged skepticism, but not by arguing with skeptics. He discussed virtue with fellow seekers of truth. In the *Gorgias* he did so by developing an account of human nature. The skeptic was Callicles. He claimed that moral standards are established by the majority who are weak and "make laws and distribute praises and censures with a view to themselves and their own interests; and they terrify the stronger sort of men, and those who are able to get the better of them, in order that they may not get the better of them. "[43] In contrast, "nature herself intimates that it is just for the better to have more than the worse, the more powerful than the weaker, and in many ways she shows, among men as among animals, and indeed among whole cities and races, that justice consists in the superior ruling over and having more than the inferior."[44]

Socrates asked whether the strong are superior simply because they are strong. Callicles said that they are. Socrates asked if the majority is therefore superior since, by Callicles' account, it can force its will and its opinions on the strong.

Callicles then changed his position. The truly superior are not "a rabble of slaves and nondescripts who are of no use except perhaps for their physical strength." The truly superior are the wiser. "By natural justice ... the better and wiser should rule and have more than the inferior."

Socrates asked in what respect they are better and wiser. Callicles answered, "I mean by superiors not cobblers or cooks but wise politicians who understand the administration of the state, and who are not only wise but valiant and able to carry out their designs, and not the men to faint from want of soul."

Socrates then asked whether such a man will "rule over others or also over himself," whether he will be "temperate and a master of himself, and the ruler of his own pleasures and passions." Callicles answered that the temperate are "fools." "I plainly assert, that he who would truly live ought to allow his desires to wax to the uttermost, and not to chastise them; but when they have grown to their greatest he should have the courage and intelligence to minister to them and to satisfy all his longings." Did Callicles believe

---

[42] *Oxyrhyncus Papyri*, ed. B. P. Grenfell, A. S. Hunt, et. al., 1364 frag. 1, in H. Diels & W. Kranz, *Die Fragmente der Vorsokratiker* (10th ed., Berlin, 1960–61), frag. 44 A, trans. Guthrie, *The Sophists* 108–09. For present purposes, it does not matter if these are the views of Antiphon himself.

[43] *Gorgias* 482–83.

[44] *Gorgias* 483.

then that all pleasures are good? He did. But is it not true that pleasure and pain come to foolish men and wise men alike, and to cowards as well as to brave men, and that it would be hard to say which experience the greater pleasure? When Callicles agreed, Socrates asked how it can then be, that the best life is lived by men who do not merely gratify their desires but are also wise and valiant. Callicles was forced to deny that all pleasure is good, and, indeed, he claimed that he had never taken that position.

Socrates had now backed him into giving an account of his own as to how one should live one's life. What mattered was not pleasure. It was to be wise and valiant and able to carry out one's own designs, regardless of what others regarded as law or morality. That was the good, and not pleasure.[45]

Socrates then probed to see where these designs were to come from. If the good man does not choose for the sake of pleasure, then pleasures are chosen for the sake of the good. Socrates then asked, "can every man choose what pleasures are good and what are evil, or must he have art or knowledge of them in detail?" Callicles answered, "He must have art." If that is so,

> will not the good man, who says whatever he says with a view to the best, speak with a reference to some standard and not at random; just as all other artists, whether the painter, the builder, the shipwright, or any other ... do not select and apply at random what they apply, but strive to give a definite form to it? The artist disposes all things in order, and compels the one part to harmonize and accord with the other part, until he has constructed a systematic whole ... Do you deny this?

"No, I am ready to admit it." There was a standard then. If there were not, the choice of how one lived would be made "at random."

Socrates explored the consequences.

SOCRATES.	Then the house in which order and regularity prevail is good, and that in which there is disorder, evil?
CALLICLES.	Yes
SOC.	And the same is true of a ship?
CAL.	Yes.
SOC.	And the same may be said of the human body?
CAL.	Yes.
SOC.	And what would you say of the soul? Will the good soul be that in which disorder is prevalent, or that in which there is harmony and order?
CAL.	The latter follows from my previous admissions.
SOC.	What is the name which is given to the effect of harmony and order in the body?
CAL.	I suppose that you mean health and strength?

---

[45] Thus, although a number of scholars take Callicles to be defending pleasure as the end of life, Callicles repudiated this position. Brian Lieter, *Moral Psychology with Nietzsche* (Oxford, 2019), 63; Scott Consigny, "Nietzsche's Reading of the Sophists," *Rhetoric Review* 13 (1994), 5 at 16–17; Tracy B. Strong, *Friedrich Nietzsche and the Politics of Transfiguration* (Berkeley, 1988), 354, n. 67.

Soc.	Yes, I do: and what is the name which you would give to the effect of harmony and order in the soul? Try and discover a name for this as well as for the other.
Cal.	Why not give the name yourself, Socrates?
Soc.	Well, if you had rather that I should, I will; and you shall say whether you agree with me, and if not, you shall refute and answer me. "Healthy," as I conceive is the name which is given to the regular order of the body, whence comes health, and every other bodily excellence: is that true or not?
Cal.	True.
Soc.	And "lawful" and "law" are the names which are given to the regular order and action of the soul, and these make men lawful and orderly: – and so we have temperance and justice: have we not?
Cal.	Granted.

It should be with the soul, then, as it is with a house or a ship: "all things in order," "one part harmonized and in accord with the other part" in a "systematic whole." There should be "harmony and order" in the soul like that of the body when it is in health.

Some scholars believe that this passage in the *Gorgias* presents the view of Plato. Yet, as in earlier dialogues, Socrates identified knowledge with virtue, and drew an analogy to the crafts. In the *Gorgias*, he used this analogy to describe the good order of the soul. It is orderly or harmonious "by reference to some standard and not at random." Its order is like that of the parts of a house or a ship or the human body.

Later dialogues such as the *Republic* often present the views of Plato rather than Socrates. Nevertheless, Socrates' final answer to Thrasymachus in the *Republic* was like his answer to Callicles in the *Gorgias*. Thrasymachus claimed that justice is the interest of the stronger. When Socrates showed that his position, like that of Callicles, led to contradictions, Thrasymachus left the discussion. Glaucon then said to Socrates, "if you really wish to persuade us ... that to be just is always better than to be unjust ... you certainly have not succeeded."[46] Glaucon told the story of how the shepherd Gyges found a ring that would make him invisible. According to Glaucon, "no man could be imagined to be of such an iron nature that he would stand fast for justice" if such a ring enabled him to "take what he liked out of the market, or go into houses and lie with anyone at his pleasure, or to kill or release from prison whom he would, and in all respects be like a god among men."[47] Was he not better off than a just man who happens to suffer every misfortune, who is "scourged, racked, bound – will have his eyes burnt out; and, at last, after suffering every kind of evil, ... will be impaled"?[48]

As in the *Gorgias*, Socrates argued that "justice and injustice ... are like disease and health, being in the soul just what disease and health are in the body"; "virtue is the health and beauty and well-being of the soul, and vice the disease and weakness and deformity of the soul."[49] Glaucon then said that his question had been answered.

[46] *Republic* 357.
[47] Ibid. 360.
[48] Ibid. 361.
[49] Ibid. 444.

[I]n my judgment, Socrates, the question has now become ridiculous. We know that when the bodily constitution is gone, life is no longer endurable ... and shall we be told that when the very essence of the vital principle is undermined and corrupted, that life is still worth having to a man, if only he be allowed to do whatever he likes with the single exception that he is not to acquire justice and virtue, or to escape from injustice and vice ... ?[50]

Lacking harmony in his soul, "the real tyrant ... can never satisfy his desires, and behind his multitudinous wants you can see ... the real impoverishment of his character: his life is haunted by fear and ... torn by suffering and misery."[51]

In response to Callicles, Socrates said that justice and virtue are to the soul what health is to the body. In response to Yang Zhu and Mozi, Mencius said that a person's inborn qualities, when developed, would lead him to benevolence, righteousness, propriety, and knowledge. Although different, each of their answers was rooted in the same claim: that the good is founded one's nature, and that consequently, to turn against the good, in pursuit of self-gratification, is self-defeating. Indeed, it is self-destructive.

IV HUMAN NATURE AS A SOURCE OF NORMATIVE STANDARDS

The classical traditions were eclipsed by the rise of the School of Principle in China and of rationalism in the West. They rejected the tenet of these traditions that normative standards are grounded in human nature and claimed instead that normative standards are grounded in eternal and invariable principles. As we will see, since then, Chinese and Western philosophers have faced a dilemma. Normative standards are either objective or subjective. If there are such principles, they are objective. Otherwise, they are not. At a later point, we will examine why either position is unacceptable and why it has been difficult to navigate between them.

Here, we will note why the two classical traditions never faced this dilemma. If normative standards are grounded in human nature, they are as universal as human nature. If Mencius is right, every human being has principles within him that develop into benevolence, righteousness, propriety, and wisdom. If Socrates is right, there is an order in every human being which is like that of the body when it is in health. For both of them, to live wrongly is like being crippled or sick. One who chooses to do so is harming himself.

Consequently, normative standards are not objective in the sense that they depend on what Rawls called "an independent order of moral values," let alone on eternal and invariable principles. They belong to human beings as much as hunger and thirst, or as Mencius said, as much as their arms and legs.

Neither are they subjective. The claim is not merely that by acting wrongly a person thinks that he is harming himself. It is not that a human being is so constructed that he cannot help but think he is harming himself. The claim is that a human being has an inborn capacity to distinguish right from wrong. A person harms himself by doing wrong.

---

[50] Ibid. 445.
[51] Ibid. 579.

Mencius' account suggests one reason for believing such a claim, and that of Socrates another. Mencius did not refute Yang Zhu and Mozi by trying to show that their accounts of normative standards were contradictory. He did so by giving his own account which, he believed, would, upon reflection, convince a person sincerely interested in the truth. If every human being has the capacity to distinguish right from wrong, that person would recognize it in himself just as he recognizes his capacity to hunger or thirst.

Mencius' account is an instance of the propensity of Chinese philosophers to submit the truth of a proposition to internal reflection. A person who, upon reflection, says "yes, I see that I can distinguish right from wrong" needs no further argument. Mencius described our moral senses but did not attempt to prove that we have them. He gave examples that were intended to illuminate them rather than to show their logical implications for human conduct. As Robert Eno observed, "though theory making was clearly an activity Mencius engaged in," "a great deal of the ethical discussion in the Mencius seems to have little explicit connection" with the theory he presented. His goal was to provide "clear insight" but not by "the articulation of coherent theory."[52]

Before Socrates attacked Callicles' claim, he asked. "Do you, Callicles, seriously maintain what you are saying?" Callicles answered that he did.[53] Socrates told him that philosophy teaches that to do injustice and escape punishment is the worst of evils. "Her you must refute, ... or, if you leave her word unrefuted, by the dog of Egypt, I declare, O Callicles, that Callicles will never be at one with himself, but that his whole life will be a discord."[54] Callicles will not simply be logically inconsistent; the inconsistency begets a disharmony in his life that he will have to live with.

Yet the point of the dialogue is that Callicles was logically inconsistent. If he had simply denied that there was any such thing as right or wrong, it is not clear Socrates could have refuted him. But he affirmed that to live rightly was to make one's own designs and have the courage and intelligence to carry them out regardless of morality and the law. He had affirmed that a certain kind of life was good. Socrates defeated him when he conceded that the choices that governed such a life could not be made "at random," and that any good design for living must aim at a harmony like that of the body when it is healthy. Aristotle called this kind of argument "dialectical." Callicles did not simply deny the truth of moral standards but offered his own account of what it meant to live rightly which Socrates could refute by showing it was contradictory.

---

[52] Robert Eno, "Casuistry and Character in the Mencius," in Alan K. L. Chan, ed., *Mencius: Contexts and Interpretations* (Honolulu, 2002), 189 at 189. According to Mary Sim, "A Confucian could profit from Aristotle's example of a more explicit metaphysics" because it would provide a justification for moral claims that would otherwise be mere assertions. Mary Sim, *Remastering Morals with Aristotle and Confucius* (Cambridge, 2007), 131;. As Ni Peimin notes, she "seems to have taken it for granted that the absence of metaphysics means the absence of a standard of justification." Ni Peimin, "How far is Confucius an Aristotelian? Comments on Mary Sim's Remastering Morals with Aristotle and Confucius," *Dao* 8 (2009) 311, 313. Mencius did not see the need for any further justification. Moreover, Aristotle did not believe one could give such a justification of the first principles of theoretical and practical reason on which all else depends.

[53] *Gorgias* 495.

[54] Ibid. 482.

Neither Mencius nor Socrates committed what since the time of David Hume has been called "the naturalistic fallacy." The fallacy, Hans Kelsen said, is to try to infer normative standards from statements – however true – about what a human nature is like.[55] As Hume said, one cannot prove an "ought" from an "is."[56]

We can now see that writers in the two classical traditions such as Mencius and Socrates never attempted to do so. Their claim was not that because a human is what he is, there are certain ways in which he ought to behave. Their claim was that a human being is so constructed that he is capable of knowing how he ought to behave. Mencius left the truth of that claim to inner reflection of people who, if he is right about how human beings are constructed, would be good and wise enough to recognize its truth. Socrates' method was to show that anyone who presented a conflicting account of normative standards would in the end contradict himself. In any event, any claim about how a person ought to behave had to be based on knowledge of right and wrong that a person already possessed. Neither tried to prove what ought to be from what is.

---

[55]   Hans Kelsen, "The Natural-Law Doctrine before the Tribunal of Science," *The Western Political Quarterly* 2 (1949), 481 at 483.
[56]   David Hume, *Treatise of Human Nature* (Oxford, 1888), 3.1.1.27.

4

A Normative Psychology

Chinese and Western classical thought began with the challenge of Confucius and Socrates to the way most people live their lives. They neglect what is "worthy." They "undervalue the greater, and overvalue the rest."

When asked why any life was worthy or of value, philosophers in both traditions said that normative standards are grounded in human nature. Yet if it is so, why do people neglect what is worthy and undervalue what is good? Why should human beings have any difficulty living the life that is natural to them? All human beings have desires and fears that are obstacles to living a good life. If these desires and fears also arise from human nature, they would seem to be part of that nature as much as inclinations toward good. Why would an evil life be any less human?

Answering those questions required an account of human psychology that explained why there are inclinations of both kinds. Such an account would be both descriptive and normative. It would describe how human inclinations actually arise. It would be normative in that it would recognize that some of them are good and others evil.

It would be different than that of Sigmund Freud. In his account, fears and desires arise from the id. To an extent, a person's conscious mind (ego) can deal with them. Yet he may be unaware of some of the most disturbing. Among them are some of the most terrible that can be imagined: a desire for sex with one's mother; a fear of being castrated by one's father. The repression of these feelings may be crippling. To deal with them, the ego must bring them to consciousness. At the same time, a person must deal with prohibitions and values that have their source in the superego. They are a source of guilt, which again can be crippling. A therapist can help a patient deal with repressed desires and guilt, and so promote a state of psychological health in which the id, the ego, and the superego are kept in balance.

As we will see, although the classical accounts of the personality are quite different, they assign roles to three similar elements: fears and desires, a conscious mind that can play a role in directing thought and action, and normative standards. Unlike Freud, they maintained that a human being could recognize that life should be lived according to these normative standards; that he can develop the ability to deal with the fears and desires that stand in the way, and that by doing so he is better off and living in harmony with his own nature.

From their point of view, Freud was wrong about human beings and psychological health. They might have said that he did not describe a human being but a monstrosity, plagued by potentially uncontrollable desires too terrible to be easily acknowledged and subservient to normative standards that he had internalized without understanding their contribution to a good and healthy life. Or they might have said that Freud gave a good description of how the world would look to someone suffering from a severe psychological disorder. Such a person might feel pursued by fears and desires which he could not understand and possibly could not control. These fears and desires might be unrelated to anything that could harm or benefit him, and in that sense, have no basis in reality. Such a person might feel chained by moral standards that had no relationship, so far as he could see, to living a genuinely good or healthy life, and yet which he could not throw off. When he violated them, he might feel an irrational sense of guilt. It would be irrational because it would not be based on an understanding of how he might have harmed himself by acting wrongfully, and consequently, it might be out of proportion to any harm he had done. According to Freud, however, that is the state of a normal person who must deal as best as he can with his repressions and his sense of guilt.

Philosophers in the classical traditions explained the fears and desires that are obstacles to living a good life in three ways. One was to deny that they had their source in human nature. That was the view of Mencius. Another was to say that there was a conflict within human nature: in order to live a good life, these desires had to be restrained. That was the view of Socrates and Plato. A third was to say that although these fears and desires could be obstacles to living a good life, they could be reshaped, harmonized or trained to contribute to it. That approach was taken by Xunzi, Dai Zhen, and Aristotle. They did not subscribe to a single account of human nature but gave different accounts, no one of which was characteristically Chinese or characteristically Western.

I NOURISHING INNER GOODNESS: MENCIUS

Mencius believed that human nature is good and the feelings proper to human nature are good.[1] All of them contribute to living rightly. They need only be allowed to develop. "From the feelings proper to him, man is constituted for the practice of what is good. This is what I mean in saying that the nature is good. If men do what is not good, the blame cannot be attributed to their natural powers."[2]

According to Mencius, as noted earlier, a good person possesses four attributes: benevolence (仁 *ren*), righteousness (義 *yi*), propriety (禮 *li*), and wisdom (智 *zhi*). They grow from inborn capacities for compassion, shame, respect and "sense of right and wrong."[3] "[M]en have these four capacities just as they have their four limbs."[4]

---

[1] Mencius rejected the view of Confucian writers who had said that human nature is both bad and good. Wang Chong (王充), writing in the first century AD, mentioned some of those with whom he disagreed: Shi Shi, Fu Tzu-Chien, and [Gongsun] Ni. Alfred Forke, *Essays of Wang Ch'ung, Lun Heng Part 1* (New York, 1962), 384. If the tendencies that lead to evil belonged to human nature, they would be as natural as those that lead to good.
[2] *Mencius* 6A6.5–6.
[3] Ibid. 6A6.7.
[4] Ibid.

For a person to possess these four attributes, all that is necessary is that these feelings be allowed to develop, as Mencius said, like the growth of barley. If the development of a human being is warped or stunted, as with barley, that result is not due to his nature but the conditions in which he develops. With barley, "[a]lthough there may be inequalities of produce, that is owing to the difference of the soil, as rich or poor, to the unequal nourishment afforded by the rains and dews, and to the different ways in which man has performed his business in reference to it."[5]

The source of evil, then, is not to be found in human nature, but in the adverse conditions in which human beings may be nurtured and the external forces that may stunt their growth. "[I]f it receives its proper nourishment, there is nothing which will not grow. If it loses its proper nourishment, there is nothing which will not decay away."[6] Mencius used the analogy of a once beautiful mountain. "The trees of the Ox Mountain were once beautiful. Being situated, however, in the borders of a large state, they were hewn down with axes and bills, how could they retain their beauty?"[7]

Consequently, people are initially alike. "[A]ll things which are the same in kind are alike to one another. . . . The sage and we are the same in kind."[8] The difference is in the development of the capacities that all people have in common.

There are two faculties that protect and nourish the development of these capacities. One is *xin* (心) which is sometimes translated as "mind." The other is *zhi* (志) which is sometimes translated as "will." The trouble with these translations is that Mencius was not contrasting "knowing" and "willing." As we will see later, he did not separate cognition and volition. For Mencius, as Kwong-loi Shun noted, the mind (心 *xin*) is "the seat of both affective and cognitive activities."[9] It is attracted to the good and also understands the good. Consequently, *xin* is a hard word to translate. It is sometimes translated not as "mind," but as "heart and mind" or "heart." There is a similar difficulty translating word *zhi*. Sometimes it is translated as "will," and some as "the directions of the mind."

Xin enables a person to protect the growth of feelings that are proper to humanity from others which are not. *Zhi* enables one to be steadfast. It fosters and directs the spirited part of a person from which he derives his courage.

By attending to the feelings that it approves, which are proper to humanity, *xin* wards off desires and aversions that could stunt the growth of these feelings. A person wards them off, as David Nivison put it, by "cognitively focusing attention on the mind's moral object."[10] Mencius said,

---

[5] Ibid. 6A7.2.
[6] Ibid. 6A8.3.
[7] Ibid. 6A8.1–2.
[8] Ibid. 6A7.3.
[9] Kwong-loi Shun, *Mencius and Early Chinese Thought* (Stanford, 1997), 48; Donald J. Munro, *The Concept of Man in Early China* (Stanford, 1989), 50. Similarly, as David Nivison said, for Mencius, "thinking is a voluntary seeking as well as a cognitive focusing on the good." David S. Nivison, "Weakness of the Will in Ancient Chinese Philosophy," in David S. Nivison, *The Ways of Confucianism Investigations in Chinese Philosophy* (Chicago, 1996), 79 at 87.
[10] *Mencius* 7A3.l.

[I]n the calm air of the morning, just between night and day, the mind feels in a degree those desires and aversions which are proper to humanity, but the feeling is not strong, and it is fettered and destroyed by what takes place during the day. This fettering taking place again and again, the restorative influence of the night is not sufficient to preserve the proper goodness of the mind; and when this proves insufficient for that purpose, the nature becomes not much different from that of the irrational animals, and when people now see it, they think that it never had those powers which I assert. But does this condition represent the feelings proper to humanity?[11]

For Mencius, the "desires and aversions which are proper to humanity" are harmonious. They need to be protected by xin from others that can "fetter and destroy" them.

Zhi, the will or the directions of the mind, enables one to remain steadfast. It can do so because it governs qi (氣). Qi is a force that enables a person to avoid weakness, whether in his own conduct or in governing others. Mencius borrowed the idea of qi from The Doctrine of the Mean, ascribed to Confucius' disciple Zisi, where it is said: "The superior man cultivates a friendly harmony, without being weak. How firm is he in his qi! He stands erect in the middle, without inclining to either side. How firm is he in his qi!"[12]

For Mencius as well, qi is a force associated with courage. It needs to be "skillfully nourished" so that it becomes "vast" and "flowing."[13] Qi is not like the four feelings that develop into benevolence, righteousness, propriety and wisdom. Those feelings, if nourished, grow in a definite direction like grains of barley. Qi must be directed by zhi – the will, or the direction of the mind. "The zhi is the leader of the qi." "The zhi is first and chief, and the qi is subordinate to it."[14] If the qi is not subordinate, it will take its own course and move the zhi along with it, instead of the other way around.[15] Mencius said, "keep the zhi firm."[16]

A difficulty with Mencius' solution is that it did not explain where the desires and fears that thwart human development come from, if not from human nature. Some later Confucians rejected it. In the Han dynasty, Yang Xiong (揚雄) said that human nature is a combination of good and evil. He pointed out that in Mencius' own account, not all of one's inborn tendencies tend toward good. Qi does not. It tends toward good or evil depending on how it is directed.[17]

In the Song dynasty, the scholar-statesman Wang Anshi (王安石) said that both good and evil tendencies belong to human nature, presenting this view as an interpretation of Mencius.[18] Mencius had said that when one turns toward evil, one is scarcely human. One is like the irrational animals. Wang concluded: "It is all right to say that when one

---

[11]   Mencius 6A8.1–2.
[12]   Doctrine of the Mean X.5.
[13]   Ibid. 2A2.11.
[14]   Ibid. 2A2.9
[15]   Ibid. 2A2.10.
[16]   Ibid. 2A2.9.
[17]   Fang yan (方言) 3:2, quoted in Wing-tsit Chan, "Taoistic Confucianism: Yang Hsiung," in Wing-tsit Chan, ed., A Source Book in Chinese Philosophy (Princeton, 1963), 289.
[18]   Peter K. Bol, "This Culture of Ours": Intellectual Transitions in T'ang and Sung China (Stanford, 1992), 226.

leaves the good for the evil, his nature (*xing*) is lost ... One may say that he has lost his nature but not that his nature has no evil."[19]

For Mencius, however, it was critical that human nature is good. If it were a combination of good and evil tendencies, the evil ones would be as much a part of human nature as the good. One could no longer maintain that by following his good tendencies, a person completes his nature and that "his nature is lost" by following his bad ones. Mencius might have answered Yang that *qi* is not bad in itself but should be fostered, and that it leads to good when directed by *zhi* – the will or directions of the mind.

II MASTERING INNER CONFLICT: SOCRATES AND PLATO

In the *Gorgias*, as we have seen, Socrates said that in the "good soul" there is "harmony and order," and in the bad soul there is "disorder." This harmony is achieved when one is "master of himself, and the ruler of his own pleasures and passions." Are pleasures and passions part of one's soul or not? If not, then to be master of oneself is to resist their influence, and to rule them is to bring them under one's control, as one would threatening forces that are outside oneself. Or is the source of pleasure and passion within one's soul although they must be mastered? Both images of the soul figure in the *Phaedo*, the *Phraedrus*, and the *Republic*. All three dialogues were written after the *Gorgias*, but so close to each other in time that one cannot tell in what order they were written. It is hard to tell how much of the thought is that of Socrates or of Plato.

The *Phaedo* is set in Socrates' prison cell as he awaits death. Death, he says, is the separation of the soul from the body. The body is the source of the pleasures and passions that interfere with the operations of the soul. "Real philosophers" understand

> that while we are in the body, our desire will not be satisfied, and our desire is for the truth. For the body is a source of endless trouble to us by reason of the mere requirement of food; and is liable also to diseases which overtake and impede us in the search after true being; it fills us full of loves, and lusts, and fears, and fancies of all kinds, and endless foolery, and, in fact, as men say, takes away the power of thinking at all. ...[B]y reason of all these impediments we have no time to give to philosophy; and last, and worst of all, even if we are at leisure and betake ourselves to some speculation, the body is always breaking in upon us, causing turmoil and confusion in our enquiries, and so amazing us that we are prevented from seeing the truth.[20]

Since the soul is better off without the body, death is a blessing "[f]or then, and not til then, the soul will be parted from the body and exist in herself alone."[21]

In contrast, in the *Republic* it is said that "in the human soul there is a better and also a worse principle; and when the better has the worse under control, then a man is said to be master of himself."[22] It is impossible that "the same thing, in the same part or in relation to

---

[19] Bol, *"This Culture of Ours"* 226 n. 74.
[20] *Phaedo* 66.
[21] Ibid. 66–67.
[22] *Republic* 431.

the same thing, can act or be acted upon in contrary ways."[23] Part of the soul must therefore seek pleasure because the soul can be drawn to opposite courses of action, for example, to drink or eat, or not to do so, by desire and reason, respectively. There must also be a third part, which is passionate or spirited, which sometimes goes against desire and sometimes against reason. It goes against desire when one rouses oneself to resist indulging in food or drink. Sometimes, it goes against reason, as when one acts out of anger.[24]

Earlier in the *Republic*, Plato described the "perfectly adjusted nature" as one in which these three elements are "bound together" so that a person "is no longer many, [he] has become one entirely temperate and perfectly adjusted nature."[25] Yet later in the *Republic*, Plato had Socrates say that we cannot believe "the soul, in her truest nature, to be full of variety and difference and dissimilarity. ... The soul ... being ... immortal must be the fairest of compositions and cannot be compounded of many elements."[26]

In the *Phaedrus*, he explained "in what way the mortal differs from the immortal soul." When "perfect and fully winged, she soars upward"; the "imperfect soul, losing her wings" comes to down earth, "receives an earthly frame ... and this composition of soul and body is called a living and mortal creature."[27] He also described the soul "in a figure:" "let the figure be composite – a pair of winged horses and a charioteer."[28] The charioteer and two horses are like the three elements of the soul described in the *Republic*: reason, desire, and the spirited part. For reason, for "the human charioteer," "driving them gives a great deal of trouble."[29]

Plato may have described the soul in inconsistent ways because he believed that the true nature of the soul could not be described. In the *Phaedrus*, he spoke "in a figure." He said that "the nature of the soul" and "her true form" is "ever a theme ... of more than mortal discourse."[30] In the *Republic*, he said "we have seen her in a condition which may be compared to the sea-god Glaucus, whose original image can hardly be discerned because his natural members are broken off and crushed and damages by the waves in all sorts of ways, and incrustations have grown over them of seaweed and shells and stones, so that he is more like some monster than he is to his own natural form."[31]

The descriptions of the soul are not only various but attuned to the dialogues in which they appear. In the *Phaedo*, in which Socrates awaited death, the discussion concerned the afterlife in which the soul would be separated from the body. The *Republic* dealt with the just constitution of the state in which the citizens are divided into three classes which correspond to three parts of the soul. The *Phraedus* concerned *eros*, a love which animates the charioteer and leads him toward an earthly beauty which resembles eternal beauty. It is a love that may be perfected or corrupted depending on whether the unruly horse is kept under control.

---

[23] Ibid. 436–37.
[24] Ibid. 439–41.
[25] Ibid. 443.
[26] Ibid. 611.
[27] *Phaedrus* 246.
[28] Ibid.
[29] Ibid.
[30] Ibid.
[31] *Republic* 611.

Having conceived of the problem as he did, it is not surprising that Plato found no single coherent description of how the soul was constituted. Desires and passions are not, as they were for Mencius, tendencies toward the good that needed only to ripen. They do not seem to belong to the order that Socrates described in the *Gorgias* which is like that of the parts of a ship, a house, or the human body in which each part contributes to the good of the whole. It is hard to see what they contribute.

III ACHIEVING HARMONY

i *Xunzi*

Xunzi (荀子) wrote in the generation after Mencius. He believed that Mencius was mistaken to think that a person's inborn tendencies need only to be nourished for him to flourish like grain or the trees on the Ox Mountain. "Those who maintain that nature is good praise and approve whatever has not departed from the original simplicity and naïveté of the child, that is, they consider that beauty belongs to the original mind in the same way that clear sight is inseparable from the eye and keen hearing from the ear."[32] If that were so, it would be enough to protect the child's original simplicity and naïveté from outside influences.

Mencius' mistake was that "he has not ... distinguished properly between basic nature and conscious activity." A person is born with tendencies that could only lead to evil unless shaped by conscious activity. In Xunzi's vocabulary, these tendencies belonged to a person's "basic nature" or "human nature." He concluded "human nature is evil."

> Human nature is such that people are born with a fondness for profit. If they indulge this fondness, wrangling and strife will arise, and all sense of courtesy and humility will perish. People are born with feelings of envy and hate, and if they indulge these, violence and crime will arise, and all sense of loyalty and honesty will disappear. People are born with the desires of the eyes and ears, with a fondness for beautiful sights and sounds. If they indulge these, prurience and chaos will arise, and all sense of propriety, righteousness, form, and principle will be lost. Hence, anyone who follows their nature and indulges their emotions will inevitably become involved in wrangling and strife, will violate norms in social division and order, and will end up a criminal. Therefore, people must first be transformed by the instructions of a teacher and guided by principles of propriety, and only then will they be able to observe the dictates of courtesy and humility, obey the norms and rules of society, and achieve order. It is obvious from this, then, that human nature is evil, and that any goodness is the result of conscious effort.[33]

His statement that "human nature is evil" is easy to misunderstand. As Donald Munro noted, Xunzi did not mean that human nature is evil without qualification.[34] "[T]here must be

---

[32] *Xunzi* 23. Again, I thank Tong Xu, with whom I discussed the original text (http://ctext.org/xunzi/zh). Throughout, translations are based on her suggestions and on Hsün Tzu, *Basic Writings*, trans. Burton Watson (New York, 1963), and *Xunzi: A Translation and Study of the Complete Works*, trans. John Knoblock (Stanford, 1988).

[33] Ibid.

[34] Munro, *Concept of Man* 178.

a potentiality in man that emerges … when one has taken the necessary steps to draw it out."[35] One's nature is "that part of man which cannot be learned or acquired by effort." Another "part of him" is "conscious activity" which can be acquired by learning and brought to completion by effort." Both are parts of a human being, and both are necessary for human perfection, even though Xunzi uses the word "nature" to describe only the first.

Both are necessary because "nature" is the raw material which "conscious activity" shapes by providing form and principle. According to Xunxi:

> Inborn nature is the root and beginning, the raw material and original constitution. Conscious activity is the form and principle of order, the development and completion. If there were no inborn nature, there would be nothing for conscious activity to improve; if there were no conscious exertion, then inborn nature could not refine itself. Only after inborn nature and conscious exertion have been conjoined is the concept of the sage perfected, and the merit uniting the world brought to fulfillment.[36]

He did not suggest, as some scholars have thought, that human nature also includes tendencies toward good[37]; nor, as others have said, that natural feelings are merely to be overridden or restrained.[38] They need to be shaped. Other scholars have observed that it is hard to see how conscious thought can reshape these tendencies if they are morally neutral.[39] Xunzi, at any rate, regarded them as potentially good, and able to assume the form provided by conscious activity.

---

[35] Ibid. Similarly, according to A. S. Cua, Xunzi thought that the "feelings and desires" that comprise one's nature "themselves are morally neutral." "To characterize man's nature as 'bad' is, in effect, a short-hand way of asserting the nature of the consequences" that can result if it is not restrained. A. S. Cua, "The Conceptual Aspect of Hsŭn Tsu's Philosophy of Human Nature," *Philosophy East and West* 27 (1977), 373 at 378.

[36] *Xunzi* 19.2d. Thus the world can be brought to a fulfillment which is harmonious and good. It is hard to see a conflict, as Derk Bodde does, between this view and the "Chinese conviction … that the universe is a harmony, the basic principle of which is … one of goodness." Derk Bodde, "Harmony and Conflict in Chinese Philosophy," in Arthur F. Wright, ed., *Studies in Chinese Thought* (Chicago, 1953), 19 at 39.

[37] D. C. Lau, *Mencius* (New York, 1970), 21; see A. C. Graham, *Disputers of the Tau* (La Salle, 1989), 250. They suggest that he did not really disagree with Mencius. But Xunzi did not mention these good tendencies, and as Bryan Van Norden noted, it would surprise Xunzi greatly to learn that he and Mencius did not really disagree. Bryan W. Van Norden, "Mengzi and Xunzi; Two Views of Moral Agency," *International Philosophical Quarterly* 32 (1992), 161 at 161. Andrew Cheng tried to soften Xunzi's position by claiming that "[h]e conceive-[d] of evil as a moral failure instead of innate wickedness." Andrew Cheng, *Hsŭn Tsu's Theory of Human Nature and Its Influence on Chinese Thought* (Peking, 1928), 42. As A. S. Cua noted, Cheng merely substituted the phrase "moral failure" for "evil." Cua, "Conceptual Aspect of Hsŭn Tsu's Philosophy" 378.

[38] Homer H. Dubs, "Mencius and Sun-tzu on Human Nature," *Philosophy East and West* 6 (1956), 213.

[39] According to Van Norden, "the beginner in moral cultivation … is capable of making herself do what she does not yet desire to do" but he did not explain why she wants to do what she does not yet desire. Van Norden, "Mengzi and Xunzi" 183. P. J. Ivanhoe said that for Xunxi "we begin life in a state of complete moral blindness" which raises a similar problem. P. J. Ivanhoe, "Human Nature and Moral Understanding in Xunzi," *International Philosophical Quarterly* 34 (1994), 167 at 173. David Nivison thought that Xunxi envisioned a sort of utilitarian calculus. Xunzi meant that "if prudent and intelligent, one will see that one must be conditioned and changed in education before one can live that life, and will submit oneself to the necessary conditioning." Nivison said so because he believed that "for Xunzi, in the end, the good is good because it is satisfying and we are predisposed to seek satisfaction; whereas for Mencius, the good is satisfying because it is good, and we are predisposed to like the good." Nivison, "Weakness of the Will" 86–87. On the contrary, for Xunzi, as for Mencius, the good is satisfying because it is good.

Conscious activity provides form through *li* (禮), one of the moral qualities described by Mencius. It was translated "propriety." The rules of *li* govern conduct in recurring social situations: for example, greeting another, showing respect, marrying, burying the dead, and honoring one's ancestors.[40] The rules that govern these situations are formal. Thus *li* is often translated as "ritual" or "rites." According to Xunzi, they are "the highest expression of order and discrimination."[41] In the beginning, the emotions are coarse, but "all rites begin with coarseness, are brought to fulfillment with form, and end with pleasure and beauty. Rites reach their highest perfection when both emotion and form are fully realized."[42] "It is through rites that the individual is rectified. It is by means of a teacher that rites are rectified. . . . When you make so in your own conduct what ritual mandates, your emotions will find peace in rites."[43]

The result will be delight. "When [the worthy man] has reached the limit of such perfection, he finds delight in it."[44] "When a man sees good, being filled with delight, he is sure to preserve it within himself."[45] So for Xunzi, as for Mencius, the good is satisfying because it is good. As for Mencius, human beings are so constituted that they can recognize the good and pursue it, although he uses the term "human nature" to refer only to those tendencies which are the raw material for a good life. "Fire and water possess energy but are without life. Grass and trees have life but no intelligence. Birds and beasts have intelligence but no sense of duty. Man possesses energy, life, intelligence, and, in addition, a sense of duty. Therefore he is the noblest being on earth."[46]

Li prescribes, for example, how a person should respond to joyful occasions such as the birth of a child or to sad ones such as the death of a parent. It can "trim or stretch," "broaden or narrow" the feelings of joy or sorrow so as to "express them completely and properly, fully and beautifully."[47]

Similarly,

> Music is joy, an emotion which man cannot help but feel at times. Since man cannot help feeling joy, his joy must find an outlet in voice and an expression in movement. The outcries and movements, and the inner emotional changes which occasion them, must be given full expression in accordance with the way of man. Man must have his joy, and joy must have its expression, but if that expression is not guided by the principles of the Way, then it will inevitably become disordered.[48]

Xunzi objected strongly to the teachings of Mozi. "The Confucians make it possible for a man to satisfy . . . both his human desires and the demands of *li*; the Mohists cause him to

---

40 Shun, *Mencius* 52.
41 *Xunzi* 15.4.
42 Ibid. 19.2c.
43 Ibid. 2.11.
44 Ibid. 1.14.
45 Ibid. 2.1.
46 Ibid. 9.
47 Ibid. 19.
48 Ibid. 20.

satisfy neither."[49] Mozi was "obsessed by utilitarian considerations and did not understand the beauties of form."[50] The same considerations explain the value of music. "And yet," Xunzi repeatedly objected, "Mozi criticizes it? Why?"[51]

ii *Dai Zhen's Reconstruction of Mencius*

The Place of Dai Zhen in the Confucian Tradition

Chung-ying Cheng (成中英 *Zhongying Cheng*) observed: "There are four stages in the development of Confucian thought that should command our attention. The first stage concerned the formulation of Classical Confucianism in the works of Confucius, Mencius and [Xunzi]."[52] This is the stage we have considered so far. We will now skip to the fourth, which culminated in the reconstruction of the philosophy of Mencius by Dai Zhen (戴震) (1724–77).

Were we writing a history of Chinese philosophy, we would not reach Dai Zhen until nearly the end of the book. As we noted at the outset, however, our concern is with how thinkers in different times and places, sometimes building on each other's work and sometimes working independently, faced and resolved similar ethical and political problems. Dai Zhen, like Mencius and Xunzi centuries before, was working on a problem that arose because he, like them, grounded normative standards on human nature. Consequently, like them, he needed to account for the desires and fears that are obstacles to a good life.

Before examining how he did so, a word is in order first about what happened in the second and third stages of the development of Confucian thought which, for the present, we are bypassing.

In the second stage, Confucianism was accepted as the official philosophy of the Han dynasty. Dong Zhongshu (董仲舒) (c. 197–104 BC) and others reshaped that philosophy into what Anthony Hulsewé called "Imperial Confucianism."[53] Cheng described it as "a closed and stratified system of five agencies and two forces (陰陽 *yin-yang*) which was "pseudoscientific in the sense of being explanatory, even capable of providing predictions, but without being founded on experimentation."[54] As Cheng noted, despite the "cosmological elaborations," Han Confucianism preserved "the Classical Confucian ideal of man's nature and its fulfillment."[55] Nevertheless, as it did little to interpret or develop this ideal, Han Confucianism will not play a part in our narrative.

In a third stage,[56] the works of Confucius and Mencius were reinterpreted by the School of Principle founded by Cheng Yi (程頤) (1033–1107) and Zhu Xi (朱熹) (1130–1200). Their

---

[49] Ibid.
[50] Ibid. 21.
[51] Ibid. 20.
[52] Chung-ying Cheng, "Introduction," to Tai Chên, *Inquiry into Goodness* (Honolulu, 1971), 3 at 4.
[53] A. F. P. Hulsewé, *Remnants of Han Law* (Leiden, 1985), 5.
[54] Cheng, "Introduction" 8.
[55] Ibid.
[56] Ibid. 9–10.

work, as we will see, rejected the classical Confucian ideal of human nature and its fulfillment, as did its chief adversary, the School of Universal Mind (陸王心學 *Lu-Wang xin xue*), founded by Lu Xiangshan (陸象山) (1139–93) and Wang Yangming (王陽明) (1472–1529). We will discuss the work of these two schools, often called "neo-Confucian," when we describe the eclipse of the classical tradition.

According to Cheng, the "final and fourth stage of Confucian development … was a critical one, because it was in this stage that serious criticism was launched against the orthodox Neo-Confucianism … of the Cheng-Zhu school."[57] It began in the late Ming dynasty and was marked by a renewed concern with human nature. As Cheng noted, it "was not given an explicit, systematic and comprehensive formulation and justification" until a "positive Confucian philosophy was formulated by [Dai Zhen] … who represents the culmination of the movement against Neo-Confucianism" and "the constructive apex of the critical Confucianism of the Ming-[Qing] Era."[58]

We will skip, then, to the work of Dai Zhen. Although he based his account of human nature on Mencius, it was a reconstruction and reinterpretation of Mencius' teachings. In Cheng's view it was a successful one:

> [That it is a] restoration may be disputed were it to be understood in a literal sense; if, however, the restoration were to be understood as an attempt to reconstruct and reinterpret Classical Confucianism in the spirit of Confucius, Mencius, and other authors of the Classical Confucian writers, I cannot but admire [Dai Zhen's] ingenuity and his original contribution to Confucian thought.[59]

Dai Zhen wrote at a time when the Cheng-Zhu School remained orthodox, and most philosophically minded scholars accepted its teachings. Scholars who were less interested in philosophy developed the so-called Han Learning (漢學), a great intellectual innovation of the Qing dynasty, in which ancient texts were studied with techniques of philology like those developed in the West by the Renaissance humanists. Their method was to compare each instance in which a particular word or phrase was used in a text or series of texts with every other. The objective was to arrive at the meaning of the texts to their authors.

Much of Han Learning concerned the historical development of Chinese characters and the correction of ancient texts. Its practitioners produced authoritative versions of these texts that are still in use. Throughout the eighteenth and nineteenth centuries, there was a tension between their work and the tenets of the School of Principle. Adherents of the School claimed that their account was not only philosophically correct but a faithful interpretation of the teachings of Confucius and Mencius. As Torbjörn Lodén observed, the new "textual criticism tended to undermine the authority of [their] philological scholarship. … It is hard to believe that the philological criticism … did not also to some degree undermine the philosophical authority of Neo-Confucian scholars" of the School of Principle. Nevertheless, rather than taking issue with the tenets of the School, many of the critics dismissed "philosophical

---

[57] Ibid. 12.
[58] Ibid. 13.
[59] Ibid. 30.

questions as inviting 'empty talk' in this age of 'seeking truth from facts.'"[60] They lived in an intellectual world of their own in which philosophical questions were not their concern.

The great exception, as Lodén noted, was Dai Zhen. "He saw textual criticism as a *means* for clarifying philosophical questions." Yet, although he was recognized as a leading textual critic, "his sharp criticism of *li xue* [the School of Principle] alienated even some of his closest friends and admires and was never much commented on by Dai Zhen's contemporaries. It was really only after the major crises in the 19th century that Dai Zhen's philosophy began to attract attention."[61]

Like other practitioners of Han Learning, and like the Renaissance humanists, Dai Zhen studied ancient texts in context, by comparing each instance in which a particular word or phrase was used with every other. It is not surprising that his reading of Mencius was more faithful to the original texts than that of Cheng Yi or Zhu Xi. Dai Zhen made one assumption, however, that a modern philologist would not. He believed that words and phrases were used consistently in all of the pre-Qin dynasty texts. A word or phrase in the *Mencius* must be consistent with its meaning in the *Analects*, compiled by the disciples of Confucius, and the *Doctrine of the Mean*, attributed to his grandson Zisi (c. 481–402 BC). A modern philologist might make this assumption in dealing with texts written by a single author such as Cicero, but he would be wary when the texts were written by several authors, particularly by authors centuries apart. Dai Zhen's assumption led him to integrate the meaning of *Mencius* with that of the *Analects* and the *Doctrine of the Mean*. He produced a philosophically coherent whole, a task that owed as much to his philosophical insight as to his skill in philology. It also owed much to the renewed concern with human nature.

Principle (*li* 理) and Desire (欲 *yu*)

For the School of Principle, as we will see, normative standards were grounded on eternal and immutable principles – *li* – hence the name of the School. *Li* (理), meaning principle, is pronounced the same way as *li* (禮), meaning propriety, but the Chinese characters are different and unrelated. For Dai Zhen, there were no eternal and immutable principles but only the principles of "concrete objects or affairs."[62]

Each thing had its own principle. Dai Zhen said:

> The word "principle" is a name assigned to the arrangement of the parts of anything which gives the whole its distinctive property or characteristic, and which can be observed by careful examination of the parts down to the most minute detail. ... When proper differentiation is made, there will be order without confusion. This is called "order and arrangement" (条理 *tiao li*).[63]

[60] Torbjörn Lodén, "Dai Zhen and the Question of the Social Dynamics of Confucian Thought," *Cina* No. 21, *XXXth European Conference of Chinese Studies Proceedings* (1988), 205 at 213.

[61] Ibid.

[62] Wolfgang Ommerborn, "Dai Zhens Konzeption des 'li' und seine Kritik an der 'Li'-Theorie der Cheng-Zhu-Schule," *Archiv für Begriffsgeschichte* 42 (2000), 9 at 29, 31.

[63] Dai Zhen 1. art. 1.1; *Tai Chen on Mencius* art. 1, p. 69. Again, I thank Tong Xu, with whom I discussed the original text (http://ctext.org/wiki.pl?if=gb&chapter=554927). Throughout, translations are based on her

The principle is the pure and correct order of a thing when it is "realized." "[B]y returning to what is necessary, the principles of Heaven, earth, men, things, and affairs are realized."[64]

Dai Zhen noted that "the word 'principle' does not often appear in the Six Classics, in the works of Confucius and Mencius, or in commentaries or in other historical records."[65] Mencius said, "the mind of all men approves the principles (理 *li*) of our nature, and the determinations of righteousness (義 *yi*)."[66] In the *Doctrine of the Mean*, Zisi used the metaphor of the ax handle from the *Book of Odes*.

> It is said, "In hewing an ax handle, the pattern (理 *li*) is not far off." We grasp one ax handle to hew the other; and yet, if we look from the one to the other, we may consider them as apart. Therefore, the worthy man governs men, according to their nature, with what is proper to them, and as soon as they change what is wrong, he stops.[67]

Zisi spoke of "the nature of animals and things" which can also reach "full development."[68]

According to Dai Zhen, in these passages, *li* referred to the principle of concrete things such as human beings, animals, and axes. A huge mistake had been made when the founders of the School of Principle regarded *li* as an eternal principle that transcends concrete things and has a mode of existence of its own. Dai Zhen asked, "[i]n the Classics, Confucius and Mencius, how could you take *li* as if it were an object that is outside the emotions and desires manifested by human nature?"[69] Certainly, the School of Principle had done so. Had they not, however, Dai Zhen might not have brought *li* down from the sky, so to speak, and concluded that there was a *li* of concrete things.

To live rightly is to live in accord with principle. The *li* of human nature governs the order that should prevail among human desires (欲 *yu*). "Heavenly principle (天理 *tian li*) refers to desires being restrained, not overly indulged. . . . To have desires but at the same time to monitor them so that they do not become excessive or insufficient – can one say that this is not in accord with Heavenly principle?"[70]

On the negative side, desires must be monitored so that they accord with principle.

> Human nature may be compared to water, and desires to the flow of water. If one keeps one's desires within bounds, he is acting in accordance with Heavenly principle (天理 *tian li*). . . . When a man indulges his desires to the point where his mind becomes rebellious and deceitful so that he commits wicked acts and causes disturbances, his actions are analogous to a flood out of control inundating the Middle Kingdom.[71]

---

suggestions and on *Tai Chen on Mencius*, trans. Ann-ping Chin and Mansfied Freeman (New Haven, 1990). Since the citation system differs, parallel citations will be given to that translation.

[64] Dai Zhen 1. art. 1.1; *Tai Chen on Mencius* art. 1, p. 69.
[65] Dai Zhen 1. art. 1.9; *Tai Chen on Mencius* art. 5, p. 74.
[66] *Mencius* 6A7.8.
[67] *Doctrine of the Mean* X.2.
[68] Ibid. XXII.
[69] Dai Zhen 1. art. 1.19; *Tai Chen on Mencius* art. 1, p. 70.
[70] Dai Zhen 1. art. 1.25; *Tai Chen on Mencius* art. 11, p. 86.
[71] Dai Zhen art. 1.21, *Tai Chen on Mencius* art. 11, pp. 85–86.

On the positive side, desires contribute to a good life.[72] Their contribution is indispensable. Mencius said that benevolence, righteousness, propriety, and wisdom develop from inborn capacities to feel compassion, shame, respect, and "sense of right and wrong." Dai Zhen concluded that, in the view of the "ancient worthy sages ... benevolence, righteousness, propriety and wisdom were never sought outside of what they called desires."[73] He went further. The entire range of human desires is necessary for the development of these virtues.

> If one were to eliminate all that moves us such as eating, drinking and relations between the sexes, in order to return to quietness and oneness, then how could there be shame and dislike, deference, and right and wrong ...? From this it is clear that what we call benevolence, righteousness, propriety and wisdom is nothing more than cherishing life and fearing death, eating, drinking relations of the sexes, and everything that stimulates us – which cannot be eliminated.[74]

Consequently, "[w]hat the ancient virtuous sages called the virtues of benevolence, righteousness, propriety and wisdom were never sought outside of what they called desires."[75]

iii The Aristotelian Tradition

Aristotle's place in the classical Western tradition is different than that of Socrates or Plato. In the ancient world, Aristotle was one philosopher among many. In the medieval world, he was, in the words of Thomas Aquinas, "the philosopher," and in the words of Dante, "the teacher of those who know." He retained that status for a long time. Hugo Grotius (1583–1645), the founder of the northern natural law school, said that "among philosophers, Aristotle takes the foremost place."[76] Thomas Hobbes (1588–1679) complained that Aristotle's teachings dominated "the Philosophy-schooles, through all the Universities of Christendome."[77] Samuel Pufendorf (1632–94) lamented the belief of most educated people that Aristotle had reached a summit beyond which the human mind could not advance.[78] The tradition that Aristotle founded and that others shaped became preeminent in the West and, indeed, as close to orthodox as any Western philosophy ever was. Here and in the following chapters, when we speak of Western classical thought, we will be describing a tradition that began with Socrates and Plato but of which Aristotle became the chief representative.

In the world of Aristotle, as in that of Dai Zhen, the world consists of individual things or substances. People, animals, and plants are substances, as are the inorganic elements which he took to be earth, air, fire, and water. Each has a nature or essence which makes it what it is.

---

[72] Ying-shih Yü, "Dai Zhen and the Zhu Xi Tradition," in Josephine Chiu-Duke and Michael S. Duke, eds., *Chinese History and Culture: Seventeenth Century Through Twentieth Century* (New York, 2016), 40 at 48.
[73] Dai Zhen 2, art. 2; *Tai Chen on Mencius* art. 21, p. 120.
[74] Dai Zhen 2, art. 2; *Tai Chen on Mencius* art. 21, p. 120.
[75] Dai Zhen 2, art. 2; *Tai Chen on Mencius* art. 21, p. 120.
[76] Hugo Grotius, *De iure belli ac pacis libri tres* (Amsterdam, 1646), *Prolegomena* 42.
[77] Thomas Hobbes, *Leviathan* (Cambridge, 1935), I.i.2.
[78] Samuel Pufendorf, *De iure naturae et gentium libri octo* (Amsterdam, 1688), I.ii.1.

Dai Zhen was reacting against the School of Principle which taught that the *li* or principles of things were eternal and immutable and had a mode of existence of their own, distinct from that of the concrete things in which they were instantiated. He thought the School was in error, but, as mentioned earlier, had it not been for this error, he might never have concluded that the world consists of individual things, each with a *li* or principle which can be separated from its concrete existence only in thought. Similarly, Plato had believed in transcendent Forms, of which the things around us are replicas. It has been said that Aristotle brought Plato's essences down from the sky, so to speak, and found them in concrete things. Aristotle thought that Plato was mistaken, but again, if so, had it not been for his error, Aristotle might not have arrived at a conclusion like that of Dai Zhen.

To complete the parallel, a pioneer in the study of Chinese philosophy, Fung Yu-lan, called the School of Principle the "School of Platonic Ideas."[79] The Western rationalist Gottfried Wilhelm Leibniz was called "the German Plato." The principles of the School and the concepts of the rationalists do look like a reified version of Plato's transcendent Forms.

For Dai Zhen, "the word 'principle' is a name assigned to the arrangement of the parts of anything which gives the whole its distinctive property or characteristic. . . . This is called 'order and arrangement' (条理 *tiao li*)."[80] For Aristotle, there was, indeed, an order and arrangement in things, but that order was based on its "final cause" or "end" (*telos*). Each thing tends to behave in a definite way: for example, pear trees have a tendency to produce pears and no tendency to chase cats. If something had no tendency to behave in any definite fashion, it would not be an individual thing. The way in which a thing tends to behave is termed its "final cause" or "end." The end of a thing, in this sense, is not a conscious purpose. The end of a pear tree is neither a conscious purpose of the pear tree nor that of people who like to eat pears. Its end is the manner of growth and reproduction characteristic of a pear tree.

Each thing behaves as it does because of something within it. If it behaved as it did because of something outside it, the behavior in question would not be that of the individual thing but of the something outside it. That within a thing which is responsible for how it behaves is its "nature." Things with the same nature are the same kind of thing. They have the same "substantial form" or "essence." Pear trees are one kind of thing, and cats are another.

A thing may have many parts and many activities, and yet, to be a single thing, it must have a single substantial form and a single end. It can do so because of the way that its parts or activities are related. Each part has an end or activity of its own which contributes to the end or activity which is the end of the whole. Each part of the pear tree contributes to the characteristic manner of growth and reproduction that is the end of the pear tree. Anything attached to the tree which does not contribute to its end, such as a pebble embedded in its bark, is not, properly speaking, a part of the tree. Thus the order or arrangement of its parts is based on their ends which in turn contribute to its ultimate end. As Aquinas explained at the beginning of his *Commentary* on Aristotle's *Nicomachean Ethics*, there are two types of order to be found in

79 Fung Yu-lan, *A Short History of Chinese Philosophy* (New York, 1948), 294; see H. G. Creel, *Chinese Thought from Confucius to Mao Tsê-tung* (Chicago, 1953), 208.

80 Dai Zhen 1. art. 1.1; *Tai Chen on Mencius* art. 1, p. 69.

things, the order of part to whole and the order of means to ends, and the first is based on the second.[81]

Consequently, for Aristotle, it cannot be, as Plato thought, that the body is the source of passions that are alien to the soul or that "in the human soul there is a better and also a worse principle; and when the better has the worse under control, then a man is said to be master of himself." Nor can it be, as Xunzi thought, that one's nature, before it is given form by conscious thought, tends toward evil. Nor can it be as Yang Xiong and Wang Anshi thought, that human nature combines good and evil. It must be, as Dai Zhen believed, that one's capacities and feelings are related as parts of one whole and contribute to its development. The reason, for Aristotle, is that they all must be capable of contributing to an ultimate end. Otherwise, a human being would not be a single entity but a sort of monster with different, conflicting, and ultimately irreconcilable tendencies toward different ends. He would be like a fish that happened to have the nesting instincts of a bird.

Aristotle called this ultimate end for which a human being acts *eudaemonia*. It is difficult to translate. It means "living well and doing well." It is commonly translated as "happiness," which is misleading. In English, "happiness" commonly refers an agreeable state of mind which is the opposite of sadness. Yet a person could be living well and doing well when he attends the funeral of a friend or when he suffers in a good cause. To pursue *eudemonia* is to pursue what one thinks to be worthwhile.

Eudaemonia is to live a life in accord with the "rational principle" which is what distinguishes a human being from plants and other animals. A pear tree, living in the manner characteristic of a pear tree, is unaware of the ends served, for example, by putting out roots and leaves. A cat, living in the manner characteristic of a cat, is aware, for example, of a mouse, and desires to eat it. A human being, in contrast, can understand the ends for which he acts. He can understand the contribution that a course of action can make to living a distinctively human life. He can choose that course of action because of its contribution. He acts by reason and will, that is, as Aristotle said, in accord with "rational principle."

The passions are such feelings as "appetite, anger, fear, confidence, envy, joy, friendly feeling, hatred, longing, emulation, and in general the feelings that are accompanied by pleasure and pain."[82] They can possess a rational principle "in the sense of being obedient to one" even though they do not "possess or exercise thought."[83] Some virtues are "states of character" by which "we stand well or badly with reference to the passions."[84] The passions obey the rational principle when they lead a person to do what is appropriate under the circumstances.

One cannot simply command the passions to obey. They need to be trained.

[T]he virtues we get by first exercising them, as also happens in the case of the arts as well. For the things we have to learn before we can do them, we learn by doing them, e.g. men

---

[81]   Thomas Aquinas, *In decem libros Ethicorum Aristoteles ad Nicomachum exposition*, Angelo Pirotta, ed. (Turin, 1934), I, lec. 1, no. 1.

[82]   *Nicomachean Ethics* II.v 1105b.

[83]   Ibid. I.vii 1098a.

[84]   Ibid. II.v 1105b.

become builders by building and lyre-players by playing the lyre; so too we become just by doing just acts, temperate by doing temperate acts, brave by doing brave acts.[85]

The passions can be trained to respond to the rational principle in the way that a horse can be trained to perform the precise and elegant movements of dressage. The horse has not merely learned to restrain its own impulses to walk or run or to eat grass. It has learned to move in accordance with the requirements of dressage although it has not learned, and has no capacity to learn, why to do so is of any value. The parallel is inexact because learning dressage has a different relationship to the horse than training the passions does to a human being. Learning dressage serves the purposes of the trainer and serves those of the horse, which are to grow and reproduce, only indirectly because the trainer feeds and breeds the horse. The passions of a human being serve his purpose because when they are trained they contribute to a life well lived.

When a passion has been trained, a virtue has been acquired. Virtue is a mean. It is "what is intermediate and best." Virtue is "intermediate and best" because the passions are felt, not only to an appropriate degree, but at a time and in a way that is appropriate under the circumstances.

> "For instance, both fear and confidence and appetite and anger and pity and in general pleasure and pain may be felt both too much and too little, and in both cases not well; but to feel them at the right times, with reference to the right objects, towards the right people, with the right motive and in the right way is both what is intermediate and best, and this is characteristic of virtue."[86]

The temperate person is moderate, for example, in what he eats, and the courageous person is neither rash nor cowardly. Moreover, the temperate person desires "things that, being pleasant, make for health or for good condition . . . and . . . are not hindrances to [his] ends, or contrary to what is noble, or beyond his means."[87] The courageous person is "the man . . . who faces and who fears the right things and from the right motive, in the right way and at the right time, and who feels confidence under the corresponding conditions."[88]

In these respects, Aristotle's understanding of the passions was like Dai Zhen's. For Aristotle as for Dai Zhen, all feelings and desires contribute to living a good life when they are in proper order, an order which in Dai Zhen's words, corresponds to "the arrangement of the parts of anything which gives the whole its distinctive property or characteristic."[89] For Aristotle, the order is in accord with "rational principle," or as Dai Zhen said, with "principle."[90] According to Aristotle, when one's desires are in order, they correspond to "what is intermediate and best." According to Dai Zhen, so that "they do not become excessive or insufficient."[91]

---

[85] Ibid. II.i. 1103a.
[86] Ibid. II.vi 1106b.
[87] Ibid. III.xi 1119a.
[88] Ibid. III.vii 1115b.
[89] Dai Zhen 1. art. 1.1; *Tai Chen on Mencius* art. 1, p. 69.
[90] Dai Zhen 1. art. 1.1; *Tai Chen on Mencius* art. 1, p. 69; Dai Zhen 1. art 1.3; *Tai Chen on Mencius* art. 2, p. 70.
[91] Dai Zhen 1. art. 1.25; *Tai Chen on Mencius* art. 11, p. 86.

5

The Universality of Normative Standards

In both classical traditions, human nature is a source of normative standards. Human nature is universal. Normative standards may not be the same for different individuals, in different times and places, or under different circumstances. Normative standards must be as invariable as human nature and yet they must vary. How is that possible?

I MENCIUS

One answer, which was given by Dai Zhen and writers in the Aristotelian tradition, was that the mind could apply the normative standards grounded in human nature by taking account of differences among people, times, places, and circumstances. In contrast, Mencius did not ascribe knowing the good and desiring it to separate faculties. To put it another way, he did not distinguish those faculties that are cognitive from those that are volitional. David Wong said that his failure to do so distinguished his account from "the Western ethical tradition."[1] It also distinguished his account from that of Dai Zhen. Consequently, Mencius had no trouble explaining why a person who knows how to act is motivated to do so. To know the good is to desire it. He did have to explain how normative standards varied with the circumstances. He could not say that the mind took these circumstances into account.

Alasdair McIntyre, as noted earlier, thought that Confucian and Western thought are "incommensurable" and cannot be compared. In this instance, however, he found early Confucian thought, including that of Mencius, to be distinctly inferior. It is "pretheoretical," unlike the "well-developed, theoretically informed views of, say, Aristotle or Kant."[2] Because it does not use "any close counterpart of human reason," "it does not possess anything like the conception of human beings as rational agents which has informed so much theoretical and practical inquiry in

---

[1] David B. Wong, "Is There a Distinction between Reason and Emotion in Mencius?," *Philosophy East and West* 41 (1991), 31 at 31.

[2] Alasdair MacIntyre, "Questions for Confucians: Reflections on the Essays in Comparative Study of Self, Autonomy, and Community" in Kwong-loi Shun and David B. Wong, eds., *Confucian Ethics: A Comparative Study of Self, Autonomy, and Community* (Kindle ed., Cambridge, 2004), loc. 2802 at locs. 2841–45.

the course of the moral history of the West."[3] "'[X]*in*' is used both of the heart and the mind."[4]

MacIntyre neglected the extent to which, as we have seen, Chinese philosophers expected their readers to discern the truth through inner reflection rather than demonstrative argument. They do not use what Henry Rosemont called "the hypothetico-deductive, adversarial style of discourse common in Western analytic philosophy" and so, he said, Westerners often fail to appreciate their work.[5] As we will see later, a little inner reflection, as practiced by the Chinese philosophers, would cast more doubt on Kant's claims about how a sense of duty can motivate than Kant's argumentation can dispel. Moreover, MacIntyre neglected the reason that the mind or reason did not play the same role in Mencius' account of a human being. Mencius had a sophisticated explanation of how the various human faculties could respond to the circumstances without the direction of reason.

According to Mencius, a good person possesses four attributes: benevolence, righteousness, propriety, and wisdom. They grow from inborn capacities for sympathy, shame, respect, and "approving of right and wrong."[6] For a person to possess these four attributes, all that is necessary is that these feelings be allowed to develop, as Mencius said, like the growth of barley. Their growth is protected against external influences that might stunt or warp their growth by *xin* and *zhi*. *Xin* wards off undue desires. *Zhi* enables one to remain steadfast. It can do so because it governs *qi*, a force within one associated with courage.

Xin and *zhi* are both cognitive and volitional. *Xin* can be translated as "mind" but also as "mind and heart" or "heart." *Xin* understands the good and is attracted to the good. As Kwong-loi Shun said, for Mencius, it is "the seat of both affective and cognitive activities."[7] Mencius said, "To *xin* belongs the office of thinking. By thinking, it gets the right view of things; by neglecting to think, it fails to do this."[8] He also said, "In the calm air of the morning, just between night and day … *xin* feels those desires and aversions which are proper to humanity." Then it can discard the influence of what happened during the day."[9] People abandon the good when "they allow their minds to be ensnared and drowned in evil."[10] But *xin* does not instruct the four inborn feelings how to

[3] Ibid. loc. 2827.
[4] Ibid. loc. 2836.
[5] Henry Rosemont, Jr., "Whose Democracy? Which Rights? A Confucian Critique of Modern Western Liberalism," in Shun and Wong, *Confucian Ethics* loc. 664 at loc. 703.
[6] *Mencius* 6A6.7.
[7] Kwong-loi Shun, *Mencius and Early Chinese Thought* (Stanford, 1997), 48; so also Donald J. Munro, *The Concept of Man in Early China* (Stanford, 1989), 50. Similarly, as David Nivison said, for Mencius, "thinking is a voluntary seeking as well as a cognitive focusing on the good." David S. Nivison, "Weakness of the Will in Ancient Chinese Philosophy," in David S. Nivison, *The Ways of Confucianism Investigations in Chinese Philosophy* (Chicago, 1996), 79 at 87.
[8] *Mencius* 6A.15.2.
[9] Ibid. 6A8.1–2.
[10] Ibid. 6A7.1.1.

grow into benevolence, righteousness, propriety, and wisdom.[11] The inborn feelings do not need to be taught how to develop any more than barley needs to be taught how to grow. Like barley, they naturally grow in the right way.

Similarly, their natural growth is protected but not directed by *zhi*, which can be translated as "will" or as "directions of the mind." *Zhi* governs *qi*, which is a force that enables a person to avoid weakness, whether in his own conduct or in governing others. It keeps a person on the right path. It is cognitive inasmuch as it is aware when a person is going astray and volitional inasmuch as it encourages a person not to do so.

For Mencius, then, to know the good is to desire it. He had no difficulty explaining why a person who knows how to act is motivated to do so. He did have to explain how a person knew how to act when circumstances made one action appropriate rather than another. He could not say that the mind took these circumstances into account. He did so by explaining the interactions of the four attributes of benevolence, righteousness, propriety, and wisdom.

Benevolence is concern for others. It is attracted to its proper object but not invariably. Mencius reassured a king that he had the capacity to be benevolent by pointing out that he had once refused to sacrifice an ox since he could not "bear its frightened appearance, as if it were an innocent person going to the place of death."[12] He had sacrificed a sheep instead. If this concern were extended to the sufferings of all people, his benevolence would be sufficient to rule a kingdom.[13] The king's compassion led him in the right direction, but not in precisely the right direction. There was no good reason for sparing the ox and sacrificing a sheep. Mencius told the king: "Your conduct was an artifice of benevolence. You saw the ox, and had not seen the sheep. So is the worthy man affected towards animals, that, having seen them alive, he cannot bear to see them die; having heard their dying cries, he cannot bear to eat their flesh. Therefore he keeps away from his slaughter-house and cook-room."[14] Thus even the worthy man must avoid situations in which his benevolence would be misplaced.[15]

Righteousness is right conduct toward another. Although a person's benevolence might be misplaced, Mencius maintained that he should always act according to righteousness.

---

[11]　Thus "ancient Chinese normative thought does not use any close counterpart of human 'reason.'" Chad Hansen, "The Normative Impact of Comparative Ethics: Human Rights," in Shun and Wong, *Confucian Ethics* loc. 996 at loc. 1035.

[12]　*Mencius* 1A7.4. Mencius was not arguing, as some modern scholars have thought, that a person distressed at a child falling into a well or an ox being led to slaughter is required as matter of logical consistency to feel distress at other misfortunes. Liu Shu-hsien, "Some Reflections on Mencius' Views of Heart-Mind and Human Nature," *Philosophy East and West* 46 (1996), 143 at 152; Nivison, "Mencius and Motivation." The point of Mencius' argument, as he says himself, is that the feeling of sympathy belongs to human nature because every human being has it. See Irene Bloom, "Mencian Arguments of Human Nature (Jen-Hsing)," *Philosophy East and West* 44 (1994), 19 at 31. Similarly, David Wong observes that Mencius was not trying to convince the king by logical argument but trying to change the king by beginning with a feeling that was "'already there'" and channeling "into practical deliberation." Wong, "Reason and Emotion in Mencius" 39.

[13]　*Mencius* 1A7.4–5.

[14]　Ibid. 1A7.8.

[15]　As Manyul Im noted, the story illustrates the difference between Mencius' account of moral qualities and Aristotle's. For Aristotle, as we will see, when a person has perfected a virtue, his attitudes and actions will be appropriate to each situation. Manyul Im, "Emotional Control and Virtue in the 'Mencius,'" *Philosophy East and West* 49 (1999), 7.

He said that Confucius, "in order to obtain the throne, would not have committed one act of unrighteousness, or put to death one innocent person."[16] One should prefer righteousness to life itself. "I like life, and I also like righteousness. If I cannot keep the two together, I will let life go, and choose righteousness."[17] For Mencius, it would be better to starve than to accept food offered in an insulting voice.[18]

Nevertheless, what accords with righteousness may depend on the circumstances. Righteousness then needs guidance, and the guidance is provided, not by mind (心 *xin*) but by wisdom (智 *zhi*). Mencius likened it to the skill of an archer that enables him to direct an arrow toward the target. "Let us analogize wisdom to skill, and sageness to strength. When aiming at a mark a hundred steps away, whether you reach the mark is determined by strength, but whether you hit it is not."[19] For Mencius, to become righteous or even to become a sage one did not need to depend on wisdom. Wisdom adds a degree of fine-tuning. Sages such as Bo Yi (伯夷), Yi Yin (伊尹), and Liu Xia Hui (柳下惠) were benevolent[20] and righteous.[21] Yet Confucius had wisdom as well. In taking office, Bo Yi followed a fixed rule: "In a time of order he took office, and in a time of disorder he retired."[22] So did Yi Yin, although the rule was a different one: "In a time of order he took office, and in a time of disorder, he also took office."[23] So did Liu Xia Hui, although his rule was that he "was not ashamed to serve a corrupt ruler, nor did he consider it lowly to be an inferior officer."[24] Confucius adapted his behavior to the situation. "When it was proper to act quickly, he did so; when it was proper to delay, he did so; when it was proper to retire, he did so; when it was proper to serve, he did so."[25] His conduct was like the "harmony" of a "concert," unlike theirs, which was like a single instrument. Achieving that harmony is the work of wisdom.[26]

Li (禮), often translated as "propriety," concerned how one should behave in recurring social situations such as attending a funeral, meeting with a person of higher rank, greeting a guest, or giving or receiving an object from a person of the opposite sex.[27] Although a person must always act righteously, there are circumstances in which the rules of *li* can be overridden. For example, *li* prescribes "that males and females shall not allow their hands to touch in giving or receiving anything." Mencius was asked, "if a man's sister-in-law is drowning," should he break this rule and "rescue her with his hand?" Mencius answered that one who does not do so "is a wolf." The rule about touching hands "is the general rule;" to rescue one's sister-in-law "is a peculiar exigency."[28]

---

[16]   *Mencius* 2A2.24.
[17]   Ibid. 6A10.1.
[18]   Ibid. 6A10.6.
[19]   Ibid. 5B1.7.
[20]   Ibid. 6B6.1–2.
[21]   Ibid. 2A2.24.
[22]   Ibid. 5B1.1.
[23]   Ibid. 5B1.2
[24]   Ibid. 5B1.3.
[25]   Ibid. 5B1.4.; similarly, 2A2.22.
[26]   Ibid. 5B1.6.
[27]   Shun, *Mencius* 52.
[28]   *Mencius* 4A.17.1.

Similarly, one need not follow the rules "if the result of eating only according to the rules of propriety will be death by starvation, while by disregarding those rules we may get food." One need not follow them if "according to the rule that he shall go in person to meet his wife a man cannot get married, while by disregarding that rule he can get married." As Mencius explained, "Gold is heavier than feathers, but does that saying have reference, on the one hand, to a single clasp of gold, and, on the other, to a wagon-load of feathers?" One could recognize exceptions and still maintain that "the observance of the rules of propriety in regard to eating" is "more important" than "merely eating," and that "the observance of the rules of propriety" "in gratifying the appetite of sex" is more important that merely gratifying the appetite.[29]

For Menicus, a person acts rightly because he has the traits of benevolence, righteousness, wisdom, and propriety. The mind does not need to teach him how to act. Yet they interact to ensure that an action is not only right in general but right in the circumstances.

II DAI ZHEN

For Dai Zhen, as we have seen, all desires belong to human nature. All of them are good but become destructive when they exceed their proper bounds. Moral development requires not only the nourishment but also the right ordering of human desires.

As we have seen, Dai Zhen's term for this right order was principle (理 *li*). A principle can be understood. "I have never heard of any principle which cannot be articulated."[30] Consequently, Dai Zhen conceived of the role of the mind differently than Mencius. Principle, correctly understood, is a standard for the realization of one's humanity. The "sage . . . has fulfilled the principle of man."[31] Consequently, "when we speak of a sage, we speak of a model to follow."[32] "Only if [men and things] are in accord with their principles as straightness is in accord with a plumb line, levelness with water, roundness with a compass, squareness with a square, do they then become a standard for the world and ten thousand generations."[33]

When the feelings that motivate a person are in accord with principle, they do not lead one astray. "Principles exist where feelings do not err."[34] A human being is motivated either by selfishness or by benevolence. "A lack of selfishness is benevolence."[35] Desires are selfish when they deviate from principle. "When feelings are balanced, this means that likes and dislikes are properly restrained and that one is in accord with the principles of Heaven." In contrast, "When a person . . . follows [his own likes and dislikes] and ignores the likes and dislikes of others, he will frequently injure others in order to satisfy his selfish desires."[36]

There are two sources of evil. One is selfish desires which deviate from principle. The other is a misconception of principle itself. "Selfishness concerns desires and

---

[29] Ibid. 6B.1.
[30] Dai Zhen 1. art 1.25; *Tai Chen on Mencius* art. 13, p. 89.
[31] Dai Zhen 1. art. 1.25; *Tai Chen on Mencius* art. 13, pp. 89–90.
[32] Ibid.
[33] Dai Zhen 1. art. 1.25; *Tai Chen on Mencius* art. 14, p. 89.
[34] Dai Zhen 1. art 1.3; *Tai Chen on Mencius* art. 2, p. 70.
[35] Dai Zhen 3. art. 5.1; *Tai Chen on Mencius* art. 10, p. 83; see art. 40, p. 165.
[36] Dai Zhen 1. art. 1.3; *Tai Chen on Mencius* art. 2, p. 71.

misconception concerns the knowledge of the mind."[37] "The sources of the suffering of people are selfishness and misconception."[38] A lack of misconception is wisdom.[39] Consequently, for Dai Zhen, unlike Mencius, there are two great virtues: benevolence and wisdom. A person is benevolent when his desires do not deviate from principle; he is wise when he is not mistaken about principle.

If a person's desires are selfish, he can rectify them by recourse to principle. A selfish person accords an undue preference to his own desires. The principle by which he can rectify them is "reciprocity" (*shu* 恕). Dai Zhen quoted Confucius: "the one word which may serve as a rule of practice for all one's life is 'reciprocity': 'What you do not want done to yourself, do not do to others.'"[40] "Though the word 'principle' is not expressly stated in these passages," Dai Zhen said that "it is implied completely."[41] Consequently:

> "When I do something to others, I should examine myself and think quietly: Would I accept it should someone do the same thing to me? When I demand something from others, I should examine myself and think quietly: Were this demanded of me, could I do it? When I gauge the response of others by my own the principle of Heaven will become clear."[42]

It is especially important to consider the feelings of the weak and powerless. "If we honestly reflect on the weak, the deprived, the dull, the fearful, the sick, the old, the young, and the lonely and think about their feelings, how are they different from our own?"[43]

The principle of reciprocity also serves as a guide to action. Even a person who is unselfish and not a prey to evil tendencies may confuse principle with his subjective personal opinion. Such people are dangerous. "There is nothing worse than for a man to be obsessed and to think that he is wise; to trust in his own opinions and cling to them as being principle and righteousness. I fear that those who seek principle and righteousness may substitute for them their own opinions. Who knows to what extent people have suffered."[44]

One way to check the correctness of one's opinions is to compare them with long-standing conventional opinions about what is right and wrong. What is agreed upon by all and throughout the ages is likely to be in accord with principle. "Only what minds all agree upon we call principle and righteousness. Then what is not agreed on belongs to the realm of opinion and is neither principle nor righteousness. When a person regards something as true, and the world all says it is so, and it cannot be changed, this is what it means to agree upon something."[45]

Yet that which has been believed by many people for a long time may still be wrong because circumstances change. Principle itself is unchangeable since it is founded on human nature. But to decide whether conduct is in accordance with principle, one must

---

[37] Dai Zhen 3. art. 5.1; *Tai Chen on Mencius* art. 10, p. 83; see art. 40, p. 165.
[38] Ibid.
[39] Ibid.
[40] *Analects* 15.24.
[41] Dai Zhen 1. art. 1.9; *Tai Chen on Mencius* art. 5, p. 75.
[42] Dai Zhen 1. art. 1.3; *Tai Chen on Mencius* art. 2, p. 70.
[43] Dai Zhen 1. art. 1.3; *Tai Chen on Mencius* art. 2, p. 71.
[44] Dai Zhen 1. art. 1.7; *Tai Chen on Mencius* art. 4, p. 73.
[45] Dai Zhen 1. art. 1.7; *Tai Chen on Mencius* art. 4, pp. 72–73.

weigh what is important against what is unimportant. What is important and unimportant may change with the times and the circumstances.

> Weighing is how the important and unimportant are distinguished. If for thousands of years, what is called important and unimportant does not change, that is constancy. If something is constant, then it should be commonly obvious that for thousands of years what is important and unimportant have not changed. When the important became unimportant and the unimportant became important, change has occurred. In case of change if one does not fully utilize his wisdom to distinguish and observe things accurately he will not be able to understand change.[46]

Consequently, one source of error is to fail to take account of what is important and unimportant in the particular situation one is confronting.

> In ancient and modern times, there is no lack of stern upright men who despise evil and uphold what they consider right as right and what they consider wrong as wrong. They insist on what is obviously important and unimportant to them as common knowledge when in fact they do not know sometimes what they consider important is unimportant and what they consider unimportant is important. Their mistake in right and wrong, important and unimportant, causes irreparable harm to the world. How is it the result of human desires that cause the error? What they believe to be the principle is not the principle.[47]

Dai Zhen presented his work as an interpretation of Mencius. For Mencius, wisdom was one of the four key attributes of a good person. It fine-tunes the others by enabling a person to do the right thing at the right time. Because Confucius was wise in this way, Mencius likened him to the "harmony" of a "concert" in comparison with others were like single instruments.[48] Dai Zhen gave a different explanation of that passage. "Harmony" means "order and arrangement" (条理 *tiao li*) in accordance with principle. Confucius was wise because he could create an orderly arrangement like that of a concert. According to Dai Zhen "[s]ageness and wisdom reached perfection in Confucius, yet Mencius in this passage used only the words 'orderly arrangement' to describe his achievement."[49] Because the mind played a different role for Dai Zhen than for Mencius, wisdom had a different significance.

Dai Zhen presented his work as a restoration of Mencius' thought. As Chung-ying Cheng said, he was correct only if "restoration were to be understood as an attempt to reconstruct and reinterpret Classical Confucianism in the spirit of Confucius, Mencius, and other authors of the Classical Confucian writers."[50]

III THE ARISTOTELIAN TRADITION

Aristotle founded a tradition which, as shaped by others, became not only preeminent in the West but as close to orthodox as any Western philosophy ever was. In medieval Europe,

---

[46] Dai Zhen 3. art. 5.1; *Tai Chen on Mencius* art. 40, p. 163.
[47] Dai Zhen 3. art. 5.1; *Tai Chen on Mencius* art. 40, p. 166.
[48] *Mencius* 5B1.6.
[49] Dai Zhen 1, art. 1.1; *Tai Chen on Mencius* art. 1, p. 69.
[50] Chung-ying Cheng, "Introduction," to Tai Chên, *Inquiry into Goodness* (Honolulu, 1971), 30.

his philosophical ideas were used by Albertus Magnus and his pupil Thomas Aquinas to explain how ethical choices are made. Their explanation outlasted the Protestant Reformation, and, indeed, was widely accepted by philosophically minded Protestants of all major denominations.

For Dai Zhen, as we have seen, "the word 'principle' is a name assigned to the arrangement of the parts of anything which gives the whole its distinctive property or characteristic. . . . This is called 'order and arrangement' (条理*tiao li*)."[51] The principle is the pure and correct order of a thing when it is "realized."[52] To live rightly was to live in accord with principle.

For Aristotle, the order and arrangement in things is based on its "final cause" or "end" (*telos*). To live rightly, a human being must pursue the ends that are his by nature. To realize them is to live rightly.

He pursues these ends by using practical reason (*phronēsis* for Aristotle, *prudentia* for Aquinas). Theoretical reason proceeds deductively from first principles to arrive at truth. Practical reason proceeds from first principles concerning the ultimate ends that are worthy of pursuit to conclusions about how these ends can best be attained. These ultimate ends are good in themselves, not because they are a means to other ends. Human beings can recognize that they are good without proof from higher principles. They can recognize, for example, that it is good to seek knowledge, to live in society, and to help others. Actions are good when they best contribute to these ends and bad when they do not.

The action that best contributes to an end may depend on the circumstances. Because practical reason must take these circumstances into account, it does not proceed deductively like theoretical reason. Consequently, although theoretical reason reaches its conclusions with certainty, practical reason does not.

Nevertheless, some ends or actions are invariably wrong whatever the circumstances. They are in conflict with the ultimate ends for which one should act. It may be good to pursue wealth in order to sustain life, to provide leisure time to seek knowledge, or to have the means to help others. It is always bad to pursue wealth as an end in itself. Seeking wealth for its own sake contributes nothing to a good life. Aristotle said that some "passions . . . have names that already imply badness" such as "spite, shamelessness, envy."[53] It is always bad to bear a grudge, to have no aversion to one's own morally repugnant actions, or to feel oneself diminished by another's good fortune.

According to Aristotle, the same can be said of actions such as "adultery, theft, murder; for all of these things imply by their names that they are bad . . . It is not possible, then, ever to be right with regard to them; one must always be wrong."[54] Actions such as these, according to Aquinas, are defined by their incompatibility with a good life. One cannot explain what adultery, theft, or murder are without including that incompatibility in their definition. It is as we just saw with the definitions of avarice, spite, shamelessness, and envy.

---

[51] Dai Zhen 1. art. 1.1; *Tai Chen on Mencius* art. 1, p. 69.
[52] Ibid.
[53] *Nicomachean Ethics* II.vi 1107a.
[54] Ibid. II.vi 1107a.

As John Finnis noted, there are two common ways of misunderstanding Aquinas' account of why some actions are invariably wrong. One is "to deny that Aquinas held the thesis, or at least to deny that it is compatible with his own deeper principles."[55] The "deeper principles" are supposedly revealed by texts in which Aquinas said that sometimes the goodness or badness of some actions does depend on the circumstances. Others "have claimed ... that these norms are exceptionless only because they contain a moral qualifier which makes them true tautologously," for example, "'adultery' *means* a married person's *unjustified* extra-marital intercourse."[56] Therefore, by definition, adultery is always wrong.

For Aquinas, however, an action is defined by the end for which it is performed.[57] In that respect, an action, such as swimming, is like a man-made thing, such as a house. Swimming is a way of moving through water. A house is a structure that provides shelter. Actions such as swimming are not defined by the relationship to a person's ultimate end. Aquinas' examples are "walking in the field" or "picking up a straw."[58] Others are defined by their relationship to this ultimate end.[59] Actions such as adultery, theft, and murder are incompatible with living a good life for the same reason that disease is incompatible with health, capitulation is incompatible with victory, and traffic accidents are incompatible with traffic safety.

Such definitions are not tautological. Whether an action is incompatible with living a good life, and therefore can be characterized as adultery, murder or theft, depends on the purposes of marriage, private property, and respect for the life of others, and their contribution to living a good life.

For Aquinas, there was no way that marital infidelity could be compatible with the purposes of marriage. Consequently, every act of that extramarital intercourse constituted adultery. In contrast, a person in urgent need could use another's property without committing theft because the owner's rights were limited by the reasons why private property is established.[60] Following Aristotle, Aquinas believed that these reasons were to avoid the disadvantages of common ownership: people would not work, and there would be endless quarrels over the use of things.[61] Similarly, a person might kill another without committing murder. Killing another person in order to bring about his death is justifiable only as a punishment which serves the public good, and therefore, criminals can be executed only by the public authority charged with promoting the public good. A private person who kills in self-defense is not killing in order to bring about the attacker's death but to ward off the attack.[62] One has to understand what sexuality, property, and the protection of human life contribute to a life well lived in order to

[55] John Finins, *Aquinas Moral, Political and Legal Theory* (Oxford, 1998), 163.
[56] Ibid. 165.
[57] *Summa theologiae* I-II, Q. 18, aa. 4, 6, 8. Therefore, in Aquinas' vocabulary, an action can be good or bad in its species. Ibid. a. 5.
[58] *Summa theologiae* I-II, Q. 18, a. 8.
[59] Ibid. I-II, Q. 18, aa. 5–8.
[60] Ibid. II-II, Q. 66, a. 7.
[61] Ibid. II-II, Q. 66, a. 2.
[62] Ibid. II-II, Q. 64, aa. 2–3.

understand what actions are opposed to them, just as one has to understand what health is in order to understand what counts as a disease.[63]

Finnis himself, along with Germain Grisez and Robert George, gave a quite different account of why some actions are invariably wrong. It is important to understand why it is different. Like Aristotle and Aquinas, they regarded some ends as good in themselves rather than because they are a means to other ends. Human beings can recognize that they are good without proof from higher principles. Unlike Aristotle and Aquinas, they tried to enumerate them. According to Finnis, there are seven basic goods: life, knowledge, play, aesthetic experience, friendship, practical reasonableness, and religion. He maintained that "one should not choose to do any act which *of itself does nothing but* damage or impede a realization or participation of any one of the basic forms of human good."[64] One may pursue some basic good, such as knowledge, even though "this inevitable concentration of effort will indirectly impoverish, inhibit, or interfere with the realization of other values."[65] But then the damage is done "indirectly" rather than "directly and immediately."[66]

It is hard to understand either this distinction or the principle on which it is founded. What if I kill in self-defense? What if I plow up a beautiful meadow to create a golf course, or destroy a golf course to build houses? Is the damage to the basic goods of life, beauty, or play direct or indirect? Moreover, this principle is said to belong to "practical reasonableness" which itself is one of the basic goods. But the value of the basic goods is supposed to be evident. This principle is not evident. Finnis tries to prove it from the proposition that basic goods are "incommensurable." "To choose an act which in itself simply (or primarily) damages a basic good is an act of opposition to an incommensurable value . . . which one treats as if it were an object of measurable worth that could be outweighed by objects of greater . . . worth."[67] One can, however, weigh one good against another without claiming that either are of "measurable worth." People do so all the time, for example when they decide to pursue some basic good, such as knowledge, even though it will "indirectly" interfere with the realization of another. Grisez, Finnis, and George avoided one extreme position, that of consequentialists who believe that nothing is invariably wrong, by going to the opposite extreme.

In the Aristotelian tradition, when an action is not invariably wrong, it belongs to practical reason to make a right estimate of the contribution that it makes to one's ultimate end.[68] For

---

[63] Finnis explained Aquinas in a different way. Aquinas, he believed, was distinguishing between "negative" moral norms, "directing us not to acts of a more or less specific type," "which can be, and a number in truth are, binding and governing on almost every occasion," and "affirmative" norms, "directing one *to do* such and such," which hold "always but not for every occasion." Finis, *Aquinas* 164. As Finis correctly stated, however, "For Aquinas, the good of virtue – any virtue . . . – is a good . . . to which we are directed by one of the first principles of practical reasonableness and natural law." Ibid. 168. I have trouble seeing the relationship between that proposition and whether a norm is "negative" or "affirmative." Moreover, often a norm can be phrased either way. One can say "an action is good in its genus: for instance to make use of what is one's own." *Summa theologiae* I-II, Q. 18. a. 2. Or one can say it is wrong "to take what belongs to another." Ibid. a. 7.

[64] John Finnis, *Natural Law and Natural Rights* (Oxford 1980), 118 (emphasis in original).

[65] Ibid. 119–20.

[66] Ibid. 120.

[67] Ibid.

[68] *Summa theologiae* II-II, Q. 49, a. 2.

example, through practical reason, one can weigh the good of spending more time in the pursuit knowledge against that of spending more time cultivating friendship. In that respect, practical reason in the Aristotelian tradition is like wisdom for Dai Zhen.

If Grisez, Finnis, and George were correct, these goods could not be weighed because they are incommensurable. Nevertheless, they recognize that in planning his own life, a person must decide to what extent to pursue each of them. According to Finnis, to do so "require[s] the harmonization of all one's deepest commitments – for which there is no recipe or blueprint."[69] There may no blueprint, but how is "harmonization" possible if one cannot compare, for example, the value of spending more time at work against that of more time with one's family? Moreover, according to Finnis, in planning one's life, there must be "no arbitrary discounting or exaggeration of any of the basic values."[70] Yet, according to Finnis, although a person should recognize the value of the basic goods, he cannot compare them. Suppose a person devotes all his time to play? Can that really be as good as a life spent pursuing objectives that most people would deem worthier?

Then there is the problem of deciding what to do when the welfare of others is at stake. R. George Wright asked Robert George how he could explain why one should break off a game of golf to save a small child from drowning in a water trap.[71] George answered, "I do not believe that the situation is controlled by a moral norm that says: In choosing between options in which competing basic norms are involved, identify and choose the one that preserves the weightier value. If, as I think, basic values, qua basic, are irreducible and therefore incommensurable ... then such a putative moral norm is incoherent."[72] He said that the golfer should save the child because of another moral norm which he and Finnis called "the Golden Rule."[73] Finnis said that it, too, belonged to "practical reasonableness" which he reckoned as one of the basic goods. It forbids "arbitrary preference among persons."[74] It is "a requirement that one's moral judgments and preferences be *universalizable*."[75]

That "requirement" is not a "good" in the sense of something worth having, such as friendship or knowledge. It is not an end to be sought. It is a principle from which rules of conduct are to be inferred. The principle is "universalizability" or impartial concern for one's own good and that of others. We have encountered it with Mozi, and we will explore its full difficulties when we encounter it again with Kant. Here it is enough to note that we have moved abruptly from the path taken by Aristotle and Aquinas, in which the rightful-ness of an action depends on what it contributes to ultimate goods or ends. We are now in a world in which its rightfulness depends on whether it conforms to a "requirement" or rule. We will also note that there is a special difficulty applying the Golden Rule if we cannot decide which is of weightier value: saving a life or finishing a game of golf. For the golfer to treat the child as he would wish to be treated, he would need to know whether to

---

[69] Finnis, *Natural Law* 104.
[70] Ibid. 105.
[71] Robert P. George, *In Defense of Natural Law* (Oxford, 1999), 92.
[72] Ibid. 95.
[73] Ibid. 97.
[74] Finnis, *Natural Law* 106.
[75] Ibid. 107 (emphasis in original).

break off a golf game if his own life were in danger, for example, from an insane killer roaming the golf course with a machine gun. How could he decide if he could not compare the importance of basic goods that are "incommensurable"?

In the Aristotelian tradition, the task of practical reason is to weigh the contribution that different courses of action make to a life well lived. It is also to determine what action can best contribute to such a life given the circumstances one is confronting. There may be no limit to the circumstances that matter. According to Aquinas, "actions are in singular matters."[76] "An infinite number of singulars cannot be comprehended by human reason."[77] In deciding how to act, a person must take the circumstances into account as best he can.

In such situations, according to Aquinas, practical reason must be aided by several kindred virtues that limit the circumstances that one takes into account. "Memory" and "experience," which are parts of practical reason, indicate "what is true in the majority of cases."[78] A person can seek advice from experienced people and, indeed, "stands in great need of being taught by others especially old folk."[79] In doing so, he employs the related virtue of *eubolia*, which is the seeking of counsel. Another virtue, *sinesis*, enables him to apply "common rules" which have been devised for similar situations. Nevertheless, he needs still another virtue, *gnome*, to make exceptions to the common rules and to "judge ... according to higher principles." *Gnome* is necessary because "it happens sometimes that something has to be done which is not covered by the common rules of actions."[80] As an example, he used a case described by Cicero and still earlier by Plato. One person entrusts his sword to another and then asks for it back when he has become insane or wishes to harm the republic. Aquinas agreed with Plato and Cicero that the person with custody of the sword should not return it.[81]

For Aquinas, one who acts in accordance with practical reason acts in accordance with natural law. Aristotle had not used the term "natural law."[82] G. E. M. Anscombe, one of the founders of so-called virtue ethics, claimed that Aristotle's ethical philosophy is incompatible with such a conception. Aristotle was concerned with whether a man is a good person, and so "[h]e has blanket terms for wickedness 'villain,' 'scoundrel'; but of course a man is not a villain or a scoundrel by the performance of one bad action, or a few bad actions." He did not have a "blanket term" such as "illicit," "unlawful," or "wrong." "How did this come about? The answer," according to Anscombe, "is in history: between Aristotle and us came Christianity, with its law conception of ethics."[83]

That account is misleading. As Anscombe acknowledged, Aristotle recognized that some actions are wrong: as we have just seen, examples are adultery, theft, and murder.[84] A person

---

[76] *Summa theologiae* II-II, Q. 47, a. 3.

[77] Ibid. II-II, Q.47, a. 3, ad 2.

[78] Ibid. II-II, Q. 49, a. 1.

[79] Ibid. II-II, Q. 49, a. 3.

[80] Ibid. II-II, Q. 51, a. 4.

[81] Ibid.

[82] He had said: "Of political justice part is natural, part legal – natural, that which everywhere has the same force and does not exist by people's thinking this or that; legal, that which is originally indifferent, but when it has been laid down is not indifferent." *Nicomachean Ethics* V.vii 1134b 19–20.

[83] G. E. M. Anscombe, "Modern Moral Philosophy," *Philosophy*, 33 (1958), 1 at 5–6, 8.

[84] *Nicomachean Ethics* II.vi 1107a.

who cheats another party to a contract violates commutative justice. So does a person who slanders someone. Moreover, according to Aquinas, "[l]aw is a dictate of practical reason."[85] Practical reason is the virtue that enables one to identify the right course of action. The other virtues enable one to act in the way that practical reason directs. It is to turn Aristotle upside down to say that action exists for the sake of virtue. The end of human life is to act virtuously. In Aquinas' vocabulary, it is to act in accordance with natural law.

Practical reason, like theoretical reason, must proceed from first principles. According to Aristotle, the first principles of theoretical reason are known by *nous*.[86] By *nous* or "intuition" we are hard-wired to know principles that cannot be demonstrated but that make demonstration possible. An example is the law of non-contradiction: the same proposition cannot be both true and false at the same time in the same way. There is no way to prove that the law of non-contradiction is true. Any proof would assume the truth of the law of non-contradiction.

Through practical reason, a person identifies the actions that contribute to the ultimate ends he is to pursue to live a distinctively human life. These ends cannot be a means to still further ends. They are like the first principles of theoretical reason. With theoretical reason, one must know these first principles in order to demonstrate anything. With practical reason, one must know that these ends are worth pursuing to decide that any action is worthwhile.

Aristotle did not explain how one knows the first principles of practical reason. Werner Jaeger, relying on an obscure passage in the *Eudemian Ethics*,[87] claimed that in this work, Aristotle took the position that one knows this ultimate end by theoretical reason.[88] If that were ever Aristotle's view, which other scholars have doubted, Jaeger himself agreed that Aristotle abandoned it in the *Nicomachean Ethics*. Aristotle did not claim that one knows what is good by a necessary inference from what is true. That idea would have put him in the same camp as the Western rationalists. He would also have committed the "naturalistic fallacy" condemned by David Hume. He would have attempted to infer what is good from a proposition about what is true.

Some modern scholars concluded that Aristotle must have thought that practical reason (*phronēsis*) enables a person to know, not only the means that contribute to an end, but the end that is ultimately worth pursuing. Yet in two passages, Aristotle denied that *phronēsis* provides a knowledge of this end. "[T]he work of man is achieved only in accordance with practical wisdom as well as with moral virtue; for virtue makes us aim at the right mark and practical wisdom makes us take the right means."[89] Again: "It is plain ... that the choice will not be right without practical wisdom any more than without virtue; for the one determines the end and the other makes us do the things that lead to the end."[90] According to these passages, to act well, one must both know the right end and choose the right means, and *phronēsis* concerns only the choice of means. But how, then, are the right ends to be known?

---

[85] *Summa theologiae* I-II, Q. 91, a. 3, citing Q. 90, a. 1, ad 2.

[86] John M. Cooper, *Reason and Human Good in Aristotle* (Indianapolis, 1986), 61–66; Takatura Ando, *Aristotle's Theory of Practical Cognition* (3rd ed., The Hague, 1971), 230–45.

[87] *Eudemian Ethics* VII.xv 1249b.

[88] Werner Jaeger, *Aristotle* (2nd ed., Oxford, 1948), 238.

[89] *Nicomachean Ethics* VI.12 1144a.

[90] Ibid. VI.14 1145a.

Other scholars have interpreted these passages to mean that the moral virtues are the source of a person's knowledge of his ultimate end.[91] Aristotle said that a morally virtuous person will know the end he should be pursuing. As noted earlier, however, the moral virtues are "states of character" by which "we stand well or badly with reference to the passions." One can see why a person without these virtues would act for the wrong ends. As Aristotle said, "wickedness perverts us and causes us to be deceived about the starting-points of action."[92] Consequently, Aquinas interpreted the first passage just quoted to mean that moral virtue gives one "a right intention toward the end . . . insofar as it inclines the appetite toward the due end."[93] Certainly, one reason a virtuous person may choose the right ends is that his vices have not led him to deceive himself about them. But that does not explain how he knows what the right ends are.

More plausibly, scholars such as John Cooper interpret Aristotle to mean that the ends of practical reason are known by an intellectual intuition, much as the premises of theoretical reason are known by *nous*.[94] By *nous* or "intuition" we are hard-wired to know the first principles that make demonstration possible. According to Cooper, by a kindred intuition we know the first principles that make practical reasoning possible.[95]

Whatever Aristotle may have thought, this position was adopted by Albertus Magnus and Thomas Aquinas. According to Aquinas, "[B]y means of those principles naturally known, we judge of those things which we have discovered by reasoning. Now it is clear that, as the theoretical reason argues about theoretical matters, so practical reason argues about practical matters. Therefore we must have bestowed on us by nature, not only theoretical principles, but practical principles."[96] He noted that according to Aristotle, the "first principles of theoretical reason bestowed on us by nature . . . belong to us . . . by *intellectus*" (the Latin word used to translate *nous*). Following Albertus, he said that "the first principles of practical reason bestowed on us by nature" belong to us . . . by *synderesis*,"[97] a term Aristotle had never used but which appeared in an early fifth-century commentary by St. Jerome on the book of Ezechiel.[98] Aquinas used the term to mean the knowledge of the first principles or ultimate ends for which one should act, and also to mean "conscience," which is "the actual application of [this] knowledge to what we do."[99]

Centuries later, conscience was still described in this way by Anglicans such as Robert Burton (1557–1640), Richard Carpenter (1575–1627), and Robert Sanderson (1587–1663), by Lutherans such as Friedrich Balduin (1575–1627) and Johannes Olearius (1639–1713), by Calvinists such as Iohann Andreas van der Meulen (1635–1702), and by Puritans such as

---

91 J. Walter, *Die Lehre von praktischen Vernunft in der greichishen Philosophie* (Jena, 1874).

92 *Nicomachean Ethics* VI.12 1144a.

93 Thomas Aquinas, *In decem libros Ethicorum Aristoteles ad Nicomachum exposition*, Angelo Pirotta, ed. (Turin, 1934), VI, lec. x, no. 1269 to VI.xii 1144a.

94 Cooper, *Reason and Human Good* 61–66; Ando, *Aristotle's Theory* 230–45.

95 Cooper, *Reason and Human Good* 65.

96 *Summa theologiae* I, Q. 79, a. 12.

97 Ibid. I, Q. 79, a. 12.

98 Actually *synteresis*. The spelling changed later. Jerome on Ezechiel I.vi.

99 *Summa theologiae* I, Q. 79, a. 13.

William Ames (1576–1633).[100] Conscience is the application to a particular action of first principles known through *synderesis* or *synteresis* or (van der Meulen) "first principles received by the light of nature." "Synteresie, or the purer part of the Conscience, is an innate habit, and doth signifie, a conservation of the knowledge of the law of God and Nature, to know good and evill,"[101] as the character Conscience said in a morality play by Thomas Nabbes (1605–41).[102] According to Ames, "the understanding of man is fitted to give assent unto Naturall principles" by *"synteresis"* on which the "practicall judgement" of "conscience" is based.[103]

Jaeger believed that Aristotle had taken such a position in the *Nicomachean Ethics*. He found it disturbing. It meant that according to Aristotle, the goodness of one's actions rested ultimately on a moral insight for which no reasons can be given.[104] Similarly, Cooper said:

> [T]his may be a disappointing conclusion to come to. For if, according to Aristotle, the practically intelligent agent only claims to "see" that his conception of how best to live is the correct one, and does not have any reason in support of his view, and against the alternatives, it might seem that one cannot expect, from the practically intelligent, or from Aristotle, any enlightenment on the fundamental principle of morality, why one ought to live (as it is said) one ought.[105]

Whether it is disappointing, however, depends on one's perspective. Certainly, some philosophers might wish that conclusions concerning how to live could be demonstrated like the conclusions of mathematics. To do so was the ideal of rationalists of the seventeenth and eighteenth centuries. Others may find it more congenial to believe all human beings have an insight into how best to live, whatever their theoretical abilities, and that to live rightly is a matter of following one's conscience, not whatever principles that moral philosophers claim to have demonstrated.

As Cooper noted, although no one can demonstrate the first principles of practical reasoning any more than the first principles of theoretical reasoning, it is still possible to respond to someone who denies them. One can do so by dialectical argument.[106] According to Aristotle, if a person denies the first principles on which theoretical reason is based, such as the principle of non-contradiction, one can ask if he believes that anything

---

[100] Richard Carpenter, *The Conscionable Christian: Or, The Indevour or Saint Paul to Have an Discharge a Good Conscience Always towards God and Men* (London, 1623), preface, "To the Reader," 2; Robert Sanderson, *De obligatione conscientiae praelectiones decem: Oxonii in schola theologica habitae anno dom. MDCXLVII* (London, 1686), *Praelectiones* I.xxxiv–xxxvi; IV.xiv; Friedrich Balduin, *Tractatus de casibus conscientiae* (Wittenberg, 1628), lib. I, cap. iii; Johannes Olearius, *Introductio brevis in theologiam casisticam, usibus studiosum Lipsiensium consecrate* (Leipzig, 1694), cap. viii.9–10; Iohann Andreas van der Meulen, *Forum conscientiae seu ius poli, hoc est tractatus theologico juridicus* (Utrecht, 1693), *Dissertatio praeliminaris* I, pp. 3, 7, 9; Guilielmus Amesius, *Conscientia et eius iure vel casibus libri quinque* (ed. nov. Amsterdam 1630), lib. I, ch. i, 1–3; ch. ii, 2–5.

[101] Robert Burton, *The Anatomy of Melancholy, What it is, With all the kindes, causes, symptoms, prgonostickes and several cures of it* (Oxford, 1621), 42.

[102] Thomas Nabbes, *Microcosmus, A Morall Maske* (London, 1637).

[103] William Ames, *Conscience with the Power and Cases Thereof. Divided into V. Bookes* (1639), lib. I, ch. i, 1–3.

[104] Jaeger, *Aristotle* 87–88.

[105] Cooper, *Reason and Human Good* 65–66.

[106] Ibid. 66–67.

is true. If he does, he cannot remain agnostic about the principle of non contradiction, for unless that principle is true, any statement that he believes to be true is also false.[107] Similarly, if a person denies that we can know what is genuinely good, one can ask if he believes anything to be genuinely right or wrong, or worthwhile or worthless, or deserving of praise or of blame. If he does, he cannot remain agnostic about whether there are moral principles concerning what is good that we can know and apply.

As we have seen, and as Aristotle recognized, this is the sort of argument that Socrates threw against the skepticism of Callicles in the *Gorgias* and Thrasymachus in the *Republic*. They did not merely remain silent but made a claim about how one should act. Callicles said that one should make one's own plans and have the courage and intelligence to pursue them despite law and conventional morality. Thrasymachus said that justice is the interest of the stronger. Socrates showed that these positions were untenable.

Unlike Mencius, Dai Zhen and Aristotle distinguished between a person's cognitive and volitional faculties, between his ability to know what is right and his willingness to do it. For Dai Zhen, to live rightly was in accord with principle. To understand principle, a person must be wise. To want to live in accordance with principle, a person must be benevolent. He is benevolent when his desires do not deviate from principle. If they do, it is because he lacks benevolence. His desires are selfish.

According to Aristotle, when practical reason indicates that some course of action is good, a person's will is drawn to it. Aquinas said that when one knows it is good, one feels desire for it; when one obtains it, one feels delight (*delectatio*).[108] "[T]he reason that a man is delighted is that he has some fitting good."[109] Consequently, he said, although every good gives pleasure, it is not true that "man's happiness consists in pleasure." One's happiness consists in choosing the fitting good, and delight – pleasure in this broad sense – is the result of having obtained it.[110]

Our nature is such that we cannot take pleasure in something unless it is in some way good. When a person acts wrongfully, the choice must attract him. What he chooses must be in some way good or it would not do so. He may choose wrongly because passion distorts his judgment.[111] Or he may choose wrongly because of "a disorder of the will." "The will is out of order when it loves more the lesser good," for example, when it "loves some temporal good, e.g. riches or pleasure" at the expense of a greater one.[112] Nevertheless, "[e]vil cannot be intended by anyone for its own sake."[113] After the Reformation, a similar account was given by Anglicans such as Richard Hooker[114] and Lutherans such as Johan Wilhelm Baier.[115]

For Aquinas, this account explained not only why a person wants to do what is good, but why his choice to do so may be not only voluntary but free. If there were only one

[107]   *Metaphysics* IV.4 1005b–1006a.
[108]   *Summa theologiae* I-II, Q. 3, a. 4.
[109]   Ibid. I-II, Q. 2, a. 6.
[110]   Ibid. I-II, Q. 2, a. 6.
[111]   Ibid. I-II, Q. 77, a. 2.
[112]   Ibid. I-II, Q. 78, a. 1.
[113]   Ibid. I-II, Q. 78, a. 1, ad 1.
[114]   Richard Hooker, *Of the Laws of Ecclesiastical Polity* (New York, 1907), I.viii.1, 3, 6, 7.
[115]   Iohannes Guilielmus Baierus, *Compendium theologiae positivae, adiectis notis amplioribus quibu doctrina orthodoxa ad ΠΑΙΔΕΙΑΝ Academicam explicatur* (Leipzig, 1750) II.iii.11–12.

right choice, if he acted rightly, he would have chosen voluntarily. Human actions are voluntary in a way that those of animals are not. For a human being, a choice is based on reason and will. A person acts voluntarily in this sense whenever he chooses what he understands to be good, even if there is only one good option.[116] We do not say that a person acts involuntarily when he saves the life of a child or uses some of his wealth to benefit others. Aquinas said that in such cases, practical reason reaches conclusions in a way that is similar to theoretical reason.[117] The conclusion that one should act in a certain way is a necessary inference.

Sometimes, there may be no one right choice even if all the circumstances that matter are taken into account. One cannot decide how to act by following the dictates of practical reason. One's decision to act in a certain way is free in the sense that it is not necessary. "[R]eason in contingent matters may follow opposite courses . . . Now particular operations are contingent, and in such matters the judgment of reason may follow opposite courses, and is not determinate to one. And forasmuch as man is rational, it is necessary that man have free will."[118] Thomas Cajetan (1469–1534) explained in his commentary to this passage:

> Reason as to contingent matters can arrive at opposite [conclusions] and therefore can do so as to particular courses of action. Therefore it does not arrive at a judgment determined to only one. . . . The root of freedom is reason, and the liberty of each person comes from this, that reason is not determinate and indifferent between this [course of action] and the opposite, and . . . this is prior to any act of the will."[119]

Even though there is no one right choice, the choice may matter very much. It may matter even though one cannot rank order the good that each course of action will achieve. For Aquinas, it matters that God created the universe, but he discussed God's freedom in the same way as that of human beings: there is no best of all possible worlds that God had to create.[120] It matters which of many possible beautiful buildings an architect chooses to build even though one cannot rank order their beauty.

Indeed, according to Aquinas, there may be no one right choice even when one is able rank order the value of the good that each course of action will achieve. Aristotle said that the highest life that one could live was that of a philosopher or that of a statesman. Their lives realized to the fullest extent two of the highest ends of human life: to acquire knowledge and to enable others to live good lives. The highest object of knowledge is studied by philosophers, and the good of everyone, the common good, is the concern of statesmen. Yet according to Aquinas, if Adam had never fallen and people still lived sinlessly in Eden, though all of them would be good, they would not be good in the same way and to the same degree. They would differ in knowledge.[121] Not everyone would have developed the virtues of a statesman, and consequently some would be

---

[116] *Summa theologiae* I, Q. 82, a. 2; Q. 83, a. 1.
[117] Ibid.
[118] Ibid. I, Q. 83, a. 1; see I-II, Q. 95, a. 2.
[119] Cajetan, *Commentaria* to Thomas Aquinas, *Summa theologica* to I, Q. 83, a. 1, no. 412 (Venice, 1580).
[120] *Summa theologiae* I, Q. 19, aa. 3, 10.
[121] Ibid. I, Q. 96, a. 3.

better qualified to govern others.[122] Some of the differences would be due to natural causes. They are the sort that we would ascribe to differences in genetic endowment, and Aquinas, following ancient philosophers, ascribed to "the climate or the movement of the stars." But some differences would be due to choice: "For man would work not by necessity but free will according to which man can apply himself to a greater or lesser extent in what is to be done or to be sought or to be known."[123] Because human beings have free will, Aquinas concluded, they would have been "unequal" even in Eden.

For Aquinas, this inequality was the consequence of diversity, and diversity had a role to play in the realization of the good. Drawing on ideas that can be traced back to Plato and forward to the eighteenth century, he envisioned all created beings, each as good in itself, but as differing from each other in their degree of perfection. Above human beings were the angels who were intelligent but whose knowledge was acquired by intuition, rather than, as with human beings, by abstracting from the information provided by our senses to form concepts. Below were the other animals, which had an awareness provided by their senses, but no ability to form concepts, and consequently, no ability to understand the ends for which they were acting. Below them were plants, which had ends to which they could adapt their behavior, but no awareness at all. Below them were inorganic things, which could act only in one invariable way. Yet each contributed in its own way to the perfection of the universe. According to Aquinas, "as the divine wisdom is the cause of the distinction of things for the sake of the perfection of the universe, so it is the cause of inequality. For the universe would not be perfect if only one grade of goodness were found in things."[124] The reason is that all good things reflect God's goodness in different ways, and it would be a less perfect universe if these many ways were not found in it. "His goodness could not be adequately represented by one creature alone." Consequently, "He produced many and diverse creatures so that what was wanting in one in the representation of divine goodness might be supplied by another."[125]

Humans are not the equals of the angels, but they have a goodness of their own which is wanting in the angels. In Eden, had Adam never fallen, those who by free choice decline to be philosophers or statesman are not their equals in that respect, yet their lives have a goodness that those of a philosopher or statesman lack. Even if everyone could be an excellent philosopher or statesman, the world would be poorer if everyone chose to do so. A person can choose a different life for the sake of the goodness which would otherwise be missing and thereby contribute to the good of society as a whole: to what, as we will see, Aquinas called the "common good." In doing so, one exercises "free will."

---

[122]   Ibid. I, Q. 96, a. 4.
[123]   Ibid. I, Q. 96, a. 3.
[124]   Ibid. I, Q. 97, a. 2.
[125]   Ibid. I, Q. 47, a. 1.

6

Justice, Propriety, and the Common Good

I *REN* (仁) AND THE COMMON GOOD

In both classical traditions, normative standards are based on human nature. To act rightly is to live a truly human life. In both traditions, the purpose of society and government is to help every person to live such a life. Part of living such a life is to help others to do so.

Confucians spoke of *ren* (仁) or benevolence. For Mencius, the object of *ren* is the well-being of others. When extended, it is the well-being of everyone in society. One of his examples of benevolence concerned a king who doubted that he had any such virtue. Mencius reminded him of the distress he had once felt seeing an ox about to be sacrificed to consecrate a bell. He spared the ox. If extended to a concern for all people, his benevolence would be sufficient to rule a kingdom.[1]

Aristotle spoke of the virtue of "general justice." The object of general justice is the well-being of everyone in society. "The form of government is best in which every man, whoever he is, can act best and live happily."[2] Speaking of general justice, he said, "we call acts just that tend to produce and preserve happiness and its components for the political society."[3] Since both traditions had similar ideas about the source of normative standards and the purpose of society and government, it is not surprising that the objects of *ren*, when it is extended, and the objects of general justice are alike. In the vocabulary of Aquinas and later writers in the Aristotelian tradition, both aim at the common good.

To seek the good of every member of society has a dual status in both classical traditions. On the one hand, to promote the good of all is the ultimate end of government. On the other, it is the highest of human virtues. Consequently, in both classical traditions, there is no conflict in principle between the pursuit of the common good and the well-being of every member of society. The common good – the object of *ren* or of general justice – is the well-being of every member of society. Moreover, every act of any member of society that promotes the well-being of others promotes his own well-being.

---

[1] *Mencius* 1A7.4–5.
[2] *Politics* VII.i 1324a.
[3] Thomas Aquinas, *In decem libros Ethicorum Aristoteles ad Nicomachum expositio* Angelo Pirotta, ed. (Turin, 1934), V lec. iii, no. 919.

According to Mencius, "benevolence is the most honorable dignity conferred by Heaven, and the quiet home in which man should dwell."[4] "Benevolence is the distinguishing characteristic of man. As embodied in man's conduct, it is called the path of duty."[5] It had a certain priority over *yi* (義), which may be translated as "righteousness" or "justice." As Kwong-loi Shun noted, *ren* "emphasizes an affective concern for others . . . . On the other hand, *yi* emphasizes a commitment to abiding by certain ethical standards."[6] Lai Chen said that *ren* "is the principle of love," and *yi* "is the principle of justice."[7] Violations of one's duties to others are instances of unrighteous conduct. It is unrighteous, for example, to impose heavy taxes,[8] to kill an innocent person,[9] or to take what belongs to another.[10] According to Mencius, one "dwells in benevolence" and "pursues the path of righteousness."[11] "Benevolence is the tranquil habitation of man, and righteousness is his straight path."[12]

Mencius regarded benevolence as the greatest of the virtues.[13] Indeed, because acts of righteousness contribute to another's well-being, they are also acts of benevolence. It is unrighteous to impose excessive taxes. Mencius said that to do so is contrary to benevolence as well.[14] To kill an innocent person is unrighteous. It, too, is contrary to benevolence, so much so that Mencius used it as an example of benevolence in contrasting benevolence and righteousness. "[T]o put a single innocent person to death is contrary to benevolence; . . . to take what one has not a right to is contrary to righteousness."[15] The force of the example is that the killing of an innocent person strongly arouses one's compassion which is the root of benevolence. Taking his property does so to a lesser extent, especially because, in Mencius' example, we are not told what was taken or how important it was to the owner. Taking his property, however, is a clear case of violating a normative standard that prescribes what is due to another person.

Aristotle said that general justice includes every other virtue. "[J]ustice in this sense" is not part of virtue but "virtue entire." "This form of justice . . . is complete virtue, but not absolutely, but in relation to our neighbor."[16] Aquinas explained, "the good of any virtue, whether that virtue directs man in relation to himself or in relation to other individuals can be referred to the common good to which justice directs: so that all acts of virtue can pertain to [general] justice insofar as it directs man to the common good."[17]

---

4 *Mencius* 2A:7.2.
5 Ibid. 7B16.
6 Kwong-loi Shun, *Mencius and Early Chinese Thought* (Stanford, 1997), 63.
7 Lai Chen, "The Basic Character of the Virtue Theory of Mencius' Philosophy and Its Significance in Classical Confucianism" *Frontiers of Philosophy in China* 9 (2013), 4 at 13.
8 *Mencius* 3B.8.
9 Ibid. 2A2.24.
10 Ibid. 7A.33.3.
11 Ibid. 4A.10; similarly 7A.33.3.
12 Ibid. 4A10.2.
13 Chen "Basic Character of Virtue Theory" 12.
14 *Mencius* 1A53.3–4.
15 Ibid. 7A.33.3.
16 *Nicomachean Ethics* V.i
17 *Summa theologiae* II-II, Q. 58, a. 5.

Mencius saw no need for a further explanation of relation of righteousness to benevolence. A person who fulfills his duties to others, as righteousness requires, is concerned about the well-being of all. Writers in the Aristotelian tradition tried to define the virtues and their relations to each other. They asked how it could be that general justice "answers to the whole of virtue" and constitutes "virtue entire." If it was a distinct virtue, how could it be all virtues?

That question was debated among the members of a school founded at the University of Salamanca by Francisco de Vitoria (1492–1546) and Domingo de Soto (1494–1560). Among its leaders were Luis de Molina (1535–1600), Leonard Lessius (1554–1623), and Francisco Suárez (1548–1617). Like the scholastic writers of the Middle Ages, they held Aristotle in high regard, and, like them, they endeavored to reconcile conflicting authorities. Consequently, historians have called them "the late scholastics."

Lessius thought that Aristotle and Aquinas must be wrong. Aquinas, he observed, thought that general justice was "a particular virtue, distinct from every other, which procures the public good." "But the whole difficulty is, what is this justice, what is its function, and in what way is it to be distinguished from other [virtues]?" "We can either discuss how the matter really is (*re ipsa*) or how it is according to the mind of Aristotle who was the first to use this term."[18] No doubt, "to wish and to procure good for the Republic is a special reason why [an act] is good and laudable which is not among the functions of the other virtues." No doubt, "every citizen, because he is part of the society and enjoys its benefits, is under a special obligation to procure what is good for the society." "If he neglects the common good when the society is in peril he sins."[19] But, "it is probable that the virtue here cannot be distinguished from that of *pietas*." That word did not have the same meaning as "piety" in English. It meant "love and service owed to the country or republic in which we live."[20] Or, Lessius said, more probably, the virtue in question is "obedience,"[21] a virtue connected with *observantia* or deference to those in authority.

According to Martha Nussbaum, when Aristotle said that general justice is "virtue entire," he meant that "true excellence of character has a relational nature: without making political and other-related concerns ends in themselves, one will lack not only justice but also true courage, true moderation, true generosity, greatness of soul, conviviality, and so forth."[22]

> The idea seems to be something like this. True courage (as opposed to mere brashness) requires an appropriate, which is to say more than merely instrumental, concern for the well-being of one's country and fellow citizens; true moderation (as opposed to crafty pleasure-seeking) requires the proper (and this is non-instrumental) respect for standing norms of convivial and sexual interaction; true generosity a non-crafty concern for the good

---

[18] Leonard Lessius, *De iustitia et iure, ceterisque virtutibus cardinalis libri quatuor* (Paris, 1628), lib. 2, cap. 1, dub. 3, no. 10.

[19] Ibid. no. 11.

[20] Ibid. no. 12.

[21] Ibid. no. 14.

[22] Martha Nussbaum, *The Fragility of Goodness Luck and Ethics in Greek Tragedy and Philosophy* (rev. ed., Cambridge, 2001), 352.

of the recipient; and so forth. In each case, one cannot choose these excellent activities as ends in themselves (as the definition of excellence requires), without also choosing the good of others as an end.[23]

Perhaps. But it is hard to see why one cannot be truly courageous, not in defense of society, but in defense of oneself or one's family, or why one cannot not be truly moderate, neither out of respect for the standing norms of society nor out of "crafty pleasure seeking," but to avoid the harm to oneself done by excess. One cannot be truly generous without a concern for the good of others, but must one be concerned the good of everyone? Yet according to Aristotle, general justice, which is "virtue entire," is directed to the "common advantage."

A sounder interpretation, and one more faithful to the tradition, is that every virtue promotes the end of society by promoting the well-being of any of its members. The reason is that the end of society is the well-being of all of its members. According to Aristotle, "a state exists for the sake of a good life," for the sake of "happiness."[24] Consequently, every virtue that contributes to the happiness of a member contributes to the end of the state.

Thus Aquinas said that "all who are included in a community stand in relation to that community as parts to a whole." Virtue is directed to the good of an individual member of the community, and hence to the good of a part: "temperance and fortitude direct man in relation to himself;" "particular justice ... direct[s] man in his relations to other individuals."[25] Yet the perfection of the part perfects the whole. "[W]hatever is the good of a part can be directed to the good of the whole."[26] Consequently, "the good of any virtue, whether that virtue directs man in relation to himself or in relation to other individuals can be referred to the common good to which justice directs: so that all acts of virtue can pertain to [general] justice in so far as it directs man to the common good."[27]

As Molina explained, "according to the mind of Aristotle" general justice "is the act of all virtue." General justice is

> an act of any virtue whatsoever, not as it is in itself, but so far as it is ordered to the common good of the multitude of which the one who exercises the virtue is a part. Or (which is to say the same thing) so far as it comes from a man, not as a person who is an individual ... but as part of the Republic, which, acting in this way, is related optimally to the whole and to the common good.[28]

Justice in this sense "is directed toward another, and indeed, to the common good and that of the Republic, and is called [general] justice."[29]

Thus, the common good is the ultimate end to which any virtuous action contributes and for the sake of which it may be performed. As Aquinas said, general justice "directs the acts of other virtues to its own end," it "moves other virtues by its command," and so is

---

23 Ibid.
24 *Politics* III.ix.
25 *Summa theologiae* II-II, Q. 58, a. 7.
26 *Summa theologiae* II-II, Q. 58, a. 5.
27 Ibid.
28 Ludovicus Molina, *De iustitia et iure tractatus* (Venice, 1614), I disp. 1 no. 1.
29 Ibid. no. 4.

"a universal cause" of all the virtues."[30] Thomas Cajetan (1469–1534) explained in his commentary on Aquinas: "[B]ecause [general justice] commands the other virtues, for example, temperance and fortitude, and orders their acts to the common good . . . ; in this relationship, justice, which commands, is said to be in the virtue commanded."[31]

To say that the common good is the ultimate end of any act of virtue does not mean that one who acts virtuously has this ultimate end continually in mind.[32] Nor does it mean an act is not virtuous at all unless it is performed for the sake of this ultimate end. Such an act is imperfectly virtuous. According to Cajetan, the relationship of general justice to the other virtues "is similar to [that of] charity [to] the other virtues . . . . They are attributed to charity because it operates by means (*mediantibus*) of the other virtues." General justice directs a person to his highest natural end: his end is to fulfill his human potential to its greatest extent, and he does so by living in and contributing to a society in which all members are fulfilling their own potential. Consequently, for Aristotle, there is no higher moral virtue than general justice. "This form of justice . . . is often thought to be the greatest of virtues, and 'neither the evening nor the morning star' is so wonderful."[33] As Christians, Cajetan, and Aquinas believed that human beings have not only a natural but also a supernatural end: to know and love God. Charity, the love of God, directs all virtues and actions toward this supernatural end[34] as general justice directs them to one's natural end. The natural end is "generically good" even if it is not "perfectly good" unless directed to this further end by charity.[35] Similarly, the virtues that general justice directs to one's natural end, such as temperance, courage, and particular justice, are generically good, though less perfectly so, if they are not performed for the sake of this natural end.

To illustrate, a carpenter might work to support his family. In doing so, he exercises the virtues of domestic prudence and care for the members of his household. His employer might pay him a just wage, and he might do a good job in return. Each would be exercising the virtue of commutative justice, which we will discuss shortly. He may find his work worthwhile because he knows that the house he helps to build will provide shelter and beauty which others can enjoy. He may be doing all of these things, however, because he wishes to live in and contribute to a society which is good for himself and all of its members. If he can no longer work, he may suffer because he is no longer a contributing member of society. In pursuing all his other ends, he is pursuing the common good. That ultimate end is not only in harmony with his private ends. Without it, they would be worthwhile but incomplete.

---

[30]   *Summa theologiae* II-II, Q. 58, a. 6.
[31]   Cajetan (Tomasso de Vio), *Commentaria* to Thomas Aquinas, *Summa theologica* to II-II, Q. 58, aa. 5–7 (Venice 1580).
[32]   Aquinas said: "One need not always be thinking of the last end, whenever one desires or does something: but the virtue of the first intention, which was in respect of the last end, remains in every desire directed to any object whatever, even though one's thoughts be not actually directed to the last end. Thus while walking along the road one needs not to be thinking of the end of every step." *Summa theologiae* I-II, Q. 2., a. 5, ad 2.
[33]   *Nicomachean Ethics* V.i.
[34]   *Summa theologiae* II-II, Q. 23, a. 7.
[35]   Ibid. a. 7, ad 1.

Mencius would have been content to say that all the acts described are good insofar as they are acts either of benevolence or of righteousness. But the root of all of them is benevolence, and benevolence extended to its utmost embraces the good of all.

II YI (義) AND DISTRIBUTIVE JUSTICE

Mencius said that it would be a violation of *yi* (義) – of righteousness or justice – to impose heavy taxes,[36] to kill an innocent person,[37] or to take what belongs to another.[38] According to Aristotle, all of these actions would violate what he called particular justice as opposed to general justice. Particular justice was of two kinds: distributive justice which promotes a fair distribution of wealth, and commutative justice which protects what belongs to each person. To impose heavy taxes would violate distributive justice. To kill another person or take what belongs to him would violate commutative justice.

The most striking difference is that writers in the Confucian traditions said much more about what the state should do to promote what Aristotelians called distributive justice. Writers in the Aristotelian tradition said much more than the Confucians about commutative justice.

Writers in the Aristotelian tradition described only the most general principles of distributive justice. Distributive justice follows a geometric proportion: each person receives according to "merit." It is the mathematics of dividing a pie. Societies with different political structures will differ as to what constitutes "merit." "Democrats identify it with the status of a freeman, supporters of oligarchy with wealth (or noble birth), and supporters of aristocracy with excellence."[39]

Mencius had much more to say. One fundamental task of government is to ensure that every member of society had a fair share of resources.

To achieve that end, the government should "make the taxes . . . light, so the people may be made rich."[40] Ideally, the amount paid in taxes would be about a tenth,[41] to limit taxes and to ensure that farmers had an adequate amount of land to farm. Mencius proposed an ideal program, the "nine squares" (井 *jing*) system, which few Chinese governments ever tried to implement. Parcels of land would be divided into nine squares, like a drawing for tic-tac-toe. One family would farm each of the eight squares. The ninth would be cultivated in common and the produce paid as taxes. "A square *li* covers nine squares of land, which nine squares contain nine hundred *mu*. The central square is the public field, and eight families, each having its private hundred *mu*, cultivate in common the public field. And not until the public work is finished, may they presume to attend to their private affairs."[42] The program required a periodic redivision of land to make sure each family was provided

---

[36] *Mencius* 3B.8.
[37] Ibid. 2A2.24.
[38] Ibid. 7A.33.3.
[39] *Nichomachean Ethics* V.3. 1131a.
[40] *Mencius* 7A23.1 See IA5.3.
[41] Ibid. 3A3.6–7.
[42] Ibid. 3A3.19.

for. The redivision had to be entrusted to officials. Mencius himself noted the danger of corruption. "If the boundaries be not defined correctly, the division of the land into squares will not be equal, and the produce available for benefits will not be evenly distributed. On this account, oppressive rulers and impure ministers are sure to slight this defining of the boundaries."[43]

Mencius was asked whether it would be better if a twentieth of the produce were collected in taxes. He answered that it would undermine the advantages of a system in which some people held a higher place than others. The principality of Mo had such a tax rate. Consequently, in Mo

> There are no fortified cities, no great houses, no ancestral temples, no ceremonies of sacrifice; there are no princes requiring coins, silks, banquets, no hundred officers with their subordinates. On that account a tax of one-twentieth is sufficient there.
>
> But now we live in the Middle Kingdom. To eliminate proper relationships among men and have no *junzi* (君子 worthy men). How could that be acceptable?
>
> With but few potters a kingdom cannot subsist. How much less can it subsist without *junzi*?[44]

Each family was to have an adequate living, but those who held a higher rank were to receive proportionately more. In the Zhou dynasty, Mencius said, the empire was divided into states of varying sizes. The amount a person received depended on the size of the state and his rank within it. For example,

> In a great State, where the territory was a hundred *li* square, the ruler had ten times as much income as his chief ministers; a chief minister four times as much as a great officer; a great officer twice as much as a scholar of the first class; a scholar of the first class twice as much as one of the middle; a scholar of the middle class twice as much as one of the lowest; the scholars of the lowest class, earn as much income as the common people employed in government offices, that is, enough income that would substitute their effort farming the fields.[45]

To jump seventeen centuries forward, the salaries paid to Ming officials ranged from 60 *shi* for a prefectural instructor, an official of the lowest rank (rank 9b), to 90 for a district magistrate (7a), 288 for a prefect (4a), 732 for a minister (2a), and 1044 for an official of the highest rank (1a).[46] Kings, officials, and scholars were deemed to be more worthy, and so they should receive more.

Yet they did not receive so much more as to shock a member of our supposedly more egalitarian society. For purposes of comparison: as of this writing, the average family income in America is just short of $60,000, and that, of course, is the median, not the bottom. If we imagine that amount to correspond to the earnings of Mencius' ordinary farmer, then, in the society he is describing, a scholar of the lowest rank would receive the

---

[43] Ibid. 3A3.13.
[44] Ibid. 6B10.6.
[45] Ibid. 5B2.6.
[46] Edward L. Dreyer, *Early Ming China: A Political History 1355–1435* (Stanford, 1982), 138.

same amount. A scholar of the next rank would receive $120,000, which is the salary of a curator at a leading art museum, and somewhat below that of a musician playing with a prominent orchestra or the average university professor or state governor, and somewhat above that of the average journalist for the *New York Times*. A scholar of the first class would receive $240,000, which is approximately the salary of the conductor of a prominent orchestra, a leading scholar at a major university, a mid-level editor of the *New York Times*, a well-known columnist, or a Supreme Court Justice. The great officers would receive $580,000, the salary of the president at a prominent university or the director of a leading museum, and nearly one and a half times that of the President of the United States. The few richest men, the chief ministers, would receive $ 2,240,000, a level reached by only the highest paid university presidents and some news anchors, a few of whom receive several times that amount. It is an unequal division of wealth but not so different than our own, so far as these occupations are concerned, although, by comparison, we grossly underpay those in government.

We have been considering, however, only jobs in education, government, art, and journalism. Top jobs in business and law pay more. The starting salary for someone with an MBA from a top school or a JD joining a top law firm is over $120,000. A salary of $2,240,000 is half the compensation of a partner at a leading law firm, and one fifth that of a CEO at a major company.

Although the Confucian tradition placed farmers, scholars, and officials on a higher moral level than those engaged in trade, Mencius thought that the goods of merchants should not be taxed. The reason was to provide an incentive for their activity and the economic benefits it conferred.

> If the shops in the market pay rent but [the goods] are not taxed or regulated then all merchants under heaven will be pleased and will wish to store their goods in his market place.
>
> If at the check-points at his borders there are inspections but no taxes, then all the travelers under heaven will be pleased and wish to be on the road.[47]

Although Mencius believed that officials should receive more than ordinary farmers, he sharply criticized those who ruined the farmers by taking still more. He quoted Confucius who said of a person in office who "exacted from the people double the grain formerly paid, 'children, beat the drum and assail him'."[48] Those in authority who impose corvee "rob their people of their time, so that they cannot plough and weed their fields, in order to feed their parents. Their parents suffer from cold and hunger. Brothers, wives, and children are separate and scatter."[49] They have "pulled down houses to make foul ponds and lakes, so that the people had no place to rest in quiet; they transformed fields into gardens and parks, so that the people could not get clothes and food."[50]

---

[47] *Mencius* 2A.5.2–3. See IB5.3.
[48] Ibid. 4A.14.1.
[49] Ibid. 1A5.4.
[50] Ibid. 3B9.5.

It is not enough to refrain from harming the people. Those in authority were responsible for promoting their welfare. Kings and officials did wrong when they failed to share with the poor.

> Dogs and pigs eat the food of men and you do not stop it. People starve and you do not give from your granaries. When people die, you say, it is not I; it is owing to the year. How is it different from stabbing and killing a man and saying, "It is not I. It is the weapon." If your Majesty stops blaming the year, then all the people under heaven will come to you.[51]

Or they may fail to take active measures to ensure that the people have enough to eat. He advised King Hui of Liang:

> If the seasons of farming are not violated, there will be more grain than can be eaten. If excessive fishing is not permitted in the pools and ponds, there will be more fishes and turtles than can be consumed. If the axes and bills enter the hills and forests only at the proper time, there will be more wood than can be used. When there are more grain and fish and turtles than can be eaten, and there is more wood than can be used, people can feed the living and mourn the dead without feeling remorse. Feeding the living and mourning the dead without feeling remorse is the first step toward way of the Kings (王道 *wang dao*).[52]

Frequently, as in one of the passages just quoted, Mencius said that when kings and officials do wrong, they are committing robbery and murder. Mencius asked King Hui of Liang,

> "Is there any difference between killing a man with a stick and with a sword?"
>
> The king said, "There is no difference!"
>
> "Is there any difference between doing it with a sword or by governing?" "There is no difference," was the reply.
>
> Mencius then said, "In your kitchen there is fat meat; in your stables there are fat horses. But your people have the look of hunger, and in the wilderness there are corpses. This leads beasts to devour men. . . . When those who are the parents of the people administer the government so that beasts devour the people, how are they the parents of the people?"[53]

Indeed, if the people wrong each other, it is likely to be the fault of the officials and kings. According to Mencius, "people who do not have a secure living . . . will not have a constant heart."[54] "In good years most of the children are good; in bad years most of the children are violent. This is not a difference coming from *Tian* [天 Heaven or God]. This is because their mind sank and drowned."[55] In times of abundance, "the strong-bodied, during their days of leisure, shall cultivate their filial piety, fraternal respect, loyalty and trustworthiness, serving their father and elder brothers at home and their elders and superiors outside."[56]

---

[51] Ibid. 1A3.5.
[52] Ibid. 1A3.3.
[53] Ibid. 1A4.2–4.
[54] Ibid. 1.1.7 20.
[55] Ibid. 6.1.7. 1.
[56] Ibid. 1.1.5.3.

In times of dearth, the people lose their "constant heart," and then "they will become lawless, wicked and extravagant, and there will be nothing that they will not do."[57]

The officials and kings who are responsible for the people's distress are therefore responsible when the people turn to evil. The passage just quoted concludes: "when they find themselves committing crimes, and then punished accordingly, the people have been led astray."[58]

III *YI* (義) AND COMMUTATIVE JUSTICE

Many Western scholars have discussed whether, in contrast to the West, the Confucian tradition failed to recognize private rights. Mencius said that it is a violation of *yi* (義) to kill an innocent person,[59] or to take what belongs to another.[60] Whether to violate *yi* in these instances is to violate one's rights to person and property depends on the meaning of "rights."

It is a violation, as Seung-Hwan Lee noted, if to have a right means to have a justified or legitimate claim against others.[61] *Yi* requires "dutifulness in discharging of one's obligation, rightfulness in respecting other's due, and righteousness in recognizing the limit of one's own desert."[62] A violation of *yi* is not a violation of rights, however, if one defines "rights" in a way that has become common in the West since the rise of liberal philosophy in the nineteenth century.

Since the nineteenth century, many Westerners have defined rights as a zone of freedom in which the right-holder exercises his will. For Kant, the right to property means that an owner may do as he chooses with what belongs to him and may exclude others from using it.[63] A promise is the expression of will of one party to a contract; a contract is the expression of will of both.[64] Nineteenth-century jurists defined rights in a similar way: property in terms of the will of the owner; contract was defined in terms of the will of the parties.[65]

That idea of right was foreign to the Confucian tradition. As Kwong-loi Shun observed:

> Confucian thinkers do ascribe to people an "autonomy" in the sense of a capacity to choose and lead their lives in a way that is not determined by external influences. On the other hand, they do not view this capacity as one of freely choosing one's own ends subject only to

---

[57] Ibid. 1.1.7 20.
[58] Ibid. 1.1.7 20.
[59] *Mencius* 2A2.24.
[60] Ibid. 7A.33.3.
[61] Seung-hwan Lee, "Was There a Concept of Rights in Confucian Virtue-Based Morality?," *Journal of Chinese Philosophy* 19 (1992), 241 at 249. See Kwong-loi Shun, "Conception of the Person in Early Confucian Thought," in Kwong-loi Shun and David B. Wong, eds., *Confucian Ethics: A Comparative Study of Self, Autonomy, and Community* (Kindle ed., Cambridge, 2004), loc. 2056 at 2750.
[62] Lee, "Concept of Rights" 249.
[63] *Die Metaphysik der Stitten Erster Theil. Metaphysische Angangsgründe der Rechtslehre* in Königlich Preussischen Akademie der Wissenschaft, ed., *Kant's gesammelte Schriften* 6 (Berlin, 1914), 203 at 245.
[64] Ibid. 272.
[65] James Gordley, *The Jurists: A Critical History* (Oxford, 2013), 222–66.

certain constraints, whether rational constraints or the constraint that one does not thereby interfere with the exercise of a similar capacity by others.[66]

Neither did the Confucians believe, like many Westerners since the nineteenth century, that a person's rights, in the sense of his legitimate claims against others, are in tension with the common good.[67] As Shun observed "there is no genuine conflict between individual interests and the public good."[68]

Although this conception of rights became common in the West since the rise of liberal philosophy, as we will see, it was not that of writers in the Aristotelian tradition. The late scholastics were the first to use the term "right" (*ius*) to refer, not to a particular right, such a right of way, but to anything a person is entitled to have or to do. But they did not define a "right" as a zone of freedom in which the right-holder exercised his will. An individual could exercise his rights as he saw fit. But the scope of a right was defined by the purpose it served, and therefore, there was no conflict between private rights and the common good.

Aristotle himself said little about commutative justice beyond identifying two kinds. In involuntary transactions, a party took or destroyed what belonged to another. Justice required that he compensate his victim for the loss. Mencius' cases of killing a person or taking his property would be examples. In voluntary transactions, the parties exchanged property or services. Justice required that they exchange at a price that enriched neither party at the other's expense. Mencius did not discuss when an exchange violates *yi*. He merely noted why it is of value for people to exchange: "If there is no division of labor and exchange of services, so that one from his surplus complements the deficiency of another, then farmers will have surplus grain and the women surplus cloth. If there is such an exchange, carpenters and carriage-wrights may all be well fed."[69] For Aristotle, the principle at stake in both kinds of commutative justice was equality. Neither party should be enriched at another's expense. Writers in the Confucian tradition laid down a general principle: *shu* (恕) or reciprocity. In the words of Confucius, "What you do not want done to yourself, do not do to others."[70]

The most striking difference is that, in discussing duties to others, writers in the Aristotelian tradition said much more about commutative justice than the Confucians

---

[66]   Shun, "Conception of the Person" locs. 2721–28. See Henry Rosemont, Jr., "Whose Democracy? Which Rights? A Confucian Critique of Modern Western Liberalism," in Shun and Wong, *Confucian Ethics* loc. 664 at loc. 729.

[67]   Lee, "Concept of Rights" 250; David B. Wong, "Rights and Community in Confucianism," in Shun and Wong, *Confucian Ethics* locs. 429–433.

[68]   Shun "Conception of the Person" locs. 2750–53.

[69]   *Mencius* 3B4.3.

[70]   *Analects* 15.24. Mencius said: "If one follows reciprocity with great effort, then his path to seeking *ren* (仁) could not be shorter." *Mencius* 7A4.3. He speaks of *ren* rather than *yi*, but as we have seen, to violate *yi* is also to violate *ren*. There is another passage in Mencius which is not clear. Literally, it reads: "Not doing what is not to be done, and not wanting what is not to be wanted; that is all." Ibid. 7A17. Legge translates it: "Let a man not do what his own sense of righteousness tells him not to do, and let him not desire what his sense of righteousness tells him not to desire; – to act thus is all he has to do." Nevertheless, the word "righteousness" (*yi*) does not appear in the passage, and, as Legge notes, there are other translations. Still, the sense of the passage, according to Legge, is that "a man has but to obey the law in himself." James Legge, trans. *The Works of Mencius* (New York, 1970), 457 note to 7A17.

said about *yi*. They were the heirs, not only of Greek philosophy but of Roman law. The late scholastics wrote volumes about commutative justice in which they synthesized the principles of Aristotle with Roman and Canon law.

The Roman jurists developed an intellectually sophisticated and comprehensive body of law, the like of which the Western world, at least, had never seen. When it was rediscovered in the twelfth century, Roman legal texts became the basis of instruction in law schools first in Italy, then in France, and eventually throughout Europe. Roman law, as interpreted by medieval jurists, was adopted as a *ius commune,* or common law, by continental courts. In the twelfth century, Canon law was taught along with Roman law based on a set of texts taken from the Bible, Church Councils, the writings of saints, and other sources authoritative for Christians which were collected in the *Decretum* or *Concordance of Dissonant Canons,* traditionally ascribed to Gratian. The same methods were used to interpret Canon law as to interpret Roman law, and the doctrines of the one often influenced those of the other.

In the ancient world and throughout the Middle Ages, the study of law was for the most part independent of the study of philosophy. Roman law was so sophisticated that many historians have thought that the Romans borrowed from Greek philosophy. Nevertheless, as I have described elsewhere,[71] and as one can see from a few comparisons, the Roman method of reasoning was quite different.

In discussing the branches of law that we call contracts and torts, Greek philosophers were concerned not with the specifics but with the underlying principles of justice. As we have seen, Aristotle distinguished between commutative justice in involuntary and voluntary transactions. Aristotle's distinction not only resembles the distinction between torts and contracts, but may be the origin of that distinction. Gaius (fl. AD 130–180) was the first Roman jurist to distinguish between contract (*contractus*) and tort (*delictus*).[72] Historians believe that he was following Aristotle.[73] Nevertheless, the Roman jurists were concerned with what we would call particular contracts and torts, each with its own rules. Having distinguished contract and tort, Gaius immediately turned to describing the particular contracts and torts recognized in Roman law and the rules peculiar to each.

Similarly, when the Greek philosophers discussed property, they discussed the justification for it. Plato proposed that in the ideal state, there should be no private property. Aristotle argued that without private property, those who worked much would receive the same as those who worked little, and there would be constant quarrels over the use of things.[74] But the theories of Plato and Aristotle did not interest the Roman jurists. Their concern was not the principles that justify private property but with the rights that attach to various kinds of property and how these rights are acquired.

---

[71] Gordley, *Jurists* 12–18.

[72] G. Inst. III.88.

[73] Reinhard Zimmermann, *The Law of Obligations: Roman Foundations of the Civilian Tradition* (Capetown, 1990), 10–11; Max Kaser, *Römische Privatrecht* (Munich, 1959), 522; A. M. Honoré, *Gaius* (Oxford, 1962), 100; Helmut Coing, "Zum Einfluß der Philosophie des Aristoteles aud die Entwicklung des römischen Rechts," *Zeitschrift der Savigny-Stiftung für Rechtsgeschichte, Rom. Abt.* 69 (1952), 24–59.

[74] *Politics* V.ii 1263a.

Throughout the Middle Ages, although the teaching of many other subjects was based on the works of Aristotle, the teaching of law was based on Roman legal texts. Even the medieval jurists who read and admired Aristotle, did not try to integrate his philosophical ideas with Roman law. The influence was only occasional. The same can be said of the influence of Roman law on the medieval philosophers.[75]

A serious attempt to explain Roman law by Aristotelian philosophical principles was first made by the sixteenth and early seventeenth centuries by the late scholastics. They gave Roman law a systematic doctrinal structure for the first time.[76]

The task of reconciling Roman rules with philosophical principles was made easier by the distinction Aquinas had drawn between "natural" and "positive" law. Aquinas said that "[l]aw is a dictate of practical reason."[77] Practical reason identifies the actions that best contribute to the ultimate ends a person should seek. Because those ends are grounded in human nature, all law is based on natural law. Sometimes, as noted earlier, practical reason can identify a single right choice, just as theoretical reason comes to a single conclusion, albeit by a different process. At other times, practical reason cannot identify one right course of action, and yet a decision must be made. The decision (*determinatio*) is like the one an architect makes when he decides on the design of a house.[78] When a conclusion is derived from the natural law in the first way, it belongs to the natural law in a strict sense. It prescribes how one should act regardless of whether one is bound to do so by enacted law. When an individual makes a decision in the second way, as we have seen, it is an exercise of freedom. When those in authority may make such a decision they enact a positive law which ensures that the same rule will be followed by everyone. Positive law is binding only because it has been enacted by someone in authority.

Consequently, when the late scholastics could explain a rule by showing that it was based on philosophical principles of justice, they said that it belonged to natural law. When they were unable to do so, they said that the rule was one of positive law binding only where Roman law was in force. They did not need to find a philosophical justification for every Roman rule.

Their work was a turning point in the development of law. Hitherto, Roman law had been regarded as preeminently reasonable. Now those parts of it for which the late scholastics could give a principled explanation took on a life of their own. They constituted a law of nature with an authority independent of the Roman texts. The medieval professors of Roman and Canon law wrote commentaries on the authoritative texts. The late scholastics wrote treatises organized into chapters on topics such property, contract, and tort, organizing them systematically into doctrines, explaining them by philosophical principles, and citing Roman texts, and, where possible, Canon law texts as examples.

The doctrinal structure which the late scholastics developed, along with many of their conclusions, was adopted by Hugo Grotius, the founder of the northern natural law school

---

[75]   Gordley, *Jurists* 83.
[76]   Ibid. 84–101.
[77]   *Summa theologiae* I-II, Q. 91, a. 3, citing Q. 90, a. 1, ad 2.
[78]   Ibid. I-II, Q. 95, a. 2.

and by later members of the school such as Samuel Pufendorf (1632–94) and Jean Barbeyrac (1674–1744).[79] Much of it passed into modern law, although, as we will see in detail later on, some characteristically Aristotelian features did not.

The late scholastics used the Aristotelian concept of commutative justice to explain the Roman law of contracts and torts (or delicts). Roman law distinguished contracts according to how they became binding. Some were binding on consent, such as sale and lease. Others were binding only on delivery of an object, such as loans of money or goods for consumption (*mutuum*), loans of specific goods for the borrower's use (*commodatum*), and the deposit of an object for safekeeping (*depositum*). These contracts were gratuitous: nothing was charged for the object loaned or for keeping the object safe. Other contracts were binding only on completion of a formality. The all-purpose formality was *stipulatio*, replaced in the Middle Ages by notarization, which could be used to make any promise binding. A special formality was required for the promise of a gift of money or property.

The late scholastics reclassified these contracts. Only some Roman contracts fit Aristotle's description of acts of voluntary acts of commutative justice, for example, sale and lease. Following Aquinas,[80] the late scholastics explained that others were acts of another Aristotelian virtue, liberality. Liberality, according to Aristotle, is a virtue manifested "in the giving and taking of wealth, and especially in respect of giving." "[T]he liberal man will give for the sake of the noble and rightly; for he will give to the right people, the right amounts, and at the right time, with all the other qualifications that accompany right giving."[81] There were, then, two kinds of voluntary arrangements: those based on commutative justice, in which each party obtained an equivalent for what he gave, and those based on liberality.

The late scholastics concluded that in principle both of them were binding upon consent. They dismissed the Roman distinctions as to when contracts were binding as matters of Roman positive law. Cajetan, a sixteenth-century theologian and commentator on Aquinas, had suggested that as a matter of commutative justice, all contracts should not be binding upon consent. A party might be disappointed if he did not receive a benefit he was not promised, but, if the contract was not performed, as a matter of commutative justice, he had lost nothing. He should recover only if he had changed his position in reliance on the agreement.[82] The late scholastics disagreed, and Grotius followed them. By voluntarily entering into a contract, one party gave the other the right to require performance. To deny him that right is a violation of commutative justice.[83]

For the late scholastics, Aristotelian principles of commutative justice explained why a contract to exchange should not be enforced when its terms are unfair. According to

---

79 Gordley, *Jurists* 128–40.

80 *Summa theologiae* II-II, Q. 61, a. 3.

81 *Nicomachean Ethics* IV.i 1119b–1120a. A similar account was given by Aquinas. *Summa theologiae* II-II, Q. 119, aa. 2–4.

82 Cajetan, *Commentaria* to Thomas Aquinas, *Summa theologica* to II-II, Q. 88, a. 1; Q. 113, a. 1. (Venice 1580).

83 Ludovicus Molina, *De iustitia et iure tractatus* (Venice, 1614), disp. 262; Leonard Lessius, *De iustitia et iure, ceterisque virtutibus cardinalis libri quatuor* (Paris, 1628), lib. 2, cap. 18, dub. 8, no. 52; Hugo Grotius, *De iure belli ac pacis libri tres* (Amsterdam, 1646), II.xi.1.3–4.

Aristotle, when the parties exchange resources voluntarily, commutative justice requires that what each party gives is equal in value to what he receives. Following Aquinas, the late scholastics and Grotius used the principle of equality in exchange to explain a remedy developed by the medieval jurists for *laesio enormis*, or a severe discrepancy between the contract price and the fair price. One Roman text, dating from the late empire, gave a remedy to one who had sold land for less than half the "true price."[84] The medieval civilians expanded this text into a general remedy that protected sellers of things other than land, buyers as well as to sellers, and parties to leases and similar contracts as well as sales.[85] According to Aquinas, in principle, as Aristotle said, commutative justice required equality, but for pragmatic reasons, the law only gave a remedy for a deviation of more than half from the just price.[86] The late scholastics agreed.[87]

For the late scholastics, the requirement of equality in exchange also explained the terms that Roman law read into a contract when the parties had made no provision themselves. In Roman law, in sale, lease, and other contracts "of good faith" (*bonae fidei*), a party was bound to whatever terms good faith required. In Roman law as interpreted by the medieval jurists, one of these terms was that a seller was bound to warrant his goods against undisclosed defects. According to Aquinas, equality would be violated if he did not.[88] The late scholastics agreed.[89] Consequently, the parties could only exclude such a term if equality was preserved in some other way. According to Molina, the law would enforce a contract in which the seller refused to provide a warranty provided he reduced the price to preserve equality.[90]

The Romans did not have a general law of delict or tort, but a series of actions for the redress of injuries. One action was the *lex Aquilia* which the plaintiff brought against one who had caused harm to his property and, at least according to medieval jurists, his person. The harm had to be done *iniuria*, or wrongfully, which, the Roman jurists explained, meant that the perpetrator must have been at fault, either by intent or through negligence. Another was the action for *iniuria* which the plaintiff brought to redress defamation and various kinds of insult. The late scholastics explained these actions by a general principle: as a matter of commutative justice, a person who had negligently injured another's property, person or honor or similar right owed compensation. They concluded that the distinctions among the Roman tort actions were merely matters of Roman positive law.[91]

---

[84]   C. 4.44.2.

[85]   They reached this conclusion early on. The *Brachylogus*, written at the beginning of the twelfth century, does not speak of land but of objects sold. *Brachylogus* iii.xiii.8. According to the thirteenth-century jurist Accursius, it was agreed among the jurists that the remedy would be available generally in contracts *bonae fidei*. Gl. ord. to C 4.44.2 to *auctoritate iudicis*.

[86]   *Summa theologiae* II-II, Q. 17, a. 1, ad 1.

[87]   Soto, *De iustitia et iure* lib. 6 q. 2 a. 3; Molina, *De iustitia et iure* disp. 348; Lessius, *De iustitia et iure* lib. 2 cap. 21 dub. 2; Grotius, *De iure belli ac pacis* II.xii.14 and 23; Samuel Pufendorf, *De iure naturae et gentium libri octo* (Amsterdam, 1688), V.i.8.

[88]   See *Summa theologiae* II-II, Q. 77, aa. 2–3.

[89]   Soto, *De iustitia et iure* lib. 2., cap. 21, dub. 11; lib. 6, q. 3, a. 2; Molina, *De iustitia et iure* disp. 353; Lessius, *De iustitia et iure* lib. 2, cap. 21, dub. 11.

[90]   Molina, *De iustitia et iure* disp. 353.

[91]   For example, Soto, *De iustitia et iure* lib. 4, q. 6, a. 5; Molina, *De iustitia et iure* disps. 315, 724; Lessius, *De iustitia et iure* lib. 2, cap. 12, dubs. 16, 18; cap. 20, dubs. 10–11.

They founded this principle on Aristotle's account of commutative justice in involuntary transactions. In involuntary transactions, one person enriched himself by taking what belonged to another, and the law required that he restore the victim to his original position. There were two problems with doing so, both of which had been resolved to the satisfaction of the late scholastics by Aquinas.

One was that, according to Aristotle, when commutative justice is violated, "the judge tries to equalize things by means of the penalty," taking away the "gain" of one party and restoring the "loss" of the other.[92] Aristotle himself had admitted that it seems odd to speak of a "gain" when one person has wounded another. Nevertheless, he maintained that "when the suffering has been estimated, the one is called loss and the other gain."[93] The reason, according to Aquinas, is that a "person striking or killing has more of what is evaluated as good, insofar, that is, as he fulfills his will, and so is seen to receive a sort of gain."[94] "To gain," in this sense, is to fulfill one's will. A person who has voluntarily harmed another in pursuit of his own ends has "gained," and therefore must pay compensation, whether or not his ends were achieved, and whether or not he had made a financial gain by pursuing them.

A second difficulty is that Aristotle had been speaking only of intentionally inflicted harm, as my former colleague David Daube demonstrated, and as Aquinas himself noted.[95] For Aristotle and Aquinas, one could be responsible only for an action one performed voluntarily since a human being acts through reason and will. *Qua* human being, he is not the cause of chance events that do not proceed from his reason and will. Why, then, did he owe compensation for harm done negligently? According to Aquinas, a negligent person had acted voluntarily.[96] He failed to exercise *prudentia* or practical reason.[97] Like all virtues, practical reason is acquired by voluntary action: by taking the consequences of one's actions into account, and by doing so over and over until it becomes habitual. Aquinas and the late scholastics concluded that a person owed compensation for harm done negligently as well as intentionally.

Aquinas and the late scholastics accepted Aristotle's justification for private property.[98] In principle, originally, or by nature, all things are held in common. Private property was

---

92 *Nicomachean Ethics* V.iv 1132a.

93 Ibid. V.iv 1132a.

94 Aquinas, *In decem libros ethicorum Aristoteles expositio* lib. V, lectio vi, no. 952. He was following his teacher, Albert the Great, who had said that "the one who acts has more of what he wants, and the one who suffers has less … and this is appropriately designated by the name gain and loss." Albertus Magnus, *Ethicorum libri decem* lib. V, tract. ii, cap. 6, no. 25 in *Opera Omnia* 7 (A. Bourgnet ed., 1891).

95 David Daube, *Roman Law: Linguistic, Social and Philosophical Aspects* (Edinburgh, 1969), 131–56; Aquinas, *In decem libros ethicorum Aristoteles expositio* lib. V, lectio xiii, no. 1043.

96 *Summa theologiae* II-I, Q. 68, a. 8.

97 More technically, negligence (*negligentia*) was a lack of solicitude (*sollicitudo*) or diligence (*diligentia*). Solicitude or diligence was the virtue that enables the alert, adroit performance of the "chief act" of prudence, *praecipere*, which could be translated as "to command" or "to execute." Prudence required three "acts:" to take counsel or to consider what should be done (*consiliari*); to judge or decide what should be done (*iudicare*); and to execute this decision (*praecipere*). See Aquinas, *Summa theologiae* II-II, Q. 47, aa. 8–9; Q. 54, aa. 1–2; Q. 64, a. 8.

98 Aquinas, *Summa theologiae* II-II, Q. 66, a.7; Soto, *De iustitia et iure* lib. 4, q. 3, a. 1; Molina, *De iustitia et iure* disp. 20; Lessius, *De iustitia et iure* lib. 2, cap. 5, dubs. 1–2.

instituted to avoid the difficulties that Aristotle had described.[99] In the seventeenth century, Grotius repeated this account, followed by Pufendorf and Barbeyrac.[100] They used this account to explain a doctrine that one person is entitled to use the property of another in times of necessity. This doctrine had been developed by the medieval Canon lawyers based on a text by St. Ambrose.[101] They had illustrated it by a Roman rule that allowed ship-wrecked passengers to share all the provisions on board. Aquinas said that despite "the division of things ... man's needs have to be remedied by these very things." Therefore, if the need was "manifest and urgent" then "it is lawful for a man to meet his own need by means of another's property."[102] Lessius, Soto, and Molina followed Aquinas.[103] Their conclusion was accepted by Grotius and Pufendorf,[104] whence it passed into later law.

A by-product of their discussion of law was a change in vocabulary. The late scholastics were the first to use the term "rights" (*ius*) to refer generally to what person is entitled to have or to do.

In most European languages, though not in English, the word that we would translate as "law" when we speak of, for example, the law of England or the civil law is the same as the word that we would translate as "right," as when we speak of the right to person and property. Examples are the words *ius* in Latin, *droit* in French, *diritto* in Italian, and *Recht* in German. When non-English speakers want to be clear about which meaning is intended, they use "objective right" for the first meaning and "subjective right" for the second.

Roman jurists used *ius* in this second sense, to mean the right of a person to have something or to do something. When they did so, however, it was nearly always to describe a particular *ius* or right. For example, one could have a variety of rights in the land of another: the right to walk across it (*ius ambulandi*),[105] to drive animals across it (*ius agenda*),[106] to have water flow across it (*ius aquaeductus*),[107] to burn limestone on it (*ius calcis coquendae*),[108] and to take sand from a sandpit (*ius harenae foedienae*).[109] A person with a usufruct had the right to use and take produce from the land (*ius utendi fruendi*).[110] A debt was a *ius debiti*.[111] A creditor had a *ius crediti*.[112]

---

[99]   Aquinas, *Summa theologiae* II-II, Q. 66, a.7 ; Soto, *De iustitia et* lib. 4, q. 3, a. 1; Molina, *De iustitia et iure* disp. 20; Lessius, *De iustitia et iure* lib. 2, cap. 5, dubs. 1–2.

[100]   Grotius, *De iure belli ac pacis* II.ii.2; Pufendorf, *De iure naturae et gentium* II.vi.5; IV.iv.4–7.

[101]   *Gl. ord.* to D. 47 c.8 to *commune*.

[102]   *Summa theologiae* II-II, Q. 66, a.7.

[103]   Lessius, *De iustitia et iure* lib. 2, cap. 12, dub. 12; Soto, *De iustitia et iure* lib. 5, q. 3, a. 4; Molina, *De iustitia et iure* disp. 20.

[104]   Grotius, *De iure belli ac pacis* II.ii.6–7. See Pufendorf, *De iure naturae et gentium* II.vi.5.

[105]   J. Inst. 2.3.pr.

[106]   Ibid. 2.3.pr.

[107]   Ibid. 2.3.pr.

[108]   Ibid. 2.3.2.

[109]   Ibid.

[110]   Dig. 7.1.1.

[111]   Ibid. 4.2.13.

[112]   Ibid.

Aquinas, on whom the late scholastics based so much of their work, rarely used the word *ius* in this second sense. In discussing harms done to another, he had not asked whether a "right" was violated but whether the conduct in question was allowed (*licet*). For example, in discussing property, he asked whether one person is allowed to possess a thing as his own.[113] In discussing murder, he asked whether one person is allowed to kill another.[114] He used the term "thing" (*res*) when he described voluntary transactions such a buying and selling which Aristotle had called acts of commutative justice. In buying and selling, one person "voluntarily transfers his thing (*res*) to another."[115] He also used the word "thing" when he described *restitutio*. *Restitutio* was a doctrine of Canon law. According to this doctrine, a person who wished to be forgiven for injuring another had to compensate the victim for the harm he had suffered. According to Aquinas, "*restitutio* appears to be nothing else than to reinstate someone in the possession or ownership of his own thing (*res*)."[116]

The Canon lawyers had grounded the doctrine of *restitutio* on a passage in which St. Augustine said that if a person sins by taking away another's thing, "the sin is not forgiven unless *restitutio* is made of the thing (*res*) that was taken away."[117] In the twelfth century, this passage was included in the *Decretum* of Gratian, a collection of texts that became the basis of Canon law. Gratian used the same Latin word: "Penance is not done if another's thing (*res*) is not restored."[118]

"*Res*" is an awkward term to denote that-which-must-be-restored. When Aquinas and the Canonists spoke of *res*, they were not referring merely to the loss of a physical thing but to the loss of honor, reputation, and whatever else belonged to a person. When Francisco de Vitoria discussed *restitutio* in his commentary on Aquinas, he proposed using the term "right" (*ius*). "A right (*ius*) . . . is nothing other than what one is allowed to do or what the law (*lex*) allows. . . . . We say, indeed, 'I do not have the right to do this,' that is, 'it is not allowed for me to do it,' and again, 'I am using my right,' that is, 'it is allowed.'"[119] Soto said that *ius* in one sense means law (*lex*) as when we say *ius civile* or *ius canonicum*, the civil law or the canon law. In another sense it means "the legitimate power which someone exercises over some person or thing."[120] Lessius defined right, in that sense, as a "legitimate power . . . the violation of which constitutes an injury."[121] Molina said that a right is a "faculty or power to do something a man has . . . or to use something by his own right."[122]

This was the first time that *ius* was used as a generic term to refer to rights. Some modern scholars have concluded that the late scholastics invented the modern conception of rights.[123]

---

[113]　*Summa theologiae* II-II, Q. 66, a. 2.

[114]　Ibid. II-II, Q. 64, aa. 2–7.

[115]　Ibid. II-II, Q. 61, a. 3.

[116]　Ibid. II-II, Q. 62, a. 1.

[117]　C. 14 q. 6 c. 1.

[118]　*Dicta Gratiani ante* C. 14 q. 6 c. 1.

[119]　Francisco de Vitoria, *Commentarios a la Secunda Secundae de Santo Tomas* to II-II Q. 61, a. 1 (Salamanca, 1932).

[120]　Soto, *De iustitia et iure* lib. 6 q. 2 a. 3 ; lib. 4, q. 1, a. 1.

[121]　Lessius, *De iustitia et iure* lib. 1, cap. 2, dub. 1, no. 3.

[122]　Molina, *De iustitia et iure* II, disp. I, no. 2.

[123]　See Brian Tierney, *The Idea of Natural Rights Studies on Natural Rights, Natural Law, and Church Law 1150–1625* (1997), 259.

Nevertheless, as Brian Tierney observed, the change in terminology was due to the desire to more adequately express what Aquinas and the Canonists had said using a different word. To quote Tierney: "Vitoria's problem was that he could not discuss restitution adequately without considering the concept of *ius* as a subjective right. The definition he had earlier accepted from Aquinas did not include any such concept."[124]

Since the rise of liberal theories in the nineteenth century, people have become accustomed to an idea of rights that was foreign to the late scholastics. As a result, modern scholars have assumed that in speaking about rights, the late scholastics must be referring to rights as they have been understood since the nineteenth century. As noted earlier, nineteenth-century liberal philosophers commonly defined rights in terms of the will of the right-holder to do as he wished.

Writers in the Aristotelian tradition conceived of a right quite differently. They recognized that an owner could exercise his rights as he chose and that the contracting parties have the right to exchange on terms that they choose. Nevertheless, the scope of their rights is determined by justice, that is, by the reasons that it is just for a person to own property or by the equality that commutative justice requires in an exchange. The novelty of defining rights in terms of the will of the owner or the contracting parties, as liberal philosophers did, was not to introduce the concept of the will. It was to leave out the considerations of justice, anchored in the social order, that once defined the content and therefore limited the exercise of rights.

In the earlier conception, as we have seen, the doctrine of necessity was not an impairment of the right of a property owner to exclude others from using his property. The owner did not have a right to do so. His rights were limited by the purposes for which property rights are established. Similarly, to give relief for an unjust price was not to interfere with the power that the law of contract assigned to the will of the contracting parties. The purpose of the contract was to allow each party to obtain resources that he wanted more than those he gave in return without either party enriching himself at the other's expense. A party who charged an unjust price was not exercising his rights as a contracting party. He was using the institution of contract to go beyond the purposes that its rules are meant to serve. His rights as a contracting party did not extend that far.

Rights of property and contract, conceived in this way, could not be exercised by individuals except in society. Private property is established by society to avoid the disadvantages of common ownership. Commutative justice preserves the share of resources that belongs to each person. The share that each person ideally should have is a matter of distributive justice. Distributive and commutative justice both pertain to the just organization of society. As Aquinas said,

> [T]he private person . . . is related to the community as a part to the whole. Now a two-fold order may be seen in a part. The first is the order of one part to another, which is like the order of one private person to another. This order is directed by commutative justice which concerns the mutual relations of two people to each other. The other order is that of the

---

[124] Ibid. 259.

whole to the parts, and it is like that order of the community to particular people. This order is directed by distributive justice.[125]

IV PROPRIETY (*LI* 禮)

In the Confucian tradition, duties to others in recurring situations are specified by *li* (禮), often translated as propriety. They are particularly concerned with how to behave in five relationships: a minister to his ruler, a son to his father, a wife to her husband, a younger brother to an elder brother, and a friend to a friend. Many of the rules of *li* are ceremonial, and so the word *li* is also translated as "rites" or "ceremonies." There are a vast number of them. The *Doctrine of the Mean* said of *li*, "[a]ll-complete is its greatness! It embraces the three hundred rules of ceremony, and the three thousand rules of demeanor."[126]

As we have seen, the origins of Roman law lay outside the Greek philosophical tradition. Similarly, the origin of the rules of *li* lay outside the Confucian tradition. Confucius claimed to be preserving the *li* of the Zhou Dynasty, which had been based on those of the Shang (or Yin), which had been based in turn on those of the Xia.[127] Nevertheless, they became an integral part of the tradition.

Mencius believed that every human being is born with a feeling of respect (恭敬之心). When it is cultivated, a person acts in accordance with *li*.[128] Proper observance of *li* was deemed essential to moral development. All people need the "leisure to cultivate propriety and righteousness."[129]

The rules of *li*, however, are contingent in a way that the principles of benevolence and righteousness are not. As we have already seen, according to Mencius, the rules of *li* may be overridden in case of need. If a woman is drowning, one may violate the rules of propriety governing physical contact with the opposite sex in order to rescue her.

Moreover, although the feeling of respect is innate, the rules of *li* by which respect is shown are not. Innate feeling leads one to recognize, for example, that the dead should be properly buried. Yet, the rules that prescribe how to properly bury the dead are not innate. According to Mencius:

> In the most ancient times, there were some who did not bury their parents. When their parents died, they took them up and threw them into some water channel. Afterwards, when passing by them, they saw foxes and wild cats devouring them, and flies and gnats biting at them. The perspiration started out upon their foreheads, and they looked away, unable to bear the sight. It was not on account of other people that this perspiration flowed. The emotions of their hearts affected their faces and eyes, and instantly they went home, and came back with baskets and spades and covered the bodies. If the covering them thus

---

[125]   *Summa theologiae* II-II, Q. 61, a. 1.
[126]   *Doctrine of the Mean* XXVII.3.
[127]   *Analects* 2.23.
[128]   *Mencius* 6A6.7.
[129]   *Analects* 14.4.22.

was indeed right, you may see that the filial son and virtuous man, in interring in a handsome manner their parents, act according to a proper rule."[130]

Neither are the rules of *li* fixed for all time. They may change from one dynasty to the next, although each dynasty bases its rules on those of its predecessors.

> Zi Zhang asked whether the state of affairs ten generations ahead could be known. Confucius said, "The Yin [the Shang dynasty] based its propriety on that of the Xia and what it added and subtracted is knowable. The Zhou has based its propriety on that of the Yin and what it added and subtracted is knowable. The affairs of those who might follow Zhou may be known a hundred generations ahead."[131]

In principle, however, the rules of *li*, like the conventions of language, ought to be the same for everyone. According to the *Doctrine of the Mean*, "now all under Heaven have the same sized wheels; writing has the same characters; conduct has the same rules."[132] Consequently, it is important that the rules of *li* be prescribed and upheld by one in authority. According to Zisi, "No one except the Son of Heaven may ordain the rules of propriety, to fix the measures, and to scrutinize the written characters."[133] According to Confucius, when this authority is exercised at lower levels, the ruling house is in danger.[134]

Li is taught primarily by example. "If people are led by command and regulated with punishment people will avoid it and become shameless. If people are led by virtue and regulated by propriety, they will have a sense of shame and restrain themselves."[135]

Li was contrasted with *fa* or criminal law. The rules of *li* are to be obeyed out of a sense of respect for others. Confucius said, "[i]f propriety is loved, then the people will not dare to disrespect their superiors. If righteousness is loved, then people will not dare to disobey their superiors."[136] The rules of *fa* are established and enforced by the state to punish bad people who would not do what is right without the threat of punishment. It was better for those who govern to do so by instruction and the force of their own example than by punishments. Confucius said, "What we need is to have no complaints in court."[137] "If you govern the people by command and control them by punishment, they will avoid crime, but have no personal sense of shame. If you govern them by means of virtue and control them with propriety, they will gain their own sense of shame, and thus correct themselves."[138]

Like benevolence and righteousness, propriety is fundamental to the social order. *Li* was integral to the government of an empire composed of households. Of the five relationships governed by *li*, one was that of a minister to his ruler. Three were relationships within the

---

[130]   *Mencius.* 3A5.4.
[131]   *Analects* 2.23.2.
[132]   *Doctrine of the Mean* XXVIII.3.
[133]   Ibid. XXVIII.2.
[134]   *Analects* 16.2.
[135]   Ibid. 2.3.
[136]   Ibid. 13.4.3.
[137]   Ibid. 12.13.
[138]   Ibid. 2.3.

family: a son to his father, a wife to her husband, and younger brother to an elder brother. The last was the relationship to someone outside the household but not a legal one: the relationship to a friend. All except the last were vertical relationships in which one party owed deference to the other. Good government depended upon *li*. Confucius said that "there is government, when the emperor acts as an emperor, the minister acts as a minister, the father as a father, and the son as a son."[139]

A constant theme in criticisms of traditional China has been the role of hierarchical governance within the household. Modern and pre-modern literature depicts its abuses. Sun Yat Sen, the founder of the Republic of China, said that to become "a real state in the modern sense of the world," it was necessary to "substitute for the primitive notion of unity of clan or family, the notion of the population formed by these clans or families."[140] The harmonious future of humanity lies in the combination of individual and family with individual taking precedency over family."[141]

For a Confucian, it was not so. The unity of the clan or family was not primitive but the mark of a cultivated society. *Li* was the mark of a cultivated individual. Mastering *li* was the work of a lifetime. Confucius said, "the worthy man who studies all learning extensively and disciplines himself with *li* will not stray from the path."[142] The abuses were instances in which a person failed to show another proper respect. Moreover, *li* could not be disassociated from benevolence and righteousness. According to Confucius, "If a person is without *ren* (benevolence) what does he have to do with *li*?"[143] Conversely, "To overcome one's self and to return to *li* is *ren*."[144] Mencius said, "Those who converse without propriety and righteousness are said to do violence to themselves. Those who throw themselves away are impossible to do anything with."[145]

For Confucians, to follow *li* was to live a beautiful and cultivated life in harmony with others. Suppose one disagreed. A critic might claim that to follow *li* is an obstacle to fulfilling one's potential as a human being. If so, that objection, right or wrong, would be based on a core principle of the Confucian tradition itself: that a good life is one that fulfils one's potential as a human being.

Suppose the critic were right. Then it might be, as Dai Zhen said, that what was once important is not important now that times have changed. Dai Zhen said

Weighing is how the important and unimportant are distinguished. If for thousands of years, what is called important and unimportant does not change, that is constancy. If something is constant, then it should be commonly obvious that for thousands of years what is important and unimportant have not changed. When the important became unimportant and the unimportant became unimportant, change has occurred. In case

---

[139]　Ibid. 12.11.2.
[140]　See Foo Ping-Shueng, "Introduction" to *Civil Code of Republic of China*, trans Ching-ling Hsia (, 1930), xxv.
[141]　Ibid.
[142]　*Analects* 12.15.
[143]　Ibid. 3.3.
[144]　Ibid. 12.1.
[145]　*Mencius* 4A.10.1.

of change if one does not fully utilize his wisdom to distinguish and observe things accurately he will not be able to understand change.[146]

If the critic were right, what was once important in governing an empire made up of households is no longer important.

Suppose instead that the critic were wrong. Then, it might be that a life lived in accordance with *li* is a fulfilling way to live although perhaps not the only possible one. According to Aquinas, as we have seen, there may be no one right choice even when all the circumstances have been taken into account. Yet the choice may matter very much. It may be the same with cultures as with individuals.

No theory, however, could determine whether the critic is right or wrong. Peoples' knowledge of what is right or wrong does not come from theory – or at least, it does not according to the two traditions that we are studying. No theory can tell people who lived according to *li*, that they were wrong to believe that their way of life was beautiful, harmonious, and cultivated. No theory can tell them that they were right. In this sense, the Confucian tradition is incommensurable with others. But that is not what Alasdair MacIntyre meant when he said that the Confucian and the Aristotelian traditions were incommensurable. He meant that there are "no shared standards and measures, external to both systems and neutral between them, to which appeal might be made to adjudicate between" them.[147] According to both classical traditions, the standard was provided by human nature. Each human being has an ability to tell, though not infallibly, what contributes to a distinctively human life. But he has to decide what contributes, according to Dai Zhen, by exercising wisdom, and according to Aristotle, by using practical reason. Dai Zhen condemned the "stern men" who accepted traditional norms of conduct without considering whether what was once important is still important. He also condemned those whose judgment of the norms they should live by is distorted by "selfish desires" rather than based on "principle." A person faced with a moral decision may fear that he is acting too sternly or too selfishly. This person may go through a crisis of conscience. But it is not what MacIntyre called an "epistemological crisis."

A contemporary critic might make a different objection. Instead of asking what contribution the observance of *li* could make to a good life, he might object that human dignity and freedom are impaired to the extent that *li* constrains choice. A person cannot decide for him or herself how to live. *Li* prescribes how a person should behave toward others in what it identifies as the most important relationships in one's life. This sort of objection has become familiar since the rise of liberal philosophies in the nineteenth century. It is often bolstered by a suggestion that a person who "uncritically" embraces a set of norms has not really chosen, anymore that a person who unthinkingly does what he or she is told.

A Confucian would not regard the observance of *li* as a matter of doing what one is told. One must be committed to living such a life. To understand *li* required study, leisure, and

---

[146] Dai Zhen 3. art. 5.1; *Tai Chen on Mencius* art. 40, p. 163.
[147] Alasdair MacIntyre, "Incommensurability, Truth, and the Conversation between Confucians and Aristotelians about the Virtues," in Eliot Deutsch, ed., *Culture and Modernity: East-West Philosophic Perspectives* (Honolulu, 1991), 104 at 109.

continual attention and practice. Because it concerned close relations with other people, it required coordination between one's own responses to them, and their responses to oneself. Nor would a Confucian think that living such a life is inconsistent with human dignity or with the sort of freedom that is of value. A violinist must play, not only as a virtuoso, but in coordination with the rest of the orchestra. Her freedom is limited in obvious ways: her interpretation of the score must harmonize with that of others; she cannot play a piece by Chopin that she particularly likes while everyone else is playing Mozart; and she is not free to add interest to the score by playing a B flat instead of an F sharp. Yet these very limitations enable her to be a concert violinist.

Another objection, also entwined with liberal theory, is that *li* as a principle of social organization is incompatible with human dignity and freedom because it has no place for claims of right. In that respect, it is true that *li* differs from *yi* – righteousness or justice. As we have seen, to injure another by killing him or by taking what belongs to him is a violation of *yi*. The victim has a legitimate claim against whoever injured him. In that sense, his rights to person and property are protected although the Confucians did not use the term "rights." But it is not so with *li*. A person who is shown disrespect because the rules of *li* have not been observed has been treated wrongly but not unjustly. Craig Ihara drew an analogy of other situations in which people are engaged in a cooperative activity such a team sport, a ballet, or family relations. One person may treat another wrongly, by failing to pass the ball to a person who has a clear shot, neglecting to support another dancer in a pirouette, or failing to prepare a family meal on time. Those persons are rightly aggrieved but it would be odd to say that they have suffered an injustice.[148]

Aquinas drew a similar distinction between justice and virtues "annexed to justice." The duties of a family member, a subordinate or a friend are not matters of justice but of *pietas*, *observantia*, and *amicita* or *affabilitas*.[149] A person owes another a duty but not, as in the case of justice, as a matter of "legal obligation," or, as we might put it, not as a matter of right.

Few of us would think that duties between family members and friends should be a matter of legal obligation or claims of right. Although few of us have pondered the ideal relationship between an emperor and his ministers, we can imagine the difficulties of running an organization in which each member thinks of himself less as a member of a team than a holder of rights. Yet none of us would think, any more than Aquinas did, that therefore such relationships offend human dignity or freedom. *Li* was based on respect for others. As Ihara noted, it was based on the Confucian view that "human beings have a moral status deserving respect."[150]

The difference is the extent to which a person's life was governed by duties and obligations that entailed respect but not entitlements or rights. Traditional China was an empire composed of households. The key relationships were those between the emperor

---

[148] Craig K. Ihara, "Are Individual Rights Necessary? A Confucian Perspective," in Shun and Wong, *Confucian Ethics* loc. 118 at locs. 118–126, locs. 156–66, locs. 244–49.

[149] *Summa theologiae* II-II, Q. 80.

[150] Ihara, "Individual Rights" loc. 304.

and his ministers and those among family members. Neither Aquinas nor people today would think that these relationships ideally should be based on claims of rights. In traditional China, however, they were the basis of the social order. *Li* was pervasive.

V CRIME AND PUNISHMENT

It is often said that while the West recognized the rule of law, China did not. It is true, as we have just seen, that Confucians believed that it is far better that people be governed by *li*, by propriety, rather than controlled by *fa*, the rules that punish evil doers. It is also true that the administration of justice was entrusted to magistrates who had been trained in the Confucian classics but might not have any specialized legal training. These magistrates, however, were expected to decide cases according to known rules. Their decisions were subject to appeal and might be reversed if they did not.

A difference, however, is that the vast bulk of traditional Chinese substantive law concerned crimes. The vast bulk of Western substantive law concerns private law – the rules that govern relations among private citizens in matters such as contracts, torts, and property. Moreover, the primary task of substantive criminal law was seen differently. In the West, it has been to define the offenses that are subject to criminal punishment. In common and civil law systems, a criminal offense is said to require both a *mens rea* and an *actus reus* – a guilty intent and a guilty act. The law then specifies the elements of particular crimes such as murder, manslaughter, robbery, theft, embezzlement, and so forth. In traditional Chinese law, comparatively little attention was paid to identifying degrees of criminal intent or to classifying offenses. One can find occasional examples. One cannot find the same massive intellectual energy devoted to distinguishing differences in intent, differentiating one crime from another and specifying the elements of each. Instead, a great deal of energy and intellectual sophistication went into determining how severely one offense is to be punished compared with another.

Still another difference concerns the moral authority of legal rules. In the West, at least before the rise of nineteenth-century positivism, legal rules were believed to state moral principles, or as it was then said, principles of natural law. As we have seen, the late scholastics reworked Roman law to show that as many as possible rested on Aristotelian principles of commutative justice. Their conclusions were borrowed or restated by members of the northern natural law school founded in the seventeenth and eighteenth centuries.

Many scholars have said that traditional Chinese law had a similar relationship to Confucianism. The rules supposedly reflected Confucian norms of conduct. The greater part of traditional Chinese law, however, was compatible with Confucian principles but not based upon them. It was not primarily concerned with norms of conduct. As John Langlois said, "[t]he primary issue in traditional Chinese jurisprudence was the setting of punishments. . . . . The traditional statutory codes were aimed directly at this issue, for they specified punishments for specific crimes."[151]

---

[151] John D. Langlois, "'Living Law' in Sung and Yüan Jurisprudence," *Harvard Journal of Asiatic Studies* 41 (1981), 165 at 165.

This approach to law originated with the Qin whose leading philosophers belonged to the anti-Confucian Legalist school (法家 *fajia*). They taught that law was purely an instrument of power. After reunifying China, the first Qin emperor, Qin Shi Huang (秦始皇), persecuted Confucian scholars and burned their books. Surprisingly, the legal tradition that began with the Qin was principally concerned with a question of justice: the fairness of punishments. Those who built this tradition evidently did not believe that law was merely a tool for exercising power. Later, under Confucian influence, punishments were moderated and the severity of certain offenses was reevaluated to reflect Confucian norms. But the Chinese legal tradition was never reworked to synthesize it with Confucian principles in the way that the late scholastics synthesized Roman law with the principles of Aristotle.

Even if a group of Confucian scholars had tried, not merely to augment or diminish certain punishments, but to create such a synthesis, they would not have found that task easy. Perhaps, for that reason, they did not attempt it. The severity of punishments was Aquinas' example of a subject that must be dealt with by positive law because there are no principles that can determine just how severely a thief, for example, should be punished. That question could be settled in a variety of different ways, no one of which was correct. As Langlois said, the question of the appropriate degree of punishment received "the attention of the greatest legal minds and aroused equally deep intellectual discussion."[152] But Chinese scholars did not try to give a principled explanation of why a given punishment was appropriate. They weighed the gravity of the offense against the gravity of others by considering what elements would make an offense more or less serious. The result was an intellectually sophisticated body of law. It was consistent with Confucian teachings. But it was not based on them in the same way that the late scholastics based the rules of contracts, torts, and property on the ideas of Aristotelian philosophy.

We would know nothing about the origins of this tradition had it not been for the discovery in 1975 of the tomb of a third-century official who had his law book buried with him written on strips of bamboo (秦簡 *qin jian*).[153] When Liu Bang (劉邦) overthrew the Qin (秦), he promised to abolish their laws. Instead he adopted a collection of law or code that was largely based on them. According to the dynastic history of the Han, in about 200 BC, "Hsaio Ho [Xiao He] gathered together the laws of the Qin ... choosing those which were suitable for those times."[154] After the fall of the Han dynasty, the king of one of the surviving kingdoms, the Wei (魏), ordered two Confucians to revise the Han Code. He promulgated their new code, the Xin Lü (新律) or Wei Lü (魏律), which has been lost. It reduced the severity of punishments. It also added a section called the "Eight Deliberations" (八議 *ba yi*) which survived into later codes and which we will discuss later.[155] The law was modified again in the Northern Wei (北魏) dynasty (386–584) when Emperor Yuan Hong (元宏) (孝文帝*Xiao Wen Di*) modified the punishments for certain

[152]   Ibid.
[153]   A. F. P. Hulsewé, *Remnants of Ch'in Law* (Leiden, 1985), E 20, 198.
[154]   *Han shu* 23.12a, quoted in A. F. P. Hulsewé, *Remnants of Han Law* (Leiden, 1955), 26.
[155]   John W. Head and Yanping Wang, *Law Codes in Dynastic China: A Synopsis of Chinese Legal History in the Thirty Centuries from Zhou to Qing* (Durham, 2005), 109.

crimes to reflect Confucian principles: for example, breaches of filial piety were punished more severely.[156] It was modified again by the promulgation of the Kai-Huang Code (開皇 律 *Kai Huang Lü*) by Emperor Yang Jian (楊堅) (隋文帝*Sui Wen Di*) when China was reunified under the short-lived Sui (隋)dynasty (581–618). That code further reduced the severity of punishments. It added "Eight Deliberations" to the "Ten Abominations" (十惡 *shi e*).

These developments culminated in the Tang Code (唐律 *tang lü*) which, as Geoffrey MacCormack observed, "in essentials survived until the end of the imperial period."[157] As John Head and Yanping Wang noted, "[T]he Song, the Yüan, the Ming and the Qing . . . each . . . added its own stitches to the pattern set by the Tang Code."[158] As Brian McKnight said, the "laws of the Song . . . are virtually identical in style and form with their predecessors and their successors,"[159] despite reorganization and revision by the Ming (明) and Qing (清). Thirty to forty percent of the articles of the Qing Code (大清律例 *Da Qing Lü Li*) were borrowed unchanged from the Tang.[160]

We can see the influence of Qin law by comparing the provisions of Tang Code with those remnants of Qin law that survive. The drafters and commentators in the Qin and Tang dynasties put a great deal of serious thought into determining when one person was more deserving of punishment than another. In the surviving fragments of Qin law and in the Tang Code, the fruit of this thought was presented in much the same way: as a description of cases, each with a conclusion as to the appropriate punishment. There is no systematic organization in these cases. There is no attempt to group them under principles which are arranged hierarchically under higher level principles. Principles are stated infrequently, and they are not presented as reasons why one offense deserves greater punishment than another. The texts contain generalizations based on specific cases, and the results appropriate in these cases are worked out by comparison and analogy to others. Yet the texts show, not the absence of legal reasoning, but a different kind of legal reasoning.

For example, in the texts concerning theft, the punishment deemed to be appropriate depends on the "illegitimate profit (贓 *zang*)" made by the thief. The texts do not define illegitimate profit or explain how it is to be determined. They describe specific cases. They ask what is to be done if the object stolen by the accused was worth over 660 units (錢 *qian*) at the time of the theft but worth only 110 at the time of trial. The answer: the accused was to be punished for a theft of over 660 units.[161] Suppose the value was 110 at the time of the theft 660 at the time of trial. Then the accused should suffer the lesser punishment, and officials who had punished him to a greater extent were themselves to be punished for doing so.[162] The Tang Code provided more generally: "All cases of assessing the value of illicit goods do

---

[156] Ibid. 111–12.
[157] Geoffrey MacCormack, *Traditional Chinese Penal Law* (London, 1990), 13.
[158] Head and Wang, *Law Codes* 137.
[159] Brian E. McKnight, "Patterns of Law and Patterns of Thought: Notes on the Specifications (shih) of Sung China," *Journal of the American Oriental Society* 102 (1982), 323 at 323.
[160] Wallace Johnson, "Introduction," in *The Tang Civil Code* 1, Wallace Johnson, trans., (Princeton, 1979), 9.
[161] Hulsewé, *Remnants of Ch'in Law* D 27.
[162] Ibid. D 28.

so according to the value of the articles at the time and place of the offense in terms of the set price of the highest grade of silk."[163] In particular: "Assessment of the value of such things as boats, grinding mills, warehouses, and wholesale stores is according to the rent at the time of the offense."[164]

A more difficult question was whether the punishment of a thief should depend on the value of what the thief actually stole or what he intended to steal. Neither Qin law nor the Tang Code posed the question in general terms. They described how a thief was to be punished in particular cases, and their answers differed. Suppose someone stole a goat with a rope attached, and that the value of the goat warranted one punishment while the value of the goat and the rope combined warranted another more severe one. According to the Qin texts, he should receive the lesser punishment if his "attention was on the goat he stole, not the rope."[165] Suppose "there is a robbery of a mare and her foal follows her." According to the Tang Code, "the foal's value is included in the punishment."[166]

Since the punishment depended on the harm done by the perpetrator, when several perpetrators were responsible, the question arose how much of the harm to attribute to each. Suppose A and B steal 800 cash from C. According to the Qin texts, if they planned the crime together, each is to be punished as though he had stolen 800. But, if A and B each went to rob C, and met for the first time just before the robbery, and each took 400 from C, then A and B are to be punished as though each had stolen 400.[167] Suppose A, B, C, and D planned together to beat or wound someone. According to the Tang Code, the punishment of each person is based on the harm done by the heaviest blow struck. If the heaviest blow broke a limb, the one who struck that blow receives the punishment for breaking a limb, which is three years of penal servitude. For the original plotter, if he did not strike that blow, the punishment is one degree less: two and a half years. For the others, it is two degrees less: two years.[168] But suppose they did not plot together. Then, each person is liable for the harm that he did himself: the person who broke a limb is punished by three years of penal servitude, the one who broke a finger by one year; the one who beat him without causing a wound is punished with forty blows with the light stick.[169]

Most of the texts deal with how the perpetrator of a crime is to be punished. A few deal with what the perpetrator owes the victim. Again, that question was addressed by describing particular cases. A robber must give back what he stole, but suppose "he sells what he had robbed, thereby buying other things?" If so, according to the Qin texts, "all are given back to the owner" of the stolen goods.[170] Suppose the robber stole the victim's clothes, sold them for money, and used it to buy cloth. Can the owner claim both the cloth and the clothes? He can only claim the cloth.[171] According to the Tang Code, in "all cases ... in which the

---

[163] *Tang Civil Code* art. 34.1.
[164] Ibid. art. 34.3.
[165] Hulsewé, *Remnants of Ch'in Law* D 24.
[166] *Tang Civil Code* Commentary 300.2.
[167] Hulsewé, *Remnants of Ch'in Law* D 10.
[168] *Tang Civil Code* Subcommentary to art. 308.1.
[169] Ibid. to art. 308.2.
[170] Hulsewé, *Remnants of Ch'in Law* D 20.
[171] Ibid. D 20.

illicit goods are still in existence, return them to the . . . owner."[172] "If there has been an exchange for other goods . . . the illicit goods are still considered to be in existence."[173] Suppose, however, "a robber takes another's goods and articles through trade or loan and gets a profit"? The profit does not go to the original owner because "this is due to the efforts of the later possessor and not the original owner."[174]

The texts do not state the principles at stake or explain why they should be applied to reach a certain result. Yet the texts show, not the absence of legal reasoning, but a method of reasoning that rests on recognizing similarities without analyzing why they are important. Those who formulated the texts decided, after careful thought, the punishment appropriate to a particular offense by considering those prescribed for others. The magistrate deciding a new case would consider which texts described a case most like his own.

MacCormack correctly noted that the "comprehensiveness, clarity and precision" of the codes reflect "drafting techniques . . . developed principally by the legalist officials of the state of Qin." It has often been assumed that Qin law was the legal expression of the legalist philosophy endorsed by the regime.[175] Hulwesé said the "primary motive" was "raison d'état" and "maintaining the stability of government and . . . increasing its power."[176] But that motive does not explain the concern with consistency in punishment. A better explanation is a concern over fairness. It was the prime concern of the Tang Code and those of later dynasties, but it was neither in conflict with Confucian principles nor the result of their influence.

MacCormack concluded that because of "legalist influence," the codes tried to "ensure that for every situation there should be a rule specifically stated or clearly inferable" to keep "judicial discretion . . . to a minimum."[177] On the contrary, the object of the codes was not to provide rules for determining what conduct would be deemed wrongful. Indeed, one of the offenses in the Tang and later codes was "doing that which ought not to be done." According to article 450 of the Tang Code, "All cases of doing what ought not to be done are punished by forty blows with the light stick." A subcommentary explained that "If there is no provision in either the Code or the Statutes . . . and there is no text to which analogy can be made, then . . . the circumstances of the crime are weighed to decide a punishment. So this article was established with a view to supplementing omissions and deficiencies."[178] The concern of the codes was consistency in punishing different offenses.

We can now better understand the traditional Chinese view that there was no need for the people to know the provisions of the law or to consult lawyers who knew them. In the Song dynasty, private persons were prohibited from printing or copying the code or any other laws, although the prohibition was lifted by Wang Anshi (王安石). According to

---

[172]   *Tang Code* art. 33.1a.
[173]   *Tang Code* Commentary to art. 33.1a.
[174]   *Tang Code* Query and reply to art. 33.1a.
[175]   Hulsewé, *Remnants of Han Law* 13; Derk Bodde and Clarence Morris, *Law in Imperial China* (Philadelphia, 1967), 27; Head and Wang, *Law Codes* 73–75.
[176]   Hulsewé, *Remnants of Han Law* 5.
[177]   MacCormack, *Traditional Chinese Penal Law* 39.
[178]   *Tang Code* Subcommentary to art. 450.

Ichisada Miyazaki, "[t]he theory was that, if the people knew the law, they could devise ways to circumvent it. The people's duty was simply to obey the doctrines of Confucianism."[179] By consulting the code, however, a person was unlikely to find loopholes in the definitions of what conduct could be punished. There were few definitions. He could, however, calculate and minimize the risk of being severely punished. He could determine the largest amount he could steal without incurring a greater punishment, or whether he would be punished less if he stole secretly or by force or by fraud. Chinese lawmakers saw little point in informing wrongdoers how to get off more lightly. In the United States, where all laws must be made public, and ex post facto laws are constitutionally prohibited, a criminal may still receive a greater punishment prescribed by a statute enacted after the crime was committed. He has no right to know in advance how much he will be punished.

He does have a right to know in advance what conduct is prohibited, and in the United States and in many other countries, that right is regarded as part of the rule of law. The traditional Chinese attitude toward the rule of law was different. The Chinese subject was not informed in advance of what sort of wrongdoing was subject to punishment. He was supposed to know without consulting the law whether he was behaving rightly or wrongly. But by the same token, in China, unlike the United States, he was unlikely to be punished for breaking a law he had never heard of that prohibited seemingly innocent conduct, and to be told that his ignorance of that law is no excuse. According to the traditional Chinese view, to be treated fairly, a rule of law must prescribe a punishment proportional to the wrong committed. Under the traditional English common law, all felonies were punishable by hanging. In the United States, the punishment today depends on a vague set of sentencing guidelines and the discretion of a parole board, except in states that have adopted the "three strikes and you're out" rule, by which a person convicted of three felonies, even if they are comparatively minor, loses his freedom for life. Both traditions rest on underlying ideas of fairness and the need for legal rules, but these ideas are different.

Traditional Chinese law was also influenced by the Confucian principles. But too much can be made of the "Confucianisation of the law."[180] According to Tung-tsu Ch'ü (瞿同祖 *Qu Tongzu*), "[a]fter Han times, the formulation and revision of the law fell into the hands of Confucian scholar-officials who seized the opportunity to incorporate as many as possible of the essentials of Confucianism into the codes."[181] MacCormack claimed that "[i]n their content, the ... codes give effect to the Confucian system of values."[182] According to Jean Escarra, "[d]espite the influence of the Legalists, ... the Confucian conception came to dominate all ancient Chinese legislation."[183] According to Derk Bodde and Clarence Morris, "the law in imperial China became the embodiment of the ethical

[179] Ichisada Miyazaki, "The Administration of Justice during the Sung Dynasty," in Jerome Alan Cohen, R. Randle Edwards and Fu-Mei Chang Chen, eds., *Essays on China's Legal Tradition* (Princeton, 1980), 56 at 58.

[180] T'ung-tsu Ch'ü, *Law and Society in Traditional China* (The Hague, 1961) 267.

[181] Ibid. 276.

[182] MacCormack, *Traditional Chinese Penal Law* 39.

[183] Jean Scarra, "Law, Chinese," *Encyclopedia of the Social Sciences* 9 (New York, 1933), 251.

norms of Confucianism."[184] Although the Tang Code was acceptably Confucian, however, it was not tightly integrated with Confucian thought. The codes incorporated some Confucian ideals. The scale of punishment was gradually reduced. Moreover, the severity of punishment was increased or decreased to reflect Confucian ideas of the seriousness of an offense. As we have seen, the underlying idea of fairness in the severity of punishments, on which so many provisions depended, went back to the Qin dynasty.

Some modern scholars have thought this idea of fairness was due to a Confucian view of law. According to Wallace Johnson, "the purpose of law is to maintain a harmony between the human and the natural worlds." Like Hulwesé, he traces that idea to the Han Dynasty philosopher Dong Zhongshu (董仲舒). According to Johnson, "An offense was regarded as a disruption in society that must be restored by the proper punishment. But punishments in the human sphere that are too heavy can bring about a reaction in the natural world – epidemics, floods and draughts are commonly mentioned."[185] This concern, he claimed, explains the lack of flexibility afforded in sentencing by the Code. "[T]hroughout the empire a particular crime would be met with exactly the same punishment. The theory behind this is that if a certain punishment has been decided upon for a crime, then assigning a lesser punishment would not be a sufficient response and a heavier punishment might well provoke some natural disaster."[186] "In the final analysis," according to Bodde and Morris, "a disturbance of the social order really meant, in Chinese thinking, a violation of the cosmic order."[187]

MacCormack observed that "such a view of the relationship between crime and punishment is nowhere explicitly stated in the legal sources."[188] There was "a widespread belief . . . that gross cases of injustice are likely to lead to a visitation of evil on the part of Heaven." Sometimes, as Johnson noted, when natural disasters occurred, the emperor would "take steps to reduce punishments."[189] But the overriding concern, for Han, the Tang, and later dynasties was not the absolute severity of a punishment: whether, for example, a robber should be punished by a hundred blows of the heavy stick or fifty. As we have seen, the scale of punishments was changed across the board from one dynasty to the next. What mattered was consistency among the punishments administered for different offenses, so, if one offense was so grave as to merit a hundred blows with the heavy stick, equally grave offenses would be punished in the same way. The bulk of the Tang Code is concerned with determining the seriousness of an offense so that this consistency can be maintained. That concern was not the result of Confucian influence. It was the chief concern of the law under the Qin.

The traditional law was modified under the influence of Confucian principles. The severity of punishments was reduced. The Qin punished crimes by fines, mutilation – which ranged from having one's head and beard shaved off to the loss of one or both feet or

[184] Bodde and Morris, *Law in Imperial China* 5.
[185] Johnson, "Introduction" 10.
[186] Ibid. 11.
[187] Bodde and Morris, *Law in Imperial China* 4.
[188] MacCormack, *Traditional Chinese Penal Law* 42.
[189] Johnson "Introduction" 10.

castration – hard labor, exile, and death by decapitation or by "cutting asunder(斬)."[190] In later dynasties, it was said that the Qin dynasty fell because of the severity of its punishments. The Tang Code, like the Sui Code, recognized five punishments: beating with a light stick (10, 20, 30, 40, and 50 blows), beating with a heavy stick (60, 70, 80, 90, and 100 blows), penal servitude (1, 1½, 2, 2½, and 3 years), life exile (at a distance of 2000, 2500, and 3000 *li*), and death (by strangulation or decapitation).[191] Some of the lighter punishments could be "redeemed" by paying a fine. Punishments further decreased in the Song. They sharply increased during the Ming, a step which coincided, as we will see, with a retreat from Confucian principles as they had previously been understood.

Also under Confucian influence, punishments were changed to reflect Confucian ideas concerning the seriousness of an offense. Some of the punishments for particular offenses were modified, especially when they concerned family members. Various articles of the Tang Code define the punishments for "cursing with bad language," beating, wounding, or killing one's wife, one's husband, one's parent or grandparent, one's elder brother or sister, one's younger brother or sister, one's elder brother's wife or husband's younger brother or sister, a relative who is older but within the fifth degree of mourning, and so forth.[192] Nevertheless, to allow the punishment to depend on the family relationship of the parties was not a Confucian innovation. Although Qin philosophers deprecated the importance of this relationship, punishments in Qin law depended on whether a man beat one's grandparents or great-grandparents[193] or his wife,[194] or on whether a person accused another of unfilial behavior.[195] In the Tang Code, concerns with the family relationship of the parties were more pervasive.

In addition, as in the Northern Wei, the Tang Code contained "Eight Deliberations (八議 *ba yi*)"[196] or circumstances in which a punishment should be decreased, and, as in the Sui Code, "Ten Abominations (十惡 *shi e*)"[197] or particularly serious circumstances in which the punishment should be increased. They do reflect Confucian influence. The official explanations of these provisions often cite the Confucian classics. Yet in many ways, the Eight Deliberations and the Ten Abominations are not a straightforward application of Confucian teachings.

Of the Eight Deliberations, which concern the reason for reducing the normal punishment, five concern the virtues of the person guilty of an offense: the "deliberations" "for the morally worthy," "for ability," "for achievement," "for high position," and "for diligence." The others favored relatives and old retainers of the emperor and guests of state. It is hard to see on Confucian principles why the "morally worthy" should be punished less rather than

---

[190] Hulsewé, *Remnants of Ch'in Law* 14–18.
[191] Johnson, "Introduction" 14–15.
[192] *Tang Code* arts. 325–35.
[193] Hulsewé, *Remnants of Ch'in Law* D 63.
[194] Ibid. D 64.
[195] Ibid. D 85.
[196] *Tang Code* art. 7.
[197] Ibid. art. 6.

more, or why the punishment of imperial relatives and retainers or those in "high position" should be mitigated.[198]

The Ten Abominations also show a Confucian influence. They are described as "the most serious of those offences that come within the five punishments. They injure morality and destroy propriety (*li*)."[199] All but one of them are offenses against relationships that on Confucian principles were worthy of special respect: against the emperor, against hierarchical superiors, and against family members. Nevertheless, if one began with Confucian principles and considered which offenses against them should be considered the most severe, one would be unlikely to end up with the items on this particular list.[200] If there is a connection with Confucian principle, it is not one that Confucius or Mencius themselves would easily recognize.

VI FORMAL RULES

The relative merits of government by men and government by formal rules were discussed by the great Song dynasty philosopher Su Shi (蘇軾) (1037–1101) who wrote during the second golden age of Chinese philosophy. They were also discussed by Thomas Aquinas. Confucian tradition stressed the advantages of governing by virtue and example rather than by law. Aquinas lived in medieval Europe which has been described as one of the most legalistic of societies. We have just seen the great differences between formal rules in China and in the West. Yet the conclusions of Su Shi and Aquinas were much the same. We need to be governed both by men and by formal rules. We need the formal rules because we fear the rule of men.

Su Shi

"In later times," after the rule of the sage kings, according to Su, "virtue declined and governance degenerated even more. They trusted to man ever less, leaving everything up to law (法 *fa*)."[201] As they did so, crime became more frequent and punishment more

---

[198]   The Subcommentary cites the Confucian classic, the *Book of Rites* (禮記 *li ji*): "Punishments do not extend up to the great officers." *Li ki* I.53 cited in Tang Code, Subcommentary to art. 7. Yet they are the very sort of people whose misbehavior Confucius and Mencius denounced and which, they believed, had caused the ruin of dynasties.

[199]   *Tang Code* Subcommentary to art. 6.

[200]   Four concern harm or disrespect to the state or the emperor: "plotting rebellion (謀反 *mou fan*)," and "plotting treason (謀叛 *mou pan*)," "plotting great sedition (謀大逆 *mou da ni*)," and "great irreverance (大不敬 *da bu jing*)." One concerns harm or disrespect toward one's hierarchical superiors such as a department head, district magistrate, prefect, or teacher. Four concern offences within family relationships. One is "lack of filial piety (不孝 *bu xiao*)." Another is "to beat or plot to kill . . . one's paternal grandparents or parents; or to kill one's paternal uncles or their wives, one's elder brothers or sisters, or one's maternal grandparents, or one's husband, or one's husband's maternal grandparents, or his parents (惡逆 *e ni*)." Commentary to art. 7. Another is "discord (不睦 *bu mu*)" which is committed by plotting to kill relatives within the fifth degree of mourning and beating relatives within the fourth degree. Another is incest (內亂 *nei luan*). The remaining "abominations" are "unrighteousness (不義 *bu yi*)" and "depravity (不道 *bu dao*)" which is committed by killing three members of a single household, sorcery and making *ku* poison, which was used in black magic.

[201]   Peter K. Bol, *"This Culture of Ours": Intellectual Transitions in T'ang and Sung China* (Stanford, 1992), 286 n. 97.

necessary.[202] Yet the sages themselves understood that government required both the rule of men and *fa*, the rule of law. They "relied on man and law together yet relied on man to a greater extent."[203] Both were necessary. It was a question of balance.

For Su, the opposition between *li* (禮) or propriety and *fa* is one example of a broader tension between relying on men and relying on law. The tension is found throughout human affairs. Because *li* consists of rules, to govern through *li* is also a way of governing through law, even though violations of *li* are not sanctioned by punishment. In that respect, "*li* and punishment are one thing."[204] Yet punishment is more drastic. It is necessary when people are not sufficiently virtuous to be governed by *li*. "If one loses *li*, he enters the domain of punishment."[205] Yet, if people were sufficiently virtuous, they would not need *li*. "The sages introduced tools for agriculture, hunting and fishing," Su wrote, "so that man might seek benefit and satisfy his desires . . . . But profit seeking opened the gate to deceit, so the sages introduced *li*, so that men would not only think of their own convenience."[206]

The tension between relying on men and on law runs from the top to the bottom of imperial government. For Su, dynastic government is an instance of relying on law. As Bol noted,

> The benevolent government of the *Documents* is also dynastic government, and that, Su argues, creates an inevitable tension between "man" and "law." Generally, sage kings and their ministers chose man over law, but they were always being driven toward law because of the contradiction between popular desire and the claims of the royal house to all under heaven as its property.[207]

The reliance on law rather than men is also shown in the number of ministers used to govern. As Bol observed, "Su notes that from Yao and Shun on, the number of offices and bureaucrats kept increasing so that 'in later times virtue declined and governance degenerated even more. They trusted to man ever less, leaving everything up to law.'"[208]

The tension appears again in the freedom given to officials to act on their own. The officials may be instructed to follow rules or to use their own discretion. Su believed that the lower the position an official occupied, the more important it was to trust to his discretion. To quote again from Bol:

> High-ranking officials are allowed to act on their own initiative outside the rules, but if left to their own devices, they tend to usurp authority. Su's solution is to punish their abuses of privilege more severely, so that they will serve as an example to their subordinates. The low-ranking officials stick to the rules too closely because job competition keeps them from taking initiative for fear of mistakes, yet infrequent periods of service encourage graft. The

---

[202] Ibid. 286.
[203] Ibid. 287 n. 99
[204] Ibid. 287 n. 110.
[205] Ibid.
[206] Ibid. 264.
[207] Ibid. 286.
[208] Ibid.

solution: promote the low ranking only for actual achievements, so that they see that it serves their interests to take some initiative.[209]

High ranking officials are more tempted to abuse their power and so should be restrained more closely by rules. Lower ranking officials are afraid their careers may be blighted if they break a rule and so should be given more discretion.

Su concluded that there must be a balance. Trust too much to man and law disappears. Trust too much to law, and all that will count is outward compliance, not virtue. "If man dominates law, law becomes an empty device; if law dominates man, man becomes a position filler. When man and law both receive their due without one dominating the other, the world will be secure."[210]

Thomas Aquinas

Like Su, Aquinas discussed the larger issue of the tension between governance by law and by men. Again, he built on Aristotle.

Aristotle had said that "it is bad ... for a man, subject as he is to all the accidents of human passion, to have the supreme power, rather than the law."[211] "The law is reason unaffected by desire."[212] The drawback to governing by law is that "laws speak only in general terms, and cannot provide for circumstances."[213] In short, "Whereas the law is passionless, passion must ever sway the heart of man. Yes, it may be replied, but then on the other hand an individual will be better able to deliberate in particular cases."[214]

Both of these considerations figured in Aquinas' explanation of the advantages of government by men and by law. Government by men would seem to be best for the reason given by Aristotle: "laws speak only in general terms, and cannot provide for circumstances." As we have seen, for Aquinas, law is a dictate of practical reason, and the conclusions of practical reason depend upon the circumstances. There may be no limit to the circumstances that matter. Why, then, rely on enacted laws? Why not have wise people act as judges and let them decide to use their practical reason without encumbering them with enacted laws?

Aquinas answered that, nevertheless, government by law may be better for three reasons:

> First, because it is easier to find a few wise men competent to frame right laws, than to find the many who would be necessary to judge correctly in each single case. Second, because those who make laws consider long beforehand what laws to make, but judgment in each single case has to be pronounced as soon as it arises, and it is easier for man to see what is right by taking many instances into consideration than by considering one solitary event. Third, because lawgivers judge in the abstract and about future events, while those who sit

[209]   Ibid. 278.
[210]   Ibid. 259 n. 23.
[211]   *Politics* III.x. 1280a.
[212]   Ibid. III.xvi. 1287a.
[213]   Ibid. III.xv. 1286a.
[214]   Ibid.

in judgment judge of things present, towards which they are affected by love, hatred, or some kind of cupidity, by which their judgment is perverted.[215]

All three of these reasons have to do with human weakness. According to the first, we could not find enough wise judges to decide all the specific cases that arise. The number of wise decision-makers that we could put in authority is small compared with the number of decisions they would have to make.

According to the second, to get the right answer in a specific case, one needs a long period of reflection, particularly on other cases since "it is easier for man to see what is right, by taking many instances into consideration, than by considering one solitary event." The wisdom of the law can therefore surpass that of a wise man left to himself. Indeed, the wisdom of the law grows with human experience. According to Aquinas, "those who first endeavored to discover something useful for the human community could not take everything into consideration themselves, and so they set up some institutions which were deficient . . . and . . . were changed by later lawgivers."[216]

Lastly, Aquinas said that a decision is less likely to be biased by "love, hatred, or some kind of cupidity" when it is made in accordance with laws that are framed abstractly to deal with future events. That argument for the rule of law had been made by Aristotle. If a popular figure commits a crime or a member of an unpopular group is accused of having done so, the result is more likely to be fair if it is determined by law rather than by someone who decides on the spot what to do.

It is true that sometimes, because of the circumstances of a case, applying the general rule will produce the wrong result. Following Aristotle, Aquinas said that as a matter of "equity," the general rule should not be followed.

> [S]ince human actions, with which laws are concerned, are composed of contingent singulars and are innumerable in their diversity, it was not possible to lay down rules of law that would apply to every single case. Legislators in framing laws attend to what commonly happens: although if the law be applied to certain cases it will frustrate the equality of justice and be injurious to the common good, which the law has in view. Thus the law requires deposits to be restored, because in the majority of cases this is just. Yet it happens sometimes to be injurious – for instance, if a madman were to put his sword in deposit, and demand its delivery while in a state of madness, or if a man were to seek the return of his deposit in order to fight against his country. In these and like cases it is bad to follow the law, and it is good to set aside the letter of the law and to follow the dictates of justice and the common good. This is the object of *epikeia* which we call equity. Therefore it is evident that *epikeia* is a virtue.[217]

In the end, Aquinas' position is not far from that of Su Shi. We adopt the rule of law because men may be lacking in knowledge or virtue. The great concern of the Confucians was to develop wise and virtuous people. Yet, as we have seen, the administration of justice in traditional China, as in the West, relied heavily on the rules.

---

[215] *Summa theologiae* I-II, Q. 97, a. 1, ad 2.
[216] Ibid. a. 1.
[217] Ibid. Q. 120, a. 1.

7

Government

I THE ORIGIN OF GOVERNMENT

i *The Confucian Tradition*

In the Confucian tradition, there was one legitimate form of government. It was an empire to which all civilized people belonged.

In the beginning, Tian conferred the mandate to rule on the emperor Yao (堯). According to Confucius, "Great indeed was Yao as a sovereign! How lofty! Only Tian is great, and Yao modeled himself upon that."[1] Yao chose Shun (舜), a simple but virtuous farmer, to succeed him. Shun was succeeded by his minister Yu (禹). Confucius said, "How sublime was the manner in which Shun and Yu possessed the empire, and yet effortlessly!"[2] Shun passed the throne to Yu who passed it to his son, thereby founding the first dynasty, the Xia (夏).

That being so, Mencius asked, by what right did Yao give the throne to Shun, or Shun give it to Yu? By what right did Yu give it to his own son?

Mencius denied that Shun had a right to the throne simply because Yao chose him. "The Son of *Tian* (天子) cannot give the throne to another." "Tian gave it to him." "The Son of Tian can present a man to Tian but he cannot make Tian give that man the throne."

Tian gave the empire to Shun, but not by a revelation or "command" because "Tian does not speak." "Yao presented Shun to Tian, and Tian accepted him. He proffered him to the people and the people accepted him."[3]

He caused him take charge of the sacrifices, and all the spirits were well pleased with them; thus Tian accepted him. He caused him to take charge of the conduct of affairs, and affairs were well governed, so that the people were at peace under him; thus the people accepted him. Tian gave the throne to him. The people gave it to him. Therefore I said, "The Son of Tian cannot give the throne to another."[4]

---

[1] *Analects* 8.19.1.
[2] Ibid. 8.18.
[3] *Mencius* 5.1.5.1–5.
[4] Ibid. 5.1.5.6.

Indeed, Shun's acceptance by Tian and the people was only manifest after Yao's death. After Yao died, Shun withdrew to the south. "The lords of the kingdom . . . went not to the son of Yao, but they went to Shun. Those with disputes went not to the son of Yao, but they went to Shun. Singers sang not the son of Yao, but they sang Shun." "That is why," Mencius explained, "I said that Tian gave him the throne." "If he had, before these things, lived in the palace of Yao, and had pressured the son of Yao, it would have been an act of usurpation, and not the gift of Tian."[5]

After the death of Yu, according to Mencius, those with disputes did not turn to Yu's minister Yi, as they had to Yu, and singers did not make songs about Yi, as they had about Yu. They turned to Yu's son Qi saying: "He is the son of our sovereign." Indeed, the sons of Yao and Shun had not been equal to their fathers, whereas "Shun assisted Yao, and Yu assisted Shun for many years, conferring benefits on the people for a long time." Qi, however, "was able, as a man of talents and virtue, respectfully following the same way as Yu." Moreover, "Yi assisted Yu only for a few years, and had not been good for the people for long." So it was understandable that the throne should pass to Qi.

Tian had ensured that the succession had passed to right person, to Shun, to Yu, and then to Qi. "All this was from Tian, and could not be done by man." "That which is done without man doing it is from Tian. That which results without man causing is the ordinance of Tian."[6]

According to Mencius, an emperor still could pass over his son and choose a person of great virtue. "In the case of a commoner obtaining the throne, he must have virtue equal to that of Shun or Yu; and moreover, he must be commended to Tian by the preceding sovereign. It was on this account that Confucius did not obtain the throne."[7] He was a sage, but he had not been commended by the previous sovereign.

Yet in China, no practice ever developed by which the emperor would choose a person of great virtue in lieu of his own relatives. If an emperor had done so, Chinese ideas concerning the legitimacy of a ruler might have developed differently.

ii *The Aristotelian Tradition*

For Socrates, Plato, and Aristotle, civilized people lived in city states. No larger community was necessary for human beings to live a distinctively human life.

In the Middle Ages, jurists interpreted their Roman texts to mean that there was only one source of legitimate authority, the emperor, whom they identified with the Holy Roman Emperor. The jurists based this view on texts in the *Corpus iuris civilis*, stretching the meaning of the texts. In one, the Emperor Antoninus had said "I am the lord of the world," although he was contrasting the force of Roman civil law, which prevailed on land, with the

---

[5] Ibid. 5.1.5.7.
[6] Ibid. 5.1.6.2.
[7] Ibid. 5.1.6.3.

law of the sea.[8] Other texts said: "the prince is not bound by the law"[9]; "what pleases the prince has the force of law."[10]

The late scholastics agreed with Thomas Cajetan, who, in his sixteenth-century commentary on Aquinas' *Summa theologiae*, claimed that the emperor's power was derived from positive law, and could be lost by disuse and by custom. He was not emperor of the world. Francisco Vitoria said that "this contention is baseless,"[11] Domingo de Soto and Francisco Suárez that it is wrong,[12] and Luis de Molina that it is "obviously ridiculous."[13]

Their account of political authority was based on Aristotelian and Thomistic principles. A human being is a political and social animal. He cannot live a distinctively human life except as a member of society. That being so, it follows that by their very nature, human beings can form a society and institute a government.[14] Grotius agreed with their conclusion.[15]

Vitoria explained that the people must be able to form a society because "[a]s Aristotle has shown in the *Politics*, man is naturally social and civic."[16]

> I, indeed, would say that they are beasts, and not even human, who say that they ought to live so that they care for no one, acknowledge duties to and take trouble over no one, take no pleasure in the good of another, are not bitter over the perversity of others, love no one, and wish to be loved by no one. Accordingly, as human society is instituted so that each assumes duties to every other, and of all societies, civil society is that which most abundantly provides for human needs, it follows that this community is a most natural union and most in agreement with nature.[17]

"Through nature," Soto said, human beings have a "faculty of conserving themselves," both as to their "temporal welfare" and "their spiritual prosperity." "Men could not well exercise this faculty dispersed," and so they have "an instinct to live gregariously such that each would be a sufficient help to each other."[18] According to Molina, "Unless he is situated in a community of many families, he ... could not be instructed and imbued with skill and *mores* befitting a free and honest man and so develop friendship

[8]   Dig. 13.2.9.
[9]   Ibid. 1.2.31.
[10] Ibid. 1.1.1.
[11] Francisco de Vitoria, *De Indis insulanis relectio prior* (2nd. ed.), no. 25, in *Relecciones Teológicas del Maestro Fray Francisco de Vitoria*, Luis Alonso Getino, ed., 2 (Madrid, 1934), 348.
[12] Domenicus Soto, *De iustitia et iure libri decem* (Salamanca, 1553), lib. 4, q. 4, a. 2; Franciso Suárez, *Defensio fidei catholicae et apostolicae adversus Anglicanae errores* (Coimbra, 1613), lib. 3, cap. 2.
[13] Ludovicus Molina, *De iustitia et iure tractatus* (Venice, 1614), II, disp. 30.
[14] Vitoria, *Relectio de potestate civili* nos. 3–4, in *Relecciones Teológicas*, 293; Soto, *De iustitia et iure* lib. 4, q. 4, a. 1; Molina, *De iustitia et iure* II, disp. 22; V, disp. 3; Suárez, *Defensio fidei* lib. 3, cap. 2. Annabel Brett is correct that one cannot conclude that they thereby adopted "the modern concept of the State." Annabel Brett, "Scholastic Political Thought and the Modern Concept of the State," in Annabel Brett and James Tully, eds., *Rethinking the Foundations of Modern Political Thought* (Cambridge, 2006), 130 at 147.
[15] Grotius, *De belli ac pacis.*
[16] Vitoria, *Relectio de potestate civili* no. 5, 297 in Luis Alonso Getino, ed., *Relecciones del Maestro Fray Francisco de Vitoria* (Madrid, 1933).
[17] Vitoria, *Relectio de potestate civili* no. 5, 297.
[18] Soto, *De iusitia et iure* lib. 4, q. 4, a. 1.

and other virtues."[19] Grotius said that the source of the social order and law is man's "impelling desire for society."[20]

According to Quentin Skinner, in passages like these the late scholastics anticipated the concept of the social contract.[21] It depends what one means by a social contract. We associate the theory of social contract with John Locke. As Charles Taylor summarized Locke's view, each person "can be a fully competent human subject outside of society."[22] People enter into a social contract "for mutual benefit, both in providing security and in fostering exchange and prosperity."[23] Later we will see that this was not Locke's view but one that has often been attributed to him by liberal philosophers in search of a pedigree. For present purposes, the important point is that it was not the view of the late scholastics or Grotius.

For the late scholastics, people must live in society to live well. They did so by their own consent, but the choice was a necessary one. As described earlier, according to Aquinas a person may act voluntarily even if there is only one right choice. He acts voluntarily in the sense that he chooses what he understands to be good. He consents to live in society because he cannot be a fully competent human outside of society. Aristotle said, "he who is unable to live in society, or who has no need because he is sufficient for himself, must be either a beast or a god."[24]

In contrast, sometimes there may be no one right choice. The decision is free in the sense that it is not necessary. According to the late scholastics, the society must make such a decision as to what kind of government to establish. While the need for a government exists by nature, there is no one form which uniquely fulfills that need and does so under all circumstances. Consequently, the people must determine what form of government to institute.[25]

They may institute any of the three forms of legitimate government that Aristotle had described: "monarchy, which is, the rule of one, aristocracy, that is, the rule of the best, and democracy, that is, popular rule or that of the multitude."[26] They may institute a mixed form of government or limit its powers. They may do so by tacit agreement or custom. They may do so by majority vote. Vitoria said it would be sufficient "if the greater part agrees,"[27] Molina that "it would be enough if the greater part of the republic consents."[28] The

---

[19]   Molina, *De iustitia et iure* II, disp. 22, no. 8.

[20]   Grotius, *De iure belli ac pacis, Prolegomena* vii–viii.

[21]   Quentin Skinner, *The Foundations of Modern Political Thought* 2 (Cambridge, 1978), 174. See John Neville Figgis, *Studies of Political Thought from Gerson to Grotius 1414–1625* (Cambridge, 1956), 154–55.

[22]   Charles Taylor, *Modern Social Imaginaries* (Durham, 2004), 19.

[23]   Ibid. 20.

[24]   *Politics* I.ii.f

[25]   Thus while human beings are born into society with others, they must institute a form of government by agreement or custom. Harro Höpfl is correct that before they do so, they are not in a "state of nature" as Hobbes or Locke envisioned it. But they are in a pre-civil state in the sense that they do not yet have a form a government, a point on which Skinner was right although Höpfl believed that he was wrong. Harro Höpfl, "Scholasticism in Quentin Skinner's *Foundations*," in Brett and Tully, *Rethinking the Foundations* 113 at 127.

[26]   Molina, *De iustitia et iure* II. disp. 23 pr.

[27]   Vitoria, *Relectio de potestate civili* no. 13, 303.

[28]   Molina, *De iustitia et iure* II disp. 23, no. 15.

alternative would be to require "the consent of all" which "in a multitude rarely or never happens."[29]

Once the people institute a form of government, they cannot alter it at will. If they choose to be ruled by a king, they cannot take back his power later unless he has become a tyrant. Otherwise, as Molina said, "the rule of kings would not be a monarchy, which is reduced under one supreme head, but a democracy, which is ultimately reduced to the multitude of the republic."[30] Grotius warned that "no wise person fails to see" "how many evils" would arise if it were "permissible for the people to restrain and punish kings whenever they make a bad use of their power."[31] They can only alter or abolish it, as we will see, when it ceases to govern for the common good. Then the people may institute whatever new form they choose.

As we have seen, had Chinese history taken a different course, emperors might have claimed legitimacy in the way Mencius described: on the grounds of merit, and thorough the nomination by an emperor confirmed by the people. Had Western history taken a different course, rulers might still be chosen, as they were in China, by dynastic succession. With the founding of the American Republic, however, the ideas of the Western classical tradition which we have just discussed were put to use.

II THE ARCHITECTURE OF GOVERNMENT

In the Confucian tradition, the right form of government was ruled by an emperor with the help of an elite of wise and good officials for the benefit of the people. In the Aristotelian tradition, there are three good forms of government: the rule of one (monarchy), the rule of an elite of the wise and good (aristocracy), and rule by the people (the good kind of democracy). Writers in both traditions discussed the proper role in government of a single ruler, of an elite, and of the people. They all believed that these roles were shaped by the purpose that government should serve. It was to enable each member of the society to flourish by living a distinctively human life.

i. *The Monarch*

Mencius said, "If the ruler is benevolent, all will be benevolent. If the ruler is righteous, all will be righteous."[32] Aristotle said that if there were one person of supreme virtue, then the government should be entrusted to him.[33] Nevertheless, writers in both traditions recognized that he might not be benevolent or virtuous or might not remain so.

According to some people, Aristotle observed, "it is bad in any case for a man, subject as he is to all the accidents of human passion, to have the supreme power, rather than the law."[34]

---

[29]   Vitoria, *Relectio de potestate civili* no. 13, 303. Similarly, Molina, *De iustitia et iure* II disp. 23, no. 15.
[30]   Molina, *De iustitia et iure* II disp. 23, no. 9. Similarly, Vitoria, *Relectio de potestate civili* no. 13, 303.
[31]   Grotius, *De iure belli ac pacis* I.iii.8.1.
[32]   *Mencius* 4.2.5.
[33]   *Politics* III. xvii.1288a.
[34]   Ibid. III.x.1281a.

According to Aquinas, "a kingdom is the best form of government of the people if it is not corrupt. But because of the great power that is given to a king, it easily degenerates into tyranny, unless the one to whom this power is given be a completely virtuous man."[35]

Even if he were, what about his successor? Aristotle said, "[e]ven supposing the principle to be maintained that kingly power is the best thing for states, how about the family of the king? Are his children to succeed him? If they are no better than anybody else, that will be mischievous." Although he could pass over his children and hand on his power to a virtuous person, that "is hardly to be expected, and is too much to ask of human nature."[36] Menicus, as we have seen, described how, ideally, a new emperor should not be chosen by birth but according to virtue and the acclamation of the people. But ever since Shu had passed the empire to his son, and thereby founded the Xia dynasty, the new emperor had always been chosen by birth.

According to the Confucian tradition, the result had been that although the mandate of Tian fell upon a worthy man who became emperor, his successors proved to be unworthy men. The result was disastrous for the people. Tian would then transfer his mandate to a new and worthy person who would then become emperor. And the cycle would begin again.

One solution proposed by writers in the Aristotelian tradition was to establish a mixed form of government. Although Aquinas described a monarchy as the best form of government in a letter to the King of Sicily, later, he explained in the *Summa theologiae* that it might be better to combine monarchy with aristocracy and democracy.

> Two points are to be observed concerning the right ordering of rulers in a state or nation. One is that all should take some share in the government. In this way peace is preserved among the people, and all love and protect this form of government as said in the *Politics* II. vi. The other point to be observed concerns the kinds of government or order or the state. These differ in kind, as the Philosopher explains. The first place is held by the kingdom, where one person rules according to virtue; and aristocracy, where a few rule according to virtue. Accordingly, the best form of government is in a state or kingdom, where one is given the power to preside over all; while under him are others who have governing powers: and yet a government of this kind is shared by all, both because all are eligible to govern, and because the rulers are chosen by all.[37]

He concluded:

> [T]his is the best form of polity: a mixture of kingdom, in as much as one is preeminent, and aristocracy, in as much as a number of persons have authority on account of virtue, and of democracy, that is, government of the people, inasmuch as the rules may be chosen from the people, and the selection (*electio*) of the rulers pertains to the people.[38]

He cited the authority of Aristotle who noted that "[s]ome indeed, say that the best constitution is a combination of all existing forms" of monarchy, aristocracy, and

---

[35] *Summa theologiae* I-II, Q. 105, a. 1, ad 2.
[36] *Politics* III.xv.1286b.
[37] *Summa theologiae* I-II, Q. 105, a. 1.
[38] Ibid.

democracy. "[T]hey are nearer the truth who combine many forms; for the constitution is better which is made up of more numerous elements."[39]

Molina said and Vitoria implied that monarchy is the best form of government. They claimed that as long as a monarch governs for the common good, there is no less liberty than in other regimes, and a monarchy best avoids seditions.[40] Nevertheless, Molina noted, the king's power might be limited.

> The power conceded to kings may be greater or lesser so that something is permitted to them, or not permitted, or they are bound to something, or not bound. Thereafter it is to be accepted that whatever power was first conceded to a king, remains as constituted. ... [T]he prince ... cannot increase his power nor transgress that which to the prince was constituted.[41]

He presented favorably the opinion of his colleague at Salamanca, Alfonsus à Castro: it should be presumed that the king's power is limited, and, indeed, that he cannot make laws without the assent of the people.

> With the power of a king in a republic is, in moderation, joined the power to make laws by which one is governed. ... If usage (*usus*) has it that such laws do not have force unless the people approve, then it is deemed that the republic did not concede its kings greater power than to make laws dependent on the approval of the people. It is most likely, if the people advert to it, that they did not concede a greater power to the kings; indeed, if they did not advert to it, that would seem to be the intention of those who constituted the king of the republic, for when something is not expressed, it is always the stronger presumption that the king would augment his own power by his own power, the subjects not daring to resist, than that the subjects would restrict their power once conceded. Wherefore it is right that republics do not accept laws that burden them notably, when they are not in all ways necessary for the public good. If the prince forces them to do so, he commits injustice.[42]

As these passages suggest, when the late scholastics spoke of limitations on the king's power, they meant that the king's power was limited as a matter of law not simply as a matter of morality. As mentioned earlier, Aquinas had distinguished duties that were owed as a matter of legal obligation from duties that are not. The duty to pay a debt is a matter of legal obligation. The duty to respect those in authority (*observantia*) is not.[43] The late scholastics were discussing the limits within which a ruler's laws were binding,[44] about "laws that ... limit, extend or diminish his power,"[45] and about how it was "lawful" for his subjects to make him observe those limits.[46] A ruler who transgresses them has violated the "right" of his subjects. "[S]uch a right be sufficiently shown by ancient and definite

---

[39]   *Politics* II.vi.1265b–1266a.
[40]   Molina, *De iustitia et iure* II disp. 23, no. 14. Vitoria, *Relectio de potestate civili* no. 11, 303.
[41]   Molina, *De iustitia et iure* II disp. 23, no. 5.
[42]   Ibid. no. 6. He was paraphrasing, not quoting, Alfonsus a Castro, *De potestate legis poenalis libri duo* (Salamanca, 1550), lib. 1, ch. 1. ff. 7r–7v.
[43]   *Summa theologiae* II-II, Q. 80.
[44]   Vitoria, *Relectio de potestate civili* no. 23, 311.
[45]   Molina, *De iustitia et iure* V, disp. 3, no. 2.
[46]   Soto, *De iusitia et iure* lib. 4, q. 4, a. 1.

documents or by immemorial custom."[47] There might be no institution, such as a court, that could call the ruler to account. Nevertheless, his violation of limits set to his power would be unlawful in the same way as it would be unlawful to refuse to pay a debt.

In the Confucian tradition, the emperor was supposed to rule with the support of his ministers. The ministers were supposed to rebuke an emperor who acted wrongfully, and he was supposed to listen. Moreover, only some matters were the proper concern of the emperor. The ministers were supposed to tell the emperor what they were.

As we will see, in the Song dynasty, which has been called "the most Confucian of dynasties," the emperor' officials regularly played these roles. There were institutional and customary safeguards on their ability to do. For example, there were organs of the administration with the task of criticizing imperial policies. The education of a future emperor was entrusted to Confucian scholars who would teach him about the emperor's proper role. Nevertheless, as we saw earlier, the relationship between the emperor and his ministers was one of the five relationships governed by propriety or *li*. It was based on the respect that that they should show each other. We can speak about a Song constitution under which the emperor's powers were limited. But the limitation was not formal and legal but moral.

One limitation was that if the emperor turned to evil, it was the duty of his ministers to correct him. Mencius said that when "the advice of a minister is not acted on, and his words are not listened to, . . . no good comes to the people."[48] According to Confucius, if a ruler is wrong, his officials should "withstand him to his face." "Do not deceive him; but do not be afraid to offend him."[49] Mencius said, "Is it a fault to restrain one's ruler? He who restrains his ruler loves his ruler."[50]

> Therefore, it is said, "To urge one's sovereign to difficult achievements may be called showing respect for him. To set before him what is good and repress his perversities may be called showing reverence for him. He who does not do these things, saying to himself 'my sovereign is incompetent for this,' may be said to play the thief with him."[51]

"It is not enough to criticize those who are wrongly appointed to office; it is not enough to criticize mistakes made in political affairs. It is only the great man who can rectify what is wrong in the sovereign's mind."[52] The ruler should listen. Confucius said, "if you are evil, and no one disagrees with you, perhaps you could destroy the country with a single utterance."[53]

If the emperor did not listen, a minister faced the difficult decision of whether he should resign. Confucius said, an official "serves his lord according to the Way and . . . resigns when this is no longer possible."[54] He also said, "[w]hen the government is just, you may

[47] Suárez, *Defensio fidei* III.iii, no. 3.
[48] *Mencius* 4.2.3.4.
[49] *Analects* 14.22.
[50] *Mencius* 1B.4.10.
[51] Ibid. 4A1.13.
[52] Ibid. 4.1.20.
[53] *Analects* 13.15.
[54] Ibid. 11.24

speak boldly . . . ; when you have an unjust government, . . . be careful of what you say."[55] But a ruler is in danger if his officials fear to disagree with him. "[I]f you are evil, and no one disagrees with you, perhaps you could destroy the country with a single utterance."[56]

Another limit to how the emperor should act concerned how his role was conceptualized. Here, Confucians disagreed. The end of government was, of course, to rule benevolently for the good of the people. In the Sung dynasty, Sima Guang (1019–86) claimed that the way to pursue that goal was not to transform society but to preserve it. Wang An-shih (1021–86) said that the government should not merely preserve order but should take active measures to benefit the people. These conceptions of the goal of government had different implications for the role that the emperor should play.

A contemporary scholar, Xiao-bin Ji, described Sima Guang's reluctance for the government to take an active role. "[W]hile it was very difficult to surpass one's predecessors, one could easily do worse if one was not careful. Consequently, in his thought on government policy, the concern to prevent disaster outweighed the desire for outstanding improvement."[57] To preserve society, nothing is more essential than the subordination of those who are ruled to those who rule. Political authority must "make the people accustomed to the role of superior and inferior."[58] As Peter Bol noted, for Sima, "[t]he ruler's task is to keep men to their appointed roles."[59]

Some scholars, such as Frederick Mote, regarded Sima's ideas as "the most important political expression" "promoting the emperor to new heights of unquestioned authority, and the demands upon the servitor to new degrees of unquestioned loyalty."[60] William Sariti was right that this view is a "misunderstanding."[61] The reason is that Sima had a limited idea of what the government should do. It should preserve stability. If everyone maintained proper subordination, there would be nothing left for the emperor to do. As Sima said, "Let the ruler only stand by with folded hands."[62]

Although he said that he was following traditional Confucian principles, Sima reinterpreted them rather drastically. He reconceptualized the Confucian virtue of *li*, meaning "ritual" or "propriety," in terms of subordination. As we have seen, for Confucius and Mencius, *li*, like benevolence and righteousness, is essential to a person's moral development. Subordination is one element in four of the five relationships it governed: those of a minister to his ruler, or a son to his father, a wife to her husband, and a younger brother to an elder brother. For Sima, however, *li* is of prime importance because subordination is of

[55] Ibid. 14.3.
[56] Ibid. 13.15.
[57] Xiao-bin Ji, *Politics and Conservatism in Northern Song China: The Career and Thought of Sima Guang (AD 1019–1086)* (Hong Kong, 2005), 50.
[58] From Peter K. Bol, *"This Culture of Ours": Intellectual Transitions in T'ang and Sung China* (Stanford, 1992), 222, n. 40.
[59] Ibid. 220.
[60] F. W. Mote, "The Growth of Chinese Despotism: A Critique of Wittfogel's Theory of Oriental Despotism as Applied to China," *Oriens Extremus* 8 (1961), 1 at 13.
[61] William Sariti, "Monarchy, Bureaucracy, and Absolutism in the Political Thought of Ssu-Ma Kuang," *Journal of Asian Studies* 32 (1972), 53 at 53; see Bol, "Government, Society, and State" 158.
[62] Sima Guang, *Wen-kuo Wen-cheng Ssu-Ma Kung Chi (The Collected Papers of Sima Guang)* (Ssu-pu ts'ung-k'an ed.), 514–16S6 quoted in Sariti, ""Monarchy, Bureaucracy, and Absolutism" 56, n. 10.

prime importance. He believed that "of the Son of Heaven's responsibilities, none is greater than *li*, that in *li* nothing is greater than roles, and that in roles, nothing is greater than names."[63] "Only after there are names to command them and accoutrements [devices to make clear their rank and position] to differentiate them will the proper places for superior and inferior be clear. This is the great constant of *li*."[64]

For Wang Anshi, the task of government is not merely to preserve order but to take action. Its programs should be designed, however, not by the emperor himself, but by talented officials. As Peter Bol said, in Wang's theory of government, "[t]he ruler and dynastic house are not functionally necessary."[65] "All that Wang requires of the ruler is that he support the program."[66]

Even the talented officials to be entrusted with designing and implementing the program should not be personally chosen by the emperor. "[T]he emperor cannot possibly investigate the character and ability of each and every one individually." Those who have already been selected for their "good character and great ability should be entrusted with the task of selecting men of like qualifications."[67]

As a practical matter, however, Wang's ability to implement his policies depended entirely on the backing of Emperor Shenzong, who put him in power in 1069. In 1085, the empress dowager dismissed him and appointed his opponent, Sima Guang. Yet his partisans resumed power in 1093 and held it almost until 1125, two years before the fall of the Northern Song Dynasty to foreign invaders.

ii *The Worthiest*

Writers in both traditions agreed that some, because of their greater wisdom or virtue, are better qualified to govern than others.

According to Confucius, the emperor should rule through officials chosen on the basis of merit. He should "raise to office the virtuous and capable,"[68] "employ the upright and put aside all the crooked."[69] According to Mencius, he should "give honor to men of talents and virtue and employ the able, so that offices shall all be filled by outstanding individuals."[70] Those qualified to govern are the *junzi* (君子) or *shi* (士), those who are noblemen or virtuous men by merit and not by descent.

Aristotle said that politics is a "master art" concerned with "the good for man."[71] The "true student of politics is thought to have studied virtue above all things for he wishes to make his fellow citizens good."[72] According to Aquinas, a monarchy could best pursue

[63] Bol, *"This Culture of Ours"* 238.
[64] Ibid. 241, n. 187.
[65] Ibid. 217.
[66] Bol, "Government, Society, and State" 160.
[67] Wang Anshi "The Ten Thousand Word Memorial" 5.
[68] *Analects* 13.
[69] Ibid. 2.
[70] *Mencius* 2.1.5.1.
[71] *Nicomachean Ethics* I.i.1094a.
[72] Ibid. I.xiii.1102a.

a unified policy.[73] An aristocracy, it would seem, could best pursue one that is wise and good. By aristocracy, Aristotle meant rule by the worthiest. A hereditary aristocracy, for Aristotle, would have been one of the bad forms of government – an oligarchy – which is rule by the well-born or the rich.

Writers in the Confucian and Aristotelian traditions held different opinions as to the origins of this inequality. According to Confucius, all men are the same at birth. Neither the intellectual nor moral capabilities of those who prove worthier are part of their natural endowment. Confucius said, "by nature, men are nearly alike; by practice, they get to be wide apart."[74] Mencius said, "All men may be Yaos and Shuns."[75] "The disciple Gong Du said, 'All are equally men, but some are great men, and some are little men; how is this?' Mencius replied, 'Those who follow that part of themselves which is great are great men; those who follow that part which is little are little men.'"[76]

According to Aristotle, some free men, such as laborers and mechanics (for example, artisans), lack the leisure for liberal activities such as the pursuit of knowledge and politics. "No man can practice virtue who is living the life of a mechanic or laborer."[77] John Grey thought he must be contradicting his "central thesis" that "each of us has a nature or essence and that goodness or virtue consists in bringing that essence or nature to realization." Yet although "the life of contemplation is beyond that of most human beings, Aristotle has no doubt that it is *the best life for man*. Conversely, though any other sort of life is inferior to that of the contemplative man, Aristotle insists that the good life for the mass of men is precisely to bring to realization their admittedly inferior natures."[78]

According to Aquinas, as we have seen, even if Adam had never fallen and humanity had lived sinlessly in paradise there would still be some more capable of government than the rest. Part of the difference would be due to what we would call natural endowment. Part of it would be due to choice. "For man would work not by necessity but free will according to which man can apply himself to a greater or lesser extent in what is to be done or to be sought or to be known."[79] Some by their own free choice might decide not to be philosophers or statesman but to pursue activities of less preeminent value. They would not be equal in that respect, but their lives would have a goodness than those of the philosopher or statesman lack. In so choosing, they contribute to the common good, which is the ultimate natural end of moral choice. The world would be poorer if everyone became a philosopher or statesman. For some to be governed by others would not diminish

---

[73] *De regno* I.iii.18.

[74] *Analects* 17.2. Although he also said:

> Those who are born with the possession of knowledge are the highest class of men. Those who learn, and so readily get possession of knowledge, are the next. Those who are dull and stupid, and yet compass the learning, are another class next to these. As to those who are dull and stupid and yet do not learn; – they are the lowest of the people.
> Analects 16.9.

[75] *Mencius* 6.2.2.1.

[76] Ibid.

[77] *Politics* III.v.1278a.

[78] John Gray, *Liberalisms: Essays in Political Philosophy* (London, 1989), 255.

[79] *Summa theologiae* I, Q. 96, a. 3.

"liberty" which is "one of the greatest goods."[80] Even in this fallen world, "[i]f ... a multitude of free men is ordered by the ruler towards the common good of the multitude, that rulership will be right and just, as is suitable to free men."[81]

According to Aristotle, however, there is only one sort of person who lacks a fully human nature: a slave lacks a "rational principle" that would enable him to decide what is best for himself. He "participates in a rational principle enough to apprehend, but not to have, such a principle."[82] Consequently, for their own preservation and protection, natural slaves are better off when they "wholly belong" to a master whose ends they serve.[83]

The late scholastics rejected this claim because they agreed that it is inconsistent with Aristotle's central thesis that each of us has the same nature or essence. Lessius said that "no one by nature is a slave." "All men according to their natural condition are equal; as they are of the same nature, of the same parents, and constituted for the same end."[84] Since a human being is a rational animal, directed to his end by reason, it is not possible, according to Vitoria and las Casas, that a large part of the human race is born defective in intellect.[85]

In the Confucian tradition, the relationship between the *shih* and the people was symbiotic. Confucius said, "the people may be made to follow a path of action, but they may not be made to understand it."[86] A *shi* will be able to maintain his moral balance even in times of adversity. Mencius said, "as to the people, if they have not a certain livelihood, it follows that they will not have a fixed heart (恆心 *heng xin*)."[87] Consequently, they should instruct those who have less wisdom. Although they will not do wrong even in times of adversity, they should not expect the same of others. Mencius said that if people who "do not have a fixed heart, there is nothing which they will not do, in the way of self-abandonment, of moral deflection, of depravity, and of wild license." To punish them is to "entrap them."[88] Thus those who govern have two duties: to see to the people's welfare and to instruct them. Confucius was asked "what should be done for the people?" He answered, "enrich them." "'And when they have been enriched, what more shall be done?' The Master said, 'Teach them.'"[89]

In turn, those who govern depend on the people for their support. As Mencius said, "[i]f there were not men of a superior grade, there would be none to rule the country-

---

[80] Ibid. I Q. 94, a. 4 obj. 3.

[81] *De regno* I.ii.10.

[82] *Politics* I.v.1254b.

[83] Ibid. I.iv 1254a.

[84] Lessius *De iustitia et iure* lib, 2, cap. 4, dub. 9, no. 54.

[85] Vitoria said that "God and nature are not deficient in that which is necessary for a large part of the species: in man, however, the foremost is reason." Vitoria, *De Indis*, in 1 in *Relecciones Teológicas* 361, no. 23. Las Casas made the same argument: "By nothing other than the intellect is the nature of man perfected." Therefore, to be born with a defective intellect must be, like any other birth defect, "most rare." Bartolomaeus de las Casas, *Apologia o Declaración y Defensa Universal de los Derechos de Hombe y de los Pueblos*, Vidal Abril Castelló et al. eds. (Junta de Castilla, 2000) cap. iii p. 25 (in Latin and Spanish).

[86] *Analects* 8.9.

[87] *Mencius* 1.1.7 20.

[88] Ibid. 1.1.7 20.

[89] *Analects* 13.9.

men. If there were not country-men, there would be none to support the men of superior grade."[90]

Both need each other.

> Then, is it the government of the kingdom which alone can be carried on along with the practice of husbandry? Great men have their proper business, and little men have their proper business. Moreover, in the case of any single individual, whatever articles he can require are ready to his hand, being produced by the various craftsmen: if he must first make them for his own use, this way of doing would keep all the people running about upon the roads. Hence, there is the saying, "Some labour with their minds, and some labour with their strength. Those who labour with their minds govern others; those who labour with their strength are governed by others. Those who are governed by others support them; those who govern others are supported by them." This is a principle universally recognized.[91]

The relationship is symbiotic.

For Aristotle, it was far from obvious that free men such as the laborer or craftsman would like to be ruled even by the worthiest. For Aristotle, "citizens" are those who have "power to take part in the deliberative or judicial administration of any state."[92] "[I]s he only a true citizen who has a share of office, or is the mechanic to be included?"[93] "May we not reply, that . . . the best form of state will not admit them to citizenship."[94] One difficulty is that for the good to rule and have supreme power "everybody else, being excluded from power, will be dishonored."[95] Another is that those excluded are free men. "A state is a community of free men."[96]

Aristotle concluded that the best form of government will depend on the sort of people to be governed. Those who can "submit to be ruled as freemen by men whose virtue renders them capable of political command are adapted for an aristocracy."[97] They will be governed as free men seeking ends of their own; not as slaves who serve the ends of their masters. They will themselves submit to being governed by others. They will submit because those who govern are best able to govern. Writers in the Confucian tradition expected that as long as the people were well governed, they would do so.

In contrast, "the people who are suited for constitutional freedom are those among whom there naturally exists a . . . multitude able to rule and to obey in turn by a law which gives office to the well-to-do according to their desert."[98] For this government to be the best, there must be a multitude capable of both of ruling and obeying. The multitude must also be capable of observing a law or procedure that does select people for offices according to their desert.

---

[90]   *Mencius* 3.1.3.14.
[91]   Ibid. 3.1.4.6.
[92]   *Politics* III.i.1275b.
[93]   Ibid. III.v.1277b.
[94]   Ibid. III.v.1278a.
[95]   Ibid. III.x.1281a.
[96]   Ibid. III.vi.1279a.
[97]   Ibid. III.xvii.1288a.
[98]   Ibid.

iii *The People*

Confucius said, "When the Way prevails in the realm, the common people do not debate politics among themselves."[99] It is not their role to decide what the government should do. Nevertheless, the object of government is the welfare of them all. When the government is good, the people will know that it is.

As we have seen, according to Mencius, in the time of the sage kings, to be entitled to the throne, an emperor had to be accepted by the people. In the *Analects*, Yao is said to have advised Shun: "Value the common people . . . If you are generous you will gain the hearts of the people; if you are trustworthy, they will rely on you; if you are diligent, you will get results; if you are fair, they will be happy."[100] The people will also know when a government is bad. Then they will talk, and the government would be ill-advised to try to stop them. It should reform, and if it does not, they will no longer obey.

A leading political theorist of the Song dynasty, Su Shih (1037–1101), thought that the people should play a more active part. With the death of his mentor Ouyang Xiu, he became the leading literary figure of the age. Su believed in Confucian ideals of the cultivation of virtue, both as an end of government and as a means of ruling. In contrast to Sima Guang, whose concern was that order be preserved though obedience, or Wang Anshi whose concern was that the right programs be devised and implemented by talented officials, Su thought that a key role in government must be played by those lower down, by local officials and by the people.

Unlike Sima and Wang, he set out a clear statement of the goals that government should achieve. As he described it, "[T]he role of the ruler . . . is simply to desire to 'accomplish something' (有為 *you wei*); the minister . . . need only consider ways to 'acting on the world' (*wen tian xia*); and the *shi* . . . need only achieve something at the local level."[101]

How, then, is a decision to be made on what should be accomplished? Su thought, in large part, decisions should be made at the lowest level: by the local officials and by the people. "If the ruler favors accomplishing something, he will encourage his ministers to speak their minds and will support them in fully realizing their plans. If the court (rulers and ministers) wants to act, it will learn what needs to be done from the *shi* who execute policy."[102]

As Bol noted: "Thus Su comes full circle; the *shi* who execute policy are ultimately the source of policy."[103] Nevertheless, the ultimate judge of what the government should do is the people. According to Su, "the sages thought that popular opinion determined whether the state would survive."[104] "Those in antiquity who were good at governing never competed with the people. Instead, they allowed them to choose for themselves, and thereupon guided them to it [their choice]."[105] When the Shang king P'an-keng prepared to move the

99   *Analects* 16.2.
100   Ibid. 20.1.
101   Bol, *"This Culture of Ours"* 263.
102   Ibid. 263.
103   Ibid.
104   Ibid. n. 105.
105   Ibid. n. 83.

capital to Yin, "the populace gathered together to express its resentment." His response was to say, "'Let none of you dare to suppress the remonstrances of lesser men.' He feared that the various officers and responsible officials would . . . forbid the populace to speak."[106]

He opposed Wang Anshi's program in which policies should be developed by the elite and implemented top-down. When critics claimed that the people objected to his reforms, Wang had answered that if the state "decided every matter according to moral principles (*i-li*), then popular sentiment ought eventually to change of its own accord."[107] According to Su, "the people should speak, and the government should listen."[108] He said, in a veiled attack on Wang:

> An unbenevolent man despises the populace. He says, "the populace can share in the success; it is difficult to plan the beginning with them." Thus in all aspects of governing, he is like thunder and ghosts, keeping the populace from knowing where [political change] is coming from. How would he be willing to reveal his true feelings and plan together with the populace?[109]

The Confucians were describing the role of the people within a government ruled by the emperor with the support of scholar-officials. In the Aristotelian tradition, democracy is one of the three good forms of government along with monarchy and aristocracy. Translation is difficult because in English, there is only one word for rule by the people – democracy. For Aristotle, there was a good form of democracy which, like any good form of government, ruled for the common good. There was a bad form, in which who ruled did so in their own interest. We might translate the bad form of democracy as "interest group pluralism."

Aristotle regarded even the good form of democracy as the least desirable. Consequently, it is surprising that he said so much about its positive side.

He said that the decisions of a multitude may actually be sounder than those of a few wiser people:

> For the many, of whom each individual is but an ordinary person, when they meet together may very likely be better than the few good, if regarded not individually but collectively, just as a feast to which many contribute is better than a dinner provided out of a single purse. For each individual among the many has a share of virtue and prudence, and when they meet together, they become in a manner one man, who has many feet, and hands, and senses; that is a figure of their mind and disposition. Hence the many are better judges than a single man of music and poetry; for some understand one part, and some another, and among them they understand the whole.[110]

A multitude may be harder to corrupt and less susceptible to passion:

> Again, the many are more incorruptible than the few; they are like the greater quantity of water which is less easily corrupted than a little. The individual is liable to be overcome by

[106] Ibid. n. 86.
[107] Ibid. n. 211.
[108] Ibid. n. 87.
[109] Ibid.
[110] *Politics* III.xi1281a–1281b.

anger or by some other passion, and then his judgment is necessarily perverted; but it is hardly to be supposed that a great number of persons would all get into a passion and go wrong at the same moment."[111]

Moreover, "a state in which many poor men are excluded from office will necessarily be full of enemies." The solution is to allow everyone to share in government, for example, by electing the officials who govern and removing them from office:

> The only way of escape is to assign to them some deliberative and judicial functions. For this reason, Solon and certain other legislators give them the power of electing to offices, and of calling the magistrates to account, but they do not allow them to hold office singly. When they meet together their perceptions are quite good enough, and combined with the better class they are useful to the state ... but each individual, left to himself, forms an imperfect judgment."[112]

As we have seen, in the mixed form of government that Aquinas favored the people would elect their rulers.

Aristotle also gave advice as to how to preserve a democracy. One should prevent extreme poverty.

> [T]he true friend of the people should see that they be not too poor, for extreme poverty lowers the character of the democracy; measures therefore should be taken which will give them lasting prosperity; and as this is equally the interest of all classes, the proceeds of the public revenues should be accumulated and distributed among its poor, if possible, in such quantities as may enable them to purchase a little farm, or, at any rate, make a beginning in trade or husbandry."[113]

Also, democracies should avoid

> a false idea of freedom which is contradictory to the true interests of the state. For two principles are characteristic of democracy, the government of the majority and freedom. Men think that what is just is equal; and that equality is the supremacy of the popular will; and that freedom means the doing what a man likes. In such democracies every one lives as he pleases, or in the words of Euripides, "according to his fancy."[114]

On Aristotelian principles, living as one likes may not contribute to the preservation of a democracy or to a person's well-being or to the common good. It depends on how a person likes to live.

III THE CONSEQUENCES OF MISRULE

According to writers in both traditions, people needed government in order to live rightly. The purpose of government was to enable them to do so. Writers in both traditions

---

[111]   Ibid. III.xv1286a.
[112]   Ibid. III.xi1281b.
[113]   Ibid. VI.v1320a.
[114]   Ibid. V.ix1310a.

concluded that when a government ceased to pursue its purpose, it lost its legitimacy. According to Confucians, the "mandate of Heaven" would change, the government would fall, and a new one would take its place. Writers in the Aristotelian tradition concluded that the people had a right to overthrow such a government and to replace it with one of their own choosing.

i *The Confucian Tradition*

Earlier we saw that in the Confucian tradition, the dynastic principle was not the only way in which an emperor might be chosen. Mencius had suggested others. But there was never a time in Chinese history when these suggestions were institutionalized.

The same is true of the removal of an emperor for misrule. From the beginning of the tradition, it was clear in principle that the emperor's right to rule lasted only so long as he ruled for the benefit of the people. But there was never a time in Chinese history when a procedure was institutionalized for removing him.

In the Confucian tradition, the emperor ruled by the decree of Tian (天). If he became corrupt, Tian could confer the mandate to rule on someone else. Tian had commissioned the founder of the Shang dynasty to overthrow the Xia, and the founder of the Zhou dynasty to overthrow the Shang. Throughout Chinese history, when dynasties tottered or fell, would-be emperors would claim that the decree of Tian had fallen on them. But there was never a procedure for testing that claim other than to see whether they held on to power. In most cases, even if they succeeded in doing so, it seemed unlikely that Tian had chosen them for their surpassing virtue. They were consolidators of power, not exemplars of virtue.

Yet Mencius had suggested that a corrupt king could be dismissed like anyone else who failed to do his job.

> Mencius said to the king Xuan of Qi, "Suppose that one of your Majesty's ministers were to entrust his wife and children to the care of his friend, while he himself went into Chu to travel, and that, on his return, he should find that the friend had let his wife and children starve and freeze; how ought he to deal with him?" The king said, "He should be abandoned."
>
> Mencius proceeded, "Suppose that a superior officer could not regulate the officers under him, how would you deal with him?" The king said, "Dismiss him."
>
> Mencius again said, "If governance is lacking within the four borders of your kingdom, what is to be done?" The king looked to the right and left, and spoke of other matters.[115]

Did anyone, however, have the authority to remove the king? In one passage, Mencius suggested that that the high ministers could do so. Here, he drew a distinction. The high ministers who had this power were relatives of the king. Those who had been appointed to their positions by merit alone did not. Mencius told king Xuan of Qi:

> "There are the high ministers who are noble and relatives of the prince, and there are those who are of a different surname." The king said, "I beg to ask about the high ministers who

---

[115] *Mencius* 1.2.6.1–4.

are noble and relatives of the prince." Mencius answered, "If the ruler has great faults, they ought to remonstrate with him, and if he does not listen to them after they have done so repeatedly, they ought to dethrone him."

The king on this looked moved, and changed countenance.

Mencius said, "Let not your Majesty be offended. You asked me, and I dare not answer wrongly."

The king's countenance became composed, and he then begged to ask about high ministers who were of a different surname from the prince. Mencius said, "When the prince has faults, they ought to remonstrate with him; and if he does not listen to them after they have done this again and again, they ought to resign from the State."[116]

In one passage, Mencius explained that when Wu killed the unrighteous King Zhou of Shang he did not kill a ruler. King Xuan asked:

"May a minister then put his ruler to death?"

Mencius said, "He who betrays the benevolence proper to his nature, is called a robber; he who betrays righteousness, is called crooked. The robber and crooked we call just a man. I have heard of the putting to death of the man Zhou, but, in his case, I have not heard of killing a ruler."[117]

Chinese institutions might have developed differently if, during an institutional crisis, an emperor had been deposed, and his deposition had been justified by principles drawn from these texts. But such an event never occurred.

ii *The Aristotelian Tradition*

The late scholastics concluded that when any government becomes subversive of the ends for which it is constituted, the people have the right to resist. Government is constituted for the common good. When it becomes subversive of the common good, the people have the right to alter or abolish it and institute what they deem to be a better form of government.

Again they drew on Aristotle and Aquinas. According to Aquinas, "A tyrannical government is not just, because it is directed, not to the common good, but to the private good of the ruler, as the Philosopher [Aristotle] states."[118] His immediate disciple Ptolemy da Lucca added a conclusion to *De regimine principum* which, in the sixteenth century, was ascribed to Aquinas. It contained this passage:

A kingdom does not exist on account of the king, but the king on account of the kingdom since for this God has provided for kings that they should guide and govern their kingdom and preserve everyone in his own rights, and this is the end of rule. But if they do otherwise, by turning everything to their convenience, they are not kings but tyrants.[119]

---

[116] *Mencius* 5.2.9.1–4.
[117] *Mencius* 1.2.8.1–3.
[118] *Summa theologiae* II-II, Q. 42, a. 3, ad 3.
[119] *De regimine principum* III, 2 (by Ptolemy da Lucca).

Aquinas concluded that those who revolt against a tyrant are not guilty of sedition since "sedition is contrary to unity" and "it is evident that the unity to which sedition is opposed is the unity of law and common good."[120] In *De regimine principum*, he said:

> If it belongs to the right of a certain multitude to provide itself with a king, it is not unjust that those who instituted the king may depose or limit his power if he tyrannically abuses the royal power. Such a multitude is not to be deemed to be acting unfaithfully in deposing him from the office of king even if it has previously subjected itself to him in perpetuity because he has not kept his pact (*pactus*) with his subjects.[121]

Similarly, according to Vitoria, a tyrant's laws are not binding.[122] According to Soto, a tyrant "may have his kingship lawfully taken away by the republic."[123] Molina said that "if the king fell into tyranny or attempted to do that which in no way benefitted the republic, "it would be the same as if the throne fell vacant. "[T]he entire right and power of the republic would devolve on the republic itself that it previously had to constitute [a government] … It could constitute a new king, who it wished, or laws that it wished to limit, extend or diminish his power, or to choose whatever other kind of regime it wished."[124]

The people would have that same right, according to Molina and Suárez, if the king overstepped whatever limits the people had set to his power when they constituted the government. Beyond those limits, "it remains as it would have been before power was conceded to him." A king who crossed those limits was, "in that respect, a tyrant."[125] According to Suárez,

> [I]f the people transfer power to the king, reserving it to themselves in certain grave cases or transactions, they can lawfully use it in these and so preserve their right. It is enough that such a right be sufficiently shown by ancient and definite documents or by immemorial custom. If the king turns his just power into tyranny and abuses it to the manifest harm of the polity, the people can use their natural power to defend themselves, for of this they can never deprive themselves.[126]

As Quentin Skinner noted, "by drawing on their Thomist heritage, the counter-reformation theorists [his term for the late scholastics] … served as the main channel through which the contractarian approach to the discussion of political obligation came to exercise its decisive influence in the course of the following century."[127] When a government was unfaithful to the ends for which it was constituted, it could legitimately be overthrown. That position was taken by Calvinists such as Theodore Beza[128] (1519–1605), Calvin's successor at Geneva, and the author of the anonymous tract *Vindiciae contra*

---

[120] *Summa theologiae* II-II, Q. 42, a. 3.
[121] Thomas Aquinas, *De regno ad regem Cypri* Joseph Kenny, ed. (Toronto, 1949), I.vii.
[122] Vitoria, *Relectio de potestate civili* no. 23, *Relecciones Teológicas* 311.
[123] Soto, *De iusitia et iure* lib. 4, q. 4, a. 1.
[124] Molina, *De iustitia et iure* V, disp. 3, no. 2.
[125] Ibid. disp. 23, no. 10.
[126] Suárez, *Defensio fidei* III.iii, no. 3.
[127] Skinner, *Foundations of Modern Political Thought* 2:174.
[128] Theodore Beza, *De jure magistratuum* (1574), qu. 6, trans. Henry-Louis Gonin, *On the Rights of Magistrates*, www.constitution.org/cmt/beza/magistrates.htm.

tyrannos (1579).[129] As Skinner noted, "[t]hey rejected the characteristically Protestant tendency to suppose that God places all men in a condition of political subjection as a remedy for their sins."[130] "[W]e may say with very little exaggeration that the main foundations of the Calvinist theory of revolution were in fact constructed entirely by their Catholic adversaries"[131] of the School of Salamanca.

In *Patriarcha*, his notorious defense of the divine right of kings published posthumously in 1680, Bishop Filmer denounced the "perilous Conclusion, which is, *That the People or Multitude have Power to punish, or deprive the Prince, if he transgress the Laws of the Kingdom.*"[132] It was founded "upon this ground of Doctrine": "Mankind is naturally endowed and born with Freedom from all Subjection, and at liberty to choose what Form of Government it please; And that the Power which any one Man has over others, was at first bestowed according to the discretion of the Multitude."[133] This doctrine, he said, was "first hatched in the Schools," meaning by the scholastics, and then "entertained" by "the Divines of the Reformed Churches."[134] It had also been disseminated by Hugo Grotius.[135]

As noted earlier, principles do not of themselves create governments. Neither do they bring them down. Yet this principle was at hand when the Stuart monarchy fell in 1688, and when thirteen English colonies declared their independence in 1776. Later we will see how the English Whigs and the founders of the American Republic put it to use.

---

[129] *Vindiciae contra tyrannos* (Basel 1579), trans. *Vindiciae contra tyrannos: A Defence of Liberty against Tyrants, or The lawful power of the Prince over the People and of the People over the Prince* (London, 1689), III.ii. A similar position was taken by other Protestant authors such as John Ponet (1514–56), *A Short Treatise on Political Power, and of the true obedience which subjects our to kings and other civil governors, with an Exhortation to all true and natural English men* (1556), chs. i, vi and George Buchanan (1506–82), *De iure Regni apud Scotos Dialogus*, critical edition and translation, *A Dialogue on the Law of Kingship among the Scots*, Roger A. Mason and Martin S. Smith eds. (Aldershot, 2004), 55, 153. I suggested elsewhere that they may have arrived at similar views by parallel evolution as much as by direct borrowing from the late scholastics. "'Revolutionary Principles': From the Late Scholastics to the Declaration of Independence," presented at the Max Planck Institute für Rechtsgeschichte, Frankfurt, Germany, July 26, 2017, manuscript available from the author.

[130] Skinner, *Foundations of Modern Political Thought* 2:320.

[131] Ibid. 321.

[132] Sir Robert Filmer, *Patriarcha: of the Natural Power of Kings* (London, 1680), 2–3

[133] Ibid.

[134] Ibid.

[135] Sir Robert Filmer, *Observations Concerning the Originall of Government upon Mr Hobs* Leviathan, *Mr Milton against* Salmasius, *H. Grotius* De Iure Belli (1652), in Sir Robert Filmer, *Patriarcha and Other Writings*, Johann P. Sommerville, ed. (Cambridge, 1991).

PART II

THE FORMATION OF TWO CONSTITUTIONS

Although principles do not of themselves create governments, two thorough-going efforts were made to organize governments on the principles of the classical traditions. One was that of Emperor Taizu (960–76), the first emperor of the Song dynasty, and his immediate successors to found a state based on Confucian principles. The other was that of the founders of the American Republic.

Circumstances had given the architects of each constitution an unusual freedom to design institutions that they believed would serve the common good. Neither faced opposition from a hereditary aristocracy or from military commanders.

They did so in different ways. Taizu and his successors created a new ruling class of scholar-officials chosen by examinations in the Confucian classics. The former colonists created a mixed form of government in which legislators and a president were elected by the people.

Without understanding the classical traditions on which the founders of the Song China and the American Republic drew, one cannot understand their achievements. Principles do not of themselves create governments. But they were the *sine qua non* of these constitutions.

8

A Confucian Empire: Song Dynasty China

In 960, when the army of Zhao Kuangyin (趙匡胤), a military commander, was camped by the Chen Bridge, a dozen miles from the capital, the rumor spread among his soldiers that a portent had occurred. A prophet had seen two suns in the sky. It was believed to be a sign that the mandate of Tian (天) had changed. Tian had conferred the empire on their commander. Zhao was awakened from his sleep a few days later by soldiers who demanded that he accept the title of Son of Heaven (天子). He was asked three times and accepted only after his officers swore unconditional obedience. That, at least, is the story.

He ruled for sixteen years (960–76) as Emperor Taizu (宋太祖), the first emperor of the Song dynasty. He ended the political influence of military leaders, it is said, in a single evening. He invited his leading officers to a drinking party. He told them that despite their protestations of loyalty, one day, as it had happened to him, their soldiers might insist that they take power, and they would be unable to refuse. He asked them to lay down their military commands and to receive in return governorships and palaces in the provinces. Every one of them accepted. As the philosopher Zhu Xi (朱熹) observed two centuries later, "Our dynasty brought warlordism to an end."[1] As Dieter Kuhn noted, "the priority of the civil over the military principle – a fundamental ideal of Confucianism – became the ideal of the Song dynasty."[2]

After the fall of the Han Dynasty in AD 220, China had been divided for centuries. Power was exercised by great hereditary clans and military strongmen. China was reunified under the short-lived Sui Dynasty and then under the Tang. As Peter Bol noted, "At its upper reaches, the Tang government was dominated by an oligarchy of great *shi* clans, the *shi-zu*, something close to a state-sponsored aristocracy. These were families who had served at court for centuries and had intermarried with other families of equal stature."[3] As the central government weakened, power was dispersed among military governors. The power of the aristocracy and of the military governors disappeared when Taizu reunified China and centralized authority. Taizu did not have to establish his government in cooperation

---

[1] Zhu Xi, *Zhuzi yulei* (Beijing, 1986), 12997, cited in Dieter Kuhn, *The Age of Confucian Rule: The Song Transformation of China* (Cambridge, 2009), 31, n. 11.

[2] Kuhn, *Age of Confucian Rule* 31.

[3] Peter K. Bol, *Neo-Confucianism in History* (Cambridge, 2008), 31.

with them, or with the military leaders who had helped him to power, or with a hereditary ruling class. He could build anew.

He put into practice Confucian principles which supposedly had been the basis of government since the Han. He was succeeded by Emperors Taizong (宋太宗) (976–97) and Zhenzong (宋真宗) (997–1022). In Dieter Kuhn's words, "Under the leadership of these three men – all lovers of learning – Song China came closer to the ideal of Confucian rule than any other dynasty in Chinese history."[4]

They gave China a constitution based on Confucian principles. In its adoption and in its subsequent growth, this constitution reflected not only these principles but pragmatism, personalities, political interests, and chance. Yet, as one could say of the American constitution, without the principles on which it was founded, the enterprise could not have succeeded and cannot be understood.

I THE ARCHITECTURE OF GOVERNMENT

i *The Creation of a Governing Elite*

One principle is that, as Confucius said, the ruler should "raise to office the virtuous and capable"[5] and "employ the upright and put aside all the crooked."[6] The Han Dynasty had adopted Confucianism as its official philosophy. Yet Emperor Wu was admonished by his Confucian advisor Dong Zhongshu: "the reason you have not yet . . . obtained any reward for your effort is because hitherto, scholars have received no encouragement."[7] "The senior officials are for the most part . . . chosen from the sons of officials with a salary of 2,000 piculs, and are not necessarily worthy because they are rich."[8] The Tang dynasty had been governed by "an oligarchy of great *shi* clans, the *shi-zu*, something close to a state-sponsored aristocracy."

As Bol noted, the foundation of the Song dynasty could have been followed by "the creation of a new state aristocracy. . . . . It did not happen because in practice, a consensus formed around an alternative model: those who governed should be the most talented men, talent could be cultivated through schooling, and competitive examinations should be used to select the best."[9] Taizu and his successors ruled through an elite selected by merit. They did so by choosing its members by competitive examinations in the Confucian classics. The recruits came for the most part from the educated strata of the population, but few possessed the great wealth and hereditary status of their aristocratic predecessors.[10] A new ruling class was created from scratch.

---

4   Kuhn, *Age of Confucian Rule* 29.
5   *Analects* 13.
6   Ibid. 12.
7   Dong Zhongsu, *Three Memorials* in David John Helliwell, *Tung Chung-shu and the New Text Confucian victory, with a translation of his three memorials to Emperor Wu* (Durham theses, Durham University, available at Durham E-Theses Online http://etheses.duham.ac.uk./7447 (1981)), 72 second memorial 2512.2.
8   Dong, *Three Memorials* 73–74 second memorial 2513.1–2513.2.
9   Bol, *Neo-Confucianism* 35.
10 Lau Nap-yin and Huang K'uan-chun, "Founding and Consolidation of the Sung Dynasty under T'ai-Tsu (960–976), T'ai-Tsung (976–997), and Chen-Tsung (997–1022)," in Denis Twitchett and Paul Jakov Smith,

Emperors had used state examinations during the Tang dynasty to recruit officials who would be loyal to themselves. Only a minority of appointments went to those who had passed them. Graduates formed factions whose members were loyal to each other. Candidates would get to know examiners before their examinations, leading to a master–disciple relationship between the examiner and those who passed which lasted for life.[11] The officials appointed through examinations jousted for power with those who belonged to other factions and with the hereditary nobility.[12]

In 962, two years after the founding of the Song dynasty, examiners and examinees were forbidden to claim a patron- protégé relationship.[13] Examinations were graded anonymously. After 1037, they were recopied to ensure that the candidate's handwriting would not give away his identity.[14] Each examination was read by three examiners. The first two read it independently and assigned it a tentative grade. If there was a discrepancy, the third examiner acted as umpire.[15]

There were other ways to become an official. One could be recommended or nominated by a high-ranking relative who himself might owe his position to the examinations. But, as John Chaffee noted, "examination success conferred the greatest prestige and offered the best chances for bureaucratic advancement. . . . [E]xaminations were transformed under the Song emperors . . . to a major, at times dominant, way of selecting officials."[16] According to one estimate, in the twelfth century, 72 percent of chief counselors and assistant counselors held the *jinshi* (進士) degree,[17] that is, they had passed the final examination in the capital which was the prerequisite for an appointment. During Taizu's reign, only 350 candidates passed this examination. As the thirteenth-century scholar Wang Yung explained, the examination system was then expanded to fill the large number of administrative posts that became available with the reunification of China.[18] More than 5,000 passed during the reign of Taizu's brother and successor Taizong.[19] In 1000, in the reign of Taizong's successor Zhenzong, 1,538 candidates passed in a single year, the largest number in one year before or since.[20]

---

eds., *The Cambridge History of China*, vol. 5, pt. 1, *The Sung Dynasty and its Predecessors* (Cambridge, 2010), 206 at 237–38.

[11] Ichisada Miyzaki, *China's Examination Hell: The Civil Service Examinations of Imperial China*, Conrad Shirokauer, trans. (New Haven, 1981), 114.

[12] David McMullen, *State and Scholars in T'ang China* (Cambridge, 1988), 6–7; Denis Twitchett, "The Composition of the T'ang Ruling Class: New Evidence from Tunhuang," in Arthur F. Wright and Denis Twitchett eds., *Perspectives on the T'ang* (New Haven, 1973), 47 at 48–51; Miyzaki, *China's Examination Hell* 113–14.

[13] Lau and Huang "Founding and Consolidation" 237–38.

[14] Thomas H. C. Lee, *Government Education and Examinations in Sung China* (Hong Kong, 1985), 155.

[15] Winston W. Lo, *An Introduction to the Civil Service of Sung China with Emphasis on Its Personnel Administration* (Honolulu, 1987), 90.

[16] John Chaffee, *The Thorny Gates of Learning in Sung China: A Social History of Examinations* (Cambridge, 1985), 4.

[17] Ibid. 29.

[18] Ibid. 50.

[19] Lau and Huang, "Founding and Consolidation" 237–38; Peter K. Bol, "Review Article: The Sung Examination System and the Shih," *Asia Major, Third Series* 3 (1990), 149 at 163.

[20] Kuhn, *Age of Confucian Rule* 39.

The founding emperors put in place a set of institutions that was to endure until the end of the empire in 1912. As John Chaffee said,

> It might seem presumptuous to claim a special Song role for the Confucian literati, scholar-officials, examinations and schools ... so central were all of them in the Chinese tradition. None was a Song creation and all flourished to the end of the imperial age. Yet the Song role was special, for it was then that the constellation of values, institutions, and social structures centering on the examinations assumed much of the shape that it was to have throughout the late imperial period.[21]

ii *The Role of the Scholar-Officials*

According to Confucius, if a ruler is wrong, his officials should "withstand him to his face." "Do not deceive him; do not be afraid to offend him."[22] Mencius said, "Is it a fault to restrain one's ruler? He who restrains his ruler loves his ruler."[23]

> Therefore, it is said, "To urge one's sovereign to difficult achievements may be called showing respect for him. To set before him what is good and repress his perversities may be called showing reverence for him." He who does not do these things, saying to himself "my sovereign is incompetent for this, may be said to play the thief with him."[24]

Under the Song, the scholar-officials assumed this role. The emperor was to govern with the help and advice of his officials, and they were to remonstrate when they thought that he was wrong.

Strenuous objections were raised by ordinary ministers when emperors issued direct decrees, bypassing their advisors.[25] When Zhenzong did so within a few months of his accession, he received a remonstrance from Han Wei (1017–98): "The hundred affairs of government each have their appropriate officials, who exercise their utmost skills to fulfill their duties. There can be no greater sacrifice of the essence of government than for the monarch to take over from his officials in the management of affairs."[26] Two months later, Sima Guang, who had just been appointed chief censor, urged the emperor not to concern himself with "the many bothersome details of government." Four months later Sima Guang complained that the emperor was bypassing normal administrative procedures by sending his own agents to investigate officials in the provinces. The emperor persisted, but he respected his critics and tried to keep them in government.[27] "I want Sima Guang by my

---

[21] Chaffee, *Thorny Gates* 182.

[22] *Analects* 14.23.

[23] *Mencius* IB.4.10.

[24] Ibid. 4A1.13.

[25] James T. C. Liu, "An Administrative Cycle in Chinese History: The Case of Northern Sung Emperors," *The Journal of Asian Studies* 21 (1962), 137 at 143.

[26] Quoted in Paul Jakov Smith, "Shen-Tsung's Reign and the New Policies of Wang An-Shih, 1067–1085" chapter 5 of *The Cambridge History of China*, vol. 5, pt. 1, *The Sung Dynasty and its Predecessors* (Cambridge, 2010), 347 at 355–56.

[27] Smith, "Shen-Tsung's Reign" 356.

side," he said, "not for his opinions on affairs of state [but] because of his moral power (*dao-te*) and learning."[28] As Edward Kracke observed, the emperor usually "restricted his actions" to avoid antagonizing "the bulk of officialdom, on whom his power depended."[29] As Jaeyoon Song described the normal working of the empire:

> [T]he primary sources of the Song dynasty present powerful ministers, rather than emperors, as heroes of imperial politics. On page after page, we find countless examples of ministers proposing plans and discoursing on the ways of government. In the memorials of high-ranking Song ministers, we find that they were free enough, even encouraged, to speak out on the "sovereign's way" (君道 *jundao*) or the virtue of the sovereign (君德 *junde*). They called upon emperors to set moral examples before the population, using hackneyed, yet poignant, words of moral restraint. They advised the emperor on what should be done and avoided. They preached on the ways of emperorship by drawing on specific cases of constrained kingship from the Classics. They routinely pointed out the dangers of "judgment by one man" (獨斷 *duduan*) and called for "public deliberation" (公論 *gonglun*) on state affairs through an open discussion among statement and literati.[30]

Indeed, one difficulty was that the emperor received too much advice. He had trouble keeping up with the sheer volume of memorials he was expected to read. As early as 999, Emperor Zhenzong (真宗) was receiving 100 memorials per day.[31]

The alternative was to allow decisions to be made by officials themselves. Some emperors, such as Emperor Zhenzong, delegated considerable authority to their officials although even he claimed that he discussed all matter of state with them, large or small.[32] Nevertheless, decisions were rarely entrusted to one official alone. If the emperor could not make a decision without consulting his officials, it seemed wrong to consult a single official. The practice was to divide responsibilities among several. They would have to read the relevant memoranda prepared by others, to confer, and to try to reach consensus. Liu pointed out the difficulties that arose.

> Conferences for mutual consultation were time-consuming. A matter on which opinions differed would be held over from one meeting to another, sometimes as long as half a year, without reaching a conclusion. .... A councilor usually read thirty to over a hundred documents every working day. .... In this bureaucratic maze, some documents were simply filed away, a step officially termed *sung shal* or "sent to a dead end."[33]

One might wonder how government could be carried on. Yet it was, and in a very large country, by a centralized government, using a small number of officials. As Peter Bol observed, the "the fact that Song could govern a population of between 60 and 100 million with between 10 and 20 thousand civil officials" was a "success" that is not easily explained.[34]

---

[28] Quoted in Smith, "Shen-Tsung's Reign" 357.
[29] E. A. Kracke, Jr., *Civil Service in Early Sung China, 960–1067* (Cambridge, 1953), 3, 29.
[30] Jaeyoon Song, *Traces of Grand Peace Classics and State Activism in Imperial China* (Cambridge, 2015), 156.
[31] Lau and Huang, "Founding and Consolidation" 273.
[32] Ibid. 261.
[33] Liu, "Administrative Cycle" 150.
[34] Bol, "The Sung Examination System" 151.

The role of the scholar-officials was not only to advise but to remonstrate. That role was institutionalized. In 1017, the Censorate was enlarged with six new posts and the Remonstrance Bureau (*jian yuan*) was established. As Paul Smith noted, its members "were responsible for informing the emperor and the central authorities of local conditions and government effectiveness throughout the empire, for providing a channel for complaints and suggestions from all sources, and for criticizing policy recommendations and, where deemed necessary, returning them to the council for reconsideration."[35] One of the duties of its six remonstrators was to criticize proposals and policy decisions. Kracke said that "[t]he institutional expression of the information and rectification functions, and the protection afforded those performing the functions, formed the closest Chinese parallel to the constitutional separation of powers."[36]

The scholar-officials' position was also strengthened by their influence on the selection and education of emperors. In the Song dynasty, the eldest son of the emperor was not entitled to succeed him. The throne passed to a relative named by the emperor as his heir apparent. As Jayeyoon Song and James Liu observed, the scholar-officials played a key role in influencing the emperor's choice.[37] For example, Taizu died survived by two sons, and yet his brother, who became the Emperor Taizong, did so with the approval and perhaps the connivance of Zhao Pu (趙普), one of Taizu's counsellors who claimed credit for the official acceptance of Confucian principles.[38] After Taizong's death, Chief Counsellor Lu Tuan ensured that the emperor's choice of a successor was respected. He prevented the emperor's eldest son from taking the throne, thus foiling the plans of the Empress Li and two officials who supported her.[39]

iii *Selection by Examination*

The members of the new ruling elite were chosen largely by examinations. "At the beginning," Liu noted, "the stress was upon the memorization of the ancient classics and their official commentaries as well as upon the composition of poems and poetic-prose in the parallel style." The parallel style was a highly stylized form of composition. To master it had been a sign of cultivation in upper-class families before the Song.[40] By the mid-eleventh century, examinations were written in the so-called ancient prose style. It was like the style of Confucius and Mencius; less formal and focused on the expression of ideas than literary style. There seems to have been no set form for the essays.[41] Under Wang Anshi, the candidates were required, not to show that they had memorized the classics, but

---

[35] Smith, "Shen-Tsung's Reign" 373–74.
[36] Kracke, *Civil Service in Early Sung* 33
[37] Song, *Traces of Grand Peace* 157; Liu, "Administrative Cycle" 140.
[38] Lau and Huang, "Founding and Consolidation" 242.
[39] Ibid. 260.
[40] Liu, "Sung Roots" 460–61.
[41] Ching-I Tu, "The Chinese Examination Essay: Some Literary Considerations," *Monumenta Serica* 31 (1974–1975), 393 at 396.

to write exegetical essays on passages chosen from them.[42] They were also required to write essays proposing the solution to five complex problems.[43]

As time went on, however, the prose expected of an examinee became more stylized. In the Southern Song, the examinations "reverted to the original emphasis on poetry and poetic-prose," as Liu noted, "in part because such compositions were capable of demonstrating a thorough mastery of their rigorous rules as well as an artful creativity in spite of them. They were a test of skill and intelligence."[44] In the Ming and Qing dynasties, examinees were expected to write "eight-legged essays" (八股文 *baguwen*) with a strict literary form that prescribed the number of characters and the order and manner in which ideas were to be presented. It would be like requiring a candidate to write a series of sonnets on how a political or economic problem should be resolved. Nevertheless, when thousands and eventually hundreds of thousands of essays had to be read and graded, it became hard to judge them on the basis of the candidate's understanding of ancient teachings or his ability to apply them to such problems. The merit of the essay would depend on the judgment of the examiner. As Elman noted, "the requirement of balanced clauses, phrases and characters provided examiners with a simple, impartial standard for ranking essays."[45] It was easier to grade but also less relevant to what a candidate had learned from Confucian teachings. Nevertheless, successful candidates had to be both intelligent and masters of the Confucian classics.

The examination system has been blamed for the weakness of China in the nineteenth century, as compared to the strength of the West. It did not test administrative and technical skills or knowledge of the natural sciences.[46] The same objection could be made, however, to liberal education as it had been understood in the West since the Renaissance.[47] Such an education was meant to inculcate moral virtue, practical wisdom, and a correct and eloquent command of language through the study of classical literature. The leaders who built the British Empire had that sort of education. So did most of the founders of the American republic.

The West achieved its technical superiority in the nineteenth century through the discoveries of the mechanical engineers who were responsible for the first industrial revolution – the inventors of steam engines, railroads, steam ships, machine driven looms, cotton gins, breach-loading rifles, and interchangeable parts. They were not using skills they acquired in universities. Natural science was not married to technology until what some have called the second industrial revolution in chemistry and electronics.

In the West, no one thought that the purpose of a liberal education was to enable graduates to invent things. Neither did the Confucian scholars of the Song Dynasty.

---

[42] Ibid. 395.

[43] Ibid. 301.

[44] Liu, "Sung Roots" 460–61. On the controversy over this change, see Benjamin A. Elman, *A Cultural History of Civil Examinations in Late Imperial China* (Berkeley, 2000), 25–29.

[45] Benjamin A. Elman, *Civil Examinations and Meritocracy in Late Imperial China* (Cambridge, 2013), 62.

[46] Elman, *Cultural History* xii (criticizing this view).

[47] Benjamin A. Elman, "Political, Social, and Cultural Reproduction via Civil Service Examinations in Late Imperial China," *The Journal of Asian Studies* 50 (1991), 7 at 10.

Yet during that dynasty, advances in technology were so rapid that some have spoken of a proto-industrial revolution. They included the military use of gunpowder, moveable type printing, cultivation of early ripening rice, the invention of mechanical clocks, and an improved method of making steel. If Jurchen invaders had not conquered northern China in 1127, the Mongols had not conquered the rest 1279, and if the pace of technological change had continued, a Chinese fleet of steel ships might have arrived in Europe just as Columbus set sail hoping to reach China.

II THE EMERGENCE OF A CONFUCIAN SOCIETY

A candidate was unlikely to pass the examinations because of family influence but more likely to do so if he came from a family had the means to give him a Confucian education. E. A. Kracke's study of the biographies of degree holders from 1148 and 1246 showed that 57 percent of the successful candidates did not have a father, grandfather, or great grandfather who held an official position.[48] Robert Hartwell has shown that almost all Song graduates had a relative who did.[49] Elman said that "[s]uch collaterals and/or affines could be decisive in determining the likelihood of academic success of those who at first sight seem to be commoners."[50] But it is hard to see how they could have directly influenced whether a candidate passed the examinations when his own father and grandfather could not, particular since examinations were graded anonymously. A family, however, could see that he received the education necessary to be well prepared. It is not surprising that members of such a family succeeded in passing the examinations more often.

Education began early, at home or in informal family or community schools. A child started to master characters at the age of five. Ideally, over the next six years he learned the Four Books and the Five Classics by heart. He then studied the Dynastic Histories, of which there were seventeen in the Song Dynasty, and learned to compose poetry and to write essays.[51] As Elman noted,

> Frequently, the rites of passage from child to young adult in wealthy families were measured by the number of ancient texts that were mastered at a particular age. "Capping" of a young boy between the ages of sixteen and twenty-one, for example, implied that he had mastered all of the Four Books and one of the Five Classics, the minimum requirement for any aspirant to compete in the civil service examinations.[52]

As Elman observed, "the actual process of education in classical Chinese and training for the examinations" drifted "out of state schools into the private domain of tutors, academies, or lineage schools."[53] Lee noted,

---

[48] E. A. Kracke, Jr., "Family versus Merit in Chinese Civil Service Examinations under the Empire," in John L. Bishop, ed., *Studies of Governmental Institutions in Chinese History* (1968), 103–23.

[49] Robert M. Hartwell, "Demographic, Political and Social Transformations of China 750–1550," *Harvard Journal of Asiatic Studies* 42 (1982), 365 at 417–18; 48–55.

[50] Elman, "Political, Social, and Cultural Reproduction" 18.

[51] Chaffee, *Thorny Gates* 5–7; Elman, "Political, Social, and Cultural Reproduction" 16.

[52] Elman, "Political, Social, and Cultural Reproduction" 17.

[53] Ibid. 10–11.

Boys of wealthier families were sent to study with other children in the neighborhood. Some luckier members of the Song elite could provide their children with tutors. . . . . Most people, however, simply sent their children to local small gatherings of pupils, where they worked with a private teacher. . . . . The wealthier children might be asked to pay a little more; the poor parents had to ask their rich clansmen for the favor of letting their children join in the study.[54]

Even if poor parents had the chance to send their children to such a school, the children of farmers began to help in the fields when they were only five or six.[55] Their parents would be making an economic sacrifice on the slim chance that their child would do well. There were cases of poor boys who passed the examinations and became leading officials. It could happen, just as, in America, a boy born in a log cabin could become president, or, in medieval Europe, a peasant's son who learned Latin from his parish priest could study in one of the great universities and become a cardinal. It did not happen often.

The examination system transformed society in a different way. Within a few decades, throughout the empire, those who were able to do so put years of study into preparing for examinations even though they had little chance of passing them and becoming officials. For a person to be considered well educated and, indeed, for him to be considered a *shi* or worthy man, he must have this preparation. As Ye Shi, a late Song writer on statecraft, observed: "All the common people can become *shi*, but not all do so; nor do all *shi* become officials."[56]

This rapid and widespread transformation was made possible by printing, which had been invented at the beginning of the ninth century.[57] Woodblock printing had been in use since the Tang dynasty. Moveable type was invented in the eleventh century, and books became accessible to the less wealthy.[58] In Western history, the development of printing is associated with the dissemination of pamphlets and newspapers such as those in which the founders of the American Republic criticized the English Parliament and Crown. In China, as Kuhn observed, the "economic success and general acceptance of printing in Song society" made possible the "revival of Confucian learning on a nation-wide basis, at a price within reach of most who aspired to become civil servants."[59] In 996, the emperor Taizong ordered a commission of scholar-officials to prepare an authoritative edition of the Confucian classics; seven were finished by 1001 and thirteen by 1011. The official version became the common resource and indispensable tool for candidates preparing for the examinations.

---

[54] Lee, "Government Education" 46–47.

[55] Ibid. 46.

[56] Quoted in Bol, *Neo-Confucianism* 36 n. 65.

[57] L. Carrington Goodrich, "The Development of Printing in China and its Effects on the Renaissance under the Sung Dynasty (960–1279): A Lecture Delivered on 3 September, 1962," *Journal of the Hong Kong Branch of the Royal Asiatic Society* 3 (1963), 36 at 39; Bol, *Neo-Confucianism* 39.

[58] James T. C. Liu, "How Did a Neo-Confucian School Become the State Orthodoxy?" *Philosophy East and West* 23 (1973), 483 at 483.

[59] Kuhn, *Age of Confucian Rule* 42.

The odds that a candidate would pass the examinations diminished as the education necessary to take them became more widespread. To be eligible for the metropolitan examination, which was held in the capital every three years, candidates first had to pass prefectural examinations, which were held every year. By the mid-twelfth century, there were 100,000 candidates per year, by the mid-thirteenth century, 400,000.[60] Zhenzong introduced quotas on the number who could pass the prefectural examinations. In 1106, only 3 percent did so, in the thirteenth century, only 1 percent. A small fraction of these passed the metropolitan examination and became eligible for an official position.[61] As Bol noted, "the chance of one of the 400,000 candidates passing in any one year between 1208 and 1223, when on the average 434 degrees were granted at each triennial exam, was 1:816."

The odds were so poor that Bol doubted that the vast majority of candidates studied for the examinations in order to pass them. The odds against doing so "might be acceptable in a lottery, but I find it difficult to equate a system that demanded years of preparation and considerable investment with a lottery, which promises great rewards for minimal effort."[62] Those who passed the lower-level examinations could be employed as teachers in local or family schools, as administrators of granaries or temples, as sub-official local administrators.[63] But Bol concluded that most candidates were seeking "to secure a preeminent social good in Song society: recognition by elite and state that the participant was one of the *shi* versus merely one of the *min* (民), the commoners, or a farmer, craftsman, or merchant." There was "a shift in the primary function of the examination system from the government's mechanism for recruiting *shi* for office to an institution maintained at government expense to acknowledge the elite status of *shi* families who could no longer secure official careers for all their male descendants."[64]

Indeed, as De Weerdt observed, "[i]ntellectually, the civil service examinations defined educational standards for literate elites across the empire."[65] The effect, according to Elman, was to "create a national curriculum that consolidated gentry families all over the empire into a culturally defined class. By requiring mastery of archaic forms of classical Chinese, state authorities initiated young males into a select world of political and moral discourse drawn primarily from the *Confucian* Classics and Four Books."[66] As Bol explained, "[l]ocal elites could remain entrenched in local society, and, although they did not actually take part in the affairs of the nation unless they became officials, their education encouraged them to see themselves as similar to the elites of other regions and as cultural kin to officials in the post-aristocratic age."[67]

What it meant to be a *shi* had changed. Participation in the examinations provided "well-to-do families without *shi* traditions with a means of transforming themselves into

[60] Ibid. 122.
[61] Ibid. 123.
[62] Bol, "Sung Examination System" 165–66.
[63] Kuhn, *Age of Confucian Rule* 122.
[64] Bol, "Sung Examination System" 155; Similarly, Hilde De Weerdt, *Competition over Content Negotiating Standards for the Civil Service Examinations in Imperial China (1127–1279)* (Cambridge, 2007), 2.
[65] De Weerdt, *Competition over Content* 6.
[66] Elman, "Political, Social, and Cultural Reproduction" 19.
[67] Bol, "Sung Examination System" 167.

shi." "[L]ocal elites who chose to be *shi* found themselves reading the same books, practicing on the same questions, [and] learning the same methods of composition, knowing about the same great men, discussing the same ideas, practicing the same rituals, [and] sharing the same aspirations." "Among other things their education taught them what it meant to be *shi.*"[68] "By 1100," Elman noted, "the *shi* had accumulated enough independence and power for their role as local elites to outshine their role as bureaucrats. Their domination of local society based on *shi* educational and cultural qualifications was one of the unforeseen outcomes of the court's enfranchisement of the *shi* in the Song political order."[69]

The relationship with the imperial government was symbiotic. As Chaffee observed, "local officials relied on the local elite for information, support and philanthropy, and since the elite generally dominated its locality economically and socially and virtually dominated entry into the bureaucracy, its support was generally forthcoming."[70]

III PRINCIPLES COMPROMISED

i *The Examination System*

Mencius said that the *shi* should be "men of education."[71] Confucius described himself as "simply a man, who in his eager pursuit of knowledge forgets his food, who in the joy of its attainment forgets his sorrows."[72] Yet the purpose of study was moral development. Moral development was the reason the ruler's officials were qualified to govern others. As critics pointed out, from a Confucian perspective, the difficulty with the examination systems was that a person who is not particularly virtuous might well succeed in passing them, and a more virtuous person might not.[73]

"Why," Chaffee asked, "did the Song give up such eminently Confucian considerations as an individual's character and reputation?" The reason, he answered, was that "the early Song emperors' concern for impartiality and fairness (公 *gong*) meant that character could not seriously be considered in the examinations," however "un-Confucian" that might be.[74]

The emperor Zhenzong declared that "we must strive for the utmost fairness and select the cultivated among the poor landlords [i.e. humble scholars.]."[75] An alternative would be to require a candidate for an official position to be recommended for his character in addition to or instead of passing an exam. Yet, to do so might lead to bias and favoritism. As Liu noted:

> Originally, the Confucian philosophy placed its emphasis not so much upon literary skills as moral conduct. Yet a brief attempt by Ts'ai Ching in late Northern Song to have the local

---

[68]　Ibid. 167.

[69]　Elman, *Cultural History* 15.

[70]　Chaffee, *Thorny Gates* 19.

[71]　*Mencius* 1.1.7.20.

[72]　*Analects* 8.18.2.

[73]　Lee, *Government Education* 231–33; Lo, *Introduction* 102.

[74]　Chaffee, *Thorny Gates* 49.

[75]　Ibid. 51.

government recommend candidates according to eight specific categories of exemplary behavior degenerated into a miserable failure of abusive favoritism. The written examinations, being impersonal and objective, remained far more satisfactory.[76]

The leading scholar-statesmen of the dynasty, Su Shi, Sima Guang, and Wang Anshi, who agreed about little else, all criticized the examination system because success was no guarantee of good character. Su Shi accepted the examination system *faute de mieux*. As Bol noted, he argued that "to admit men to the metropolitan examinations on the basis of 'ethical conduct' would encourage excessive displays of self-sacrificing and poverty as *shi* competed to prove their incorruptibility and filiality."[77]

Sima Guang proposed that a candidate should only be allowed to take the examinations if he was sponsored by an official, with a preference to be given to those with the greater number of sponsors.[78] He proposed the appointment of "intelligent and impartial officials [to] find out and elect" people of high character. Those who recommended the most reliable and trustworthy people should be rewarded.[79] The risk was that officials would appoint not men of character, but their own protégés.

Wang Anshi said of the examination system:

> The present method of selecting officials is as follows: If a man has a colossal memory, can repeat extensive portions of the classics, and has some skill at composition, he is termed specially brilliant or worthy, and chosen for the highest grades of state ministers. .... It should need no discussion to show that the knowledge and skill which these men display in no sense of itself fits them for such places of authority and distinction.[80]

ii *The Political System*

The Song Constitution was based on the Confucian principle that the emperor should rule with the aid of elite officials chosen for their merit. The role of these officials was both to design and to implement policy. The design of a good policy requires the wisdom of all and the freedom to criticize both the views of others and the working of whatever policy is adopted. Nevertheless, the implementation of policy requires unity. It requires a commitment by those in charge to making it work.

The conflict between these roles led Wang-An Shih to compromise Confucian principles and bypass constitutional restraints in order to implement his own policies. He needed unity and could not achieve it by a consensus of the best qualified.

As noted earlier, he believed that the government should play an active role in the two tasks that the Confucian tradition assigned it: to ensure the people's livelihood and to provide for their education. To do so, he launched an ambitious program known as the

[76] James T. C. Liu, "Sung Roots of Chinese Political Conservatism: The Administrative Problems," *The Journal of Asian Studies* 26, (1967), 457 at 460–61.
[77] Peter K. Bol, *"This Culture of Ours": Intellectual Transitions in T'ang and Sung China* (Stanford, 1992), 271.
[78] Ibid. 252.
[79] Lee, *Government Education* 242.
[80] Wang Anshi, "The Ten Thousand Word Memorial" 10.

New Policies (新法 *xin fa*). He did so with the support of the emperor Zhenzong, who put him in power in 1069. In 1085, the empress dowager dismissed him and appointed his opponent, Sima Guang. Yet his partisans resumed power in 1093 and held it almost until 1125, two years before the fall of the Northern Song Dynasty to foreign invaders.

One goal of Wang's New Policies was to increase agricultural production. The Regulations on Agriculture set rules for recovering fallow land, instituting projects for irrigation, and the preservation of waterways. The Green Shoots Policy allowed the government to make loans to farmers. Another goal was to make greater use of markets while regulating them more closely. The Equitable Transport Policy allowed the government to buy and sell provisions on the market. State Trade Policy allowed it to bypass wholesalers and deal with small merchants. Another goal was economic equity. His policies were intended to benefit the poor at the expense of the local rich whom Wang called the *jianping*, whom he regarded as profiteers who lent at a high interest rate and set high prices in times of scarcity.[81] A further step toward this goal was a progressive land tax, the Land Survey and Equitable Tax Policies. Still another goal was public education. Wang proposed establishing village and district schools and established a national university in the capital providing instruction for 2,400 students at a time. Graduates could enter the civil service with the same standing as those who took the imperial examinations.[82] Wang believed that officials should be selected based on the recommendations from these schools and personal observation. Recruitment through the schools would supplement or replace recruitment through competitive examinations.

The New Policies were not endorsed by a consensus of the scholar-officials after open discussion. His critics charged that by implementing the program despite opposition, he was violating Confucian principles as to how power should be exercised. One Confucian principle was that power should be exercised by common consent. His critics accused him of violating the principle of "collaborative government" (公治 *gong zhi*).

Another principle was that officials should be selected and promoted on merit. To implement his policies Wang Anshi delegated tasks to new institutions outside the administrative hierarchy.[83] Since the New Policies did not meet with the approval of many senior officials, the dissenters were forced out. In 1070, Tseng Kung-liang told the emperor "it is important to have people of different opinions stirring each other up, so that no one will dare to do wrong." Wang Anshi disagreed:

> If everyone at court agitates one another with different opinions then how will it be possible to govern? This minister humbly believes that if the court ministers in charge of affairs of state do not share one mind and one morality (同心同德 *tong xin tong de*) nor cooperatively strive for unanimity, then none of the tasks facing the empire can be accomplished.[84]

---

[81]   Bol, *"This Culture of Ours"* 249–50.

[82]   Ichisada Miyazaki, "The Administration of Justice during the Sung Dynasty," in Jerome Alan Cohen, R. Randle Edwards, and Fu-Mei Chang Chen, eds., *Essays on China's Legal Tradition* (Princeton, 1980), 56 at 116.

[83]   Smith, "Shen-Tsung's Reign" 378.

[84]   Quoted in ibid. 363.

Wang's opponents were not beaten or killed. But many of them were dismissed or exiled from the capital or resigned in protest.[85] The Council of State controlled administration and policy making. Wang packed it with his own supporters. Many of the empire's senior statesmen were forced into early retirement, including Ouyang Xiu (age 65), Sima Guang (age 50), Wang Tao (age 50), Fan Chen (age 63), Lü Hui (age 58), and Fu Pi (age 68).[86]

Wang silenced the Censorate and the Remonstrance Bureau. In 1069, Lü Hui, a member of the Censorate, submitted a memorial denouncing Wang. Among other offenses,

> Wang An-shi has appointments entirely on his own authority, transferring court officers who were not of his own party to outside positions. For these, he professed to have the Emperor's authority, but actually issued the orders in his own name. He has thus exceeded the bounds of his legitimate authority, and broken long-established precedent. By his arrogance and assumption in this matter he has violated the principles of good government. . . . [He] brooks no opposition.[87]

Soon after, Lü and three other censors were dismissed for resisting Wang's policies.[88] In 1070, Chen Qian, the acting director of the Censorate, was fired simply because he was expected to oppose the promotion of one of Wang's protégés to a position as investigating censor.[89] Vacancies throughout the administration were filled with new men whom Wang could count on for support.[90] According to Sima Guang, "Those who agreed with him were given his help in rising to the sky, while those who differed with him were thrown out and cast down into the ditch."[91]

Moreover, the Confucian tradition had been an open one in which each scholar reflected on the truths contained in the Classics. Wang came close to having his own interpretation of Confucianism adopted at the expense of every other. Wang believed that his policies were based on Confucian principles. Therefore those who disagreed with him must have misunderstood these principles.

> To push benevolence to the level of the sage and then to *tian-dao* [the way of Heaven], is the task of scholars [*shi-xue zhe*]. The people who made the books in the past told us so based on fact. To know what is above and to not know what is below, to see what is beginning and not to see what ends – that is why the Way (*dao*) is so scattered, and also why the hundred schools prospered, and also why the scholars dispute. What is study? It is to unify the scholars under heaven until all disputes end.[92]

[85] Bol, *Neo-Confucianism* 76.
[86] Smith, "Shen-Tsung's Reign" 373.
[87] Lü Hui, "Impeachment of Wang An-Shih," trans. H. R. Williamson, in John Meskill, ed., *Wang An-Shih Practical Reformer?* (Boston, 1963) 19 at 20.
[88] Smith, "Shen-Tsung's Reign" 373–74.
[89] Ibid. 375.
[90] Smith, "Shen-Tsung's Reign" 377.
[91] Sima Guang, "Petition to Do Away with the Most Harmful of the New Laws," in Meskill, ed. *Wang An-Shih* 25 at 25.
[92] Bol, *"This Culture of Ours"* 218 n. 19.

Wang thought that to arrive at this intellectual harmony, scholars merely needed to study the Classics. "We learn from the sages and that is all. When we learn from the sages, our friends and teachers will necessarily be men who also learn from the sages. The words and actions of the sages are uniform; of course [our friends and teachers] will resemble each other."[93]

If other scholars persisted in their misunderstanding, the difference of opinion should be suppressed. Sometimes he suggested the reason was simply to ensure the implementation of uniform polices. As he told the emperor, "one may see an issue as right or wrong, but if one sees it as wrong when the court disagrees and deems it right, then one must obey the court's commands."[94] Sometimes, however, he suggested that "the cacophony of opinion" is a sign of the emperor's failure "to succeed in transforming civic culture by unifying morality."[95]

Su Shi objected that Wang's New Policies rested on a particular interpretation of the Confucian classics that Wang insisted everyone must accept. Even a sage would not try to make everyone the same.

> There has never been a decline in cultivation (*wen zi*) such as that of today. The source of this is really Mr. Wang. . . .. The problem is that he likes to make others the same as himself. Ever since Confucius was unable to make others achieve the same benevolence as Yen Hui or the same courage as Zi Lu, it has not been possible to move others toward each other. Yet with his learning Mr. Wang would make all under heaven the same. The goodness of the earth is uniform in bringing things into being; it is not uniform in what it brings into being.[96]

According to Su, "Confucius must have thought that the one sentence that could lose the state was this: 'All the people should be like me.'"[97] The government ordered the destruction of the printing blocks of the writings of Su Shi.[98]

In the end, Wang Anshi's program was discredited by a problem no statesmen could have resolved: the massive military expenses necessary, despite his policies, to defend against invaders, and the invaders' ultimate success. The empire could not defend itself against the Jurchens, or later, the Mongols. They had one advantage that tribal peoples had always enjoyed in their many centuries of conflict with the Empire. The number of their warriors was equal to the male population of their tribes. They had overcome traditional disadvantages. They were well organized. They fought on horseback in disciplined formations with compound bows that could penetrate armor. They could ride around the static defenses of the Chinese, around the forts and the hundreds of thousands of infantry, which were costing the Northern Song 80 percent of its tax revenue.

---

[93] Ibid. 189 n. 72.
[94] Smith, "Shen-Tsung's Reign" 366.
[95] Ibid. 365.
[96] Bol, *This Culture of Ours* 273 n. 50.
[97] Ibid. 287 n. 108.
[98] Bol, *Neo-Confucianism* 76.

Had it not been for the military threat, that problem would not have arisen. Another problem, however, was inherent. It was the tension between the procedures for making decisions, which were founded on Confucian principles, and the need for a unified policy to implement the very goals which, according to Confucian principles, the government should promote: economic welfare, a fair distribution of resources, and the education of the people. To secure that unity, Wang forced out many of the wisest and the best and bypassed the procedures that had been put in place to secure them a voice.

9

A Democratic Republic

The United States of America

In 1776, representatives meeting in Philadelphia as a congress "of the thirteen united States of America" unanimously adopted a Declaration of Independence, which stated that "these United Colonies are, and of Right ought to be Free and Independent States."

The former colonies fought and won a war for their independence, recognized by the Treaty of Paris in 1783. In that year, a group of officers of the Continental Army planned to march on Congress to demand their back pay and guarantees for the future. George Washington met with them and persuaded them not to do so. Later that year, he resigned as Commander-in-Chief. He did not impose a military government as Oliver Cromwell had done. He did not try to make himself king, which George III said marked him "as the greatest man in the world."

In 1789, "the people of the United States" adopted a constitution. They had great esteem for the constitution of England. Their complaint was that they had been denied the rights of Englishmen. In the English constitution, however, power was divided among a hereditary monarch, a heredity House of Lords, and a House of Commons whose members were elected in a way that reflected entrenched privilege. The American colonies had no monarch, no heredity nobility, and no similarly entrenched privilege. They could build anew.

They self-consciously built according to principles which, as we will see, they regarded as ancient and well-established, although they knew that they were putting them into practice almost for the first time. The adoption and subsequent development of their constitution reflected not only principle but pragmatism, personalities, political interests, and chance. Yet, as one can say of the Song constitution, without the principles, the enterprise could not have succeeded and cannot be understood.

These principles concerned the right of resistance to authority, the common good, and the merits of different forms of government, and particularly of limited government. According to the once conventional view, the American Republic was founded on the liberal principles of the Enlightenment. These principles were found *par excellence* in the work of John Locke. We quoted earlier a summary of Locke's view by the leading philosopher Charles Taylor. Each person "can be a fully competent human subject outside of society."[1] They enter into a social contract "for mutual benefit, both in providing security and in fostering exchange and prosperity."[2]

On the contrary, the principles of the founders of the American Republic were not the fruit of the Enlightenment. As we will see, they were gleaned from the classical tradition that stretched back to Aristotle. They were adopted by the English Whigs in their attacks on the Stuart monarchy with the exception of John Locke. The principles of the founders were not those of Locke but of the other English Whigs. Moreover, the principles of Locke were not those that are often ascribed to him, for example, by Charles Taylor. Locke was not the progenitor of political liberalism. As others have noted, he attained that status only when nineteenth-century liberal theorists in search of a pedigree read their ideas into his work.[3] Yet many historians today take Locke's influence on the founders for granted.

I THE RIGHT OF RESISTANCE

i *The English Whigs*

As noted earlier, in his defense of the divine right of kings, Bishop Filmer denounced an idea that he believed had been too widely accepted: that "Mankind is naturally . . . at liberty to choose what Form of Government it please."[4] Upon the ground of this Doctrine" its proponents "have built a perillous Conclusion, which is, *That the People or Multitude have Power to punish, or deprive the Prince, if he transgress the Laws of the Kingdom.*"[5] He said that this doctrine was "first hatched in the Schools" and then "entertained" by "the Divines of the Reformed Churches."[6]

Filmer's treatise was published posthumously in 1680 during the reign of Charles II. Responses were written by such leading Whigs as Algernon Sidney (1623–83), James Tyrell (1642–1718) and John Locke (1632–1704). In the following century, the arguments of Sidney and Tyrell were repeated by Whigs such as John Trenchard (1662–1723) and Thomas Gordon (1691–1750), the authors of *Cato's Letters*, to justify the Glorious Revolution of 1688.

They had all drawn the "perillous Conclusion" of which Filmer complained. Government is instituted by the people for certain ends, and if it becomes destructive of them, the people may abolish it. They maintained that the people had the right to resist oppression because government is established to serve the public or common good, and, with the exception of Locke, they understood the common good in much the same way as the late scholastics. Government is established to serve the "publik advantage," "the profit

---

[1]   Charles Taylor, *Modern Social Imaginaries* (Durham, 2004), 19.
[2]   Ibid. 20.
[3]   Alexander S. Rosenthal, *Crown Under Law: Richard Hooker, John Locke and the Ascent of Modern Constitutionalism* (Lanham, 2008), 221.
[4]   Sir Robert Filmer, *Patriarcha: Of the Natural Power of Kings* (London, 1680), 2–3.
[5]   Ibid.
[6]   Ibid.

of the governed," "the public good," "the good of those who are under it."[7] People needed society to live well and to acquire and exercise the virtues that living well entailed. "[T]he ends of instituting of Commonwealths," Tyrrell said, were that the people "might more safely and with more leasure live after the Laws of Nature, and Virtue."[8] According to Sidney, "liberty produceth virtue"[9] – "great virtue," according to Gordon. "Every private man upon earth has a concern" in government, Gordon said, which encompasses "his virtue, his property, and the security of his person: And where all these are best preserved and advanced, the government is best administered."[10] These principles, according to Sydney, were those of Aristotle as well as the "Schoolmen."[11] They all agreed that a ruler who does not govern for that end but for ends of their own is a tyrant, and can be resisted or overthrown.[12]

ii *The Founders*

The American Declaration of Independence, written by Thomas Jefferson, set forth the principles that justified the American Revolution.

> We hold these truths to be self-evident that all men are created equal, that they are endowed by their Creator with certain unalienable Rights, that among these are Life, Liberty and the pursuit of Happiness, – That to secure these rights, Governments are instituted among Men, deriving their just powers from the consent of the governed, – That whenever any Form of Government becomes destructive of these ends, it is the Right of the People to alter or to abolish it, and to institute new Government, laying its foundation on such principles and organizing its powers in such form, as to them shall seem most likely to effect their Safety and Happiness.

According to Jefferson,

> [T]he Declaration of Independance ... neither [aiming at] originality of principle or sentiment, nor yet copied from any particular and previous writing, ... was intended to be an expression of the american mind, and to give to that expression the proper tone and spirit called for by the occasion. All its authority rests then on the harmonising sentiments

---

7 Algernon Sidney, *Discourses Concerning Government*, Thomas G. West, ed. (Indianapolis: 1996), ch. II, sec. 30; James Tyrrell, *Patriarcha non monarcha* (London, 1681), ch. 3, p. 129; John Locke, *Two Treatises of Government*, Peter Laslett, ed. (New York, 1960), II.xviii § 199; Thomas Gordon, *Cato's Letters*, vol. 1, November 5, 1720 to June 17, 1721 (1724). No. 38. July 22, 1721. *The Right and Capacity of the People to judge of Government.*
8 Tyrrell, *Patriarcha non monarcha* ch. 4, pp. 240–41.
9 Sidney, *Discourses* ch. II, sec. 11.
10 Gordon, No. 38. July 22, 1721. *The Right and Capacity of the People to judge of Government.*
11 Sidney, *Discourses* ch. 1, sec. 5.
12 Sidney, *Discourses* ch. II sec. 30; Tyrell, *Patriarcha non monarcha* ch. 3, p. 129; Locke, *Two Treatises of Government* II.xix §§ 221–22; John Trenchard, *Cato's Letters* No. 14. Jan. 28, 1721. *The unhappy State of despotick Princes, compared with the happy Lot of such as rule by settled Laws. How the latter, by abusing their Trust, may forfeit their Crown*; Gordon, *Cato's Letters* No. 38. July 22, 1721. *The Right and Capacity of the People to judge of Government.*

of the day, whether expressed, [in conversations,] in letters, printed essays or in the elementary books of public right, as Aristotle, Cicero, Locke, Sidney Etc."[13]

John Adams had called these "revolution principles" when he defended them in 1774.[14] Neither Adams nor Jefferson thought that these principles were new or original, and indeed they were not. We have seen how they were formulated in the sixteenth century on the basis of Aristotelian principles, adopted by Protestant writers, attacked by Bishop Filmer in his defense of the divine right of kings, and defended by seventeenth- and eighteenth-century Whigs.

Adams thought that they went back to Aristotle and Plato.

> They are the principles of Aristotle and Plato, of Livy and Cicero, and Sidney, Harrington and Locke; the principles of nature and eternal reason; the principles on which the whole government over us now stands. It is therefore astonishing, if any thing can be so, that writers, who call themselves friends of government, should in this age and country be so inconsistent with themselves, so indiscreet, so immodest, as to insinuate a doubt concerning them.[15]

When he invoked these principles to defend the Boston Tea Party, he claimed to be presenting the accepted view of the best authorities.

> If there is any thing in these quotations, which is applicable to the destruction of the tea, or any other branch of our subject, it is not my fault; I did not make it. Surely Grotius, Pufendorf, Barbeyrac, Locke, Sidney, and Le Clerc, are writers of sufficient weight to put in the scale against the mercenary scribblers in New York and Boston, who have the unexampled impudence and follow, to call these, which are revolution principles, in question."[16]

iii *The Myth of the Influence of John Locke*

When the founders cited Locke, it was, most often, for principles accepted by writers in the Aristotelian tradition with which Locke's fellow Whigs agreed. Locke, too, believed that government is instituted by the people for certain ends, and if it becomes destructive of them, the people may abolish it.[17] He also believed, like writers in the Aristotelian tradition, that there is no one legitimate form of government. The people may place power "in the

---

[13] Letter from Thomas Jefferson to Henry Lee, 8 May 1825, in Adrienne Koch and William Peden, eds., *The Life and Writings of Thomas Jefferson*, (New York, 1944), 719.

[14] Adams was attacking David Leonard, who, writing under the name Massachusettensis, criticized those who hold "that all men by nature are equal; that kings are but the ministers of the people; that their authority is delegated to them by the people, for their good, and they have a right to resume it, and place it in other hands, or keep it themselves, whenever it is made use of to oppress them." John Adams, *Novanglus; or, A History of the Dispute with America, from its Origin in 1754, to the Present Time* in *The Works of John Adams* 4 (Boston, 1856), No. I.

[15] Adams, *Novanglus* No. I.

[16] Ibid. No. VII.

[17] Locke, *Two Treatises of Government* II.xix §§ 221–22.

hands of one person, or a few people, or retain it themselves, or they may institute a mixed form of government."[18] He did not believe that because government is instituted by the people, the people must institute a democratic government.

Locke's innovation concerned the ends for which people enter into society. Whigs such as Tyrell, Sidney, Trenchard, and Gordon argued that Charles II and James II had overstepped the wise limits that the English constitution had imposed on royal power. Locke's approach was different. In the *Two Treatises of Government*, he argued that these kings had overstepped limits that were not only wise but that were necessary features of any legitimate government. To do so, he tailored his account of the reasons people form a government to fit the misdeeds of Charles and James.

He argued from the premise that "[t]he great and *chief end* ... of men's uniting into common-wealths, and putting themselves under government, *is the preservation of their property*," a term which Locke used broadly to include rights in general: life, liberty and whatever else belongs to a person. He did not say that men unite into commonwealths because a human being is a social political animal, or because one cannot live a fully human or a virtuous life on one's own. Instead, he identified the "publick good" or "the good of the people" or the "common good" as the preservation of life, liberty, and property.[19]

That was his first break with the Aristotelian tradition. Another was his account of the origin of property. As we have seen, in the Aristotelian tradition, private property was instituted by society to avoid the disadvantages of a state of common ownership. In Locke's account, people acquire property first, and then they form commonwealths in order to protect it. A person does so by mixing his labor with the object he thereby acquires:

> Though the Earth, and all inferior Creatures be common to all Men, yet every Man has a Property in his own Person. This no Body has any right to but himself. The Labour of his Body, and the Work of his Hands, we may say, are properly his. Whatsoever then he removes out of the State that Nature hath provided, and left it in, he hath mixed his Labour with, and joyned to it something that is his own, and thereby makes it his Property. It being by him removed from the common state Nature placed it in, hath by this labour something annexed to it, that excludes the common right of other Men. For this Labour being the unquestionable Property of the Labourer, no Man but he can have a right to what that is once joyned to, at least where there is enough, and as good left in common for others.[20]

The argument is not that the institution of private property provides an incentive for people to labor. That was the argument made by writers in the Aristotelian tradition. The argument is that by "removing" a thing "out of the State that Nature ... left it in," it

---

[18] Ibid. II.x § 132.

[19] For example, when he said that "the Power" of government "in the utmost Bounds of it, is limited *to the publick good* of the Society," he contrasted it an "Arbitrary Power over the Life, Liberty or possession of another." Locke, *Two Treatises of Government* II. xi § 135. When he said that the "Laws ought to be designed for no other end but *the good of the people*," he had previously explained that the government must rule the people by "declared Laws, or else their Peace, Quiet, and Property will still be in the same uncertainty, as it was in the state of Nature." Ibid. § 142.

[20] Ibid. II.v § 27.

becomes one's own, whatever its magnitude, whatever the effort involved, because the "removing" counts as "labor" which is a person's own just as his body is his own.

Although these two propositions break with the Aristotelian tradition, they fall far short a new theory of human nature and human society. John Dunn claimed that Locke's "intellectual system" is one of "radical individualism, an individualism as radical as that of Hobbes and in its potential social implications more subversive."[21] For that reason, according to Edward Feser, "[o]f all modern philosophers, John Locke has had the profoundest influence on the world we live in, and most embodies its guiding principles."[22] Unfortunately, Dunn notes, "[t]he philosophy embodied in these beliefs is nowhere systematically developed in Locke's works." "It is possible, nevertheless, to discern in these works at least the outlines of an intellectual system."[23] To find this "radical individualism," however, one must read it into passages which had no such significance for Locke. As Alexander Rosenthal noted "The misreading of Locke in terms of Hobbes – or for that matter in terms of the later developments in liberalism – has been an obstruction to understanding Locke's political theory in its own terms."[24]

Locke used his account of the purposes of government and of the origins of property to condemn specific misdeeds of the Stuart kings. These accounts were custom-made to support that indictment. His readers were not supposed to accept them because he proposed a new theory of human nature and human society. They were supposed to agree that commonwealths were founded to protect property without concerning them-selves with whatever else commonwealths were founded to do. They were supposed to agree that "Man has a Property in his own Person" because it seems obvious that a person has a right to his own body. Therefore they were to conclude that a person owns whatever "he hath mixed his Labour with." It would have defeated Locke's purpose to begin with premises that seemed controversial, let alone which seemed to contradict mainstream political thought. The success of his arguments would then have depended on persuading his readers to accept this new theory.

From these premises, however, he moved swiftly to his conclusion that the Stuarts had overstepped the boundaries that all commonwealths must observe. Property is insecure without a government because "[t]here wants an *established*, settled, known *law*, received and allowed by common consent to be the standard of right and wrong ... for though the law of nature be plain and intelligible to all rational creatures; yet men being biased by their interest, as well as ignorant for want of study of it, are not apt to allow of it as a law binding to them in the application of it to their particular cases." Also, "there wants *a known and indifferent judge*, with authority to determine all differences according to the established law." Finally, "there often wants power to back and support the sentence when right, and to give it due execution."[25]

---

[21] John Dunn, "The Politics of Locke in England and America in the Eighteenth Century,' in John W. Yolton, ed., *John Locke: Problems and Perspectives: A Collection of New Essays* (Cambridge, 1969), 45 at 51.

[22] Edward Feser, *Locke* (Oxford, 2007), 1.

[23] Dunn, "Politics of Locke" 51.

[24] Rosenthal, *Crown Under Law* 221.

[25] Locke, *Two Treatises of Government* II.ix §§ 124–26.

It followed, Locke said, that even the "supreme authority" (which Locke called "the legislative") cannot "rule by extemporary arbitrary decrees" and must "decide the rights of the subject by promulgated standing laws, and known authorized judges."[26] "The legislative cannot transfer the power of making laws to any other hands: for it being but a delegated power from the people, they who have it cannot pass it over to others."[27] The "prerogative" was a "power to act according to discretion, for the public good, without the prescription of law" because the "lawmaking power is not always in being." Consequently, "they have a very wrong notion of government, who say, that the people have incroached upon the prerogative, when they have got any part of it to be defined by positive laws."[28]

Locke thus arrived at the Whig position on the monarch's authority. The king must respect the independence of the common law courts and the laws made by Parliament. He could not rule by prerogative or by decree. The royal prerogative does not extend to making law or departing from law or appointing ministers to do so, even if a friendly parliament should authorize it. It only gives the king discretion as to matters not covered by law, and then only in unforeseen emergencies, and only so long as Parliament permits. It requires him to allow disputes about the law to be decided by known and indifferent judges.

One of the powers of Parliament was to enact laws. Another, which had been a mainstay of parliamentary authority throughout the struggle with the Stuarts, was the power to tax. Because of this power, kings could not rule without parliaments, even though Charles II and James II tried to do so. According to Locke, it followed from the very reasons that government was instituted that the power to tax could not belong to the king. Commonwealths were founded for the preservation of property. Consequently, "the prince, or senate, however it may have the power to make laws, for the regulating of property ... yet can never have a power to take to themselves the whole, or any part of the subjects property, without their own consent: for this would be in effect to leave them with no property at all."[29] Therefore, the legislative or supreme power "must not raise taxes on the property of the people, without the consent of the people, given by themselves, or their deputies." That was so even though, as we have seen, Locke believed that the government need not be democratic. When they institute government, the people may place power "in the hands one person, or a few people, or retain it themselves, or they may institute a mixed form of government."[30]

For the argument to work, however, people must enter into society to preserve private property. Locke introduced his theory of the origin of private property to show that they did.

Locke had broken with the Aristotelian tradition to reach these conclusions. But one cannot find a new theory of human nature and human society without going beyond what he wrote and what, for his own purposes, he needed to say. Locke's theory of the origin of property was based on a proposition he took to be obvious: that we have a right to our own

[26] Ibid. II.xi § 136.
[27] Ibid. II. xi § 141.
[28] Ibid. II.xiv § 163.
[29] Ibid. II.xi § 139.
[30] Ibid. II.x § 132.

bodies. Michael Zuchert, however, interpreted that proposition as a liberal expression of the importance of self. "The prerequisite for the discovery of self-ownership for Locke, is the discovery of the self. And the prerequisite for the discovery of the self is a thoroughgoing critique of the typical ways the human person was understood in previous thought – as God's created image, as rational soul, or as thinking substance."[31] Kevin Cope interpreted Locke's argument as a liberal expression of the importance of property. It shows that "the amalgamation of property is at the center of Locke's thinking."[32] "Assaulting or stealing property is tantamount to assaulting or abducting the person whose labor is intermixed with it."[33] But Locke did not say that stealing is as bad as assaulting a person, nor did he set out to prove that it was. He set out to prove that that no legitimate government can permit taxation without representation. To do so, he first had to establish that people enter into government to protect property that they already have.

Locke said that the chief end of forming commonwealths is the protection of property. But in the *Two Treatises of Government*, he does not present, as Taylor maintained, a theory of human nature according to which "one can be a fully competent human subject outside of society."[34] He described human nature, not in the *Two Treatises*, but in his *Essay Concerning Human Understanding*. There, he also broke with the Aristotelian tradition, but not in a way that supports philosophical liberalism or the importance of liberty or any of the propositions he defends in the *Two Treatises*.

He broke with the Aristotelian tradition by denying that moral reasoning begins with an innate knowledge of first principles that are not demonstrable. His "assault on 'innate ideas and principle'" "shocked" conventional opinion.[35] As John Yolton showed, Locke attacked the generally held belief as to how moral knowledge is possible. Locke's English contemporaries who held this belief sometimes spoke, as Aquinas had done, of *synderesis* and sometimes said that "conscience" rests on an inborn knowledge of good and evil.[36]

Having broken with the classical view of the roots of morality, Locke briefly sketched three different and mutually inconsistent views of his own. The first was proto-rationalist: to act morally means to conform to rules that can be derived from definitions. The second was proto-utilitarian: good and happiness are identified with pleasure. The third view was squarely within the Aristotelian tradition, and, indeed, paraphrased Richard Hooker: "we should . . . suit the relish of our minds to the true intrinsic good or ill that is in things."[37] To do so is to pursue "true and solid happiness" which is "[t]he highest perfection of

---

[31] Michael P. Zuckert, *Launching Liberalism: On Lockean Political Philosophy* (Lawrence, 2002), 194.
[32] Kevin L. Cope, *John Locke Revisited* (New York, 1999), 108.
[33] Ibid. 109.
[34] Taylor, *Modern Social Imaginaries* 19.
[35] Alexander Campell Fraser, "Prolegomena" xi to John Locke, *An Essay Concerning Human Understanding* (New York, 1959), xlii.
[36] John W. Yolton, *John Locke and the Way of Ideas* (Oxford, 1956), 26–48.
[37] John Locke, *An Essay Concerning Human Understanding*, Alexander Campbell Fraser, ed. (New York, 1959), II.xxi.54.

intellectual nature."[38] Taking a step beyond Hooker, he said: "The necessity of pursuing true happiness is the foundation of liberty."[39]

According to the first or proto-rationalist view, to act morally means to follow a law that can be demonstrated in the same way as the theorems of mathematics. According to Locke, "the idea of a Supreme Being ... and the idea of ourselves, as rational creatures"

> would, I suppose, if duly considered and pursued, afford such foundations of our duty and rules of action a: wherein I doubt not, from self-evident propositions, by necessary consequences, as incontestable as those in mathematics, the measures of right and wrong might be made out, to anyone that will apply himself with the same indifferency and attention to the one as to the other.[40]

An example is the proposition that "where there is no right there is no injustice" "for the idea of property being a right to anything, and the idea to which the name 'injustice' is given being the invasion or violation of that right," the proposition "is as certain as any demonstration in Euclid." It is as certain as "that a triangle has three angles equal to two right ones."[41]

In the *Two Treatises of Government*, he did not present his conclusions as deductions from abstract concepts of "right" and "justice." In the *Essay*, moreover, though he said that one "might place *morality* amongst the *sciences capable of demonstration*," he did not say that he has succeeded in doing so. Nor did he link his proto-rationalist account to human liberty. Indeed, if moral action merely means conforming to rules as demonstrable as the conclusions of mathematics, it is hard to see the place of liberty.

Locke's second view was like that of utilitarians such as Jeremy Bentham. He defined good and happiness in terms of pleasure. "Happiness ... in its full extent, is the utmost pleasure we are capable of, and misery the utmost pain. ... [W]hat has an aptness to produce pleasure in us is that we call good, and what is apt to produce pain in us we call evil."[42] What gives people pleasure varies as much as does their taste in food.

> The mind has a different relish, as well as the palate; and you will as fruitlessly endeavour to delight all men with riches or glory (which yet some men place their happiness in) as you would to satisfy all men's hunger with cheese or lobsters; which, though very agreeable and delicious fare to some, are to others extremely nauseous and offensive: and many persons would with reason prefer the griping of an hungry belly to those dishes which are a feast to others. Hence it was, I think, that the philosophers of old did in vain inquire, whether summum bonum consisted in riches, or bodily delights, or virtue, or contemplation: and they might have as reasonably disputed, whether the best relish were to be found in apples, plums, or nuts.[43]

[38] Ibid. II.xxi.52.
[39] Ibid.
[40] Ibid. IV.iii.18.
[41] Ibid.
[42] Ibid. II.xxi.43.
[43] Ibid. II.xxi.56.

Locke did not try to link "goodness" or "happiness" in this sense with liberty. Indeed, unlike the utilitarians, he thought it was a pity that humans were doomed to pursue whatever happened to give them pleasure in this life "like a company of poor insects; whereof some are bees, delighted with flowers and their sweetness; others beetles, delighted with other kinds of viands, which having enjoyed for a season, they would cease to be, and exist no more for ever."[44] Fortunately, according to Locke, God had decreed punishments in the next world so terrible that during this life people will shun pleasures that they would otherwise pursue.[45]

Modern scholars have found it difficult to reconcile Locke's account of happiness in terms of pleasure and pain with his account of moral knowledge in terms of deduction and demonstration.[46] Be that as it may, it difficult to see any relationship between liberty and either account.

Locke discussed liberty only in connection with a third account of morality. Remarkably enough, this account makes sense only from the Aristotelian point of view, which he discarded.[47] His immediate source seems to have been Richard Hooker whose immediate sources were Aquinas and Aristotle.

In this account, Locke spoke of the pursuit of "true happiness." As we have seen, when Aristotle spoke of "happiness," he did not mean an agreeable state of mind which is the opposite of sadness. He meant to live well and to do well, pursuing what is worthwhile. Hooker used the word "felicity" in the same way. It is "the utmost good and greatest perfection whereof nature hath made [us] capable."[48] According to Locke, a "steady prosecution of true felicity" requires that human beings choose those things that "lie in

---

[44]   Ibid.

[45]   Ibid. II.xxi.62, 72. Despite these statements in the *Essay*, in an entry in his private journal, Locke had suggested that human beings are so constituted as to take greater pleasure in objects of choice which are actually are better. He said that "happiness and misery seem wholly to consist in ... pleasure and pain." Nevertheless, "God has so framed the constitutions of our minds and bodies that several things are apt to produce in both of them pleasure and pain, delight and trouble, ... for ends suitable to His wisdom and goodness." John Locke, "Journal for 16 July 1676," M.S. Locke f. 1, p. 325, in John Locke, *Essay on the Law of Nations and Associated Writings*, W. von Leyden, ed. (Oxford, 1954), 263 at 266, at *335–36. "[N]ature for wise ends of her own had made us so that we are delighted with the very being of our children. Some wise minds are of a nobler constitution, having pleasure in the very being and happiness of their friends, and some yet of a more excellent make are delighted with the existence and happiness of all good men. " Locke, "Journal" 266 at *330. If it were so, then one would choose for the sake of pleasure, but find pleasure by choosing what is good. In these notes his second view of human nature seemed to blend with the third.

[46]   For example , Richard I. Aaron, *John Locke* (2nd ed., Oxford, 1955), 257; Gideon Yaffee, *Liberty Worth the Name: Locke on Free Agency* (Princeton, 2000), 67; Zuckert, *Launching Liberalism* 26; Huyler, *Locke in America* 91; Ruth Grant, *John Locke's Liberalism* (Chicago, 1987), 44

[47]   The reemergence of an Aristotelian viewpoint can be seen in other passages. For example:

> [W]e can infer the principle and a definite rule of our duty from man's own constitution and the faculties with which he is equipped. For since man is neither made without design nor endowed to no purpose with these faculties, his function appears to be that which nature has prepared him to perform. ... [H]e feels himself not only impelled by life's experience and pressing needs to procure and preserve a life in society with other men, but also to be urged to enter into society by a certain propensity of nature."

Locke, *Essay Concerning Human Understanding* 157.

[48]   Richard Hooker, *Of the Laws of Ecclesiastical Polity* (Dutton, 1907), I.viii.1.

the way to their main end, and make a real part of that which is their greatest good."[49] "[W]e should take pains to suit the relish of our minds to the true intrinsic good or ill that is in things."[50] "[T]he highest perfection of intellectual nature lies in a careful and constant pursuit of true and solid happiness."[51]

Locke explained why we sometimes choose what is evil in the same way as Hooker and Aquinas. According to Aquinas, something purely evil cannot attract us. What a person chooses must be in some way good or it would not do so. He may choose wrongly because passion distorts his judgment.[52] Or he may choose wrongly because of "a disorder of the will." "The will is out of order when it loves more the lesser good," for example, when it "loves some temporal good, e.g. riches or pleasure" at the expense of a greater one.[53] Nevertheless, "[e]vil cannot be intended by anyone for its own sake."[54]

Similarly, according to Hooker, "evil as evil cannot be desired; if that be desired which is evil, the cause is the goodness which is or seemeth to be joined with it."[55] One sins by choosing the lesser good. "For there was never sin committed, wherein a less good was not preferred to a greater, and that wilfully." The greater good can be known by reason. "There is not that good which concerneth us, but it hath evidence enough for itself, if Reason were diligent to search it out."[56] One may reject this greater good because "the hastiness of our Wills prevent[s] the more considerate advice of sound Reason" or "the very custom of evil making the heart obdurate."[57] Or one may reject it because the will follows "that inferior natural desire which we call Appetite." "Affections such as joy, and grief, and anger, with such like" are "sundry fashions and forms of Appetite."[58]

Similarly, according to Locke, "by a due consideration, and examining any good proposed, it is in our power to raise our desires in a due proportion to the value of that good, whereby in its turn and place it may come to work upon the will, and be pursued."[59] "Power to suspend the prosecution of any desire makes way for consideration," "[f]or, during this suspension of any desire, before the will be determined to action, and the action . . . done, we have opportunity to examine, view, and judge of the good or evil of what we are going to do."[60]

We may reject the greater good because of "the uneasinesses of hunger, thirst, heat, cold, weariness, with labour, and sleepiness" that arise from "the ordinary necessities of our lives" as well as "the fantastical uneasiness (as itch after honour, power, or riches, &c.) which acquired habits, by fashion, example, and education, have settled in us."[61] Then, the

---

49 Locke, *Essay Concerning Human Understanding* II.xxi.53.
50 Ibid. II.xxi.54.
51 Ibid. II.xxi.52.
52 *Summa theologiae* I-II, Q. 77, a. 2.
53 Ibid. I-II, Q. 78, a. 1.
54 Ibid. I-II, Q. 78, a. 1, ad 1.
55 Hooker, *Laws of Ecclesiastical Polity* I.vii.6.
56 Ibid. I.vii.7.
57 Ibid.
58 Ibid. I.vii.3.
59 Locke, *Essay Concerning Human Understanding* II.xxi.47.
60 Ibid. II.xxi.48.
61 Ibid. II.xxi.46.

"absent good, though thought on, confessed, and appearing to be good . . . is justled out . . . till due and repeated contemplation has brought it nearer to our mind, given some relish of it, and raised in us some desire: . . . and so, according to its greatness and pressure, comes in its turn to determine the will."[62]

Going beyond Hooker, Locke said: "The necessity of pursuing true happiness is the foundation of liberty. As therefore the highest perfection of intellectual nature lies in a careful and constant pursuit of true and solid happiness; so the care of ourselves, that we mistake not imaginary for real happiness, is the necessary foundation of our liberty."[63] One who mistakes imaginary for real happiness is not free. "To be determined by our own judgment, is no restraint to liberty. . . . Nay, were we determined by anything but the last result of our own minds, judging of the good or evil of any action, we were not free; the very end of our freedom being, that we may attain the good we choose."[64]

Zuchert acknowledged that "the natural law" in the tradition of Aquinas "can generate a version of the right to liberty." Liberty would then be a right "to adhere to the natural law mandate in a truly human way, through the use of one's reason and will." "[T]hat right," he said, "is far different" than "a right to do or not to do, as each agent determines," which, he claimed, is "the right to liberty as affirmed, for example, in the Declaration of Independence" and by Locke. Locke's description, however, sounds more like a natural law mandate in the tradition of Aquinas than like Zuchert's description of Locke. Liberty rests on a mandate to pursue "true and solid happiness" which is "the highest perfection of intellectual nature." To do so, "we should take pains to suit the relish of our minds to the true intrinsic good or ill that is in things." "[P]ursuing true happiness is the foundation of liberty." The characteristic features of the Aristotelian understanding of human nature are united with the concern for which Locke is chiefly famous: the value of liberty. He expressed that value in words like those that Thomas Jefferson was to make famous: "the pursuit of true happiness." Zuchert observed that "[t]he natural law" in the tradition of Aquinas "does not imply a libertarian society."[65] Zuchert was correct, but neither does the idea of liberty as described by Locke. Unlike Zuchert, Locke did not confuse a free society with a society that libertarian philosophical principles can explain.

The founders of the American Republic certainly were familiar with the writings of Locke. But they made little use of any of Locke's view that was specifically Lockean. Huyler looked for passages in the writings of the founders in which Locke himself was cited or paraphrased. He found what we might expect, given what we have seen of Locke's political philosophy. Sometimes Locke was cited for the "revolutionary principles" which were common to other Whigs: for example, "power-as-a-trust, popular political judgment, and the 'dissolution of government' and the reversion of the supreme constituent power to the people."[66]

---

[62] Ibid.

[63] Ibid. II.xxi.52.

[64] Ibid. The last part of this passage, appearing after the words "we were not free," was added in Coste's French version of the *Essay*. Coste was Locke's literary assistant and prepared it under Locke's direct supervision. It was published after the four English editions.

[65] Zuckert, *Launching Liberalism* 185.

[66] Dworetz, *Unvarnished Doctrine* 95.

Sometimes he was cited for the principle of no taxation without representation,[67] an issue on which, as we have seen, he did make a unique contribution. The American revolutionaries quoted him to show that virtual representation in Parliament was not enough. But that is a far cry from philosophical liberalism.

II PRIVATE RIGHTS AND THE COMMON GOOD

According to the once conventional view, the American Republic was founded on the liberal principles of the Enlightenment. This view was challenged over four decades ago by the now classic work of Gordon Wood, *The Creation of the American Republic*. He observed that "No phrase except 'liberty' was invoked more often by the Revolutionaries than 'the public good.'"[68]

> To make the people's welfare – the public good – the exclusive end of government became for the Americans, as one general put it, their "Polar Star" [69] [quoting Horatio Gates], the central tenet of Whig faith, shared not only by Hamilton and Paine at opposite ends of the Whig spectrum, but by any American bitterly opposed to a system which held "that a Part is greater than its Whole; or, in other words, that some individuals ought to be considered, even to the Destruction of the Community, which they compose."[70]

John Adams wrote,

> A government has a constitution, like a person, or a clock, and so it has an end. "These parts, therefore, are the essentials and fundamentals of a clock. Let us now inquire whether the same reasoning is not applicable in all its parts to government. For government is a frame, a scheme, a system, a combination of powers for a certain end, namely, – the good of the whole community. The public good, the salus populi, is the professed end of all government.[71]

The *salus populi* was the end of government "as much as grinding corn is the use of a mill, the transportation of burdens is the end of a ship, the mensuration of time the scope of a watch, or life and health the designation of the body."[72]

According to Thomas Jefferson, this was the one point on which he and Adams agreed, despite their bitter differences in the presidential election of 1800. During the controversy, Jefferson wrote to Adams' wife Abigail, "Both of our political parties, at least the honest portions of them, agree conscientiously in the same object, the public good: but they differ essentially in what they deem the means of promoting that good."[73]

---

[67] Dworetz, *Unvarnished Doctrine* 75–94.
[68] Gordon S. Wood, *The Creation of the American Republic 1776–1787* (Chapel Hill, 1998) (first published 1968), 55.
[69] Citing Letter from Horatio Gates to Thomas Jefferson (Feb. 2, 1781), in Julian P. Boyd, ed., *The Papers of Thomas Jefferson* 4 (Princeton, 1951), 502.
[70] Wood, *Creation* 55, citing Gates, Letter to Jefferson (Feb. 2, 1781)
[71] John Adams, 27 January 1766, No. III, "The Earl of Clarendon to William Pym, " in Robert J. Taylor, ed., *The Adams Papers, Papers of John Adams* (Cambridge, 1977), 164–70.
[72] Ibid.
[73] Letter from Thomas Jefferson to Abigail Smith Adams, 11 September 1804, in James P. McClure, ed., *The Papers of Thomas Jefferson* 44, (Princeton, 2019), 379–80.

The puzzle for historians is how to reconcile this idea of the common good with the protection of private rights. Although the founders believed in both, historians have seen a contradiction between two incompatible conceptions of government. They have called the first conception "classical republican" and the second "liberal." According to Lance Banning, "[t]he two philosophies begin with different assumptions about human nature and develop a variety of different ideas."[74] Steven Dworetz called the classical republican idea "life-threatening": it "cut[s] the historical grounds of legitimacy ... of constitutional politics by denying that liberalism was an essential ideological component of the founding doctrine."[75] Jerome Huyler asked:

> How could as astute a thinker as John Adams entertain so obvious a contradiction of basic values as in his pronouncement [in a single paragraph] that "each individual of the society has a right to be protected by it in the enjoyment of life, liberty and property ... And government is instituted for the common good ... not for the profit, honor or private interest of any one man, family or class of men"?[76]

Some scholars have said that the founders held these incompatible views because they were pluralistic thinkers,[77] or because their thought was complex,[78] or because they had creatively combined the two in some unspecified way,[79] or because these views are ideal types that capture implicit tendencies immanent in the thought of a single person.[80]

Wood correctly observed that the founders' idea of the public or common good cannot be understood from a modern perspective. It "embodied the idea of the good society as it had been set forth from antiquity through the eighteenth century."[81] Their idea was neither Lockean nor liberal nor modern.

Wood himself did not discuss the history of that idea before the time of the founders. J.G. A. Pocock tried to do so in his study *The Machiavellian Moment* but, in my view, he followed a false trail. He sought the ideas that influenced the founders in the thought of the Italian civic humanists and particularly that of Niccolo Machiavelli. Although the civic humanists, like the founders, attached great importance to civic virtue, that does not show that the founders were influenced by their work or that of authors they had directly influenced. John Adams studied the history of the Italian republics[82] but seems to have

---

[74] Lance Banning, *Founding Visions: The Ideas, Individuals and Intersections that Created America* (Lexington, 2014), 44.

[75] Steven M. Dworetz, *The Unvarnished Doctrine: Locke, Liberalism and the American Revolution* (Durham, 1990), 5.

[76] Jerome Huyler, *Locke in America: The Moral Philosophy of the Founding Era* (Lawrence, 1995), 224.

[77] Alan Gibson, "Ancients, Moderns and Americans: The Republicanism–Liberalism Debate Revisited," *History of Political Thought* 21 (2000), 261 at 261–62; Rogan Kersh, "The Founding: Liberalism Redux," *The Review of Politics* 55 (1993), 729 at 729.

[78] Saul Cornell, "Liberal Republicans or Republican Liberals? The Political Thought of the Founders Reconsidered," *Reviews in American History* 21 (1993), 26 at 26–27.

[79] Gibson, "Ancients, Moderns and Americans" 264.

[80] Morton J. Horwitz, "History and Theory," *Yale Law Journal* 96 (1987), 1825 at 1833–36.

[81] Wood, *Creation* 59.

[82] Letter from Abigail Adams to Richard Cranch (10 May 1787), in C. James Taylor et al., eds., *The Adams Papers*, Adams Family Correspondence March 1787–December 1789 8 (Cambridge, 2007), 42–43 .

bypassed the writings of the civic humanists. An exception was Machiavelli, whose work on Roman virtue was known and respected by many of the founders. Benjamin Franklin sent the editor of the *London Chronicle* "an extract from Machiavell's discourses on Livy" in a letter criticizing the Stamp Act.[83] More often, references to Machiavelli's work were anecdotal.[84]

In any event, Pocock's concern was less with the influence of Machiavelli or other Renaissance writers on the founder's conception of civic virtue than with what he called a "Machiavellian moment." It is a crisis that arises from a commitment to the ideal of civic virtue. At times, the founders, and particularly John Adams, were very concerned about the virtue of the citizenry. But to speak of a "Machiavellian moment" is not an interpretation of how Machiavelli influenced them. It is a critique of classical republicanism used to diagnose an unease they supposedly must have felt. Moreover, it does not illuminate their ideas about private rights, the public good, and how the two are related.

The correct path toward understanding these ideas was marked out by Quentin Skinner when, as we have seen, he showed that the idea that the people establish the government to serve the common good was not formulated in the eighteenth century but by the late scholastics.[85]

One source of the problem, as we can now see, is that, with the exception of Locke, private rights were not conceived in the same way before the nineteenth century. For Locke, people first acquired property rights and then formed society to protect them. Later, liberal philosophers defined rights in terms of the will of the right holder to do as he wished. Property, for example, was defined as the right of the owner to do as he willed with what he owned. Writers in the Aristotelian tradition recognized that a right holder can exercise his right as he chooses. Nevertheless, the content of rights is determined by justice, for example, by the reasons that it is just for

---

[83] Letter from "N.N." to "the Printer of the London Chronicle" (7–9 January 1766), in Leonard W. Labaree, ed., *The Papers of Benjamin Franklin January 1 through December 31, 1766* 13 (New Haven, 1969), 26–28 (attributed to Franklin because he used the signature N.N. in other letters to the same editor).

[84] Major General John Sullivan quoted Machiavelli's advice to George Washington; "Always beware of the Man, that flatters you, and appears to Coincide with your Sentiments, on all Occasions." Letter from Major General John Sullivan to George Washington (1 December 1779), in William M. Ferraro, ed., *The Papers of George Washington, Revolutionary War Series, 22 October–31 December 1779* 23 (Charlottesville, 2015), 503–06. John Adams complained that people honored the "ribbons" of the Order of the Cincinnati, founded by Revolutionary War soldiers, while neglecting true merit, which showed: "true are those Words of Machiavel 'Not Ingratitude, but too much love is the constant Fault of the People.'" Letter from John Adams to Elbridge Gerry (25 April 1785), in Gregg L. Lint et al., eds, *The Adams Papers, Papers of John Adams, April–November 1785* 17 (Cambridge, 2014), 39–44. Speaking of the Terror in France, Adams said that "Macchiavels Advice to cutt off a numerous Nobility had more weight than mine to preserve them." Letter from John Adams to Abigail Adams, 3 February 1793, in *The Adams Papers*, in *Adams Family Correspondence, January 1790–December 1793* 9 (Cambridge, 2009), 389–91. George Joy warned James Madison that some were saying that the English "will think us weak, which, says Machiavelli, derogates from a Government much more than wickedness." Letter from George Joy to James Madison (19 May 1812), in J. C. A. Stagg et al., eds., *The Papers of James Madison, Presidential Series, 5 November 1811–9 July 1812 and Supplement 5 March 1809–19 October 1811* 4 (Charlottesville, 1999), 399–402.

[85] Quentin Skinner, *The Foundations of Modern Political Thought* 2 (Cambridge, 1978), 321.

a person to own property. Private property was instituted by society to remedy the disadvantages of holding property in common.[86] Consequently, the owner's rights were not absolute. For example, another person could use his property without his consent in time of necessity.[87] This account of property rights, formulated by late scholastics, was adopted by Hugo Grotius and Samuel Pufendorf,[88] who also used them to explain the doctrine of necessity.[89] Both authors were well known to the revolutionary generation in America. Adams cited them alongside Locke.[90] Neither he nor others discussed the break Locke had made with the classical conception of rights.

Moreover, in the classical tradition on which the founders drew, the public or common good was not conceived in the same way. Wood correctly noted that "[t]he common interest was not, as we might today think of it, simply the sum or consensus of the particular interests that make up the community."[91] He concluded, incorrectly, that "[f]or the republican patriots of 1776 the common-weal was all-encompassing – a transcendent object with a unique moral worth that made private considerations fade into insignificance."[92] "Ideally republicanism obliterated the individual."[93]

His remarks illustrate the modern tendency to take one of two extreme views of the relationship of private rights and the public good. Either the end of society is an aggregate of particular interests or a consensus on how best to promote them, or else it is an end that transcends and therefore disregards the interests of individuals. Having recognized that eighteenth-century Americans did not believe in the first of these alternatives, Wood concluded that they must have believed in the second. In support, he quoted such passages as these:

> True liberty is "natural liberty restrained in such manner, as to render society one great family; where every one must consult his neighbor's happiness as well as his own." In a republic "each individual gives up all private interest that is not consistent with the general good, the interest of the whole body" [citing a contemporary sermon[94]].
>
> . . .

[86] Domenicus Soto, *De iustitia et iure libri decem* (Salamanca, 1553), lib. 4, q. 3, a. 1; Ludovicus Molina, *De iustitia et iure tractatus* (Venice, 1614); Leornardus Lessius, *De iustitia et iure, ceterisque virtutibus cardinalis libri quatuor* (Paris, 1628), disp. 20; lib. 2, cap. 5, dubs. 1–2.

[87] Lessius, *De iustitia et iure* lib. 2, cap. 12, dub 12; Soto, *De iustita et iure* lib 5, q. 3, a. 4; Molina, *De iustitia et iure* disp. 20.

[88] Hugo Grotius, *De iure belli ac pacis libri tres* (Amsterdam, 1646), II.ii.2; Samuel Pufendorf, *De iure naturae et gentium libri octo* (Amsterdam, 1688), II.vi.5; IV.iv.4–7.

[89] Grotius, *De iure belli ac pacis* II.ii.6–7; Pufendorf, *De iure naturae* II.vi.5.

[90] Adams, *Novanglus* No. VII.

[91] Letter from Thomas Jefferson to John Adams, 14 October 1816 in J. Jefferson Looney, ed., *Papers of Thomas Jefferson, Retirement Series* 10 (Princeton, 2013), 458–61.

[92] Wood, *Creation* 61.

[93] Ibid. 61.

[94] Edward Payson, "Sermon Preached May 27, 1778," in John Wingate Thornton, ed., *The Pulpit of the American Revolution* (Boston, 1876), 332.

"A Citizen," said Samuel Adams, "owes everything to the Commonwealth."[95] "Every man in a republic," declared Benjamin Rush, [96] "his public property. His time and talents – his youth – his manhood – his old age – nay more, life, all belong to his country."[97]

The passages puzzled Banning. He noted, correctly, that "the Revolutionary thinkers . . . seldom hoped that individuals would not pursue their own self-interests. A vigorous and vigilant defense of one's own liberties was widely thought of as a necessary characteristic of the citizen of a republic – the contribution of his virtue to the public."[98] Banning concluded that the passages quoted by Wood must be atypical.[99] Adams and Rush, however, saw no conflict between their sentiments and contemporary ideas of what the private and public interest entailed.

Wood was closer to the truth when he said that for eighteenth century Americans, "what was good for the whole community was ultimately good for all the parts."[100] John Adams said that "all divines and moral philosophers" will agree that "the happiness of society is the end of government [and] the happiness of the individual is the end of man. From this principle it will follow, that the form of government, which communicates . . . happiness to the greatest number of persons, and in the greatest degree, is the best."[101] As we have seen, this idea of the relationship between the common good and the happiness of each citizen was also a product of the classical tradition of political though that goes back Aristotle.

By understanding this idea, we can understand why there is no contradiction between the passages Wood quoted and a belief in the value of asserting one's private rights and in acting for common good. Samuel Adams said that "a citizen owes everything to the commonwealth." He does. Only as a member of society can he live a truly human life. Rush said that "his time and talents – his youth – his manhood – his old age – nay more, life, all belong to his country." True enough. If he uses his time and talents well, in youth, manhood and old age, whatever he does will promote not only his own well-being but the welfare of his country. But his ends as an individual human being are thereby promoted, not disregarded.

The anonymous Protestant minister quoted by Wood had said that in a republic, "each individual gives up all private interest that is not consistent with the general good, the interest of the whole body." For John Adams, to assert private interests inconsistent with the public good is to overstep one's rights. To assert one's rights is to act from a "resentment of injury, and indignation against wrong," through a "love of virtue truth and a veneration for virtue," through "understanding, seeing and feeling the difference between true and false,

---

95 Citing Letter of Samuel Adams to Caleb Davis (April 3, 1781) in Harry Alonzo Cushing, ed., *The Writings of Samuel Adams* 4 (New York, 1904), 255.

96 Citing Benjamin Rush, *On the Defects of the Confederation* (1787), in Dagobert D. Runes, ed., *The Selected Writings of Benjamin Rush* (New York, 1947), 31.

97 Wood, *Creation* 61.

98 Banning, *Founding Visions* 67.

99 Ibid. 86 n. 20.

100 Wood, *Creation* 58.

101 John Adams, III. Thoughts on Government, April 1776," in C. James Taylor, Gregg L. Lint, and Celeste Walker, eds., *Adams Papers* 4 (1979), 86–93.

right and wrong, virtue and vice," and so to defend the liberty that the society should protect. Such sentiments are rooted "in human nature."[102] In contrast, a person who seeks unjust advantages, "extravagant and unconstitutional emoluments," is motivated by "excessive ambition and venality." These are the "unhappy imperfections in human nature" which "will, in spite of all human precautions, creep into government." We must "never relax our attention, or our resolutions, to keep them out."[103] To assert one's rights contributes to society. To seek more undermines it. There is a harmony between asserting one's true rights and the common good.

III THE ARCHITECTURE OF GOVERNMENT

i *A Mixed Form of Government*

Like the founders of the Song dynasty, the American revolutionaries looked to the past for guidance. The founders of the Song saw a cycle in which the virtuous governed, became corrupt, and then lost power; eventually good government was reestablished. So it had been with the Xia, Shang, and Zhou Dynasties, and later the Han. The founders of the American Republic saw a perpetual struggle for liberty and against despotism. As Gordon Wood observed, "[t]he theory of government that the Americans clarified in their reading and discussion possessed a compelling simplicity: politics was nothing more than a perpetual battle between the passions of the rulers, whether one or a few, and the united interest of the people."[104] According to Adams,

> Liberty ... has always been surrounded by dangers ... Consider the commonwealths of Greece. Were not the wisest of them so sensible of it as to establish a security of liberty, I mean the ostracism, even against the virtuous of their own citizens ... ? ... In Rome, how often were the people cheated out of their liberties, by kings, decemvirs, triumvirs, and conspirators of all denominations.[105]

Liberty had been threatened throughout history, in the ancient world and later by the kings who had consolidated their power in modern Europe.

> "The same game, with the same success, has been played in all ages and countries," ... When a favorable conjuncture has presented, some of the most intriguing and powerful citizens have conceived the design of enslaving their country, and building their own greatness on its ruins. Philip and Alexander are examples of this in Greece; Caesar in Rome; Charles V, in Spain; Louis XII. in France, and ten thousand others.[106]

---

[102] John Adams, "To the Inhabitants of the Colony of Massachusetts-Bay" (23 January 1775), in ibid. 2: 226–33.
[103] John Adams, "'U' to the *Boston Gazette*" (29 August 1763) in ibid. 1: 76–81.
[104] Wood, *Creation* 18.
[105] John Adams, "Governor Winthrop to Governor Bradford," 9 February 1767 in *Adams Papers* 1 (Taylor, Lint, and Walker eds.), 198–202.
[106] Adams, *Novanglus* No. I.

The English Civil War was a struggle for liberty although "it is true, and to be lamented, that Cromwell did not establish a government as free as he might."[107]

History furnished not only examples of how liberty might be lost but models of how it might be protected. The models were the English constitution and the ancient republics of Greece and Rome. "Let us study the law of nature," Adams said, "search into the spirit of the British constitution; read the histories of ancient ages; contemplate the great examples of Greece and Rome; set before us the conduct of our own British ancestors, who have defended for us the inherent rights of people against foreign and domestic tyrants and usurpers."[108]

Their struggles had produced the English constitution. According to Adams, "here lies the difference between the British constitution and [despotic] forms of government, namely, that liberty is its end, its use, its designation, drift and scope."[109] Jefferson, though he later changed his mind, said in 1776 that the spirit of republicanism "so far from being incompatible with the British constitution, ... is the greatest glory of it."[110] In the *Declaration of Independence*, he said not that the English constitution was oppressive, but that the English government was attempting, despotically, to deprive the colonists of their liberties. His draft included a line eliminated in the final version: "we might have been a great and free people together." As Wood observed, "[f]or the Americans the English constitution was always 'the glorious fabrick of Britain's liberty,' 'the palladium of civil liberty ... that firm foundation of the nation's peace,' 'the monument of accumulated wisdom, and the admiration of the world.'"[111] The colonists protested that they were being deprived of the rights of Englishmen.

The strength of the English constitution, it was thought, was that it was a mixed or balanced form of government, combining the three Aristotelian forms of monarchy, aristocracy, and democracy, represented, respectively, by the king, the House of Lords, and the House of Commons. "Were I to define the British constitution," Adams said,

I should say it is a limited monarchy, or a mixture of the three forms of government commonly known in the schools, reserving as much of the monarchical splendor, the aristocratical independency, and the democratic freedom, as are necessary that each of these powers may have a control, both in legislation and execution, over the other two, for the preservation of the subject's liberty.[112]

---

[107] Ibid.
[108] John Adams, "A Dissertation on the Canon and the Feudal Law," No. 4, 21 October 1765, *Adams Papers* 1 (Taylor, Lint, and Walker eds.) 123–28.
[109] Adams, 27 January 1766, No. III, in "The Earl of Clarendon to William Pym" in *Adams Papers* 1 (Taylor, Lint and Walker eds.), 164–70.
[110] Thomas Jefferson, "Summary View" in *Papers of Thomas Jefferson* 1 (Boyd ed.), 131; *Philadelphia Pennsylvania Gazette*, Oct. 8, 1776, from Wood, *Creation* 45 n. 110.
[111] Wood, *Creation* 11 quoting James Wilson, "Considerations on the Nature and Extent of the Legislative Authority of the British Parliament" (Philadelphia, 1774) in Bird Wilson, ed.,*The Works ... of James Wilson* 3 (Philadelphia, 1804), 220.
[112] 27 January 1766, No. III, in "The Earl of Clarendon to William Pym" in *Adams Papers* 1 (Taylor, Lint and Walker eds.), 164–70.

Ironically, this interpretation of the English constitution had first appeared in a response drafted by the ministers of Charles I to the "Nineteen Propositions made by Both Houses of Parliament" in 1642. According to the response, the principles of the English mixed constitutions are violated when Parliament attempts to rule without the king's assent.

> There being three kindes of Government amongst men, Absolute Monarchy, Aristocracy and Democracy, and all these having their particular conveniencies and inconveniencies. The experience and wisdom of your Ancestors hath so moulded this out of a mixture of these, as to give to this Kingdom (as far as human prudence can provide) the conveniencies of all three, without the inconveniencies of any one, as long as the Balance hangs even between the three Estates, and they run jointly on in their proper Chanell (begetting Verdure and Fertilitie in the Meadows on both sides) and the overflowing of either on either side raise no deluge or Inundation. The ill of absolute Monarchy is Tyrannie, the ill of Aristocracy is Faction and Division, the ills of Democracy are Tumults, Violence and Licentiousnesse. The good of Monarchy is the uniting a Nation under one Head to resist Invasion from abroad, and Insurrection at home. The good of Aristocracie is the Conjuncion of Counsell in the ablest Persons of a State for the publike benefit. The good of Democracy is Liberty, and the Courage and Industrie which Libertie begets.[113]

As Lance Banning noted, "the theory of the mixed and balanced constitution … acquired a virtually unchallenged hold. By the eve of the American Revolution, the theory was so solidly entrenched and seemed so characteristically British that one of its best known proponents [William Blackstone] could forget its ancient roots."[114] According to Wood, "the Americans to the very end of the imperial controversy justified their constitutional opposition to English policy not by abjuring the theory of mixed government but by using and affirming it."[115]

> Not surprisingly, then, most Americans set about the building of their new states in 1776 within the confines of this theory of mixed government, for independence and the abolition of monarchy had not altered the basic postulates of the science of politics.[116] In Adams' mind, and in the minds of most of the framers in 1776, it was not a question of whether there would be a mixture or not, but rather a question of what sort of mixture. . . .
>
> The issue separating a conservative Whig, like Carter Braxton, from a Revolutionary Whig, like Richard Henry Lee, was not the theory of mixed government itself, but the proportion of power to be allotted to each of the elements in the constitution.[117]

Consequently, as Wood observed, "republicanism as the Americans expressed it in 1776 possessed a decidedly reactionary tone. It embodied the idea of the good society as it had been set forth from antiquity through the eighteenth century."[118] Its roots in antiquity have been neglected by standard histories in which the Constitution is "located" in the words of

---

[113] His Majesties Answer to the Nineteen Propositions of Both Houses of Parliament in John Rushworth, *Historical Collections of Private Passages of State* 4 (London, 1692), 731.

[114] Lance Banning, *The Jeffersonian Persuasion: Evolution of a Party Ideology* (Ithaca, 1978), 33.

[115] Wood, *Creation* 201.

[116] Ibid. 202.

[117] Ibid. 203–04.

[118] Ibid. 59.

Jack Rakove "in the Enlightened world of Locke and Montesquieu, Hume and Blackstone,"[119] a world that he believed (with some unfairness to Blackstone) had turned its back on the past. Rakove spoke of "the colonists' rejection of monarchy, aristocracy, and much (if not quite all) of the theory of mixed constitution."[120] Wood's work has been a valuable corrective.

In England, the theory was used to explain existing institutions, but the attempt to do so produced only a rough fit. The English monarchy and Parliament were originally feudal institutions. The monarchy was hereditary, and, according to Aristotle, that was an understandable but defective way to choose a monarch. The House of Lords was hereditary. According to Aristotle, government by those of good birth is an oligarchy, not an aristocracy, which is government by the wise and virtuous. The House of Commons was not chosen from "the multitude."

In the newly independent American states, however, where there was neither a hereditary monarch nor a hereditary nobility, the theory became an architectural plan for building new institutions.

ii *The Constitution of the United States of America*

According to J. G.A. Pocock and Gordon Wood themselves, the framers of the Constitution, and James Madison in particular, abandoned the classical principles of a mixed constitution. Here I believe that they were wrong.

Madison followed the classical theory of a mixed constitution but changed the terminology. He did not use the terms "monarchy" and "aristocracy" to describe role of the President and the Senate. At the time he was writing, "monarchy" and "aristocracy" had become terms of abuse, or, at least, terms that suggested a hereditary monarch and hereditary lords. Nevertheless, he attributed to the President, the Senate, and the House of Representatives the characteristics traditionally ascribed to the monarchical, aristocratic, and democratic elements of a mixed constitution. He redefined the term "republic" as government by elected representatives. He expected it to combine the advantages of superior wisdom and popular rule, the advantages that were traditionally ascribed to aristocracy and democracy,

The president was to have an executive power independent of the two branches of the legislature. Madison explained the need for entrusting this power to a single individual with the traditional argument in favor of monarchy: it enables unity of action. He said, in the passage just quoted: "The energy in government requires not only a certain duration of power, but the execution of it by a single hand."[121]

The Senate would ensure the pursuit of the public good despite the tendency of the popularly elected branch of government, the House of Representatives, "to yield to the impulse of sudden and violent passions, and to be seduced by factious leaders into

---

[119] Jack N. Rakove, *Original Meanings: Politics and Ideas in the Making of the Constitution* (New York, 1996), 7.
[120] Ibid. 2.
[121] Madison, *Federalist* no. 37.

intemperate and pernicious resolutions." It would provide men of greater wisdom, and so compensate for the "deficient wisdom" and "important errors" to be expected of members of the House, who would be "called for the most part from pursuits of a private nature, continued in appointment for a short time, and led by no permanent motive to devote the intervals of public occupation to a study of the laws, the affairs, and the comprehensive interests of their country."[122] Wisdom and temperance were the advantages traditionally ascribed to an aristocracy.

By "republic," Madison said, "I mean a government in which the scheme of representation takes place."[123] The representatives chosen by the people are likely to be wiser and more concerned with the public good than the people themselves. Representation will

> refine and enlarge the public views, by passing them through the medium of a chosen body of citizens, whose wisdom may best discern the true interest of their country, and whose patriotism and love of justice will be least likely to sacrifice it to temporary or partial considerations. Under such a regulation, it may well happen that the public voice, pronounced by the representatives of the people, will be more consonant to the public good than if pronounced by the people themselves, convened for the purpose.[124]

Madison believed that the advantage of representative government was a modern discovery.[125] As we have seen, however, for Aristotle, although in a pure democracy the people would govern or the leaders would be chosen by lot, in a mixed form the "multitude" by law "gives office to the well-to-do according to their desert."[126] According to Aquinas "the best form of polity" is a "mixture" in which "one is preeminent," "a number of persons have authority on account of virtue," and the "government" is "of the people, inasmuch as the rules may be chosen from the people, and the selection (*electio*) of the rulers pertains to the people."[127]

As Banning noted, "Madison and others . . . had decided that there was a fundamental difference between a mixed monarchy and a republic. Still, they were determined to secure all of the benefits traditionally attributed to balanced states." They did not imagine the society as composed of separate estates, such as nobles and commons, but then neither did Adams. "[T]hey retained the largest portion of the superstructure of eighteenth-century constitutional ideas. They defended the new government in terms that could be difficult to distinguish from the old."[128]

In contrast, Pocock and Wood interpreted Madison's account of representative government as a break with classical principles. One source of confusion is the change in terminology. Another, for them and for others, is Madison's discussion of interests in his account of representative government.[129]

---

[122]   Ibid. no. 62.
[123]   Ibid. no. 10.
[124]   Ibid.
[125]   Ibid. no. 14.
[126]   *Politics* III. xvii. 1288a.
[127]   *Summa theologiae* I-II, Q. 105, a. 1.
[128]   Banning, *Jeffersonian Persuasion* 100.
[129]   Isaac Kramnick, "The 'Great National Discussion': The Discourse of Politics in 1787," *The William and Mary Quarterly* 45 (1988), 3 at 4–5; Colleen A. Sheehan, "The Politics of Public Opinion: James Madison's 'Notes

According to Pocock,

As Federalist thought took shape, and the people were less and less seen as possessing virtue in the classical sense, it is not surprising to find, in Madison's writings, and those of others – the tenth issue of *The Federalist* is the locus classicus – an increasing recognition of the importance and of the legitimacy, in human affairs of the faction pursuing collective but particular interests.

Indeed, "there are passages which strikingly indicate that the capacity of this structure for reconciling conflicting interests is without limits. There is no interest which cannot be represented and given its place in the distribution of power."[130]

If so, Madison would have broken with the classical idea that the purpose of the government was to pursue the common good, which meant the welfare of every citizen, not the interest of a particular group. According to Madison, however, "[t]he aim of every political constitution is, or ought to be, first to obtain for rulers men who possess most wisdom to discern, and most virtue to pursue, the common good of the society."[131] Pocock and Wood rely heavily on *Federalist* no. 51 which certainly does not recognize the "legitimacy, in human affairs, of a faction pursuing collective but particular interests."

It is of great importance in a republic not only to guard the society against the oppression of its rulers, but to guard one part of the society against the injustice of the other part. Different interests necessarily exist in different classes of citizens. If a majority be united by a common interest, the rights of the minority will be insecure. ... There are but two methods of providing against this evil: the one by creating a will in the community independent of the majority that is, of the society itself; the other, by comprehending in the society so many separate descriptions of citizens as will render an unjust combination of

on Government'," *William and Mary Quarterly*, 49 (1992), 609 at 609–10 (speaking of Martin Diamond, Joyce Appleby, and John Patrick Diggins). There are also scholars who, again, interpret the work of Madison as a liberal break with classical republicanism. See Saul Cornell, "Liberal Republicans or Republican Liberals? The Political Thought of the Founders Reconsidered," review of Richard C. Sinopoli, The Foundations of American Citizenship: Liberalism, the Constitution, and Civic Virtue in *Reviews in American History* 21 (1993), 26 at 27. According to some, Madison was a liberal because he "looked to individual rights, especially religious freedom," thus "[t]urning decisively away from civic religion, value homogeneity, and an exclusive reliance on strong citizenship." See Andreas Kalyvas and Ira Katznelson, "The Republic of the Moderns: Paine's and Madison's Novel Liberalism" *Polity* 38 (2006), 447 at 466. The Constitution reflects this liberalism because it "places little emphasis on promoting virtue through religion, the arts, a system of education, or by requiring the contemplation of the good society and government." See James D. Savage, "Corruption and Virtue at the Constitutional Convention Source," *The Journal of Politics* 56 (1994), 174 at 176. As before, these scholars are reading distinctions between "ancient" and "modern liberty," drawn by nineteenth-century liberals such as Constant, into eighteenth-century sources. Some scholars have rejected the dichotomy between liberalism and classical republicanism only to reinstate it. Andreas Kalyvas and Ira Katznelson "claim the development of liberalism ... was the unplanned result of actors and thinkers situated within classical republicanism." Kalyvas and Katznelson, "Republic of the Moderns" 474–75. Isaac Kramnick described the confusion in terminology as a "full-blown the confusion of idioms, [an] overlapping of political languages, in 1787." Isaac Kramnick, "The 'Great National Discussion'" 12.

[130] J. G. A. Pocock, *The Machiavellian Moment: Florentine Political Thought and the Atlantic Republican Tradition* (Princeton, 1975), 522. As authority, Pocock cites "Wood, [*Creation of the American Republic 1776–1787*] pp. 605–10, relying largely on *The Federalist*, no. 51." 522 n. 29.

[131] Madison, *Federalist* no. 57.

a majority of the whole very improbable, if not impracticable. . . . The second method will be exemplified in the federal republic of the United States. Whilst all authority in it will be derived from and dependent on the society, the society itself will be broken into so many parts, interests, and classes of citizens, that the rights of individuals, or of the minority, will be in little danger from interested combinations of the majority.

Thus the advantage of a large republic is not that it "reconcil[es] conflicting interests" or "gives each private interest its place in the distribution of power." The advantage is that makes it hard for private interests to have their way. Madison explained in *Federalist* no. 10 that a faction is "a number of citizens . . . united and actuated by some common impulse of passion, or of interest, adverse to the rights of other citizens, or to the permanent and aggregate interests of the community." In a "pure democracy" in which all the citizens "assemble and administer the government in person . . . [a] common passion or interest will, in almost every case, be felt by a majority of the whole." The majority will "sacrifice to its ruling passion or interest both the public good and the rights of other citizens." The sacrifice of the public good to private interests is less likely in a representative system of government and still less likely when the republic is large.

Wood claimed that by making the purpose of government the reconciliation of private interests "(t)he Federalists hoped to create an entirely new and original sort of republican government – a republic which did not require a virtuous people for its sustenance."[132] To the contrary, Madison said, in the debates over ratifying the Constitution, "Is there no virtue among us? If there be not, we are in a wretched situation. No theoretical checks, no form of government, can render us secure. To suppose that any form of government will secure liberty or happiness without any virtue in the people is a chimerical idea."[133]

Wood believed that Madison presented a new theory of politics. It was "a kinetic theory of politics," "a crumbling of political and social interests," an "atomization of authority."[134]

Madison would not have understood that description. What Madison said was that in a large republic it would be hard for any particular interest to command a majority. Consequently, it would be easier to pursue the acknowledged end of government: the common good. In claiming that "this revolution marked the end of the classical conception of politics," Wood described the classical conception in a way that no defender of mixed government would have recognized: it was "an integrated, ordered changeless ideal of the totality and complexity of the world," an "ideal [in which] there could be only potential energy, no kinetic energy, only a static equilibrium among synthetic orders, and no motion among the particular, miscellaneous parts that made up the society."[135] What Madison described was how representative government better served the classical ideal of the common good.

---

[132] Wood, *Creation* 475.
[133] James Madison, *The Debates in the Several State Conventions, on the Adoption of the Federal Constitution, as Recommended by the General Convention at Philadelphia, in 1787* 3, Joseph Elliot ed. (2nd ed., Washington, 1836), 536–37 (hereinafter cited as *Elliot's Debates*).
[134] Wood, *Creation* 605.
[135] Ibid. 606.

Although Madison defended the principles of a mixed constitution while changing the terminology, others had attacked these principles. Thomas Paine rejected the theory of the mixed constitution in his pamphlet *Common Sense*, but few readers agreed with him.[136] During the "critical period" from 1776 to the late 1780s, as Wood has shown, "radical Whigs" challenged not only the principles of mixed government, but the traditional understanding of what it means to say that government is instituted by the people. According to the traditional understanding, accepted even by Locke, the people had the power to institute whatever form of government seemed most likely to preserve their safety and happiness: a monarchy, an aristocracy, a democracy, or a mixed form of government. Unless they instituted a pure democracy, they did not retain the power to govern. According to the "radical Whigs," the people could not divest themselves of the power to govern.

Among Wood's many examples of "radical Whiggism" are the "instructions" to their delegates given by the "radical counties of Orange and Mecklenburg, North Carolina" in 1776: "Political power is of two kinds, one principal and superior, the other derived and inferior ... The principal supreme power is possessed by the people at large, the derived and inferior power by the servants which they employ."[137] Another example is the declarations of the freeholders of Albemarle County, Virginia and of the mechanics of New York City, also in 1776, both of which maintained that the power of "approving and disapproving their own laws ought forever to remain with the whole body of the people."[138] The cconstitution of Pennsylvania provided that "the Grand Legislative Council of the People ... had a right to approve or disapprove every bill" passed by the legislative assembly, a provision, one critic charged, that "destroys all ideas of representation."[139] Other radical Whig proposals were to allow the electorate to bind their representatives by instructions or by the decisions of popular conventions.

Their opponents, Wood noted, "thrust in the way of these radical constitutional developments" "the orthodox notion of sovereignty, the most important doctrine of 18th century political science."[140] As Noah Webster explained, "s]overeignty consists in the understanding and will of the political society," which, admittedly, was originally in the people. When the government was formed, however, the people vested the sovereignty "where and in what manner" they pleased; "he or they to whom it is delegated is the sovereign, and is thus vested with the political understanding and will of the people, for their good and advantage solely."[141] According to Wood, "beginning in the late seventies and continuing on through the eighties opponents of all these radical extensions of Whiggism – the mobbing and electioneering, the proliferation of conventions, the broadened use of instructions, the actualization of representation – repeatedly fell back upon this doctrine of sovereignty as the final, best rebuttal they could offer."[142]

---

[136] Banning, *Jeffersonian Persuasion* 81.
[137] Wood, *Creation* 364–65.
[138] Ibid. 366.
[139] Ibid.
[140] Ibid. 372.
[141] Ibid.
[142] Ibid.

In was during this period that the United States Constitution was adopted. According to Banning, "the triumph of the Constitution in the midst of a ferocious party conflict is to be explained, in no small part, as a consequence of the persistent influence of received ideas." Its ratification "that many of the central concepts of the eighteenth-century balanced constitution ... persisted in America long after 1789."[143]

Banning spoke of the "triumph of the Constitution." Michael Klarman spoke of the "framers' coup." He asked, "how were the supporters of the Constitution able to convince the nation, in the course of a reasonably democratic (for the era) ratifying process to approve a document that was severely constrain of popular influence on government?"[144] Klarman described the astute political maneuvering of the Constitution's supporters. He described the relative difficulties that farmers and backwoodsmen would have voting. He noted that many people voted for ratification because of their respect for the opinions of those who were better educated, or who drafted or endorsed the proposed constitution – although that consideration might indicate that they did prefer less direct popular control over government. One is at a loss, after reading this very long book, to find evidence of a "coup," or, for that matter, of intimidation, fraud, or corruption.

According to Klarman, the limits the constitution set to popular influence on government were "vastly different from what most Americans would have expected or wanted."[145] His evidence of what the people wanted is that some state constitutions contained some provisions that assigned a greater role to popular government than the federal constitution. Wood acknowledged, however, that the Massachusetts constitution, and "the revisions of the other state constitutions in the late 1780s and early 1790s" which "decisively affected the nature of the national Constitution of 1787" were "largely but certainly not entirely the work of Adams," and who eulogized virtue and the mixed constitution.[146]

In any event, none of the ratifying conventions proposed adopting the purer form of democracy advocated by the radical Whigs, for example, by vesting all power in a single assembly, by binding representatives by instructions given them by their constituents, by requiring legislation to be ratified by the people, or by allowing conventions of the people to tell the legislature what to do. When the question of popular influence arose in the ratification debates, the discussion concerned how extensive it should be in a mixed constitution. When the anti-federalists attacked the "aristocratic" character of the Constitution, the context was either completely general – any rule by a strong federal government was aristocratic – or it concerned two issues: the size of the House of Representatives and the terms of senators. The question was not whether to have a mixed constitution but how strong the democratic element should be.

Discussions and debates over the rule of the few versus of the many were rare during the state nominating conventions. The issue was raised during the New York convention by Melancton Smith who said that the size of the House of Representatives presented the

---

[143]   Banning, *Jeffersonian Persuasion* 92.
[144]   Michael J. Klarman, *The Framers' Coup* (Oxford, 2016), x.
[145]   Ibid. 540.
[146]   Gordon Wood, *Friends Divided: John Adams and Thomas Jefferson* (Kindle ed., 2017), 172.

larger question of "the qualifications which this house ought to possess, in order to exercise their power discreetly for the happiness of the people."[147] He claimed that unless the membership of the House was increased, "this government is so constituted that the representatives will generally be composed of the first class in the community, which I shall distinguish by the name of the natural aristocracy of the country."[148] "The Author of nature has bestowed on some greater capacities than others; birth, education, talents, and wealth, create distinctions among men as visible, and of as much influence, as titles, stars, and garters."[149] They are a "natural aristocracy."

He did not wish to "exclude the first class in the community from any share in legislation." "But my idea is, that the Constitution should be so framed as to admit this class, together with a sufficient number of the middling class to control them. You will then combine the abilities and honesty of the community, a proper degree of information, and a disposition to pursue the public good."[150] His argument is what one would expect in a debate over the respective importance of aristocracy and democracy in a mixed constitution. All agreed that those who govern should use "their power discreetly for the happiness of the people" and "pursue the public good." The question was whether the few or the many were more likely to do so.

Pauline Maier believed that "Smith's position was the direct opposite of James Madison's." "To Madison, rule by the talented, disinterested few was most likely to serve the public good. Smith believed "the people themselves – that is the mass of ordinary, middle-class Americans" were most likely to do so.[151] She underestimates the extent to which, on the one hand, Madison also believed in "the genius of republican liberty" and, on the other, Smith believed in the contribution to be made by a "natural aristocracy." What the two had in common were the principles of a mixed constitution.

iii *Jeffersonian Democracy*

After the outbreak of the French Revolution, a debate over which principles are truly "republican" split the Republic into two antagonistic parties, the "republicans" led by Thomas Jefferson, and the "federalists" led by John Adams. Their opposition made the presidential election of 1800, in which Jefferson defeated Adams, one of the bitterest in American history. Jefferson called the election "the revolution of 1800," "as real a revolution in the principles of our government as that of 76."[152]

Both parties believed that the purpose of the government was to promote the common good. In 1804, Jefferson wrote to Adams' wife Abigail that this was the one principle on which he and her husband agreed. "Both of our political parties, at least the honest portions

---

[147] *Elliot's Debates* 245.
[148] Ibid. 245–46.
[149] Ibid. 246.
[150] Ibid. 248.
[151] Pauline Maier, *Ratification: The People Debate the Constitution 1797–1788* (New York, 2010), 355.
[152] Letter from Thomas Jefferson to Spencer Roane, 6 September 1819, *Papers of Thomas Jefferson, Retirement Series* 15 (Looney ed.), 16–19.

of them, agree conscientiously in the same object, the public good: but they differ essentially in what they deem the means of promoting that good."[153] Writers in the classical tradition had rested this principle on the rational and social nature of human beings. So did Jefferson. A human being is "formed for society,"[154] he said in 1799, and in 1814, "[t]he Creator would indeed have been a bungling artist had he intended man for a social animal, without planting in him social dispositions."[155]

They disagreed over another classical idea: the value of a mixed constitution which Adams defended and Jefferson attacked.

Along with Benjamin Rush, Jefferson accused Adams of abandoning the principles he championed in 1776. Adams answered that he believed and had always believed that "the best republic" was one of "Equal Laws resulting from a Ballance of three Powers the Monarchical, Aristocratical & Democratical."[156] The "three ballanced Branches, ought to be at Stated Periods elected by the People."[157] Because of its three balanced branches, the English constitution was superb. In one of his letters to Rush, he said: "I deny, that there is or ever was in Europe a more free Republic than England, or that any Liberty on Earth ever equaled English liberty, notwithstanding the defects in their Constitution."[158]

It was Jefferson, not Adams, whose opinions had changed. Gordon Wood noted, in 1776, "[f]or the Americans the English constitution was always 'the glorious fabrick of Britain's liberty,' 'the palladium of civil liberty ... that firm foundation of the nation's peace,' 'the monument of accumulated wisdom, and the admiration of the world.'"[159] "The Americans to the very end of the imperial controversy justified their constitutional opposition to English policy not by abjuring the theory of mixed government but by using and affirming it."[160] Lance Banning observed that "the theory of the mixed and balanced constitution ... acquired a virtually unchallenged hold."[161]

---

[153] Letter from Thomas Jefferson to Abigail Smith Adams, 11 September 1804, *The Papers of Thomas Jefferson* 44 (McClure, ed.), 379–80.

[154] Letter from Thomas Jefferson to William G. Munford, 18 June 1799, *The Papers of Thomas Jefferson, 1 February 1799–31 May 1800*, Barbara B. Oberg, ed. (Princeton, 2004), 126–30.

[155] Letter from Jefferson to Thomas Law, June 13, 1814, in Thomas Jefferson, *Writings*, Merrill Peterson, ed. (New York, 1984), 1335–37. Similarly, "Man was destined for society. His morality therefore was to be formed to this object. He was endowed with a sense of right and wrong merely relative to this. This sense is as much a part of his nature as the sense of hearing, seeing, feeling." Letter from Thomas Jefferson to Peter Carr, 10 August 1787, *Papers of Thomas Jefferson* 12 (Boyd ed.), 14–19.

[156] Letter from John Adams to Benjamin Rush, 4 April 1790, *Founders Online*, National Archives, http://founders.archives.gov/documents/Adams/99-02-02-0903.

[157] Letter from John Adams to Benjamin Rush, 24 July 1789, *Founders Online*, National Archives, http://founders.archives.gov/documents/Adams/99-02-02-0700.

[158] Ibid.

[159] Wood, *Creation* 11 quoting James Wilson, "Considerations on the Nature and Extent of the Legislative Authority of the British Parliament" (Philadelphia, 1774) in *The Works ... of James Wilson* 3, Bird Wilson, ed. (Philadelphia 1804), 220.

[160] Wood, *Creation* 201.

[161] Ibid. 201.

Jefferson was no exception. In 1776, he said that the spirit of republicanism "so far from being incompatible with the British constitution, ... is the greatest glory of it."[162] In the *Declaration of Independence*, he said, not that the English constitution was oppressive, but that the English government was attempting, despotically, to deprive the colonists of their rights. When the French Revolution broke out in 1789, while acknowledging its defects, he urged his French friends to take the English constitution as their model.[163] Two years later, he described the English constitution as a "Half-way house" and the idealization of it as a danger to the American Republic.[164]

Similarly, Jefferson turned against the principle of a mixed constitution only after 1790. In 1787, Adams had defended the principles of a mixed constitution in a book he sent Jefferson, the first volume of *Defence of the Constitutions of Government of the United States of America*. Jefferson commended the book warmly. In the preface, Adams said that "the nature of monarchy, aristocracy, and democracy, and the advantages and inconveniences of each" had been understood since ancient times, and a "variety of mixtures of these simple species were conceived and attempted, with various success, by the Greeks and the Romans."[165] "There can be no free government without a democratical branch in the constitution."[166] Yet the power of the "democratical" branch must be balanced by those of the monarchical and aristocratic.[167] Jefferson wrote to Adams, objecting to a minor point in the conclusion, but assuring him "I have read your book with infinite satisfaction and improvement. It will do great good in America. Its learning and its good sense will I hope make it an institute for our politicians, old as well as young."[168] He promised to help with a French translation.[169] Adams replied: "The approbation you express in general of my poor Volume, is a vast consolation to me."[170]

[162] Thomas Jefferson, "Summary View" in *Papers of Thomas Jefferson* 1 (Boyd ed.), 131; *Philadelphia Pennsylvania Gazette*, Oct. 8, 1776, cited in Wood, *Creation* 45 n. 110.

[163] Wood, *Friends Divided* 225. In 1789, he wrote to Edward Bancroft, "The National assembly are wise, firm and moderate. They will establish the English constitution, purged of its numerous and capital defects." Letter from Thomas Jefferson to Edward Bancroft, 5 August 1789 in *Papers of Thomas Jefferson* 15 (Boyd ed.), 332–33.

[164] Letter from Thomas Jefferson to George Mason, 4 February 1791 in ibid. 19:241–243. Similarly see Letter from Thomas Jefferson to Lafayette, 16 June 1792, *The Papers of Thomas Jefferson* 24, John Catanzariti ed. (Princeton, 1990), 85–86.

[165] John Adams, *Defense of the Constitutions of the United States*, in *The Works of John Adams* 6, Charles Francis Adams, ed. (Boston 1856), 284.

[166] Ibid. 289.

[167] Ibid. 291.

[168] Letter from Thomas Jefferson to John Adams, 23 February 1787, *Papers of Thomas Jefferson* 11 (Boyd ed.), 176–77.

[169] In *The Creation of the American Republic*, published in 1998, Wood said that "[a]fter only a cursory, reading, Jefferson told Adams that 'it would do a great deal of good.'" Wood, *Creation of the American Republic* 581. Wood cited not Jefferson's letter in response to the first volume, but one he wrote months later after receiving the second volume. In the later letter he said that the pressure of other business "has only permitted me to look into it a little. I judge of it from the first volume." Letter from Thomas Jefferson to John Adams, 28 September 1787 in *Papers of Thomas Jefferson* 12 (Boyd ed.), 189–90. In *Friends Divided*, published in 2017, Wood said that "[l]ike most people receiving a gift from a friend of such a dense and massive tome, Jefferson was eager to assure the author that he actually had dipped into the book, and the best way to do that was to object to a minor point in the conclusion." Wood, *Friends Divided* 217. The argument is conclusory. Wood's only reason for thinking Jefferson did not even read the Preface is his premise that Jefferson would have disagreed with it.

[170] Letter from John Adams to Thomas Jefferson, 1 March 1787, *Papers of Thomas Jefferson* 11 (Boyd ed.), 188–90.

According to Gordon Wood, "it's clear that Jefferson did not read the book from cover to cover – who could blame him? – for if he had, he would have been deeply disturbed by so much that ran against the grain of his own thinking, indeed, that challenged almost everything that he believed."[171] As we will see, a more plausible explanation is that during the course of the French Revolution, Jefferson changed his mind. He no longer held the view of mixed government that he did in 1787.

In the 1790s, Jefferson began to sound like Thomas Paine. Paine had written *The Rights of Man* in response to Edmund Burke's *Reflections of the Revolution in France*. Burke praised the English constitution and attacked that of revolutionary France. According to Paine, Burke was wrong. Unlike the English constitution, the French assemblies represented the people. One source of the error was the theory of mixed government. According to Paine, "[i]n a well constituted republic, the parts are not foreigners to each other, like democracy, aristocracy and monarchy." Though powers may be "arranged into legislative and executive, they all have one natural source" which is "representation."[172]

> [W[hen Government is mentioned under the distinct, or combined heads of monarchy, aristocracy, and democracy, what is it that reasoning Man is to understand by the terms? If there really existed in the world two, or more, distinct and separate elements of human power, we should then see the several origins to which those terms would descriptively apply; but as there is but one species of man, there can be but one element of human power; and that element is man himself. Monarchy, aristocracy, and democracy, are but creatures of imagination; and a thousand such may be contrived, as well as three.[173]

In the 1790s, Jefferson, like Paine, abandoned the idea that there are three legitimate forms of government. As he later explained, the ancient city states knew only "democracy" on the one hand and "aristocracy" or "tyranny" on the other.

> I think little edification can be obtained from their writings on the subject of government. They had just ideas of the value of personal liberty; but none at all of the structure of government best calculated to preserve it. they knew no medium between a democracy (the only pure republic, but impracticable beyond the limits of a town) and an abandonment of themselves to an aristocracy, or a tyranny, independant of the people.[174]

Jefferson concluded that little could be learned from "the political writings of Aristotle, or of any other antient."[175]

Paine and Jefferson defined a "republic" as government by representatives of the people. According to Paine, it is a "government by election and representation."[176] According to Jefferson, it means a government, by its citizens, in mass, acting directly and personally,

---

[171]   Wood, *Friends Divided* 217.
[172]   Thomas Paine, *The Rights of Man; Being an Answer to Mr. Burke's Attack on the French Revolution* (London, 1817), 94.
[173]   Ibid. 94.
[174]   Letter from Thomas Jefferson to Isaac H. Tiffany, 26 August 1816 in *Papers of Thomas Jefferson*, Retirement Series 10 (Looney ed.), 349.
[175]   Ibid.
[176]   Paine, *Rights of Man* 92.

according to rules established by the majority: and that every other government is more or less republican in proportion as it has in its composition more or less of this ingredient of the direct action of the citizens."[177] The "controul of the people over the organs of their government" is "the measure of its republicanism."[178]

Although Madison had also defined a "republic" as "a government in which the scheme of representation takes place,"[179] and contrasted it with a "pure democracy" in which the citizens govern directly, his views were not those of Paine. They "sharply diverged," as Andreas Kalyvas and Ira Katznelson noted. "For Madison, [representation] was, among other purposes, a check on pure majoritarianism and on unbridled passion. For Paine it was a means to better actualize democratic values." "Madison ... understood representation as a limiting corrective to democracy, whereas Paine thought representation to be the key means by which to enhance democracy."[180] The views of Jefferson were like those of Paine. As Gordon Wood observed, *The Rights of Man* "opposed much of what Adams favored and said everything Jefferson believed in. Indeed, if Jefferson had every systematically written out his thoughts on government, the book would have resembled *The Rights of Man*."[181]

After Jefferson's election in 1800, the federalist party withered. Though it had revived briefly during the War of 1812, by 1817, the federalists were competitive only in Massachusetts and Delaware. They lost both those states to the republicans by 1823.[182] The battle was over. An Era of Good Feeling began. John Adams' son, John Quincy Adams, declared his conversion to republican principles. As Wood noted, in the nineteenth century, the distinctions between the three forms of government and their place in a mixed constitution, which had figured in political thought from Aristotle to Adams, fell out of political discourse. These ideas began to do so with Jefferson's electoral victory. In 1813, after Jefferson and Adams had renewed their friendship, Adams wrote Jefferson of his surprise when an anonymous author published "an Attack by name for the doctrines of Aristocracy in my 3 Volumes of 'Defence.'" "I thought my Books as well as myself were forgotten."[183]

To the puzzlement of later historians, this great political battle, one of the bitterest in American history, was fought between two parties, each defending a constitution that the United States had already adopted, which neither party seriously proposed to change. Adams would have been happier with an executive veto on legislation,[184] but he never sought one, even when his party was in power. He never proposed instituting a hereditary

---

[177] Letter from Thomas Jefferson to John Taylor, 28 May 1816 in *Papers of Thomas Jefferson* 10 (Looney ed.), 86–90.

[178] Ibid. 86–90.

[179] Madison, *Federalist* no. 10.

[180] Kalyvas and Katznelson, "Republic of the Moderns" 461, 466.

[181] Wood, *Friends Divided* 257.

[182] Richard P. McCormick, *The Second American Party System: Party Formation in the Jacksonian Era* (Chapel Hill, 1966), 23

[183] Letter from John Adams to Thomas Jefferson, 15 September 1813 in *Papers of Thomas Jefferson* 6 (Looney ed.), 503–05.

[184] Wood, *Friends Divided* 135.

monarch or aristocracy, and if he had, he would have failed, as Jefferson was well aware. Jefferson described those who were "preaching up and panting after an English constitution" as "preachers without followers," as the "people are firm and unanimous in their principles of republicanism."[185]

Jefferson said the Constitution contained a variety of "heresies,"[186] but never proposed to abolish them even after his party triumphed. He insisted that

> "the party called republican is steadily for the support of the present constitution. They obtained at it's commencement all the amendments to it they desired. these reconciled them to it perfectly, and if they have any ulterior view, it is only perhaps to popularise it further, by shortening the Senatorial term, and devising a process for the responsibility of judges more practicable than that of impeachment."[187]

After the fight was over and they had become friends and correspondents, Jefferson wrote to Adams that at least they agreed

> a constitution has been acquired which, tho neither of us think perfect, yet both consider as competent to render our fellow–citizens the happiest and the securest on whom the sun has ever shone. if we do not think exactly alike as to it's imperfections, it matters little to our country which, after devoting to it long lives of disinterested labor, we have delivered over to our successors in life, who will be able to take care of it, and of themselves.[188]

He had said that a constitution is republican to the degree that it allows for popular control of the government. He said that the fundamental issue at stake in the election of 1800 was who should rule: the people, or the upper classes:

> [A]fter all it is but a truth which exists in every country where not suppressed by the rod of despotism. men, according to their constitutions, and the circumstances in which they are placed, differ honestly in opinion. some are whigs, liberals, democrats, call them what you please; others are tories, serviles, aristocrats E^{t}C. the latter fear the people, and wish to transfer all power to the higher classes of society. the former consider the people as the safest depository of power, in the ultimate, they cherish them therefore, and wish to leave in them all the powers to the exercise of which they are competent. this is the division of sentiment now existing in the US. it is the common division of whig and tory, or, according to our denominations, of Republican and Federalist.[189]

Even on this point, his views had changed after 1790. In 1776, he had criticized the draft of a constitution for Virginia for allowing the people to elect the upper house or senate

---

[185] Letter from Thomas Jefferson to Lafayette, 16 June 1792 in *Papers of Thomas Jefferson* 24 (Catanzariti ed.), 85–86; Letter from Thomas Jefferson to Thomas Paine, 19 June 1792 in *Papers of Thomas Jefferson* 20 (Boyd ed.), 312–31.

[186] Letter from Thomas Jefferson to John Taylor, 28 May 1816 in *Papers of Thomas Jefferson* 10 (Looney ed.), 86–90.

[187] Letter from Thomas Jefferson to John Melish, 13 January 1813 in ibid. 5: 562–66.

[188] Letter from Thomas Jefferson to John Adams, 28 October 1813 in ibid. 6: 562–68.

[189] Letter from Thomas Jefferson to William Short, 8 January 1825, *Founders Online*, National Archives, http://founders.archives.gov/documents/Jefferson/98-01-02-4848. He concluded with the charitable sentiment, that it "is the most salutary of all divisions. it ought therefore to be fostered, instead of being amalgamated."

directly.[190] One needed "to get the wisest men chosen . . . I have ever observed that a choice by the people themselves is not generally distinguished for its wisdom."[191] When he received a draft copy of the United States Constitution in 1787, he expressed his fear that "house . . . chosen by the people directly . . . will be very illy qualified."[192]

Yet, after his victory in 1800, he did not propose that the Constitution be changed to reflect the suggestions of the "radical Whigs" of the late 1770s and 1780s: that all power be vested in a single assembly, that representatives be bound by instructions given them by their constituents, or that legislation should be ratified by the people. Yet the "radical Whigs" advocated these measures because they claimed, as Jefferson did, that the only legitimate source of political power was the will of the majority.

The disagreement between Adams and Jefferson was not over the Constitution that was already in place. It was over the principles on which government and the Constitution ultimately rested. For Adams, the best republic was one of "Equal Laws resulting from a Ballance of three Powers the Monarchical, Aristocratical & Democratical."[193] The "three ballanced Branches, ought to be at Stated Periods elected by the People."[194] The strength of the United States Constitution was that it effected such a balance. As we have seen, Madison also described the merits of the Constitution as a balance among these three elements although Madison did not use the terms "monarchy" and "aristocracy." Jefferson thought that the "controul of the people over the organs of their government" is "the measure of its republicanism."[195]

Ironically, Jefferson could have used the theory of mixed government to attack the English constitution. He could have defended the rule of the people against that of the upper classes without discarding that theory.

---

[190] *Notes on the State of Virginia* in *Writings* (Peterson, ed.), 123, 244–45.

[191] Letter from Thomas Jefferson to Edmund Pendleton, 26 August 1776, *Papers of Thomas Jefferson* 1 (Boyd ed.), 503–06.

[192] Letter from Thomas Jefferson to James Madison, 20 December 1787, in Robert A. Rutland, Charles F. Hobson, William M. E. Rachal and Frederika J. Teute, eds., *The Papers of James Madison* 10 (Chicago, 1977), 335–39. Gordon Wood placed a different construction on Jefferson's letter. "In his response, Jefferson scarcely acknowledged Madison's sophisticated account of the thinking behind the Constitution. Instead, he set forth his objections to a president who could be continually reelected, and reaffirmed his 'principle that the will of the Majority should always prevail'" – precisely the point that Madison had most systematically questioned. Wood, *Friends Divided* 221–22. In the passage quoted, however, Jefferson had said, "After all, it is my principle that the will of the Majority should always prevail. If they approve the proposed Convention in all it's parts, I shall concur in it chearfully, in hopes that they will amend it whenever they shall find it work wrong." Jefferson was saying that the will of the majority should prevail in the ratification of the Constitution, not that that the Constitution did or should establish government by the majority. Adams had expressed the same view. "[I]f the House should establish a single Assembly as a Legislature, I confess it would grieve me to the very Soul. . . . However, the Right of the People to establish such a Government, as they please, will ever be defended by me, whether they choose wisely or foolishly." Letter from John Adams to Francis Dana, 16 August 1776, in *Adams Papers* 4 (Taylor, Lint, and Walker eds.), 465–67.

[193] Letter from John Adams to Benjamin Rush, 4 April 1790, *Founders Online*, National Archives, http://founders .archives.gov/documents/Adams/99-02-02-0903.

[194] Letter from John Adams to Benjamin Rush, 24 July 1789, *Founders Online*, National Archives, http://founders .archives.gov/documents/Adams/99-02-02-0700.

[195] Letter from Thomas Jefferson to John Taylor, 28 May 1816, *Papers of Thomas Jefferson* 10 (Looney ed.), 86–90.

As we have seen that theory of mixed government had been used to explain the role of the English monarchy and Parliament. These were originally feudal institutions which did not fit easily within the theory. For Aristotle, hereditary succession was an understandable but defective way to choose a monarch. A government by those of good birth is an oligarchy, not an aristocracy, which is government by the wise and virtuous.

One could defend a larger role for the people without questioning the theory. Some members of Jefferson's party said that their program was to strengthen the democratic part of the constitution against the monarchical and aristocratic parts. According to a pro-republican series of articles called "The Watchman":

> The great danger to be apprehended at present to our government is that the democratical part, that is the people, will lose their due and proper influence in the government. The sources of this danger are various: ... the influence made and increasingly in favor of the executive, the monarchical part, by the multiplicity of officers; ... the vast accumulation of property occasioned by the funding system, etc. in the hands of those who have been called the natural aristocracy.[196]

Jefferson's "republican principles" have shaped the way Americans think about their form of government. Popular representation is not regarded as one element in a constitution which is also monarchic and aristocratic. As for Jefferson, the cause of liberty has been identified with representative government. This conviction that the American Republic is founded on Jeffersonian principles is often taken for granted. Wood had to remind us that they were not the principles of the American revolutionaries. Neither were they the principles of the framers of the Constitution.

One effect of Jeffersonian principles was to promote an increase in popular participation in government. In 1800, the electors who chose the president were chosen by the state legislatures in ten states, and in only two states by popular vote. By 1824 they were chosen by the legislature in only six states, and after 1832 only in South Carolina. Typically, the electors were pledged in advance to vote for a certain candidate. Between 1800 and 1824, qualifications to vote were liberalized in several states; by 1824 all adult white males were entitled to vote except in three states. At the state level, more offices were made elective instead of appointive, and the size of election districts was reduced so that people traveled shorter distances to vote.[197] Moreover, more people voted. In the election of 1828, voter participation was double that of 1824: 57 percent compared with 27 percent.[198] Nearly a century later, in 1913, the 17th amendment to the Constitution provided that senators were to be elected by popular vote rather than appointed by state legislatures. In making use of their increased influence, the people did a far better job than Adams might have expected.

An increase in popular participation, however, was compatible with a theory of mixed government. Given the character of the American people, it would most likely have

---

[196] "The Watchman," no. 2, *Independent Chronicle*, Sept. 8, 1791, quoted in Banning, *Jeffersonian Persuasion* 139.

[197] McCormick, *The Second American Party System* 28–29.

[198] Lynn Hudson Parsons, *The Birth of Modern Politics: Andrew Jackson, John Quincy Adams, and the Election of 1828* (Oxford, 2009), 184

occurred without Jefferson's theory of democracy. In other ways, the enduring influence of this theory has created difficulties.

It became more difficult for Americans to understand their own constitution which was not founded on the principle that "controul of the people over the organs of their government" is "the measure of its republicanism."[199] It was founded on Madison's adaptation of the principles of a mixed constitution. There are more conflicts between a Madisonian Constitution and Jeffersonian principles than Jefferson himself was willing to admit.

More generally, Jeffersonian principles make it difficult to evaluate the proper role of nondemocratic features of government, many of which have arisen since Jefferson's times. We have seen the growth of new elites of professional politicians and administrative appointees. We have seen a growth in executive power. It is not helpful either to accept these changes uncritically or to reject them because they are undemocratic. It would be better to consider when a decision requires wisdom or ability that is less likely to be possessed by the people than by professionals appointed for their expertise. It would be better to consider when a decision requires the decisiveness and coherence that executive power can provide. In doing so, we will again be thinking in terms of a mixed constitution in which different roles are best played by the people, an elite, and a single person.

Another unfortunate consequence has been to mislead Americans about their contribution to the cause of liberty. They can be proud of their constitution. According to Jefferson and Paine, however, their form of government is republican rather than despotic because it is based on principles that were unknown before 1776. In fact, Jefferson and Paine formulated these principles in the 1790s. The principles on which the American Republic was founded belong to a classical tradition that can be traced at least to Aristotle. The framers believed, like many writers in the classical tradition, that a mixed form of government is better than any other. They did not believe that "control by the people" is "the measure of the republicanism" of any government, or that any government that is not republican is despotic.

The totalitarian governments that the United States has opposed were indeed despotic. On Aristotelian principles, totalitarianism might well be considered the simultaneous corruption of all three legitimate forms of government. A totalitarian government is based on a perverted idea of the common good which is not the pursuit of happiness as classically understood. It concentrates power in a leader whose qualification is to unite the nation in a struggle against ideological enemies. It creates a ruling elite distinguished, not by its wisdom, but by its commitment to that ideology and its support for the leader. It denies the people a voice in government while demanding that their open, unambiguous, and enthusiastic support.

On Aristotelian principles, however, not all monarchies are tyrannies and not all aristocracies are oligarchies. Popular government may take good and bad forms. Before condemning a government as despotic, Americans would do well to face the possibility that Jefferson was wrong. Woodrow Wilson probably did not do so when he called World War

---

[199] Letter from Thomas Jefferson to John Taylor, 28 May 1816 in *Papers of Thomas Jefferson* 10 (Looney ed.), 86–90.

I a war to "make the world safe for democracy" and supported peace terms that dethroned two dynasties and created short-lived republics. Americans condemn national chauvinism. But the Jeffersonian persuasion can become a chauvinism of principles in which the American mission is to mold the world in its own image. One can be proud of oneself without thinking that everyone else ought to be the same.

In any event, Jeffersonian principles triumphed at the expense of one classical idea: the theory of mixed government. Neither Jefferson nor anyone else questioned another classical idea: that the purpose of government is to pursue the common good, and that the inclination to pursue it, as Jefferson said, is grounded in human nature.

IV THE EMERGENCE OF A DEMOCRATIC SOCIETY

After Jefferson's term of office, he and Adams again became friends and correspondents. In one letter, Jefferson tried to sum up their differences, "not with a view to controversy, for we are both too old to change opinions which are the result of a long life of enquiry and reflection; but on the suggestion of a former letter of yours that we ought not to die before we have explained ourselves to each other."

> I agree with you that there is a natural aristocracy among men. the grounds of this are virtue & talents. .... the natural aristocracy I consider as the most precious gift of nature, for the instruction, the trusts, and government of society. .... may we not even say that that form of government is the best which provides the most effectual[ly] for a pure selection of these natural aristoi into the offices of government?[200]

He said that, unlike Adams, he believed that the people were the best judges of who the natural aristocrats were.

> [O]n the question, What is the best [pro]vision? you and I differ; but we differ as rational friends, using the free exerci[se] of our own reason, and mutually indulging it's errors. ... I think the best remedy is exactly that provided by all our constitutions, to leave to the citizens the free election and separation of the aristoi from the pseudo–aristoi, of the wheat from the chaff. in general they will elect the real good and wise."[201]

The "pseudo-aristoi" were those called oligarchs in the Aristotelian tradition: those whose claim to govern was based on birth. In the same letter to Adams, Jefferson said that in Virginia, they had "laid the axe to the root of Pseudo–aristocracy" in 1776 by enacting "laws, drawn by myself" that abolished entailed estates and primogeniture. "[H]ad another which I prepared been adopted by the legislature, our work would have been compleat."

This other, "A Bill for the More General Diffusion of Knowledge," would have ensured that the natural aristocrats could be educated to rule from their youth even if they came

---

[200]   Letter from Thomas Jefferson to John Adams, 28 October 1813 in *Papers of Thomas Jefferson* 6 (Looney ed.), 562–68.

[201]   Ibid.

from poor families.[202] It would have established "free schools to teach reading, writing, and common arithmetic."[203] "[A]fter the most diligent and impartial examination and enquiry ... some one of the best and most promising genius and disposition" would be chosen to attend the district schools where they would learn Latin, Greek, English grammar, and more advanced mathematics.[204] "A certain number of the most promising" would be admitted to a "University, where all the useful sciences should be taught. worth and genius would thus have been sought out from every condition of life, and compleatly prepared by education for defeating the competition of wealth & birth for public trusts."[205] The goal, according to the Preamble, was to secure "wise and honest" lawmakers and administrators by providing a "liberal education" to those persons, "whom nature hath endowed with genius and virtue" and so "promot[e] the publick happiness."

For Adams, the natural aristocrats were gentlemen, by which he meant the well-educated. They might be born into any social class.

> By gentlemen are not meant the rich or the poor, the high-born or the low-born, the industrious or the idle: but all those who have received a liberal education, an ordinary degree of erudition in liberal arts and sciences. Whether by birth they be descended from magistrates and officers of government, or from husbandmen, merchants, mechanics, or laborers, whether they be rich or poor.[206]

Nevertheless, Adams believed, "leisure for study must ever be the portion of the few." "With all the encouragements, public and private, which can ever be given to general education ... the laboring part of the people can never be learned." Gentlemen were therefore an aristocracy, albeit a natural aristocracy. In a mixed constitution, both of "[t]hese parties will be represented in the legislature, and must be balanced, or one will oppress the other."

Although Jefferson believed that the "controul of the people over the organs of their government" is "the measure of its republicanism,"[207] he expected the people to elect the natural aristocrats. For Adams, in contrast, although gentlemen might come from any social class, they were a natural aristocracy, but an aristocracy nonetheless.

To the generation of Jefferson and Adams, entrusting government to gentlemen distinguished by education and not by birth was a republican ideal. Moreover, it was one which seemed to have been realized within their own lifetimes. As Gordon Wood observed, this

---

[202] It was presented in the Virginia House of Delegates in 1778 and 1780, but it did not pass either then or when Madison presented it several more times while Jefferson was in Paris, although a revised version did pass in 1796.

[203] 79. A Bill for the More General Diffusion of Knowledge, 18 June 1779, sec. VI, *Papers of Thomas Jefferson* 2 (Boyd ed.), 526–35.

[204] Ibid. secs. XIII, XVI.

[205] Sec. XIX of the Bill was more specific: "after diligent examination and enquiry as before directed, shall chuse one among the said seniors, of the best learning and most hopeful genius and disposition, who shall be authorised by them to proceed to William and Mary College, there to be educated, boarded, and clothed, three years."

[206] Adams, *Defense* 185.

[207] Letter from Thomas Jefferson to John Taylor, 28 May 1816 in *Papers of Thomas Jefferson* 10 (Looney ed.), 86–90.

ideal had a particular appeal in the American colonies. "America, 'just emerging,' as William Livingston said, 'from the rude unpolished Condition of an Infant Country,' was primed to receive these new republican standards of gentility. The colonists were eager to create a new kind of aristocracy, based on principles that could be learned and were superior to those of birth and family, and even great wealth."[208]

One could become a gentleman, then, in a single generation, and many in the generation of the founders of the Republic had done just that. Wood observed: "It is extraordinary, to say the least, to realize what a high proportion of the revolutionary leaders were first-generation gentlemen. That is to say, many were the first in their families to attend college, to acquire a liberal arts education, and to display the marks of an enlightened eighteenth-century gentleman."[209] He added: "We shall never understand the unique character of the revolutionary generation until we appreciate the seriousness with which they took these new republican ideas of what it was to be a gentleman. No generation in American history has ever been so self-conscious about the moral and social values necessary for public leadership."[210]

These leaders had defied Britain, led the colonies to independence and to unity, debated the principles of liberty and good government, and framed constitutions. They seemed to have realized an ancient ideal of what a gentleman should be. It was Cicero's ideal of a *vir virtutis*, a complete man, cultivated and fit for an active role in public life. It was the Renaissance ideal of a gentleman formed by the *studia humanitatis*, an education that would inculcate moral virtue, practical wisdom, and a correct and eloquent command of language through the study of classical languages and authors. That ideal was accepted by the hereditary elite of England. But, as Wood noted, it "had special appeal for the outlying provinces of the greater British world . . . [which] lacked the presence of the great hereditary noble families that were at the controlling center of English life."[211] Government was now in the hands of a natural aristocracy, not one based on birth. The qualifications for leadership, they assumed, would be the same in every generation as long as the Republic endured.

To the wonderment of their fellow citizens, Jefferson and Adams died with a few hours of each other on July 4, 1826, fifty years after the Declaration of Independence was signed. By that date, the influence of the federalists had disappeared. Leadership remained in the hands of an elite, albeit an elite committed to Jeffersonian principles. Presidential candidates were chosen by a caucus of congressional leaders. With its blessing, James Madison and then James Monroe were nominated for president. Candidates for other offices, state and national, were "self-nominated, or were put forward by 'friends,' and voters responded as individuals rather than in terms of party identities,"[212] and in which "those who were recognized at the time as 'gentry' wielded decisive influence."[213]

---

[208]   Gordon S. Wood, *The Radicalism of the American Revolution* (New York, 1991), 195.
[209]   Ibid. 197.
[210]   Ibid.
[211]   Ibid. 195.
[212]   McCormick, *Second American Party System* 20.
[213]   Ibid. 30.

In 1824, the republicans were unable to unite behind a single candidate. John Adams' son, John Quincy Adams, was supported by northern voters, but the south favored Andrew Jackson, and the west favored Jackson or Henry Clay. Adams became president. Jackson then defeated Adams in 1828 in the bitterest election since 1800.

The contest between Adams and Jackson turned on the characters of the two men, on regional loyalties, and on alternative ideas about the role of government. It was also a referendum on rule by a "natural aristocracy" of the well-educated. An opponent of Jackson asked: "What will the English malignants ... the Edinburgh and Quarterly reviewers ... say of a people who want a man to govern them who cannot spell more than about one word in four?"[214] The *Washington Journal* conceded, "Mr. Adams is a scholar. Is he to be superseded by a man of no education?" It answered: Yes. "[A] close application to books, and a consequent banishment from society and neglect of living models render a man ignorant of human nature." Nevertheless, "[h]e may be a philosopher, a lawyer, an elegant scholar, and a poet ... yet the nation may be little better off for all these endowments and accomplishments." "[N]o person can have a correct knowledge of mankind who has led a life of abstraction from the great body of the people, and who relies for this information on the books he has read. "[215]

In fact, Adams had as much experience with men as with books. He had been a successful diplomat since his youth. But the fear of the *Washington Journal* was like that of Melancton Smith: a member of the elite would be out of touch with the feelings of the common man. Unlike Smith, however, the *Washington Journal* thought such a man was suitable for President.

As Lynn Parsons observed:

> The emerging egalitarian rhetoric of second-generation American republicanism suggests that voters were more comfortable with candidates who were closer to them in education and experience. No one in the earlier generation claimed that Washington, Jefferson, Adams or Madison was an ordinary American. The letters that passed between John Adams and Thomas Jefferson in their old age were sprinkled with passages in French, Latin, and even in Greek. Most voters were unversed in those languages and might even be suspicious of a candidate who was. It was more important in this, the second quarter of the 19th century, to be, or at least to appear to be, closer to the electorate.[216]

One reason for the change may have been that popular participation in government had increased. But that change would not have mattered but for a shift in popular opinion as to who is best qualified to govern. According to Gordon Wood, "[e]verywhere in the early republic northern aristocrats were besieged relentlessly, mercilessly, in print and in speeches ... by countless numbers of common ordinary people who had never been to

---

[214] Anonymous, *An Impartial and True History of the Life and Services of Major General Andrew Jackson* (n.p., n. d.) 40 quoted in Parsons, *Birth of Modern Politics*, 165.

[215] Quoted in ibid. 166–67.

[216] Ibid. 91.

college – artisans, traders, and businessmen – and who . . . had felt the deprivations of being common and ordinary."[217]

Wood maintained that this change was the direct consequence of the American revolution although he acknowledged that "the American revolutionaries . . . could scarcely have imagined . . . how much of their society they would change."[218] "Here in this destruction of aristocracy, including Jefferson's 'natural aristocracy,' was the real American Revolution – a radical alteration in the nature of American society whose effects are still being felt today."[219] "The Revolution brought respectability and even dominance to ordinary people."[220] "By the early years of the nineteenth century the Revolution had created a society fundamentally different from the colonial society of the eighteenth century. It was in fact a new society unlike any that had ever existed in the world."[221] "And this astonishing transformation took place without industrialization, without urbanization, without railroads, without the aid of any of the great forces we usually invoke to explain 'modernization.' It was the Revolution that was crucial to this transformation."[222]

It would have been a different republic if the majority of Americans had continued to choose "gentlemen" for their leaders. Had the people done so, the political leaders of the United States, like those of Song China, would have been chosen from an elite who had received an education in classics which, for Western humanists, as for Chinese Confucians, was the defining characteristic of a gentleman and believed to be the best preparation for public life. These American gentlemen, however, would have been answerable to the majority of the people; in Song China, they were answerable to the emperor.

Principles matter, but it is a mistake to think that there was a logical progression from the principles of American revolutionaries and of the framers of the Constitution, to the principles of Jefferson, to the "destruction of aristocracy" described by Wood. Had it not been for the French Revolution, Jefferson might not have arrived at his principles. His election was followed, not by the destruction of aristocracy, but by the election of Madison and Monroe at the federal level and at the state and county level by the "decisive influence" of "those who were recognized at the time as 'gentry.'"[223]

The transformation that Wood described was not the consequence of the principles of the Revolution, of the framers of the Constitution, or of Jefferson. It was the response of Americans to the opportunity that these principles afforded them to participate in government. It is remarkable that that this response came as such a surprise to Jefferson and other leaders of the American Revolution. Adams had written to John Dickenson Sergeant in 1776, "It grieves me to hear that your People have a Prejudice against liberal Education." To "Soften and eradicate this Prejudice" "Gentlemen of Education" should "lay aside Some of their Airs, of Scorn, Vanity and Pride, which it is a certain Truth that they

---

[217] Wood, *Radicalism of the American Revolution*, 275.
[218] Ibid. 5.
[219] Ibid. 276.
[220] Ibid. 7–8.
[221] Ibid. 6.
[222] Ibid. 7.
[223] McCormick, *Second American Party System* 30.

Sometimes indulge themselves in."[224] If this "prejudice" was widespread in 1776, was it realistic for Adams or Jefferson to expect the people to accept the leadership of an educated elite indefinitely?

Aristotle, as we have seen, suggested that whether an aristocracy or a democracy is the best form of government depends what the people are prepared to accept. A people who can "submit to be ruled as freemen by men whose virtue renders them capable of political command are adapted for an aristocracy."[225] In contrast, "people who are suited for constitutional freedom are those among whom there naturally exists a ... multitude able to rule and to obey in turn by a law which gives office to the well-to-do according to their desert."[226]

Americans did not submit to government by "natural aristocrats." Yet, although the seeds of change had been sown by the American Revolution, they ripened only in the early years of the nineteenth century. By the time Jackson was elected, Americans had fifty years of experience with self-government. They had learned by experience to exercise power. They had become, in their own judgment, "a multitude able to rule." "To rule and obey in turn," however, is not an option except in Greek city states. The question arose, how are leaders to be chosen when they are no longer members of an identifiable elite? The answer, we will see, was the development of political parties.

V PRINCIPLES COMPROMISED

i *Violations of Principle: Slavery and Conquest*

As we have seen, the principles on which the American Republic was founded belonged to a classical tradition that can be traced back to Aristotle. There were two violations of these principles that Americans were to remember with shame. One was to permit slavery, which writers in the Aristotelian tradition had condemned though Aristotle had not. The other was to deprive indigenous peoples of their land and their independence, which had been condemned by the late scholastic critics of the Spanish expansion in the New World.

It is not an anachronism to see slavery as violating not only the words but the principle of the Declaration of Independence that "[a]ll men are created equal." In the Aristotelian tradition, as we have seen, all human beings are equal in that they all have the same end: the pursuit of a distinctively human life. Two centuries before the foundation of the American Republic, writers in the Aristotelian tradition had concluded that Aristotle himself was wrong to believe that some are natural slaves.[227] Lessius said, "All men according to their natural condition are equal; as they are of the same nature, of the same parents, and constituted for the same end." He concluded that "no one by nature is a slave."[228] Since a human being is

---

[224] Letter from John Adams to Jonathan Dickinson Sergeant, 21 July 1776, *Adams Papers* 4 (Taylor, Lint, and Walker eds.), 397–98.
[225] *Politics* III. xvii. 1288a.
[226] Ibid.
[227] Ibid. I.v.1254b.
[228] Lessius *De iustitia et iure* lib, 2, cap. 4, dub. 9 no. 54.

a rational animal, directed to his end by reason, it is not possible, according to Vitoria and las Casas, that a large part of the human race is born defective in intellect.[229]

Vitoria and las Casas concluded that it was it was unjust for the Spaniards to enslave the indigenous peoples in the New World. Indeed, it was unjust to deprive them of their property or their independence. Since people could only live a distinctively human life by living in society and instituting government, they said that the governments of the indigenous peoples were legitimate. They were entitled to form governments of their own whatever their state of civilization and whatever their religion might be.[230] They had the same right as anyone else to the land that they possessed. The Spanish Empire in the New World was illegal.

The Spanish did not give up their empire. The American Republic did not recognize that the indigenous peoples had any rights that the government could not take away. The question came before the United States Supreme Court in 1823 in *Johnson* v. *M'Intosh*.[231] The plaintiff had purchased land from the Piankeshaw Indians. Later, the defendant had purchased the same land from the United States. Justice Marshall held that the United States held title to all the lands occupied by Indians, and therefore the Piankeshaw could not convey title to the plaintiff. The Indians had merely a right to occupy land until the United States granted it to someone else.

> While the different nations of Europe respected the right of the natives, as occupants, they asserted ultimate dominion to be in themselves; and claimed and exercised, as a consequence of this ultimate dominion, a power to grant the soil, while yet in possession of the natives. These grants have been understood by all, to convey a title to the grantees, subject only to the Indian right of occupancy.[232]
>
> Conquest gives a title which the Courts of the conqueror cannot deny, whatever he private and speculative opinions of individuals may be, respecting the original justice of the claim which has been successfully asserted. … The title by conquest is acquired and maintained by force."[233]

Vitoria and las Casas would have disagreed. Vitoria is called the founder of international law because he recognized that if, as Aristotle said, people must live in society, then every society has the right to establish a government of its own consistent with the good of that society. The American Republic had declared its independence on the basis of that right.

---

[229] Vitoria said that "God and nature are not deficient in that which is necessary for a large part of the species: in man, however, the foremost is reason." Francisco de Vitoria, *De Indis*, in Alonso Getinao, ed., *Relecciones del Maestro Fray Francisco de Vitoria* 1 (Asociación Franciso de Vitoria, 1933) 348 at 361, no. 23. Las Casas made the same argument: "By nothing other than the intellect is the nature of man perfected." Therefore, to be born with a defective intellect must be, like any other birth defect, "most rare." Bartolomaeus de las Casas, *Apología o Declaración y Defensa Universal de los Derechos de Hombe y de los Pueblos* Vidal Abril Castelló et al. eds. (Junta de Castilla, 2000), cap. iii p. 25 (in Latin and Spanish).

[230] Vitoria, *De Indis* no. 7.

[231] 21 U.S. 543 (1823).

[232] Ibid. 574.

[233] Ibid. 589.

ii *The Party System*

The compromises we have just described were violations of principle. If all men are created equal, no one should be a slave. If the American colonists have a right to a government of their own choosing, so should the indigenous peoples of North America.

Another sort of compromise does not violate a principle but endeavors to make it workable at the cost of diluting or distorting it. That sort of compromise had to occur to make electoral democracy workable. As the society and its government became more democratic, the question arose, how are leaders to be chosen when they are no longer members of an identifiable elite? As Adams had observed:

> How shall the men of merit be discovered? When the government of a great nation is in question, shall the whole nation choose? Will such a choice be better than chance? Thirty millions of votes, for example, for each Senator in France! It is obvious that this would be a lottery of millions of blanks to one prize, and that the chance of having wisdom and integrity in a senator by hereditary descent would be far better. There is no individual personally known to a hundredth part of the nation.[234]

The rise of political parties was, in part, an answer to that question. In the new era of popular participation in government, parties played a different role than when Jefferson squared off against Adams. As Richard McCormick said, they became "electoral machines, engaged in nominating and electing candidates."[235] "It was recognized very early," he observed, "that if a party did not concentrate its vote behind a single candidate for each office, it would dissipate its strength and risk defeat."[236] A procedure was needed to secure agreement on a single candidate. That procedure was the nominating convention, which appeared in the mid-Atlantic states after 1824 and became universal by 1840.[237] As described by Parsons,

> [C]ounty "committees of correspondence" ... organized carefully staged county "conventions," consisting of delegates elected from the towns, often made up of as many as could afford the trip. The county conventions in turn chose delegates to state conventions, whose numbers were calculated according to the state's population or congressional representation or some combination thereof. ...
>
> The conventions tended to follow an established pattern that would be repeated for generations to come. First the faithful would sit through a number of speeches ... Resolutions would be proposed and adopted. Toasts would be offered, followed by dinner. Then speeches and resolutions would be reported and approved in friendly presses and denounced, dismissed or ridiculed by their opponents.[238]

---

[234] John Adams, *Discourses on Davila: A Series of Papers on Political History* in *The Works of John Adams* 6, Charles Francis Adams, ed. (Boston, 1851), 223 at 249–50.

[235] McCormick, *Second American Party System* 4.

[236] Ibid. 23.

[237] Ibid. 346; Parsons, *Birth of Modern Politics* 195.

[238] Parsons, *Birth of Modern Politics* 137–38.

Having nominated a candidate, the party's next task was to garner support from the voters. Campaigns were organized and often dramatic. To quote McCormick, the formation of parties

> brought into vogue a new campaign style. Its ingredients can scarcely be described with precision, but they included an emphasis on dramatic spectacles – such as the mass rally, the procession, and the employment of banners, emblems, songs, and theatrical devices – and on club-like associations, colorful personalities and emotionally charged appeals to party loyalty. Politics in this era took on a dramatic function. It enabled voters throughout the nation to experience the thrill of participating in what amounted to a great democratic festival."[239]

A candidate for office needed the support of a party to be nominated and elected. The party expected loyalty from the candidates it supported. The *National Intelligencer* accused Jackson's successor, Martin van Buren, who pioneered the development of political parties, of creating a "system of party discipline [that] procure[s] the rejection of nominations, not upon the question of honesty or fitness for trust, but upon the test of persons' having voted one way or another at a preceding election." The result is "to substitute the regular operation of the Government, and to control the popular election by means of organized clubs in the States, and organized presses every where."[240]

The newly formed parties sought and obtained the allegiance of voters, not simply to the candidates they nominated, but to the parties themselves. As McCormick observed "voters everywhere thought of themselves as Whigs or Democrats."[241]

According to McCormick, the people "eagerly assumed the identity of partisans, perhaps for much the same reasons that their descendants were to become Dodger fans, Shriners or rock-and-roll addicts. In this guise, at least, campaigns had little to do with government or public policy, or even with the choice of officials."[242] If that were so, the party system would be unfaithful to any version of the principles on which the Republic was founded, whether those of mixed government embraced by the framers or the "republican principles" of Jefferson. The party programs would not be coherent, thus defeating the advantages traditionally ascribed to the unified direction of an executive. The candidates chosen would not be the best, thus forfeiting the advantages traditionally ascribed to the wisdom and virtue of an elite. Popular participation would be blind. These advantages, however, still could be obtained, but now in large part through the competition between parties.

To be successful, each party had to claim that it had the best approach to government and public policy and that it had nominated the best of candidates. The Whigs were committed to one approach to government, the Democrats to another. Each party wished to select a candidate whom the voters would believe to be better than the nominee of the other party. Nevertheless, the people's choices were limited by the decisions of the party as

---

[239] McCormick, *Second American Party System* 349–50.
[240] Quoted in Parsons, *Birth of Modern Politics* 130.
[241] McCormick, *Second American Party System* 342.
[242] Ibid. 350.

to the proper approach to government and the candidates to nominate. Those restrictions on the options of the voters were inherent in the party system.

The Whigs and Democrats were committed to different approaches to government. In Parson's words: "One perspective, put forth by Adam's annual message of 1825, maintained that it was the function of government to improve the economic, educational, and moral condition of the citizenry. The other, that of most Jacksonians, was that the government's sole function was to protect liberty against power."[243]

Suppose a citizen believed that neither program addressed the true problems of the Republic. For example, neither addressed the issue of slavery. Or suppose a citizen believed that the value of either party's program depended on how it was executed: on the wisdom of measures adopted to improve the economic, educational, and moral condition of the citizenry or to protect liberty. That citizen would be reluctant to vote for either party and would not be nominated by either as a candidate.

The parties themselves were constrained as to the definiteness of the principles of government to which they could be committed. To be successful, the principles had to be sufficiently definite to inspire support. Nevertheless, they had to be sufficiently indefinite not to alienate too many voters whose opinions differed. They also had to be sufficiently indefinite to be endorsed by candidates of various opinions whom the party might wish to support because of their appeal to the voters.

The parties' nominations did not depend entirely on whom the party members or party leaders thought the majority of the people would consider to be the best qualified for office. Party loyalty mattered. So did consistency of the policies that a given candidate favored with the principles to which the party was committed. Having nominated a candidate, however, the party had to endorse the policies that candidate favored.

In 1828, Martin van Buren organized the first partisan convention to nominate a presidential candidate. Of the runners-up in the 1824 election, he eliminated John Calhoun and Henry Clay because Calhoun's (then) commitment to federalism and Clay's commitment to the "American system" conflicted with his party's commitment to a limited role for government. He eliminated William Crawford because he was too bland to appeal to the voters. The remaining candidate was Jackson.[244] So Jackson was nominated. The party was then committed to Jackson's policies of hostility to paper money, the Bank of the United States and to special corporate charters. One who opposed these policies might vote for Jackson because he favored the Democrats' approach to government and had no better choice. Had there been another popular military hero the Democrats could nominate, a Democratic victory would not have meant the endorsement of Jackson's policies.

The first Whig victory was in the presidential election of 1840. The Whigs had to choose between nominating Clay, who was committed to the American system, and William Henry Harrison, who was committed to very little. As Michael Holt has shown, support for the Whigs waxed and waned in proportion to the difficulties of the economy, which they

---

[243] Parsons, *Birth of Modern Politics* 187.
[244] Ibid. 125–26.

blamed on the incumbent Democrats. Clay, because he endorsed a definite policy, was in a better position than Harrison to claim that he could turn the economy around. On the other hand, his very commitment to a definite policy would alienate voters who did not share it. Harrison was nominated because the convention was held during a brief economic recovery.

> Support for Clay surged in 1837–38 but 1838–39 the economy recovered, and the Whigs held their convention before the impact of the price slump in late 1839 had been felt. Had they convened in May, 1840, when the Democratic national convention met, the results would probably have been different. The Whigs would have chosen someone with clear policies over a "noncommittal" military hero.[245]

Having nominated Harrison, the party was not committed to Clay's American system. Those who believed in the Whig approach to government and would have preferred Clay had little choice but to vote for Harrison.

The party system necessarily constrains the will of the majority which the framers' regarded as a necessary element in government and Jefferson regarded as its foundation. Yet the party system resolved a problem with representative government that Adams had described when he criticized the French National Assembly. "How shall the men of merit be discovered?" "There is no individual personally known to a hundredth part of the nation."[246]

One way to prevent the election from becoming a lottery would be for the people to accept nominations made by an elite, as they did before the Jacksonian era when candidates for president were nominated by congressional caucus and for local office by the local gentry. But when that alternative was rejected, political parties provided an alternative. Their function was to cull through potential candidates and decide whom to nominate, and then to conduct campaigns to convince voters of the merits of the nominee.

With the advent of the party system, according to Meyers, "[t]he winning of elections became to an unprecedented degree the business of professionals who managed powerful machines. Nevertheless

> they brought a novel intimacy to the relation between the people and politics. The political machine reached into every neighborhood, inducted ordinary citizens of all sorts into active service. Parties tended to be lively two-way channels of influence. Public opinion was heard with a new sensitivity and addressed with anxious respect. The bureaucratic science of machine politics was effective only in association with the popular art of pleasing the many. As never before, the parties spoke directly, knowingly, to the interests and feelings of the public.[247]

He may be right that, as never before, parties spoke to the interests and feelings of the people. To the degree that the parties interacting with the people provided coherent programs of action and selected the best candidates, the party system not only reflected

[245] Holt, *Political Parties* 187–88.
[246] Adams, *Discourses on Davila* 223 at 249–50.
[247] Meyers, *Jacksonian Persuasion* 7–8.

the people's interests and feelings but provided the unity and the wisdom also sought by the framers. Consider the alternative. To the extent that the electorate cannot not judge a candidate for office by his party allegiance or by the information about him that his party provides, the candidate must inform the public about himself. That requires resources. Where are they to come from? A definite possibility is that they will be supplied by the very special interests whose influence Madison wished to minimize, interests that are advanced at the expense of the common good. To make themselves known to the electorate, candidates must cater to them. And so the weakening of the traditional party system, with all of its undemocratic features, places power in the hands of those who are least likely to speak for the people.

To that degree, the traditional party system was faithful to the principles of the founders, although in a way that was as distant from what they had envisioned as the selection of the worthy by competitive examinations was distant from the thoughts of Confucius or Mencius. It was distant, but a workable compromise.

PART III

THE ECLIPSE OF CLASSICAL THOUGHT

In China and the West, the classical traditions we have described gave way to philosophies that grounded normative standards, not on human nature, but on eternal and immutable principles. This step was taken by the School of Principle whose most prominent members were Cheng Yi (1033–1107) and Zhu Xi (1130–1200). It was taken by Western rationalists, among them Francisco Suárez (1548–1611), Gottfried Wilhelm Leibniz (1646–1716), and Christian Wolff (1679–1754).

In China and the West, these philosophers were seeking a stronger foundation for normative standards. The founders of the School of Principle were responding to the intellectual challenge of Buddhism. Western rationalists were seeking a certainty comparable to that of mathematics.

These eternal and immutable principles were conceived differently in China and the West. For the School of Principle, all principles were ultimately one transcendental principle. As Angus Graham explained, although there is a difference in principle (理 *li*) whenever there is a difference among actions or objects, nevertheless "principle seems to be conceived as a network of veins: ... the veins prove ... to be one."[1] For the Western rationalists, immutable moral principles were necessary consequences of the definitions of concepts such as man and the good.

In both cases, these principles were believed to have a mode of being of their own. Considered in themselves, they are what they are, and exist eternally. Considered in another way, a principle or concept exists only when it is actualized: when it comes to exist in something that is not a concept. For the School of Principle, a principle exists, in this second sense, when it is embodied in *qi* or material. For the Western rationalists, the concept exists as a possible being. When actualized, it is a being that actually is. On account of these similarities, both philosophies can be described as forms of rationalism.

In neither case were normative standards grounded in human nature as the classical traditions had conceived it. The founders of the School of Principle claimed that they were faithful to the teachings of Mencius. Yet, for them, as Graham noted, human nature is not "the distinctive principle of man." "[N]ature is principle in general, and it includes within it the principles of all things."[2] The Western rationalists defined the good for a human being, or any other thing, as its "perfection." Unlike Aristotle and Aquinas, they did not

---

[1] A.C. Graham, *Two Chinese Philosophers: The Metaphysics of the Brothers Ch'êng* (La Salle. 1992), 13.
[2] Graham, *Two Chinese Philosophers* 56.

describe perfection in terms of human capacities to be perfected, or describe human capacities in terms of the ultimate end of leading a good life. Wolff claimed that his philosophy preserved the best insights of Aristotelian and scholastic philosophy. Yet for them, as Kant was later to claim, human perfection had become an abstract and empty concept.

Consequently, in both cases, a gap opened between cognition and motivation. Knowledge of these principles was regarded as a necessary and sufficient condition for moral action. The ultimate reason why a person should act in a certain way is that principle so demands. Why a person would want to do so was not clear. Writers in both classical traditions had examined the tension between desire and right action. They all had assigned a role to human desire in moral life, although their accounts differed. These philosophies did not.

The School of Principle and the Western rationalists held different views as to how principles are known. The School of Principle, drawing on Buddhism, thought that they could be known by meditation. If one investigated things, "[a]fter long thought, insight comes spontaneously;"[3] "penetration will come as a sudden realization."[4] Western rationalists, drawing on Western geometry, claimed that these principles could be derived from the definitions of concepts by deductive logic.

Writers in both classical traditions had tried to explain how human nature, which is invariant, can be the source of normative standards which can vary with convention and circumstance. For the School of Principle and for Western rationalists, the principles are invariant. The objects and events that compose our world are instantiations or actualizations of principles which are intelligible without it. A gap emerged between moral principles, which are static and unchanging, and the world of complex and constantly changing circumstances in which these principles were supposed to apply.

Because of these gaps, a problem arose concerning normative standards that had not existed in the classical traditions. If, as the School of Principle and the Western rationalists claimed, they are absolute, eternal, and invariable they seem to be divorced from human motivations and the contingencies of the world in which we act. The other possibility would seem to be that they are individual and subjective. That conclusion seems to call into question whether there is any real difference between right and wrong.

In China, the dichotomy between immutable principle and desire was attacked by Lu Hsiang-Shan (1139–93) and Wang Yangming (1472–1529). They attacked the School of Principle and founded what has been called the School of Universal Mind. They tried to close the gap by identifying principle with mind, and thought with desire and action. They denied that principles have, so to speak, an existence of their own. They exist in the mind, and the mind is principle. They denied that one first knows how to act and then acts in conformity to what he knows. Thought cannot be separated from desire or desire from action.

---

[3]　*Ho-nan Ch'êng-shi yi-shu.* BSS. 207/12f, from Graham, *Two Chinese Philosophers* 78.
[4]　Zhu Xi, *Complete Works* 44:13a–b.

The question then was whether, if principle is identical with mind, moral principles still should be regarded as immutable, as the School of Principle had taught. If so, morality is still a matter of following immutable principles. If not, moral standards are the result of thoughts and desires which do not correspond to immutable principles. If they are not grounded in such principles, then, it would seem, they are subjective. Some members of the School of Universal Mind concluded that they were.

In the West, David Hume showed that rationalism had created an unbridgeable gap between concept and motivation. A proposition about moral law, as the rationalists conceived it, merely described the relationship among concepts. It could not provide a motive for action. He described all motivations, including the motivation to do what is right, as feelings. "To have a sense of virtue," he said, "is nothing but to *feel* a satisfaction of a particular kind."[5]

Western thinkers then faced a dilemma like the one that had arisen in China. If, as Hume claimed, there are no universal and immutable standards of right and wrong, then, it seemed, there can only be subjective opinions. The last part of this book will describe how liberal political theorists in the West have tried to escape this dilemma.

---

[5]   *Treatise of Human Nature* (Oxford, 1888), 3.1.2.3, 471.

10

Neo-Confucianism

In China, the classical tradition was eclipsed by the rise of those whom Chung-yin Cheng called the "later Neo-Confucians": adherents of the School of Principle founded by Cheng Yi and Zhu Xi, and of the School of Universal Mind founded by Lu Hsiang-Shan and Wang Yangming. In the late Song dynasty, the School of Principle was declared to be the orthodox interpretation of Confucianism. The School of Universal Mind was its leading opponent. Nevertheless, "[it] is natural," as Cheng said, to consider them a group apart. They both "deviated from Classical Confucianism in two important respects; First, they completely objectified human reason into a nonhuman order of things" – a doctrine that the School of Principle formulated and "Wang Yangming subjectivised" by identifying principle with the mind. "A second deviation concerned the status of human nature in relation to its ideal of perfection and development."[6] Both schools lost track of human nature as Mencius understood it.

I BEYOND HUMAN NATURE: THE SCHOOL OF PRINCIPLE

Traditional Confucianism was concerned with nature and above all with human nature. The founders of the School of Principle, Cheng Yi (程颐) and Zhu Xi (朱熹), were later said to have blended Confucianism with Buddhism. Buddhism, like the Abrahamic religions, looked beyond nature to an ultimate reality: in Abrahamic religions, to God, a supreme Being and the architect of nature; in Buddhism, to non-being, either as ultimate reality – strange as that may sound – or as that which must be realized to arrive at ultimate reality. It seemed to give a more complete account of why things are as they are. Moreover, as William Theodore de Bary put it, Buddhism had "a way of dealing with the inner world of the spirit" that "Confucianism lacked." Confucianism, unlike Buddhism, had always been concerned "with the outer world of human affairs."[7]

In de Bary's opinion, Cheng Yi "succeeded in reconciling the two" traditions.[8] That was not his intention. Cheng Yi and Zhu Xi thought that Buddhist doctrine was false and

---

[6] Chung-ying Cheng, "Introduction," to Tai Chên, *Inquiry into Goodness* (Honolulu, 1971), 3 at 9–12.
[7] William Theodore de Bary, *Neo-Confucian Orthodoxy and the Learning of the Mind-and-Heart* (New York, 1981), 68.
[8] Ibid.

dangerous.[9] They wished to refute it, as Mencius had refuted Yang Zhu and Mozi. According to Cheng Yi:

> [Buddhist] doctrine has already become a fashion throughout the Empire; how can this situation be remedied? . . . [A]s things are going today, even if there were several men each as great as Mencius, they would be helpless. Consider the time of Mencius; the harm done by Yang Zhu and Mozi did not amount to much, and compared with the situation today it was negligible. And, of course, this matter is connected with the failure or success of the state.[10]

The Buddhists were wrong because they thought that the world is neither real nor intelligible. They had ignored *li* (理), which means "pattern" or "principle." The world is real on account of *li*.

As Peter Bol noted, Cheng Yi and Zhu Xi "made three crucial claims":

> 1. Every single thing (such as a tree) or an affair (such as being a child to one's parents) has its *li*, by which they meant that there is a norm or standard for every single thing.
> 2. It is possible for the mind to see the *li* of something absolutely, with total certainty.
> 3. All *li* are one *li*.[11]

We will consider the first and third of these propositions and then return to the second.

Li

Everything has a *li* or principle which Bol also translates as a "coherence." As Barry Keenan explained "[t]he Neo-Confucian assumption regarding principle" is that "there is a reason why all things are as they are."[12] Cheng Yi said, "Where there is a thing there must be a rule (則 *ze*). One thing must have one principle."[13] Zhu Xi said: "As far as the things in the universe go, we can be certain that each has a reason why it is as it is and a rule to which it should conform. This is what is meant by principle."[14]

According to Zhu Xi, "nature consists of innumerable principles."[15] Animals have their principle. So do non-living things such as the primary elements of which other things are composed which were thought to be Metal, Wood, Water, Fire and Earth.[16] Zhu Xi was

9   Graham, Two Chinese Philosophers. See Carson Chang, *The Development of Neo-Confucian Thought* (New York, 1957), 28–29, 43; Joseph S. Wu, "Zhu Xi" in Ian P. McGreal, ed., *Great Thinkers of the Eastern World* (New York, 1995), 116 at 118–19 (agreeing that this was their view of Buddhism, but denying it was true of most Buddhist sects).

10   *Ho-nan Ch'êng-shi yi-shu.* BSS. 24/1–6, from Graham, *Two Chinese Philosophers* 83.

11   Peter K. Bol, *Neo-Confucianism in History* (Cambridge, 2008), 163.

12   Barry C. Keenan, *Neo-Confucian Self-Cultivation* (Honolulu, 2011), 10–11.

13   Cheng Yi, *I-shu* 18:9a.

14   *Ta-hsüeh hwo-wen* 15a:3 in Daniel K. Gardner, *Chu Hsi and the Ta-hsueh: Neo-Confucian Reflection on the Confucian Canon* (Cambridge, 1986), 90.

15   Zhu Xi, *Complete Works* 42:6b. Again, I thank Tong Zu, with whom I discussed the original text (http://ctext.org/wiki.pl?if=gb&res=315560). Throughout, translations are based on her suggestions and on *Reflections on Things at Hand*, trans. Wing-tsit Chan (New York, 1967), and Chu Hsi, *Learning to be a Sage*, trans. Daniel K. Gardner (Berkeley, 1990).

16   Zhu Xi, *Complete Works* 42:25a.

asked: "Do things without feelings also possess principle?" He answered: "They of course have principle. For example, a ship can go only on water while a cart can go only on land."[17] "There is not a single thing in the universe that is outside nature. Thereupon [he] walked up the step and said, 'the bricks of these steps have in them the principle of bricks.' Then he sat down and said, 'a bamboo chair has in it the principle of the bamboo chair.'"[18]

Li are eternal and unchanging. As Chen Zhong, a disciple of Zhu Xi wrote: "What does not change for innumerable ages is principle."[19] According to Cheng Yi:

> "The decree of *Tian*, how profound it is and unceasing" [quoting the *Odes*[20]] means simply that the principles continue of themselves without ceasing, and are not made by man. If they could be made, even if they were improvised in hundreds and thousands of ways, there would still be a time when they would stop. It is because they are not made that they do not stop.[21]

Cheng Yi explained the sense in which the *li* of a cooking pot or tripod is eternal.

> The construction of the vessel is derived from its image (像 *xiang*). . . . It may be objected that there can be no natural (自然 *zi ran*) image since the tripod was made by man. The answer is that certainly it is man-made, but the fact that things can be made edible by cooking, and that its use depends on certain form and construction, is not man-made but natural.[22]

The *li* of the cooking pot is eternal: people make the pot, but they do not make the reason why the pot must be constructed in a certain way in order to cook food.

Everything, in order to exist, must not only have a *li* or principle; it must also have *qi* in which this principle is embodied. There is no English equivalent for the word *qi*. It has been translated as "material," "material force," "psychophysical stuff," "stuff," "ether," "energy," and "vital energy." Cheng Yi said: "To talk about nature and not *qi* is incomplete; to talk about *qi* and not nature is unintelligible. It would be wrong to consider them as two."[23] Zhu Xi explained, "Nature is principle only. However, without *qi* . . . principle would have nothing in which to inhere."[24]

Nevertheless, *li* have a mode of existence that is independent of that of the things in which they are embodied. Zhu Xi said: "There are *li*, even if there are no things. In that case there are only such-and-such *li*, but no such-and-such things." "Question: 'Before Heaven and Earth had yet come into existence, were all the things of later times there?' Answer: 'Only the *li* were there.'" Fung Yu-lan, a great historian of Chinese thought, believed that the members of the School conceived of *li* or principle as Plato conceived of Forms or

---

[17]   Ibid. 42:30a.
[18]   Ibid. 42:29b–30a.
[19]   Ch'ên Chun, *Pei-ch'i tzŭ-yi. Hsi-yin hsüan ts'ung-shu* 2/5B from Graham, *Two Chinese Philosophers* 14.
[20]   Ode no. 267, L 570/1-575/1.
[21]   *Ho-nan Ch'êng-shi yi-shu*. BSS. 248/9f, from Graham, *Two Chinese Philosophers* 13.
[22]   *Yi-ch'uan Yi-chuan. Êrh Ch'êng ch'üan-shu*, 4/12B/4-7, in Graham, *Two Chinese Philosophers* 20.
[23]   Cheing I, *I-shu* 6:2a.
[24]   Zhu Xi, *Complete Works* 43:2b–3a.

Ideas. According to Fung, like Plato's Forms, "there are the *li* for things already before the concrete things exist."[25]

Some passages, however, seem to say the opposite. For example, according to Zhu Xi, "[i]n the universe, there has never been any material force without principle or principle without material force."[26] There are similar statements by Cheng Yi.[27] Kirill Thompson concluded that *li* must have no existence apart from the things in which they are imminent.[28] According to Carsun Chang and Walter Watson, *li* must be like the forms of Aristotle which are universal but instantiated only in matter.[29]

Then there are mysterious passages in which they say that *li* neither exist nor do not exist. According to Cheng Yi, "existence or non-existence, addition or reduction, cannot be postulated about *li*."[30] Zhu Xi said, "Fundamentally, principle cannot be interpreted in the sense of existence or non-existence. Before Heaven and Earth came into being, it already was as it is."[31]

Thus in one sense, then, *li* preexist everything in the universe; in another sense they do not exist at all. To say they exist would be misleading since they do not exist without *qi*. Yet to say that they do not exist would be misleading since the *li* are eternal, innumerable, and include every distinction that ever could exist among things. They have a mode of being of their own. They are real when we think of them as they are in themselves, without considering whether or not they are embodied in *qi*.

A better parallel than that of the Platonic Forms, as we will see later, is the *essentia realis* of Francisco Suárez which rationalists such as Gottfried Wilhelm Leibniz and Christian Wolff incorporated in their metaphysics. *Essentia realis*, according to Suárez, is the mode of being that a thing possesses "prescinding from [its] actual existence or being as actual existence."[32] Leibniz explained that concepts (*rationes*) have a similar mode of existence. "[T]he concepts (*rationes*) of numbers are true even if there were no one to count and nothing to be counted, and we can predict that a house will be beautiful, a machine efficient, or a commonwealth happy if it comes into being even if it should never do so."[33] Like *li*, the *essentiae* of Suárez and *rationes* of Leibniz are eternal. Etienne Gilson objected that "[t]he Mattheus Passion was not an essence hovering in a limbo of possible essences where Johann Sebastian Bach caught it, so to speak, on the wing."[34]

[25] Fung Yu-lan, *A Short History of Chinese Philosophy* (New York, 1948), 294; see H. G. Creel, *Chinese Thought from Confucius to Mao Tsê-tung* (Chicago, 1953), 208.

[26] Zhu Xi, *Complete Works* 49:1a.

[27] He said, "The Way is that through which [the material force of] yin and yang operate." *I-shu* 15:13b. Also: "there is no Way independent of *yin* and *yang*. Yin and *yang* are both *qi*." Yet in the same paragraph: "Material force is what exists after physical form, whereas the Way is what exists before physical form." Cheng Yi, *I-shu* 15:15b.

[28] Kirill Thompson, "Li and Yi as Immanent: Chu Hsi's Thought in Practical Perspective," *Philosophy East and West* 38 (1998), 30 at 32–33.

[29] Carsun Chang, *Neo Confucian Thought* 1 (New Haven, 1957), pp. 243–331; Walter Watson, "Chu Hsi, Plato, and Aristotle," *Journal of Chinese Philosophy*, 5 (1978), 149.

[30] Quoted in Fung, *Short History* 286.

[31] Zhu Xi, *Complete Works* 49:6a.

[32] Francisco Suárez, *Disputationes metaphysicae* in Vivès ed., *Opera omnia* 25 (1861), disp. 2, sec. 4, no. 9.

[33] Gottfried Wilhelm Leibnitz, *Elementa juris naturalis* in Akademie der Wissenschaften der DDR ed., *Philosophische Schriften Erster Band 1663–1672* (Berlin, 1990), 459 at 460.

[34] Etienne Gilson, *Being and Some Philosophers* (Toronto, 1952), 211.

Gilson would have been as skeptical of Cheng Yi's suggestion that the poems of Tu Fu exist independently of the mind of the poet, the readers of the poem, or the pages on which the poem is written.

> There was a man who had been completely illiterate all his life, and yet one day when he fell ill he was able to recite a volume of Tu Fu's poems. There is nothing impossible in this. [literally: Nevertheless, there is this principle.] There are only two alternatives: the activities between heaven and earth either are or are not. When they are they are; when they are not they are not. As for Tu Fu's poems, these poems really exist in the world. Therefore, since there is such a *dao-li*, the man's mind, refined and concentrated by sickness, of itself reacted to and penetrated it.[35]

Another difference between *li* and both Platonic Forms and Aristotelian essences is that, for Plato and Aristotle, things with the same Form or essence are the same kind of thing. Human beings are one kind of thing and cats are another. As Angus Graham observed, Cheng Yi and Zhu Xi were not concerned with "the problem of universals and particulars."[36] He noted:

> *Li* is in fact conceived in such a way that the problem does not arise; there are different *li* wherever there are differences, just as there is the same *li* whenever there are similarities. Principle seems to be conceived as a network of veins; however much they diverge from each other, the veins prove when we "extend" them to be one; on the other hand we can also go on indefinitely making finer and finer distinctions among them, finding as we proceed that not only classes but individuals and parts of individuals have *li* which distinguish them from each other.[37]

He quoted this passage from Zhu Xi:

> There is only one principle (道理 *dao li*), but its divisions are not the same ... Thus there is only one for this board, but the grain runs one way here and another way there; one of a single house, but it has different sorts of rooms; one for plants, but they include both peach and plum trees; one for mankind, but there is Mr. A and Mr. B. Mr. A cannot become Mr. B. Mr. B cannot become Mr. A.[38]

The passage suggests that where there is a difference among things, there must be a *li* or reason for the difference. Otherwise, in their view, there would not be a difference that is intelligible and real. Not only do human beings, animals, and plants, the elements, and man-made things such as ships, carts, and chairs have a *li*. So does a single house, its parts, and Mr. B and Mr. A. In contrast to Platonic Forms and Aristotelian essences, Graham notes that "what distinguishes the principles ... is not generality but permanence."[39] The *li* are eternal.

---

[35]   *Ho-nan Ch'êng-shi yi-shu.* BSS. 49/1-6, from Graham, *Two Chinese Philosophers* 16.
[36]   Graham, *Two Chinese Philosophers* 13.
[37]   Ibid.
[38]   Zhu Xi, *Sayings of Zhu Xi, Chu-tzŭ yü-lei, Ying-yüan shu-yüan* (1872), 6/ 3B/8, 4A/3 from Graham, *Two Chinese Philosophers* 12.
[39]   Graham, *Two Chinese Philosophers* 13.

Ultimate Principle

According to Cheng Yi and Zhu Xi, all *li*, although they are innumerable, are ultimately one *li*, or, as Bol would translate it, one "coherence." To use Graham's metaphor, the many *li* are like a network of veins: "however much they diverge from each other, the veins prove when we 'extend' them to be one."[40] Thus according to Cheng Yi: "The principle of one thing is one with the principle of all things."[41] Zhu Xi said, in a passage quoted earlier: "There is only one principle (道理 *dao li*) but its divisions are not the same."[42]

For Cheng Yi, the fact that one can "extend" *li* indefinitely, making finer and finer distinctions, proved that all of these distinctions belong to one *li* which is eternal, and are not arbitrary human inventions.[43] Zhu Xi called the one *li* the Great Ultimate. "When all principles of heaven and earth and the myriad things are put together, that is the Great Ultimate."[44] "The Great Ultimate is nothing other than principle."[45] Cheng Yi and Zhu Xi sometimes referred to the one principle as the Principle of Heaven (天理 *tian li*) or, using the ancient terms, the Way (道 *dao*) or the decree of Heaven (天命 *tian ming*). Tian can be translated as Heaven or as God. As Graham noted, "The great innovation . . . is to claim that 'the innumerable principles amount to one principle,' for which 'heaven,' the 'decree,' and the 'Way' are merely different names, thus transforming a natural order conceived after the analogy of human society into a rational order."[46] "Before the Song the central place in the Confucian world-picture had been occupied by *tian*, 'heaven,' which was conceived as a very vaguely personal power controlling nature as the Emperor, the 'Son of Heaven,' controls men."[47]

Tian became an impersonal principle.[48]

Because the *li* are eternal, the Buddhists were wrong to think the world is an illusion. "[T]he only difference between the Confucianists and the Buddhists," Zhu Xi said, is that "whereas the Buddhists talk about non-being, the Confucianists talk about being."[49] "What we Confucianists regard as real, they deny."[50] "*Li* is a reality of which the Buddhists are ignorant."[51]

Zhu Xi maintained that the one *li* is omnipresent. It is embodied in every thing. "Each and every person has in him the Great Ultimate and each and every thing has in it the Great

---

40   Ibid.
41   Cheng Yi, *I-shu* 2A:1a.
42   Zhu Xi, *Sayings of Zhu Xi, Chu-tzǔ yü-lei, Ying-yüan shu-yüan* (1872), 6/ 3B/8, 4A/3 in Graham, *Two Chinese Philosophers* 12.
43   *Ho-nan Ch'êng-shi yi-shu.* BSS. 248/9f, from Graham, *Two Chinese Philosophers* 13.
44   Zhu Xi, *Complete Works* 49:14b–15a.
45   Ibid. 49:8b.
46   Graham, *Two Chinese Philosophers* 11, see 23.
47   Ibid. 23.
48   When, occasionally, they speak of yin and yang, Cheng Yi and Zhu Xi describe them as operations or manifestations of the ultimate principle Cheng Yi, *I-shu* 15:14a; Zhu Xi and LüTsu-ch'ien, *Reflections on Things at Hand*, trans. Wing-tsit Chan (New York, 1967), I.1, 8, pp. 5–7, 10.
49   Zhu Xi, *Complete Works* 60:14b.
50   *Chu-tzu yu-lui* Book 126, about Buddhism, quoted in Chang, *Development of Confucian Thought* 271–72.
51   Ibid.

Ultimate."[52] Although "there is only one Great Ultimate, yet each of the myriad things has been endowed with it and each possesses the Great Ultimate in its entirety."[53]

Things differ because their *qi* limits the extent to which the Great Ultimate – the one principle – is received by them. "The principle is received by things in precisely the same degree as the material force received by them. For example, the physical constitution of dogs and horses being what it is, they know how to do only certain things."[54] When Zhu Xi was asked whether one therefore should say that each thing possesses the Great Ultimate in its completeness or only partially, he answered: "You may consider it complete or you may consider it partial. From the point of view of principle, it is always complete, but from the point of view of material force, it cannot help being partial."[55] "It is like the light of the sun and the moon. In a clear, open field, it is seen in its entirety. Under a mat-shed, however, some of it is hidden and obstructed so that part of it is visible and part of it is not."[56]

As Graham said, "nature is therefore the same in all things; animals differ from men only in that the impurity of their [material force] is permanent, and so great that it prevents them from showing more than a few practically negligible traces of moral principle (such as the loyalty of ants to their ruler, and the otter's practice of sacrifice)."[57] In contrast, for Mencius, as we saw earlier, human beings differed from animals because they possessed certain qualities: the feelings which, when developed, would grow into benevolence, righteousness, wisdom, and propriety.

According to Cheng Yi, a person's goodness depends on his *qi*, which may be clear or turbid.[58] This idea was developed more elaborately by Zhu Xi. He said, "in its original state, heavenly principle (天理 *tian li*) is free from human desire."[59] The desires that corrupt a human being come from the impurity of *qi* which prevents *li* from being perfectly received. "[M]an loses his original nature and beclouds it by habits engendered by material (*qi*). It is not that nature fails."[60] "Nature is like water. If it flows in a clean channel, it is clear, if it flows in a dirty channel, it becomes turbid. When physical nature that is clear and balanced is received, it will be preserved in its completeness."[61] Zhu Xi concluded that, in the case of a bad man, "the objective of learning is to transform this material endowment."[62] As he acquires knowledge of principle, his *qi* changes.

[52] Zhu Xi, *Complete Works* 49:11b.
[53] Ibid. 49:10b–11a.
[54] Ibid. 42:26b–27a.
[55] Ibid.
[56] Ibid. 42:27a–b.
[57] Graham, *Two Chinese Philosophers* 57.
[58] Cheng Yi, I-shu 18:17b.
[59] Zhu Xi, *Complete Works* 42:14b–15a.
[60] Ibid. 42:21b.
[61] Ibid. 43:7a–b.
[62] Ibid. 43:4b.

Knowledge

Cheng Yi and Zhu Xi maintained that the human mind can grasp ultimate reality. Cheng Yi said, "[t]he mind of one man is one with the mind (心 *xin*) of Heaven and Earth. The *li* of one thing is one with the *li* of all things."[63] According to Zhu Xi, "[t]he mind embraces all *li*, and all *li* are complete in this single entity, the mind."[64] They were ascribing to the mind a knowledge which, according to monotheists such as Averroes, Maimonides, and Aquinas, belongs only to God.

To grasp ultimate principle, one must begin by understanding the *li* of particular things. Cheng Yi said, "[a]ll things under heaven can be understood in the light of their principles."[65] "If you want to make sense of a thing, where do you start? You should start by figuring out its *li*. It is not the thing that is disordered. It is you that are disordered."[66]

One cannot know the principles of all particular things since they are innumerable. According to Cheng Yi: "In investigating things to exhaust their *li*, the idea is not that one must exhaust completely everything in the world. ... The reason why they cannot be exhausted is simply that there is one *li* in all innumerable things, and even a thing or activity however small, has this *li*."[67] Nevertheless, because the many *li* are extensions of the one *li*, according to Cheng Yi, "[i]f they are exhausted in only one matter, the rest can be inferred by analogy."[68] "[A]ll have this *li*. If there were not this *li*, the inferences would not be successful."[69]

According to Cheng Yi, "If one cannot exhaust the principle of one thing, start with something easier."[70] According to Zhu Xi, one must begin with what is "already known and make efforts to go beyond it."[71] Then, in Graham's words, in the "investigation of a thing ... thinking [is] followed by a sudden insight into its principle."[72] As Cheng Yi said: "After long thought, insight comes spontaneously."[73] According to Zhu Xi: "When the principles of things are investigated most thoroughly, penetration will come as a sudden realization."[74]

By this method, one is to investigate natural things. According to Cheng Yi, "[a] single tree and a single blade of grass both have principle which must be investigated."[75] "A wide acquaintance with the names of birds, animals, grasses and trees' is a means of understanding

---

[63] Cheng Yi, *I-shu* 2A:1a.
[64] Zhu Xi, *Complete Works* 2:4b.
[65] Cheng Yi, *I-shu* 18:9a.
[66] Ibid. 18:10b.
[67] Cheng Yi, *Ho-nan Ch'êng-shi yi-shu.* BSS. 174/2-4, from Graham, *Two Chinese Philosophers* 9–10.
[68] Ibid. 10.
[69] Ibid.
[70] Cheng Yi, *I-shu* 2A:22b.
[71] Zhu Xi, *Complete Works* 3:22b–23a.
[72] Graham, *Two Chinese Philosophers* 78.
[73] Cheng Yi, *Ho-nan Ch'êng-shi yi-shu.* BSS. 207/12f, from Graham, *Two Chinese Philosophers* 78.
[74] Zhu Xi, *Complete Works* 44:13a–b.
[75] Cheng Yi, *Ho-nan Ch'êng-shi yi-shu.* BSS. 313/3, from Graham, *Two Chinese Philosophers* 79.

principle."[76] The same method was to apply to moral questions such as those involving filial piety.[77]

Although Cheng Yi and Zhu Xi claimed that this method would lead to an understanding of *li*, they did not explain how it could. To know *li*, according to Zhu Xi, is to know the "reason why [each thing] is as it is, and a rule to which it should conform;"[78] "the reason things are as they are;"[79] "the reason for which things and affairs are as they are and the reason according to which they should be."[80] But how could one acquire such knowledge by observing and reflecting on a thing, or even related things?

The question is all the more difficult because it is not clear in what sense *li* are coherent either in themselves or in relation to other *li* or in relation to the one ultimate *li*. For Zhu Xi, as we have seen, Mr. A and Mr. B have different *li*. He likened the relationship of *li* to each other as that of grain running in different directions in a single board. Graham's metaphor was a network of veins. Zhu Xi is right that there must be an intelligible distinction between Mr. A. and Mr. B. and the grains running in different directions. Otherwise we could not tell that they are different. But any principle that distinguishes the two is neither conceptual, like the difference between a triangle and a square, nor functional, like the difference between organs of the body. It is hard to envision the distinction as a difference in coherent principle.

Bol's explanation of how *li* were supposed to be coherent was Aristotelian although he did not mention Aristotle. He said, "I think we can understand the Neo-Confucian use of the term *li* in the following manner."

> First, things have their distinctive structure: the structure of a tree is the interconnectedness of leaf, branch trunk, and root, in which on part depends on another as branch to root . . . Second, things have their distinctive direction and process of development; the tree goes thorough daily and annual cycles and grows through a certain life span . . . Third, this have their distinctive functions in relation to other things as part of a larger whole."[81]

According to Bol, "[k]nowledge of *li* . . . is knowledge about how something is put together, how it develops over time, and what role it should play."[82] "[T]he *li* of every thing is alike in that it plays the same role in every thing."[83]

Bol described the way in which, in the Aristotelian tradition, part is related to whole and both are related to final cause or end. If Zhu Xi thought of *li* in that way, he would not have spoken of the *li* of Mr. A. and Mr. B. nor of the *li* of the grain in a board. Moreover, he and his followers would have tried to explain plants, animals, human beings, and social and political relations as Aristotle did, by identifying their end or final cause, distinguishing their parts, and describing the contribution that each part made to achieving that end.

---

76   Cheng Yi, *Ho-nan Ch'êng-shih yi-shu*. BSS. 355/3, from Graham, *Two Chinese Philosophers* 79.
77   Cheng Yi, *Ho-nan Ch'êng-shih yi-shu*. BSS. 174/2–4, from Graham, *Two Chinese Philosophers* 10.
78   Zhu Xi, *Ta-hsüeh hwo-wen* 15a:3 in Gardner, *Chu Hsi* 90.
79   Zhu Xi, *Complete Works* 3:27b.
80   Ibid. 3:34a.
81   Bol, *Neo-Confucianism* 164–65.
82   Ibid. 165.
83   Ibid.

As Stephen Angle observed, "The fullness of *li* is forever shrouded in mystery. Even the strongest claims from within the Neo-Confucian tradition about the ability of the sages to grasp *li* are themselves cloaked in the language of mystical, incommunicable experience."[84] Bol said: "The core of the Neo-Confucian self is belief – a conscious commitment of faith – rather than a philosophical proposition or unarticulated assumption."[85] Angle noted that, nevertheless, the teachings of the School "sound quite different from faith: rather than being disconnected from evidence or reasoning, as we would expect from faith, we have systematic theory that rests in part on what we all can, and do, actually experience. Which is it?"[86] It is hardly surprising that Bol did not answer that question. The Neo-Confucians could not.

According to the School of Principle, *li* is the standard for what is right and wrong. The acquisition of moral knowledge is the discovery of *li*. Once this knowledge is acquired, one will not only know what is right but do it. Moral action is governed by *li* which, as we have seen, are eternal.

Cheng Yi said "[A]ll *li* are pervasively present. We cannot say that the *dao* of kingship was more when Yao ... exemplified it as a king, nor that the *dao* of sonship was more when Shun ... exemplified it as a son. These remain what they are."[87] Kingship and sonship are what they have always been, even though no one now alive exemplifies them like Yao and Shun.

Consequently, for every thing there is a rule. Moral knowledge is knowledge of that rule. Cheng Yi said:

> If there is a thing there must be a rule. The father rests in compassion, the son in filial piety, the ruler in benevolence, the minister in reverence. Each thing and every activity has its proper place; if it gets it there is peace, if not disorder. The reason why the sage can bring the Empire good government is not that he can make rules for it, but that he makes each rest in its proper place.[88]

People do not make the rules that prescribe how person must act to be a father, a son, a ruler or a minister, any more than they make the rules as to how a pot must be constructed in order to cook food. The rules prescribe the proper place for each thing. When things do not rest in their proper place there is disorder. But the rules do not change.

To understand things around us, we must know their *li*. To act rightly, we must apply *li* to our own situation. It is hard to see how, by reflecting on an eternal moral principle, one could tell in a difficult case what to do. Zhu Xi acknowledged that what to do may depend on the circumstances. "As for moral principle, each [manifestation of it] has its own spot. You can't talk about it from one perspective only. When it's there, you should talk about it

---

[84] Stephen C. Angle, *Sagehood: The Contemporary Significance of Neo-Confucian Philosophy* (Oxford, 2009), 88–89.

[85] Bol, *Neo-Confucianism* 195.

[86] Stephen C. Angle, review of Peter K. Bol, Neo-Confucianism in History, *Journal of Chinese Studies* 50 (2010), 345 at 350.

[87] Quoted in Fung, *Short History* 286.

[88] Cheng Yi, *Yi-ch'uan Yi-chuan. Êrh Ch'êng ch'üan-shu*, 4/20B/7–9, from Graham, *Two Chinese Philosophers* 17.

that way. Its relative circumstances are different in every case."[89] As Bol noted, correct judgment "depends on seeing it in context rather than sticking to a rigid definition."[90] Bol concluded that Zhu Xi recognized the importance of "thinking for oneself" despite his "great reluctance to allow that non-sages may vary from the 'constant' (*jing*) and exercise their own judgment at variance from the norm (*quan*)."[91]

Perhaps. But this "thinking for oneself" was not to fine-tune one's actions through wisdom, as Mencius believed, or as Dai Zhen believed, to weigh what is important and what is not, or, as Aristotle believed, to exercise one's practical reason. It was to grasp an eternal principle. There must be an eternal principle that prescribes the right action to take under any circumstances that may arise. Moreover, until one grasps that principle, one must defer to *jing*. As Donald Munro noted, "[t]he preference is for obedience to the proper authorities ... until such time as the right actions emerge spontaneously, without deliberate choice making." There is a "denegration of deliberation." The "ramifications" of this "difference ... between many European ethical systems and that of Ch'eng-Chu [Cheng-Zhu] Confucians on the matter of choice" are "enormous."[92] Munro contrasted the importance of choice in Western philosophy and the Christian religion. He could equally well have contrasted its importance to Mencius or Dai Zhen.

For Cheng Yi and Zhu Xi, knowledge of principle enables one not only to know but also to do what is right: to overcome selfish desires, to acquire benevolence, righteousness, wisdom, and propriety. Indeed, to act rightly "[t]here is nothing for the student to do except to examine all principles with his mind. Principle is what is possessed by the mind. Always preserve this mind to examine all principles. These are the only things to do."[93] "If the Principle of Nature exists in the human mind, human selfish desires will not exist, but if human selfish desires win, the Principle of Nature will be destroyed. There has never been a case where both the Principle of Nature and human selfish desires are interwoven and mixed."[94]

When selfish desires are destroyed, the result is an outpouring of love or concern for others (*ai*). The source of this love or concern is *ren* or benevolence which Zhu Xi identified as "the principle of love."[95] "[I]f we can overcome and eliminate selfishness and return to the principle of nature (天理 *tian li*), then the substance of the mind (that is, *ren*) will be present everywhere and its function will always be operative."[96]

In these passages, Zhu Xi suggested that knowledge of principle will give rise to unselfish feelings: to *ren*, which is the principle of love, and to the other qualities mentioned by Mencius: righteousness, wisdom, and propriety. In other passages, Zhu Xi suggested that knowledge of principle will overcome selfish desires by indicating what is right and wrong.

---

[89] Zhu Xi, *Complete Works* 8.2a:1.
[90] Bol, *Neo-Confucianism* 180.
[91] Ibid. 179.
[92] Donald J. Munro, *Images of Human Nature: A Sung Portrait* (Princeton, 1988), 172.
[93] Zhu Xi, *Complete Works* 1:19a.
[94] Ibid. 3:3a.
[95] Zhu Xi, *A Treatise on Jen*, in Chan, *Source Book*, 593 at 595.
[96] Ibid. 594.

Thinking will overcome feeling. "As things and affairs approach, the mind can clearly see which is right and which is wrong. . . . What is right is the principle of nature and what is wrong is in violation of the principle of nature. If one can always collect the mind like this, it would be as if one holds the scale and balance to measure things."[97] When asked about Cheng Yi's comment that "only thinking can control desires,"[98] Zhu Xi said: "Thinking is the same as examining. It means that when one is angry, if one can directly forget his anger and examine the right and wrong according to principle, then right and wrong will be clearly seen and desires will naturally be unable to persist."[99] If a person can clearly see what is right and wrong, then he will act rightly.

For Zhu Xi, these suggestions were not inconsistent. One who returns to principle is for that very reason impartial. To be impartial is to be unselfish. To be unselfish is to possess *ren* which is the principle of all other good qualities. Zhu Xi said, "impartiality is the principle of *ren*. Therefore, if there is impartiality there is *ren*, and if there is *ren*, there is love."[100] Moreover, "whenever and wherever benevolence (仁 *ren*) flows and operates, righteousness will fully be righteousness and propriety and wisdom will fully be righteousness and wisdom."[101] "*Ren* embraces them all."[102]

As Keenan noted, Mencius "claimed that inherent in human nature are the four sprouts, or capacities, to develop into four lived moral virtues . . . Instead of a developmental model in which nurturing is necessary to make the sprout grow," Zhu Xi taught that if "principle," which is "embedded in our material nature" can "shine forth," these virtues will be acquired.[103] In Kennan's words, principle will shine forth when, after exerting oneself to understand the principles of things, "the individual will one day experience a breakthrough to integral comprehension" in which "the qualities of all things, whether internal or external, refined or coarse, will be apprehended and . . . all will be clearly manifested."[104] One can then "rectify one's mind, cultivate the person, regulate the family, order the state, and bring peace to all."[105]

If we grant that all of these virtuous actions are in conformity with principle, the question still remains, why does a grasp of principle motivate a person to live virtuously, or, indeed, to do anything at all? Zhu Xi's answer relies on what we have called the principle of impartial concern. *Li* is impartial. "Impartiality is the principle of *ren*. Therefore, if there is impartiality there is *ren*, and if there is *ren*, there is love."[106] As always with the principle of impartial concern, the difficulty is to move from the principle that all should be treated alike to a desire to do so, in Zhu Xi's words, to benevolence and love.

---

[97] Zhu Xi, *Complete Works* 2:2a.
[98] Cheng Yi, *I-shu* 25: 3a–b.
[99] Zhu Xi, *Complete Works* 3:3b.
[100] Ibid. 47:6b.
[101] Ibid. 47:3a.
[102] Zhu Xi, *Treatise on Jen* in Chan, *Source Book* 593–94.
[103] Keenan, *Neo-Confucian Self-Cultivation* 16.
[104] Ibid. 43 (quoting Zhu Xi).
[105] Ibid. 40.
[106] Zhu Xi, *Complete Works* 47:6b.

As Stephen Angle and Justin Tiwald explained, the difficulty was to avoid either of two unacceptable alternatives. One is that normative standards are external to ourselves, in which case we have no motivation to follow them. The other is that these standards depend on our own motivations, and so are contingent and subjective "For many Daoxue [School of Principle] Confucians, an appealing way to avoid both of these unhappy alternatives was to maintain ... that, in some sense, the mind is identical to principle."[107] As Bol described their position, "[r]ealizing morality in the world thus depends on becoming conscious of something in our own persons."[108] We need "a *theory* about how to understand, cultivate and realize in practice something that we humans can experience personally because we possess it innately."[109] The theory, however, tells us "[m]an's nature is nothing but principle,"[110] that the principle in question is not the distinctive principle of man but includes within it the principles of all things. Why this knowledge should lead to action is as obscure with the School of Principle as it is with the Western rationalists. Still more obscure is why a being that can grasp the principles of all things, like the God of monotheistic religions, behaves like a mere human.

Adherents of the School of Principle, however, had no doubt that ultimate principle could be known through reflection and meditation. Those who had done so had a capacity for moral action that transcended other men. As Bol noted, they believed it "possible for the mind to see the *li* of something absolutely, with total certainty."[111] Moreover, knowledge of principle was a *sine qua non* condition for moral action. Only action which is taken on account of principle can be good.

They concluded that an intellectual and moral dark age separated the time of Mencius from the advent of their own school. During this period, no one understood principle as Cheng Yi and Zhu Xi did. Knowledge of principle had therefore disappeared. They grafted this idea onto a claim, made by the Tang dynasty philosopher Han Yu, that true learning had been passed down by tradition from the sage emperors in a line of succession that ended with Mencius.[112] According to Zhu Xi,

> After the death of the Mencius, the Way of the Sages was not handed down. Scholars occupied themselves with writing in a literary style, and mixing their knowledge with the theories of Lao-tzu and the Buddha. Moreover, their way of cultivation was motivated by their own selfish desires. There was a great departure from the orthodox path. ... This continued for more than a thousand years.

True learning was revived in the time of Cheng Yi. "Now," Zhu Xi said, "scholars could free themselves from the vulgarity of ordinary essay writing and the enticement of heretics. Henceforth personal cultivation and public administration went beyond the mere acquisition of selfish ends and aspired toward the ideal kingship of Yao and Shun."[113]

---

[107]   Angle and Tiwald, *Neo-Confucianism* loc. 2642.
[108]   Bol, *Neo-Confucianism* 157.
[109]   Ibid. 157–58.
[110]   Zhu Xi, *Complete Works* 42:5a.
[111]   Bol, *Neo-Confucianism* 163.
[112]   Quoted in Chang, *Development of Neo-Confucian Thought* 58.
[113]   Quoted ibid.

His friend and critic Chen Liang disagreed in a series of letters he exchanged with Zhu Xi. How can it be, he asked that "the world for fifteen centuries has lived in a vacancy of the Way ... But how can beings in such a world prosper, and how can the Dao be everlasting?"[114] His mistake, according to Zhu Xi, was in "letting the mind of the Way become mixed with the human mind. ... [O]ne should be single in the purpose of maintaining the supremacy of heavenly reason over desire."[115] "[W]ith the moment that marked the first absence of mind from the morally right, the Way among mankind stopped."[116] "Your proposal is mixing gold, silver, copper and iron in order to make the expedient and practical. Your mind is undoubtedly utilitarian."[117] Unless actions proceed from principle, they are corrupt. There can be no middle way.

The Break with the Past

Bol contrasted the teachings of the School with the idea that ethical beliefs are acquired through "internalization."

> In asking what Neo-Confucians meant by learning, it will be useful to begin by distinguishing what we, as observers on the past, think Neo-Confucians were actually doing and what the Neo-Confucians claimed to be doing. Historians are inclined to assume that culture forms the person, that people internalize what they are taught, that they adopt the values of the group they wish to belong to, and that the choices that are available to them are defined by the society in which they live. To state this in an extreme form: people are blank slates on which society writes its culture, and because people internalize what they are taught, they come to believe the way they behave is somehow natural to themselves.[118]

Bol is correct that modern Western historians are inclined to assume that ethical values are acquired only through internalization. The popularity of that idea is one response to the eclipse of the Western classical tradition. It seems to be neutral: the historian can know how values are acquired without having to determine whether those values are right or wrong.

It is not neutral. It assumes that the School of Principle and both classical traditions are wrong about how ethical values are acquired. Bol contrasted "internalization" with what the Neo-Confucians claimed to be doing, which, he implied, was much better. They recognized the "need for self-reflection or awareness of one's own moral conscience" and the relevance of "the goodness of human nature." It is not enough for a student merely to "emulate his teacher's model." Both of the classical traditions recognized the need for reflection and awareness and the goodness of human nature.

Nevertheless, the School of Principle broke with the past. It did so precisely by distorting traditional Confucian teaching about the purpose of reflection and the goodness of human

---

[114] *Lung-chuan wen-chi* Book 20, in Chang, *Development of Neo-Confucian Thought* 316.
[115] Ibid. 323.
[116] Ibid. 324.
[117] Ibid. 325.
[118] Bol, *Neo-Confucianism* 153–54.

nature. Bol defanged and declawed the teachings of the School of Principle by failing to recognize the distortion.

"Self-reflection or awareness" for Mencius meant a collected state of mind in which one became attuned to those desires and aversions which are proper to humanity. Human nature, for Mencius, meant that everyone was born with a distinctively human potentiality to care for others, to act fairly, to behave respectfully, and to act wisely. Later in the Confucian tradition, Dai Zhen, like Mencius, grounded ethical norms on human nature. He taught that everyone has the capacity to order his desires rightly and to weigh what is important and unimportant in deciding how to act.

For the School of Principle, "self-reflection" or "awareness" meant a capacity to grasp the one principle underpinning everything in the universe including the eternal and invariable principles of right conduct. "Man's nature," Zhu Xi said, is nothing but principle,"[119] meaning the principle that includes within it the principles of all things. As Cheng Yi said, "[t]he mind of one man is one with the mind (心 *xin*) of Heaven and Earth. The *li* of one thing is one with the *li* of all things."[120] A human being can act rightly, not because each human being can distinguish right from wrong, but because some human beings have a theory which enables them, after considerable effort, to grasp with certainty the one principle. That theory is indispensable for moral action. It was lost for 1400 years until the founders of the School of Principle rediscovered it.

An historian is not really being neutral when he assumes that all ethical thought is the result of "internalization." Similarly, it is hard to describe neutrally the teachings of the School of Principle. If there were such principles, their discovery would have been, as they claimed, the turning point of human history. From then on, the enlightened people who grasped all things would have been infallible guides for the conduct of governments and individuals.

If there are no such principles to be grasped, their claim was not simply mistaken but radically wrong and dangerous. Zhu Xi said, in a passage quoted by Bol,

> All affairs in the world have their basis in one man, and the person of that one man has its master in one mind. Thus once the mind of the ruler of men is correct, then all affairs in the world will be correct; but once the mind of the ruler is deviant, then all affairs in the world in world will be deviant.[121]

Bol noted correctly that what this passage "cannot mean is that the ruler has moral authority simply by virtue of his political position."[122] Instead it confers ultimate authority on the person with the correct mind, even if he has no other claim to rule. If the School of Principle is correct, such a person is infallible. If the School is not correct – if there is no one *li* and no eternal principles for the mind to grasp – the person who makes that claim has delusions of grandeur. His followers are deluded as well.

---

[119]   Zhu Xi, *Complete Works* 42:5a.
[120]   Cheng Yi, *I-shu* 2A:1a.
[121]   Zhu Xi, *Zhu Xi ji* 12.490 from 1189 quoted by Bol, *Neo-Confucianism* 133.
[122]   Bol, *Neo-Confucianism* 133.

Cheng Yi and Zhu Xi were among the greatest philosophers who ever lived. Otherwise they would have been dismissed as cranks peddling a panacea. But brilliant people can be very wrong, and their brilliance makes their ideas all the more dangerous.

II THE RESPONSE: THE SCHOOL OF UNIVERSAL MIND

From the Ming dynasty to the end of the empire, the alternative to the School of Principle, for most scholars, was the School of the Universal Mind founded by Wang Yangming (1472–1529). He borrowed some of his ideas from Lu Hsiang-Shan (1139–93) who challenged Zhu Xi in his own lifetime.

Mind

According to Lu and Wang, all principle is to be found within oneself. "All things are complete in oneself," Lu said. "It is only necessary to understand principle."[123] According to Wang, "Man is the mind of Heaven and Earth."[124] "The innate knowledge of my mind is the same as the Principle of Nature."[125] As Julia Ching put it, "the ability of the mind to 'know the good' is somehow identical with the mind itself, with nature, with 'being' or 'virtue' and even with *Tian li*, heavenly [or ultimate] principle."[126]

They drew the radical conclusion that nothing exists apart from the mind. Lu said, "[a]ll things are luxuriantly present in one's mind. What permeates the mind, emanates from it, and extends to fill the universe is nothing but principle."[127] "The universe is my mind, and my mind is the universe."[128] According to Wang, "Separated from my clear intelligence, there will be no heaven, earth, spiritual beings or myriad things, and separated from these, there will be no clear intelligence."[129]

A pupil said, "Heaven, earth, spiritual beings, and the myriad things existed from great antiquity. Why should it be that if my clear intelligence is gone, they will all cease to exist?" Wang answered, "Consider the dead man. His spirit has drifted away and dispersed. Where are his heaven and earth and myriad things?"[130] "A friend pointed to flowering trees on a cliff and said, '[You say] there is nothing under heaven external to my mind. These flowering trees on the high mountains blossom and drop their blossoms by themselves. What have they to do with my mind?'" Wang answered, "Before you look at these flowers, they and your mind are in the state of silent vacancy. As you come to look at them, their

---

[123] *Complete Works of Lu Hsiang-Shan* 35:7b-8a.
[124] Wang Yangming, *Instructions for Practical Living* § 337. Again, I thank Tong Zu, with whom I discussed the original text (http://ctext.org/wiki.pl?if=gb&res=667533). Throughout, translations are based on her suggestions and on Wang Yangming, *Instructions for Practical Living*, Wing-tsit Chan, trans. (New York, 1962).
[125] Ibid. § 135.
[126] Julia Ching, *To Acquire Wisdom: The Way of Wang Yang-ming* (New York, 1977), 107(for purposes of consistency, *hsin*, which Ching translates as "mind-and-heart" had been translated as "mind.")
[127] Lu, *Complete Works* 34:21a.
[128] Ibid. 22:5a.
[129] Wang, *Instructions for Practical Living* § 337.
[130] Ibid. § 337.

colors at once show up clearly. From this you can know that these flowers are not external to your mind."[131]

Wang believed that the School of Principle had never explained how one could understand *li*, or how, if one did, understanding *li* could motivate action. Both problems were resolved if principle was identical with one's own mind, and understanding was identical with action.

He described how he first recognized that it is impossible to grasp the *li* of things by observation and reflection.

> People merely say that in the investigation of things we must follow Zhu Xi, but when have they carried it out in practice? I have carried it out earnestly and definitively. In my earlier years my friend Qian discussed the idea that to become a sage or worthy one must investigate all things in the world. ... I therefore pointed to the bamboos in front of a pavilion and told him to investigate them and see. Day and night Mr. Qian went ahead to try to investigate to the utmost the principles in the bamboos. He exhausted his mind and thoughts and on the third day he was tired out and took sick. At first I said that it was because his energy and strength were insufficient. Therefore I went myself to try to investigate to the utmost. From morning until night I was unable to find the principles of the bamboos. On the seventh day I also became sick because I thought too hard.[132]

The story may have been composed as satire, but Wang said that this experience led him to reject the method of Cheng Yi and Zhu Xi. He concluded that principle and mind cannot be separate. If they were, the gap between them could never be bridged.

Lu believed that virtue was found within. "When I should be commiserative, I am naturally commiserative. When I should be ashamed, liberal, generous, affectionate, tender, or strong, and firm, I am naturally so."[133] In 1175, a celebrated meeting was arranged between Lu and Zhu Xi at the Goose Lake Temple to allow them to discuss their differences. According to Lu's account: "On the way I wrote a poem:

> Simple work has endless strength, unlimited, unbound.
> The mind immersed in many things can only drift and drown.[134]

When I recited my poem up to these lines, [Zhu Xi's] face turned pale."[135]

Wang took this idea further. He said that knowledge cannot be separated from action.

> The mind is naturally able to know. When it perceives the parents, it naturally knows that one should be filial. When it perceives the elder brother, it naturally knows that one should be respectful. And when it perceives a child fall into a well, it naturally knows that one

---

[131]   Ibid. § 275
[132]   Ibid. § 319.
[133]   Lu, *Complete Works* 35:18a.
[134]   Or: "The mind entranced by subleties ... " "the mind entranced by many things ...." Literally: "Work that is simple and easy will in the end be lasting and great/ Understanding that is devoted to isolated details will end up in aimless drifting ...."
[135]   Lu, *Complete Works* 34:24a–b.

should be commiserative. This is innate knowledge of good (良知 *liangzhi* which can also be translated as "conscience") and need not be sought outside.[136]

Wang concluded that Zhu Xi was wrong to think that one first knows a principle and this knowledge then leads one to act. Knowledge and action are one. "Knowledge is the beginning of action and action is the completion of knowledge. Learning to be a sage involves only one effort. Knowledge and action should not be separated."[137]

He observed that there are things that one loves or hates as soon as one knows them.

Seeing beautiful colors appertains to knowledge, while loving beautiful colors appertains to action. However, as soon as one sees that beautiful color, he has already loved it. It is not that he sees it first and then makes up his mind to love it. Smelling a bad odor appertains to knowledge, while hating a bad odor appertains to action. However, as soon as one smells a bad odor, he has already hated it. It is not that he smells it first and then makes up his mind to hate it. ... Suppose we say that so-and-so knows filial piety and so-and-so knows brotherly respect. They must have actually practiced filial piety and brotherly respect before they come to know them. It will not do to say that they know filial piety and brotherly respect simply because they show them in words.[138]

Objectivity versus Subjectivity

According to Wang, "innate knowledge of good (*liangzhi*) need not be sought outside" the mind.[139] He also said that "the innate knowledge of my mind is the same as the Principle of Nature"[140] The difficulty was to explain the relationship between the principle of nature, which is invariable principle, and the moral standards that guide one's actions. If the moral standards depend on principle, then, it would seem that the principles of moral action are eternal and invariable, just as Cheng Yi and Zhu Xi maintained. The principles had been relocated to within one's mind. If so, the same difficulties would arise as for Cheng and Zhu: moral action would still presuppose knowledge of such a principle. If instead the principle of nature is eternal but the standards that should guide moral action are not, what is the source of these moral standards? If each person makes them up himself, they are individual and subjective.

When this problem was put to Wang, his solution, to put it generously, was ambiguous.

A dispute between two of his disciples and recounted by Huang Zongxi (黃宗羲) (1610–95) concerned meaning of a passage in his work known as the "Four Sentences." According

---

[136] Wang, *Instructions for Practical Living* § 8.
[137] Ibid. § 26.
[138] Ibid. § 5.
[139] Ibid. § 8.
[140] Ibid. § 135.

to Wang, "In the original substance of the mind there is no distinction between good and evil. When the will is active, however, the distinction [between good and evil] exists. The faculty of innate knowing is to know good and evil. Doing good and removing evil is 'the rectification of external affairs.'"[141] One student, Wang Chi, pointed to the first sentence: "in the original substance of the mind there is no distinction between good and evil." He concluded, "When a person awakes to the understanding that mind is neither good nor evil, he also realizes that intention, knowledge, and things are neither good nor evil." Another disciple, Qian Dehong, questioned that interpretation. He pointed to the last two sentences which said that "the faculty of innate knowing" (*liangzhi*) enables one to distinguish "good and evil"; "doing good and removing evil is 'the rectification of external affairs.'"[142]

> Together, the two disciples questioned Wang Yangming about it. Wang said: "I actually have two ways of teaching. The Four Negatives [meaning Wang Chi's interpretation] are for men of superior gifts of understanding. The Four Postitives [meaning Qian Dehong's intepretation] are for men of medium gifts or less. The superior gifts refer to the understanding that reality itself (*ben ti*) is nothing but its manifestation (*gong fu*) or effort. This is the teaching of sudden enlightenment. Those with medium gifts should devote themselves to the effort of doing good and ridding themselves of evil, in order to recover gradually the original reality (*ben ti*) [within themselves]."[143]

According to Huang, who reported this conversation, Wang Chi inferred that "one should fix one's roots in the mind,"[144] which meant that "one need not worry about intention, and that to fix one's roots in intention is meant for those of medium gifts or less." Therefore "one can naturally manifest emotions without deliberation." "Thus self-realization can happen all at once, without reliance on effort or cultivation. By the same reasoning the extension of *liangzhi* [knowledge of the good] was taught for the sake of those who had not yet attained enlightenment." Wang Chi concluded that "earnest fidelity and cautious behavior, as well as all action that flows from concern for reputation, are to be considered artificial behavior."[145]

"When such tenets spread throughout the country," Huang said, "scholars could not overlook certain difficulties." For Wang Yangming, the mind was ultimate reality. By Wan Chi's interpretation, good and evil have no root in reality. As Huang noted, "[s]uch teaching is necessarily close to Chan [Zen] Buddhism."[146] Unlike the Buddhists, however, Wang Yangming identified reality with principle (*li*) or Heavenly principle (*tian li*), and principle with the mind.

---

[141] Wang, Instructions for *Practical Living*, 243–44.
[142] Ibid.
[143] Huang Tsung-hsi, *The Records of Ming Scholars: A Selected Translation*, Julia Ching, ed. (Honolulu, 1987), 115 (life of Wang Chi).
[144] Ibid.
[145] Ibid. 116 (life of Wang Chi).
[146] Ibid. 117.

Qian Dehong recalled that in the 1520s, Wang Yangming had received a letter from Chan Jo-shui asking about the relationship between *liangzhi* and *tian li*. "[D]eclining to answer the letter, Wang Yangming had told Qian that the issue needed to be most carefully explicated and that a hasty response would lead to controversy."[147] Willard Peterson noted the dilemma raised by the question:

> If Wang had conceded that "innate knowing" was identical to "universal coherence," then there was little reason to reinterpret [Zhu Xi's] call for the investigation of things in order to fathom coherence, [since Zhu] included meditation and introspection as methods; if Wang denied the identity to pursue his original contribution, then his concept of "innate knowing" contained the possibility of being relativized, particular to each individual.[148]

Consequently, many of Wang Yangming's followers "relativized" morality. According to Peterson:

> When Qian came to call twenty years later, Chan Jo-shui pointed out that this is exactly what had happened. "Nowadays followers of your school say that 'innate knowing' does not entail learning or thinking, and they act on it by relying on their own wills and knowledge." How, Chan asked, could this be called "innate knowing" of moral good? And Qian Dehong, ever accommodating, even in his own telling, could only agree.[149]

Yen Ch'ün, for example, taught:

> Human nature is like a bright pearl, without any defilement originally. ... On ordinary days one need only follow one's nature, acting completely spontaneously and naturally. This is called the Way. Only in moments of excess need one practice caution, fear and apprehension in order to rectify it. All experiences, doctrines and formulas practiced by earlier scholars can become hindrances to the achievement of the Way.[150]

One of the most extreme proponents was Li Zhi (1527–1602), also known as Li Zhouwu. He wrote: "Yesterday's right is today's wrong. Today's wrong is right again tomorrow. Even if Confucius reappeared today, there is no means of knowing how he would judge right and wrong, so how can we arbitrarily judge everything as if there were a fixed standard?"[151] As Shi Meng-li reported his lectures:

> When [he] discoursed in Nanking on the philosophy of mind, all his directions to his pupils consisted in "living in the present" and spontaneity. He said that every single man is a perfectly ready-made sage. When he heard about loyal, chaste, filial, or righteous people, he said that all this was artificial and that loyalty, chastity, filial

[147]   Willard Peterson, "Confucian Learning in Late Ming Thought," in Denis C. Twitchett and Frederick W. Mote, eds., *The Cambridge History of China* Volume 8: *The Ming Dynasty, Part 2: 1368–1644* (Cambridge, 1998), 708 at 720.
[148]   Ibid.
[149]   Ibid.
[150]   Huang, *Records* 165–66 (the T'ai-chou School).
[151]   Li Chih, "Ch'ien lun," Ts'angshu, p. 7, in Peterson "Confucian Learning in Late Ming Thought" 749.

piety, and righteousness are foreign to the nature of the inner essence. The students were pleased by this easy formula and flocked to him like mad."[152]

Not all adherents of the School of the Universal Mind accepted the subjective interpretation of the teachings of Wang Yangming. But those who did found a vast audience. Peterson noted that Lo Ju-fang, travelling "north to Shantung, south to Kwangtung, west to Hu-kuang, east along the River to Nanking and Yang-chou, ... lectured and directly influenced an important segment of the next two generations of intellectuals."[153] Lo "told a dozen or so of his followers that, just as with his learning he had inspired ten friends ... they could, in turn, each inspire ten more, and each of the hundred could inspire ten more, and so on, until hundreds of thousands were implementing the teachings of Lo Ju-fang."[154] He did succeed in giving "discourses on learning before audiences of hundreds of thousands of men."[155] Lo did not try to turn his following into a political movement. Nevertheless, his teachings and audiences alarmed the Grand Secretary Zhang Juzheng who sent Lo to serve as a magistrate in remote provinces. In the 1570s Zhang became the most serious opponent of proponents of the subjective interpretation. In 1579, Zhang ordered the closing of private academies as part of his effort to discourage large gatherings for discussing philosophical issues.[156]

Very likely, Wang Yangming himself wanted it both ways. One modern scholar not only believed that he did but found this interpretation appealing. According to Ching:

> [O]n the one hand, the notion that the Absolute is neither good nor evil is liberating to the human spirit, who realises that value judgments are man-made whereas the real Good is supra-human. On the other hand, any doctrine of pure enlightenment, when adhered to by an "unenlightened" person, may result in a complete disregard of all known criteria of truth and of moral behaviour. In this regard, the history of spirituality in both East and West can supply us ample evidence.[157]

It may be liberating to believe that value judgments are man-made. It may be reassuring to think that people cannot disregard all known criteria of truth and of moral behavior. Nevertheless, it should be possible to feel both liberated and assured without embracing contradictory propositions. The intellectual history of both East and West show the futility of trying to have it both ways.

---

[152] *Ming-ju hsüeh-an*, ch. 60 (XII, 6), in Heinrich Busch, "The Tung-Lin Academy and its Political and Philosophical Significance, *Monumenta Serica*, 14 (1949–1955), 1 at 89.
[153] Peterson, "Confucian Learning in Late Ming Thought" 730–31.
[154] Ibid. 731.
[155] Ibid. 734.
[156] Ibid. 738.
[157] Julia Ching, "Beyond Good and Evil: The Culmination of the Thought of Wang Yang-ming (1472–1529)," *Numen*, 20 (1973), 125 at 133–34.

11

The Path to Orthodoxy

The School of Principle was recognized as the correct interpretation of Confucianism from the late Song dynasty until the end of imperial China.

When it first appeared, the School was regarded as dangerous. The works of Cheng Yi were prohibited most of the time from 1103 to 1155. It is said that only four people were brave enough to go to his funeral.[1] Zhu Xi was dismissed from office several times on account of his philosophical views. In 1196, his teachings were prohibited, and there was a call for his execution. One contemporary described his funeral as "a gathering of heretics from all over the empire to follow the arch-heretic to the grave."[2]

In the end, however, the School of Principle prevailed. It was recognized as orthodox toward the end of the Song dynasty. In 1313, Emperor Renzong of the Mongol (Yuan) dynasty decreed that the imperial examinations would no longer be based on the Book of Odes and other traditional classics. They would be based Zhu Xi's commentaries to the Four Books (as they were later called) to which Zhu Xi had attached particular importance: the *Analects*, the *Mencius*, the *Doctrine of the Mean*, and the *Great Learning*. So it remained until the examinations were abolished in 1905.

Paradoxically, the School of Principle rose to orthodoxy in the late Song because of its detachment from the business of government. Its members formed fellowships dedicated to their own moral improvement through reflection and meditation on *li* and bound together by personal, political, and ritual ties. Members regarded involvement with the examination or the government as morally compromising. The School was declared orthodox in the last years of the dynasty because their commitment inspired admiration and because all else had seemingly failed.

Its independence from government allowed the School to flourish during the early years after the Mongol conquest when they examination system was abolished. Its traditional opponents had been Confucians who were committed to the examination system and to public service. These opponents were gone. When the Mongols recognized the need to placate their Chinese subjects, and, indeed, to enlist them in government, many of the

[1] Wing-tsit Chan, *A Sourcebook in Chinese Philosophy* (Princeton 1963), 546.
[2] W. Theodore de Bary, "A Reappraisal of Neo-Confucianism," in *Studies in Chinese Thought*, Arthur F. Wright, ed. (Chicago, 1953), 81 at 87.

Confucian scholars to whom they turned for help were affiliated with the School of Principle.

The School of Principle had flourished, not only because of the intellectual brilliance of its founders, but also because of the admiration inspired its all-or-nothing commitment to moral purity in which contact with government was regarded as sullying. It is deeply paradoxical that this school became the official philosophy of the Ming and Ching dynasties in which the emperors claimed and exercised near-absolute power. They were assisted by Confucian scholars who compromised their principles by serving such emperors. The constitutional balance between the emperor and the scholar-officials that had been struck in the Song dynasty was never restored.

One cannot blame the School of Principle for Ming and Ching despotism, any more than one can blame Rousseau for the Terror in the French Revolution or Hegel, von Treitschke or Nietzsche for Nazi totalitarianism. The Ming and Ching emperors as thoroughly misunderstood the teachings of the School as Robespierre did Rousseau or the Nazis the teachings of these German philosophers. Nevertheless, one can say of the School of Principle, as one might of Rousseau and these German thinkers, that they set ideas loose in the world which the proponents of absolutism found it easy to use.

We have seen that the School of Principle believed that a moral dark age ended in their lifetimes with the rediscovery of the significance of ultimate principle, a truth which had been lost since the time of Confucius and Mencius. One who thoroughly grasped ultimate principle would do no wrong. The Ming and Ching emperors claimed to have grasped ultimate principle; therefore, they were the equals of the sage kings and possessed ultimate moral authority. They could do no wrong. As Donald Munro noted, Zhu Xi would not have accepted "the elevation of emperors to the role of the highest moral authority." Yet there are "textual justifications" in Zhu's work for such a conclusion.[3]

The School of Principle claimed that the basis of every moral judgment was unchanging *li*, and that *li* was grasped by a kind of moral insight one attained by concentration of the mind. In the Ming and Ching dynasties, orders and decisions came to be justified by an invocation of *li*, not only by the emperor but by the scholar-officials who served him.

The belief of the School of Principle that virtue is acquired by reflection on *li* sometimes produced people who, with a detachment from their personal feelings like that of Buddhists, could act heroically. It did not produce those people best able to play a political role in bad times. Neither did the all-or-nothing morality of the School produce people with a gift for principled compromise.

Towards the end of the Ming dynasty, an unsuccessful attempt to curb absolutism was made by affiliates of the Dong Lin Academy (or Tung-lin Academy) (東林書院). As part of that attempt, they tried to reestablish the links between Confucian philosophy, human nature, and political morality. They did so despite the teachings of the School of Principle and the School of Universal Mind.

---

[3] Donald J. Munro, *Images of Human Nature Sung Portrait* (Princeton, 1988), 168.

I THE LATE SONG DYNASTY

In the late Song dynasty, the adherents of the School of Principle, or, as they called it, the Learning of the Way (道學 *daoxue*), put their philosophy into practice. They adopted a program of moral regeneration through reflection on principle.

The Confucian tradition had always taught that moral development comes through learning. For those committed to the Learning of the Way, the learning was of a different kind. It followed the program of the School of Principle: lectures, writing, and meditation on the ultimate principle underlying all things. That program was not the traditional one of studying of the Classics and cultivating virtue in everyday life and government. As Peter Bol noted, "In theory, one could engage in the learning of the Dao [the Way] without the mediation of the Classics and ancient models, which in turn made possible the conception of a non-constructed moral self. For the Neo-Confucians, Confucius was less important for compiling ancient texts than for teaching men how to connect sagehood to its natural basis."[4] According to a contemporary critic,

> How can we not be delighted about people being outspoken regarding their learning? However, [the true] Dao is essentially in everyday conduct; recent scholars contrarily limit it to one activity [abstract philosophizing], so the name inflates an empty reputation and exceeds reality. This causes people to be uneasy. Therefore, those who use the expression Dao-xue [the Learning of the Way] are certain to be profoundly rejected and vigorously censured. As soon as this wind prevails, won't it be fearful?[5]

"In this embattled condition," as William Theodore de Bary observed, "the School of the Way, in its struggle for survival, readily acquired a kind of 'paranoid style'. ... Their enemies were out to get them ... and the experience of genuine persecution left is mark of the Cheng-Zhu followers, reinforcing the paranoid style to which their view of the Way's endangered state easily led them." Thus the School "exhibited much of the zeal and dynamism of a religion of the oppressed. ... Messianism and martyrdom came naturally to these high-minded believers, whose sense of dedication always demanded much sacrifice."[6] Membership in the school was both an intellectual and a spiritual commitment. Zheng Yu recalled:

> When I was in my teens and still ignorant, having not settled on any "former sayings and past deeds" as my guide, I heard others reciting the Master's [Zhu Xi's] words and felt as if they were coming from my own mouth. When I heard them speaking of his Way, I felt as if it was expressed from my own mind. Since I liked it so much, I gave it everything I had.[7]

---

[4]   Peter K. Bol, "'Neo-Confucianism and Local Society' Twelfth to Sixteenth Century: A Case Study," in Paul Jakov Smith and Richard von Glahn, eds.,*The Song-Yuan-Ming Transition in Chinese History* (Cambridge, 2003), 241 at 247.

[5]   Lu Chiu-yuan, *Lu Chiu-yuan chi* (Peking, 1980), 35/437 quoted in Hoyt Cleveland Tillman, "A New Direction in Confucian Scholarship: Approaches to Examining the Differences between Neo-Confucianism and Tao-hsüeh," *Philosophy East and West* 42 (1992), 455 at 464.

[6]   William Theodore de Bary, *Neo-Confucian Orthodoxy and the Learning of Mind-and-Heart* (New York, 1981), 16, 17.

[7]   Zhu Yu, *Shishan xiansheng wenji* quoted in Bol, "Neo-Confucianism" 242.

Members of the School cultivated moral principle in fellowship with each other. John Dardess described them as "a sectarian 'fellowship' that was at once intellectual (its claim to represent absolute moral truth), social (with its local academies, rural compacts, and community graineries), and political (with its factional struggle to secure imperial endorsement)."[8] They did not have an organization like that of a society or a political party. By calling them a "fellowship," Hoyt Tillman said,

> I mean that [*Daoxue*](Learning of the Way) Confucians had a network of social relations and a sense of community with a shared tradition that was distinct from other Confucians of their era. Personal, political, ritual, and intellectual ties bound members of the group together in such common undertakings as reforming Song political culture, reviving ethical values, and rectifying Confucian learning. Bonding was fostered in institutions, such as academies, and in rituals, such as the rites performed by students for their teachers.[9]

De Weerdt described them as "a community characterized by a cluster of identity-forming discursive practices – habits of thinking, speaking, writing and acting that form a systematic whole."[10]

One of these practices, she noted, was "hierarchical authority" which "prioritized personal contact between teacher and disciple." "The moral authority accorded leading thinkers in the geneology of the Way and the teachers who followed in their wake was based on a new image of a teacher. . . . [T]eachers emerge as transmitters of the Way."[11]

According to De Weerdt, these practices included expressions of commitment, that is, "the personal and explicit identification of the individual with the Learning of the Way."[12] "The performance of rites . . . participation in the promotion of the transmission through study, teaching and publishing, and the use of distinctive dress, speech and behaviors were all read as signs of commitment."[13] Liu noted,

> Among other features, they chose to wear a tall hat with a pointed top, a beret like gear for casual wear, a roomy gown with broad sleeves, and a fine white-gauze shirt underneath. Their mannerism was strict: they sat squarely with their back erect, walked in measured steps looking straight ahead, bowed slowly and deeply to express sincere propriety, spoke in a dignified way with few gestures and carefully made at that.[14]

To outsiders, "their lofty air" appeared "strange, stupid, snobbish, arrogant, or more like a Daoist than a Confucianist."[15] According to one contemporary critic, if one saw "a doltish

---

[8] John W. Dardess, "Did the Mongols Matter? Territory, Power and the Intelligentsia in China from the Northern Song to the Early Ming," in Paul Jakov Smith and Richard von Glahn, eds., *The Song-Yuan-Ming Transition in Chinese History* (Cambridge, 2003), 111 at 129.

[9] Tillman, "New Direction" 459.

[10] Hilde De Weerdt, *Competition over Content: Negotiating Standards for the Civil Service Examinations in Imperial China (1127–1279)* (Cambridge, 2007), 42.

[11] Ibid. 43.

[12] Ibid. 44.

[13] Ibid.

[14] James T. C. Liu, "How Did a Neo-Confucian School Become the State Orthodoxy?" *Philosophy East and West* 23 (1973), 483 at 497.

[15] Ibid. 497.

schoolmaster type, dressed in rags and poorly fed, [wearing] a high head-cloth but with holes in his shoes [o]thers only needed to look at him to know he was a *Daoxue* (Learning of the Way) virtuous man."[16]

Their commitment to their program of moral regeneration was coupled with a contempt for those who competed in the imperial examinations and held official positions. As Liu noted, they disparaged those who "excelled in examinations as *wen-shi* or literati, implying that they were writers rather than genuine Neo-Confucianists with proper understanding of the principles."[17] Some thought that taking the examinations compromised one's moral integrity, although Zhu Xi said it need not do so. According to Chen Chun, a member of the School,

> The only purpose of exam writing is to oppose the enemy. Its strengths and weaknesses depend upon this. If we strive for more artistry on top of this and make calculations for gain, we will be misled. Principle and rightness reside in our bodies and minds, and we cannot be without them for even a single day. If we abandon them for a single day, we will lead a meaningless life, like a lost people, like ordinary men and vulgar fellows.[18]

Members of the School feared that an active role in politics might also be morally compromising. Indeed, according to their critics, they despised it:

> All who managed resources and revenues, they regarded as aggrandizers of wealth; those who served as attendants in the palace or as soldiers on the frontier, they regarded as scum; those who read books and engaged in literary composition, they regarded as dilettantes bereft of any sense of purpose; and those who devoted their attention to government affairs, they regarded as petty clerks.[19]

Underlying and sustaining this commitment was the belief described earlier: true learning which had been passed down from the sage kings to Confucius and Mencius had been lost for a thousand years until it was revived in the time of Cheng Yi. As Peter Bol observed, "[i]ntegral to the claim that 'we can be sages' were the assertions . . . that there had not been a sage since Confucius and that the traditions that had emerged from the time of Confucius and Mencius had led the literati astray."[20] Consequently, "Neo-Confucians saw their own claims as totalizing. Theirs was not a position that allowed for its own inclusion as part of a pluralistic whole."[21] As a contemporary critic said:

> They read only the Four Books [and the Cheng-Zhu literature]. They pretended that their learning corrected the mind, cultivated the self, ordered the state, and brought peace to the world. Therefore they took the following slogan for their guide: "Be the ultimate standard for the populace, establish the mind of Heaven-and-Earth, inaugurate the Great Peace for a myriad of generations, and continue the lost learning of the former sages."[22]

---

[16] Zhou Mi, *Guixin dashi* (Beijing 1980), 69, quoted in Bol, "Neo-Confucianism" 256.
[17] James T. C. Liu, "Neo-Confucian School" 496.
[18] Chen Chun, *Beixi daquan ji*, 34.7a, quoted in De Weerdt, *Competition over Content* 252.
[19] Zhou Mi, *Guixin dashi* (Beijing 1980), 69, quoted in Bol, "Neo-Confucianism" 255.
[20] Bol, "Neo-Confucianism" 246.
[21] Ibid. 254.
[22] Zhou Mi, *Guixin dashi* (Beijing 1988), 69, quoted in Bol, "Neo-Confucianism" 255.

As Peter Bol observed, the School of Principle brought with it a vision of politics in which, instead of flowing downward from the emperor, political initiative was in principle to come from such local groups.[23] He was sympathetic to the movement because in that way it provided an alternative to and a safeguard against autocracy. One might question the desirability of this alternative: power sought by tightly knit, hierarchically ordered groups who claimed to have a unique insight into truth and whose leaders claimed to have the mind of sage kings.

Previously, the Confucian tradition had been open to different interpretations. Wang Anshi had believed that his own interpretation was correct, and that those who diligently studied the Classics would support both it and his programs. Yet there had been no ban on other interpretations, and some thought that Wang's insistence on his own was a sign of arrogance. The claim of the Learning of the Way movement to have found the one right interpretation alarmed other Confucians.[24] In 1188, Lin Li submitted a memorial attacking Zhu Xi for claiming that the Learning of the Way was the single correct Confucian tradition.[25] In 1195, an imperial ban was placed on the Learning of the Way. In 1197, the works of fifty-nine scholars were censured.[26]

The ban was lifted in 1202. Three decades later, for reasons no one understands, the government recognized the teachings of the School of Principle as the true interpretation of the Confucian tradition. In 1237, in a eulogy supposedly written by the emperor, its teachings were praised. In 1241, this eulogy was released to the country, and the School was formally proclaimed to be the state orthodoxy. The eulogy officially confirmed that the transmission of true Confucian principles had been interrupted for a thousand years after the death of Mencius and rediscovered in the time of Cheng Yi who passed it on to Zhu Xi.

The change did not come about because of the convictions of the emperor. As de Bary said, "[a]fter making ritual obeisance to the memory of [Zhu Xi] and other Neo-Confucian patriarchs at the temple of Confucius, the emperor [Duzong] (r. 1225–1264) went back to the business of enjoying himself in his palace and letting the dynasty run off to its doom."[27]

James Liu thought that the official endorsement of the School of Principle was a response to the threat of a Mongol invasion. The Mongols conquered northern China in 1234. They built a temple to honor Confucius. In 1237, they held examinations in the Chinese classics. According to Liu, the Song endorsed the School of Principle to show "that no matter how Confucian the Mongol empire might become, the legitimate line of transmitting the orthodoxy and the true way of Confucianism rested with the Southern Song alone." The dynasty was trying "to boost its political prestige by cultural propaganda."[28] Perhaps. But the Mongols did not conquer the south by winning a propaganda war, and it is hard to think that the Song thought that its cultural claim to legitimacy was threatened by the Mongols, of all people.

---

[23] Peter K. Bol, *Neo-Confucianism in History* (Cambridge, 2008), 249.
[24] Tillman, "New Direction" 464–65.
[25] De Weerdt, *Competition over Content* 38.
[26] Tillman, "A New Direction" 464–65.
[27] de Bary, *Neo-Confucian Orthodoxy* 1; similarly Liu, "Neo-Confucian School" 503.
[28] Liu, "Neo-Confucian School" 502.

The explanation may be simpler. The emperor may have switched his support to the comparatively few officials who subscribed to the School of Principle because times were desperate, and he thought that they could do a better job. They pushed for the School of Principle to be declared orthodox because they thought its teachings were right. The ban on its teachings had made their status an either-or question: either its claim to exclusive truth was false, in which case the School should be banned, or true, in which case its claim should be officially recognized.

In any event, as de Bary noted, during the Song dynasty "[n]othing significant was done to institutionalize Zhu's teaching in the one form essential to the implementation of state orthodoxy: prescribing it for the civil service examinations, which tended also to determine the school curriculum. But in the deteriorating condition of the Song dynasty, even this would have been a meaningless gesture."[29]

II THE MONGOLS

During the Song dynasty, those committed to the Learning of the Way had been criticized for their clannishness, their exclusive claim to truth, and their disdain for the civil examinations, for those in authority, and for the analysis of policy in the pragmatic terms. These features of their movement, however, suited it for survival when the dynasty fell to the Mongols. Their version of Confucianism was less dependent on civil institutions.

After the disappearance of the Song officials and the Song examination system, many of the educated Chinese who were keeping Confucian traditions alive were affiliated with the School. According to Benjamin Elman, "[t]he [*Daoxue*] literati in local society had gained control of the examination debate while the Mongols hesitated to reinstate examinations for fear of the vast Han majority. In effect, the examination system, by its very absence as an institutional bulwark favoring [literary studies] had become irrelevant to the battle over its future content." The Mongols wanted the support of the educated Chinese and their help in ruling China. When they reinstituted civil examinations in 1313 and based them on the teachings of the Learning of the Way, they "accomodate[d] their most influential literati constituency of the time, the [*Daoxue*] fellowship. What [Zhu Xi] and his followers could not accomplish in Song times, their later disciples achieved under the watchful eye of a Mongol court seeking literati support for its legitimacy."[30]

According to Elman, "In the thirteenth and fourteenth centuries, 'Way learning' remained a widespread but still local literary persuasion, enough so, however, that it was one of the major candidates to become the Ming's mainstream vision of itself. . . . [I]t took Ming historical events to forge and consummate the supremacy of 'Way learning.'"[31]

The Mongols, however, did revive the civil service examinations and base them on the teachings of the School of Principle. In 1267, a scholar who had passed the Song imperial examinations in 1224 proposed that examinations be reinstituted, citing the precedent of

---

[29] de Bary, *Neo-Confucian Orthodoxy* 1.
[30] Benjamin A. Elman, *A Cultural History of Civil Examinations in Late Imperial China* (Berkeley, 2000), 32–33.
[31] Benjamin A. Elman, *Civil Examinations and Meritocracy in Late Imperial China* (Cambridge, 2013), 16.

earlier dynasties and the examinations in the Chinese classics that the Mongols had introduced in 1237. Members of the School had qualms. As de Bary noted, they were "ambivalent about examinations. In the past the most they had been willing to concede was that they were not necessarily opposed. ... For the Neo-Confucians the highest priority went to the precondition of any effective recruitment system at all – education in character formation and public morality."[32] In 1313–15, one of Kubilai's successors reintroduced the examinations as the method of recruiting state officials. "[T]hough a great deal of outward tribute was paid to virtue – the hallowed Neo-Confucian idea of the selection of candidates on the basis of character – there is little to indicate that this was more than a preliminary screening device."[33]

The examinations were based on the Four Books to which Zhu Xi had attached special importance and on his commentaries to these books. The course of study necessary to prepare for the examinations was far narrower than the course of study that Cheng Yi and Zhu Xi themselves had proposed as ideal. "Rather than a [*Daoxue*] manifesto," Elman noted, Cheng Yi's proposal for the education of the scholars "affirmed the entire classical and historical repertoire of texts that had accrued in the literati tradition since antiquity."[34] Zhu Xi proposed a curriculum that was more partisan, De Weerdt observed, but it was inclusive. It included the works of scholars he had criticized such as Wang Anshi.[35] Moreover, under the Mongols, the import of Zhu Xi's commentaries was now simplified to what de Bary called "the lowest common denominator of educated leadership among Mongols, Central Asians, and Chinese, it being understood that graduates of this system would enter official service."[36] Teaching manuals had titles such as "The General Significance of the Elementary Learning," "The *Great Learning* Reduced to its Essentials," "A Straightforward Explanation of the *Great Learning*," and "A Straightforward Explanation of the *Mean*."[37] De Bary described the new course of study as "a stripped down version of [Zhu's]."[38]

According to de Bary, this simplification was an "adaptation to the requirements of the Yuan situation" which was "worlds away from the high culture of the Song." But he also observed that it was "the product of a long process of distillation in the School of the Way."[39] For members of that school, what mattered was clarity in the rectification of one's mind. "In theory," Peter Bol noted, the Learning of the Way did not require "the mediation of the Classics."[40] As Yu Zhi (1271–1348) summarized the teachings of Tu Pen (1276–1350), "what was called 'learning' among the ancients was simply the Learning of Mind-and-Heart

---

[32] de Bary, *Neo-Confucian Orthodoxy* 44.
[33] Ibid. 55.
[34] Elman, *Cultural History of Civil Examinations* 28
[35] Hilde De Weerdt. "Changing Minds through Examinations: Examination Critics in Late Imperial China," *Journal of the American Oriental Society* 126 (2006), 367 at 373–74; see de Bary, *Neo-Confucian Orthodoxy* 57–59.
[36] de Bary, *Neo-Confucian Orthodoxy* 49.
[37] Ibid. 137.
[38] Ibid. 61.
[39] Ibid.
[40] Bol, "Neo-Confucianism" 247.

and nothing else." He was quick to add that as "we are imperfect ... study is indispensable."[41] Still, it is not surprising that when the teachings of Zhu Xi were distilled, much that had been regarded as the core of Confucian learning evaporated

III THE MING DYNASTY

i *Orthodoxy and Absolutism*

The Mongols were overthrown, and the Ming dynasty founded by Zhu Yuanzhang, a rebel leader who reigned as the Hongwu Emperor from 1368–98. As de Bary noted,

> He had in his service representatives of the [Cheng-Zhu] school who played a leading role in setting the cultural direction of the new dynasty. They included Xu Yuan, who "would not read anything but the five Classics and Four Books and would not teach anything but the learning of the Cheng-Zhu school," ... Chang I (1314–1369), spoken of as someone holding the highest respect for [Zhu Xi's] teachings; Chu Lien, a deep student of [Zhu Xi's] Classified Dialogues; Sung Lien (1310–1381), widely known as an ardent admirer of [Zhu Xi]; Wang Wei (1323–1374), who held to the orthodox tradition from the Song school; and [Liu Ji] (1311–1375), who though not formally identified with this school, was influenced by its Learning of the Mind-and-Heart.

The "examination system in essentially Yuan form" was resumed "almost [as] a matter of course." "[N]o alternative was consciously considered and rejected. 'Orthodoxy' won without a struggle."[42]

In the late Song dynasty, the School of Principle was declared to be orthodox, but dissenters had not been persecuted. In the Yuan and early Ming dynasty, scholars sometimes preferred their own interpretations of a text to those of Zhu Xi. In the reign of the Yongle emperor (1402–24), other interpretations were proscribed. As John Dardess noted,

> In 1404, the Yongle emperor made it clear that this kind of intellectual inquiry, which compromised the integrity of the Cheng-Zhu interpretations, would be severely punished. For demonstration effect, he sent home in shackles the hapless Zhu Jiyou who had come to Nanking to present with pride the fruit of his researches to the throne. The poor fellow was arrested and marched back to his home in Jiangzi province where his house was ransacked and his papers burned. He was flogged a hundred strokes for good measure. The intimidation effect worked. Yongle's enshrinement of the Cheng-Zhu orthodoxy lasted through the Ming and most of the Qing.[43]

Another change concerned the relationship the emperor and the officials. The Ming dynasty began with a bloodbath. Benjamin Elman noted, "Estimates vary but by [Zhu Yuanzhang's] own estimate perhaps 50,000 to 70,000 people were executed."[44]

The emperor killed some and humiliated others. According to Frederick Mote,

---

[41] Yü Chi, "Ssu-hsüeh-chai chi," in Ssu, *Yüan wen-lei* 30:3a in de Bary, *Neo-Confucian Orthodoxy* 151–52.
[42] de Bary, *Neo-Confucian Orthodoxy* 153–54.
[43] John W. Dardess, *Ming China, 1368–1644: A Concise History of a Resilient Empire* (Lanham, 2012), 88.
[44] Elman, *Civil Examinations* 20; Elman, *Cultural History* 83.

[H]e added to this his personal delight in humiliating high officials, and keeping them in terror of his temper. His sudden outbursts of wrath were so real a threat that the court became accustomed to watching his countenance for indications of his mood, and officials are said to have fainted from fright on hearing him raise his voice to a shout, without waiting to hear what he said. Eunuchs, despised by the Confucian literati, were given the responsibility for supervising the decorum of ministers in the daily audience, and for administering beatings with heavy clubs in the presence of the court on a signal from the emperor, to any official who incurred his displeasure. These beatings at court introduced by [Zhu] became a most notorious feature of Ming government, and in later reigns were a chief means by which eunuchs came to intimidate the officialdom.[45]

"During the Tang dynasty," Elman noted, "high officials sat with the emperor as social equals. Beginning with the Song dynasty, they stood in front of a seated emperor."[46] Wang Anshi, it is said, even refused to stand in the emperor's presence, and so was charged by Lu Hui with "ignorance of correct distinctions" and "a tendency to self-glorification."[47] "Beginning with the Ming and continuing under the Qing, officials were required to prostrate themselves and kneel before him."[48]

The founder of the Song dynasty had established two bureaus whose task was to admonish the emperor. In contrast, the Hongwu emperor established the Jin Yi Wei or Embroidered Uniform Guard, which Mote described as "a secret police unit which had the power to arrest any person at any time, incarcerate him for any length of time, and inflict any manner of torture on him in order to prepare a case against him."[49] The emperor also established the Eastern Depot, another such police unit run by eunuchs. He instituted "the literary inquisition, which ... was not 'legalized' ... but which was simply a direct expression of the emperor's power. It was a most convenient device for getting rid of a man and simultaneously terrorizing others."[50]

In the Song dynasty, the punishments for crimes had been reduced. Death sentences were infrequent and amnesties common. Those executed were either strangled or decapitated. In the Ming dynasty, Mote noted,

Many new means of slowly and painfully separating the body from the spirit were made regular punishments; they included beating the victim with sand bags without breaking his skin until his whole body was a balloon of jelly, inducing a lingering and painful death; alternate scaldings with boiling water and scrubbings with wire brushes; and [*ling chi*] which meant slowly slicing a man to pieces with a prescribed 3,357 strokes of the knife, with a pause after each ten strokes to permit him to recover his feelings. Never before had such cruelties been widely practiced as legitimate means of execution.[51]

---

[45] F. W. Mote, "The Growth of Chinese Despotism: A Critique of Wittfogel's Theory of Oriental Despotism as applied to China," *Oriens Extremus* 8 (1961), 1 at 27.

[46] Elman, *Civil Examinations* 21.

[47] Lü Hui, "Impeachment of Wang An-shih" 5, in John Meskill, ed., *Wang An-Shih Practical Reformer?* (Boston, 1963), 19 at 19.

[48] Elman, *Civil Examinations* 21.

[49] Mote, "Growth of Chinese Despotism" 28.

[50] Ibid. 29.

[51] Ibid. 28.

Mote concluded, "[Zhu Yuanzhang] established a reign of terror that more or less persisted throughout the 277 years of the Ming dynasty."[52] He characterized the dynasty as "an age of terror."[53]

The autocratic character of the regime was mitigated only by the fact that beyond the reach of the emperor and his police, the institutions established in the Song dynasty still functioned. The empire was governed by officials chosen by competitive examinations and promoted according to achievement and seniority. The laws remained in place. David Robinson said of the officials, their "faith in the imperial vision of order" led them to believe that they could "restore order to the court, the realm and the cosmos ...an understanding [that] was simultaneously empowering and optimistic."[54] As Mote noted, the Ming Code "had a daily influence on the whole government and society at large, even if [Zhu] could execute persons by the thousands without reference to the code."[55]

For the Ming emperors, the recognition of the School of Principle and the assumption of autocratic power reinforced each other. They claimed to be the equals of the sage kings. According to the School of Principle, the sage kings, Confucius and Mencius, had grasped ultimate principle, and so they had acquired ultimate moral authority. The Ming emperors claimed to have done so as well. In 1404, in the palace examinations which were given in the presence of the emperor, Teng Ch'i said:

> Your humble servant recognizes that the emperor's mind is the mind of Yellow Emperor, Yao and Shun. Those sages before and after have all had this mind. The Paramount Ancestor [i.e. [Zhu Yuanzhang]], as sage and worthy, wisely wielded both civil and military power. The exalted Ming was set in motion and great virtue was accomplished. He was the esteemed ruler who unified heaven and magnified filial piety and thereby exemplified in reality this mind-heart.[56]

Teng was ranked first on the examination. As Elman noted, he had set "a precedent for linking the [*Daoxue*] (Learning of the Way) focus on the moral cultivation of the mind to discussion of the sagely qualities of the Ming emperors . . . that would be produced over and over again in examination essays, becoming in the Qing dynasty a mantra about the emperor's cultural prestige."[57] Indeed,

> By the mid-Ming, the emperors were said by civil service candidates to have unified the *dao-t'ung* [succession to the *dao* or Way] and *chih-tung* [political succession]. The emperor also took precedence over his literati in reestablishing the "orthodox transmission of the *Dao*," a position never granted him by literati in Song or Yuan times. Hu Cheng-meng, the tertius [third-ranked candidate in the examinations] in 1547, wrote on his palace essay, for example, that "the rulers in Han, Tang, and Song had positions but no learning, while

---

52   Ibid. 31.
53   Ibid. 20.
54   David M. Robinson, "The Ming Court," in David M. Robinson, ed., *Culture, Courtiers, and Competion The Ming Court (1368–1644)*, (Cambridge, Mass. 2008), 21 at 29.
55   Mote, "Growth of Chinese Despotism" 34.
56   *Huang-Ming chuan-yuang ch'üan-ts'e* (1591 ed.) 2.18a–19b, 36a–b, quoted in Elman, *Cultural History* 68.
57   Elman, *Cultural History* 69.

[Zhou Dunyi] (1017–73), Cheng Yi, [Cheng Hao] (1032–85) and [Zhu Xi] as the four Song masters had learning but no achievements. That is why in the preceding hundreds and thousands of years the transmission of the *dao-t'ung* had been interrupted." Only the early Ming emperors had for the first time successfully combined *dao-xue* morality and imperial governance simultaneously.[58]

Consequently, the Ming emperors expected people to obey them as if they were sage kings. The Yongle emperor explained:

When a ruler becomes like Yao and Shun, the people become like the people of Yao and Shun. . . . Therefore, in upholding high principles without submitting to threats, nothing is greater than loyalty. Those who receive their positions and salaries from the ruler should concern themselves with the dynasty as they do with their families. They should forget about themselves and follow the dynasty.[59]

Contemporary scholars who are sympathetic to the School of Principle have described it as antithetical to autocracy because of its high regard for moral principle. According to Allen Wood, "[t]he close correspondence held to exist by the neo-Confucian metaphysical thinkers between the nature of man's being (and therefore of political society) and the nature of the universal order" implied "protection against arbitrary rule," "strengthening the obligation of the ruler to obey universal moral laws, of which the ruler himself was regarded as merely the instrument."[60] According to Peter Bol, one result of Neo-Confucianism was that "the ruler became a more human figure, who was expected to cultivate himself through learning in the style of the literati and whose ability to maintain the support of the populace depended on his success in managing the government so that it served the common good."[61] Both descriptions fit the role of the emperor in classical thought and the role he was expected to play in the Song dynasty. What Neo-Confucianism added was not the idea that the emperor was subject to moral law. It was the idea that the knowledge of moral law was possessed by those who had grasped ultimate principle and thereby acquired the mind of a sage king. Any limit it could have placed on autocracy ended when the emperor claimed the mind of a sage king.

As Elman noted, "the emperor could not have made such a claim without literati support."[62] One cannot know what would have happened if the Confucian scholars had taken seriously the teachings of Mencius on the consequences of misrule. When Mencius was asked, "'May a minister put his ruler to death?'" he answered,

He who betrays the benevolence proper to his nature, is called a robber; he who betrays righteousness, is called crooked. The robber and crooked we call just a man. I have heard of the putting to death of the man Zhou [the last Shang emperor killed by Wu who established the Zhou dynasty], but, in his case, I have not heard of killing a ruler.[63]

---

[58]   Ibid. 69.
[59]   Chu Ti, *Sheng-hsueh hsin-fa* "Hsu" 24b–25a, quoted ibid. 113.
[60]   Alan T. Wood, *Limits to Autocracy: From Sung Neo-Confucianism to a Doctrine of Political Rights* (Honolulu, 1995), 111.
[61]   Bol, *Neo-Confucianism in History* 119.
[62]   Elman, *Cultural History* 97.
[63]   *Mencius* 1.2.8.1–3.

In another passage, Mencius suggested that if a king has "great faults," relatives who are high ministers "ought to remonstrate with him, and if he do not listen to them after they have done so repeatedly, they ought to dethrone him."[64]

These passages were taken seriously by the Hongwu emperor. He ordered Mencius' tablet to be removed from the temple of Confucius, and passages such as these to be eliminated from the works of Mencius. His minister Qian Tang agreed, and an expurgated version was prepared in by Liu San-wu in 1394, which became the standard text until 1414–15, when the Yongle emperor allowed the passages to be restored. He may have thought that they provided some justification for his own conduct in usurping the throne from his nephew, Jianwen, the grandson of the Hongwu emperor.[65] Nevertheless, as Elman noted, "Hu Kuang [the compiler of the official version] chose commentators who stressed that that Mencius' words applied only to the chaotic historical situation of the Warring States period. Accordingly, Mencius stood as a guide to the past, not a model to the present."[66]

Elman explained succinctly why the Ming scholars and officials submitted: they "acquiesced to this betrayal of their ideals or they lost their heads."[67] There was no chance of resisting an emperor like Hongwu or Yongle. These emperors denied them even the traditional recourse of refusing to serve a ruler whose actions they could not support. A law added to the Ming Code provided: "Scholars anywhere in the realm who refuse to enter the ruler's service are to be executed."[68]

In the later Ming dynasty, as Julia Ching noted "a succession of mediocre, pleasure-loving sovereigns increased the abuses of total power with the assistance of a 'secret police force' conducted by eunuchs, while also enforcing a strict official orthodoxy of thought through a rigid civil service examination regulating both the content of the syllabus as well as the form of expression of ideas."[69] As John Dardess observed, "[t]he enshrinement of the Cheng-Zhu orthodoxy lasted through the Ming and most of the Qing."[70]

Some scholar-officials began using the teachings of the School of Principle to justify their own arbitrary exercise of power. In the Qing dynasty, Dai Zhen claimed that the teaching of the School of Principle had infected those in authority. They invoked principle (*li*) to justify arbitrary decisions which they could not otherwise defend. He said of "those who are presently in a ruling position"

> when it comes to reproving others on the basis of "principle," it is easy for them to point out what is considered the highest standard in the whole world [principle] and then to condemn others in the name of "righteousness." The exalted reprove their inferiors on the basis of "principle"; the elders reprove their juniors on the basis of principle; the noble

[64] Ibid. 5.2.9.1–4.
[65] Elman, *Cultural History of Civil Examinations* 102.
[66] Ibid. 117; similarly, Elman, *Civil Examinations* 40.
[67] Elman, *Civil Examinations* 21.
[68] Mote, "Growth of Chinese Despotism" 36.
[69] Julia Ching, "Beyond Good and Evil: The Culmination of the Thought of Wang Yang-ming (1472–1529)," *Numen* 20 (1973), 125 at 125.
[70] John W. Dardess, *Ming China, 1368–1644: A Concise History of a Resilient Empire* (Lanham, 2012), 88.

reprove the ordinary folk on the basis of principle. Although they are wrong, they insist that they are following principle. The inferiors, the juniors and the ordinary folk protest this by appealing to principle, but even when these people of lower status are right, they are judged to be against principle. Thus those below are unable to reach those above on the basis of shared feelings and desires. . . .

When men die because they have violated the law, there are those who have pity for them, but when men die because they have violated principle, who has compassion for them? Alas! To mix Daoist and Buddhist ideas with those of the sages can result only in calamities worse than were ever inflicted by Shen Pu-hai or Han Feizi.[71]

De Bary observed that some "modern writers" have said that the School of Principle "bore the seeds of such despotism in its own 'dogmatism' and authoritarian ways." "Still others" blame the School "for almost opposite reasons, citing their impractical idealism, naïve optimism, and simple moralistic approach to politics."[72] Both views are correct. As Dai Zhen said, those who claimed to have grasped principle were dogmatic and authoritarian. Yet, as he also noted, the School had incorporated Daoist and Buddhist ideas. It regarded ultimate principle – the principle underlying all principles – as ineffable. Those who are dedicated to an ineffable principle may often behave heroically since they are unattached to mundane life. But their approach to politics may be simple, naïve, and impractical. They may be both more willing to die for a principle and also more likely to be mistaken as to which principles are worth dying for. It is striking that, until the protests associated with the Dong Lin Academy, which will be described later, when scholar-officials defied the emperor, few of their protests were directed at absolutism or the institutional roots of absolutism.

It is true that Lin Zu-ning had protested the arbitrary execution of talented officials when he took the palace examination in the Hongwu emperor's presence.[73] The emperor not only spared Lin, but ranked him second in the examination and appointed him to office. Lin died, however, for a quite different principle. He was killed for objecting to the Yongle emperor's usurpation of the throne from his nephew, Jianwen, the grandson of Hungwu. The Yongle emperor had violated the rule of primogeniture. But that rule was not at the heart of the Confucian tradition. It had been established by Hongwu. To cement his power, the emperor killed, not only Lin, but thousands and perhaps tens of thousands of officials and their family members and friends who remained loyal to Jianwen.[74]

On several occasions, officials gathered to protest an imperial decision. Sometimes the protest was successful and sometimes the officials were flogged or killed. One, in 1506, was a demonstration at the Meridian Gate outside the Forbidden City demanding that a clique

[71] *Tai Chen on Mencius: Explorations in Words and Meaning. A Translation of the Meng Tzu tzu-i shu-cheng*, trans. Ann-ping Chin and Mansfield Freeman (New Haven, 1990), art. 10 pp. 84–85. Shen Pu-hai and Han Feizi were exponents of the "legalist" philosophy endorsed by the Qin dynasty and anathematized by the Confucians. It taught that the ultimate goal of politics was to strengthen the state.

[72] William Theodore de Bary, *The Trouble with Confucianism* (Cambridge, 1991), 54.

[73] For his answer, see *Lin Chung-ch'eng Chin-ch'uan chi* (1762 ed,) 2,1a–7b, quoted in Elman, *Cultural History* 87.

[74] John W. Dardess, *Ming China, 1368–1644: A Concise History of a Resilient Empire* (Plymouth, 2012), 34.

of seven eunuchs close to the emperor surrender to the courts for trial. The demonstration was crushed and those who participated blacklisted. When a follow-up demonstration was held the next year in Nanjing, the officials who participated were brought to the capital and flogged.

That demonstration was one of the few that concerned the arbitrary exercise of political power. Others, like Lin's protest over the succession, did not. In 1468, a successful protest stopped the secondary consort of a deceased emperor from preventing his principal consort from being buried by his side. In 1519, officials knelt by the Meridian Gate to protest the emperor's plan to abandon his responsibilities in the capital and take an extensive trip of southern China. The demonstration was broken up by arrests and floggings in which twelve officials died. In 1521, Jiajin, who succeeded to the throne when the Hongzhi emperor died without offspring, refused to be adopted posthumously by Hongzhi out of filial respect for his own father. "[N]early all of Beijing officialdom dropped what they were doing and mounted an impromptu demonstration, wailing and kneeling outside the Meridian Gate, placing their careers and lives on the line in an emotionally supercharged effort to compel the ruler to change his mind."[75]

These protests concerned succession, correct ritual practice, and where the emperor should reside. For the scholar-officials who engaged in them, their protest showed their dedication to the dynasty and dynastic succession. They wished to serve the dynasty even at the risk of their lives.

An opposition party that appealed to higher principles that limit the power of the emperor formed only late in the dynasty. It was called the "Dong Lin party" by its adversaries – "party" because it was a pejorative term connoting factionalism, and "Dong Lin" because its leaders were associated with the intellectual activities of the Dong Lin Academy.

ii *The Dong Lin Academy*

Politically, the objective of those associated with the Dong Lin Academy was to curb absolutism by increasing the influence of scholar-officials, and to ensure that they were selected and promoted according to merit rather than political loyalty. Intellectually, their objective was to reestablish the links between Confucian philosophy, human nature, and political morality.

The founders of the Dong Lin Academy had opposed the absolutism that peaked under Zhang Juzheng. He became Grand Secretary in 1572 when the Wanli emperor was only ten years old. Until his death in 1582, he ruled, in Heinrich Busch's words, as an "absolute dictator,"[76] and an extremely effective one. He diverted power from the ordinary organs of the civil service and concentrated it in his own hands. His critics were flogged in court and threatened with death. He complained that he was criticized

---

[75] Dardess, *Ming China* 49.
[76] Heinrich Busch, "The Tung-Lin Academy and its Political and Philosophical Significance," *Monumenta Serica*, 14 (1949–1955), 1 at 16.

as an enemy of learning.[77] Nevertheless, he wrote a commentary on the Four Books to supplement that of Zhu Xi which did not deviate significantly from his teachings.[78]

Those who opposed him called themselves "the righteous circles." Zhang had five of them flogged before the court when they opposed his decision to remain in power after his father died rather than to observe the customary period of mourning. He persuaded the fourteen-year-old Wan-li emperor to threaten to execute anyone else who complained.

When Zhang died, the young emperor had a change of heart. He removed Feng Pao, the Chief Eunuch who had abetted Zhang. He had Zhang posthumously disgraced. The "righteous circles" continued their campaign against Zhang's successors as Grand Secretary. They demanded that power be decentralized, that officials be chosen by merit, and that there be an end to "suppression of freedom of speech" (literally "cutting the path of speech").[79]

In the ensuing power struggle, members of the righteous circles tried to gain control of the official scrutiny into the conduct of metropolitan officials which was held every six years. In 1581, Zhang had used it to oust his opponents. In 1587, a member of the righteous circles, Hsin Tzu-hsiu, secured the emperor's permission to have it be conducted in strict accordance with law. Nevertheless, a friend of the Grand Secretary saw to it that ten corrupt officials were retained. Hsin was forced to resign, and those who protested his resignation were punished. In 1593, the reformers were in control and purged the government of incompetent and corrupt officials, many of whom were friends of Grand Secretaries. In retaliation, their opponents managed to have two leaders of the righteous circles cashiered. The political struggle continued for the next two decades.

Gu Xiancheng (1550–1612) was a leader of the righteous circles and, after leaving office, the co-founder of the Dong Lin Academy. He had been transferred to a minor post for protesting the resignation of Hsin, recalled in 1592, and played an active role in the scrutiny of 1583. His official career ended in 1594 when he opposed a candidate for Grand Secretary whom the emperor favored.

Out of office, Gu lectured on philosophy at local temples. He, his brother, and Gao Panlong raised the funds to build and endow a permanent site for such lectures. It opened in 1604. They called it the Dong Lin or Eastern Grove Academy. Its purpose was to promote discussion of the philosophical principles on which self-cultivation and the reform of the state should be founded. Gu believed that without such discussion, the political struggle was futile.

The Academy was not a school or house of study. It was a center for meetings: a large one every year, and smaller ones every month. The Academy had no formal membership, only a guest book to keep track of those interested in its work. Its objectives and procedures were stated in a document Gu drafted with the help of friends: the *Statutes or Convention*

---

[77] Willard Peterson, "Confucian Learning in Late Ming Thought," in Denis C. Twitchett and Frederick W. Mote, eds., *The Cambridge History of China 8The Ming Dynasty Part 2: 1368–1644* (Cambridge, 1998), 740. Peterson, "Confucian Learning" 740 at 741.

[78] David E. Mungello, *Curious Land: Jesuit Accommodation and the Origins of Sinology* (Honolulu, 1989), 270.

[79] Heinrich Busch, "The Tung-Lin Academy and its Political and Philosophical Significance," *Monumenta Serica* 14 (1949–1955), 1 at 20.

Concerning the Tung-lin Meetings. The document described "Two Illusions" to be avoided and "Four Essentials" to be observed. The Two Illusions were that the "investigation of philosophy" is "remote from practical life and too idealistic," and that it is "without influence on practical morality." The first of the Four Essentials was "to know nature," which meant, according to Henrich Busch, "to have the correct notions about human nature, which is essentially identified with the fundamental moral relations, and about the way to acquire an adequate understanding of these relations or duties, and to carry them out in one's actions, motives, and relations to others."[80]

The Academy did not have a political program other than that government be conducted by men of character in accordance with Confucian principles. It did not have an official philosophy other than "to respect the Classics and acquire the right principles by a sound study of them," which was the second of the Four Essentials. Most affiliates of the Academy adhered to the School of Principle, and some to the School of Universal Mind. Yet, as the language of the First Essential suggests, adherents of each school tried to find, despite its teachings, correct ideas about human nature, especially by studying the works of Confucius and Mencius.

Their task was not easy because, as we have seen, both schools had lost track of the idea of human nature as understood by Mencius. Those committed to the work of the Academy did not consider scrapping the teachings of these schools. Nevertheless, they found the teaching of both of them, in its original and pure form, unacceptable.

Thomas Lee found it "remarkable" that Gu wished "to restore the academy to the teaching of Ch'eng I and Chu Hsi scholarship, against the dominant intellectual trend of Wang Yang-ming thought."[81] Gu's reason was that the objective of the Academy was to find sound principles for living that could be used to reform the government. This objective seemed impossible if all moral values are subjective, as some members of the School of Universal Mind maintained. Gu said that "the danger of following . . . Wang Yangming is dissolution,"[82] by which he meant the loss of moral standards.

> Does Wang Yangming not teach men to do good and remove evil? . . . When, having first said, "There is no good and no evil", he then says also, "Do good and remove evil", the scholars, adhering to his first sentence, cannot but pay little heed to the second. What is the reason? When mind in itself is not good and not bad, then the so-called good and evil are both not firmly rooted in us. If both are not firmly rooted in us, both are arbitrary acts dictated by our subjective judgment."[83]

If so, "one is released from all obligations . . . This will lead to such extreme views wherein love and righteousness are considered as fetters and handcuffs; the rules of propriety as dirt and straw."[84]

---

[80]   Ibid. 35.
[81]   Thomas H. C. Lee, "Academies: Official Sponsorship and Suppression," in Frederick P. Brandauer and Chun-Chieh Huang, eds., *Imperial Rulership and Cultural Change in Traditional China* (Seattle, 1994), 117 at 132.
[82]   Ku Hsien-ch'eng, *Hsiao-hsin chai chai cha-chi*, ch. 3, 5–6, in Busch, "Tung-Lin Academy" 100.
[83]   Ku Hsien-ch'eng, *Ming-ju hsüeh-an*, ch. 58 (XI, 64–65), in ibid. 106.
[84]   Ku Hsien-ch'eng, *Hsiao-hsin chai cha-chi*, ch. 18, 2a-b and 3a-b, in ibid. 110–11.

On the other hand, Gu thought that the School of Principle had inhibited the questioning of moral judgments. He believed that no one should accept a moral judgment unless he is satisfied of its truth, even if that judgment had been made by Confucius. He quoted with approval two sentences from Wang Yangming:

> When we apprehend [what is moral] after seeking it in our own heart, we dare not consider it not so even though the words we put to it are not to be found among those of Confucius. When we do not apprehend [that it is morally good] after seeking it in our own heart, we dare not consider it so even though the words put to it are to be found among those of Confucius.

Other affiliates of the Academy charged that according to the teachings of the School of Principle, a human being is at war with his own nature, a good part of him fighting against a bad part. Qian Yipen (1539–1610) accused the School of bifurcating human nature into "an ideal or abstract nature,"[85] which was due to *li*, and a "special material nature," which was due to *qi*.[86] He maintained that "there is no natural power but that is good." Sun Shengxing (1565–1636) blamed the School for concluding that some men are virtuous and others foolish because of a difference in *qi* since "if pure (*qi*) makes virtuous, turbid (*qi*) foolish, then, while part (of their natures) is good, part of them is also bad."[87]

Affiliates of the Academy saw these features of the School of Principle as an obstacle to the kind of philosophy they were looking for. They did not want a combination of intellectualism and mysticism that aimed at the grasp of an ineffable principle estranged even from a desire for what is good. They were interested in goodness, in oneself and in government, and this interest led them to a concern for human nature. As Willard Peterson noted, "Gu sought to elucidate the teachings in a manner which would avoid the recklessness (*tang*) of later followers of Wang without reverting to the restrictiveness (*chu*) often associated in Ming times with Zhu Xi's teachings. In part, Gu's solution was to reassert that goodness (*shan*) is in every person as part of his human nature (*xing*)."[88]

At the beginning of a book of philosophical musings, Gu wrote: "One can talk about 'learning' only after he knows about human nature; one can talk about 'human nature' only after he knows about [true] learning."[89] His philosophical motto was "the goodness of nature." He wrote,

> Somebody asked me: "In recent times philosophical lecturers always lay down a basic principle; how is it that you alone do not have one? You put greatest emphasis on asserting that nature is good; is this, then, not your guiding principle?" I answered: "For some years, I, too have pondered on this a good deal; having thought about it from all sides I feel there are no better words than 'nature is good.'"[90]

85   Busch, "Tung-lin Academy" 93.
86   Ch'ien Yi-pen, *Ming-ju hsüeh-an*, ch. 59 (XI, 1) in ibid. 93–94.
87   Sun Sheng-hsing, *Ming-ju hsüeh-an*, ch. 59 (XI, 107–08) in ibid. 95–96.
88   Peterson, "Confucian Learning" 756.
89   Ibid. 757.
90   Ku Hsien-ch'eng, *Hsiao-hsin chai cha*-chi, ch. 7, 1a, in Busch, "Tung-Lin Academy" 112.

When Gu died in 1612, his successor as head of the Dong Lin Academy was its co-founder Gao Panlong (1562–1626). For Gao, as Busch observed, "the Wang School [was] on a level with Chan [Zen] Buddhism."[91] While professing his allegiance to the School of Principle,[92] Gao said, "The beginning of learning and inquiry is knowing nature, followed in the middle by recovering nature, ending with the extension of nature to the utmost."[93] The wise man spends his life "solely talking about the one word nature."[94] "What is knowing good? Goodness is nature."[95]

So began a philosophical enquiry that outlasted the Dong Lin Academy. As On-cho Ng observed, scholars of the late Ming and early Ching adopted a philosophical agenda that "reasserted the centrality and primacy of *xing* [nature]."[96] They deemphasized a transcendent ultimate principle and emphasized the principles of concrete things. Ng saw this tendency in two notable Qing dynasty scholars, Lu Shiyi (1611–72) and Li Guangdi (1642–1718). Guandi's work, in particular, was "transformative and critical: he employed Cheng-Zhu resources to reconceptualize the nature of *xing*."[97] Others such as Wang Fuzhi (1619–92), Yan Yuan (1635–1704), and Dai Zhen (1724–77) went further. They broke with both the School of the Mind and the School of Universal Principle. They said that there is no ultimate principle, whether without or within the mind. There are only the principles of concrete things. According to Chung-ying Cheng, their work marked the "final and fourth stage of Confucian development" which "was a critical one, because it was in this stage that serious criticism was launched against the orthodox Neo-Confucianism ... of the Cheng-Zhu school."[98] We have already examined the work of Dai Zhen, which Cheng described as "the culmination of the movement of against Neo-Confucianism" and "the constructive apex of the critical Confucianism of the Ming-[Qing] Era."[99]

The Academy's objective, however, was to find sound principles for living that could be used to reform the government. The hope of reforming the government ended when the Dong Lin Academy was closed and its buildings destroyed, but until then its success in conveying its message to the learned elite was impressive. To quote Busch:

> The newly founded Dong Lin Academy enjoyed the favor of the local and provincial authorities. ... This attitude of the authorities, together with the renown of Gu and his friends, gave the Academy from the beginning a more than local prestige. Large gatherings from among the gentry of the closer surroundings in Kiangsu and Chekiang appeared at the meetings. Some came even from remoter parts .... Ere long Tung-lin [Dong Lin] was the most famous Academy in the empire.[100]

---

[91] Busch, "Tung-Lin Academy" 123–24.

[92] Ibid. 123–24.

[93] Gao Panlong, *Gaozi yishu* 8 (shang)/61a in On-Cho Ng, *Cheng-Zhu Confucianism in the Early Qing Li Guangdi (1642–1718) and Qing Learning* (Albany, 2001), 33.

[94] Ibid. 3/17a in ibid. 34.

[95] Ibid. 3 /26b-27a in ibid. 35.

[96] Ng, *Cheng-Zhu Confucianism* 26.

[97] Ibid. 101.

[98] Chung-ying Cheng, "Introduction," to Tai Chên, ed., *Inquiry into Goodness* (Honolulu, 1971), 3 at 12.

[99] Ibid. 13.

[100] Busch, "Tung-lin Academy" 42–44.

According to John Dardess, the Academy's teachings "c[aught] on among the students and junior officials of the late Ming as though it were a wind-driven blaze through dry grass."[101]

As Busch noted, part of the attraction of the Academy was its role in politics. "Within a short time, Tung-lin became the rallying point of the 'righteous circles' to which many dismissed officials flocked."[102] Political opponents began to speak of a "Dong Lin party," the word "party" being a term of opprobrium. But the lectures or "pure discussions" rarely concerned politics.[103] Part of the attraction was that the Academy presented an alternative to the Cheng-Zhu and Lu-Wang schools. As we have seen, the alternative the Academy provided was neither an endorsement nor a repudiation of either school. It was an attempt to navigate between the shoals of each.

Politically, the Dong Lin party faced two obstacles: the enmity of Grand Secretaries and their coteries of friends, and the weak character of the emperors. Under strong and supportive emperors such as the founders of the Song dynasty, they would have triumphed. Under strong and hostile emperors such as the founders of the Ming, they would never have had a chance.

The Wan-li emperor was so ineffective that the official history of the Ming dynasty blamed him for its fall. His agents illegally extorted a fortune for him. Otherwise, he withdrew from official life while positions went unfilled, and the memorials to the throne by which important business was transacted went unanswered. In 1606, when the emperor offered the position of Grand Secretary to a candidate favored by the Dong Lin party, its members hoped for a new era of reform. The candidate, however, Wang Hsi-chüeh, was an old man with no taste for a battle, who declined the appointment despite the urging of Gu Xian Cheng.

The Wan-li emperor died in 1620, and was succeeded by his oldest son who became the Taichang emperor. He may have owed his succession to the Dong Lin party which had protested the attempt of Lady Zheng, the emperor's favourite consort, to put her son on the throne. For a time, it seemed that the party had won. The new emperor was a dissolute alcoholic, but he was open to their advice. In the late summer of 1620, Dong Lin adherents recalled many officials who had previously been dismissed and began to refill the ranks of the civil service.

Then, in Dardess' words, "the unbelievable happened." Within a month of his enthronement, the Taichang emperor died of unknown causes.[104] His heir was fourteen years old and deemed a minor. To prevent Lady Zheng and the dead emperor's consort Lady Li from declaring a regency, Yang Lian, a Dong Lin partisan, organized an invasion of the Forbidden Palace, off-limits to civil officials, captured the heir, and had him proclaimed the Tianchi emperor before a hastily assembled group of officials.

The eunuch Wei Zhongxian, however, had gained a psychological hold over the emperor. A struggle broke out between him and the Dong Lin party. In 1624, Yang Lian

---

[101] Dardess, *Ming China* 100.
[102] Busch, "Tung-lin Academy" 49.
[103] Ibid. 48.
[104] Dardess, *Ming China* 56.

protested Wei's encroachments in a memorial listing twenty-four of his crimes, a memorial followed by a flood of others. As a result, Yang Lien, Gao Panlong, and other Dong Lin leaders were dismissed. In 1625, members of the Dong Lin party and their friends were purged. All future memorials to the throne were required to mention Wei favorably, and all rescripts were to be issued in the name of the emperor and the "Depot Minister," which was Wei's title as head of the Eastern Depot, the eunuch-run police unit. A general order was issued "to suppress throughout the empire the Academy of Dong Lin for the investigation of philosophy." An imperial rescript was issued ordering that the Dong Lin Academy and affiliated academies "be demolished and their buildings and houses sold at their estimated value." Yang Lien and five other Dong Lin leaders were arrested and died while incarcerated. In 1626, five more met the same fate. Gao drowned himself to avoid it. A list of 300 Dong Lin party members was promulgated, all of whom, if still alive, were to be demoted to the status of commoners. On May 23, 1626, shortly after Gao's suicide, the last buildings of the Dong Lin Academy were torn down.

So ended what Dardess called the "Ming experience with literati self-organization." The Manchus, who conquered China and founded the Qing dynasty, "prohibited all such activities as threats to security and order."[105]

Huang Zongxi (1610–95), whose father had been imprisoned and killed when the Tung-lin movement was broken, wrote in his *Records of the Ming Scholars*:

> Today, when people talk about Dong Lin, they associate the Dong Lin party's political disaster with the fate of the Ming house. So mediocre men use this as an excuse to accuse Dong Lin for causing the loss of our country to the Manchus . . .
>
> The critics say that Dong Lin attracted disaster by its promotion of "pure discussion." Confucius said, "The way of government may be compared to dikes conserving that in which the people are deficient." Those engaged in pure discussion were like the dikes of the world. . . . [M]ediocre men hated pure discussions just as the Yellow River dislikes Mount Ti-chu for standing in its way. . . .
>
> The loyalty and righteousness we witnessed [when the dynasty was falling] surpassed that which was ever manifested during the earlier dynasties. All this was the result of the lasting influence and example of Dong Lin. That a group of teachers and disciples belonging to one academy should give their blood to purify Heaven and Earth and that fools should criticize them in secret is a cause for lament.[106]

iii *Waiting for Dawn*

In his book, *Waiting for Dawn*, Huang Zongxi wrote, "I set about itemizing the essentials of a grand system of governance."[107] His book is regarded by some modern scholars as a classic of Chinese political philosophy. It describes the purposes of government in much the same

---

[105] Ibid. 102.

[106] Huang, *Records* ch.16, 223–24 (Tung-lin School).

[107] Huang Tsung-hsi, *Waiting for Dawn: A Plan for the Prince Huang Tsung-hsi's Ming-i-tai-fang lu*, trans. Wm. Theodore de Bary (New York, 1993), 90.

way as did Confucius and Mencius. It condemns absolutism. It outlines a form of government that looks like an idealized version of the Song constitution modified by the experience of the Dong Lin Academy.

According to Huang, government is instituted for the common benefit.

> In the beginning of human life each man lived for himself and looked after his own interests. There was such a thing as the common benefit, yet no one seems to have promoted it; and there was common harm, yet no one seems to have eliminated it. Then someone came forth who did not think of benefit in terms of his own benefit but sought to benefit all-under-Heaven from harm. Thus his labors were thousands of times greater than the labors of ordinary men.[108]

"With those who later became princes it was different. They believed that since they held the power over benefit and harm, there was nothing the matter with taking for themselves all the benefits and imposing on others all the harm." "In ancient times all-under-Heaven were considered the master, and the prince was the tenant. . . . . Now the prince is master, and all under Heaven are tenants." "Thus he who does the greatest harm in the world is none other than the prince."[109]

The task of "true ministers" was not "to act solely for the prince and his dynasty."[110] "If I come to serve him without regard for serving all-under-Heaven, then I am merely the prince's menial servant or concubine. If, on the other hand, I have regard for serving the people, then I am the prince's mentor and colleague."[111]

Huang's description of how government should be conducted to avoid these evils was quite short. There should be a prime minister so that "even though the sons of emperors [are] not worthy to rule . . . worthy prime ministers [can] make up their deficiencies."[112]

> Each day . . . state matters should be discussed, with the emperor seated facing south, and the prime minister, six ministers of state, and censors seated in order facing east and west. All those who participate in these deliberations should be scholar-officials (*shi*). The presentation of all memorials to the emperor should be handled by the supervising secretaries of the Six Offices of Scrutiny. They should explain matters to the prime minister, and the prime minister should explain them to the emperor. After consultation between them as to approval or disapproval of these memorials, the emperor should endorse them in red; or, if he is unable to go through them all, the prime minister should endorse them, after which they should go to the Six Ministries for execution.[113]

Scholar-officials should be selected through the examination system, but the questions should require a candidate to show both a mastery of past learning and a capacity for original thought.

---

[108] Ibid. 91.
[109] Ibid. 92.
[110] Ibid. 95.
[111] Ibid. 96.
[112] Ibid. 101.
[113] Ibid. 103.

After listing one by one what is said by the various Han and Song scholars [on the classics], the candidate should conclude with his own opinion, there being no necessity for blind acceptance of one authority's word. Through the first part, those who are ignorant [of the classics and commentaries] will be failed, and through the second part those who show themselves dull in reasoning.[114]

Some scholar-officials should also be selected by recommendation and from the Imperial University.[115]

Thus far, Huang's plan of governance is an idealized version of the Song constitution. His innovation was to supplement it with schools which were to play the role of late Ming academies.

Schools are for the training of scholar-officials. But the sage-kings of old did not think this their sole purpose. .... Indeed, schools were meant to imbue all men, from the highest at court to the humblest in country villages, with the broad and magnanimous spirit the Classics. What the Son of Heaven thought right was not necessarily right; what he thought wrong was not necessarily wrong. And thus even the Son of Heaven did not dare to decide right and wrong for himself, but shared with the schools the determination of right and wrong.[116]

"The place of schools [had] been taken by academies" until "the academies were suppressed [in the Ming]."[117] That place should be restored. At the highest level, "[t]he libationer [rector] of the Imperial College should be chosen from among the great scholars of the day. He should be equal in importance to the prime minister."[118]

On the first day of each month, the Son of Heaven should visit the Imperial College, attended by the prime minister, six ministers, and censors. The libationer should face south and conduct the discussion, while the Son of Heaven too sits in the ranks of students. If there is anything wrong with the administration of the country, the libationer should speak out without reserve.

When they reach the age of fifteen, the sons of the emperor should study at the Imperial College with the sons of high ministers. They should be informed of the real conditions among the people and be given some experience of difficult labor and hardship. They must not be shut off in the palace, where everything they learn comes from eunuchs and palace women alone, so that they get false notions of their own greatness.[119]

At a lower level, district and prefectural schools should be under the direction of superintendents who are not appointed by the court.[120] In less populous areas, "wherever there are ten or more young boys among the people," teachers should be appointed for them.[121]

---

[114] Ibid. 113.
[115] Ibid. 119–20.
[116] Ibid. 104.
[117] Ibid. 105.
[118] Ibid. 107.
[119] Ibid.
[120] Ibid. 106.
[121] Ibid.

In the various prefectures and districts, on the first and fifteenth of each month, there should be a great assembly of the local elite, licentiates, and certified students in the locality, at which the school superintendent should lead the discussion. The prefectural and district magistrates should sit with the students, facing north and bowing twice. Then the teacher and his pupils should bring up issues and discuss them together.[122]

Huang wrote: "Old as I am, it may be that I . . . could still be visited by [an enlightened ruler seeking wisdom]. 'Dawn is just breaking and the light is still quite faint,' but how could I, on this account, keep my opinions to myself."[123] The dawn, however, did not break.

[122] Ibid. 107.
[123] Ibid. 91.

12

The Rise and Fall of Western Rationalism

I THE RISE OF RATIONALISM

Rationalism flourished in the seventeenth and eighteenth centuries. As John Finnis and Germain Grisez noted,[1] its metaphysics can be traced to the theologian Francisco Suárez (1548–1617). He was one of the last of the late scholastics.

Suárez, unlike Aristotle and Aquinas, believed that that the concepts of all things that are or could be are timeless and invariable. Consequently, so are the precepts of natural law. Moral knowledge is knowledge of these precepts. Moral action is conformity to them. In reaching those conclusions, he broke with the way human nature had been understood in the Aristotelian tradition. In these respects, he was followed by two of the most influential rationalist philosophers, Gottfried Wilhelm Leibniz (1646–1716) and Christian Wolff (1679–1754).

These tenets were so different from those of the Aristotelian tradition that one might have expected an intellectual battle. The battle was never fought. Suárez claimed to be interpreting Aristotle, much as Cheng Yi and Zhu Xi claimed to be interpreting Mencius. As Leroy Loemker noted, in the seventeenth century, "Suárez's *Disputationes Metaphysicae* had become the academic standard of doctrine for Protestant and Catholic Europe alike."[2] Wolff said that it "must be agreed, among the scholastics" it was Suárez who "most profoundly meditated matters of metaphysics."[3] What is more surprising is that, according to Wolff, his conception of being was that of Aquinas.[4] The actual position of Aquinas had dropped off the radar screen. As Etienne Gilson said, "Suárezianism has consumed Thomism."[5]

For many people, rationalism came to epitomize the natural law tradition. For many people it still does. Finnis, Grisez, and Gilson stressed the difference between the philosophy of Aquinas and Suárez, in part, because many Catholic writers neglected it. We noted

---

[1] For example, John Finnis, *Natural Law and Natural Rights* (Oxford, 1980); Germain Grisez, *Christian Moral Principles* (Quincy, 1997), 104. See also Pauline C. Westerman, *The Disintegration of Natural Law Theory: Aquinas to Finnis* (Leiden, 1998), 101.

[2] Leroy E. Loemker, "Introduction" to *Gottfried Wilhelm Leibniz Philosophical Papers and Letters* 1, Leroy E. Loemker, ed. (Chicago, 1956), 1 at 17.

[3] Christian Wolff, *Philosophia prima sive ontologia*, Johannes Ecole, ed. (Helesheim, 1962), § 169.

[4] Ibid. § 169.

[5] Etienne Gilson, *Being and Some Philosophers* (Toronto, 1952), 118.

earlier that Roberto Unger cited Christian Wolff as exemplifying "the metaphysical systems of ancient and medieval Europe" and "Aquinas' theory of natural law."[6] John Rawls used the term "rational institutionalism" to describe what he apparently regarded as the traditional approach to natural law. As we have seen, its features are the very ones that distinguish rationalist moral philosophy from that of Aristotle and Aquinas.

i *Reality*

Suárez maintained that the natural law consists of "principles which are known of themselves or those which are necessarily inferred from them."[7] Unlike Aquinas, he believed that these principles are timeless and invariable. "The law of nature is always the same, and made up of the same precepts, because they are either principles or conclusions necessarily elicited from them."[8] As Finnis said, using "φ" to denote any action,

> Suárez maintained that in discerning the content of natural law, reason's decisive act consists in discerning precepts of the form "φ is unfitting to human, i.e. rational nature and thus has the quality of moral wrongfulness" or "φ befits human, i.e. rational nature and thus has the quality of moral rectitude, and if φ is the only such act possible in a given context, the additional quality of moral necessity or dueness."[9]

For Aquinas, the principles of natural law were not timeless and invariable. He believed, as we have seen, that law is a dictate of practical reason. Natural law is the application to one's own situation of innate first principles concerning the good which are the starting point for practical reason. Thus while some precepts of natural law are always to be followed, others depend on the circumstances. His example was a person who refuses to return a sword to its owner. According to the natural law, Aquinas said, he should do so under normal circumstances but not if the owner has become insane or wishes to use it to harm his country. Aquinas concluded that the natural law is the same for all people only as to its "general" principles: the first principles known through *synderesis* and those that follow immediately from them. The conclusions of the natural law may be different for people acting under different circumstances.[10]

Suárez agreed that the sword should not be returned to the insane or dangerous owner. But the reason, he said, is not that the natural law varies with the circumstances in which a person finds himself. "[G]ranted that in this case [the sword] is not to be returned, the reason is not that the natural precept has changed, for the principle was not posited for this case but for others . . . "[11]

> "And therefore it is no objection that the matter is variable. . . . For [natural law] prescribes one thing as to the material in one situation, and another for that in another, and so in itself

---

[6] Roberto Mangabeira Unger, *Knowledge and Politics* (New York, 1975), 30–31, 31, n. 1.

[7] Francisco Suárez, *Tractatus de legibus et de legislatore deo* (Coimbra, 1612), lib. 2, cap. 13, no. 3.

[8] Ibid. lib. 2, cap. 8, no. 9.

[9] Finnis, *Natural Law* 45.

[10] Aquinas, *Summa theologiae* I-II, Q. 94, a. 6.

[11] Suárez, *Tractatus de legibus et de legislatore deo* lib. 2, cap. 13, no. 6.

it remains always unchanged, although according to our way of speaking and when it is spoken of extrinsically, it seems as though it varies."[12]

"Some," he said – meaning Aquinas – thought that the natural law is the same for all people only as to its "universal principles" but not as to the "conclusions" to be drawn from these principles. It is true, he said, that only the universal principles are known by everyone everywhere. Some of the conclusions are widely known, and some are known less widely since they are "in greater need of discussion." Nevertheless, the natural law is always the same.[13]

The source of the disagreement was that they had different ideas of natural law. For Aquinas, as we have seen, the natural law is the application of its most general principles by a person who is deciding how to act. One cannot speak of what the natural law is apart from the decision a person is making as to what he should do. The correct application of the natural law may depend upon his circumstances, and so it may be different from one person to the next. For Suárez, the natural law prescribes the right course of action for a given set of circumstances, whether or not anyone is trying to apply the law under those circumstances, and whether or not those circumstances have yet arisen. It is always true that the sword should be returned under one set of circumstances but not under another, and that truth is independent of whether any actual person is now contemplating, or ever has contemplated, when he should return a sword to its owner. The precept is the same although, when it is fully stated, it requires persons under one set of circumstances to act one way, and those under another set of circumstances to act differently.

The contrast can be seen in their discussions of societies that are ignorant of some precept of natural law. They each used the example of the ancient Germans, who, according to Caesar, did not know that it is wrong to steal. Aquinas and Suárez agreed that the Germans were mistaken as to what the natural law requires of them, although they might not be to blame for being mistaken.[14] For Aquinas, however, the natural law is the application of its most general principles by a person who is deciding how to act. Although the general principles are known to all people, even to the ancient Germans, the "second-ary precept" prohibiting theft was not known by them and could not be applied by them. They were not aware of that secondary precept. It had therefore been "abolished" or "blotted out from their hearts."[15] For Suárez, the natural law prescribes that theft is wrong. The precept prohibiting theft had not been abolished. It could not be. The existence of the precept did not depend on whether or not the Germans were or could have been aware of it.[16]

Suárez' view that the natural law is invariable and immutable was shared by some of his contemporaries such as Luis de Molina[17] and Gabriel Vasquez.[18] But it raised a difficulty

[12]   Ibid. lib. 2, cap. 13, no. 9.
[13]   Ibid. lib. 2, cap. 8, no. 7.
[14]   Aquinas, *Summa theologiae* I-II, Q. 94, a. 4; Suárez, *Tractatus de legibus et de legislatore deo* lib. 2, cap. 8, no. 7.
[15]   Aquinas, *Summa theologiae* I-II, Q. 94, a. 6.
[16]   Suárez, *Tractatus de legibus et de legislatore deo* lib. 2, cap. 8, no. 7.
[17]   Ludovicus Molina, *De iustitia et iure tractatus* (Venice, 1614), V, disp. 49, no. 3.
[18]   Gabriel Vasquez, *Commentariorum ac disputationum in primam partem sancti Thomae* (most recent edition, Lyon, 1631), disp. 231, cap. 4, no. 16.

which Suárez dealt with more cleverly than they. How or in what way does a precept of the natural law exist when no one is aware of it? According to Aquinas, the natural law could not exist apart of the human mind. According to Suárez, it could.

For Aquinas, as for Aristotle, the world consists of things, each with a tendency to behave in a certain way which, in this sense, is its "end." A bird builds nests, which is itself a means to the life characteristic of its species. A person acts in a way that contributes to his ultimate end which is the life characteristic of a human being. One could say that each of them is following a natural law that prescribes how they must act to reach their ends. The person does so consciously, by following the dictates of practical reason, and the bird does not. But the natural law can no more exist apart from the person than the nesting instinct can exist apart from the bird. The precepts of the natural law are "in us."[19] The natural law is an "act" which occurs when the bird is actually building the nest, or the person is deciding what to do. Apart from this act, the natural law exists only as a "habit,"[20] that is, as a person's capacity to know and apply the first principles when he makes a decision, or a bird's capacity to build nests when the occasion requires.

For Suárez the precepts of natural law can exist in a way that is neither in act nor in habit. He agreed with "the common opinion of the Thomists" that, most properly speaking, the natural law is an "act." "The natural law exists most properly in an actual judgment of the mind."[21] Yet, as we have seen, Suárez also thought that the natural law was the same even though the actual judgment of the mind of one person, acting under one set of circumstances, differs from that of another person acting under a different set. For the natural law to be the same for both, it must have some sort of reality apart from those who are trying to apply its precepts to decide how to act. According to Suárez, it does: "[I]t is one thing," he said,

> to speak of the existence of precepts ... and another to speak of their actual obligation or exercise. Therefore, although one can postulate a state in which one precept is in use and another is not, nevertheless, the law of nature is always the same, and made up of the same precepts, because they are either principles or conclusions necessarily elicited from them which are not defective in any situation.[22]

For Suárez, then, these precepts exist even when they are not "exercised" by anyone. Although that claim is not possible in Aquinas' metaphysics, it is in the metaphysics of Suárez. According to Suárez, "being ... has a double meaning, by which it signifies either being as prescinding from actual existence or being as actual existence."[23] "[B]eing primarily seems to signify a thing having a real and actual existence ... thence the word was transferred to signify that which has a real essence (*essentia realis*)."[24] As a result, Suárez could say that immutable and invariable precepts of natural law exist in this secondary

[19]   Aquinas, *Summa theologiae* I-II, Q. 91, a. 2.
[20]   Ibid. Q. 94, a. 1.
[21]   Suárez, *Tractatus de legibus et de legislatore deo* lib. 2, cap. 5, no. 14.
[22]   Ibid. lib. 2, cap. 8, no. 9.
[23]   Francisco Suárez, *Disputationes metaphysicae* in *Opera omnia* 25 (Vivès ed., Paris, 1861), disp. 2, sec. 4, no. 9.
[24]   Ibid. disp. 2, sec. 4, no. 9.

sense although they exist "actually" intermittently and partially in the minds of actual human beings. The precept requiring one to return a deposit under some circumstances and not under others, with a full specification of the circumstances that could matter, exists in this secondary sense even though no one actually has the complete precept in mind. This idea of a real essence or *essentia realis*, as José Pereira noted, "is original in Suárez."[25]

In metaphysics and in their idea of natural law, Leibniz and Wolff followed Suárez. Leibniz claimed that as a student, he had read Suárez like a novel.[26] His metaphysics owed much to Suárez' concept of possible being. According to Leibniz, there are certain propositions that are "absolutely necessary, whose contrary implies contradiction [such as] occurs in the eternal verities like the truths of geometry."[27] These propositions will be valid in any possible world.[28] Which possible world comes into actual existence depends upon God. Because God is good, however, he will call into existence the best of all possible worlds.[29] Which world is the best depends upon "principles of goodness, of justice and of perfection that follow from his understanding, and do not depend upon his will any more than does his essence."[30]

Before Leibniz incorporated these ideas in his system of metaphysics, he had already accepted the proposition of Suárez that concerns us here. Leibniz worked out his system from 1680 to 1697.[31] Years before, in 1666–67, he wrote in an essay on *The Elements of Natural Law*:

> The doctrine of law (*doctrina iuris*) belongs to those sciences that depend on definitions and not on experience, on demonstrations of reason and not of sense, and are matters of law, one can say, and not of fact. As, indeed, justice consists in some congruity and proportionality, we can understand that something is just even if there is no one who is acting justly, or who is being treated justly, in the same way that the concepts (*rationes*) of numbers are true even if there were no one to count and nothing to be counted, and we can predict that a house will be beautiful, a machine efficient, or a commonwealth happy if it comes into being even if it should never do so. We need not wonder, therefore, that the principles of these sciences possess eternal truth.[32]

Leibniz wrote this passage at the age of twenty.

---

[25] José Pereira, "The Existential Integralism of Suárez' Reevaluation of Gilson's Allegation of Suarezian Essentialism," *Gregorianum* 85 (2004), 660 at 667.

[26] See Suárez in Stuart Brown and N. J. Fox, *Historical Dictionary of Leibniz's Philosophy* (Lanham, 2006), 221.

[27] Gottfried Wilhelm Leibniz, *Discours de métaphysique* (Paris, 1907), xiii.

[28] Ibid. iii.

[29] Ibid. i–iii.

[30] Ibid. ii.

[31] C. D. Broad, *Leibniz: An Introduction* (Cambridge, 1975).

[32] Gottfried Wilhelm Leibniz, *Elementa juris naturalis* in Gottfried Wilhelm Leibniz, *Philosophische Schriften Erster Band 1663–1672*, Akademie der Wissenschaften der DDR, ed. (Berlin, 1990), 459 at 460. Loemker notes that this passage "already presupposes the distinction between possibility and existence made in his later thought." Gottfried Wilhelm Leibniz, *Philosophical Papers and Letters* 1, Leroy E. Loemker, trans. & ed. (Chicago, 1956), 138 n. 5. Leibniz wrote several short treatises with the title *Elementa iuris naturalis*. Two will be cited here: this one, which appears at p. 459 of *Philosophische Schriften Erster Band 1663–1672*, and another which appears at p. 433. They will be cited by the first page followed by the page on which the reference is to be found.

"And then," as Etienne Gilson said, "Suárez begat Wolff."[33] In his work *First Philosophy or Ontology*, published in 1730, Wolff explained:

> Being is what can exist, and consequently, that with which existence is not incompatible ... [A] right triangle with acute angles drawn on paper is a being, as it exists in act, but no less is a triangle that can be drawn a being, because it exists when it is first drawn, and therefore it can exist. If a stone is exposed to fire or to the rays of the sun in summer, it is hot. Therefore, a hot stone can exist, and therefore it is a being, not inasmuch as it exists in act, but inasmuch as existence is not incompatible with it. The idea of being taken generally scarcely involves existence but only a lack of incompatibility with existence, or, which is the same, the possibility of existing. Because what is possible can exist, what is possible is a being.[34]

Gilson objected that in this metaphysics, in contrast to that of Aquinas, there is no place for anything new and original. The rationalists failed to recognize that "there are no such things as fully determined essences prior to their existential actualization ... The Mattheus Passion was not an essence hovering in a limbo of possible essences where Johann Sebastian Bach caught it, so to speak, on the wing."[35] If the rationalists were right, they would have to regard the Mattheus Passion of Bach as Cheng Yi regarded the poems of Tu Fu: as having a mode of existence of its own independent of the mind or the poet or paper on which they were written.

The idea of *essentia realis* was an innovation of Suárez. Yet, as we have seen, it is like the mode of existence which Cheng Yi and Zhu Xi ascribed to *li* or principles. To say they exist would be misleading since they do not exist without *qi* or material in which they are embodied. Yet to say that they do not exist would be misleading since the *li* are eternal, immutable, and include every distinction that ever could exist among things. They are real when we think of them as they are in themselves, without considering whether or not they are embodied in *qi*. Similarly, Suárez' *essentia realis* exists when we think of a thing as it is in itself, prescinding from whether a being with that essence actually exists. Cheng Yi and Zhu Xi concluded that *li* are eternal and include every distinction that ever could exist among things. Suárez concluded that the precepts of natural law are eternal and provide for every circumstance that could affect the right way to act.

ii *Ethics*

Knowledge

Suárez rejected an idea that had been of great importance in the Aristotelian tradition: that practical reason operates differently than theoretical reason and does not reach its conclusions with the same certainty. Suárez continued to speak of theoretical and practical reason. But he believed that they both reached their conclusions with certainty and in basically the same way. "The law of nature" consists "of principles [and] conclusions necessarily elicited

---

33 Gilson, *Being and Some Philosophers* 112.
34 Wolff, *Philosophia prima* §§ 134–35.
35 Gilson, *Being and Some Philosophers* 211.

from them." These conclusions are certain and immutable. Since the "natural law ... is posited by right reason ... [it] cannot deviate from the truth, for if it does deviate, it is not right reason."[36] That is so, at least, when all of the circumstances on which these conclusions depend are specified. It is the same, not only with "moral and practical science" but with the propositions of physics dealt with in "natural and speculative science."[37]

For Suárez, a precept of natural law, fully and correctly stated, takes account of all the circumstances that matter. For Aquinas, the judgment of practical reason might depend on more circumstances than a person could take into account. Therefore, as we have seen, a person needs the assistance of kindred virtues such as "memory" and "experience," *eubolia* or the willingness to seek counsel, *sinesis* or the ability to apply "common rules" devised for similar situations, and *gnome*, the ability to make exceptions to the common rules and "judge according to higher principles."[38] As an example, of *gnome*, Aquinas used the case described earlier in which one person entrusts a sword to another and then asks for it back when he has become insane or dangerous. The common rule would be to return property when the owner asks for it, but under these circumstances, the sword should not be returned.[39]

For Suárez, since the natural precept takes account of all the relevant circumstances, no virtue such as *gnome* was needed to make an exception when new circumstances arise. Suárez did not discuss *gnome*. He did discuss the related virtue of *epikeia* or "equity." According to Aristotle and Aquinas, *epikeia* corrects the application of a human law when the law fails to take account of some circumstance.[40] Aquinas' example, again, was the return of the sword to a lunatic or malefactor.[41] According to Suárez, there is no place for *epikeia* in natural law. "[N]atural law cannot be corrected, as it is posited by right reason, which cannot deviate from the truth, for if it does deviate, it is not right reason."[42] To see that the sword should not be returned to the lunatic or malefactor requires, not *epikeia*, but interpretation.[43]

Suárez did not say whether he believed, as Aquinas did, that the circumstances that might matter are infinite in number. It is doubtful, however, that he thought that they were. The examples he gave are cases in which it would seem that only a few circumstances would matter, such as whether the return of the sword is demanded by a lunatic or malefactor. He did not discuss cases in which the circumstances that could matter are many and complex.

---

36   Suárez, *Tractatus de legibus et de legislatore deo* lib. 2, cap. 16, no. 9.
37   These sciences are distinguished ibid. lib. 2, cap. 16, no. 9.
38   Aquinas, *Summa theologiae* II-II, QQ. 49, 51.
39   Ibid. Q. 51, a. 4.
40   Aristotle, *Nicomachean Ethics* V.x.
41   Aquinas, *Summa theologiae* II-II, Q. 120, a. 1.
42   Suárez, *Tractatus de legibus et de legislatore deo* lib. 2, cap. 16, no. 9.
43   Ibid. lib. 2, cap. 16, no. 9. Farrell seems to think, I believe incorrectly, that Aquinas looked at the precepts of natural law in the same way, that "a full statement of the precept" would include the way it would be applied under different circumstances. Walter Farrell, *The Natural Moral Law According to St. Thomas and Suarez* (Ditchling, 1930), 116.

Aquinas put such a case. Suppose that one person has a high opinion of another and wishes to become friends. Should he tell that person just how high his opinion is? As a general rule, Aquinas observed, to do so would promote friendship. Sometimes, however, it would reinforce conceit or arouse a suspicion of flattery.[44] Any number of circumstances might affect what one ought to say. Finding the right words would be easier for a person with more experience, sound advice, a familiarity with common rules of social intercourse, and an ability to apply them flexibly. Suárez did not mention this case. It may be that he did not think that precepts of natural law apply in situations of this complexity.[45] If he did, his immutable precepts would have been extraordinary. They would prescribe, immutably, what to say to another person under all the circumstances that could matter: the situation, their previous relationship, and the possibilities for that relationship to develop fruitfully. There would have to be as many precepts as there are friendships or love stories, and, indeed, as many precepts as there are possible friendships or possible love stories.

As we have seen, Suárez maintained that the natural law consists of principles which are known of themselves or those which are necessarily inferred from them."[46] Nevertheless, he was not clear about the method to be followed to identify these principles or to draw the necessary inferences. Some scholars have said that "Suárez narrows down the scope of reason to that of theoretical reason only . . . overlook[ing] the importance of practical reason as distinct from theoretical reason."[47] Yet, as we have seen, Suárez never clearly distinguished between theoretical and practical reason.[48] He seemed to think that they worked in basically the same way, although he did not explain how they worked.

Leibniz and Wolff did explain how necessary inferences were to be drawn. The method was the same as in mathematics. Here they followed the seventeenth-century philosopher René Descartes, despite a fundamental difference in their metaphysics. As a young man, Descartes came to doubt that philosophy contained any truth. "[P]hilosophy," he found, "has been cultivated for many centuries by the best minds that have ever lived, nevertheless, no single thing is to be found in it which is not an object of dispute, and in consequence which is not doubtful."[49] Yet he was "pleased above all" by one branch of study: "mathematics because of the certainty of its demonstrations and the evidence of its reasoning."[50] He

---

[44]   Aquinas, *Summa theologiae* II-II, Q. 49, a. 7.

[45]   Because of its failure to take account of more complex situations in which an action contributes to human flourishing, Suárez' account has been attacked by natural law scholars such as Germain Grisez and John Finnis. Grisez criticizes its "negativism and minimalism," its concern with "issuing a few prohibitions [rather] than at directing people's lives toward growth and flourishing," its failure to recognize that "although essential human nature does not change, in the course of human history new possibilities do open up and humankind acquires powers to act in new, more complex ways." "[I]t is too much concerned with laws and too little with persons." Germain Grisez, *Christian Moral Principles* 104–06. See John Finnis, *Natural Law* 45.

[46]   Suárez, *Tractatus de legibus et de legislatore deo* lib. 2, cap. 13, no. 3.

[47]   Westerman, *Disintegration of Natural Law Theory* 97.

[48]   According to Germain Grisez and John Finnis, Suárez' precepts concern "theoretical" or "self-evident relations of conformity or non-conformity to human nature." Grisez, *Christian Moral Principles* 104; John Finnis, *Natural Law* 48.

[49]   René Descartes, *Discours de la méthode pour bien conduire sa raison et chercher la vérité dans les sciences* in *Oeuvres philosophiques* 1, Ferdinand Alquié, ed. (Paris, 1963), 567, at 576.

[50]   Ibid. 574.

concluded, as he said in his first work, published anonymously in 1637, that he could obtain certainty "in all those things which fall under the cognizance of man" only by "accepting nothing as true which I did not recognize to be so" and then employing those "chains of reasoning, simple and easy as they are, which geometricians use to arrive at the most difficult demonstrations."[51] Four years later he published his *Meditations on First Philosophy* in which he sought certainty by doubting everything that could be doubted, including the existence of the physical world, and then drawing inferences from the one proposition he could not doubt: that, indeed, he was doubting.

Although Leibniz' metaphysics was like that of Suárez, and quite different from that of Descartes, he claimed that one can arrive at certainty in the same way. One can do so in law. In 1667, at the age of twenty-one, he published a book entitled *A New Method of Learning and Teaching Jurisprudence*. "Demonstration (*analytica*) or the art of judging," he explained, "seems to me to be almost completely reducible to two rules: (1) no word is to be admitted unless it is explained, (2) and no proposition unless it has been proven."[52] By the use of these rules, it would be possible, he said, to arrive at the "elements" of "didactic jurisprudence" consisting of "the explication of terms or definitions" and of "propositions or precepts" – "aptly called by the name of elements in imitation of Euclid,"[53] In this way, "an infinity of special rules would be learned at once by means of general ones," and one "would descend in order from the premises of genera to species" through "an accurate definition of terms." "The way would be open for undecided cases in law to be determined by universal principles (*rationes*)."[54]

For Suárez, as we have seen, a precept of natural law, properly interpreted, took account of every circumstance that could matter. For that reason, he seems to have thought that the number of circumstances that could matter was limited. For Leibniz, "an infinity of special rules" can be derived from the "general ones" in the same way that the definition of a triangle or a circle or a prime number can lead to innumerable conclusions.

Wolff, like Leibniz, was a mathematician. He was appointed a professor of mathematics at the University of Halle although he lectured there on philosophy as well. His method was like that of Leibniz. He described it in the Preface to his treatise *Institutions of the Law of Nature and of Nations*:

> As the love of truth was instilled in me as it were by nature, as I have often taught, I applied my mind to the study of mathematics for no other reason than to understand the great certainty to be found in geometry. I had nothing more at heart than once having known it, to put its truth in plain light, and to yield to it not as one persuaded but convinced. In that spirit I turned to the explication of law. The source of every law is in human nature, as the ancients taught and the moderns have repeated though not demonstrated. . . .
>
> All of this can only be put in the light by following in the track of Euclid . . . that is, explaining each term by an exact definition, and making a sufficient determination of the

---

[51]   Ibid. 587.
[52]   Gottfried Wilhelm Leibniz, *Nova methodus discendae docendaeque jurisprudentia* in Leibniz, *Philosophische Schriften Erster Band* I, § 25.
[53]   Ibid. II. § 6.
[54]   Ibid. II, § 11.

meaning of each proposition, and arranging the definitions so that those that come before allow one to fully understand those that follow.[55]

As Claes Peterson said, what Wolff meant "is clearly not that logic is an analytic disentangling of legal argument. Instead, logic is the way to a synthetic understanding of the legal system. With the help of logic, a logically coherent system of norms can be constructed and even the norms can be derived from it."[56]

Moral Law

In the Aristotelian tradition, practical reason enables a person to choose those actions that contribute to living the distinctively human life that is his ultimate end. Law is a dictate of practical reason. For Leibniz and Wolff, the natural law consists of conclusions that can be drawn from definitions by deductive logic. To act morally is to act in conformity with these conclusions.

They attempted to derive these conclusions from a definition of the good. They defined the good in terms of perfection. "The true good," Leibniz said, "is whatever serves the perfection of intelligent substances."[57] According to Wolff, "every man as an ultimate end should seek his perfection and that of others."[58]

They then tried to derive the moral law from the concept of "perfection." Their problem was not only that they were attempting to do moral reasoning by deductive logic. It was that, to draw inferences about what is necessary for human perfection, they would have needed a thicker idea of human nature. Instead, they could say little more about a human being than that he is capable of defining concepts and deducing conclusions, and that he is in need of perfection.

They concluded that natural law is based on the principle that everyone should do whatever he can to perfect both himself and everyone else. According to Leibniz, "[t]he true good . . . is merely whatever serves the perfection of intelligent substances."[59] "Justice" is "charity," which is "universal benevolence."[60] Borrowing from Leibniz,[61] Wolff said, "[w]ithout doubt, every man as an ultimate end should seek his perfection and that of

---

55   Christian Wolff, *Institutiones juris naturae et gentium*, in Christian Wolff, *Gesammelte Werke* 26, M. Thomann, ed. (Hildescheim, 1972), *Prefatio*.

56   Claes Peterson, "Zur Anwendung der Logik in der Naturrechtslehre von Christian Wolff," in Jan Schröder, ed., *Entwicklung der Methodenlehre in Rechtswissenschaft un Philosophie vom 16. bis zum 18. Jahrhundert* (Stuttgart 1998), 177 at 177.

57   Gottfried Wilhelm Leibniz, "Reflections on the Common Conception of Justice," in Leibniz, *Philosophical Papers and Letters* 911 at 917.

58   Christian Wolff, *Jus naturae method scientific pertracta*, published as *Jus naturae* in Christian Wolff, *Gesammelte Werke* 17–24: I, § 609.

59   Gottfried Wilhelm Leibniz, "Reflections on the Common Conception of Justice" in 917.

60   Gottfried Wilhelm Leibniz, "Codex iuris gentium diplomaticus," *Praefatio* in Leibniz, *Philosophical Papers and Letters* 690 at 690. Similarly, "the good man is one who is benevolent toward all . . . The ultimate rule of law is everything is directed to the maximum general good or common happiness." "De tribus juris praeceptis sive gradibus," in Gottfried Wilhelm Leibniz, *Textes in édits*, Gaston Grua, ed. (New York, 1985), 606 at 607.

61   Clemens Schwaiger, "Ist Wolffs Ethik leibnianisch? Ein Beitrag zur Wiederbelebung der Glücksthematik," in *Leibniz und Europa VI. Internationaler Leibniz-Kongress* (Langenhagen, 1994), 727 at 728

others, and therefore to make all use of his faculties that is required for this end to be pursued. The perfection of others, then, should be no less dear and of concern to us than our own."[62]

They were unable to move by deduction from this principle to conclusions about how one should act. To do so, as Klaus Luig observed, was "the most difficult task" Leibniz confronted.[63] Hans-Peter Schneider noted that Leibniz did not genuinely make the attempt, although it was required by the rationalist program, and if he had, he could not have succeeded.[64] The same can be said of Wolff.

Instead, they drew a radical distinction between the pursuit of perfection and the exercise of private rights. The ultimate principle of moral law was the pursuit of perfection. It was purely altruistic. The perfection of another person should be as important as one's own. They defined a private right negatively, by its contrast to altruism. Private rights were self-regarding. Although a person should seek his own perfection and that of others, within the sphere of his own rights, he could do as he willed. His only moral duty was to respect the rights of others.

The rationalists launched an idea that outlasted them and, as we will see, proved hard to kill: the idea that rights can be defined in terms of will, and, so defined, are conceptually unlimited. We noted earlier that this concept of rights appeared in liberal theories built in the nineteenth century and in the "will theories" of nineteenth-century jurists who subscribed to will theories of property and contract. Writers in the Aristotelian tradition conceived of a right quite differently. They recognized that a right holder can exercise his rights as he chooses. Nevertheless, the content of his rights is determined by considerations of justice, anchored in the social order. To determine the scope of rights to property or contract, one must understand the purposes that these rights are instituted to serve. For the rationalists, rights were not defined in terms of purposes that they served any more than mathematical figures.

The private rights that Leibniz and Wolff discussed were those rights familiar in private law: property, contract, and the right to compensation for injury (tort or delict). They defined them in terms of will.

Rights to property arise by an act of will: the will to appropriate what no one else yet owns. Leibniz said, "[i]f one begins to possess a thing then belonging to no one, he acquires it."[65] According to Wolff, anyone, acting in his own interest, could take possession of goods, or cultivate land, and thereby acquire a perfect right to what he possessed.[66]

Once this right is created, it is conceptually unlimited. As Klaus Luig observed, in Leibniz' view, "the thing [is] the object of an absolute right."[67] Wolff said as much. "[T]

---

[62] Christian Wolff, *Jus naturae* I, § 609.

[63] Klaus Luig, "Leibniz als Dogmatiker des Privatrechts," in Okko Behrends, Malte Diesselhorst, and Wulf Eckart Voss, eds., *Römishes Recht in der europäischen Tradition Symposion aus Anlass des 75 Geburtstages Franz Wieacker* (Ebelsbach, 1985), 213 at 220.

[64] Schneider, *Justitia Universalis* 366.

[65] Leibniz, "Annotationes ad methodi vigelianae librum de rerum dominio" *Textes inédits* 2: 858 at 858.

[66] Wolff, *Jus naturae* I, § 609, cited II, § 496; II, §§ 171–73.

[67] Klaus Luig, "Leibniz als Dogmatiker" 231.

he owner has the right to dispose of rights over a thing subjected to him according to his own judgment (*arbitrio*)." The right "of disposing of a thing by one's own decision, indeed, as one sees fit, we call ownership."[68] "By nature, no one is held to give another a reason concerning in what way a thing is used, nor does anyone have the right to impede an abuse of things, so long as whoever is abusing the thing does nothing against the right of another."[69] In the Aristotelian tradition, the owner's rights were limited by the purposes served by the institution of private property. For example, a person in urgent need could use another's property without his consent and even against his will. For the rationalists, the rights of an owner were unlimited.

Leibniz and Wolff defined contracts as rights created by promises.[70] Promises are declarations of will. According to Leibniz, a promise is a "declaration that something to your benefit is to be done by me." According to Wolff, "A promise ... is a declaration of our will to perform to another joined to the right to require the transfer of that to be performed."[71]

Thus defined, the freedom of the parties to contract on any terms they choose is conceptually limitless. In Leibniz' view, Luig observed, contract law is "fundamentally governed by the principle of the freedom and equality of the citizens. This equality is also realized in the freedom to make a law for one's own contractual relations through the *lex contractus* [the law of the contract]"[72] For Leibniz "in contracts we have the right to gain ... according to the principle that it is licit for the parties to circumvent each other,"[73] citing a maxim of Roman law. According to Wolff, "one can charge the other as much of a price as he wishes."[74] In the Aristotelian tradition, contracts of exchange were an act of commutative justice. A party could not enrich himself at another's expense by charging an unjust price. For the rationalists, parties' right to contract on any terms they chose was unlimited.

Leibniz and Wolff defined the duty to compensate for injury, known in private law as tort or delict, in terms of harm done to another, which means depriving someone of what he ought to have, the deprivation of private right. Leibniz said that a person is harmed if he is deprived of whatever he has whether acquired by "fortune or industry."[75] According to Wolff, "[t]he one to whom harm has been done has less than he ought to have."[76] They had defined rights in terms of the will of the right holder. They now defined tort in terms of the violation of a right so defined. In the Aristotelian tradition, rights such as property had been defined by the reason such rights should be protected.

---

[68] Wolff, *Jus naturae* I, § 609, cited II, § 496; II, § 118.
[69] Ibid. II, § 169.
[70] Leibniz, "Definitionum iuris specimen" *Textes inédits* 2: 721 at 733.
[71] Wolff, *Jus naturae* III, § 361.
[72] Luig, "Leibniz als Dogmatiker" 239.
[73] Leibniz, "Varia" *Textes inédits* 2: 811 at 814.
[74] Wolff, *Jus naturae* IV, § 319.
[75] Leibniz, "De tribus juris praeceptis sive gradibus," *Textes inédits* 2: 606 at 607.
[76] Wolff, *Jus naturae* II, § 580.

II RATIONALISM DISCREDITED: THE CRITIQUE OF DAVID HUME

For the Western rationalists as for the School of Principle, a gap emerged between cognition and volition. Right action was a matter of knowing a precept of natural law or a principle (*li*) and then acting accordingly. Why one would want to conform to that precept was not explained. This gap had not existed for Aristotle and Aquinas, Mencius, or Dai Zhen, despite the differences in their philosophies. For Aristotle and Aquinas, practical reason enables a person to know the good; his will is then attracted to it. A person's desires can be directed to the good, and so participate in the rational principle, but only when they are trained to respond appropriately. For Mencius, the mind does not prescribe how to act but nourishes inborn tendencies toward benevolence, righteousness, propriety, and wisdom. These qualities are both cognitive and volitional: they are directed toward the good, and they motivate a person to seek it. For Dai Zhen, human nature has its own principle which, when correctly understood, serves as a standard for the realization of one's humanity. A person is benevolent when his desires do not deviate from principle; he is wise when he is not mistaken about principle.

This gap between cognition and volition was the focus of the attack on the School of Principle by Lu Hsiang-Shan and Wang Yangming, the founders of the School of the Universal Mind. In the West, it was the focus of the attack on rationalism of David Hume. Hume said, "reason alone can never ... give rise to volition."[77]

The way in which Lu and Wang resolved this problem was diametrically opposite to that of Hume. As we have seen, they identified *li* or immutable principle with the mind, and the mind with action and feeling. According to Wang, it is wrong to think that one first knows a principle and then acts on it. "Knowledge and action should not be separated."[78] They are one. "Seeing beautiful colors appertains to knowledge, while loving beautiful colors appertains to action. However, as soon as one sees that beautiful color, he has already loved it."[79] Knowledge and action are one with feelings.

Hume took the opposite course. The gap between cognition and volition cannot be closed. It is an unbridgeable chasm. In the words of Derek Parfit, "Hume claimed that, since reasoning is entirely concerned with truth, and desires cannot be true or false, desires cannot be supported by or contrary to reason."[80] Hume argued succinctly:

> Reason is the discovery of truth or falsehood. Truth or falsehood consists in an agreement or disagreement either to the *real* relations of ideas, or to *real* existence and matter of fact. Whatever, therefore, is not susceptible of this agreement or disagreement, is incapable of being true or false, and can never be an object of our reason. Now 'tis evident our passions, volitions, and actions, are not susceptible of any such agreement or disagreement; being original facts and realities, compleat in themselves, and implying no reference to other passions, volitions, and actions. 'Tis impossible, therefore, they can be pronounced either true or false, and be either contrary or conformable to reason.[81]

---

[77] David Hume, *Treatise of Human Nature* (Oxford, 1888), 2.3.3.4, 414–15.
[78] Wang Yangming, *Instructions for Practical Living* § 26.
[79] Ibid. § 5.
[80] Derek Parfit, "Reasons and Motivation," *Proceedings of the Aristotelian Society* 71 (1997), 99 at 128.
[81] Hume, *Treatise of Human Nature* 3.1.1.9, 458.

Since moral convictions motivate, they must be feelings or passions. "To have a sense of virtue, is nothing but to *feel* a satisfaction of a particular kind."[82] "An action, or sentiment, or character is virtuous or vicious ... because its view causes a pleasure or uneasiness of a particular kind."[83] "In feeling that [an action] pleases after such a particular manner, we in effect feel that it is virtuous."[84] "We do not infer a character to be virtuous, because it pleases: But in feeling that it pleases after such a particular manner, we in effect feel that it is virtuous."[85]

Since "reason is the discovery of truth or falsehood," passions or feelings cannot "be pronounced either true or false," it follows that reason cannot tell us about virtue. To try to derive a proposition about what we ought to do from a proposition about what it is to commit what has since been called the "naturalistic fallacy." Hume said:

> In every system of morality, which I have hitherto met with, I have always remark'd, that the author proceeds for some time in the ordinary way of reasoning, and establishes the being of a God, or makes observations concerning human affairs; when of a sudden I am surpriz'd to find, that instead of the usual copulations of propositions, *is*, and *is not*, I meet with no proposition that is not connected with an *ought*, or an *ought not*. This change is imperceptible; but is, however, of the last consequence. For as this *ought*, or *ought not*, expresses some new relation or affirmation, 'tis necessary that it shou'd be observ'd and explain'd; and at the same time that a reason should be given, for what seems altogether inconceivable, how this new relation can be a deduction from others, which are entirely different from it.[86]

Consequently,

> 'Tis not contrary to reason to prefer the destruction of the whole world to the scratching of my finger. 'Tis not contrary to reason for me to chuse my total ruin, to prevent the least uneasiness of an *Indian* or person wholly unknown to me. 'Tis as little contrary to reason to prefer even my own acknowledg'd lesser good to my greater, and have a more ardent affection for the former than the latter. A trivial good may, from certain circumstances, produce a desire superior to what arises from the greatest and most valuable enjoyment.[87]

Reason can influence the passions in only two ways. It can point out the existence of some object which is an object of a desire. Or it can point out the means by which some object of desire may be obtained.[88] Hume concluded: "Reason is, and ought only to be the slave of the passions, and can never pretend to any other office than to serve and obey them."[89] Consequently, it is not contrary to reason to prefer what is "ruinous" or of "lesser" or "trivial" value to what is "greater" or "most valuable." Indeed, there is no measure or standard except the "passions" to determine what is ruinous or trivial or valuable.

[82] Ibid. 3.1.2.3, 471.
[83] Ibid.
[84] Ibid.
[85] Ibid.
[86] Ibid. 3.1.1.27, 469.
[87] Ibid. 2.3.3.6, 416.
[88] Ibid. 3.1.1.12, 459.
[89] Ibid. 2.3.3.4, 415.

Hume's critique set bounds that later Western philosophers were unable to escape. It is important to take a close look at its presumptions, its strength, which lay largely in its coherence, and its weaknesses, which lay largely in what it could not explain.

We have seen that in attacking the School of Principle, Lu and Wang borrowed one of its distinguishing features: the idea of *li* or principle. They identified principle with the mind. Having done so, their school was never able to return to Mencius' idea of human nature as a source of normative standards. In attacking the rationalism, Hume borrowed one of its distinguishing features. He identified reason with the ability to show from an uncontestable starting point that a proposition is true or false. For the rationalists, the uncontestable starting points were definitions of concepts. For Hume, they were either definitions of concepts or sense perceptions and feelings. "Reason is the discovery of truth or falsehood. Truth or falsehood consists in an agreement or disagreement either to the *real* relations of ideas, or to *real* existence and matter of fact."[90]

In describing the "real relations of ideas," Hume sounded like the rationalists.

> All the objects of human reason or enquiry may naturally be divided into two kinds, to wit, *Relations of Ideas*, and *Matters of Fact*. Of the first kind are the sciences of Geometry, Algebra, and Arithmetic; and in short, every affirmation, which is either intuitively or demonstratively certain. *That the square of the hypothenuse is equal to the square of the two sides*, is a proposition, which expresses a relation between these figures. *That three times five is equal to the half of thirty*, expresses a relation between these numbers. Propositions of this kind are discoverable by the mere operation of thought, without dependence on what is any where existent in the universe. Though there never were a circle or triangle in nature, the truths, demonstrated by Euclid, would for ever retain their certainty and evidence.[91]

In contrast, our knowledge of matters of fact depends on our sense perceptions and feelings. Reason can examine what perceptions we encounter and the relationships among them. Perceptions can be related by resemblance or continuity or by the regularity with which one follows the other. When we say that a thing exists, we can make no further claim about its existence than that we have observed a set of sense perceptions related in these ways. When we say that one thing causes a change in another, we have no further knowledge about causation than that we have observed that one set of perceptions regularly follows another. This approach to knowledge has been called "empiricism" as distinguished from "rationalism." Rationalists start with definitions that are uncontestable and try to derive our knowledge from them. Empiricists start with perceptions such as shape or color or relations among perceptions and try to derive our knowledge of matters of fact from them. Whatever cannot be derived in these ways cannot be known.

If Hume's conception of reason were correct, it would follow that the truth or falsity of moral convictions could not be shown by reason, and that one could never infer what ought to be from what is. But it all depends on whether his conception of reason is correct. Elijah Millgram observed that Hume's arguments about morality depend upon "the major

---

[90]   Ibid. 3.1.1.9, 458.
[91]   David Hume, *Enquiry Concerning the Principles of Human Understanding, and Other Essays* (New York, 1963), 4.1.

premise . . . that all reasoning is either mathematical or empirical."[92] Millgram concluded, "This is a terrible premise to use in an argument whose conclusion is that there is no such thing as practical reasoning: anyone who needed to be persuaded of the conclusion would be extremely unlikely to concede it. (After all, why isn't practical reasoning a third kind of reasoning?)"[93] Millgram called it "question-begging."[94] Parfit rejected Hume's argument on similar grounds.[95] For Hume, however, as for the rationalists, nothing could be known unless it could be derived from some uncontestable starting point, whether definitions of concepts or sense perception. How else could anything be known?

In the Aristotelian tradition, practical reason does not proceed by deductive reasoning. Neither is it solely concerned with deciding which means would work instrumentally to accomplish a given end. It is a power of moral appraisal and judgment. It does not infer what ought to be from propositions about what is. Its inferences are drawn from innately known first principles concerning what is good: for example, that it is good to pursue knowledge, appreciate beauty, or help others rather than harm them. The first principles can be demonstrated only dialectically. If a person were to deny that anything is good or evil, better or worse, more or less worthwhile, there is no way to refute him until he says or does something inconsistent with his claim. He must affirm that something he is doing is indeed worthwhile.

For Hume, moral convictions are feelings which cannot be true or false. Consequently, it is hard to explain how they can be convictions. As Barry Stroud observed, when we say "that was a vicious act done by a vicious man" we are not "merely saying" we have "a sentiment of disapprobation towards it,"[96] as when we say we do not like olives, nor are we "merely reporting the feeling, as when [we] cheer."[97] Even "Hume thinks of a moral conclusion or verdict as a 'pronouncement' or 'judgment' – something put forward as true."[98]

The difficulty is how, on Hume's premises, one can explain why we regard a moral conclusion as a judgment, as a proposition with a truth value. One answer would be that although one cannot know such a judgment is true, human beings are so constructed that they must believe that they know what they know they cannot know. Stroud and Elizabeth Radcliffe suggested that believing an action or character is virtuous or vicious is like the believing that one event causes another. For Hume, we arrive at the idea of causation by observing that one event invariably follows another. What we call causation does not occur outside of our mind, or at least, we have no evidence that it does. Yet we form the idea within our mind and project it on the external world. This is the view Sophie Botros called "projectionism."[99] As Radcliffe put it, "We do use ideas of virtue and vice in our moral

---

[92] Elijah Millgram, "Was Hume a Humean?" *Hume Studies* 21 (1995), 75 at 80.
[93] Ibid. 80.
[94] Ibid.
[95] Parfit, "Reasons and Motivation" 128.
[96] Barry Stroud, *Hume* (London, 1977), 180.
[97] Ibid. 181.
[98] Ibid. 182.
[99] Sophie Botros, Review of Rachel Cohon, Hume's Morality: Feeling and Fabrication in *The Philosophical Review* 121 (2012), 131 at 131–32.

judgments, but those ideas are Humean fictions . . . which are invented by the imagination and have no source in experience. We conjure up something that we do not find in experience, analogously to the way in which the idea of necessary connection is conjured by the imagination in causal reasoning."[100] According to Stroud, for Hume, moral judgments could be similar. A moral judgment is

> the attribution of a certain characteristic – virtue or goodness – to an action or character. Although there is in fact no such characteristic in actions or characters, the feelings we get on contemplating them inevitably lead us to ascribe it to them. The acceptance or assertion of the moral judgment is thus a reaction to or a result of the feeling, but it does not merely evince the feeling as does a cry or a cheer. We express the feeling by making an assertion about the contents of our own minds. Our moral judgments, like our causal judgments, are projections.[101]

"It must be admitted," Stroud noted, "that this sketch goes beyond anything expressly stated in Hume's morality, but it is on all fours with his treatments of other topics in the science of man, and it coheres better that any alternative with his philosophical goals."[102]

One problem with this view is the analogy to causation. We arrive at that idea by observing that one event invariably follows another. We do not seem to arrive at a moral judgment by projecting an idea on any such pattern in what we observe.

Another problem, as Radcliffe observed, is that this approach this approach "implies we have moral beliefs, but they all turn out to be false." One could call it an "error theory."[103] Radcliffe added, "I see no reason for treating moral beliefs employing fictions as a denial of moral beliefs."[104] The reason it is a denial is, in Stroud's words, that "a moral claim is a 'pronouncement' or 'judgment' – something put forward as true."

Were we to acknowledge that our moral beliefs are not true, or, at least, that we have cannot know whether they are true, we could not say that anything is good or evil, better or worse, or more or less worthwhile. In the Aristotelian tradition, there is no way to refute that claim until the person who makes it affirms that something he does is indeed worthwhile. For many centuries, that argument was considered sufficient to counter claims of moral agnosticism

Hume's intention, however, was not to explain whether moral beliefs were true or false. It was to develop an account of how people develop the moral beliefs that they do. He claimed that the fact that a person has some moral feelings rather than others can be explained psychologically. Later authors had cultural and economic explanations. As Russell Hardin noted, these explanations concern why one holds moral views, but do not justify holding them.

> Hume's account does not tell us what is right or wrong, good or bad. It explains moral views; it does not justify them or even argue for them beyond fitting them to the actual

---

[100] Elizabeth S. Radcliffe, "Moral Internalism and Moral Cognitivism in Hume's Metaethics," *Synthese* 152 (2006), 353 at 360.
[101] Stroud, *Hume* 184–85.
[102] Ibid. 185.
[103] Radcliffe, "Moral Internalism" 360.
[104] Ibid.

psychology of people. Hume has no moral theory, only a theory of the psychology of our moral views. A purely psychological theory cannot be satisfactory for anyone who seeks "true" moral positions.[105]

In so doing, Hume committed himself to a non-normative psychology. Suppose he were to say that the reason human beings seek truth is that they value truth, that the reason they appreciate beauty is that they value beauty, and that the reason that they care about others is that they value the well-being of others. He would be giving an account of human psychology, but it would be a normative account. He would be explaining our moral views by what we believe to be good. In a non-normative account, there must be some other explanation.

He said of the desire for truth:

> The first and most considerable circumstance requisite to render truth agreeable, is the genius and capacity, which is employ'd in its invention and discovery. What is easy and obvious is never valu'd; and even what is *in itself* difficult, if we come to the knowledge of it without difficulty, and without any stretch of thought or judgment, is but little regarded.[106]

Then, too, "[t]he truth we discover must also be of some importance,"[107] although "'tis not on account of any considerable addition, which of itself it brings to our enjoyment, but only because 'tis, in some measure, requisite to fix our attention."[108] "[T]here is likewise requir'd a degree of success in the attainment of the end, or the discovery of that truth we examine."[109] He concluded, "there cannot be two passions more nearly resembling each other, than those of hunting and philosophy ... 'Tis evident, that the pleasure of hunting [also] consists in the action of the mind and body; the motion, the attention, the difficulty, and the uncertainty."[110] "If we want another parallel to these affections, we may consider the passion of gaming, which affords a pleasure from the same principles as hunting and philosophy."[111]

Similarly, he explained our appreciation of beauty as the indirect result of other desires. "Beauty is such an order and construction of parts, as either by the *primary constitution* of our nature, by *custom*, by *caprice*, is fitted to give a pleasure and satisfaction to the soul." It does so, in large part, because of an association with utility in the sense of usefulness. "[A] great part of the beauty, which we admire either in animals or in other objects, is deriv'd from the idea of convenience and utility." Thus "the rules of architecture require, that the top of a pillar shou'd be more slender than its base, and that because such a figure conveys to us the idea of security, which is pleasant; whereas the contrary form gives us the apprehension of danger, which is uneasy."[112] It is the same with symmetry. "There is no rule

[105]   Russell Hardin, *David Hume: Moral and Political Theorist* (Oxford, 2007).
[106]   Hume, *Treatise of Human Nature* 2.3.10.3, 449.
[107]   Ibid. 2.3.10.4, 449.
[108]   Ibid. 2.3.10.6, 450.
[109]   Ibid. 2.3.10.7, 451.
[110]   Ibid. 3.10.8, 451.
[111]   Ibid. 2.3.10.9, 452.
[112]   Ibid. 2.1.8.2, 299.

in painting more reasonable than that of balancing the figures, and placing them with the greatest exactness on their proper centers of gravity. A figure, which is not justly ballanc'd, is disagreeable; and that because it conveys the ideas of its fall, of harm, and of pain."[113] Nothing, it would seem, could be more beautiful than a concrete pillbox.

It is the same with concern for others. Hume recognized that there is a psychological mechanism he calls "sympathy." Sympathy is "that propensity we have ... to receive by communication [the] inclinations and sentiments [of others]."[114] "As in strings equally wound up, the motion of one communicates itself to the rest; so all the affections readily pass from one person to another, and beget correspondent movements in every human creature."[115] Sympathy, in this sense, is not a concern for another's happiness. Moreover, a concern for another's happiness is a different feeling than "love." When feelings are distinct, as when perceptions are distinct, one can only say that a person experiences first one and then another. For example, one can say that the set of perceptions we call "wood" is followed by those we call "fire" which is followed by those we call "ash." One cannot say that the fire caused the wood to burn to ash. Similarly we can say "[l]ove is always follow'd by a desire of the happiness of the person belov'd, and an aversion to his misery."[116] But because the feelings are different, there is no reason why one should follow the other. It is a quirk of our psychological make-up that it is so.

> [B]enevolence and anger are passions different from love and hatred, and only conjoin'd with them, by the original constitution of the mind. . . . This order of things, abstractedly consider'd, is not necessary. Love and hatred might have been unattended with any such desires, or their particular connexion might have been entirely revers'd. If nature had so pleas'd, love might have had the same effect as hatred, and hatred as love. I see no contradiction in supposing a desire of producing misery annex'd to love, and of happiness to hatred.[117]

For Hume, then, it is not the case that we seek knowledge because we desire to understand the world. Indeed, if all we can discover is that some sensations are frequently or invariably accompanied by others, but we can never know why, the world is not particularly interesting. Nor is it the case that we appreciate beauty because we can recognize it in the things around us, and once we do so, we are attracted to it. To say so would come too close to saying that there is a genuine difference between things that are beautiful and those that are not, and that we are able to recognize the difference. Nor is it the case that we are concerned about the happiness of others because we care for them.

Indeed, from Hume's perspective, it is hard to see how a person could care for his own happiness. His happiness could depend only on his desires, and desires conflict. Hume was clear that there is no way in which these feelings or desires could be summed up or aggregated so as to determine the extent of a person's happiness.[118] The only standard by

---

[113]   Ibid. 2.2.5.19, 364.
[114]   Ibid. 2.1.11.2, 316
[115]   Ibid. 3.3.1, 576.
[116]   Ibid. 2.2.6.3, 367.
[117]   Ibid. 2.2.6.6, 368.
[118]   As Dorothy Coleman pointed out: ""[M]oral motivation does not depend on an external desire for happiness to which moral action serves only as a means." A "desire for happiness" is not an "independent desire" but rather "spurious." Dorothy Coleman, "Hume's Internalism," *Hume Studies* 18 (1992), 321. The opposite

which a person's desires and feelings could contribute to his happiness is his desires and feelings themselves. They vary from one of his moods to the next.

When a person's desires are in conflict, there is no reason for identifying his happiness or welfare with the gratification of one desire rather than another. He will feel "pleasure" when he gratifies a desire and "uneasiness" when he does not, but Hume recognized that the pleasure or unease he feels on that account is incommensurable with his pleasure or unease in gratifying or failing to gratify another desire. Pleasure cannot be, as the utilitarians later claimed, a common metric of all feelings of satisfaction. "Pleasure" refers only to a resemblance among sensations that are otherwise different.

> [U]nder the term *pleasure*, we comprehend sensations, which are very different from each other, and which have only such a distant resemblance, as is requisite to make them be express'd by the same abstract term. A good composition of music and a bottle of good wine equally produce pleasure; and what is more, their goodness is determin'd merely by the pleasure. But shall we say upon that account, that the wine is harmonious, or the music of a good flavour? . . . Nor is every sentiment of pleasure or pain, which arises from characters and actions, of that *peculiar* kind, which makes us praise or condemn."[19]

Nor can one say that a person is better or worse off for having gratified a particular desire. Hume, like Aquinas, described greed as a desire for wealth for its own sake. Hume said that the "avaricious man" is one who seeks wealth for no further reason, even though "there scarce is a probability or even possibility of his employing [it] in the acquisition of the pleasures and conveniences of life."[120] For Hume, greed is a psychological fact due to an "association of ideas," not a vice. A person is attracted to the "pleasures and conveniences" which wealth can buy. Consequently, he associates wealth with that to which he is attracted, and becomes attracted to wealth independently of the pleasures and conveniences it can buy. From Hume's perspective, there is no way of saying that gratifying this desire is pointless, or that one would be better off without it.

Hume, like Aquinas, said that envy arises from a feeling that another's good fortune diminishes one's own. Hume said: "So little are men governed by reason in their sentiments and opinions that they always judge more of objects by comparison than from their intrinsic worth and value. When the mind considers . . . any degree of perfection, whatever falls short of it, though really estimable, has really the same effect on the passions as what is defective and ill."[121] Envy, like greed, is a psychological fact, not a vice. A person is greedy because of a psychological mechanism: a trick of perspective which leads him to think he has less because another person has more.

Hume, like Aquinas, explained how wrath could thwart the pursuit of other ends. Hume said: "When I receive any injury from another, I often feel a violent passion of resentment, which makes me desire his evil and punishment, independent of all considerations of

---

position was taken by Charlotte Brown, "Is Hume an Internalist?" *Journal of the History of Philosophy* 26 (1988), 82.
[119]   *Treatise of Human Nature* 3.1.2.4, 472.
[120]   Ibid. 2.2.5.
[121]   Ibid. 2.2.8.

pleasure and advantage to myself." An angry person has a "violent emotion" that leads him, while his anger lasts, to desire to injure others even at the cost of the pleasure or advantage he would prefer if "calm passions" prevailed.[122]

> Both the *causes* and *effects* of these violent and calm passions are pretty variable, and depend, in a great measure, on the peculiar temper and disposition of every individual. Generally speaking, the violent passions have a more powerful influence on the will; tho' 'tis often found, that the calm ones, when corroborated by reflection, and seconded by resolution, are able to controul them in their most furious movements.[123]

With some people, the violent passions do not prevail because they have an equitable temperament or can moderate their force by reflection and resolution. As Paul Guyer noted, "while Hume does stand by his theory that our ends are always determined by our passions, he also supposes that most of us are ultimately motivated by a passion for calm or tranquility, or a passion for freedom, at least in the negative sense of freedom from domination by importunate desires."[124] Guyer is pleased that it is so. But in Hume's world, one cannot say that these people have done well. There is no standard for judging which desires to gratify except one's desire to gratify them. The desire that one most wishes to gratify is different when one is furious than when one is calm. Indeed, if "by reflection, seconded by resolution," a person desires to gratify the desires he has when his passions are calm, his desire to do so would be merely one more desire, no more worth gratifying than any other.

According to the classical traditions of China and the West, a person lives a truly human life by cultivating those desires which contribute to such a life and restraining the others. The desires that contribute to such a life support each other. Those that do not pull a person in different directions. Hume's account of the normal state of the human personality resembles Xunzi's description of its original unformed state. A person has a liking for profit that leads to wrangling and strife, feelings of envy and hate that lead to violence and crime, and desires of the eyes that lead to license and wantonness and no conscious activity has yet reshaped these desires. Hume's account resembles Socrates' description of the human personality in its pathological state, that of a tyrant plagued by desires he cannot control or reconcile. Of course, the extent of the conflict that a person actually experiences will depend, in Hume's words, on his "peculiar temper and disposition," and few people actually experience the perpetual struggle among their desires described by Xunzi and Socrates. Those who do not can feel relieved. But their relief, from Hume's perspective, is one more feeling which is of no more significance than any other.

---

[122]　Ibid. 2.3.3.9, 417–18.
[123]　Ibid. 2.3.8.13, 437–38.
[124]　Paul Guyer, "Passion for Reason: Hume, Kant, and the Motivation for Morality," *Proceedings and Addresses of the American Philosophical Association* 86 (2012), 4 at 5.

13

The Search for Alternatives

I POSITIVISM

By the nineteenth century, nearly everyone agreed that the rationalist program had failed. In Section II, we will consider how liberal philosophers responded. In this section, we will see how, in the nineteenth century, jurists tried to opt out of the philosophical enterprise entirely. We will also see how some contemporary liberal thinkers such as Dworkin and Rawls have revived that approach. They have said that their conclusions do not rest on the principles of any particular philosophy.

The jurists claimed to be talking about law, not morality, although these contemporary philosophers have applied their approach to moral questions. The jurists claimed that the law was to be found in authoritative legal texts. These texts were supposed to contain the entire law of a particular jurisdiction, and the law was to be derived from them alone. The texts were to be interpreted without regard to any higher principles of justice, or, for that matter, the principles of any particular philosophy. Their approach to law has been called "legal positivism." It should not be confused with the "positivism" of thinkers such as Auguste Comte.

The legal positivists developed "will theories" of private law which bore a remarkable resemblance to those of the rationalists, although they claimed to find them in their legal texts. They defined property in terms of the will of the owner to do as he willed with his own, and contract in terms of the will of the contracting parties. Liability in tort depended on one person's violation of another's rights, which were themselves defined in terms of will. Though the positivists claimed to have reached these conclusions without the benefit of philosophy, they were congenial to nineteenth-century liberal philosophy, so congenial that historians have often thought that the jurists must have been drawing, for example, on Immanuel Kant or Jeremy Bentham. The positivists, however, rejected all philosophical commitments, including commitments to philosophical liberalism.

We will examine the enterprise of the nineteenth-century positivists, how it was rejected by jurists in the late nineteenth century, and then how it has attracted some contemporary liberal thinkers.

i *Nineteenth-Century Legal Positivism*

Method

The legal positivists claimed that their conclusions followed logically from authoritative texts. In Germany, the authoritative texts were still those of Roman law contained in the *Corpus iuris civilis* of Justinian, where they had not been displaced by codes or statutes. They remained in force until the enactment of the German Civil Code of 1900. In France, the authoritative texts were those of the French Civil Code of 1804. In England and the United States, they were the decisions of judges. In the nineteenth century, jurists in these jurisdictions adopted methods which, they claimed, allowed an interpreter to proceed with certainty from the authoritative texts to a legal conclusion. The conclusion was authoritative because it was already implicit in the texts.

According to the German jurist Friedrich Carl von Savigny and his followers, the legal rules of each people were expressions of its *Volksgeist*, the mind or spirit of that people. Despite the apparent paradox, the Roman texts were expressions of the German *Volksgeist*, which is why the Germans had accepted them as law for centuries.[1] There were no higher universal principles on which these texts were based. Savigny considered and rejected the idea that all law might be based on a *Menchengeist*, a mind or spirit of humanity. He thought that any law stemming from that source would be too vague.[2]

For Savigny, because the Roman texts were expressions of the German *Volksgeist*, the law was to be found, not by the exposition of abstract philosophical ideas, but by the exegesis of these texts. Yet, he believed that underlying the texts was a system of fundamental legal concepts united by logical implication. "In every triangle," he said, "there are certain given features from the relations of which all the rest are deducible … In like manner, every part of our law has points by which the rest may be given: these may be termed leading axioms."[3] The difficulty" was that "to distinguish them, and to deduce from them the internal connection … is one of the most difficult problems of jurisprudence. Indeed, it is peculiarly this that gives our work a scientific character."[4] Consequently, although Savigny denied the existence of a natural law to be found outside these texts, as Karl Wieacker noted, his method was like that of the rationalists:

> The … school … borrowed the method of forming a system and concepts as well as the logical deduction of legal decision from the system and concepts from the earlier Christian Wolff. … The subsequent development of Pandectist legal science shows that it never surrendered in principle the formalism of natural law, descending *more geometrico* from axioms to general concepts and from these to particular concepts and particular principles.[5]

---

[1] Friedrich Carl von Savigny, *Vom Beruf unsrer Zeit für Gesetzgebung und Rechtswissenschaft* (Heidelberg, 1840).
[2] Friedrich Carl von Savigny, *System des heutigen römischen Rechts* 1 (Berlin, 1840), §8, pp. 20–21.
[3] Savigny, *Vom Beruf* 38.
[4] Ibid.
[5] Karl Wieacker, *Privatrechtsgeschichte der Neuzeit* (2nd ed., Göttingen, 1967), 373–74. Christoph-Eric Mecke, *Begriff und System des Rechts bei Georg Friedrich Puchta* (Göttingen, 2009), 594. Bohnert noted that despite all the debate over the work of Savigny and his followers, one point of agreement has been its resemblance to that

We can describe Savigny's method as "inverse rationalism." The rationalists began, as in mathematics, with higher concepts and principles. Savigny said that one must begin with the texts and then identify concepts and formulate principles by which they could be explained. Then, like the rationalists, a jurist could pursue the logical implications of these concepts.

In France, the authoritative texts were those of the French Civil Code. Two-thirds of its provisions and nearly all those that deal with the law of obligations, were taken more or less verbatim from two jurists of the Old Regime, Jean Domat and Robert Pothier, who were commenting on Roman law as received in France, but who were strongly influenced by Grotius and Pufendorf. These provisions of the code reflected neither eighteenth-century rationalism nor nineteenth-century liberalism.[6]

Jean-Étienne-Marie Portalis, the chairman of the committee that drafted the French Civil Code, was not a legal positivist. He denied that exegesis of its provisions could resolve all or even most of the cases that came before French courts. "[N]o one pleads against a clear statutory text."[7] He believed that "[l]aw (*droit*) is universal reason, supreme reason founded on the very nature of things. Enacted laws (*lois*) are or ought to be only the law (*droit*) reduced to positive rules, to particular precepts."[8] Consequently, to interpret the code, judges should return to natural law. They were to apply "equity,"[9] "universal equity,"[10] "natural reason,"[11] "principles,"[12] "doctrine,"[13] and "the natural light of justice and good sense"[14] – in short, they were to apply that "equity" which was "a return to the natural law in the silence, obscurity, or insufficiency of the texts."[15] They could also consult "the learning of the entire class of men" trained in legal science who had produced "compendia, digests, treatises, and studies and dissertations in numerous volumes."[16] Portalis was referring to compendia, digests, treatises, and studies and dissertations that had already been written on the Roman law previously in force in France, not to new ones that were yet to be written and based solely on the texts of the Civil Code. Portalis did not expect the Civil Code to be the sole authoritative source of French law. He thought the judge must look to natural law and to Roman law as well. "Few cases are susceptible of

of the rationalists. Joachim Bohnert, *Über die Rechtslehre Georg Friedrich Puchtas (1798–1846)* (Karlsruhe, 1975), 125.

[6] James Gordley, "Myths of the French Civil Code," *The American Journal of Comparative Law* 42 (1994), 459.

[7] Corps législatif, Discours prononcé par Portalis, séance du 23 frimaire, an X (14 déc. 1801), in P. A. Fenet, *Recueil complet des travaux préparatoires du Code civil* 6 (1827; reprinted 1968), 269.

[8] Portalis, Discours préliminaire prononcé lors de la présentation du projet de la Commission du gouvernement, in Fenet, *Recueil* 1: 467.

[9] Présentation au Corps législatif. Exposé des motifs, par Portalis, séance du 4 ventose, an XI (23 fév. 1803), in Fenet, *Recueil* 6: 359; Portalis, Discours préliminaire in Fenet, *Recueil* 1: 474; 6: 51.

[10] Portalis, Discours préliminaire in Fenet, *Recueil* 1: 475.

[11] Présentation au Corps législatif. Exposé des motifs, par Portalis, séance du 4 ventose, an XI (23 fév. 1803), in Fenet, *Recueil* 6: 359; Portalis, Discours préliminaire in Fenet, *Recueil* 1: 469.

[12] Portalis, Présentation au Corps législatif, séance du 4 ventose, an XI (23 fév. 1803), in Fenet, *Recueil* 6: 360.

[13] Ibid.; Portalis, Discours préliminaire in Fenet, *Recueil* 1: 474.

[14] Portalis, Présentation au Corps législatif, séance du 4 ventose, an XI (23 fév. 1803), in Fenet, *Recueil* 6: 359.

[15] Ibid.

[16] Ibid.

being decided by a statute, by a clear text. It has always been by general principles, by doctrine, by legal science, that most disputes have been decided. The Civil Code does not dispense with this learning but, on the contrary, presupposes it."[17]

Nevertheless, in the nineteenth century, the conviction grew that the Code should be interpreted exegetically without looking beyond its own texts. And so, strangely enough, the Code was treated as self-sufficient even though its drafters had not intended it to be.[18] Demolombe took as his motto: "The texts before all else."[19] From the point of view of a jurist, he explained, there is only one true law, the positive law.[20] Troplong praised the jurist who measured his writings by the inflexible text of the Code.[21] Valette advised restraint in using principles of equity to interpret it.[22] Laurent claimed that the jurist should merely note defects in the Code, thus leaving to the legislator the task of bringing it into accord with natural law.[23] Aubry and Rau gave an account of interpretation which made no reference to natural reason or equity.[24] The method that these jurists claimed to be using was like that of the rationalists, with the provisions of the Code taking the place of higher principles. They said that they reached their conclusions by deductions from the Code, just as the rationalists claimed to do so by deduction from higher principles.

In England and the United States, the authoritative texts were the decisions of judges. Like the continental lawyers, the Anglo-American jurists also sought a legal science, and one that owed its certainty to its grounding in authoritative texts. The decided cases were the law. Judges and commentators only explained what the cases meant, and if they did more, they would be making law themselves.

The texts were to be explained without reference to higher principles concerning human nature or the end of society. According to Christopher Columbus Langdell, "Law, considered as a science, consists of certain principles or doctrines. To have such a mastery of these as to be able to apply them with facility and certainty to the ever tangled skein of human affairs, is what constitutes a true lawyer."[25] The principles of this science were to be found in the decided cases. Sir Frederick Pollock thought that principles or purposes beyond the law as declared by the state were of no concern to jurists. "Their business is to learn and know, so far as is needful for their affairs, what rules the State does undertake to enforce or administer, whatever the real or professed reasons for these rules may be."[26]

---

[17] Portalis, Discours préliminaire, in Fenet, *Recueil* 1: 471.

[18] See André-Jean Arnaud, *Les Juristes face à la société du XIXe siècle à nos jours* (Paris, 1975), 53–60.

[19] Charles Demolombe, *Cours de Code Napoleon* 1 (Paris, 1854–82), 1st preface, p. vi.

[20] Ibid. § 8.

[21] Raymond-Théodore Troplong, *De la vente* 1 (Paris, 1837), preface, p. viii.

[22] Auguste Valette, *Cours de Code Civil* 1 (Paris, 1872), 4. While acknowledging that the judge must consult general principles of law to find a solution when statutory provisions are absent, Valette maintained that it would be astonishing to find a case in which these provisions were wholly lacking given the legislation enacted in the previous 70 years (1: 34–35).

[23] François Laurent, *Principes de droit civil français*, 1 (Paris, 1869–78, 1875), §§ 5, 30. For a judge to decide a case by natural law is permissible only when the texts are insufficient, and then it is a necessary evil (§§ 256–57).

[24] Charles Aubry and Charles Rau, *Cours de droit civil français d'après la méthode de Zachariae*, 1 (4th ed., Paris, 1869–71), §40–41.

[25] Christopher Columbus Langdell, *A Selection of Cases on the Law of Contract* (Boston, 1879), viii.

[26] Frederick Pollock, *A First Book of Jurisprudence for Students of the Common Law* (London, 1896), 26–27.

In the nineteenth century, the attempt to explain the cases by concepts or principles of any sort was new to the common law. Traditionally, the common law had not been organized by categories such as tort, property, and contract, nor by concepts such as fault, ownership, possession, and consent. It had been organized by writs. To prevail, the plaintiff had to bring his case within the scope of an appropriate writ. Its scope was not determined by general principles of substantive law but by bodies of lore that had developed around each writ as cases had been decided over the course of time.

The great historian Frederic William Maitland once said that when the history of the common law is finally written, we will understand how the common lawyers arrived at "the great elementary conceptions, ownership, possession, contract, tort and the like."[27] Historians now recognize that these ideas did not come from the common law. As I have described elsewhere, treatise writers rationalized the common law by borrowing from civilian writers.[28] They claimed to be explaining what the judges had done all along. Even after the writs were abolished in the nineteenth century, supposedly, judges were still to give relief in the same cases as before. Nevertheless, the common law treatise writers explained relief by ideas borrowed from a different legal tradition. They were so successful in reading new ideas into older cases that most common lawyers today still imagine that the amalgam of civil and common law they created is the traditional common law.

This transformation in the common law was made possible by a method of interpreting precedent in which the results of past cases were assumed to be correct, but the principle or rule for which case stands might be one never envisioned by the judge who decided that case. Suppose there are two cases. In one, the facts were a, b, and c, and the plaintiff prevailed. In the other, the facts were a, b, and d, and the plaintiff did not. If to follow precedent is to follow a rule consistent with what judges did in the previous cases, then there are two possibilities: the rule that outcome x should be reached when the facts are a, b, and c, or the rule that outcome x should be reached when the facts are a, b, and not d.[29] Americans have been fonder of this explanation of the force of precedent than the English, who attach far greater importance to the rule as stated by the prior judge. Yet the transformation of English law in the nineteenth century was only possible because both the English and Americans read principles into decided cases that judges before 1800 did not have in mind. As long as these principles explained the results in the previous cases, they were said to be based on precedent.

This method can also be called "inverse rationalism," like the method by which Savigny and his school interpreted Roman texts. Both identified concepts and formulated principles by which they explained the results particular cases, according to the common lawyers, or particular Roman texts, according to Savigny. Those principles are then to be applied to new cases. The results fit into a logically coherent structure. This structure, however, was

---

[27] Frederic Willian Maitland, "Why the History of English Law is Not Yet Written," in *The Collected Papers of Fredric William Maitland*, ed. H. A. L. Fisher 1 (1911, repr. Buffalo, 1981), 480 at 484.

[28] James Gordley, *The Jurists: A Critical History* (Oxford, 2013), 204–12.

[29] This example is taken from Karl N. Llewellyn, *The Bramble Bush: Some Lectures on Law and its Study* (New York, 1930), 52. Llewellyn used it to show that the positivists were wrong. One could not get from precedent to the result appropriate in a new case in which the facts were even slightly different by logic alone.

not established by first moving downward from higher principles, like the rationalists, or from code provisions, like the French, but rather by moving upward from common law cases or Roman texts.

The methods of the positivists were like those of the rationalists except that the rationalists claimed to be deriving their conclusions from definitions and concepts as certain as those of mathematics, and the positivists claimed to be doing so from authoritative texts. The rationalists claimed that their conclusions had the same certainty as their definitions and concepts. The positivists claimed that their conclusions had the same authority as their texts.

For a rationalist, to add anything that did not follow logically from a definition would destroy the certainty of his conclusions. For a positivist, if a judge or jurist were to add anything that did not follow from the texts, he would destroy the authority of his conclusions. He would be usurping authority by making law.

The Will Theories of Private Rights

Supposedly, the German jurists derived their conclusions from the Roman texts, the French from their Civil Code, and the common lawyers from their decided cases. Yet they defined the basic concepts of private law in much the same way. Indeed, they defined them in much the same way as the rationalists. In Germany, France, England, and the United States, property was defined as the will of the owner to do as he chooses with what belongs to him.[30] Contract was defined in terms of the will of the parties.[31] Tort law was defined in terms of a violation of another's rights, which were themselves defined in terms of will.

These ideas of private rights were congenial to the liberalism of the nineteenth century. Many historians have assumed that the jurists arrived at these principles through the influence of liberal philosophies. There is no reason to think that they did.

On even a cursory view, the will theories seem different than other intellectual movements that stressed individual choice. The views of philosophers, economists, and political liberals were the subject of endless disputes, no single view winning out. The will theories, in contrast, enjoyed an easy and universal acceptance. They were espoused by both liberal and traditionally minded jurists.

Moreover, liberal philosophers discussed at length what choice is and why it is important. Their views were as different as those of Bentham and Kant. In contrast, the will

---

[30]   For example, Christopher Columbus Langdell, "Classification of Rights and Wrongs" (pt. 1), *Harvard Law Review* 13 (1900), 537, 537–38; Pollock, *First Book of Jurisprudence* 160; Aubry and Rau, 2: § 190; Laurent, *Principes* 6: § 101; Demolombe, *Cours* 9: § 543; Bernhard Windscheid, *Lehrbuch des Pandektenrechts* 1 (7th ed., Düsseldorf, 1891), § 167.

[31]   For example, Christopher C. Langdell, *A Summary of the Law of Contracts* (2nd ed., Boston, 1880), 1–21; Stephen Leake, *Elements of the Law of Contracts* (London, 1867), 7–8; Frederick Pollock, *Principles of Contract* (London, 1885), 1–9; Demolombe, *Cours* 24: § 12; Léon Larombière, *Théorie et pratique des obligations* 1 (Paris, 1857), § 41; Laurent, *Principes* 15: §§ 424–27; Georg Friedrich Puchta, *Pandekten* (Leipzig, 1844), §§ 49, 54; Savigny, *System* 3: § 134; Windscheid, *Lehrbuch* 1: § 69. See generally Gordley, *Philosophical Origins* 161–213.

theorists defined contract and property in terms of will and tort in terms of fault without explaining what the will is or why fault matters.

In Germany, Savigny, who was one of the principal architects of the will theories, was also one of the most philosophical of German jurists. He gave an account of law that owed a good deal to Kant. Law exists to protect freedom.[32] But neither he nor his followers rested their theories on a specifically Kantian conception of will. Indeed, Savigny sharply distinguished the legal concept of will from any philosophical conception: "We in the area of law are not at all occupied with the speculative difficulties of the concept of freedom. For us, freedom is based simply on the appearance, that is, on the capacity, of making a choice among several alternatives."[33]

Similarly, Valérie Ranouil observed in her study of the French will theorists that they appeared to be hostile to philosophy, that they never cited Kant, and that, until the end of the nineteenth century, they never even spoke of the autonomy of the will.[34] She concluded, nevertheless, that the will theorists must have been using the concept of autonomy of the will "as Monsieur Jourdan used prose – without perceiving it."[35] It would be more reasonable to conclude that the will theorists were not drawing on the ideas of Kant or any other philosopher as to why the will was important.

In England and the United States, it is hard to see the influence of any fashionable nineteenth-century school of thought. Sir Frederick Pollock, who built the most elaborate will theory, said that jurists should leave alone "topics which . . . may be philosophical, or ethical, or political, but are distinctly outside the province of jurisprudence."[36] The "business" of jurists is simply "to learn and know . . . what rules the State does undertake to enforce and administer, whatever the real or professed reasons for those rules may be."[37]

Indeed, positivism was not based on a liberal theory. It was an effort to do law without embracing any philosophical theory. The jurist's task was merely to interpret authoritative legal texts, and that task was deemed to be philosophically neutral.

As we have seen, the nineteenth-century jurists described the basic principles of property, contract, and tort in the same way as eighteenth-century rationalists such as Leibniz and Wolff. The rationalists were not liberals. The jurists were not directly influenced by the rationalists except possibly in Germany. It is likely that they all reached similar conclusions because they all faced similar intellectual problems. They were trying to define legal institutions without regard to the purposes that these institutions are established to serve. By definition, promises are to be kept, and the owner has the exclusive right to the use of his property; it is axiomatic that compensation is due when one person's rights are violated. When legal institutions are defined as without regard to their purposes, one cannot explain, as writers in the Aristotelian tradition did, why there are exceptions when the purposes of

---

[32] Savigny, *System* 1: 331–32.

[33] Ibid. 3: 102.

[34] Valérie Ranouil, *L'Autonomie de la volonté: Naissance et évolution d'un concept* (Paris, 1980), 9, 53–55, 79.

[35] Ibid. 70.

[36] Sir Frederick Pollock, "The Nature of Jurisprudence Considered in Relation to Some Recent Contributions to Legal Science," in Sir Frederick Pollock, *Essays in Jurisprudence and Ethics* (London, 1882), 19–20.

[37] Pollock, *First Book* 26–27.

the rules are not served. There is no way to explain, in terms of the purposes of these institutions, why sometimes a promise need not be kept because of changed circumstances or because it is unfair, or why sometimes one may use another's property even against his will because of urgent necessity, or why some rights are protected.

For the rationalists, rights could not be defined in terms of purposes any more than the definitions of mathematical figures. If one tried to do so, conclusions could no longer have the certainty of mathematics. For the positivists, legal conclusions must follow logically from the authoritative texts if they are to have the same authority. If one were to ask about the purposes that legal institutions are meant to serve, application of the texts could no longer be a matter of logical inference or possess the same certainty. A rule that works well in one situation may not work well in another, and logic alone will not explain the difference.

ii *Its Rejection by Jurists*

The jurists turned against positivism in the late nineteenth and early twentieth centuries.

One reason was that the unqualified rights of which the positivists spoke did not correspond to the law actually in force. The positivists, like the rationalists before them, defined rights in a way that is conceptually unlimited. Yet rights of property and contract were not unlimited in the law that the jurists were trying to explain even in their own day. The law does not allow an owner to do as he wishes with his property. The German Civil Code and the common law recognized a doctrine of necessity which allows a person in danger to use another's property to rescue himself, even against the owner's will.[38] Contract law does not recognize an unlimited right of the parties to do what they will. If the terms the parties agreed on are unfair, relief was sometimes given even in the nineteenth century. In the twentieth century, in Germany, a party is given relief when the values exchanged are disproportionate, and in the United States, when a contract is "unconscionable."[39]

Moreover, the parties are often bound by terms they did not will or even contemplate. Nineteenth-century jurists had difficulty explaining why the parties should be bound by them at all. Critics, such as Oliver Wendell Holmes, rejected the will theories in favor of "objective theories" in which a contract was simply a set of legal consequences assigned by the law to the words of the parties.[40] But they had trouble explaining why the law should assign one set of legal consequences rather than another. None of the nineteenth-century jurists had a theory to explain which substantive rights should be protected by tort law.

As we have seen, these were precisely the issues that the late scholastics could address because they had a different conception of rights. The contents of rights were determined

---

[38]   German Civil Code (*Bürgerlichesgesetzbuch*) § 904; *Vincent v. Lake Erie Transportation Co.*, 124 N.W. 221 (Minn. 1919); *Ploof v. Putnam*, 71 A. 188 (Vt. 1908).

[39]   German Civil Code (*Bürgerlichesgesetzbuch*) § 138; Uniform Commercial Code § 2–302; Restatement (Second) of Contracts § 208.

[40]   S. Schlossman, review of E. Zitelmann, *Irrthum und Rechtsgeschäft*, in *Zeitschrift für das Privat- und öffentliche Recht der Gegenwart* 7 (1880), 543 at 560–61; Samuel Williston, *The Law of Contract* 2 (New York, 1920), § 615.

by justice: by the reasons that it was just for a person to own property or by the equality that commutative justice requires in an exchange. The doctrine of necessity was not an impairment of the right of a property owner to exclude others from using his property. The owner did not have a right to do so. His rights were limited by the purposes for which property rights are established. To charge an unjust price was to contravene the purpose of contract law, which was to allow the parties to exchange without either enriching himself at the other's expense. The unexpressed terms by which the parties were bound were those that ensured the justice of the exchange. The rights protected by tort law depended on the purposes which those rights served. Fault mattered because a human being acts through reason and will.

Critics of the nineteenth-century jurists did not turn back to Aristotelian theories of private property and commutative justice. Yet they saw clearly that the underlying difficulty was the conceptualism of the positivists and will theorists. It depended on deductive logic. It ignored purposes. The mistake of "the traditional method," according to François Gény, was the idea "that the whole positive legal system is enclosed in a number of logical categories which are essentially predetermined, basically immutable, governed by inflexible dogmas, and therefore not susceptible of adjustment to the varied and changing exigencies of life."[41] To maintain that the law should consist of categories whose "consequences should be deduced by logically necessary reasoning, could not be justified unless law were an exact science, such as mathematics."[42] Rudolf von Ihering wrote a satire in which he visited the heaven of the jurists, which contained concepts so rarefied that they could never exist in our world, and devices for exploring them such as a hair-splitting machine. As Matthias Reimann observed, Holmes' position was like that of Ihering.[43] Holmes denied that legal questions can be "settled deductively, or once for all."[44] He criticized those who think "that the only force in the development of law is logic," "that a given system, ours, for instance, can be worked out like mathematics from some general axioms of conduct."[45]

Gény and Julian Bonnecasse[46] denied logic was sufficient to interpret the provisions of the French Civil Code. Members of the *Freijuristenschule* said the same of the German Civil Code, which had come into force in 1900. Portalis had made this point long before in explaining his objectives in drafting the French Civil Code. Any case in litigation cannot be decided by logical inference since no one pleads against a clear text. The American Legal Realists, a school that flourished in the 1930s, denied that one could, by logic alone, derive a rule from precedent that could then be applied to new cases. Karl Llewellyn, a leading member of that school, illustrated the problem with the hypothetical cases

---

[41] François Gény, *Method d'interpretation et sources en droit privé positif* (Paris, 1899), no. 62.

[42] Ibid. no. 64.

[43] Mathias W. Reimann, Holmes's *Common Law* and German Legal Science," in *The Legacy of Oliver Wendell Holmes, Jr.* (Robert W. Gordon, ed., Stanford, 1992), 72 at 101–03.

[44] Oliver Wendell Holmes, Jr., *The Path of the Law*, in *Collected Legal Papers* (New York, 1920), 167 at 182.

[45] Ibid. 180.

[46] Julian Bonnecasse, *L'Ecole de l'exégèse en droit civil: les traits distinctifs de sa doctrine et de ses méthodes d'après la profession de foi de ses plus illustres représentants* (Paris, 1924).

described earlier. In one, the facts are *a*, *b*, and *c*, and the outcome is *x*; in the other, the facts are *a*, *b*, and *d*, and the outcome is *y*. "How, now," Llewellyn asked, "are you to know with any certainty whether the changed result is due in the second instance to the absence of fact *c* or to the presence of the new fact *d*?" Certainly, a court could not get from the first result to the second by formal reasoning.[47] The problem also arises with statutes even though one might think that "statutory rules with their fixed words take us wholly outside the ... problem." One must nevertheless decide what the words of statutes mean. "Made without any particular case in mind – or in some instances, with a singular case too much in mind – and without the caution drilled by experience into judges, the language is faced now with a succession of particular cases." One cannot decide, by formal logic, whether cases with "new ambiguous concrete facts ... fit into the statutory boxes."[48]

To claim that the law could be interpreted by formal logic was to ignore the purposes that rules serve. "Jhering invincibly demonstrated," Gény said, that "legal rules and the solutions they provide are essentially determined by the practical purpose and the social goal of the institutions. Here is their source, and, one may say, here also is their logic."[49] "Purpose," Ihering maintained, "is the creator of the entire law: that there is no legal rule which does not owe its origin to a purpose, *i.e.*, to a practical motive."[50] Similarly, according to Holmes, "every rule [the law] contains is [to be] referred articulately and definitely to an end which it subserves and ... the grounds for desiring that end are [to be] stated or are ready to be stated in words."[51]

The revolt against conceptualism raised questions that have never been put to rest among jurists. If rational argument in law does not mean logical deduction, what does it mean? Is it even possible? If the law is to be understood in terms of purposes, how are these purposes related to the concepts in which legal rules and doctrines were framed? What purposes is the law to serve and how are their implications to be determined? Suppose that rational argument is impossible, that the purposes to be pursued are decided arbitrarily, and that the means to pursue them are decided ad hoc according to what seemed best in a particular case. Wouldn't the rule of law be impossible? Some of the extreme *freie Juristen* and American Legal Realists made exactly that claim.

Challenges to the rule of law like those of the *frei Juristen* were rarely heard after 1945. They were recognized as dangerous. The doubts raised by the American Legal Realists were never successfully answered but allowed to sleep until the advent of the Critical Legal Studies movement in the 1970s. As we have seen, Roberto Unger, one of the founders and foremost spokesmen of the movement, traced the rise of positivism and conceptualism (which he called "formalism") to the demise of "the metaphysical systems of ancient and medieval Europe [which] accepted the view that all things in nature have intelligible essences. ... [T]he supporters of the doctrine of intelligible essences have gone on to hold that the standards of right and wrong also have essences

---

[47]   Llewellyn, Bramble Bush, 52.
[48]   Ibid. 79.
[49]   Gény, *Methode* no. 68.
[50]   Rudolph von Ihering, *Der Zweck im Recht* (Leipzig, 1884), liv.
[51]   Holmes, *Path* 186.

which thought can comprehend."[52] As we have seen, that statement was true of the rationalists. Unger illustrated that view by citing Christian Wolff.[53]

He said that with positivism, as we have described it, "the resort to a set of public rules as the foundation of order and freedom, is a consequence of the subjective conception of value."[54] But

> a difficulty arises. If there are no intelligible essences, how do we go about classifying facts and situations, especially social facts and social situations. Because facts have no intrinsic identity, everything depends on the names we give them. The conventions of naming, rather than any perceived quality of "tableness" will determine whether an object is to count as a table. In the same way, convention rather than contract will determine whether a particular bargain is to be treated as a contract.[55]

Critics of positivism had said that the alternative was to ask about the purposes that rules serve. Unger pointed out why the same difficulty arises. If values are subjective, then interests and ends are those of individuals. "[S]ociety is artificial: groups are the products of the will and interests of individuals. For the individual, the group is characteristically a means to the satisfaction of ends that he could not achieve except through membership."[56] But then "the purpose theory" of how law should be applied "leaves the regime of legal justice hanging in the air."[57]

> [T]he purpose theory of law needs some way of defining the values, policies or purposes that are to guide the judge's work. In general a rule will be thought to serve many purposes. Moreover, a judge deals with a whole system of rules, from which he must select the rule appropriate to the case before him. When he applies one of these rules to the case, he must weigh the policy of the rule he is choosing against the policies he might have applied to the case with a different result. Thus, the purpose theory of adjudication requires not only a criterion for the definition of controlling policies, but also a method for balancing them off against one another. In the absence of a procedure for policy decision, the judge will inescapably impose his own subjective preferences, or somebody else's, on the litigants.[58]

He did not propose returning to the earlier view of human nature. One reason, he said, is that that the earlier "doctrine denies any significance to choice rather other than the passive acceptance or rejection of independent moral truths. Our experience of moral judgment, however, seem to be one at least contributing to shape the ends we pursue." Another reason is "the inability of the theory objective value to determine how we should act in particular situations."[59] Both of these criticisms are telling objections against the rationalist version of natural law theory advanced by Suárez and developed by Leibniz and Wolff. In their

---

[52] Roberto Mangabiera Unger, *Knowledge and Politics* (New York, 1975), 30–31.
[53] "For the development of this view see Christian Wolff, *Philosophia Prima sive Ontologia* § 143." Ibid. 31, n. 1.
[54] Ibid. 80.
[55] Ibid.
[56] Ibid. 81.
[57] Ibid. 94.
[58] Ibid. 94–95.
[59] Ibid. 77–78.

version of natural law, there is one right answer to every moral question. They expected, implausibly, that the natural law could prescribe how to act in every situation that can arise. That was not the moral philosophy of Aristotle or Aquinas. Yet, as we have seen, their moral philosophy had dropped out of sight in the eighteenth century when, in the words of Etienne Gilson "Suárezianism consumed Thomism."[60]

iii *Its Revival by Contemporary Philosophers*

Since the publication of H. L. A. Hart's book *The Concept of Law*, some contemporary legal philosophers have made their peace with positivism. Liberal philosophers such as Ronald Dworkin and John Rawls embraced their own version of it. They have done so with a confidence that would have astonished an American Legal Realist, a German *Freijurist*, or a disciple of Gény. "In contemporary Anglo-American legal philosophy," Andrew Altman noted, "little attention has been paid to the work in legal theory carried out in this country during the first half of the century. Indeed, it would be only a slight exaggeration to say that legal theory prior to the publication of H. L. A. Hart's classic, *The Concept of Law*, is generally treated as belonging to a kind of prehistorical legal philosophy."[61] In his book *Taking Rights Seriously*, Dworkin mentioned Legal Realism only once, noting that although it was "a powerful intellectual movement," the reason that "[l]awyers have argued . . . for decades" about the uncertainty of legal rules is "because they are unclear about what the concept of following rules really means."[62]

For the nineteenth-century jurists, as we have seen, positivism and conceptualism went together. They believed that to understand the authoritative texts, one must define concepts implicit in the texts and derive conclusions from these definitions. Hart believed that the reason that the meaning of legal texts could be uncertain was simpler than that. Language is open textured, and so the meaning of words in any natural language is uncertain. For Hart, Altman noted, "all general terms have a penumbral range in which it is unclear and irresolvably controversial whether the term applies to some particular. Yet this penumbral range of extensional indeterminacy is necessarily much smaller than the core extension in which the term's application is clear and uncontroversial."[63] Hart concluded that although "there is no single method of determining the rule for which a given authoritative precedent is an authority . . . in the vast majority of decided cases, there is very little doubt. The headnote is usually correct enough."[64]

If so, one wonders why the vast majority of decided cases were litigated. "No one pleads against clear text," as Portalis and later Gény pointed out. Moreover, in the unclear cases, if the problem is an unresolvable ambiguity in language, it is strange that so much legal

[60] Etienne Gilson, *Being and Some Philosophers* (Toronto, 1952), 118.
[61] Andrew Altman, "Legal Realism, Critical Legal Studies, and Dworkin," *Philosophy & Public Affairs* 15 (1986), 205 at 205.
[62] Ronald Dworkin, *Taking Rights Seriously* (Cambridge, 1977), 3–4.
[63] Altman, "Legal Realism" 207. See H. L. A. Hart, *The Concept of Law* (Oxford, 1961), 119, 123–25.
[64] Hart, *Concept of Law* 131.

training and legal argument is invested in resolving it. A law student would make a serious mistake if he imagined that knowing the headnote of a case is usually enough.

Although in legal language as in natural language, some cases will be clear and others not, with legal language the reason is that words are crafted to reach what is deemed to be the right result in the cases to which they are applied. In any case in litigation, whether the words apply is unclear. As Llewellyn said of statues, "Made without any particular case in mind – or in some instances, with a singular case too much in mind – and without the caution drilled by experience into judges, the language is faced now with a succession of particular cases." How is one to decide whether "new ambiguous concrete facts . . . fit into the statutory boxes?"[65] The answer cannot be found by asking how a word such a "contract" is used in non-legal contexts. In legal contexts, "contract" might have a different meaning in one statute than in another. So we are back to the problem of how the language should be interpreted. Certainly not by deductive logic, as Llewellyn pointed out. If by purpose, one has to face Unger's questions about which purpose matters.

Ronald Dworkin himself had a more sophisticated idea of interpretation and one which, as he observed, resembles that later proposed by Rawls, although for Dworkin, unlike Rawls, it applies to all questions of law and ethics. Beginning with propositions that we accept, some of which are general and some specific, we try to find a consistent set of principles from which they can be reconciled. In *Justice for Hedgehogs*, he explained:

> We need . . . detailed moral opinions when we actually confront a wide variety to moral challenges in family, social, commercial and political life. We form these through an interpretation of abstract concepts that is mainly unreflective. We unreflectively interpret each in the light of others. That is, interpretation knits values together. We are morally responsible to the degree that our various concrete interpretations achieve an overall integrity so that each supports the others in a network of value that we embrace authentically.[66]

For Dworkin, as for the rationalists, moral reasoning is reasoning about the consistency of concepts. "Moral reasoning is . . . conceptual interpretation."[67] Nevertheless, while the rationalists began with definitions and axioms and reasoned downward to moral conclusions, Dworkin's method is to begin with moral convictions and connect them into a consistent system of principles and ideas.

> If you organized all your moral convictions . . . they would form a large interdependent and interconnected system of principles and ideas. You could defend any part of that network only by citing some other part, until you had somehow managed to justify all of the parts in terms of the rest. . . . There is no hierarchy of moral principles built on axiomatic foundations.[68]

---

[65] Llewellyn, *Bramble Bush* 79.
[66] Ronald Dworkin, *Justice for Hedgehogs* (Cambridge, 2011), 101.
[67] Ibid. 157.
[68] Ibid. 117.

His approach is like that of the nineteenth century German and Anglo-American positivists. We have called it as "inverse rationalism." The German jurists began with the Roman legal texts, and the Anglo-Americans with decided cases, and tried to identify concepts and formulate principles that would explain them all as completely as possible.

Dworkin himself noted the similarity to legal analysis in Anglo-American law. In his earlier work, *Taking Rights Seriously*, he said that this "constructive model is not unfamiliar to lawyers. It is analogous to one model of common law adjudication."[69] The ideal judge, whom he called "Hercules," must "develop his concept of principles that underlie the common law by assigning to each of the relevant precedents some scheme of principle that justifies the decision of that precedent."[70] "He must construct a scheme of abstract and concrete principles that provides a coherent justification for all common law precedents and, so far as these are to be justified on principle, constitutional and statutory provisions as well."[71] That was the method of Anglo-American legal positivism which was discredited by the American legal realists.

John Rawls proposed a similar method to answer a narrower question: what "list of liberties" would be "the most appropriate one for a democratic society marked by the fact of reasonable pluralism"?[72] Beginning with settled convictions, one tries to identify the ideas and formulate the principles implicit in them into a coherent system.

> We collect such settled convictions as the belief in religious toleration and the rejection of slavery and try to organize the basic ideas and principles implicit in these convictions into a coherent political conception of justice. These convictions are provisional fixed points that it seems any reasonable conception must account for. We start, then, by looking to the public culture itself as the shared fund of implicitly recognized basic ideas and principles. We hope to formulate these ideas and principles clearly enough to be combined into a political conception of justice congenial to our most firmly held convictions.[73]

We thus arrive at a "publicly recognized point of view" which enables citizens to "examine . . . whether their political and social institutions are just. It enables them to do so by citing what "are . . . valid and sufficient reasons singled out by this conception itself."[74] The goal is to find "a fundamental organizing idea within which all ideas and principles can be systematically connected and related."[75]

Dworkin noted that while "Rawls aimed at a kind of integrity among abstract and concrete convictions about justice," his own goal was "more ambitious and more hazardous." Instead of "bracket[ing] philosophical issues . . . that can be seen as distinctly political," he proposed "a theory of moral and interpretative truth" with "no such limitation as to its scope."[76]

---

[69] Dworkin, *Taking Rights Seriously* 159–60.
[70] Ibid. 116.
[71] Ibid. 116–17.
[72] John Rawls, *Political Liberalism* (New York, 1993), 95.
[73] Ibid. 8.
[74] Ibid. 9.
[75] Ibid.
[76] Dworkin, *Justice for Hedgehogs* 263–64.

Dworkin and Rawls claimed the same advantage for their methods as the nineteenth-century legal positivists. These methods are supposedly free from a commitment to any philosophy. Dworkin said that his "model of reasoning does not require" what he called "moral ontology" because its requirements are independent of it."[77] Rawls, as we will see, tried to identify political principles on which people can agree whatever their philosophical commitments may be.

Their methods raise the same problems as the inverse rationalism of nineteenth-century legal positivists. One is the problem of how one is supposed get from the starting points – be they Roman texts, Anglo-American cases, or the "settled convictions" of some indeterminate group of people – to a system of coherent ideas and principles supposedly implicit in them. The problem is like that posed by Llewellyn. Suppose that in one case, the facts are a, b, and c, and the outcome is x; in the other, the facts are a, b, and d, and the outcome is y. "How, now, are you to know . . . whether the changed result is due in the second instance to the absence of fact c or to the presence of the new fact d?"[78] One can explain the outcomes consistently in either way. As Larry Alexander said of Dworkin, "no matter how extensive the data – the community's judgments, particular and theoretical – there are an infinite number of political moralities that can be constructed that will fit the data perfectly."[79] The same can be said of Rawls.

Llewellyn and Alexander are surely right if the goal is logical consistency among cases or convictions. Dworkin said that when a system of ideas or principles is coherent, "you could defend any part of that network . . . by citing some other part, until you had somehow managed to justify all of the parts in terms of the rest."[80] If, however, defense or justification does not mean that one part of the network logically implies the other, what could it mean? Rawls' method is supposed to arrive at political "conceptions" which provide "valid and sufficient reasons singled out by this conception itself" for holding a political conviction. If a "valid and sufficient reason" is not a logical inference, what could it be?

Could it be a sense of fit or harmony among the parts, or between conceptions and convictions? An interpreter's sense of fitness would, then, determine, for Dworkin, the rights, and for Rawls, the liberties that his fellow citizens enjoy, and the reason is supposed to be that he has faithfully interpreted their views. As Rawls said, "the public political culture may be of two minds at a very deep level."[81] The interpreter is to reconcile these opposing views or provide an alternative of his own. It is quite possible for a citizen to be told that his own view has been ruled out by an interpreter's sense of fitness. That conclusion is hard to accept if one believes in government by the people.

Another criticism of nineteenth-century positivism, as we have seen, was that it ignored the purposes that rules serve. For Rawls and for Dworkin, it is hard to see how coherence in

---

[77] Dworkin, *Taking Rights Seriously* 162.
[78] Llewellyn, *Bramble Bush* 52.
[79] Larry Alexander, "Striking Back at the Empire: A Brief Survey of Problems in Dworkin's Theory of Law," *Law and Philosophy*, 6 (1987), 419 at 435.
[80] Dworkin, *Justice for Hedgehogs* 117.
[81] Rawls, *Political Liberalism* 9.

a system of rules and principles could be based on purpose. Dworkin said that the scope of rights must depend on "principles" instead of "policies."[82]

> An argument of principle can supply a justification for a particular decision, under the doctrine of responsibility, only if the principle cited can be shown to be consistent with earlier decisions not recanted, and with decisions that the institution is prepared to make in the hypothetical circumstances. That is hardly surprising, but the argument would not hold if judges based their decisions on arguments of policy. They would be free to say that some policy might be adequately served by serving it in the case at bar, providing, for example, just the right subsidy to some troubled industry, so that neither earlier decisions nor hypothetical future decisions need be understood as serving the same policy.[83]

According to Rawls, as we will see, the list of liberties belonging to the citizens is to be drawn up by their hypothetical representatives behind a "veil of ignorance" which prevents them from knowing what purposes the members that they represent wish to pursue. The liberties on the list cannot be chosen to further any substantive purpose.

Moreover, positivists could not be philosophically neutral if they did wish to interpret law and legal institutions in terms of the purposes which they serve, whether they are nineteenth-century jurists or contemporary liberal philosophers. Suppose, as Roberto Unger observed, the only purposes that matter arethose of individuals. If so, "society is artificial: groups are the products of the will and interests of individuals. For the individual, the group is characteristically a means to the satisfaction of ends that they could not achieve except through membership."[84] But then "the purpose theory" of how law should be applied "leaves the regime of legal justice hanging in the air."[85]

Positivists would be making a philosophical commitment if they believed, like writers in the Aristotelian tradition, that the purpose of law and legal and political institutions is to do justice and serve the common good. They would then be making a philosophical commitment if, in Unger's words, they believe that "society is artificial: groups are the products of the will and interests of individuals."[86] Philosophical commitments are hard to escape.

Moreover, the legal positivists claimed that their conclusions had authority because they were based on legally authoritative texts. According to Dworkin, the conclusions of moral reasoning are based on "organiz[ing] ... moral convictions" in general.[87] According to Rawls, they are based on "looking to the public culture itself as the shared fund of implicitly recognized basic ideas and principle" which can "be combined into a political conception of justice congenial to our most firmly held convictions."[88]

Whose convictions are to be the starting points for this effort to arrive at moral conceptions or political conceptions supposedly acceptable to everyone? According to Dworkin,

---

[82]   Dworkin, *Taking Rights Seriously* 87.
[83]   Ibid. 88.
[84]   Unger, *Knowledge and Politics* 81.
[85]   Ibid. 94.
[86]   Ibid. 81.
[87]   Dworkin, *Justice for Hedgehogs* 117.
[88]   Rawls, *Political Liberalism* 8.

"It falls to moral and political philosophers though not only to them – to construct self-conscious articulate systems of value and principle out of widely shared but disparate moral inclinations, reactions, ambitions and traditions. They must try to find connections and winnow out inconsistencies . . . ."[89]

"[A] school or group of philosophers who share roughly similar general moral attitudes might hope together to provide a template of what responsibility requires for people with those general attitudes: a template of liberal responsibility for example."[90]

These philosophers are not merely to systematize everyone's moral convictions. They collect them. Presumably, they cannot collect them all. Moreover, they can "winnow out" the ones they believe to be inconsistent. Dworkin does not explain, when different convictions are inconsistent with each other, how they decide which to winnow out. Nevertheless, they are to condemn even widely held moral convictions if they find no justification for them within their network of concepts. "We can count a great proportion of the substantive claims other cultures make about justice as mistakes; we do this when we assume that the best available justification of the paradigms of attribution and response we share justifies rejecting those claims."[91]

As Dworkin seems to acknowledge, which convictions they winnow out and which they regard as central will depend on their "general moral attitudes." People who are liberals will look to liberal philosophers to provide them with "a template or liberal responsibility." It would be no great surprise if political liberals collecting, winnowing, organizing, and accepting or rejecting moral attitudes arrived at conclusions congenial to political liberalism. Conservatives would do the opposite. As we will see, Dworkin based his defense of liberal institutions on the principles that each person's moral conclusions are entitled to equal respect and that each person should act only according to those moral conclusions that he personally can endorse. These principles are in tension with a theory of moral reasoning that leaves so much to the philosophers. For present purposes, the important point is that though we have spoken of Dworkin's theory as a form of positivism, unlike legal positivism it is not based on legally authoritative texts. It is based on reasoning from whatever moral convictions the reasoners select as starting points. People are to defer to claims based on moral convictions that may or may not be their own, whether they are politically liberal or conservative, which the people or their representatives never enacted into law.

One can say the same of Rawls. He claimed that his method of reasoning can produce a "publicly recognized point of view" which enables citizens to "examine . . . whether their political and social institutions are just." It enables them to do so by citing what "are . . . valid and sufficient reasons singled out by this conception itself."[92] Like Dworkin, his goal is "to do this by using a fundamental organizing idea within which all ideas and principles can be systematically connected and related."[93] Whoever does the collecting, decides what

---

[89] Dworkin, *Justice for Hedgehogs* 209.
[90] Ibid. 209–10.
[91] Ibid. 171.
[92] Rawls, *Political Liberalism* 9.
[93] Ibid.

principles are implicit in people's actual convictions, and welds them into a coherent political conception of justice gains the right to speak for the people. He can present his view as a "publicly recognized point of view," even though the members of public have not recognized it but merely expressed the convictions that he, to his own satisfaction, has interpreted.

In *Political Liberalism*, Rawls made it clear that the "public" which is to share this "recognized point of view" and whose convictions contribute to shaping it is not, as Bruce Douglass observed "'humanity as a whole.' It was only people of the sort who inhabited modern democratic societies (or even an idealised version of such people)."[94] Which people are they? Do they belong to a neighborhood in Chicago, a city such as Berkeley or Sioux Falls, a state such as Texas or Massachusetts, a nation such as the United States, or all nations embracing the same "political culture?"

They cannot, without circularity, be the citizens of a hypothetical democratic society embracing idealized democratic principles, or we will be identifying the principles by looking to the views of such a society, and identifying the society by its allegiance to certain principles. Nevertheless, it is likely that the views said to represent the political culture will be those congenial to whoever is expounding what is supposed to be "the recognized point of view." As Bruce Ackerman said,

> John Rawls quite correctly expects his particular readership to be drawn from that large group of middle-class Americans . . . They hate racism; they like free speech, free religion (and free love?) and are suitably ambivalent about the place of achievement and compassion in social affairs. These aspirations, moreover, are transparently the product of a given social structure and cultural situation. Nonetheless, Rawls takes these intuitions as given in his exercise in reflective equilibrium.[95]

If we wish to know what the public in a democratic society thinks, we can hold elections. It would be more democratic than trusting someone to expound, on their behalf, what he takes to be the "publicly recognized point of view."

II PHILOSOPHICAL LIBERALISM

After the fall of rationalism, moral and political philosophers wrote in the shadow of David Hume. They did not retrace the path that would have led back to reason and human nature as understood by the classical tradition. Yet, unlike Hume, they tried to defend normative standards rather than merely explain their psychological origin. Some, such as Hegel, set ideas loose that were later coopted to justify totalitarianism, although Hegel himself would have recognized Nazism as a perversion of his philosophy. Other philosophers tried to justify liberal democratic institutions. The rest of this book concerns their attempt to do so.

Here we must distinguish between liberal democratic institutions themselves and modern attempts to justify and explain them. Democratic institutions were in place before

---

[94]   R. Bruce Douglass, "John Rawls and the Revival of Political Philosophy: Where Does He Leave Us?" *Theoria: A Journal of Social and Political Theory* 59 (2012), 81 at 86.
[95]   Bruce Ackerman, *Social Justice in the Liberal State* (New Haven, 1980), 353.

liberal philosophers made these attempts – unless one counts Locke as a founder of modern liberal philosophy, which, we have seen, he was not. Liberal philosophy has two salient features. One, as John Gray said, is that it places a special value on "liberty" which "is accorded priority over other political goods or values."[96] The other is a denial that human nature can be a source of normative standards. If there is such a thing as human nature, it is too unknowable or indeterminate. According to George Santayana,

> [T]he liberal view implies a certain view of the relation of man in the universe. It implies that the ultimate environment, divine or natural, is either chaotic in itself or undiscoverable by human science, and that human nature, too, is either radically various or only determinable in a few essentials, round which individual variations play *ad libitum*. For this reason, no normal religion, science, art or way of happiness can be prescribed. These remain always open, even in their foundations, for each man to arrange for himself.[97]

As we have seen, for Mencius and for Socrates, the idea that human nature is a source of normative standards was the alternative to the claims of Mozi, Yang Zhu, and the sophists that there were no standards of conduct, or, at least, none beyond one's own desires. Hume drew a similar conclusion, that virtue was a feeling of a certain kind. Yet the object of modern liberal philosophy is to defend the value of human liberty. The difficulty is to make such a claim successfully if there are no values implicit in human nature.

One liberal response has been to maintain that the satisfaction of human desires is good, whatever those desires may be. Freedom is the freedom to do as one desires. This path was taken by utilitarians such as Jeremy Bentham and John Stuart Mill, and later by economists who speak of "preference satisfaction."

A second response has been to maintain that each person, in pursuing his own ends, should accord equal respect to others who are pursuing theirs, whatever their ends may be. Freedom is to pursue one's ends subject to the same rules or limitations that one would wish others to adopt. A progenitor of this approach was Immanuel Kant. He thought that moral law could be inferred from a categorical imperative: one must act according to a maxim that one would will to be universal law. A free and rational being would obey this law because he is free and rational. Neo-Kantians have changed the starting point. Ronald Dworkin and John Rawls defended liberal institutions by ascribing a normative value to a human being's capacity to form a conception of the good. They maintained that, at least so far as politics is concerned, each citizen's conception of the good must receive the same respect as every other.

A third response has been to identify freedom with self-expression, and to maintain that self-expression is of value for its own sake. To be free is to make a choice that is dictated neither by desire nor by reason. Such choices are creative, like the work of an artist. This view was developed in response to Kant by German writers of the late nineteenth and early twentieth century such as Friedrich Schiller and Wilhelm von Humboldt. It inspired John

---

96 John Gray, *Liberalisms: Essays in Political Philosophy* (London, 1989), 140.
97 George Santayana, "Liberalism and Culture," in *Soliloquies in England and Later Soliloquies* (Ann Arbor, 1967), 174.

Stuart Mill. It is a major theme in some contemporary theories. For Joseph Raz, it explains the value of "autonomy."

We have seen approaches like these before. Yang Zhu identified the good life with the gratification of desire. Mozi believed it is a mistake to regard one's own desires as more important because from an objective point of view, they are not, and because to do so one must apply a different standard to himself than to others. Callicles admired a person who was bold enough to scorn convention and act according to his own designs. These approaches face the same difficulties today as they did then. Indeed, they face one difficulty more. Modern philosophers accept many of Hume's premises. On these premises, none of these approaches is viable.

Utilitarians attribute a normative significance to the satisfaction of desire. More desire satisfied is better than less. On Hume's principles, one cannot say so. One cannot say what is better. Desires are mutually inconsistent and incommensurable. For Kant and the neo-Kantians, it would not accord with reason to apply one standard to oneself and a different standard to others. On Hume's principles, reason cannot be the foundation of morality. Freedom of expression is regarded as a choice that is made neither for the satisfaction of a desire nor in obedience to reason. On Hume's principles, all choices are made out of desire and none in obedience to reason.

Each of these three approaches presupposes that there is a gap between reason and desire: utilitarians define the good in terms of desires satisfied, Kantians in terms of reason, and those committed to self-expression in terms of choices dictated neither by reason nor desire. In Hume's world, the gap is unbridgeable. There can be no reason to satisfy a desire, no desire impelled by reason, and no choice that is not due to desire. Liberal philosophers try to bridge the gap and fail.

Moreover, each of these three versions of liberalism has led to results that are at odds with common sense. Their proponents have had to choose between common sense and consistency. As we will see, whenever they opted for common sense, they reintroduced, though often veiled, Aristotelian ideas of human nature and rationality.

i *Utilitarianism*

Classical Utilitarianism

Jeremy Bentham said that in reading the work of Hume, I "felt as if scales had fallen from my eyes."[98] Hume had said that some feelings were pleasurable and others "uneasy." Bentham concluded that one acts to obtain pleasure and to avoid uneasiness or pain. He defined happiness in terms of experiencing pleasure and avoiding pain. He defined right and wrong in terms of happiness: "it is the greatest happiness of the greatest number that is the measure of right and wrong."[99] Bentham named this philosophical approach

---

[98] Jeremy Bentham, *A Comment on the Commentaries and A Fragment on Government* (J. H. Burns and H. L. A. Hart, eds., Oxford, 1977), 440.

[99] Jeremy Bentham, *A Fragment on Government* (London, 1776), Preface, 2nd par.

"utilitarianism" after a dream he had in 1781. He dreamed that he was "a founder of a sect; of course a personage of great sanctity and importance. It was called the sect of the *utilitarians*."[100]

He explained the value of freedom by its contribution to happiness. In general, utility is maximized by allowing people to choose for themselves since "no man can be so good a judge as the man himself, what gives him pleasure or displeasure."[101] The ultimate good is pleasure, and freedom to choose is a means by which the pleasure of individuals will be increased.

One can see the debt that he owed to Hume. For Hume, one is motivated by desire but one cannot be motivated by reason. The only role that reason could play is to identify outcomes that one might desire and the means by which they may be obtained. There is no reason why one desire is more worth gratifying than another. If that is so, then one can see why, for Bentham, the only normative standard could be the pleasure that comes with the gratification of desire. Yet, the moment he elevated pleasure to a normative standard, he stepped outside Hume's world, in which right or wrong, virtue or vice, are merely feelings of approbation or disapprobation of a certain kind. He depended upon Hume's premises but then ignored their implications.

Individuals are always gratifying one desire or another. If Bentham had gone no further than to say that it is right for them to do so he would have violated Hume's rule that one cannot derive an "ought" from an "is." He would have moved from the proposition that people do take pleasure in gratifying their desires to the proposition that they should.

He would also have rejected Hume's distinction between the desire to act rightly or virtuously and other desires. If Bentham were correct, when a person acts because he feels that an action is right or virtuous, it must be that the amount of pleasure he derives from so acting is greater in amount than the pleasure he would derive from not doing so. But that is not consistent with what seems to be distinct about feelings of right and wrong even if, as Hume said, they are merely feelings of approbation and disapprobation. Kant, like Bentham, defined "happiness" in terms of agreeableness or pleasure.[102] Kant observed, however, that to make "the principle of one's own happiness" "the determining ground of the will" is "the direct opposite of the principle of morality."[103] The person who claims to be acting rightly would not say that he does so to obtain more pleasure for himself although he does take pleasure in acting rightly. If Bentham were correct, he must be acting for the sake of pleasure. In Hume's world, he is acting out of a feeling of approbation that is different from other pleasurable feelings.

If Bentham had gone no further than to say that it is right for people to seek pleasure by gratifying their desires, his position would have been like that of Yang Zhu. It is right to be

---

[100] Quoted in J. E. Crimmins, *Secular Utilitarianism: Social Science and the Critique of Religion in the Thought of Jeremy Bentham* (Oxford, 1990), 314.

[101] Jeremy Bentham, *Principles of Morals and Legislation* (J. H. Burns and H. L. A. Hart, eds., Oxford, 1970), XIII. iv, 159.

[102] Immanuel Kant, *Kritik der praktischen Vernunft in Kant's gesammelte Schriften*, Königlich Preussischen Akademie der Wissenschaft (5th ed., Berlin, 1913), 1 at 22.

[103] Ibid. 35.

"gratifying your wishes and cherishing your days."[104] But then Bentham would have had to accept Yang Zhu's conclusion that it is right for a person to care only about gratifying his own desires and not to care about anyone else. Bentham wanted a normative standard by which it is right to care about others. He therefore defined happiness in terms of the amount of pleasure a person experiences, and "the measure of right and wrong" as "the greatest happiness of the greatest number." In Hume's world, that conclusion is impossible, and for two reasons.

One is that, according to Hume, it is not possible to compare the amounts of pleasure that different people experience. It is not even possible to compare the amounts of pleasure that a single person derives from different pleasures. "[U]nder the term *pleasure*, we comprehend sensations, which are very different from each other, and which have only such a distant resemblance, as is requisite to make them be express'd by the same abstract term."[105] One can use the word "pleasure" to describe the agreeable feelings I have listening to music, reading a mystery, accomplishing some task, or helping a friend. But, if Hume is correct, one cannot conclude that the agreeableness or pleasure of these feelings has a common metric. Bentham did not explain why he thought Hume was wrong. He assumed Hume was wrong, and he needed to make that assumption to introduce normative standards into a Humean world.

Moreover, Hume refuted the rationalists by showing that that no one can be motivated by a proof that an action is right or wrong. Reason can identify outcomes that one might desire and the means by which they may be obtained. But reason cannot motivate. Bentham's definition of "the measure of right and wrong" as the "greatest happiness of the greatest number" is subject to the same criticism. It is not a statement about what actually gives people pleasure, although some people do take pleasure in the pleasure of others. It is a claim about what is right or wrong whatever people actually desire. It depends on what we have called the principle of impartial concern: it cannot be right to treat the desires of one person as more important than those of another. In that respect, it is like Mozi's principle of "universal love," or, as it might better be translated, equal concern for others. As David Nivison observed, Mozi, unlike Mencius, expected people to observe that principle because it is rational to do so, not because they are naturally inclined to do so.[106] We will defer discussion of whether the principle of impartial can concern can be rationally defended until we encounter the more sophisticated version of it formulated by Kant. In Hume's world, however, even if it were a rational and coherent principle, it could not motivate anyone to act in accordance with it.

Bentham spent much of his life trying to persuade governments to shape policy according to the principle of the greatest happiness for the greatest number. He, at least, thought that governments could be motivated to follow this principle. Yang Zhu would have asked why the motivations of those in government would be any different than those of anyone

---

[104] A. C. Graham, *Disputers of the Tao Philosophical Argument in Ancient China* (La Salle, 1989), 108.

[105] David Hume, *Treatise of Human Nature* (Oxford, 1888), 3.1.2.4, 472.

[106] David S. Nivison, "Weakness of the Will in Ancient Chinese Philosophy," in David S. Nivison, ed., *The Ways of Confucianism: Investigations in Chinese Philosophy* (Chicago, 1996), 79 at 87.

else: to gratify their own desires. Indeed, they might develop new desires to exert power at the expense of other people. There is nothing in Bentham's philosophy to explain why that fear would be unjustified if, indeed, all people act for the sake of pleasure. But for Bentham those in power had to be motivated to carry out his program.

Mozi believed governments could take measures to change what people desire. He wished to reduce their desires to the minimum so that all desires could be satisfied. By prohibiting the gratification of certain desires, the government could reduce their intensity or even make them go away. Bentham wished to maximize the pleasure people receive from gratifying their desires. Suppose, however, by changing peoples' desires, some would lose pleasure that they would otherwise obtain but others would have the resources to gratify their own desires. There might be a net gain in pleasure satisfied. Utilitarianism would the clash with liberalism. It would justify a state as authoritarian as the one envisioned by Mozi in which state-imposed restrictions on consumption would be a feature of ordinary life. But Bentham did not want an authoritarian state.

We have discussed why Bentham's utilitarianism would not make sense in the world of Hume, whose writings, Bentham said, removed the scales from his eyes. From the perspective of either of the classical traditions, it would not make sense because it ignores the possibility that one is making a choice on the basis of what is genuinely right or wrong. The result is often pleasurable. But the choice is not made for the sake of pleasure.

In both classical traditions, as we have seen, a person is able by conscious effort to affect what he desires and consequently what gives him pleasure. Indeed, he must if he wishes to live rightly. Mencius believed that bad desires could be fended off by focusing the mind. Xunzi believed that bad desires could be consciously reshaped so as to become the raw material for a good and beautiful life. Dai Zhen taught that selfish desires could be rectified by recognizing that they are out of harmony with the principle by which life should be lived. According to Aristotle, all desires can contribute to a good life, but to do so they must be properly trained. A person does not choose to live a good life for the sake of pleasure, but rather the choice of how to live affects what gives him pleasure.

Moreover, a person may give thought to what course of action contributes to a good life. Dai Zhen said one must use "wisdom" to weigh what is important against what is unimportant. In the Aristotelian tradition, one must use practical reason to make a right estimate of the contribution that an action makes to one's ultimate end.[107] The result of a good choice will normally be pleasure. But the criterion by which the choice is made is not the strength of a feeling but a judgment concerning the contribution that an action makes to a good life. Any pleasure a person experiences depends on his belief that he has chosen rightly. Pleasure, in the ordinary sense of an agreeable feeling, is therefore the consequence of his belief that he has made the right choice, not his reason for making the choice that he did.

The answer a utilitarian might make depends on what he means by pleasure. He might respond that such a person does not really seek to live a good life but rather the pleasurable feeling that comes from leading a good life. In that event, he would have to explain why the

---

[107] *Summa theologiae* II-II, Q. 49, a. 2.

desire to live a good life cannot be a sufficient motivation, whatever pleasure comes from it, and why the sources of pleasure is the belief that one has chosen rightly. Or a utilitarian might answer that by definition, a person chooses the course of action that would give him the most pleasure because if another course of action were more attractive to him, he would choose it instead. In that event, pleasure has become an empty concept. It no longer means a feeling with a certain intensity and magnitude. It merely means that a peron prefers one course of action to another. To "maximize" pleasure merely means to choose what one prefers.

John Stuart Mill recognized that people do not always choose the course of action that will give them the most intense pleasure. They seek beauty or knowledge in preference to gratifying "animal appetites." Mill answered that human beings are capable of pleasures of "much higher value"[108] because they "have faculties more elevated than the animal appetites" and desire a "manner of existence which employs [their] higher faculties."[109] People will choose a pleasure with higher value provided that they are "competently acquainted" with it.[110] To do so they must cultivate their higher faculties. "Capacity for the nobler feelings is in most natures a very tender plant, easily killed, not only by hostile influences, but by mere want of sustenance."[111] If, however, one chooses a pleasure of higher "quality," even though it is no more pleasurable, then a person's sole end cannot be pleasure. As G. E. Moore observed, "if you say, as Mill does, that quality of pleasure is to be taken into account, then you are no longer holding that pleasure *alone* is good as an end, since you imply that something else, something which is *not* present in all pleasures, is *also* good as an end."[112]

Contemporary Economic Liberalism

Modern economics, though launched by Adam Smith, for a long time was wedded to classical utilitarianism. Alfred Marshall, one of the leading economists at the turn of the twentieth century, described the utilitarian economist Henry Sidgwick[113] as his "spiritual mother and father."[114] According Marshall, "The total utility of a thing to anyone (that is, the total pleasure or benefit it yields him) increases with every increase in his stock of it, but not as fast as his stock increases."[115] Marshall used this proposition to derive "the general law of demand": "The greater the amount to be sold, the smaller must be the price at which it is offered to find purchasers."[116] Francis Edgeworth mathematized the principles of Bentham.[117] The Nobel prize-winning economist Amartya Sen believes that classical utilitarianism still colors the thought of economists.

---

[108]   John Stuart Mill, *Utilitarianism* 1.
[109]   Ibid. 11.
[110]   Ibid. 12.
[111]   Ibid. 14.
[112]   G. E. Moore, *Principia Ethica* (Cambridge, 1959), 81.
[113]   See Henry Sidgwick, *Principles of Political Economy* (London, 1883).
[114]   Phyllis Deane, "Sidgwick, Henry," in John Eatwell, John Murray Milgate, and Peter K. Newman, eds., *The New Palgrave: A Dictionary of Economics* 4 (2nd ed., London, 1987), 328–29.
[115]   Alfred Marshall, *Principles of Economics* (8th ed., London, 1962), 79.
[116]   Ibid. 84.
[117]   *F. Y. Edgeworth: Mathematical Psychics and Further Papers on Political Economy*, ed. Peter Newman (Oxford, 2003).

Nevertheless, early in the twentieth century, for quite different reasons, modern economists repudiated classical utilitarianism. As Paul Samuelson observed, they rejected the idea that pleasures are commensurable and that, in principle, a quantity of pleasure is measurable. They "ceased to believe in the existence of any introspective magnitude or quantity of a cardinal, numerical kind."[118] They also discovered that they did not need to do so to build their economic models. To draw a demand curve, they merely needed to assume that people do prefer some courses of action to others. One could speak of preferences and preference satisfaction without imagining, as Marshall did, there is some quantity that people are maximizing when they choose what they prefer. Indeed, as Samuelson noted, economists now define a "preference" as what a person actually chooses, regardless of why he chooses it. "Thus, the consumer's market behavior is explained in terms of preferences, which are in turn defined only by behavior. The result can very easily be circular."[119]

J. R. Hicks claimed that the new approach had liberated economists from philosophical commitments. They no longer needed to be utilitarians.[120] That is not quite true. Some of them still make normative claims. These claims are based on a weaker form of utilitarianism than those we previously considered. Though they have dropped the term "pleasure" and speak only of "preferences," they attach a normative value to the satisfaction of preferences just as the classical utilitarians attached a normative value to pleasure.

When the classical utilitarians spoke of "maximizing utility" they meant maximizing the amount of pleasure that people experience. Economists still speak of "maximizing utility" or "maximiz[ing] their desired ends."[121] Nevertheless, it is only in a figurative sense that a person who satisfies his preferences maximizes anything. Suppose, for example, that this morning, in order of preference, I would like to wear my blue, my brown, and my green sports jacket. Suppose that this afternoon, I will go to a committee meeting, because it needs to be done; if there were no meeting, I would shop for groceries, because that needs to be done, too; and if neither needed to be done, I would read a book. The new approach, in effect, assigns numbers to each of these possible choices. The numbers do not indicate the quantity of utility I derive from these choices but the order in which I prefer them. Assigning these numbers says nothing about how or why I make these choices or how much of anything I get out of them. I am not maximizing anything, except in the sense that I am choosing what I prefer. Sen made a similar point:

> The binary relation underlying choice ... has sometimes been described as the person's "utility function." Needless to say, by construction, a person can be seen as maximizing that "utility function." But this is not adding more to what we already knew, and, in particular, it

118 Paul Anthony Samuelson, *Foundations of Economic Analysis* (enlarged edition, Cambridge, 1976), 91 (the passage quoted appeared in the first edition of 1947).

119 Ibid. 91. Similarly, Arthur Leff said that it is "definitionally circular" to say "what people do is good, and its goodness can be determined by what they do." Arthur Allen Leff, "Economic Analysis of Law: Some Realism about Nominalism," *Virginia Law Review* 60 (1974), 451, 458.

120 J. R. Hicks, *Value and Capital: An Inquiry into Some Fundamental Principles of Economic Theory* (2nd ed., Oxford, 1946), 18.

121 For example, Michael Trebilcock, *The Limits of Freedom of Contract* (Cambridge, 1993), 2–3 ("[E]conomics assumes that individuals ... attempt to maximize their desired ends (which may be of infinite variety.").

is saying really nothing about what it is that the person is trying to maximize. Calling that binary relation the person's "utility function" does not tell us that it is his or her utility in any independently defined sense (such as happiness or desire-fulfilment) that the person is in fact trying to maximize.[122]

A result is "efficient" when at least one person is better able to satisfy his preferences without anyone else becoming less able to do so. To attach a normative value to efficiency and hence to preference satisfaction has the same difficulties as the empty form of utilitarianism mentioned earlier in which utility or pleasure merely means preference.

According to that approach, a person who satisfies his preferences is better off by definition. If he chooses to tear the wings off flies, he is by definition better off. Sen pointed out that the same is true if he chooses to cut off his own toes.

> Consider the person we find busy cutting off all his toes with a blunt knife. We ask him why he is being so imprudent and he replies that it is indeed his goal to get rid of his toes because that is what he "feels like." "Have you examined," we ask him, "what the consequences of not having toes would be?" He replies, "No, I have not, and I am not going to, because cutting off my toes is definitely what I desire; it is my principal objective and I understand I am entirely rational so long as I pursue any objective intelligently and systematically."[123]

Since he is doing what he prefers, his conduct is not only rational but efficient. By the economists' definition of efficiency, a sufficiently lazy person could "efficiently" starve to death if he chose to do so rather than to do a minimal amount of work.

To retell a story, I put a hypothetical case to seven well-known economists and members of the law and economics movement, one of whom won the Nobel prize. A man whose yacht was sinking radioed his position to the Coast Guard and was told that, for whatever reason, it could not reach him for six days. He got into a lifeboat with a six-pack of beer, which is all that he had on the yacht to drink. He knew (never mind how) that if he drank one can each day, he would survive. Instead, he drank four cans the first day, two the second, and was found dead on the sixth. Is this efficient? Six economists said yes. The seventh (as it happens, the Nobel prize winner), said that it couldn't happen.

One might say that preference satisfaction is good only so long as the preferences of a person are not self-destructive but contribute to a good life. Each person is often the best judge of whether they do.[124] But at that point, one has returned to the classical tradition. The satisfaction of preferences is good provided each person acts with wisdom, as understood by Dai Zhen, or practical reason, as understood by Aristotle.

---

[122]   Amartya Sen, *On Ethics and Economics* (Oxford, 1987), 14–15.
[123]   Amartya Sen, *Rationality and Freedom* (Cambridge, 2002), 39.
[124]   See James Gordley, "Morality and Contract: The Question of Paternalism," published with the proceedings of the conference on Law and Morality, held at the William and Mary School of Law, March 2006, 48 *William and Mary Law Review* 1733 (2007).

As Sen noted: "That income or wealth is an inadequate way of judging advantage was discussed with great clarity by Aristotle in Nicomachean Ethics: 'wealth evidently is not the good we are seeking; for it is merely useful for the sake of something else.'"[125] Aristotle's "analysis of development ... treats the freedom of individuals as the basic building blocks. Attention is thus paid particularly to the expansion of the 'capabilities' of persons to lead the kind of lives they value – and have reason to value."[126]

According to Martha Nussbaum, "Sen is explicitly interested in the full range of capabilities that make up good human functioning in all areas."[127] Nevertheless:

> Sen needs to be more radical than he has been so far in his criticism of utilitarian accounts of well-being, by introducing an objective normative account of human functioning and by describing a procedure of objective evaluation by which functionings can be assessed for their contribution to the good human life. I think that Aristotle will provide substantial assistance in this task. For Aristotle's ethical thought contains an account of human functionings (of the diverse activities whose excellent performance constitutes the good human life) that is non-external, but still objective – and objective in a way that still leaves room for a certain sort of sensitivity to cultural relativity.[128]

The Law and Economics Movement

The discrediting of the nineteenth-century will theories of law left an intellectual vacuum that the law and economics movement has tried to fill. Here I will sketch the reasons I have given elsewhere[129] why it has been unable to do so successfully.

Its goal is to explain why the law is or can be efficient. A result is Pareto efficient or efficient in the strict sense, a result is "efficient" if at least one person's ability to satisfy his preferences is increased and no one's is diminished. According to what is called Kaldor-Hicks efficiency, a result is efficient if those who become better able to satisfy their preferences would be willing to compensate those who become less able, even if they never actually do so. Richard Posner has spoken of "wealth maximization," which, he explained, is formally identical to Kaldor-Hicks efficiency.[130]

Aristotle distinguished between distributive justice which concerns fairness in the distribution of resources and commutative justice which concerns fairness in transactions between one person and another. Partisans of the law and economics movement are not concerned with the distribution of wealth. The efficiency of the transaction is independent

---

125 Amartya Sen, *The Idea of Justice* (Cambridge, 2009), 253 citing Aristotle, *Nicomachean Ethics* I.5. Similarly, Sen, *On Ethics and Economics* 3.

126 Amartya Sen, *Development as Freedom* (New York, 2000), 18.

127 Martha C. Nussbaum, "Nature, Function, and Capability: Aristotle on Political Distribution" (Wider Working Papers, WP 31, December 1987), published in *Oxford Studies in Ancient Philosophy* (Oxford, 1988), 26.

128 Ibid. 34.

129 James Gordley, *The Jurists: A Critical History* (Oxford, 2013), 300–09.

130 Richard A. Posner, "The Value of Wealth: A Comment on Dworkin and Kronman," *Journal of Legal Studies* 9 (1980) 243, 244.

of the way resources are distributed. A purchase and sale between any two people satisfies the preferences of both. Therefore, it is efficient even if purchasing power were almost entirely concentrated in a few families and the rest were close to starvation. At that point, although a contract between the two parties makes both better off, one wonders if a still better result would be for someone like Robin Hood to steal from the rich party and give the poor one what he needs but cannot easily afford.

According to Posner, if the goal is wealth maximization, anyone whose "net social product is negative" may have to starve. "[H]e would have no right to the means of support though there was nothing blameworthy in his inability to support himself." That conclusion "grates on modern sensibilities," Posner admits, and yet he "see[s] no escape from it that is consistent with any major modern ethical theory."[131]

The only way in which one initial distribution of resources could be less efficient than another is if it led to additional "transactions costs," that is, the party who did not receive a resource would have to incur the otherwise unnecessary expense of buying it back. Posner asked why our initial distribution of resources is such that a person has the right to sell his own labor and a woman the right to choose her sexual partners. He answered that otherwise there would be transactions costs: the people lacking these rights would want to buy them back from the other people to whom they have been assigned, and that would entail the costs incident to repurchasing them. There would be no transaction costs, and presumably, no inefficiency if the persons lacking these rights were also so utterly impoverished that they had no resources with which to repurchase them. Hereditary slavery would not be inefficient if the slave had no means of purchasing his freedom. If the master's initial endowment of resources included, among other rights, the right to beat his slave without cause, his choice to do so out of sheer cruelty would be one more preference.

For Aristotle, commutative justice concerns the fairness of transactions between the parties. A right is defined by asking about the purpose served by recognizing such a right. The rationalists and the will theorists defined rights in terms of the will of the parties. The economists define efficiency in terms of the protection and exchange of whatever rights the parties have. But like the rationalists and will theorists, they do not ask why, as a matter of justice, the parties should have them in the first place. Consequently, they encounter similar problems.

For the rationalists and the will theorists, property is an unconditional right. Yet, as we have seen, the law gives relief in cases of urgent necessity. A leading American case is in *Ploof* v. *Putnam*, where a pier owner was held liable when his employee cut loose the plaintiff's ship which the plaintiff had tied to the pier to save it in a storm.[132] Writers in the Aristotelian tradition explained the doctrine by saying that the rights of an owner should extend no further than the purposes served by private property, which are to give an incentive to labor and to avoid quarrels. Posner noted that in *Ploof*, it was the pier owner's employee who cut loose the plaintiff's ship. The pier owner was not there and so

---

[131] Richard A. Posner, "Utilitarianism, Economics and Legal Theory," *Journal of Legal Studies* 9 (1979), 103 at 128.

[132] *Ploof* v. *Putnam*, 71 A. 188 (Vt. 1908).

"negotiations were, in the circumstances, infeasible."[133] The negotiations would have led to an efficient result. Suppose, however, that the owner had been there and had cut the ship loose out of sheer cussedness after the plaintiff offered him a fortune to refrain. Would that result be efficient? I think Posner would have to say so. He defines efficiency in terms of preference satisfaction, whatever the preference may be, and cussedness is as much a preference as any other.

For the will theorists, contract is the will of the parties. Consequently, they found it hard to explain why the law gives relief from an extremely unfair bargain. Writers in the Aristotelian tradition said that such a bargain violates commutative justice. Suppose that in *Ploof*, the owner had been present and allowed the plaintiff to tie up to his pier but only in return for a fortune. Would that result also be efficient? In an article on rescue at sea, Posner found a reason why it would not. Under admiralty law, a ship that rescues the property of a ship in distress can charge only a reasonable amount for doing so. According to Posner, this rule is efficient because otherwise shipowners will overinvest in safety equipment to avoid the need for a rescue.[134] That is imaginative. Suppose that no investment in safety equipment and no reasonable degree of extra care would have prevented the need for a rescue. Why, then, shouldn't the bargain stand?

In his seminal treatise *Economic Analysis of Law*, Posner suggested a different explanation. Although any price higher than the cost of rescue and lower than the value of the ship and its cargo will make both parties better off, "[a]scertaining this range may be costly, and the parties may consume much time and resources in bargaining within the range. Indeed, each party may be so determined to engross the greater part of the potential profits from the transaction that the parties never succeed in coming to terms."[135] Suppose, however, that the parties waste little time negotiating while the ship is sinking and that neither is so blind to self-interest as to let it sink rather than agree. Should the agreement be enforced when, to give Posner's example, they agreed on "a price equal to 99% of the value of the ship and its cargo"?[136]

One of the strengths of the law and economics movement is that it is supposed to explain the law. As we have seen, it cannot do so in the cases that caused difficulty after the eclipse of the classical tradition.

ii *Kantianism*

Immanuel Kant

Kant said that reading the work of David Hume first roused him from his dogmatic slumber. It was Christian Wolff who lulled him to sleep.

For rationalists such as Wolff, as we have seen, a gap opened between cognition and volition, between reason and desire, that Hume declared to be unbridgeable. According to

133 Richard A. Posner, *Economic Analysis of Law* (5th ed., New York, 1998), 190.
134 William M. Landes and Richard A. Posner, "Salvors, Finders, Good Samaritans and Other Rescuers: An Economic Study of Law and Altruism," *Journal of Legal Studies* 7 (1978) 83. The same explanation is given by F. H. Buckley "Three Theories of Substantive Fairness," *Hofstra Law Review* 19 (1990) 33, 40–48.
135 Ibid. 62.
136 Ibid.

Hume, the definitions and proofs of the rationalists only tell us about the relationship among concepts. Kant agreed that one cannot derive moral rules, as Wolff thought, from concepts like that of "perfection."[137] That concept "turns in a circle and inevitably though clandestinely presupposes the morality that it ought to explain."[138]

Moreover, according to Hume, even if reason could establish a moral rule, that rule could not motivate a person to follow it. Motivations arose from desire, not reason. Kant accepted Hume's account of motivation. He agreed that "the faculty of desire" is "determined" by "a feeling of agreeableness the subject expects from the reality of an object." He called this agreeable feeling "pleasure." Kant also agreed that reason does not lead a person to desire one object rather than another. "Pleasure," he said, "belongs to sense (feeling) and not to the understanding."[139]

He tried to bridge the gap by overcoming two obstacles. He tried to find a concept from which moral rules could be derived that was not empty. He tried to show that it could motivate even though it was a concept and not a desire. He undertook the first by formulating the categorical imperative, which was supposed to depend on reason alone and yet could be the measure of moral action. He undertook the second by formulating conception of *Achtung*, which might be translated as attentiveness to duty, which was supposed to motivate although it was not a desire.

The categorical imperative is the most sophisticated version we have yet encountered of what we have called the principle of impartial concern. It can be formulated:: "So act that the maxim of your will could always hold at the same time as a principle in a giving of universal law."[140] Or: "I ought never to act otherwise than in such a manner that I could also will that my maxim should become a universal law."[141] Kant's hopes for this principle were greater than those of Mozi or Bentham. They began by explaining what a person wanted or should want for himself, and then claimed that he should want the same for others. Mozi said that it was good for no one to have ungratified desires. He then claimed that a person should be as concerned about the good of others as for his own good. Bentham defined happiness in terms of pleasure. He then claimed that the measure of right and wrong was

---

[137] Immanuel Kant, *Kritik der praktischen Vernunft* in *Kant's gesammelte Schriften*, Königlich Preussischen Akademie der Wissenschaft (5th ed., Berlin,1913), 1 at 40.

[138] Immanuel Kant, *Grundlegung zur Metaphysik der Sitten* in *Kant's gesammelte Schriften* 4: 385 at 443.

[139] Kant, *Kritik der praktischen Vernunft* 21–22.

[140] Ibid. 30.

[141] Kant, *Grundlegung* 492. Some of Kant's readers have been happier with a second formulation that he offered: "So act that you always treat humanity, whether in your own person or in the person of any other, never merely as a means but always at the same time as an end." According to Allan Wood, it depends on "something more substantive" than the first and is "richer in content." Allan W. Wood, *Kant's Ethical Thought* (Cambridge, 1999), 111, 186. They should recognize, as Kant did, that the content of this formulation is equivalent to the first. Christian Schnoor, *Kants Kategorischer Imperativ als Kriterium der Richtigkeit des Handelns* (Tübingen,1989), 47, 54–55; Kenneth R. Westphal, "How 'Full' is Kant's Categorical Imperative?" *Jahrbuch für Recht und Ethik/Annual Review of Law and Ethics* 3 (1995), 467. If I act out of self-love, I am treating others as a means to satisfying my own desires. If I act by the categorical imperative, I cannot be doing so because I am acting without regard to my desires and those of others. I am treating others in the same way I treat myself, as an end. Mary Gregor, "Kant on Obligation, Rights and Virtue," *Jahrbuch für Recht und Ethik/Annual Review of Law and Ethics* 1 (1993), 69 at 84; Heiner Bielefeldt, "Hegelianizing Kant? Allan W. Wood's Interpretation of Kant's Ethical Thought," *Canadian Journal of Philosophy*, 31 (2001), 445 at 448.

the greatest happiness of the greatest number. Kant said that a rational being should wish to act according to a law that would apply universally. That law was formulated independently of any account of what a person should or might want for himself. The question arose, what criteria should specify the way in which people should universally act?

Three ways of answering that question should be ruled out by the very nature of Kant's project. One is to try to deduce the universal law from definitions of moral concepts which apply universally. That was the way of the rationalists, and Kant, like Hume, rejected it. Another is to say that the universal law promotes pleasure or the gratification of human desire, like Bentham's principle of the greatest happiness of the greatest number. Like Bentham, Kant defined "happiness" in terms of agreeableness or pleasure.[142] But he regarded obtaining pleasure as an end of no moral significance. A third way is to say that the universal law prescribes that all human beings should live a life in which the potentials of human nature are realized. That was the way of the classical tradition. Had Kant followed it, he would have been grounding normative standards, not on the categorical imperative, but on human nature.

Nevertheless, when Kant illustrates how moral standards depend on the categorical imperative, he goes in all three of these directions. Christian Schnoor and Kenneth Westfall suggested that the reason that Kant's examples seem plausible is that if we look at them closely, we find beneath the surface an independent reason supporting his conclusions, a reason that does not depend on the categorical imperative but can be formulated without regard to it.[143] Indeed, if we look still more closely we can see that these independent reasons are of the three kinds just described: deductions from abstract definitions; arguments about what will give someone pleasure; and prescriptions about how to live a good human life given the potentialities of human nature. Those are the three paths that the very nature of Kant's project forbids him to take.

As we have seen, although the rationalists tried to begin with the concept of "perfection," they derived rules of conduct from lower-level concepts such as the rights to property and contract. They defined property and contract rights in terms of the will of the owner or of the contracting parties. In discussing what he called "strict or narrow (inflexible) duties," Kant did the same.

Such duties arise, he said, "when actions are so constituted (*beschaffen*) that their maxim cannot without contradiction even be thought (*gedacht*) as a universal law of nature, let alone that one could will that it should be one."[144] Kant's illustrations include appropriating a deposit, theft, and making a deceitful promise.

Like Leibniz and Wolff, he defined property as the right of the owner to use a thing as he chooses and to exclude others from doing so. "Anything is rightfully mine (*meum juris*) when I am so connected with it, that if any other person should make use of it without my consent, he would do me an injury."[145] By definition, anyone who uses another's property

[142]   Kant, *Kritik der praktischen Vernunft* 22.
[143]   Schnoor, *Kants Kategorischer Imperativ*; Westfall, "Kant's Categorical Imperative."
[144]   Kant, *Grundlegung* 424.
[145]   Kant, *Rechtslehre* 245.

without his consent violates the owner's rights. Therefore, according to Kant, one cannot will as a universal law that a person may keep a deposit against the owner's will or to steal another's property.

His example of a deceitful promise is a person who "finds himself forced by necessity to borrow money" and "knows he will not be able to repay it . . . also sees that nothing will be lent him unless he promises firmly to repay it." Making the deceitful promise cannot be willed as universal law because "it would contradict itself"; "the promise itself would become impossible": "no one would believe that anything had been promised to him."[146]

Robert Wolff raised the wrong objection to this argument. He said that the "contradictory nature of the policy cannot possibly be demonstrated by appeal to the contingent fact – if, indeed, it is a fact – that people tend to disbelieve a persistent promise breaker."[147] But Kant is not advising the would-be borrower how to keep his credit rating, or, in his other examples, advising the depositee or thief that no one will trust him again. Neither is he saying that the system of promising or private ownership of property will break down if people frequently break their word or steal. That would also be an appeal to a contingent fact. As Onora Nell noted, for Kant there must be "an *inner* impossibility in non-universalizable maxims. And an inner impossibility is presumably not an incompatibility between a [supposedly universal rule] and some true, but quite extraneous, empirical premise."[148]

Kant explained the inner impossibility in *The Science of Right* (*Rechtslehre*). Like Leibniz and Wolff, he defined promise and contract in terms of will. He drew the same conclusion: that there is an unqualified obligation to keep a promise. According to Kant, a promise is the expression of will of one party to a contract; a contract is the expression of will of both.[149] Suppose the question is put: "Why should I keep my promise?" Kant answered, "It is utterly impossible to give a proof of this categorical imperative just as it is impossible for a geometrician to prove by logical inference that to make a triangle I must take three lines."[150] A promise is binding by definition, as it was for the rationalists. Kant concluded that it is a contradiction to will as a universal law that one can break a promise.

In discussing duties to others, despite what he had said about the moral irrelevance of desire, Kant took the second path described earlier. He attached a normative value to desires for happiness or pleasure. We are under a less strict duty, a "broader (meritorious)" duty of "beneficence," that is, to promote the happiness of others.[151] There is a moral duty to promote the happiness of others because the "principle of happiness" can be universalized so that each person is bound to promote the happiness of every other.

> "[M]y own happiness . . . can become an objective practical law only if I include in it the happiness of others. Thus the law to promote the happiness of others arises not from the presupposition that this is an object of everyone's choice but merely from this: that the form

---

[146] Kant, *Grundlegung* 422.
[147] Robert Paul Wolff, *The Anatomy of Reason* (New York, 1973), 166.
[148] Onora Nell, *Acting on Principle: An Essay on Kantian Ethics* (New York, 1975), 67.
[149] Kant, *Rechtslehre* 272.
[150] Ibid. 273.
[151] Kant, *Grundlegung* 423.

of universality, which reason requires as the condition of giving to a maxim of self-love the objective validity of a law, becomes the determining ground of the will."[152]

To be of moral value, then, such "actions have to be performed, not out of love to others, but out of duty, with the mortification and sacrifice of our own ends."[153] Kant's example in the *Foundations* is a person who "is doing well, while he sees that others have to struggle with great misery."[154] He is under a duty to assist them.

That claim is vulnerable to the same objections as utilitarianism. Kant defined happiness in terms of pleasure, whatever the pleasure may be. Like Bentham, he regarded all pleasures as commensurable, as "entirely of one kind."[155] Pleasures differ only in degree.

> However dissimilar the conceptions of the objects ... a feeling of pleasure ... which alone is the real determining ground of the will ... can differ from another only in degree. Otherwise how could one make a comparison with regard to magnitude between two determining grounds the ideas of which depend upon different faculties, in order to prefer the one that affects the faculty of desire to the greater extent?[156]

Consequently, there are no "higher" or "lower" pleasures, as John Stuart Mill later claimed, but only greater and lesser ones.

> The same human being can return unread an instructive book that he cannot again obtain, in order not to miss a hunt; he can leave in the middle of a fine speech in order not to be late for a meal; he can leave an intellectual conversation he otherwise values highly, in order to take his place at the gaming table; he can even repulse a poor man whom at other times it is a joy for him to benefit because he now has only enough money in his pocket to pay for his admission to the theater. If the determination of his will rests on the feeling of agreeableness or disagreeableness that he expects from some cause, it is all the same to him by what kind of representation he is affected. The only thing that concerns him, in order to decide upon a choice, is how intense, how long, how easily acquired, and how often repeated the agreeableness is.[157]

One can see, then, why Kant regarded the pursuit of one's own happiness as of no moral value. Consequently it is hard to see how he could then claim that there is a moral value in promoting the happiness of anyone else. To "universalize" concern for one's own happiness to include that of everyone seems to lead to the conclusion that at least one moral objective is, in Bentham's words, the greatest happiness of the greatest number. The difference would be that, for Kant, one could not pursue this objective while violating the "strict or narrow (inflexible) duties" whose violation "cannot without contradiction even be thought (*gedacht*) as a universal law of nature."[158] Kant's clandestine rationalism sets limits to his clandestine utilitarianism. Yet Bentham ascribed a normative value to pleasure. Kant did not. Consequently, it is hard to see how experiencing pleasure acquires a normative value when it is "universalized."

---

[152] Kant, *Kritik der praktischen Vernunft* 34.
[153] Kant, *Rechtslehre* 210.
[154] Kant, *Grundlegung* 423.
[155] Kant, *Kritik der praktischen Vernunft* 21–22.
[156] Ibid. 23.
[157] Kant, *Kritik der praktischen Vernunft* 23.
[158] Kant, *Grundlegung* 424.

Kant himself said, "a feeling of pleasure ... can differ from another only in degree."[159] Consequently, one cannot say that it is better to read an instructive book that to go hunting, or to miss an intellectual conversation to enjoy a meal.[160] How then can one distinguish assisting the destitute by giving them money from assisting them to obtain pleasure in any other way: for example, by flattering them or enabling the gluttonous or lustful to do what they find pleasurable? Kant responded, "What others may deem conducive to their happiness, is left for themselves to judge, but it pertains to me to refuse many things that they deem conducive but I do not, for they do not have a right to require them from me as their own."[161] If my duty is to promote their happiness, however, and happiness means pleasure, all that should matter to me is how much pleasure I give them.

Kant took the third path described earlier when he discussed a person's "broader (meritorious) duty" to cultivate his own talents. For example, "[a] person finds himself with a talent which, by means of some culture, might make him a man useful for many purposes. But he finds himself in comfortable circumstances and prefers to indulge in pleasure." Should he do so? According to Kant, he cannot "will that this should be a universal law of nature," "that men (like the South Sea Islanders) should let their talents rest and devote their lives merely to idleness, amusement and the propagation of the species – in a word, to enjoyment."[162] He cannot because it is contradictory to maintain that human beings have "capacities that belong to an end which nature has in view" and that they should not cultivate them.

According to Kant, "as a rational being, he naturally wills that his faculties be developed, since they are of use to him, and have been given him, for all sorts of possible purposes."[163] But to cultivate reason in order to pursue these purposes would support only a hypothetical imperative: that one ought to do so to pursue whatever purposes one happens to want to pursue. To invoke the categorical imperative, he gave a different reason but one which assumes that human nature is a source of normative values.

> The capacity to propose to one's self an end, is the characteristic of humanity, as distinguished from animality. Along with the ends of humanity in our own person there is also the rational will to which is tied the duty to make oneself deserving of humanity by general culture, to advance and acquire the capacity to pursue all ends so far as they may be encountered in humanity itself, that is, to the cultivation of the unrefined tendencies of his nature through which an animal is elevated to a man: hence, a duty to himself.[164]

Indeed, "perfection" is "the cultivation of all our capacities for the ends proposed by reason," and it is a duty to cultivate them "without regard to the advantage that they bring us."[165] Here, "perfection" is no longer the "empty and indefinite" concept of the rationalists. Human

---

[159]   Kant, *Kritik der praktischen Vernunft* 23.
[160]   Ibid.
[161]   Kant, *Tugendlehre* 388.
[162]   Kant, *Grundlegung* 422–23.
[163]   Ibid. 423.
[164]   Kant, *Tugendlehre* 392. Similarly, "perfection" is "an end that is at the same time a duty": "the cultivation of all our capacities for the ends proposed by reason" is a duty "without regard to the advantage that they bring us." Ibid. 391.
[165]   Ibid. 391.

beings, unlike animals, can act for ends that they propose to themselves, and one which "makes him deserving of humanity" is to develop the capacities that are distinctively human. That proposition would make perfect sense to an Aristotelian because he grounds normative standards on human nature. Unless one does so, however, it is hard to understand why there is a duty to act in a way that is deserving of one's humanity.

We have discussed the first obstacle the Kant had to overcome to bridge the gap Hume had described between reason and desire. He had to find a concept from which moral rules could be derived that was not empty, like those of the rationalists. To do so he formulated the categorical imperative.

The second obstacle was to show that a concept based upon reason could motivate action, which Hume thought to be impossible. Kant also agreed with Hume that reason does not lead a person to desire one object rather than another. "Pleasure," he said, "belongs to sense (feeling) and not to the understanding."[166] Yet the moral law – the categorical imperative – must be able to motivate people to act. Kant explained: "In all lawgiving (*Gesetzgebung*) . . . there are two elements: first, a law, which represents an action that is to be done as objectively necessary, that is, which makes the action a duty; and second, an incentive, which connects a ground for determining choice to this action subjectively with the representation of the law."[167] Although the moral law must motivate, the motive cannot be a desire in the ordinary sense. When reason prescribes how a person should act to obtain what he desires, it formulates a hypothetical imperative. The moral law requires a categorical imperative: reason must prescribe how a person should act independently of what he desires.

Kant's solution was to posit a motivation that functions like a desire and yet is not a desire. He called the motivation for obeying the moral law *Achtung*, which is usually translated as "respect" for the moral law. It might be translated as "attentiveness to duty." Scholars have characterized it as "a specific emotion which Kant believes to be present in actions done for the sake of duty,"[168] as "an effect of the moral law [that is] self-wrought [but which] functions like a feeling" and "is analogous to feeling" "in its effect."[169] It has been called a feeling that is "*sui generis*," that "is both intrinsically normative and conative," or which, precisely speaking, is not "any kind of feeling at all."[170] It is, at any rate, a motivation that is unlike all other motivations, and without which no action has moral value.[171]

In the classical traditions, moral actions are motivated by the will or desire for what is good. For Kant, it cannot be so because he accepted Hume's account of human desire. The

[166]   Kant, *Kritik der praktischen Vernunft* 21–22.
[167]   Immanuel Kant, *Metaphysik der Sitten*, in *Kants gesammelte Schriften* 6: 203 at 218.
[168]   H. J. Paton, *The Categorical Imperative* (5th ed. London, 1965), 63.
[169]   Chad Wellmon, "Kant and the Feelings of Reason," *Eighteenth-Century Studies* 42 (2009), 557 at 566.
[170]   Book review by David Sussman, review of Daniel Guevara, *Kant's Theory of Moral Motivation* (Boulder, 2000), in *The Philosophical Review* 111 (2002), 116 at 116.
[171]   It is not true, then, that Kant "interprets pure practical reason as will," that "reason . . . is conceived as a motivating power" and "the will is understood as a rational power." Yirmiyahu Yovel, "Kant's Practical Reason as Will: Interest, Recognition, Judgment, and Choice," *The Review of Metaphysics* 52 (1998), 267 at 267.

consequence is that a person's actions have no moral value unless they are motivated by *Achtung*.

This doctrine has sometimes been misunderstood. It does not imply that all actions are selfish unless they are done for the sake of duty.[172] A person who helps others only because he takes delight in unselfish actions is still acting on the principle of self-love. Nevertheless, as long as a person acts for the sake of duty, his action has moral value, even though he acts from other motives as well.[173] Otherwise a person who saves another's life would not be acting morally unless he did not care whether they lived or died but acted only out of duty. According to Kant, a person has a moral duty to preserve his own life, but that does not mean that, to act morally, he must eat only when he isn't hungry. Nor would Kant deny that some inclinations are valuable, not in themselves, but because they make it easier to act for the sake of duty.[174]

It is still true, however, that for Kant, all acts that are not done for the sake of duty are morally irrelevant, whatever a person's other motivations for acting may be.[175] That claim is odd because it clashes with most people's idea of what it means to act morally. Kant said that some people are so constituted that "without any other motive of vanity or self-interest, they find a pleasure in spreading joy around them, and can take delight in the satisfaction of others."[176] They are nevertheless acting out of a desire to get what they happen to want. Unless they are also acting out of *Achtung*, they are not acting morally. As Daniel Guevara said, the doctrine "is controversial because, among other things, it seems morally repugnant to maintain that, for example, all acts of self sacrifice or friendship or love are lacking in moral worth if not done for duty's sake."[177]

It is still more difficult, however, to see how *Achtung* can motivate a person to act if it is not a desire. Kant himself recognized how strange *Achtung* must be.[178] His reason for claiming that there is such a motivation is that if the only motivation were desire, there would be no moral law. Kant needed another motivation for his theory to work, and so he claimed that there must be one As Lawrence Hinman observed, Kant

> faced . . . a very serious problem: showing how pure reason can move the will to action. . . . Kant's account of this pure feeling of respect for the moral law is certainly in many ways a peculiar one, and commentators have not hesitated to level a charge of inconsistency against Kant on this point. Yet . . . there was almost nothing else that Kant could have done at this juncture in his analysis insofar as he needed to bridge the gap between the two worlds, that is, to explain – to the extent that this can be explained at all in Kant's eyes – how the moral law could have a practical effect. . . . [H]e simply could not forfeit this element in

[172] As noted by Wood, *Kant's Ethical Thought* 30–31; Christine M. Korsgaard, "Kant's Analysis of Obligation: The Argument of 'Foundations I,'" *The Monist* 72 (1989), 311at 322.

[173] As noted by Paton, *Categorical Imperative* 15, 48; Henry E. Allison, *Kant's Theory of Freedom* (Cambridge, 1990), 110; Sally Sedgwick, *Kant's Groundwork of the Metaphysics of Morals: An Introduction* (Cambridge, 2008), 68; Robert B. Louden, "Kant's Virtue Ethics," *Philosophy* 61 (1986), 473 at 476.

[174] Paton, *Categorical Imperative* 49; Sedgwick, *Kant's Groundwork* 69–70.

[175] Barbara Herman, *The Practice of Moral Judgment* (Cambridge, 1933), 1; see Paton, *Categorical Imperative* 24.

[176] Immanuel Kant, *Grundlegung zur Metaphysik der Sitten* 24, in 4 *Werke* 7.

[177] Daniel Guevara, review of Philip Stratton-Lake, Kant, Duty and Moral Worth in *The Philosophical Quarterly* 52 (2002), 643 at 643.

[178] Kant, *Kritik der praktischen Vernunft* 80.

his position without giving up completely on explaining how the moral law could move persons to act.[179]

Kant concluded that a person is free if he acts from duty because he acts according to a law given by reason itself. It is the law by which a rational being would choose to govern himself. In doing so, such a being acts autonomously, meaning, according to its own law. "The point here," Sally Sedgwick noted, "is that, were we not free, we would have to concede that we are merely complicated machines, determined in all we do by the laws of nature. ... From the standpoint of nature, the subject has no freedom. ... Considered from the standpoint of freedom, we have a pure will and are capable of giving ourselves law."[180] That will is entirely good and entirely free.

This enterprise required Kant to define "freedom" in an odd way. To be free, to most people, means to decide for oneself such matters as for whom to vote, whether to marry, whether to buy a new car, or whether to study law rather than medicine. For Kant, these choices are not free if they are made in order to have the president or spouse or car or career that one wants. Although people do make such choices to have what they want, freedom means that a person acts, not because he wants something, but because he is a free and rational being. To be free, an action must have its source in one's self as distinguished from one's inclinations.[181]

In the Aristotelian tradition, acting according to one's inclinations did not mean "we are merely complicated machines, determined in all we do by the laws of nature." Our actions are voluntary because we act by reason and will: we can understand that some ends are worthwhile and choose a course of action because it contributes to them. Sometimes only one course of action best serves these ends. Even though there is a single best option, such a choice is still voluntary. We do not say that a person acts involuntarily when he saves the life of a child or uses some of his wealth to benefit others. Sometimes, there may be no one right choice even if all the circumstances that matter were taken into account. The choice of a course of action is free in the sense that it is not necessary. In either case, we are acting because we have recognized that certain ends are good, and we choose them for that reason. We are not acting like complicated machines.

Contemporary Neo-Kantians: Ronald Dworkin and John Rawls

By the mid-twentieth century, scholars were speaking about the death of political philosophy,[182] and, in particular, about the lack of a coherent defense of liberal democracy.[183] As Allan Bloom noted, "[h]istoricism, cultural relativism, and the fact-value distinction ... eroded the bases of

---

[179] Lawrence M. Hinman, "On the Purity of our Moral Motives: A Critique of Kant's Account of the Emotions and Acting for the sake of Duty," *The Monist* 66 (1983), 251 at 254–55.

[180] Sedgwick, *"Kant's Groundwork"* 198–99.

[181] Kant, *Grundlegung* 79–80.

[182] William A. Galston, "Moral Personality and Liberal Theory: John Rawls's 'Dewey Lectures,'" *Political Theory* 10 (1982), 492 at 510.

[183] Philip Abbott, "With Equality & Virtue for All: John Rawls & the Liberal Tradition," *Polity* 8 (1976), 339 at 339; Allan Bloom, "John Rawls vs. the Tradition of Political Philosophy," *The American Political Science Review* 69 (1975), 648 at 648.

conviction that [a liberal] regime is good or just, that reason can support its claims to our allegiance."[184]

Some philosophically minded liberals believed in a vague utilitarianism: everyone's preferences should count the same as everyone else's. Some believed in a vague Kantianism: each person may claim only as much liberty for himself as he would concede to others. But as Bruce Douglass observed:

> The people who were responsible for raising questions about whether political philosophy had a future were, on the whole, figures who believed that certain developments had occurred since the days when the last great political philosophers ... had done their work that had altered fundamentally the terms on which philosophical reflection was conducted, and their contention was that the effect of those developments was to make it impossible to proceed any longer in the old way. They had in mind two developments in particular: the emergence of logical positivism in philosophy, on the one hand, and the rise of the modern "empirical" sciences of human behaviour, on the other. ... It was only natural to wonder if it still made sense to continue trying to theorise about such matters as the right form of government.[185]

As we can see, the obstacles to political philosophy that concerned these people had been put in place by David Hume before the last great political philosophers did their work. Hume taught that reason could investigate the relationship among concepts, although concepts could not motivate. It could investigate the empirical causes of motivations, but they were facts from which values could not be inferred. For a logical positivist, a statement was meaningful only if it could be verified logically or empirically. The sciences of human behavior were concerned with the causes of human motivations, whether psychological, historical, economic or cultural. Both remained within the confines of Hume's world in which a human being had values but in which it made no sense to ask whether they were genuinely right or wrong. Bentham and Kant had sought escape routes. By the mid-twentieth century, few were still looking.

Since then, political philosophy has been revived largely through the work of philosophers who reworked Kant to explain and defend liberal institutions. We will discuss the work of Ronald Dworkin and John Rawls. Dworkin has been called one of the greatest contemporary political philosophers. Credit has been given to Rawls for having "revitalised political philosophy in the West."[186] He "moved boldly to restore the legitimacy of political evaluation,"[187] and his work, Jurgen Habermas said, "marks a pivotal turning point in the most recent history of practical philosophy, for he restored long-suppressed moral questions to the status of serious objects of philosophical investigation."[188]

---

[184]   Bloom, "John Rawls" 648.
[185]   R. Bruce Douglass, "John Rawls and the Revival of Political Philosophy: Where Does He Leave Us?" *Theoria: A Journal of Social and Political Theory* 59 (2012), 81 at 84.
[186]   Douglass, "John Rawls" 81.
[187]   Galston, "Moral Personality" 510.
[188]   Jurgen Habermas, "Reconciliation Through the Public Use of Reason: Remarks on John Rawls's Political Liberalism," *The Journal of Philosophy* (1995), 109 at 109.

Neither of them conceived of law or freedom in the same way as Kant. For Kant, to act morally meant to follow, not one's desires, but a moral law determined by reason alone. They both rejected the popularized version of Kant in which each person may claim only as much liberty for himself as he would concede to others. Rawls did subscribe to this principle in *A Theory of Justice*. In his words, "each person is to have an equal right to the most extensive basic liberty compatible with similar liberty for others."[189] That principle would work if there were a way of defining liberty so as to demarcate each person's rights and duties. But, as H. L. A. Hart pointed out, there is no way. To speak of "the most extensive basic liberty compatible with similar liberty for others" is "not only indefinite but unintelligible."[190] One person's exercise of a liberty frequently limits that of another person. To give Hart's example, if I have the liberty to exclude others from trespassing on my land, they do not have the liberty to do so. There is no way to say whether the liberty granted is more or less extensive than the liberty abridged. Rawls admitted that Hart was right.[191] In *Political Liberalism*, he tried to reformulate his theory of justice so that "no priority is assigned to the exercise of liberty as such, as if the exercise of something called 'liberty' has a preeminent value and is the main if not the sole end of political and social justice."[192]

Yet their versions of liberalism have a Kantian structure. They rely on what we have called the principle of impartial concern: each person should be treated alike. As we have seen, one question that arises whenever this principle is invoked is in what respect should they be treated alike. Another is why such a principle, even if it could be rationally defended, would motivate anyone to be as concerned with others as with himself.

According to Dworkin and Rawls, each person is entitled to an equal respect for his or her beliefs as to what is right or wrong. That answer breaks with Hume's view of the world in a far more radical way than their predecessors. In both classical traditions, a person has the capacity, although it is not infallible, to know what is genuinely right and wrong. For Hume, right and wrong, virtue and vice, were merely feelings of approbation or disapprobation of a distinct kind. For Dworkin and Rawls, they are worthy of a respect that is not accorded to a person's other feelings or desires.

According to Dworkin and Rawls, each person believes that he has the capacity to distinguish right from wrong. Dworkin said that "One must believe that what one does has objective value."[193] You must believe "there is a right and wrong way for you to live."[194] According to Rawls, all human beings have "a capacity for a conception of the good."[195] A "conception of the good" is "a conception of the ends and purposes worthy of our devoted pursuit."[196] A person builds on this conception to form a "determinate conception of the

[189] John Rawls, *A Theory of Justice* (Cambridge, 1971), 60.
[190] H. L. A. Hart, "Rawls on Liberty and Its Priority," *University of Chicago Law Review* 40 (1973), 534.
[191] Rawls, *Political Liberalism* 289–91.
[192] Ibid. 291–92.
[193] Ibid. 255.
[194] Ibid. 207.
[195] Ibid. 18–19.
[196] Ibid. 104.

good." To accept a determinate conception of the good is to "take the step beyond recognizing the reasonableness of a doctrine and affirm our belief in it."[197] A political theorist cannot endorse any conception of the good but his neutrality is not skepticism. "Political liberalism ... does not argue that we should be hesitant and uncertain, much less skeptical, about our own beliefs."[198]

The classical traditions taught that there is a right and a wrong way to live, and every human being has the capacity, though it is not infallible, to tell which is which. The question is, having come this close to that postion, how Dworkin and Rawls can defend the liberal philosophical tradition that emerged in the nineteenth century. In particular, how can they claim that each person is entitled to an equal respect for his or her beliefs as to what is right or wrong whatever those beliefs may be?

It is true that in the classical traditions, every human being is worthy of respect because they are able to know, to choose, and to live a good life. The purpose of government is to help them do so. "The form of government is best in which every man, whoever he is, can act best and live happily."[199] But it did not follow that each citizen's beliefs as to what is right and wrong were entitled to equal respect.

In *Taking Rights Seriously*, Dworkin said, that because "government must ... treat people ... with equal concern and respect ... [i]t must not constrain liberty on the ground that one citizen's conception of the good life of one group is nobler or superior to another's."[200] In *Justice for Hedghogs*, he said that "each person has a special, personal responsibility to create that life through a coherent narrative or style that he himself endorses."[201] A person "does not live authentically if ... others forbid him some options otherwise available because they deem those options unworthy."[202] "Some coercive laws violate ethical independence because they deny people power to make their own decisions about matters of ethical foundation – about the basis and character of the objective importance of human life."[203]

It is not clear how it is possible to deny people the power "to make their own decisions about matters of ethical foundation." As Aquinas said, one cannot make anyone change his beliefs by the threat of force.[204] One can still deny that their decisions merit equal respect. It is impossible to convince a Nazi that he is wrong by threat of punishment, and it may be inadvisable to punish him. But one cannot be required to show equal respect for his beliefs. Nor can we imagine that the government must do so. Any government policy is based on a belief as to what is good. That is so not only in combatting racism, but in furthering knowledge or beauty or protecting the natural environment or deciding whether to spend more on guns than on butter. When the government sets policy it may accord each citizen

---

[197]   Ibid. 60.
[198]   Ibid. 63.
[199]   *Politics* VII.i 1324a.
[200]   Dworkin, *Taking Rights Seriously* 272–73.
[201]   Dworkin, *Justice for Hedgehogs* 203–04.
[202]   Ibid. 212.
[203]   Ibid. 369.
[204]   Aquinas, *Summa theologiae* II-II, Q. 10, a. 8.

an equal voice but it must prefer some citizens' beliefs as to what is right over those of others.

It is true, as the classical traditions recognized, to live a truly human life a person must not only act rightly but exercise his own capacity to understand what is right. As Dworkin put it, the value of a person's life depends not only on whether the person has the "events, experiences, associations, and achievements" that "make a life good" but also on whether he "sought them or regards them as valuable."[205] That he "endorses" "the components of a good life" is not "frosting on the cake" but "an essential part of living a good life."[206]

It does not follow that when a person has chosen wrongly, he should invariably be allowed to act wrongly, any more than it follows that he should never be allowed to do so. Two values are at stake. As T. M. Wilkinson observed, "Dworkin's arguments even go beyond those which appeal to autonomy in claiming that people gain from choosing for themselves. As mentioned earlier, the contribution of autonomy to a life can sometimes be balanced against the need to make sure someone chooses the correct options. No such balancing is possible if the constitutive view is right."[207] In Upton Sinclair's novel *The Jungle*, workers risked their lives walking on unfenced catwalks over boiling vats of meat. A worker should not be allowed to do so even if he were willing to risk his life for a small increase in his wages.

Dworkin also said: "Government must not distribute goods or opportunities unequally on the ground that some citizens are entitled to more because they are worthy of more concern." For him, that principle follows from "the liberal conception of equality."[208] In the Aristotelian tradition, that principle is the one that guides distributive justice in a democracy. In an aristocracy, in Aristotle's sense, the principle would be to distribute goods or opportunities according to merit. Although every form of government is concerned with the well-being of each citizen, in an aristocracy, the well-being of those who are better able to pursue a good life entitles them to more resources with which to pursue it. Citizens of a democracy cannot accept that principle. If they did, they would adopt an aristocratic form of government. But one cannot simply dismiss it as incompatible with the government's concern for the well-being of each citizen.

These difficulties with Dworkin's defense of liberalism arise if, in Dworkin's words, "there is a right and wrong way ... to live."[209] It follows that a person might err. If so, his beliefs are not deserving of equal respect, and he is not living a fully human life even though the beliefs are his own. Moreover, if goods or opportunities are to be distributed to enable people to pursue a good life, it is not obvious why everyone should have an equal share. Some of

[205] Ronald Dworkin, "Liberal Community," 77 *California Law Review* (1989) 479 at 485.
[206] Ronald Dworkin, "Foundations of Liberal Equality," in G. B. Peterson, ed., *The Tanner Lectures on Human Values* 11 (Salt Lake City, 1990), 50. Dworkin went a bit further. He said that that "no component may even so much as contribute to the value of a person's life without his endorsement." Ibid. That cannot be right. Diet or exercise or study or learning habits of discipline against my will might contribute to my life even if they were forced on me, and even if it were true that my life would be still better if I had been left alone.
[207] T. M. Wilkinson, "Dworkin on Paternalism and Well-Being," *Oxford Journal of Legal Studies* 16 (1996), 433 at 436.
[208] Dworkin, *Taking Rights Seriously* 272–73.
[209] Dworkin, *Justice for Hedgehogs* 207.

Dworkin's interpreters have tried to escape these difficulties by assuming Dworkin meant that no choice can be better or worse than another because all values are subjective.[210] According to Stanley Brubaker, for example, Dworkin "relies principally" on "the utter subjectivity of the good life." "[I]n the absence of knowledge about the good life, it is unfair to base public policy on one notion of it over another."[211] They rely on passages like those quoted earlier in which Dworkin describes ethical thought as a matter of finding coherence among one's own beliefs.

But Dworkin said that people must regard their own ethical beliefs as having "objective value." He did not claim people who do so are under an illusion, whereas governments know the truth: that values are utterly subjective. As we have seen, Dworkin claimed that there is a method which will lead people not only to better answers, but to the "right answer." It is the method we described earlier and characterized as "inverse rationalism." Brubaker noted that "utter subjectivity . . . stands in marked contrast to Dworkin's argument for right answers."[212] Moreover, according to Dworkin, a person's life has value because of characteristics he shares with every other human being. He asked the hypothetical question: "Do you value your life as objectively important in virtue of something special about your life, so that it would be perfectly consistent for you not to treat other human beings as having the same kind of importance? Or do you value your life in that way because you think all human life is objectively important?"[213] He could not have meant that all people are in error because nothing is objectively important. The difficulties of his theory arise because, having come that close to the standpoint of the classical traditions, he could not consistently pull back.

The same can be said of Rawls, although his defense of the principle that each person's beliefs should be given equal respect was otherwise much different. According to Rawls, governments cannot prefer one determinate conception of good to another because, in a free society, people will arrive at different determinate conceptions of the good and consequently will "remain profoundly divided by reasonable religious, philosophical and moral doctrines."[214] They are able to agree on the principles of a just political order despite their differences because they also have "a capacity for a sense of justice." "Reasonable persons will think it unreasonable to use political power, should they possess it, to repress comprehensive views that are not unreasonable, though different from their own."[215]

As we have seen, Mozi shared Rawls' concern that a diversity of beliefs would undermine the social order. His solution, however, was to have the emperor impose uniformity. "[W]hat it is that brings order to the world? It is only that the Son of Tian is able to make uniform the principles of the world?"[216] "What the Son of Tian takes to be wrong, all must

---

[210] See William Galston, "Defending Liberalism," *American Political Science Review*, 76 (1982), 624–25; Frederick Schauer, *Free Speech* (Cambridge, 1982), 62.
[211] Stanley C. Brubaker "Taking Dworkin Seriously," *The Review of Politics*, 47 (1985), 45 at 57, 58.
[212] Ibid. 60.
[213] Dworkin, *Taking Rights Seriously* 255.
[214] Rawls, *Political Liberalism* 4.
[215] Ibid. 60.
[216] *Mozi* 11.3, trans. from Ian Johnston, *The Mozi: A Complete Translation* (New York, 2010).

take to be wrong."[217] One answer would be that people thinking for themselves are more likely to arrive a correct, or at least a better, conception of the good than an authoritarian government. Another would be that even if the government's conception is good, it is better that people accept it because they think for themselves. Still another would be that there is no one right conception of how to lead a good life although there are many bad ones. All three of these reasons fit comfortably in the classical traditions. Whether Rawls could have made use of them is another question

The reason people remain profoundly divided, according to Rawls, is that irreconcilable differences arise as they develop "determinate conceptions of the good." Rawls asked, "why should free institutions lead to reasonable pluralism . . . ? Why does not our conscientious attempt to reason with one another lead to reasonable agreement?"[218] The reason concerns the "sources, or causes, of disagreement between reasonable persons." Rawls calls these sources "the burdens of judgment" which are "the many hazards involved in the correct (and conscientious) exercise of our powers of reason and judgment in the ordinary course of political life."[219]

For Rawls, it is critical, on the one hand, that people's determinate conceptions of the good diverge, and, on the other, that they do so because of a conscientious exercise of their powers of reason and judgment that other people should respect. What would a conscientious effort to arrive at conclusions about the good look like? Aristotle described how one arrives at such a conclusion by practical reason. Rawls' account of a conscientious exercise of our powers or reason and judgment look much like Aristotle's description. The resemblance is not surprising. Both were asking about how reason could arrive at conclusions about the good. Aristotle's conclusion, however, was that because practical reason could not reach its conclusions with certainty, they were open for discussion and debate. There is no reason for Rawls to think that the same process would result in divisions of opinion so deep that discussion is fruitless.

In the Aristotelian account, the first principles of practical reason are ends to be sought. A person needs to consider the best means to those ends, whether instrumentally or as a component part, under the circumstances he is facing. He will look for evidence of what those circumstances are. He will weigh good and bad consequences against each other. To do so he will need experience and ought to take counsel. Even then, he will often be unsure whether he has correctly applied the very general and common principles concerning what is good to his own situation.

Rawls gave a list, "not complete," of "the more obvious sources" of reasonable disagreement. They are: (a) "[t]he evidence . . . is confusing and complex"; (b) we may "agree fully about the kind of considerations that are relevant" but "disagree about their weight"; (c) "our concepts . . . are vague and subject to hard cases"; (d) "the way we assess evidence and weigh moral and political values is shaped by our total experience"; (e) "Often there are different kinds of normative considerations of different force on both sides of an issue and it

---

[217] Ibid. 11.4.
[218] Rawls, *Political Liberalism* 55.
[219] Ibid. 55–56.

is difficult to make an overall assessment"; (f) "any system of social institutions is limited in the values it can admit so that some selection must be made from the full range of moral and political values that might be realized."²²⁰

A comprehensive view "organizes and characterizes recognized values ... in ways that distinguish it from other doctrines, for example, by giving certain values a particular primacy and weight."²²¹ "[W]e should be able to explain the failure of our judgments to converge by such things as the as the burdens of judgment: the difficulties of surveying and assessing all the evidence, or else the delicate balance of competing reasons on opposite sides of the issue, either of which leads us to expect that reasonable persons may differ" in contrast to "a lack of reasonableness, or rationality, or conscientiousness of one or more of the persons involved."²²²

This account explains why reasonable people who start with similar conceptions of the good can reach different conclusions. Yet every factor that Rawls mentions would matter, in the Aristotelian account, to a person exercising practical reason.

Rawls not only claimed that government cannot repress any determinate conception of the good. He claimed that it cannot base its decisions on any citizen's determinate conception of the good. Arguments based on such a conception should be kept out of the public forum. Public reason must appeal to principles on which citizens can agree, whatever their determinate conception of the good may be. The force of this claim was brought home to me when I was told at a conference on fairness in contract law that it was illegitimate for me to mention Aristotle in the public forum.²²³ On the same ground, what I say in this book, or most of it, would not be allowed in the public forum.

In contrast, in the Aristotelian tradition, the differences that arise because people reach different conclusions through practical reason (or, in Rawls' terms, by assuming the burdens of judgment) are precisely those that ought to be matters of public debate. Everyone can understand the issues better when they consider other people's views. When differences remain, then a genuine problem of government arises: whose opinion should prevail when people disagree? In the Aristotelian tradition, the answer depends on the form of government. To the extent it is monarchical, the decision will be made by one person for all; to the extent it is aristocratic, by an elite which is chosen because it is deemed to have better judgment; to the extent it is democratic, by each person making the best decision he can, or, when a common rule is needed, by a majority that has listened to what the minority has to say.

Rawls gave examples of "irreconcilable differences." His examples, however, are not differences that arise from the "burdens of judgment." Neither do they stymy political cooperation in a free society. Some are religious differences. Others are philosophical differences that arose after the advent of rationalism.

---

²²⁰   Ibid. 56–57.
²²¹   Ibid. 59.
²²²   Ibid. 121.
²²³   At the suggestion of the organizers of the conference, I wrote a response: " The Just Price: The Aristotelian Tradition and John Rawls," *European Review of Contract Law* 11 (2015), 197.

The religious differences he mentioned did not arise because different people, beginning with similar conceptions of the good, encountered the burdens of judgment and arrived at different comprehensive doctrines. Jews, Christians, and Moslems differ over how God has acted in history. The Jews believe that he gave them a law as part of a covenant he made with them; Christians believe that this old law was set aside by a new covenant in Christ; Moslems believe that God inspired the prophet Mohammed. They differ as to which scriptures are divinely inspired: the Old Testament; the Old and New Testaments; the Koran. Catholics and Protestants differ as to how humanity is redeemed, how God's grace is conferred, and who can interpret scripture authoritatively. They need not regard each other's religious views as reasonable. Indeed, it would put a strain on the principle of religious toleration if, to be tolerant, they must do so. Despite these differences, however, they may have similar views of what is morally right and wrong, and of the value of political ends. In contemporary societies, they work together without political issues becoming ipso facto religious issues.

The other differences Rawls mentioned are among the philosophical doctrines such as utilitarianism and Kantianism. He also mentioned "rational intuitionalism" which, as we have seen, is a reasonably accurate description of rationalism. The differences among them, however, are not due to differences in the way different philosophers assumed the "burdens of judgment" in elaborating a conception of the good. As we have seen, they are due to different conceptions of what is meant by the good. For rationalists, it is a concept or principle to be elaborated by theoretical reason; for Hume, the object of a desire of a particular kind, of no more objective value, no worthier of gratification than any other desire; for the utilitarians, pleasure; and for Kant, a categorical imperative binding on all rational beings simply because they are rational. None of these philosophers conceived of the good in the way that Rawls did. To accept Rawls' theory, they would have to abandon their own. Rawls' theory is not neutral among opposing conceptions of what is meant by the good. Moreover, how people of these different philosophical persuasions can live in peace together is not currently a burning question. No one worries about utilitarians rioting to protest rationalism, or how many Kantians are being appointed to the Supreme Court.

Given Rawls' discussion of why people disagree, it is hard to see why their disagreements should become so profound that society cannot endorse or even publicly discuss the merits of any substantive conception of the good. Since practical reason does not reach its conclusions with certainty, there will be disagreements. But these disagreements should lead people to debate and discuss whether a given action is truly wise or just. Rawls, like Dworkin, came close enough to the classical tradition that his theory ran into trouble when he tried to stop short.

As mentioned, one difficulty with the principle of impartial concern is to determine in what respect all people should be treated alike. According to Dworkin and Rawls, their beliefs about right and wrong should receive equal respect. Another difficulty is why such a principle, even if it could be rationally defended, would motivate anyone to be as concerned with others as with himself.

That problem arises for Dworkin because of his theory of how moral judgments are made. We examined that theory when we discussed positivism. It is a form of what we have called "inverse rationalism." As with the rationalists, moral reasoning is reasoning about the consistency of concepts. "Moral reasoning is . . . conceptual interpretation."[224] Unlike the rationalists, who worked downward from definitions and axioms, Dworkin's method was to work upward from moral convictions to a consistent system of principles and ideas.

Hume would have objected that Dworkin is talking about the relationship among concepts, which cannot of themselves motivate action. Suppose a person does not care sufficiently about being a consistent thinker. Suppose he has two ends that he wishes to accomplish. If you can persuade him that one end is self-defeating or will prejudice the accomplishment of the other, he has a motive to consider what you say. But why should he listen if you tell him that although he can accomplish both ends, conceptually, according to some higher principle, to purse them both would entail a contradiction, or at least, to do so would contradict a set of principles that provide the most consistent account of everything he wants to do?

For Rawls, it is critical that people act according to the principles of a "publicly recognized point of view." As we have seen, the method by which people are to arrive at this point of view is also a form of "inverse rationalism."

> We collect such settled convictions as the belief in religious toleration and the rejection of slavery and try to organize the basic ideas and principles implicit in these convictions into a coherent political conception of justice. These convictions are provisional fixed points that it seems any reasonable conception must account for. We start, then, by looking to the public culture itself as the shared fund of implicitly recognized basic ideas and principles. We hope to formulate these ideas and principles clearly enough to be combined into a political conception of justice congenial to our most firmly held convictions.[225]

Earlier, we questioned whether this method could arrive at a point of view that is coherent or that represents the convictions of the public. Supposing it did, a further question is why anyone would be motivated to suspend their own conceptions of the good and act in accordance with it. As Brian Barry pointed out, to show that these principles are logically necessary for them to live in peace is quite different than showing that it could motivate them to do so.

> [W]e have to be clear that "the priority of the right over the good" is a theoretical proposition, forming part of the architecture of the theory of justice. It has nothing to say about the strength of the motivation to comply with the demands of justice. In particular, it does not say that the recognition of something as required by justice will provide an overriding motive for doing it.[226]

As John Gray said of Rawls,

> Why is it supposed that hypothetical choices can give us reasons to act in the real world? The fact that an abstract or artificial person, screened by an imaginary veil of ignorance

---

[224]   Dworkin, *Justice for Hedgehogs* 157.
[225]   Ibid. 8.
[226]   Brian Barry, "John Rawls and the Search for Stability," *Ethics* 105 (1995), 874 at 883.

from that knowledge of his own life that is constitutive of any real person, would choose a specific set of moral or political principles, if he were to choose anything at all, has no force for any real person. For any real person, only the values he in fact upholds, the projects and attachments he actually harbours, can generate reasons for action.[227]

Barry and Gray were making the same point as Hume. To show that a principle of morality can be logically demonstrated does not mean that anyone would be motivated to follow it.

iii *Self-Expression*

Yet another strand of liberalism identifies freedom with self-expression. Self-expression means making choices that are valuable because they are free, and free because they are compelled neither by desire nor reason.

One difficulty is to set limits to freedom once it has been so defined. The limits would have to be set by some other and higher standard than self-expression. But then someone who values acting according to self-made standards must believe that he is also bound by standards other than his own. The problem is to explain why he should be. Friedrich Nietzsche condemned Socrates and praised the sophists for "possess[ing] the courage of all strong spirits to know their own immorality."[228] His views have often been identified with those of Callicles[229] who claimed that to live rightly is to form one's own designs and to have the intelligence and courage to carry them out, regardless of conventional morality. If "self-expression" means to have such "strong spirit," boundaries to it will not be set by self-expression.

Another difficulty is to explain the value of self-expression. Socrates asked Callicles whether the person who forms his own designs does so on at random or by reference to a standard. Callicles lost the argument by saying that he does so according to a standard, since then the standard must be the true of normative values. If Callicles had answered that such a person forms his designs at random, Socrates presumably would have asked why these designs mattered to him or to anyone else.

John Stuart Mill

One of the most influential attempts to confront these difficulties, and perhaps one of the least successful, was made by John Stuart Mill in his essay *On Liberty*.

---

[227] Gray, *Liberalisms* 250–51.
[228] Friedrich Nietzsche, *The Will to Power*, Walter Kaufmann and R. J. Hollingdale, trans. (New York, 1968), 428.
[229] For example, E. R. Dobbs, *Plato Gorgias: A Revised Text with Introduction and Commentary* (Oxford, 1959), 388; W. K. C. Guthrie, *The Sophists* (London, 1971), 107; John M. Finnis, "Natural Law and the Ethics of Discourse," *American Journal of Jurisprudence* 43 (1998) 53 at 63. A standard objection is that Nietzsche would not have endorsed Callicles' hedonism. Brad Lieter, *Moral Psychology with Nietzsche* (Oxford, 2019), 63; Scott Consigny, "Nietzsche's Reading of the Sophists," *Rhetoric Review* 13 (1994, 5 at 16–17; Tracy B. Strong, *Friedrich Nietzsche and the Politics of Transfiguration* (Berkeley, 1998), 354, n. 67. See Gilles Deleuze, *Nietzsche and Philosophy* (London, 1983), 54–55 George Klosko, "The Refutation of Callicles in Plato's Gorgias'" *Greece & Rome* 31 (1984), 126 at 130. In the dialog, however, Callicles first endorsed hedonism, and then repudiated in favor of the position he that truly wished to defend which is like that of Nietzsche: those who live rightly "are not only wise but valiant and able to carry out their designs."

He explained the value of liberty in terms of self-expression. He said that the limit to a person's liberty was set by the "harm principle" or "principle of liberty."

> That principle is, that the sole end for which mankind are warranted, individually or collectively in interfering with the liberty of action of any of their number, is self-protection. That the only purpose for which power can be rightfully exercised over any member of a civilized community, against his will, is to prevent harm to others. His own good, either physical or moral, is not a sufficient warrant.[230]

As John Gray said:

> [T]here are crippling indeterminacies in the statement of the Principle of Liberty itself. It is plain that, because it always requires further principles for its application, Mill's principle does not tell us *how much* liberty may be given up *for how much* harm prevention. But what, in any case, does Mill understand by harm? It is an obvious objection to Mill's project that conceptions of harm vary with competing moral outlooks, so that no Principle of Liberty whose application turns on judgments about harm can expect to resolve disputes between proponents of opposed moral perspectives.[231]

As we have seen, H. L. A. Hart had pointed out the indeterminacy of this principle in his critique of John Rawls' early work, *A Theory of Justice*. Hart objected that "[o]ne cannot define liberty in the abstract." To speak of "the most extensive basic liberty compatible with similar liberty for others" is not only indefinite but unintelligible.[232] Rawls admitted that Hart was right.[233] Gray observed that Hart's objection "gives a death-blow to the currently fashionable neo-Kantian and Anglo-American species of liberalism in which neutrality in respect of specific conceptions of the good is specified as part of the constitutive morality of liberalism." "The upshot ... is radical indeed. It is that no Principle of Liberty of the sort assigned a constitutive place in the political morality of liberalism – be it a Harm Principle, Greatest Equal Liberty Principle, or an account of basic liberties – can be coherently or definitively stated. In this case liberalism itself becomes indeterminate and barely coherent."[234]

Mill explained the value of self-expression in two ways.

He observed that a person ought to decide for himself what is valuable rather than conforming without reflection to the opinions of others. "He who lets the world, or his own portion of it, choose his plan of life for him, has no need of any other faculty than the ape-like one of imitation."[235] Certainly, but that does not show that self-expression in itself is of value but merely that a person should pursue what he values himself.

He claimed that no one can be sure that another person's choices concerning how to live are wrong. Ideas that were once condemned are now praised, such as Christianity, and ideas that were once praised are now condemned. Nevertheless, if another person is able to

---

[230] John Stuart Mill, *On Liberty* (London, 1901), 18.
[231] Gray, *Liberalisms* 222.
[232] H. L. A. Hart, "Rawls on Liberty and Its Priority," *University of Chicago Law Review* 40 (1973), 534.
[233] Rawls, *Political Liberalism* 289–91.
[234] Gray, *Liberalisms* 231–32.
[235] Mill, *On Liberty* 109–10.

tell whether his own choices are likely to be right or wrong, it cannot be impossible for others to conclude that in certain instances he is mistaken. If, however, the other person's choices are deemed to be valuable simply because he has chosen, and without regard to whether they are right or wrong, then the value of self-expression has not been demonstrated. It has been assumed.

Wilhelm von Humboldt and Friedrich Schiller

Both the value of self-expression and the harm principle were defended more robustly by William von Humboldt. In his *Autobiography*, Mill acknowledged the debt he owed to Humboldt for the thoughts expressed in his essay *On Liberty*.[236]

Humboldt gave an account of the value of self-expression which Mill did not describe in his own essay. The "end of man" is realized through self-expression. His defense of the harm principle was that it is wrong to interfere with self-expression.

According to Humboldt, the "harm principle" or "principle of liberty" protects this sort of freedom.

> I therefore deduce, as the natural inference from what has been argued, *that true reason cannot wish any other condition of man than that in which each individual not only enjoys the most absolute freedom to develop himself in his individuality, but in which physical nature received no other form as each individual gives it of himself and his own free will, according to the measure of his wants and instincts, and restricted only by the limits of his powers and his rights*. From this principle, in my opinion, reason must never yield more than is necessary to preserve it. It must therefore be the basis of every political system.[237]

Humboldt did not have the same difficulty as Mill explaining the limits of a person's power and his rights. The limits, according to Humboldt, were those set by Kant's categorical imperative. That option was not open to Mill. In *Utilitarianism*, he said that "when [Kant] begins to deduce from this precept any of the actual duties of morality, he fails, grotesquely ... to show that there would be any contradiction ... in the adoption by all rational beings of the most outrageously immoral rules of conduct."[238] According to Humboldt, "Kant ... it may be truly said, was never surpassed in profundity."[239]

Humboldt's innovation was to place a normative value on self-expression. That might seem a difficult task for a Kantian. Humboldt agreed with Kant that the moral life is "especially the province of cold, abstract reason" and that moral laws must be obeyed "in a divine and disinterested way" with a "total disregard to happiness or misfortune."[240]

---

[236]   John Stuart Mill, *Autobiography of John Stuart Mill* (Oxford, 1975), 179–80.
[237]   Wilhelm von Humboldt, *Ideen zu einem Versuch, die Gränzen der Wirksamkeit des Staats zu bestimmen*, in Wilhelm von Humboldt, *Gesammelte Werke* 1 (Berlin, 1903), 97 at 111.
[238]   John Stuart Mill, *Utilitarianism*, in James M. Smith and Ernest Sosa, eds., *Mill's Utilitarianism Text and Criticism* (Belmont, 1969), 31 at 34.
[239]   Humboldt, *Ideen zu einem Versuch* 171.
[240]   Ibid. 172.

Kant said, however, that a person is motivated to follow these laws by *Achtung*, by attentiveness to duty, which, he claimed, was not a desire but could nevertheless be a motivation. Humboldt's first step in a new direction was to claim that reason alone is normally insufficient to motivate a person. The will must be moved by feelings.

He was following Friedrich Schiller who also accepted Kant's account of morality.[241] Schiller said:

> Reason has done what it can when it has discovered and presented the law; bold will and lively feeling must execute it. When the truth is to obtain victory in the struggle with force, it must itself become a force and find some impulse (*Trieb*) to be its agent in the realm of the sensible world (*Erscheinungen*); for impulse is the only motivating force in the world of feelings.[242]

Thus "[t]he way to the head is through the heart."[243] Humboldt agreed.

For both of them the feeling or impulse that must provide the motivation is a feeling of a special kind. It is an aesthetic sense, an impulse toward the beautiful. Here, again, they were indebted to Kant. "Truth and duty," as Kant said, "have a determining power in themselves" to motivate, but moral action "is first made possible by the aesthetic condition of our temper."[244] "[O]nly from the aesthetic condition can the moral one be developed."[245] Similarly, for Humboldt, "the idea of the sublime alone enables us to obey absolute and unconditional laws."[246]

Then they went further. The aesthetic sense did not merely motivate people to follow the moral law. It could reconcile desire and reason, elements in human nature that would otherwise be opposed. This reconciliation, for Schiller, is "the consummation of [one's] humanity" and for Humboldt, the "true end of man."

According to Schiller desire and reason are "two contrary forces" "very properly called impulses (*Treiben*)." The first is concerned with matter, the second with mind. But "[m]an, we know, is neither exclusively matter nor exclusively mind. Beauty, as the consummation of his humanity, can therefore neither be exclusively life . . . nor exclusively form."[247] "Only the perception of beauty makes a whole of [man] because through it both his natures must come together."[248] Similarly, Humboldt distinguished "the crudest matter" which "we call sensuous perception" for the "purest form" which "we call idea." Beauty or the sublime requires both. "The true end of wisdom," according to Humboldt, lies in "the eternal struggle to unite these two elements, so that each may rob as little as possible from the other."[249] "Upon this constant intermingling of form and substance, or of diversity with the

---

[241] Friedrich Schiller, *Über die ästhetische Erziehung des Menschen in einer Reihe von Briefen*, in Friedrich Schiller, *Gesammelte Werke* 8 (Berlin, 1955), 399 at 400.

[242] Ibid. 420.

[243] Ibid. 422.

[244] Ibid. 469–70.

[245] Ibid. 472.

[246] Humboldt, *Ideen zu einem Versuch* 172.

[247] Schiller, *Über die ästhetische Erziehung* 444.

[248] Ibid. 495.

[249] Humboldt, *Ideen zu einem Versuch* 169.

individual unity, depends the combination of the two natures of man, and his greatness."[250] To unite these two elements is to realize "[t]he true end of man, or that which is prescribed, not by transient desires, but by the eternal and immutable dictates of reason, [which] is the highest and most harmonious development of his powers into a whole."[251]

That last sentence was quoted by Mill in *On Liberty*. He said that "[f]ew persons, out of Germany, even comprehend the meaning of the doctrine which Wilhelm von Humboldt, so eminent both as a savant and as a politician," was expounding in that text. But Mill did not undertake a defense of Humboldt's view of the end of man.

According to Schiller and Humboldt, when a person unites these opposed elements through his aesthetic sense, his actions are free in a way that actions based on either reason or desire are not. Here Schiller and Humboldt drew on Kant's account of aesthetic judgment. Kant said, "(t)he cognitive powers . . . are here in free play, because no definite concept limits them to a particular rule of cognition."[252] Consequently, "[t]here can be no objective rule of taste which determines by means of concepts what is beautiful."[253] Our assent is "forced" when are moved either by "sense or reason." Aesthetic choices create things without following a definite rule. They require originality and genius. According to Kant, "genius is a *talent* for producing that for which no definite rule can be given, not a mere aptitude for what can be learnt by a rule. Hence *originality* must be its first property."[254]

Sabine Roehr's observation about Schiller applies equally well to Humboldt: "Schiller had to be dissatisfied with Kant's rigorist ethics, with the constraining character of the moral imperative. As he writes in 'On the Pathetic' (1793) . . . 'The fact that the will is limited to being determined in one way alone, a limitation demanded by duty, is at odds with the instinct of freedom on the part of fantasy.'"[255] She concluded that "Schiller can be credited with breaking" with Kant's conception of freedom "and thus providing a concept of a neutral will that is free to decide between different options for acting."[256] She could have said the same of Humboldt for whom "[f]reedom is the first and indispensable condition" which human development presupposes.[257]

Ursula Vogel said, "If it is incumbent on the liberal to explain why individual liberty should be given priority over other conflicting values like equality, social justice, general happiness – for the realization of which one might justifiably call for state action – then one can draw on Humboldt's book for some convincing arguments."[258]

---

[250] Ibid. 108.

[251] Ibid. 106.

[252] Immanuel Kant, *Kritik der Urteilskraft* in *Kant's gesammelte Schriften*, Königlich Preussischen Akademie der Wissenschaft ed., 5 (Berlin, 1913), 165 at 217.

[253] Ibid. 231.

[254] Ibid. 307–08.

[255] Sabine Roehr, "Freedom and Autonomy in Schiller," *Journal of the History of Ideas* 64 (2003), 119 at 126, quoting Friedrich Schiller, "On the Pathetic," in Friedrich Schiller, *Essays*, Walter Hinderer and Daniel O. Dahlstrom eds., Daniel O. Dahlstrom trans. (New York, 1993), 64.

[256] Roehr, "Freedom and Autonomy" 131.

[257] Humboldt, *Ideen zu einem Versuch* 106.

[258] Ursula Vogel, "Liberty is Beautiful: Von Humboldt's Gift to Liberalism," *History of Political Thought* 3 (1982), 77 at 81.

On reflection, the arguments are less convincing. For Humboldt as for Schiller, a free choice is one that is made neither on account of desire nor on account of reason. It is *par excellence* an aesthetic choice. It has no other purpose than beauty, which reconciles the sensuous and the rational parts of human nature. If Kant is right, to exercise this sort of freedom requires "genius," a "talent" possessed by very few. Be that as it may, it takes no account of the freedom to pursue other purposes than beauty: for example, to decide for oneself such matters as for whom to vote, whether to marry, whether to buy a new car, or whether to study law rather than medicine.

Gray remarked that "the lineage of [Humboldt's] argument is Aristotelian in that it ascribes to the human species a common nature" to be "realized."[259] In the Aristotelian tradition, however, to seek the beautiful is one of the ultimate ends of human action. Beauty is one end that is worthy of pursuit but there are others. Some things – trees, for example – are beautiful even if they are not the product of originality. Some things are ugly even if they are.

Schiller and Humboldt thought that boundaries could be set to freedom of expression by the Kantian categorical imperative. They believed that free choices – choices that are creative because they do not follow a definite rule – must be made by individuals themselves. "Each individual [must] enjoy the most absolute freedom to develop himself in his individuality."[260] To accept the first proposition one must be a Kantian. To accept the second, one must ignore the extent to which the beauty of a person's action may depend, as it does in an orchestra, on what other people are doing. Without these propositions, their positions would be less attractive to political liberals. There would be no reason to protect or prioritize the value of individual liberty.

Schiller envisioned an "aesthetic State" which he claimed was founded on individual freedom.

> Amidst the fearful realm of power and within the holy realm of law, the creative impulse unobserved builds a third joyful realm of play and appearance in which man is released from the fetters of all conditions and unbound from everything one may call constraint, whether physical or moral. . . . To give freedom through freedom is the basic law of this realm.[261]
>
> . . .
>
> Everything in the aesthetic State, even the subservient tool, is a free citizen having equal rights with the noblest, and the intellect, which forcibly molds the suffering masses to its designs, must here ask its assent. Here, then, in the realm of aesthetic appearance, is fulfilled the ideal of equality whose being the visionary would so gladly see realized.[262]

Some have praised Schiller for "advocat[ing] a new kind of politics compatible with modern individuality and its differentiated forms."[263] Others have condemned him as a progenitor of Nazism.

---

259   Gray, *Liberalisms* 254.
260   Humboldt, *Ideen zu einem Versuch* 111.
261   Schiller, *Über die ästhetische Erziehung* 494.
262   Ibid. 496.
263   Douglas Moggach, "Schiller's Aesthetic Republicanism," *History of Political Thought* 28 (2007), 520 at 527.

Walter Benjamin, in 1930, spoke of an "aesthetization of politics," "an uninhibited translation of the principles of *l'art pour l'art* to war itself," which had to be stopped. He observed prophetically, "if this corrective effort fails, millions of human bodies will indeed inevitably be chopped to pieces and chewed up by iron and gas."[264] A few years later, Hitler's propaganda minister, Joseph Goebbels, said that "Schiller, if he had lived at the time of national socialist rule, would undoubtedly have become the greatest poetic champion of our revolution."[265] Goebbels' attraction to Schiller is illuminated by the remarks of a character in a novel that Goebbels wrote:

> Art is the expression of feeling. The artist is distinguished from the nonartist by the fact that he can also express what he feels. He can do so in a variety of forms. Some by images; others by sound; still others by marble – or also in historical forms. The statesman is an artist, too. The people are for him what stone is for the sculptor. Leader and masses are as little of a problem to each other as color is a problem for the painter. Politics are the plastic arts of the state as painting is the plastic art of color. Therefore politics without the people or against the people are nonsense. To transform a mass into a people and a people into a state – that has always been the deepest sense of a genuine political task.[266]

Schiller would not have agreed.[267] For him, the state does not play an analogous role as the composer or conductor in directing the aesthetic life of its citizens.[268] Take away the assumption that the beautiful life is best achieved through the shaping hand of an individual and one can understand Benjamin's warning. People's lives may be shaped by a political leader who regards himself as a sculptor and them as clay.

Joseph Raz

For Schiller and Humboldt, one acts freely when there is no one right choice to make. Joseph Raz used the word "autonomy" to describe this kind of freedom. He faced the same problems: to set limits to the exercise of that freedom and to explain its value.

Like Mill, he claimed that limits could be set by the "harm principle" or "principle of liberty." According to Raz, "the only justification for coercively interfering with a person is to prevent him from harming others."[269] "Depriving a person of opportunities or the ability

---

[264] Walter Benjamin, "Theories of German Fascism: On the Collection of Essays *War and Warrior*," in *New German Critique* 17 (1979), 120–28, quoted by María del Rosario Acosta López, "'Making Other People's Feelings Our Own': From the Aesthetic to the Political in Schiller's Aesthetic Letters," in Jeffrey L. High, Nicholas Martin, and Norbert Oellers, eds., *Who Is This Schiller Now? Essays on His Reception and Significance* (Rochester, 2011), 187 at 187–88.

[265] Quoted by Henrik Sponsel, "Was sagte dieser Schiller (damals)? Schillers Antworten auf seine Kritiker nach 1945," in High, Martin and Oellers, *Who Is This Schiller Now?* 383 at 386.

[266] Joseph Goebbels, *Michael: Ein deutsches Schicksal in Tagebuchblatten* (Munich, 1933), 21, quoted by Elizabeth M. Wilkinson and L. A. Willoughby, "Introduction," *Schiller's On the Aesthetic Education of Man*, Elizabeth M. Wilkinson and L. A. Willoughby, ed. and trans. (Oxford, 1967), cxlii.

[267] Sponsel, "Was sagte dieser Schiller (damals)?" 390; Constantin Behler, "The Politics of Aesthetic Humanism: Schiller's German Idea of Freedom," in *Goethe Yearbook* 20 (Rochester, 2013,), 223 at 228.

[268] Acosta López, "'Making Other People's Feelings Our Own'" 190–91.

[269] Joseph Raz, *The Morality of Freedom* (Oxford, 1986), 412.

to use them is a way of causing him harm."[270] Therefore, "the harm principle allows [the government] to use coercion . . . in order to stop people from actions that would diminish people's autonomy."[271]

If one substitutes the word "liberty" for "autonomy," one can see why this argument is subject to the same objections that Gray raised against Mill, and Hart against the early work of Rawls. To allow one person to act autonomously limits another person's sphere of autonomous action. There is no way to determine if the gain exceeds the loss.

Moreover, unlike Mill, Raz did not argue that we cannot know whether a choice is morally wrong, and therefore the state should not interfere. "[P]ursuit of the morally repugnant cannot be defended on the ground that being an autonomous choice endows it with any value."[272] Raz argued instead:

> [T]he harm principle is defensible in the light of the principle of autonomy for one simple reason. The means used, coercive interference, violates the autonomy of its victim. First, it violates the condition of independence and expresses a relation of domination and an attitude of disrespect for the coerced individual. Second, coercion by criminal penalties is a global and indiscriminate invasion of autonomy. Imprisoning a person prevents him from almost all autonomous pursuits.[273]

In response, Wojciech Sadurski observed "disrespect for such an action need not imply disrespect for a person."[274] Moreover, "Raz's argument is, at best, an autonomy-based argument against the penalty of imprisonment for morally repugnant actions, but is not sufficient to justify rejection of all coercive prohibitions of immoral [though victimless] behaviour."[275] Similarly, Robert George objected that "[I]f preventing self-corruption is as valid a reason for political action as preventing theft, as Raz concedes it is, then there seems to be no moral principle that forbids the use of the criminal law to combat vice."[276]

Raz's greater contribution to political thought was his defense of the value of what he called autonomous choice: choice when there was no one right decision to be made. He avoided the difficulties that Humboldt and Schiller encountered by adopting what he called "an essentially Aristotelian account of well-being."[277] Consequently, as he acknowledged, his "defense of the traditional belief "is based on a radical departure from historically central liberal doctrines."[278]

Like Ronald Dworkin and John Rawls, Raz maintained that people "engage in what they do because they believe it to be a valuable, worthwhile activity."[279] Dworkin said that "one

---

[270] Ibid. 413.

[271] Ibid. 415.

[272] Ibid. 418.

[273] Ibid. 417–18.

[274] Wojciech Sadurski, "Joseph Raz on Liberal Neutrality and the Harm Principle," *Oxford Journal of Legal Studies* 10 (1990), 122 at 133. Robert P. George, "The Unorthodox Liberalism of Joseph Raz," *The Review of Politics* 53 (1991), 663.

[275] Sadurski, "Joseph Raz" 133.

[276] George, "Unorthodox Liberalism" 664.

[277] Joseph Raz, "Facing Up: A Reply," *Southern California Law Review* 62 (1989), 1153 at 1227.

[278] Raz, *Morality of Freedom* 17.

[279] Ibid. 298–99.

must believe that what one does has objective value."[280] For you to do so, you must believe that "there is a right and wrong way for you to live."[281] Rawls said that all human beings have "a capacity for a conception of the good,"[282] that is, of the "ends and purposes worthy of our devoted pursuit."[283] Nevertheless, Dworkin and Rawls were less than clear about whether a person's activities can be truly good, or whether it is enough that he believes so.

Raz was clear. People not only form conceptions of what they believe to be good but that is a matter about which they may be right or wrong.[284] "To the extent that their valuation is misguided it affects the success of their life."[285] "A person who spends all his time gambling has, other things being equal, less successful a life, even if he is a successful gambler, than a livestock farmer busily minding his farm."[286] Consequently, the value of what one chooses matters, not merely the fact that it is chosen. "People adopt and pursue goals because they believe in their independent value, that is, their value is believed to be at least in part independent of the fact that they were chosen and are pursued."[287] Such goals have an "impersonal value" which is "their value judged independently of the fact that this agent does or can engage in them."[288] "[A] person's well-being depends on the value of his goals and pursuits."[289]

For Raz, unlike the rationalists, the value of a course of action is not deduced from "a priori or conceptual truths." That people make choices according to what they believe is truly valuable is one of the "general features of the human experience." "[P]ervasive and unshakeable features of human practical thought need no justification," according to Raz, "though they call for an explanation."[290] Raz, like Aristotle, treats them as first principles.

As we have seen, Aquinas believed that there can be different ways to choose rightly, no one of which is best, and yet the choice may matter very much. In Raz's vocabulary, such a choice is "autonomous." It is a choice is between "incommensurables," each of which is valuable for "choice independent" or "impersonal" reasons.

His examples are the choices between a career in medicine and one in medical research, or between a career in law and one in teaching. There would be a right choice if a person had no talent for the one and great talent for the other. If he has both talents, there may be no right choice. Both alternatives are good, and one cannot rank order them. But that does not mean that a person is indifferent between them and might as well choose by flipping a coin. The choice of whom he will be matters very much although there is no one right way to make it.[291]

---

[280] Dworkin, *Justice for Hedgehogs* 255.
[281] Ibid. 207
[282] Rawls, *Political Liberalism* 18–19.
[283] Ibid. 104.
[284] Raz, *Morality of Freedom* 302 ("the satisfaction of goals based on false reasons does not contribute to one's well-being").
[285] Ibid. 302.
[286] Ibid.
[287] Ibid. 308.
[288] Ibid. 299.
[289] Ibid. 298.
[290] Ibid. 289–90. See ibid. 344.
[291] Ibid. 340–42.

For Raz "the ideal of autonomy ... holds that free choice of goals and relations are an essential ingredient of individual well-being."[292] Robert George denied that this claim can be reconciled with an Aristotelian account of well-being.

> Autonomy appears to be intrinsically valuable because something really is more perfect about the realization of goods when this realization is the fruit of one's own practical deliberation and choice. The additional perfection is provided not by autonomy, however, but by the exercise of reason in self-determination. Among the intrinsic values that one realizes in practically reasonable (i.e., morally upright) choosing is the value of practical reasonableness itself.[293]
>
> One may desire autonomy for a reason (and thus one's desire for autonomy may be rationally grounded); or one's desire for autonomy may be grounded in some nonrational factor (e.g., a merely emotional desire to do as one pleases). Autonomy does not, however, provide an ultimate reason for action.[294]

Here it is helpful to distinguish carefully between the value of creativity and the value of autonomous choice. As we will use the term, all creative activity is, in Raz's sense, autonomous. There is no one right decision as to how an architect should design a church to be built on a given site or how a writer should compose a speech to be delivered on a given occasion. A person might prefer a career as an architect or a writer because it is creative. There is, in George's words, an "additional perfection" in doing such work. It is not exercising practical reason to determine the best alternative. It is the value of making something that otherwise would not have been.

In contrast, a decision may be autonomous even though it does not entail creative activity. Examples would be the choice between a career in law or in medicine, or a choice between which of two people to marry, when there is no one right decision. In these situations, George is right. It is hard to see how autonomy adds to the value of a person's choice, or even that he is better off for having acted autonomously. Mozart's life was no poorer because his one great gift was for music. It would have been no richer if he had had the gifts of his contemporaries Captain Cook and the Duke of Wellington, and had chosen to be a composer rather than an explorer or a military leader. The life of a person whose great gift is for medicine is no poorer because he could not turn down an equally successful career in law. A person who marries may have chosen autonomously between two possible partners. But his life is no poorer if he correctly believes that he could never have been happy with anyone else.

Raz describes the autonomous shaping of one's life as a creative activity. "Personal autonomy is the ideal of free and conscious self-creation."[295] By "successive decisions throughout our lives" we "fashion" them. "In embracing goals and commitments, in coming to care about one thing or another, one progressively gives shape to one's life, determines what would count as a successful life and what

---

[292]   Ibid. 369.
[293]   George, "Unorthodox Liberalism" 665.
[294]   Ibid. 668.
[295]   Raz, *Morality of Freedom* 390.

would be a failure."[296] "The ruling idea behind the idea of personal autonomy is that people should make their own lives. The autonomous person is a (part) author of his own life. The ideal of personal autonomy is the vision of people controlling, to some degree, their own destiny, fashioning it through successive decisions throughout their lives."[297]

According to Raz, to have a successful life a person must have the opportunity to make an "adequate number" of "autonomous" choices. In *Morality of Freedom*, he seemed to claim that it is essential to well-being to live in a society like our own. "In western industrial societies a particular conception of well-being has acquired considerable popularity. It is the ideal of personal autonomy. It transcends the conceptual point that personal well-being is partly determined by success in willingly endorsed pursuits and holds the free choice of goals and relations is an essential ingredient of individual well-being."[298]

It is not even clear, however that the "free choice of goals and relations" characteristic of "western industrial societies" increases the opportunities for creative activity. Modern art or music is not more creative simply because it there are fewer rules to follow that those that guided Van Dyke or Bach.

Autonomy is not the same as self-expression. One can express oneself in traditional forms of life. As Gray said of Mill's idea of liberty:

> By its invocation of a strong conception of autonomous choice, distanced from convention, it condemns as devoid of individuality all traditional forms of life. The man who accepts the way of life into which he was born as an inheritance to be explored and enjoyed, and who has no interest in trying out alternatives to it, cannot for Mill exhibit individuality, however stylish his personality may be. In ruling out traditional conduct as incapable of embodying or expressing individuality, Mill expresses a modernist prejudice which dismisses as repressive of individuality the ways in which almost all men have always lived. The objection has a reverse side. If a post-traditional society of Millian individualists were possible, it would be one from which much variety had been drained and many options had been lost.[299]

If Gray is correct, then a life in traditional China in which the rules of *li* governed much of human life may have provided opportunities for self-expression that are ruled out by the autonomy of contemporary Western societies.

Earlier, we discussed the possibility that a life lived in accordance with *li* may be well-lived. There may be no right answer to whether such a life is better than one leaves more to autonomous choice. In a later work, Raz himself suggested this possibility. He said that he did not "regard[s] autonomy as a universal value." "People who lack personal autonomy" can be "be completely well-off, or have a completely good life."[300]

---

296 Ibid. 387.
297 Ibid. 370.
298 Ibid.
299 Gray, *Liberalism* 224–25.
300 Raz, "Facing Up" 1227.

I think that there were, and there can be, non-repressive societies, and ones which enable people to spend their lives in worthwhile pursuits, even though their pursuits and the options open to them are not subject to individual choice. Careers may be determined by custom, marriages arranged by parents, child-bearing and child-rearing controlled only by sexual passion and traditions, past-time activities few and traditional, and engagement in them required rather than optional. In such societies, with little mobility, even friends are not chosen. There are few people one ever comes in contact with, they remain there from birth to death, and one just has to get on with them. I do not see that the absence of choice diminishes the value of human relations or the display of excellence in technical skills, physical ability, spirit and enterprise, leadership, scholarship, creativity, or imaginativeness, which can all be encompassed in such lives.

Of course, to succeed in such lives one's socialisation has to succeed, and one must engage in the various pursuits wholeheartedly. But it is a mistake to think that what is chosen is more likely to attract our dedication or involvement than what is not.[301]

If Raz is right, there may be no one right answer to which sort of society is better. Nevertheless, one need not have deny that autonomy in the sense of creativity is a universal value even though in some societies, it is sacrificed for the sake of other values. The decision whether to make that sacrifice may be, for a culture, like an autonomous choice made by an individual. There may be no one right answer. The choices that fashion a culture, however, are made by all those who contribute to strengthening its norms, weakening them, or changing them. They may do so for better or for worse.

In both classical traditions, the ultimate question is whether the choices people make contribute to a life well-lived. In a democracy, Aristotle said, people value freedom but they should not confuse it with doing what one likes. Dai Zhen condemned the "stern men" in traditional China who accepted its norms without considering whether what was once important is still important. But he also condemned those whose choices were distorted by "selfish desires." Whether we value the opportunities for a good life that arise through cultural norms or those that arise by devaluing them, our choices matter because we may choose for better or for worse. If one denies or ignores that possibility, one cannot explain the value of freedom.

---

[301]   Ibid. 1227–28.

14

Conclusion

Aristotle said that the only way to establish first principles is by dialectical argument. This book has presented an extended dialectical argument. We have seen how modern philosophers have tried to justify liberal institutions. Some did so by attaching a normative value to pleasure or preference satisfaction. Yet it is hard to believe that all pleasures or preferences are worthwhile. Some embraced what we have called a principle of universal concern: one must apply the same standard to others as to oneself. They had trouble explaining what that standard should be. Some attached a normative value to self-expression but then they had to explain why, in itself, self-expression is of value.

Liberal philosophers were trying to escape the dichotomy between reason and desire which was introduced by the rationalists and described with clarity and precision by David Hume. They were not able do so by ascribing value to the gratification of desire, nor by claiming it is irrational to apply a different moral standard to others than to oneself, nor by identifying self-fulfillment with the making of choices independent of either reason or desire.

To escape these problems, some contemporary philosophers have spoken of human well-being, like Amartya Sen; some of the human capacity to form a conception of the good, like Ronald Dworkin and John Rawls; and some of the independent value of a person's goals and pursuits, like Joseph Raz. Those ideas make sense if, as the classical traditions taught, there are actions that contribute or detract to a life well lived, and if a human being, by nature, has an ability to know, though not infallibly, what they are. Otherwise, it is hard to understand or defend them.

What we have seen in the West recapitulates what we saw in China. The school of Cheng Yi and Zhu Xi, like Western rationalism, taught that moral values are eternal and unchanging, and that moral conduct means that one knows them and then acts accordingly. Like Western rationalism, this school sharply distinguished knowledge from desire. The alternative proposed by the school of Lu Hsiang-Shan and Wang Yangming identified thought, feeling, and action. Some of their followers concluded that nothing is genuinely right or wrong.

China took a different path than the West. The Cheng-Zhu school was accepted as orthodox for centuries, whereas Western philosophers rejected rationalism and tried to work with the premises of Hume. In the late Ming, political reformers, without breaking with either school, reemphasized the teachings of Mencius concerning human nature. In the eighteenth century, some philosophers tried to reconcile the teachings of the Chen-Zhu school with the school of Lu and Wang Yangming. Others, such as Dai Zhen, saw that Mencius' idea of human nature was inconsistent with the doctrines of both schools. He returned to Mencius, and reinterpreted his teachings, showing how they fit with ideas important to the later schools, such as principle or *li*. The chance for these teachings to work a political change had already ended with the suppression of the academies in the late Ming. The chance for them to work an intellectual reform was not pursued, in part because the question that attracted the attention of nineteenth-century scholars was what to do about the West. Nevertheless, they reaffirmed the classical Chinese idea of human nature as a source of normative values.

According to Aristotle, one cannot prove first principles except by a dialectical argument, that is, by showing the consequences that follow if one denies them. Suppose one denies that some actions are good for a human being and others bad according to whether they contribute or detract from a distinctively human life, and that human beings, by nature, have an ability to know which are which. The intellectual history of China and the West since the rise of rationalism shows the consequences.

In China and the West, we can learn from these consequences. China's institutions are in formation and their philosophical foundations are being worked out. The path the Chinese take will be decided by the Chinese. They may adopt the model of Western democracy. Or they may not. Whatever they do, they can learn from their own tradition of classical thought.[1] According to that tradition, those who govern should be incorruptible. They have a duty to criticize when criticism is warranted. They have a duty to help people to live better lives, but they should try to do so by example rather than reward and punishment. Their tradition can teach them, and us, not only about being authentically Chinese, but about being authentically human.

In the West, we can learn to value the Chinese classical tradition and relearn to value our own. The Enlightenment not only disclaimed respect for the classical tradition of ethical and political philosophy but for any intellectual tradition. Until the Enlightenment, each of the great intellectual movements in the West in law, politics, and ethics was a renaissance or rebirth of older thought. The past was not simply rediscovered. Its insights were developed in new ways and applied to new problems. There was a renaissance of Roman law in the twelfth century, of Aristotelian philosophy in the thirteenth, of classical rhetoric, literature, and art in the fourteenth and fifteenth, and a new rediscovery of Aristotelian philosophy in the sixteenth and seventeenth centuries. The Enlightenment – if by that we mean the philosophical movement that began with the seventeenth-century founders of rationalism such as Descartes and extended though the work of Bentham, Kant, Schiller, and Humboldt in the late eighteenth century – was not a renaissance. Descartes began by doubting everything that anyone had hitherto believed. Locke claimed that if his own book was not a work of genius, still it would do the work of "an under-labourer in clearing the ground a little and removing some of the rubbish that lies in the way to

---

[1] For some suggestions as to what they might learn, see Daniel A. Bell, *The China Model: Political Meritocracy and the Limits of Democracy* (Princeton, 2015).

knowledge," put there by "the efforts of ingenious and industrious men" whose use of "uncouth, affected or unintelligible terms" had turned philosophy into a subject "that was thought unfit to be brought into well-bred company and polite conversation."[2] He succeeded so well in convincing others that, as Peter Gay noted in his history of the Enlightenment, "[i]t was [Locke's] decisive repudiation of the Scholastics that allowed the *philosophes* to malign them in their turn without troubling to study them."[3] Hume believed that previous moral philosophers had made the mistake of thinking about what was genuinely right and wrong instead of the psychological causes of our moral beliefs. Hume's work was the starting point for Bentham and Kant, and Kant's for Schiller and Humboldt. The Enlightenment was not a renaissance. It was the eclipse of classical thought in the West.

The American Republic has been called a product of the Enlightenment. On the contrary, it was a blessing for the founders and for ourselves that they did their work before the Enlightenment discredited classical thought. The founders were as unoriginal as they claimed to be. The idea that government is instituted to serve the common good, and that when it fails to do so the people may overthrow it, and institute whatever new form seems most consistent to their safety and happiness, was developed on the basis of Aristotelian principles in the sixteenth and seventeenth centuries and restated by Whig writers in the eighteenth. Locke's break with classical principles was an exception. That break had little influence on the founders. They cited his work and that of other Whigs in support of the right of resistance and ignored him when, unlike other Whigs, he called into question the classical idea of the common good.

Patrick Deneen was mistaken, then, when he described liberalism as "a political philosophy conceived some 500 years ago, and put into effect at the birth of the United States nearly 250 years later."[4] He was correct, however, that "[l]iberalism rejects the ancient conception of liberty" which aims at "self-governance of both city and soul" and depends on "the art of virtue and self-rule." "Liberalism instead understands liberty as the condition in which one can act freely within the sphere unconstrained by positive law."[5] The result is "a liberal society – one that commends self-interest, the unleashed ambition of private individuals, an emphasis on private pursuits over a concern for public weal, and an acquired ability to maintain psychic distance from any other human, including to reconsider any relationships that constitute a fundamental limitation on our personal liberty."[6]

To some extent, we are protected against that result both by human nature and by human inconsistency. If the classical traditions are correct, human beings can distinguish right from wrong. If so, it is unlikely that philosophical liberalism will stop them from doing so. Moreover, even the most committed liberal is unlikely to abide by his philosophical principles consistently. Liberals have tacitly incorporated classical ideas into their theories of government. Moreover, whatever the principles of a liberal philosopher say concerning

---

[2]   John Locke, "The Epistle to the Reader," in *Essay Concerning Human Understanding* (New York, 1959), 7 at 14.
[3]   Peter Gay, *The Enlightenment: An Interpretation, The Rise of Modern Paganism* 1 (New York, 1966), 321.
[4]   Patrick J. Deneen, *Why Liberalism Failed* (New Haven, 2018), 1.
[5]   Ibid. 37–38.
[6]   Ibid. 165.

how other people should be governed, they will not tell him much about how to live his own life.

Ordinary people, relying on their common sense, still believe that there is a difference between common good and private interest in government. They live their own lives recognizing that there is a difference between good and evil. William James, not intending to be complimentary, spoke of the Aristotelian tradition as a philosophy of common sense. For those not-so-ordinary people who have the benefit of a university education, recognizing distinctions between good and evil is problematic. In some disciplines such as politics, philosophy, and economics, these distinctions are ignored or attacked, and in others, such as psychology, sociology, anthropology, and history, they are treated as the end result of amoral forces. If it is true, however, that a human being can distinguish good from evil, and the common good from private interest, then however great these amoral forces may be, these academic disciplines distort the study of people and societies. They give the impression that human beings have no capacity to draw such distinctions or that their ability to do so has no influence.

What has saved us so far is that we are a democracy. William Buckley once said that he would rather be ruled by the first 200 people listed in the Boston telephone directory than by the Harvard faculty. In a democracy the opinions of ordinary people count. It is a perversion of education, however, for it to leave people less able than they were before to distinguish right from wrong, and the common good from private interests, and, indeed, to leave them uncertain as to whether such distinctions are possible. A liberal education, as classically understood, was meant to develop one's insight into what it means to be a complete human being. It did so not by preaching but by imparting a knowledge of the good and evil that people had said and done. Like a classical education in China, it was intended to foster not only knowledge but wisdom, and through wisdom, character and integrity. Traditional Confucians, and even the democratic Thomas Jefferson, thought that people so educated were better able to govern. One hopes that modern education does not deprive students of their aspirations to wisdom, integrity, and character. One hopes that if the educated elite does not enlighten ordinary people, at least it will not corrupt them. We need a new renaissance.

Liberal philosophers do not provide a solution. With the exception of Raz, they do not look to human nature for substantive standards of right and wrong nor allow political decisions to rest on these standards. That is a source of danger.

One danger is that people may believe that claims about right and wrong have no truth value. Nothing is genuinely right or wrong. The nightmare scenario, described in Dostoevsky's novels over a century ago, is that they will act as though there is no difference.

Since to do so requires a consistency and a moral indifference that is rare, people are more likely to slip into a vague version of one of the modern philosophies we have described. Like the rationalists, they may think that if a moral truth cannot be demonstrated, they are free to dismiss it. Like the utilitarians, they may identify what is good with what feels good. Like the Kantians, they imagine morality as setting a boundary within which their actions are neither moral nor immoral. Within that boundary – although Kant would have disapproved – they may seek wealth, without regard to whether they are using it to help their families or others, or position, without regard to why, or admiration, regardless of why it is conferred. They may value "self-expression" without regard to the value of what they express.

Another danger is that people will misconceive the public good. As we saw, and as Gordon Wood observed, "republicanism as Americans expressed it in 1776 ... embodied the idea of the good society as it had been set forth from antiquity through the eighteenth century."[7] Wood noted that this idea is hard for us to understand. "[W]hat was good for the whole community was ultimately good for all the parts. ... The common interest was not, as we might today think of it, simply the sum or consensus of the particular interests that make up the community."[8] Conversely, the good of the community is defined in terms of the well-being of each of its citizens.

The danger, if that ideal is no longer understood, is that the goal of promoting the good of individuals is contrasted with, or set against, that of promoting the public good. Either the public good is not public: there is only an aggregate of individual interests for governments to protect. Or the public good has no clear relation to the good of the members of the public.

The nightmare scenario would be either a society that values the private interest sought by each individual without regard to any benefit conferred on anyone else, or one that values a "public good" that is to be promoted without regard to the welfare of individuals. The former recognizes no higher good than self-interest, and the latter leads to totalitarianism.

More likely, people will imagine that whether an action promotes the private or the public interest as an either-or question. A person who acts in his own interest is purely self-interested. The danger is that if a person thinks so, the significance of his own life will diminish in his own eyes. A physician, carpenter or judge may work only for pay. Nevertheless, he may work to provide for his family and others in need. He may also work because he values his skill in performing a demanding operation, doing a craftsman-like job, or writing a well-crafted opinion. He may do so to enable people to have health, shelter, or justice. A further motive may be to contribute to a society in which everyone is able to live well. He is then working to promote the public interest as classically understood. He may also be working to serve a God whose grace perfects nature but does not destroy it.

A person who regards promoting the private or the public interest as an either-or question may be repelled by living a self-interested life, and choose instead to serve the public good. But such a person may regard what promotes the public good as independent of, or perhaps opposed to, what promotes the goals that most people are pursuing. He may neglect the extent to which the pursuit of the public good, so conceived, compromises the goals of individuals. In the pathological case, such a person sees nothing valuable in the lives of his fellow citizens unless they are co-champions of the same causes.

The failure of liberal philosophers to provide a convincing defense of liberal institutions is the source of another danger. People may come to believe that liberal institutions lack

---

[7] Gordon S. Wood, *The Creation of the American Republic 1776–1787* (Chapel Hill, 1998), 59.
[8] Ibid. 58.

rational foundation. In the nightmare scenario, these institutions wither and die from lack of concern or an unwillingness to defend them. The more likely result is that people will think that there is no better reason to believe in these institutions than the fact that they believe in them. Bruce Ackerman described this attitude as "liberal skepticism."

> [C]an we *know* anything about the good? Sure, all of us have beliefs; but isn't it merely pretentious to proclaim one's *knowledge* on this subject? . . . Rather than welcoming such certainties, they should be taken as a sign that your intellectual arteries are hardening, that you are beginning to mistake your own personal musings for the unheard music of the spheres. The hard truth is this: There is no moral meaning hidden in the bowels of the universe. All there is you and I struggling in a world that neither we, nor any other thing, created.
>
> Yet there is no need to be overwhelmed by the void. We may create our own meanings, you and I; however transient or superficial, they are the only meanings we will ever know. And the first meaningful reality we must create – one presupposed by all other acts of meaningful communication – is the idea that you and I are persons capable of giving meanings to the world.[9]

"Liberal skepticism" is not liberal. It might lead a person to support liberal institutions or it might lead anywhere else. If there is no standard of good and evil except what each of us chooses in an act of self-determination, there is no reason anyone should care about anyone's rights or freedom, unless his own quest for meaning leads him to do so. Nietzsche understood that, as Ackerman recognized. Ackerman observed: "If there is no master design, the challenge is to transcend all talk of good and evil and master the universe. If God is dead, everything is permitted." He then asked, "But are you willing to say this?"[10] He allowed the answer to turn on a person's own act of self-determination.

In the end, according to Ackerman, you must "[e]ither fight for your rights or hand over the understanding that you have, with some effort, gained for yourself. If you choose to fight, your defense, quite literally, is self-defense – for if you surrender your understanding of yourself to the power of another, what do you have left?"[11] Ackerman did not appeal to any genuine truth or goodness but to one's self-understanding. The resort to arms is the only resort, and the combatants are morally and intellectual indistinguishable, except in their own eyes. The result of "liberal skepticism" is that he who opposes evil does so on the worst terrain, relying on brute strength, and having abandoned every intellectual, moral, and spiritual weapon.

---

[9]   Bruce Ackerman, *Social Justice in the Liberal State* (New Haven, 1980), 368.
[10]   Ibid. 369.
[11]   Ibid. 371.

The Encounter with the Abrahamic Religions

Over 1,000 years after Aristotle wrote, great thinkers of the Abrahamic religions tried to integrate his thought with their own traditions. Among Christians, despite initial resistance, much of Aristotelian philosophy was accepted through the efforts of Albertus Magnus (1199–1280) and Thomas Aquinas (1225–74). The influence of Aristotle outlasted the Reformation. Among Jews, Aristotle profoundly influenced Moses ben Maimon (Maimonides, 1138–1204). Despite initial resistance to Aristotelian philosophy, he became recognized as a respected teacher. Yet he did not influence Rabbinic teaching to the extent that Aquinas influenced Christian doctrine. Among Muslims, despite the efforts of Ibn Rushd (Averroes, 1126–98), and despite a tacit use of Greek philosophical ideas, the resistance to Aristotle was never overcome.

Here we will consider why. The reason was not that the ethical teachings of Aristotle were more acceptable to Christians, less acceptable to Jews, and unacceptable to Muslims. The resistance in all three religious traditions concerned the question of what God is like. Those who attacked Aristotle were afraid that his philosophy would lead to belief in an impersonal God who had no more concern for human affairs than a force of nature. That, in fact, was how God was conceived by Ibn Sina (Avicenna, 980–1037), one of the first to bring Aristotle's teaching to the Islamic world. In contrast, Ibn Rushd, Maimonides, and Aquinas believed that God created all things in wisdom and cared for them with love. They also believed that neglect of philosophy, and especially Aristotle, would lead to an anthropomorphic conception of God as very wise, powerful, and good, but in the same way that human beings can be wise, powerful, and good.

As we will see, it mattered that Muslims were the first to consider the religious significance of Aristotelian ideas, followed by Jews and then by Christians. In Islam, those who resisted the assimilation of Aristotle had won the battle before Ibn Rushd wrote. Maimonides wrote before the way in which Aristotle's ideas might be assimilated had been fully worked out. By drawing on the work of Ibn Rushd and Maimonides, Aquinas was able to make his case that Aristotle's work made it possible to understand the God of the Bible better, not to displace him.

The important point, for present purposes, is that this conflict did not concern the value of Aristotle's ethical teachings. But for the religious conflict, they might have played the role in Judaism and Islam that they did in Christianity.

We will see, however, that the history of this conflict has another bearing on the story we have told. Ibn Sina's defense of Aristotle led him to a view close to that of Francesco Suárez, who, as we have seen, was one of the founders of Western rationalism. To refute him, Ibn Sina's chief opponent Abu Hamid al-Ghazali (1058–1111) took an anti-rationalist position close to that of David Hume. Al-Ghazali's position prevailed among Muslims. Aristotelian philosophy was so thoroughly routed that Ibn Rushd's non-rationalist interpretation of Aristotle came too late.

ETHICS

Moslems such as Ibn Rushd, Jews such as Maimonides, and Christians such as Aquinas drew on Aristotle to describe what it means to live righteously and in obedience to God's will. They agreed that such a life required practicing of the moral virtues as Aristotle had explained them.

According to Ibn Rushd, because the end of man is "what God wills," the "intention" of religious laws "as regards this purpose is essentially the same as philosophy." He agreed with those who

> are of the opinion that these religious laws only follow ancient wisdom. It is obvious that Good and Evil, beneficial and harmful, beautiful and ugly are in the opinion of all these men something that exists by nature, not by supposition [or convention[1]]. This means that everything that leads to the end is good and beautiful, whereas everything that impedes it is evil and ugly. This is evident from the nature of these laws and in particular our own law.[2]

Oliver Leaman observed,

> It is very clear what Averroes [Ibn Rushd] wants to say about prophecy and shari'a here, that it provides exactly the same information as philosophy, albeit in a different form. Shari'a does have a decisive superiority, he makes it clear elsewhere[3] in that it is available to a far wider cross-section of the community than is philosophy, yet there is nothing in shari'a which contradicts "ancient wisdom", by which he means Greek thought.[4]

Ibn Rushd explained:

> That the Law calls for consideration of existing things by means of the intellect and for pursuing cognizance of them by means of it is evidence from various verses of the Book of God (may He be blessed and exalted). . . . "Consider you who have sight" [59:2] . . . "Have they not reflected upon the kingdoms of the heavens and the earth and what things God has

---

[1] *Averroes' Commentary on Plato's "Republic,"* Hebrew ed. and English trans., E. I. J. Rosenthal (Cambridge, 1956), 185 n. 6.

[2] Ibid. 185.

[3] Citing Averroes, *Tahafut Al-Tahafut,* Simon van den Bergh trans. (Oxford, 1954), 582.

[4] Oliver Leaman, *Averroes and His Philosophy* (Oxford, 1988), 124.

created?" [7:185] "Do they not reflect upon the camels, how they have been created, and upon the heaven, how it has been raised up?" [88:17]"[5]

Maimonides said, "If you consider most of the commandments . . . you will find that all of them discipline the powers of the soul."[6] Himself a physician, he drew on Aristotle to explain the "diseases of the soul" which, he said, were condemned by scripture. Scripture spoke of "[t]hose who recognize their illness and pursue their pleasures," and said of the sinner, "in the stubbornness of my heart I walk."[7] Solomon spoke of "[t]hose who do not recognize their illness." Maimonides explained the illness of the soul as a deviation from the mean as Aristotle had described it.

> Moderation is the moral habit in the mean between lust and insensibility to pleasure. . . . In like manner, liberality is the mean between miserliness and extravagance; courage is the mean between rashness and cowardice; wit is the mean between buffoonery and dullness; humility is the mean between haughtiness and abasement; generosity is the mean between prodigality and stinginess; contentment is the mean between greed and laziness, gentleness is the mean between irascibility and servility; modesty is the mean between impudence and shyness; and so, too, with the rest of them.[8]

For Maimonides, as knowledge of the truth is the highest object to which the intellectual virtues could attain, the highest object of human life is to know God, who is "the First Being, that caused all beings to be."[9] "This is what the Exalted requires . . . when He says, 'And you shall love the Lord your God with all your heart and with all your soul.'"[10] Higher, then, than "moral perfection, the highest degree of excellency in man's character," "is the true perfection of man; the possession of the highest intellectual facilities; the

---

5   Averroes, *The Book of the Decisive Treatise Determining the Connection between the Law and Wisdom*, trans. Charles E. Butterworth (Provo, 2001), 1–2.

6   Moses Maimonides, *Commentary on the Mishnah, Eight Chapters* chapter 4, in Raymond L. Weiss and Charles E. Butterworth, eds., *Ethical Writings of Maimonides* (New York, 1975).

7   Deut. 29:18.

8   Maimonides, *Eight Chapters* ch. 4. Scholars have argued over whether Maimonides believed in a natural law. Joseph E. David, "Maimonides, Nature and Natural Law," *Journal of Philosophy Law and Culture* 5 (2010), 67 (he did); S. Atlas, "The Philosophy of Maimonides and Its Systematic Place in the History of Philosophy," *Philosophy* 11 (1936), 60 at 73 (he did); Marvin Fox, "Maimonides and Aquinas on Natural Law" *Dinei Israel* 3 (1972), 5 (he did not); Michael P. Levine, "The Role of Reason in the Ethics of Maimonides: Or, Why Maimonides Could Have Had a Doctrine of Natural Law Even if He Did Not," *The Journal of Religious Ethics* 14 (1986), 279 (he could have). The question is misleading. Like Aristotle and unlike Aquinas, he did not use the phrase "natural law." Aquinas, however, gave the phrase an Aristotelian meaning, defining it in terms of the rational principle that governed the virtues according to both Aristotle and Maimonides.

   According to Marvin Fox, Maimonides "could not affirm a theory of natural law" because he believed that "moral precepts . . . are not capable of demonstration." Marvin Fox, *Interpreting Maimonides* (Chicago, 1990), 133, 141. Jonathan Jacobs objected that for Maimonides, as for Aristotle, "moral requirements are rationally grounded even if not demonstrable." Jonathan Jacobs, "Aristotle and Maimonides on Virtue and Natural Law," *Hebraic Political Studies* 2 (2007), 46 at 62. Aristotle, unlike the rationalists, believed that the conclusions of practical reason are not demonstrable like the conclusions of theoretical reason.

   For the argument that Jewish law is not only compatible with but requires a belief in natural law, see David Novak, *Natural Law in Judaism* (New York, 1998).

9   Moses Maimonides, *Mishnah Torah*, Simon Glaser, trans. (New York, 1927), Book One I.i.

10   Deut. 6:5; *Eight Chapters* chapter 5.

possession of such notions which lead to true metaphysical opinions as regards God."[11] "The prophets have likewise explained unto us these things, and have expressed the same opinion on them as the philosophers. They say distinctly ... that the knowledge of God, i.e., true wisdom, is the only perfection ... in which we should glorify ourselves."[12] That is the ultimate end in life, even though, Maimonides said, the human intellect was limited, and so one could never know God as He truly is. Not even Moses did so, although Moses was allowed to come close; God said, "And thou shalt see My back; but My face shall not be seen."[13]

For Aquinas, the ultimate end of a human being was to be united with God. The human intellect was limited, and so, in this world, one could never know God as He truly is. St. Paul said that here we see as through a glass darkly, but in the next world we will see as face to face (1 Cor. 13:12). We come to the next world only by grace, but, Aquinas said, grace perfects nature. As we have seen, he explained natural law in Aristotelian terms. According to Aquinas, "[a]ll the inclinations of any parts whatsoever of human nature ... in so far as they are ruled by reason belong to the natural law."[14] "Law is a dictate of practical reason."[15] Because God created man, and because God's "grace perfects nature" but does not destroy it, to follow the natural law is to follow the divine will.

As we have seen, Aquinas' account of natural law remained a staple of the Aristotelian tradition among Protestants. A similar account was given by Arminians such as Hugo Grotius; by Anglicans such as Richard Hooker; by Lutherans such as Johann Baier (1647–95), Johannes Olearius (1639–1713), Johann Heinrich May (1653–1719), and Johann Georg Dorsche (1597–1659); by Calvinists such as Iohann Andreas van der Meulen; and by Puritans such as William Ames (1635–1702).[16] Conscience was explained in the same way as by Aquinas, as a natural ability to apprehend what is good, by Anglicans such as Robert Burton (1557–1640), Richard Carpenter (1575–1627), Robert Sanderson (1587–1663), by Lutherans such as Friedrich Balduin (1575–1627) and Johannes Olearius (1639–1713), and, again, by

---

[11] Moses Maimonides, *The Guide for the Perplexed*, trans. M. Friedländer (2nd ed., New York, 1956), III.lii 394–95. For Maimonides, then, the moral virtues and the intellectual virtue of theoretical reason were paths to God. It is striking, and, indeed, a "cause for wonder," as Raymond Weiss observed, that in the *Eight Chapters* "practical reason is not identified as a virtue." Raymond L. Weiss, *Maimonides' Ethics: The Encounter of Philosophic and Religious Morality* (Chicago, 1991), 76–77.

[12] Maimonides, *Guide for the Perplexed* III.lii 396.

[13] Ex. 33:23. Maimonides, *Mishnah Torah*, Book One I.x.

[14] Ibid. I-II, Q. 94 a. 2 ad 2.

[15] Ibid. I-II, Q. 91, a. 3, citing Q. 90, a. 1 ad 2.

[16] Iohannes Guilielmus Baierus, *Compendium theologiae positivae, adiectis notis amplioribus quibu doctrina orthodoxa ad ΠΑΙΔΕΙΑΝ Academicam explicatur* (Lipsiae, 1750 (1st ed. 1593) II.i.4; Johannes Olearius, *Introductio brevis in theologiam casisticam, usibus studiosum Lipsiensium consecrate* (Leipzig, 1694#), cap. viii, sec. 9; Johannes Henricus Majus, *Praxi pietatis in cognition veritatis sive synopsis theologiae moralis* (Giessen, 1697), Locus XI, §4; Iohann Andreas van der Meulen, *Forum conscientiae seu ius poli, hoc est tractatus theologico juridicus* (Utrecht, 1693), *Dissertatio praeliminaris* I p. 19; Johann Georg Dorsche, *Theologia moralis ex manuscriptis edita*, ed. J. F. Mayer (Wittenberg, 1685); Disp. 1, cap. 1,§§ 3–5; Guilielmus Amesius, *Conscientia et eius iure vel casibus libri quinque* (ed. nov. Amsterdam 1630), lib. 1, ch. 1, § 11.

Calvinists such as Iohann Andreas van der Meulen and by Puritans such as William Ames.[17]

Martin Luther said that salvation must come by faith alone and not by works since after the Fall of Man, through the sin of Adam, human beings were radically depraved. Yet St. Paul had taught that all people had a law inscribed on their hearts. Lutherans such as Baier and May concluded that after the Fall, sufficient "vestiges"[18] or "relics"[19] of this law remained to guide the conscience and make possible the study of moral theology. Calvinists such as van der Meulen and Wilhelm Zepper (1550–1607) thought that this law had been obscured but not obliterated.[20] Girolamo Zanchi (1516–90) also a Calvinist, believed that "[a]fter the Fall ... natural law was almost entirely blotted out [and [p]eople became completely blind in their minds, totally depraved in their hearts, and altogether corrupted." Afterward, however, the natural law "had been inscribed and impressed on our hearts anew by God because of his goodness."[21]

In all three religious traditions, Aristotelian philosophy initially aroused suspicion. Stephen Tempier, the Bishop of Paris, condemned what he believed to be a series of Aristotelian principles in 1277. Still earlier, the Jewish scholar Judah Hallevi (1075–1141) had raised objections like those of Tempier in an imaginary dialog between a rabbi and the king of the Khazars. Still earlier, similar objections were raised by al-Ghazali.

Their attacks on Aristotelian philosophy were not directed against his ethical principles or their implications for law. The Condemnation of Paris did not mention them. Judah Hallevi acknowledged that "the social and rational laws are those generally known" without divine revelation. For example, "[w]e know that the giving of comfort and the feeling of gratitude are as incumbent on us as is chastening of the soul by means of fasting and meekness; we also know that deceit, immoderate intercourse with women, and cohabitation with relatives are abominable; that honoring parents is a duty, etc." Divine law makes these laws better known by clarifying their "scope." "The limitation of all these things to the amount of general usefulness is God's. Human reason is out of place in matters of divine action."[22] It is hard to see, however, why it would be out of place for reason to

[17] Richard Carpenter, *The Conscionable Christian: or, the indevour of Saint Paul to have an discharge a good conscience always towards God and men* (London, 1623), preface, "To the Reader," 2; Robert Sanderson, *De obligatione conscientiae praelectiones decem: Oxonii in schola theologica habitae anno dom. MDCXLVII* (London, 1686), *Praelectiones* I.xxxiv–xxxvi, IV.xiv; Friedrich Balduin, *Tractatus de casibus conscientiae* (Wittenberg, 1628), lib. I, cap. iii; Johannes Olearius, *Introductio brevis in theologiam casisticam, usibus studiosum Lipsiensium consecrate* (Leipzig, 1694), cap. viii.9–10; van der Meulen, *Forum conscientiae Dissertatio praeliminaris* I, pp. 3, 7, 9; Amesius, *Conscientia* lib. I, ch. i, 1–3; ch. ii, 2–5.

[18] Baierus, *Compendium theologiae positivae* II.i.5.

[19] Majus, *Praxi pietatis Locus* XI, sec. 4.

[20] Van der Meulen, *Forum conscientiae, Dissertatio praeliminaris* I, p. 19; Wilhelm Zepper, *Legum Mosaicarum forensium explanatio* (Herborn, 1604), Lib. 1, cap. 1.

[21] Girolamo Zanchi, *Operum theologicorum De primi hominis lapsu, de peccato, et de lege Dei* 4 (Geneva, 1617), trans. Jeffrey J. Veenstra, *On the Law in General* (Grand Rapids, 2012), X.ii thesis 8, pp. 11–12, 14.

[22] Judah Hallevi, *Kitab al Khazari*, trans. Hartwig Hirschfeld (New York, 1905), III.7, pp. 141–42.

examine the nature and end of the social and rational laws, as Maimonides tried to do.

Al-Ghazali repeated the teaching of "the philosophers" that

> The rational soul has two faculties: the theoretical, and the practical. Each one of these is called Reason, but this is so because the name is common to them. The practical faculty is the motive principle of the human body, urging to those activities that are marked by coordination, and whose coordination is derived from the deliberation characteristic of man.[23]

When al-Ghazali wrote about human happiness, according to Vincent Cornell, his "debt to Plato is clearly revealed."[24] In *The Alchemy of Happiness,*

> he states that the human self consists of three parts: spirit or ego (Arabic *tiafs*), life or vital force (Persian *fin*), and heart or inner soul (Persian *dil*). Although the vital force connects the soul to the body, for Ghazâlî, the soul is never truly embodied: "The true nature of the soul is not of this world. It has come to this world as a stranger and a wayfarer."[25]

The heart or soul must rule over appetite and anger through reason.[26]

In his writing on ethics, al-Ghazali "draws from Aristotle's *Nicomachean Ethics*,"[27] and his image of human nature is more Aristotelian. As Frank Griffel observed, "[a]t no point does al-Ghazâlî reveal the philosophical origins of his ethics." Yet, he noted, it depends on an Aristotelian account of virtue.

> [O]nly strict efforts and patient treatment can lead ... towards developing virtuous character traits.[28] The human soul ... needs to undergo constant disciplining (*riyâda*) and training (*tarbiya*) in order to keep these character traits at equilibrium. Behind this kind of ethics stands the Aristotelian notion of *entelechy*: humans have a natural potential to develop rationality and through it acquire virtuous character. ... As a result al-Ghazâlî rejected the notion, for instance, that one should try to give up potentially harmful affections like anger or sexual desire. These character traits are part of human nature, al-Ghazâlî teaches, and cannot be given up. Rather, disciplining the soul means controlling these potentially harmful traits through one's rationality (*'aql*).[29]

23 Al-Ghazali, *Thafut Al-Falsifah*, Sabih Ahmad Kamali, (Lahore, 1963), pblm. xviii, p. 199.
24 Vincent J. Cornell, "Applying the Lessons: Ideals Versus Realities of Happiness from Medieval Islam to the 'Founding Fathers,'" *Journal of Law and Religion* 29 (2014), 92 at 99.
25 Ibid. 99, quoting Abu Hamid Muhammad Ghazzätl (sic) Tösl, *The Alchemy of Happiness (Kimiyä-yi Sa'ädat)*, trans. Jay R. Crook (2nd ed. 2005, repr. Chicago, 2008), 1: 9, 6.
26 Cornell, "Applying the Lessons" 100. On the debt to Plato and Neo-Platonism, see Nicholas White, *A Brief History of Happiness* (Walden, 2006), 81–88; Taneli Kukkonen, Al-Ghazālī on the Origins of Ethics, *Numen* 63 (2016), 271 at 279–80.
27 Cornell, "Applying the Lessons" 101.
28 Citing al-Ghazali, *Ihyâ' 'ulûm al-dîn* (Cairo, 1937–38), (repr. Beirut, n.d.), book 28.
29 Frank Griffel, "al-Ghazali,"*The Stanford Encyclopedia of Philosophy* (Summer 2020), Edward N. Zalta (ed.), https://plato.stanford.edu/archives/sum2020/entries/al-ghazali.

GOD

The objections were not to Aristotle's ethics but to his metaphysics and what they believed it implied about God and God's relationship to creation. Among the propositions condemned at Paris were:

> That God cannot know contingent beings immediately except through their particular and proximate causes.
> That the world is eternal because that which has a nature by which it is able to exist for the whole future has a nature by which it was able to exist in the whole past.
> That God of necessity makes whatever comes immediately from Him.[30]

These were not the only objections. But they were among the most important.

The same objections appear in the opening paragraph of Judah Hallevi's imaginary dialog. The King of Khazar consults a "philosopher" who expounds what Hallevi took to be the principles of Aristotelian philosophy.

> When the King of Khazar ... dreamt that his way of thinking was agreeable to God, but not his way of acting, and was commanded in the same dream to seek the God-pleasing work, he inquired of a philosopher concerning his religious persuasion. The philosopher replied: There is no favour or dislike in [the nature of] God, because He is above desire and intention. A desire intimates a want in the person who feels it, and not till it is satisfied does he become (so to speak) complete. If it remains unfulfilled, he lacks completion. In a similar way He is, in the opinion of philosophers, above the knowledge of individuals, because the latter change with the times, whilst there is no change in God's knowledge. He, therefore, does not know thee, much less thy thoughts and actions, nor does He listen to thy prayers, or see thy movements. If philosophers say that He created thee, they only use a metaphor, because He is the Cause of causes in the creation of all creatures, but not because this was His intention from the beginning. He never created man. For the world is without beginning, ... Everything is reduced to a Prime Cause; not to a Will proceeding from this, but an Emanation from which emanated a second, a third, and fourth cause.[31]

Similarly, al-Ghazali charged that, according to the philosophers, God has no knowledge of particular things, or, at least that "only that he knows the particulars in a universal manner!"[32] "The philosophers believe that the world is eternal."[33] "According to the philosophers, God has not will. ... Whatever proceeds from him is a necessary consequence."[34]

If this is what "the philosophers" believed, it is no wonder that learned and pious men such as Stephan Tempier, Judah Hallevi, and al-Ghazali condemned them for rejecting the God of Abraham, the maker of heaven and earth, who shepherds his people and cares for each. He is not, as Hallevi's "philosopher" claimed, a God "above desire and intention,"

---

[30] *The Condemnation of 1277* arts. 14, 84, 20, http://faculty.fordham.edu/klima/Blackwell-proofs/MP_C22.pdf.
[31] Hallevi, *Kitab al Khazari* I.1, pp. 35–36.
[32] Al-Ghazali, *Thafut Al-Falsifah*, pblm. xiii, p. 153.
[33] Ibid. iv, p. 89; pblm. iii, p. 63.
[34] Ibid. pblm. iii, p. 63.

"who does not know thee, much less thy thoughts and actions, nor . . . listen to thy prayers." And it is not a metaphor to say, "He created thee."[35]

According to Ibn Rushd, Maimonides, and Aquinas, none of the offending propositions were true.[36] Aristotle had not believed them, or else he had not demonstrated them. God did know particular things. The mistake was to imagine that to do so, he must know them the way we do – one thing at a time – whereas he knows them all at once, and not through their effects but because he is their cause.[37] Aquinas said, "Even the Philosopher [Aristotle] considers it incongruous that anything known by us should be unknown to God."[38]

Aristotle had thought that the world was eternal, but, according to Ibn Rushd, Maimonides, and Aquinas, he had never proved that it is. God is free to create the world eternally or at a moment of time, as he chooses. In either case, the world is completely dependent on God for its continued existence.[39]

God made the world, they maintained, not by necessity, but by free choice. According to Ibn Rushd, "God's act proceeds from Him through knowledge, not through any necessity which calls for it, either in His essence or outside His essence, but through His grace and His bounty. He is necessarily endowed with will and choice in their highest form, since the insufficiency which is proper to the empirical willer does not pertain to Him."[40] Maimonides said, "We, however, hold that all things in the Universe are the result of

---

[35] Howard Kreisel, *Judaism as Philosophy: Studies in Maimonides and the Medieval Jewish Philosophers of Provence* (Boston, 2015), 3 at 3–4.

[36] Here, it is important to distinguish Averroes' own positions from those with which his name became associated in the Middle Ages.

In the Middle Ages, the following five statements were considered characteristic of this philosophy [Averroism]: (1) The world is eternal; (2) God does not know particulars and there is no Providence; (3) There is no free will; (4) The possible intellect is one numerically, as is the active intellect; hence there is no individual immorality nor individual moral responsibility; (5) Philosophy and theology are contradictory to one another and the supernatural must be rejected.

Dominique Urvoy, *Ibn Rushd (Averroes)* (London, 1991), 101. As noted in the text, he did not hold the first three positions. As to the fourth, he said that "it must be admitted that the soul is immortal, as is proved by rational and religious proofs, and it must be assumed that what arises from the dead is simulacra of these earthly bodies, not these bodies themselves, for that which has perished does not return individually." Averroes, *Tahafut Al-Tahafut*, trans. Simon van den Bergh 1 (Oxford, 1954)[stars indicate the page numbers in *Tahafut al Tahafut*, Fr. Bouyges ed., 3 *Biblioteca Arabica Scholasticorum* (Beyrouth, 1930)] *587–86, p. 362. As to the fifth, he said that "any knowledge which the weakness of the human mind is unable to grasp is bestowed on man by God through revelation." Ibid. *255, p. 152.

[37] Averroes, *The Book of the Decisive Treatise Determining the Connection between the Law and Wisdom*, trans. Charles E. Butterworth (Provo, 2001), 13; Moses Maimonides, *The Guide for the Perplexed*, trans. M. Friedländer (2nd ed., New York, 1956), III.xx, p. 292; III.xxi, p. 295; Aquinas, *Summa theologiae* I, Q. 14, a. 11.

[38] Aquinas, *Summa theologiae* I, Q. 14, a. 11.

[39] Averroes, *Tahafut Al-Tahafut* *264, p. 156; Averroes, *Tahafut Al-Tahafut* 1st discussion, *22–23, p. 12; Maimonides, *Guide for the Perplexed* II.xiii, p. 171; II.xv, p. 176. Aquinas, *Summa theologiae* I, Q. 46, a. 1.

[40] Averroes, *Tahafut Al-Tahafut* 1st discussion, *22–23, p. 12. Consequently, it is surprising that Etienne Gilson said of Averroes, "One could hardly wish for a world better made to suit the taste of abstract conceptual thinking. . . . Perfect proof against newness, it remains eternally such as it is." Étienne Gilson, *Being and Some Philosophers* (Toronto, 1952), 59. Such a world, as we will see, more closely resembles that of Avicenna, whom he congratulates for taking a step in the other direction by distinguishing existence and essence.

design, and not merely of necessity; He who designed them may change them when He changes His design."[41] He wrote of the passage, "I am the Lord which exercise loving-kindness, judgment, and righteousness in the earth" (Jeremiah 9:24):

> Another very important lesson is taught by the additional phrase, "in the earth." It implies a fundamental principle of the Law; it rejects the theory of those who boldly assert that God's providence does not extend below the sphere of the moon, and that the earth with its contents is abandoned . . . It teaches, as has been taught by the greatest of all wise men in the words, "The earth is the Lord's" (Exod. ix.29), and that His providence extends to the earth in accordance with its nature, and in the same manner as it controls the heavens in accordance with their nature.[42]

Aquinas agreed.[43]

The pious men who attacked the teachings of Aristotle feared that his philosophy would lead to belief in an impersonal God unconcerned with human affairs. The pious men who defended Aristotle's teachings feared that neglect of his philosophy would lead to an anthropomorphic conception of a God who was wise, powerful, and good but in the same way as a human being. For Maimonides, to believe that God has a physical body is "worse than the worship of idols."[44] Moreover,

> in the same way as all people must be informed, and even children must be trained to believe, that God is One, and that none besides Him must be worshipped, so must all be taught by simple authority that God is incorporeal; that there is no similarity in any way between Him and His creatures; that his existence is not like the existence of His creatures, His life is not like that of any living beings, His wisdom is not like the wisdom of the wisest of men; and that difference between Him and His creatures is not merely quantitative but absolute.[45]

One reason that the Christian West was more receptive to Aquinas' answers to these objections was that he wrote after Maimonides and Ibn Rushd, indeed, after Aristotle's *Ethics, Politics, Physics,* and *Metaphysics* made their way into Europe in the late twelfth and early thirteenth centuries. He could draw on the works of Maimonides and Ibn Rushd which were thoroughly familiar to him and well known in the West.[46] The Islamic world was not receptive because Ibn Rushd wrote too late. A decisive battle over Aristotelian philosophy had already been fought between al-Ghazali and Ibn Sina. In the view of most pious Muslims, al-Ghazli won. F. E. Peters noted,

> When a Muslim author uses the term *falsafah* [philosophy], he may mean either of two things: in its earliest acceptation it refers to the Greek and Roman thinkers and the

---

[41] Maimonides, *Guide for the Perplexed* II.xix, p. 184.
[42] Ibid. III.lii, p. 397.
[43] *Summa theologiae* I, Q. 22, a. 1.
[44] Maimonides, *Guide for the Perplexed* I.xxxvi, p. 52.
[45] Ibid. I.xxxv, p. 49.
[46] On Maimonides' influence, see Atlas, "Philosophy of Maimonides" 70–71.

systems they erected. After al-Ghazali, however, use of the word has marked a polemical tone; *falsafah* refers to a rationalism which opposes the epistemological basis of *kalam*: it means, finally, Ibn Sina.[47]

As for Ibn Rushd, as Leaman observed,

> on one occasion [he] was actually driven from the mosque in Cordoba by an angry crowd of worshippers. Indeed, his reputation within the Islamic community did not remain high after his death, and there is little evidence that he influenced the development of thought within Islam until quite recently. He had a far more successful afterlife among the Jewish and Christian communities in the medieval world, and a widespread effect upon the Christian world.[48]

Ibn Sina's interpretation of Aristotle had the very features that troubled pious Muslims, Jews, and Christians. They were the features that Ibn Rushd, Maimonides, and Aquinas denied were true implications of Aristotle's philosophy.

IBN SINA AMD AL GHAZALI

According to Ibn Sina, God "knows all things by virtue of one knowledge, in a manner which changes not according to the change in the thing known. ... His knowledge of genera, species, things with being, contingent things ... is a single knowledge."[49] But what of his knowledge of particular things?

> Particular things may be known as universal things are known, i.e., in as much as they are necessitated by their causes, as they are attributed to a principle whose species is individuated in its particulars. This is exemplified by the particular eclipse; for the occurrence of such an eclipse may be known due to the availability of its particular causes, the intellect's complete understanding of these causes, and their being known as universals are known. This is other than the temporal particular realization that judges that such an eclipse occurs now, that it occurred before, or that it will occur later.[50]

But knowing what causes eclipses to occur is not the same as knowing a particular eclipse. Al-Ghazali objected:

> Ibn Sīna assert[s] that [God] knows things by a universal knowledge which does not fall under Time, and which does not change through the Past, the Present and the Future. And in spite of this, it is asserted by Ibn Sīna ... that "nothing – not even as much as a particle of dust, in the heavens, or on the earth – is hidden from his knowledge" – only that he knows the particulars in a universal manner![51]

47 Peters, *Aristotle and the Arabs* 156.
48 Leaman, *Averroes and his Philosophy* 4–5.
49 Avicenna, *Al-Risālt al-'Arishīya*, trans. Arthur J. Arberry, in Arthur J. Arberry,*Avicenna on Theology* (London, 1951), 35.
50 Ibn Sina, *Remarks and Admonitions: Physics and Metaphysics*, trans. Shams C. Inati (New York, 2014), III.vii ch. 18.
51 Al-Ghazali, *Thafut Al-Falsifah*, pblm. xiii, p. 153.

Ibn Sina said that the world is eternal – not that it might or might not be – with the caveat that it is dependent for its continued existence on God.[52] But God did not choose to create the world. All things proceeded from God necessarily and in a necessary order.

> [God's] First Act is one. For if there had emanated from him two acts, the emanation would have been in two different manners, for duality in the act implies duality in the agent. . . . Therefore all things having being emanated from him according to a known order and known media: that which came later cannot be earlier, and that which came earlier cannot be later, for it is He Who causes things to be earlier and later. Indeed, the first thing having being that emanated from his was the noblest; thereafter came a descent from the nobler to the lower, until the lowliest of all was reached. First was Intelligence; then Soul; then the Body of Heaven; then the materials of the four Elements with their forms.[53]

Aristotle had described a great chain of being stretching from the highest to the lowest beings. In suggesting that the lower proceed by necessity from the higher, Ibn Sina was following not Aristotle himself, but neo-Platonic commentators on Aristotle who had read this idea into his works. Ibn Rushd said:

> The fundamental mistake of Avicenna [Ibn Sina] . . . was that [he] made the statement that from the one only one can proceed, and then assumed a plurality in the one which proceeds. Therefore [he was] forced to regard this plurality as uncaused. And [his] assumption that this plurality was a definite plurality which demanded the introduction of a third and fourth principle was a supposition not enforced by any proof.[54]

Ibn Sina's philosophy was also remarkable because it prefigured a philosophical movement in the West centuries later, which, as we have seen, led to the distortion and ultimately to the discrediting of the Aristotelian tradition: the rise of rationalism.

Like the rationalists, Ibn Sina believed that concepts, principles, or ideas have a manner of being of their own, independent of whether they exist in the world around us or in our minds. In this respect, Avicenna's philosophy was less like that of Aristotle, or for that matter, of Averroes, Maimonides or Aquinas, than like that of Francisco Suárez in the seventeenth century which, as we have seen, gave rise to the rationalism that dominated the eighteenth. For Aristotle, a human being, a tree or a triangle exists in the external world in which we live, or it exists in our mind when we think of a human being, a tree or a triangle. When we do so, we form a concept that corresponds to what a thing is, to its "essence" or "quiddity." For Ibn Sina, the essence or quiddity of a thing exists before the thing exists either in the external world or the mind.[55] A thing first has a "possible existence." "Whatever begins to exist must have had a possible existence before existing." When it actually comes to exist, "the

---

52 Ibn Sina, *Remarks and Admonitions* III.v, ch. 1 132.
53 Avicenna, *Al-Risālt al-'Arishīya* 35–36.
54 Averroes, *Tahafut Al-Tahafut* *250, p. 148.
55 That is so for possible being but not for things in the world around us. "Ibn Sina points out that matter cannot be free from an essential form, that the former needs the latter to be actual, and that essential forms do not exist separately from matter." Erwin Tegtmeier, "Ibn Sina on Substances and Accidents," in Christian Kanzian and Muhammad Legenhausen, eds., *Western and Islamic Traditions in Dialogue* (Frankfurt, 2007), 229 at 230.

possibility of its existence is realized."[56] A thing which possibly exists thus has "reality" even if it does not otherwise exist. It can be defined without regard to whether it otherwise exists. Ibn Sina said,

> A thing may be caused in relation to its quiddity or it may be caused in its existence. You can consider this in the triangle, for example. The reality of the triangle depends on the surface and the line which is its sides. Both the surface and the line constitute the triangle inasmuch as it is a triangle and has a reality of triangularity ... But inasmuch as the triangle exists, it may also depend on a cause other than these which is not a cause that constitutes its triangularity and is not a part of its definition.[57]

One can know what a thing is without knowing whether it exists. "You must know that you understand the concept of triangle while in doubt as to whether or not concrete existence is attributed to the triangle. This is after triangle is represented to you as constituted of a line and a surface and is not represented to you as existing."[58]

Ibn Sina had taken the first steps toward conceiving of the world as a place where nothing is ever new. All things that ever are or could be, have always been, not in the world around us, but as possible existences with a reality of their own. One can know the definitions or principles or properties of these things without knowing whether they exist in any other way or not. That knowledge is immutable. We have seen how this path was not only followed by the European rationalists but by the Chinese founders of the School of Principle who claimed it was the true interpretation of Confucianism.

A remarkable feature of al-Ghazali's attack on Ibn Sina was that it paralleled David Hume's attack on rationalism centuries later. Like Hume, al-Ghazali pointed out how far removed such a world of concepts lay from our world of sensation and change. If all one knew was the concepts of two things, and their logical implications, one could not understand change. Al-Ghazali said:

> In our view, the connection between what are believed to be cause and effect is not necessary. Take any two things. This is not That; nor can That be This. The affirmation of one does not imply the affirmation of the other; not does its denial imply the denial of the other. The existence of the one is not necessitated by the existence of the other; nor its nonexistence by the non-existence of the other.[59]

If we touch fire to cotton, we observe "blackness in cotton; ... the disintegration of its parts, and ... their transformation into a smouldering heap of ashes." That observation does not prove that the fire caused the burning of the cotton. "The only argument is from the observation of the fact of burning at the time of contact with fire. But observation only shows that one is *with* the other, not that it is by it and has no other cause than it." Al-Ghazali concluded, as Hume was to do, that no matter how frequently one observed the phenomena, one can only conclude that the one occurs with the other, not that it causes

[56] Ibn Sina, *Remarks and Admonitions* III.v, ch. 6.
[57] Ibid. III.iv. ch. 5, p. 121.
[58] Ibid. III.iv ch. 6, p. 121.
[59] Al-Ghazali, *Thafut Al-Falsifah*, Sabih Ahmad Kamali, ed. (Lahore, 1963), pblm. xvii, p. 185.

the other.[60] Hume said that was the limit of our knowledge. Al-Ghazali said, "We say that it is God who – through the intermediary of angels or directly – is the agent" of the transformation.[61]

According to Ibn Rushd, Ibn Sina and al-Ghazali misunderstood the relationship of our concepts to the world around us. Things have ends or "special functions," and it is through these special functions that we know their essences and properties.[62] Take away causation and we would have no knowledge of what any thing is.

> It is self-evident that things have essences and attributes which determine the special functions of each thing and through which the essences and names of things are differentiated. If a thing had not its specific nature, it would not have a special name and definition, and all things would be one – indeed, not even one ... for it had not special act, then the one would not be one.[63]
>
> Now intelligence is nothing but the perception of things with their causes ... and he who denies causes must deny the intellect. Logic implies the existence of causes and effects, and knowledge of these effects can only be rendered perfect by knowledge of their causes.

---

[60] Simon van den Bergh, "Introduction" to Averroes, *Tahafut Al-Tahafut* xxv; Stephen Riker, "Al-Ghazali on Necessary Causality in 'The Incoherence of the Philosophers'" *The Monist* 79 (1966) 315 at 315. Edward Moad objected that while "Stephen Riker, among others" claim that Hume denied "necessary causation," "as George Giacaman and Raja Bahlul point out, while for Hume this constitutes a wholesale denial of any meaningful concept of causation whatsoever, over and above the mere constant conjunction of impressions, al-Ghazali has in mind nothing of the sort." Edward Omar Moad, "Al-Ghazali on Power, Causation, and 'Acquisition,'" *Philosophy East and West* 57 (2007), 1 at 1–2. Nevertheless, Giacaman and Bahlul agreed that Hume's "views on causation bear a striking resemblance to those of Ghazali." George Giacaman and Raja Bahlul, "Ghazali on Miracles and Necessary Connection," *Medieval Philosophy and Theology* 9 (2000), 39 at 42. The difference, they said, is that "unlike Hume, Ghazali's intent is not primarily the analysis of the meaning of causation. Ghazali's concern is to guard against compromising divine omnipotence." Ibid. As Lenn Goodman noted, "It's natural to compare Ghazzali's critique of causality with Hume. But for al-Ghazali the 'locus' of the regularities between events that we experience is God." Lenn E. Goodman, "Ghazzali and the Philosophers: The Defence of Causality," in Ali Paya, ed., The Misty Land of Ideas and the Light of Dialogue: An Anthology of Contemporary Philosophy: Western and Islamic (London, 2013), 77.

[61] Al-Ghazali, *Thafut Al-Falsifah*, pblm. xvii, p. 186. In such passage, al-Ghazali clearly accepted some form of "occasionalism" – the belief that God intervenes when one event seems to be the cause of another. Lenn Goodman and Ilai Aron claim that his version was less strict than that of the Ash'arite school. Lenn E. Goodman, "Did Al-Ghazali Deny Causality?" *Studia Islamica* 47 (1978) 95; Ilai Alon, "Al-Ghazali on Causality," *Journal of the American Oriental Society* 100 (1980), 397. According to Michael Marmura, the passages they cite merely grant certain premises for the sake of argument. Michael Marmura, "Al-Ghazali's Second Causal Theory in the 17th Discussion of his Tahafut," in Parviz Morewedge, ed., *Islamic Philosophy and Mysticism* (New York, 1981), 85 at 98–99. For an evaluation, see Riker, "Al-Ghazali on Necessary Causality" 321–22.

[62] Frank Griffel, unlike Averroes, thought that al-Ghazali might have believed that things with essences and properties exist despite what he said about causation. By this interpretation, al-Ghazali believed that although the essence of a thing may be the same in one possible world, its causal efficacy may be different than in another. Fire burns cotton in this world, but in another possible world it does not. Frank Griffel, *Al-Ghazali's Philosophical Theology* (Oxford, 2009), 150. According to Michael Marmura, al-Ghazali mentioned that hypothesis but only for the purposes of argument. Michael Marmura, "Introduction" to Al-Ghazali, *The Incoherence of the Philosophers*, trans. Michael Marmura (Provo, 2000), xxv. In any event, that interpretation would be equally fatal for an Aristotelian or for that matter a Neo-Platonic theory of essences. To imagine a world in which fire does not burn is like imagining one in which fire is not hot. It would no longer have the essence of fire.

[63] Averroes, *Tahafut Al-Tahafut* *520, p. 318.

Denial of cause implies the denial of knowledge, and denial of knowledge implies that nothing in this world can really be known, and that what is supposed to be known is nothing but opinion, that neither proof nor definition exist, and that the essential attributes which compose definitions are void. The man who denies the necessity of any item of knowledge must admit that even this, his own affirmation, is not necessary knowledge.[64]

If you imagine that nothing in the world causes anything, you have denied the existence of things, for they would not be things if they did not have special functions. Consequently, you have denied the possibility of knowledge. If "we suppose [God] to rule existents like a tyrannical prince who has the highest power, for whom nobody in his dominion can deputize" then "there would no longer, even for the twinkling of an eye, be any permanent knowledge of anything."[65]

According to Ibn Rushd, the fundamental mistake was that "Ghazali based his discussion on the doctrine of Avicenna [Ibn Sina], and this is a false doctrine, for Avicenna believed that existence is something additional to the essence outside the soul and is like an accident of the essence."[66] By this doctrine, the essence of a thing such as a human being, a tree or a triangle has a possible existence and comes into our world if and when one additional characteristic, so to speak, is added on: existence. But essences or concepts or quiddities do not exist except outside the mind in entities that already exist, and in the mind, in which case they are true if they correspond to such entities.[67]

The appeal of this rationalist idea to Ibn Sina may have been like the appeal of the neo-Platonist idea that the world was the result, not of chance, not of choice, but of causes that operate by necessity to produce a necessary order. Once chance and choice are banished, everything can be understood. At one point, Ibn Sina suggested that the coming of the prophet Muhammed was the last logical step in the inevitable course of human history.

Now it is well known that man differs from all other animals in that he cannot enjoy a good life in isolation and alone, managing his affairs without any partner to assist him in fulfillment of his needs. . . . This being so, it is necessary for men both to associate with each other, and to behave like citizens. This is obvious; it follows that it is necessary to the life and survival of mankind that there should be co-operation between them, which can only be realized through a common transaction of business; in addition to all the other means which secure the same purpose. This transaction requires a code of law and just regulation, which in their turn call for a lawgiver and regulator. Such a man must be in a position to speak to men, and to constrain them to accept the code; he must therefore be a man. . . . It follows that there should exist a prophet, and that he should be a man; it also follows that he should have some distinguishing feature which does not belong to other men, so that his fellows may recognize him as possessing something which is not theirs, and so that he may stand out apart from them. This distinguishing feature is the power to work miracles. The fundamental principle upon which his code rests will be to teach them that

---

[64]   Ibid. *522, p. 319.
[65]   Ibid. *531, p. 531.
[66]   Ibid. *303, p. 179.
[67]   Ibid. *303–05, pp. 179–80.

they have One Creator, Almighty and Omniscient, Whose commandments must of right be obeyed.[68]

This position was unacceptable to a pious Muslim such as al-Ghazali for whom Mohammed was a prophet specially chosen and beloved by God.

Al-Ghazali's arguments, however, were like those of Hume although, for al-Ghazli, doubts about the power of nature and reason confirmed the omnipotence of God. There is only one cause: His inscrutable will. If that is so, Michael Sweeney wrote, only the norms God has revealed would be worthy of respect, or, indeed, tolerance:

> Whether Islamic reflection on revealed law can accept the Greek notion of essence is central to this debate and to the question of tolerance; indeed, the various positions taken with regard to essence determine the nature and limits of political tolerance.[69]
>
> For Al-Ghazali ... there can be no such essential or natural metaphysical limits, since there are no created limits to the divine will, but the Qur'an is a supraessential limit that guides human knowledge and action. It follows that the only epistemological limits that could ground tolerance are ignorance of the Qur'an and the degree of tolerance mandated by the Qur'an itself.[70]

Sweeny is right about the approach to moral norms that would be consistent with al-Ghazali's metaphysics. He would have grounded them in divine will alone and not in human nature. As we have seen, however, his discussion of happiness rested on a Platonic account of the soul and his discussion of ethics on an Aristotelian account of virtue. He does say that law is based only on divine will. That, indeed, was the view of the Ash'arite school of Islamic law to which he belonged. It has been called "scriptural positivism." As Anvers Emon said,

> The dominant Positivist thesis, as expressed in premodern *usul al-fiqh* or legal theory, holds that where there is no scripture on a matter, one is left in a state of legal suspension (*tawaqquf*); there is no epistemically coherent way to determine the divine law on that matter, and consequently no one is in a sufficient epistemic position to attribute to God a ruling of any nonnative force. Fundamentally, this position enshrines within Islamic law a strict scriptural positivism. Jurists argued that all determinations of God's law must find expression, either directly or indirectly, from scripture. Extrascriptural indices, whether in the form of rational proofs or references to nature, do not provide a proper basis or foundation for asserting the divine law.[71]

Nevertheless, when scripture provided no answer, al-Ghazali believed that problems must be resolved by reference to values that would be respected in any society. "These purposes or basic aims of the law consist of five values, namely the preservation of religion (*din*), life (*nafs*), reason (*'aql*), lineage (*nasl*), and property (*mal*)."[72] Certainly scriptural

---

[68] Avicenna, *Kitāb al-Najāt*, trans. Arthur J. Arberry, in Arberry, *Avicenna on Theology* 38 at 42–43.

[69] Michael Sweeney, "Greek Essence and Islamic Tolerance: Al-Farabi, Al-Ghazali, Ibn Rush'd," *Review of Metaphysics* 65 (2011), 41 at 41.

[70] Ibid. 61.

[71] Anver M. Emon, "Natural Law and Natural Rights in Islamic Law," *Journal of Law and Religion* 20 (2004), 351 at 351.

[72] Ibid. 367.

rules and provisions uphold these values. But for al-Ghazali, these values are the kinds of values that any society or legal tradition would uphold if it values the preservation and flourishing of society.[73] Al-Ghazali said: "It is impossible that any society (*milia min al-milal*) or any legal system (*shari'a min al-shara'i'*) which aims to benefit creation (*islah al-khalq*) would not include prohibitions against neglect of and restraint from these five values."[74] Al-Ghazali thought that these purposes should be considered only when the text of the law itself did not provide a solution directly or by implication.[75] However, to recognize that these are such purposes implies a good deal about how texts should be interpreted.

Al-Ghazali, then, was more concerned with the religious implications of Greek philosophy, as interpreted by Ibn Sina, than with its normative implications. Expressly or tacitly, when he discussed human happiness, ethics, and even Islamic law, he grounded norms in human nature as Plato and Aristotle had done. He did so even though he rejected Greek philosophy for reasons like those of Hume.

We have seen how modern liberal philosophers, without abandoning Hume's premises, have made use of ideas from the classical tradition that Hume would have rejected. Al-Ghazli's experience, like theirs, suggests that unless one is a consistent skeptic, like Hume, one cannot do without them.

---

[73] Ibid. 368.
[74] Ibid. 368, quoting Abu Hamid Muhmmad b. Muhammad al-Ghazali, al-Mustafa min 'Ilm al-Usul ISS (Ibrahim Muhammad Ramadan ed., Dar al-Arqam n.d.) 1: 637.
[75] Emon, "Natural Law" 352.

Index

Ackerman, Bruce, 290, 336
Adams, John
  Declaration of Independence, 158
  English constitution, 173
  liberty, 172–73
  mixed constitution, 174, 182
  natural aristocracy, 191
  public good, 167, 171–72
Adams, John Quincy, 185, 193
Adams, Samuel, 171
Albertus Magnus, 69, 75, 95
Alexander, Larry, 287
Alfonsus à Castro, 122
al-Ghazali
  attack on philosophy, 343, 346
  atttack on Ibn Sina, 346
  contrast with Aristotle, 342
  contrast with Hume, 348–49
  contrast with Ibn Rushd, 347
  contrast with Plato, 342
  contrast with positivism, 351–52
Allison,Henry E., 308
Altman, Andrew, 284
Ambrose, St., 96
American Legal Realism, 281, 282
Ames, Roger, 37
Ames, William, 76, 340, 341
Amesius, Guilielmus, 76
Angle, Stephen, 216, 219
Anscombe, G. E. M., 73–74
Antiphon, 39
Aquinas, Thomas
  choice, 77, 165
  common good, 80
  Condemnation of Paris (1277), 341, 343, 344
  conscience, 75
  contrast with Ibn Rushd, 344–45
  contrast with Ibn Sina, 347
  contrast with Maimonides, 344–45
  contrast with Raz, 327

contrast with Western rationalism, 203, 252–56, 257,
    258–59, 264
determinatio, 92
diversity, 79
freedom, 77–79, 166
government
  aristocracy, 126–27
  mixed constitution, 121–22
  monarchy, 120–21, 125
  origin, 119–20
  right of resistance, 133–34
intrinsically wrong actions, 69–71
natural law, 73–74, 92, 166, 340
positive law, 92
property, 95–96
punishment, 105
rights, 97–99
rule of law, 114–15
synderesis, 75
virtues
  affabilitas, 103
  amicitia, 103
  annexed to justice, 103
  eubolia, 73
  experience, 73
  gnome, 73
  justice, commutative, 94, 95
  justice, general, 81–84
  liberality, 93
  memory, 73
  observantia, 103
  pietas, 103
  practical reason, 69, 73, 74, 75
  sinesis, 73
will, 77
Aristotle
  Aristotelian tradition, 58
  contrast with "virtue ethics," 73–74
  contrast with Dai Zhen, 58, 61, 69, 72, 77
  contrast with Dworkin, 313

Aristotle (cont.)
    contrast with Humboldt, 324
    contrast with Kant, 306–7
    contrast with Mencius, 77, 80, 90
    contrast with modern economics, 299–301
    contrast with Plato, 60
    contrast with Rawls, 315–16
    contrast with Raz, 327
    contrast with School of Principle, 210, 211, 215
    contrast with utilitarianism, 296
    contrast with Western rationalism, 203, 252, 264
    contrast with Xunzi, 60
    dialectical argument, 13, 28, 43, 332
    essence, 58, 59
    eudaemonia or happiness, 60
    final cause or end, 59, 60, 69
    government
        aristocracy, 126, 128
        democracy, 128, 130–31
        end, 119
        mixed constitution, 121, 131
        monarchy, 120–21
    intrinsically wrong actions, 69
    law, 114
    nature, 59
    passions, 60
    property, 91
    slavery, 127
    substance, 58
    virtues
        courage, 61
        epikeia or equity, 115, 258
        justice, commutative, 85, 90, 91, 94, 95
        justice, distributive, 85
        justice, general, 80, 81–83
        liberality, 93
        practical reason, 71, 74–75, 76
        temperance, 61
    will, 77
Atlas, S., 339
Aubry, Charles, 276, 278
Augustine, St., 97
Averroes. *See* Ibn Rushd
Avicenna. *See* Ibn Sina

Bahlul, Raja, 349
Baier, Johan Wilhelm, 77, 341
Balduin, Friedrich, 75, 340
Banning, Lance, 168, 171, 174, 176, 180, 182
Barry, Brian, 318
"basic goods," 71–73
Benjamin, Walter, 325
Bentham, Jeremy, 163, 291
    contrast with Hume, 293, 294
    contrast with Mozi, 294, 295

    contrast with Yang Zhu, 293–95
    pleasure, 292–93
Beza, Theodore, 134
Bielefeldt, Heiner, 302
Bloom, Allan, 309
Bloom, Irene, 37, 64
Bo Yi, 65
Bodde, Derek, 52, 109, 110
Bohnert, Joachim, 275
Bol, Peter K.
    Confucian society, 148
    examination system, 150
    scholar-officials, 140, 143
    School of Principle
        doctrine, 208, 215–16, 217, 219, 220, 221, 232, 235
        political implications, 233
        praxis, 230
    Sima Guang, 124
    Su Shi, 113–14
    Tang dynasty, 139
    Wang Anshi, 125
Bonnecasse, Julian, 281
Boston Tea Party, 158
Botros, Sophie, 267
Braxton, Carter, 174
Brown, Charlotte, 271
Brubaker, Stanley, 314
Buchanan, George, 135
Buckley, William, 334
Buddhism
    contrast with the School of Principle, 212
    influence on the School of Principle, 208
    parallel with School of the Universal Mind, 225
    political consequences, 229
Burton, Robert, 75, 340

Cajetan, Thomas, 78, 84, 93, 118
Calhoun, John, 199
Canon law, 91, 97
Carpenter, Richard, 75, 340
Censorate, 144, 152
Ch'en Chien, 152
Chaffee, John, 141, 142, 149
Chan Jo-shui, 226
Chang I, 236
Chang, Carsun, 210
Charles I, 174
Charles II, 161
Chen Chun, 232
Chen Liang, 220
Chen Zong, 209
Chen, Lai, 81
Cheng, Andrew, 52
Cheng, Chung-yin, 207

Cheng, Chung-ying, 54, 55, 68
Ching, Julia, 222, 227
Chu Lien, 236
Cicero, 73
Clay, Henry, 199, 200
Coleman, Dorothy, 270
Compte, Auguste, 273
Confucius
    common people, 129
    duty of government, 127
    duty to criticize, 123, 142
    fa (法), 100
    human nature, 30, 31
    li (禮), 99, 100, 101
    method, 25–26
    mission, 23–24
    natural equality, 126
    reciprocity, 67, 90
    rectification of names, 26, 101
    ren (仁), 101
    worthy person (*junzi*), 24–26, 125, 127
Cooper, John, 75, 76
Cope, Kevin, 162
Cornell, Saul, 177
Cornell, Vincent, 342
Crawford, William, 199
Creel, H. G., 33
Critical Legal Studies Movement, 282
Cua, A. C., 52

Dai Zhen
    attack on School of Principle, 55, 57, 240–41, 246, 264
    contrast with Aristotle, 59, 61, 72
    contrast with Mencius, 62, 77
    desire, 58
    good and evil, 66–67
    principle (*li* 理), 56–57
    reciprocity (shu 恕), 67
    textual criticism, 56
    tradition, 68, 101–2
    virtue, 58
        benvolence (*ren* 仁), 67
        wisdom (*zhi* 智), 67
    weighing important and unimportant, 68
Dardess, John, 231, 236
Daube, David, 95
David, Joseph E., 339
de Bary, William Theodore, 230, 233, 234, 235, 236
De Weerdt, Hilde, 148, 231, 235
Declaration of Independence, 155, 157, 173, 183, 195
Decretum, 91, 97
Democratic Party, 198
Demolombe, Charles, 276, 278
Deneen, Patrick, 333
Derrida, Jacques, 11–14

Descartes, René, 259
Domat, Jean, 275
Dong Lin Academy, 242–48
Dong Zhongshu, 54, 110, 140
Dostoyevski, Fyodor, 334
Douglass, Bruce, 290, 310
Dubs, Homer, 52
Dunn, John, 160
Duzong, 233
Dworetz, Steven, 168
Dworkin, Ronald
    contrast with Aristotle, 311
    contrast with Hume, 311
    contrast with Kant, 311
    equality, 312–14
    method, 285–86, 287–89, 317–18
    principle of impartial concern, 317

Eastern Depot, 237
economic liberalism
    contrast with utilitarianism, 296–97
    efficiency, 298–99
    law and economics movement
        contrast with commutative justice, 300–1
        contrast with distributive justice, 299–300
    preference satisfaction, 297–98
Edgeworth, Francis, 296
"eight-legged essays," 145
Elman, Benjamin, 145, 146, 148, 149, 234, 235, 236, 237
Emon, Anvers, 351
"empiricism," 266
Enlightenment, 155–56, 167, 332–33
Eno, Robert, 43
epikeia, 258
Escarra, Jean, 109
essentia realis, 210, 256, 257
Euclid, 260, 266

falsafah, 345
Fan Chen, 152
Federalist Papers, 177, 178
Federalist Party, 177, 181, 185, 186, 192
Feser, Edward, 160
Filmer, Sir Robert, 135, 156
Finnis, John, 70, 259
    basic goods, 71–73
    principle of impartial concern, 72
    rationalism, 252, 253
Fox, Marvin, 339
Freijuristenschule, 281, 282
French Civil Code, 274, 275, 281
French Revolution, 183, 184
Freud, Sigmund, 45–46
Fu Pi, 152
Fung Yu-lan, 59, 209

Gao, 38
Gates, Horatio, 167
Gay, Peter, 333
Gény, Francois, 281, 282
George, Robert, 326, 328
    basic goods, 71–73
    principle of impartial concern, 72
German Civil Code, 274, 280, 281
Giacaman, George, 349
Gibson, Alan, 168
Gilson, Etienne, 252, 257, 284, 344
Goebbels, Joseph, 325
Gong Du, 126
Goodman, Lenn, 349
Gordon, Thomas, 156, 157
Graham, Angus, 7, 34, 52, 203, 211, 212, 213, 214
Gratian, 97
Gray, John, 126, 291, 318, 320, 324, 329
Gregor, Mary, 302
Griffel, Frank, 342, 349
Grisez, Germain, 259
    basic goods, 71–73
    rationalism, 252
Guevara, Daniel, 308
Guthrie, William C., 29
Guyer, Paul, 272

Habermas, Jurgen, 310
Hallevi, Judah, 341, 343
Hamilton, Alexander, 167
Han Code, 105
Han Confucianism, 54
Han learning, 55–56
Han Wei, 142
Han Yu, 219
Hansen, Chad, 64
Hardin, Russell, 268
"harm principle," 319–21, 325
Harrison, William Henry, 199, 200
Hart, H. L. A., 284–85, 311, 320
Hartwell, Robert, 146
Head, John, 106
Hicks, J. R., 297
Hinman, Lawrence, 308
Hobbes, Thomas, 160
Holmes, Oliver Wendell Jr., 280, 281, 282
Holt, Michael, 199
Hongwu Emperor, 236
Hooker, Richard, 77, 162, 164–66, 340
Höpfl, Harro, 119
Horwitz, Morton J., 168
Huang Zongxi, 224, 225
Hulsewé, Anthony, 54
Hulwesé, A. F. P., 108
Humboldt, Wilhelm von

aesthetic sense, 322–23
    contrast with Aristotle, 324
    contrast with Kant, 321–22
    freedom, 323–24
    harm principle, 321
Hume, David
    "naturalistic fallacy," 265
    beauty, 269–70
    benevolence, 270
    cognition and volition, 264–65
    contrast with rationalism, 266–67
    harmony, 271–72
    morality, 267–69
    pleasure, 270–71
    truth, 269
Huyler, Jerome, 168

Ibn Rushd
    attack on al-Ghazali, 347, 349–50
    attack on Ibn Sina, 349–50
    contrast with Aristotle, 339
    defense of philosophy, 344–45
Ibn Sina
    contrast with al-Ghazali, 346
    contrast with rationalism, 348
    neo-Platonism, 350–51
    theology, 346
Ihara, Craig, 103
Ihering, Rudolf von, 281, 282
Im, Manyul, 64
iniuria, 94
interest group pluralism, 130
ius commune, 91
"inverse rationalism," 275, 277, 286, 287, 318
Ivanhoe, P. J., 52

Jackson, Andrew, 193, 199
Jacobs, Jonathan, 339
Jaeger, Werner, 74, 76
James II, 161
James, William, 334
Jefferson, Thomas
    Declaration of Independence, 157–58
    influence, 188–90
    mixed constitution
        earlier view, 186–87
        later view, 184–85, 186
    natural aristocracy, 190–91
    public good, 167
Jerome, St., 75
Ji, Xiao-bin, 124
Jin Yi Wei (Embroidered Uniform Guard), 237
jinshi degree, 141
Johnson, Wallace, 110

Kai-Huang Code, 106
Kaldor-Hicks efficiency, 299
Kalyvas, Andreas, 177, 185
Kant, Immanuel
  Achtung, 307–9
  categorical imperative, 302–7
  cognition and volition, 307–9
  contrast with Aristotle, 306–7
  contrast with Bentham, 303
  contrast with Hume, 302
  contrast with Mozi, 302
  contrast with rationalism, 303–4
  contrast with utilitarianism, 304–6
  freedom, 309
  principle of impartial concern, 302
Katznelson, Ira, 177, 185
Keenan, Barry, 208, 218
Kelsen, Hans, 44
Kennan, Barry, 218
Kersh, Rogan, 168
Klarman, Michael, 180–81
Korsgaard, Christine M., 308
Kracke, Edward, 143, 144, 146
Kuhn, Dieter, 139, 140, 147

laesio enormis, 94
Lai, Whelan, 38
Langdell, Christopher Columbus, 276, 278
Langlois, John, 104, 105
Larombière Leon, 278
las Casas, Bartolomé de, 196
late scholastics, 82
  government
    emperor, 117–18
    monarchy, 122–23
    origin, 118–20
    right to resist, 133–34
  justice, commutative, 92–96
  justice, general, 82–84
  rights, 96–98, 280–81
  Roman law, 92–96
  slavery, 127
Lau, D. C., 52
Lau, Nap-yin, 143
Laurent, François, 276, 278
Leake, Stephen, 278
Leaman, Oliver, 338, 346
Lee, Richard Henry, 174
Lee, Seung-Hwan, 89
Lee, Thomas H.C., 146
Leff, Arthur, 297
Legalist school, 105, 108, 109
Legrand, Pierre, 11–14
Leibniz, Gottfried Wilhelm, 6, 12, 59, 203, 210–11, 256, 260, 261–63

Lessius, Leonard, 82, 96, 97, 127, 195
Levine, Michael P., 339
lex Aquilia, 94
Li Zhi (Li Zhouwu), 226
"liberal skepticism," 336
Lin Li, 233
Liu Bang, 105
Liu Ji, 236
Liu Shu-hsien, 37, 64
Liu Xia Hui, 65
Liu, James T.C., 144, 145, 149, 231, 232, 233
Livingston, William, 192
Llewellyn, Karl N., 277, 281, 285
Lo Ju-fang, 227
Locke, John
  contrast with liberalism, 160
  government
    end, 159
    forms, 158–59
    powers, 160–62
    taxation without representation, 161
  influence, 166–67
  morality
    neo-Aristotelian, 164–66
    protorationalist, 163
    protoutilitarian, 163–64
  property, 159–60, 161–62
Lodén, Torbjörn, 55
Loemker, Leroy, 252
Louden, Robert B., 308
Lu Hui, 152, 237
Lu Tuan, 144
Luig, Klaus, 262, 263
Luther, Martin, 341

MacCormack, Geoffrey, 106, 108, 110
Machiavelli, Niccolo, 168–69
MacIntyre, Alasdair
  inadequacy of Confucian philosophy, 62–63
  incommensurability of the Confucian and
    Aristotelian tradition, 14–17, 102
Madison, James
  mixed contitution, 178
  private interests, 177–78
  public good, 177–78
  virtue, 178
Maier, Pauline, 181
Maimonides, Moses
  contrast with Aristotle, 339–40
  defense of philosophy, 344–45
Maitland, Frederic William, 277
Marmura, Michael, 349
Marshall, Alfred, 296
Marshall, John, 196
May, Johann Heinrich, 340, 341

McCormick, Richard, 197, 198
McKnight, Brian, 106
Mencius
  cognition and volition, 62–66
  contrast with Aristotle, 77, 80, 90
  contrast with Dai Zhen, 66, 68, 77
  contrast with Socrates, 42
  government
    common people, 127–28
    duty to criticize, 123
    legitimacy, 116–17, 132–33
    persons of merit (*junzi*), 125
  human nature, 36–38, 46–47, 49
  method, 43, 62–63
  natural equality, 126
  principle, 57
  qi (氣), 48, 64
  virtues, 36–37
    benevolence *ren* (仁), 36–37, 64, 80, 81
    propriety *li* (禮), 36, 65–66, 99–100, 101
    righteousness *yi* (義), 36, 64–65, 81, 82, 85–89, 90
    wisdom *zhi* (智), 36, 65
  xin (心), 47–48, 63
  zhi (志), 47, 48, 64
Meng Sunyang, 32
Mill, John Stuart
  "harm principle," 319–21
  pleasure, 296
Millgram, Elijah, 266
Ming Code, 238
Miyazaki, Ichisada, 109
Moad, Edward Omar, 349
Moggach, Douglas, 324
Molina, Luis de, 82, 83, 94, 96, 97, 118, 119, 120, 122, 134, 254
Monroe, James, 192
Moore, G. E., 296
Morris, Clarence, 109, 110
Moses ben Maimon. *See* Maimonides, Moses
Mote, Frederick, 124, 236, 237, 238
Mozi
  contrast with Bentham, 295
  contrast with Kant, 303
  contrast with Rawls, 314–15
  pleasure and pain, 33–34
  principle of impartial concern, 35
  unanimity, 35–36
  unselfishness, 34–35
Munro, Donald, 51, 63, 217, 229

Nabbes, Thomas, 76
Native Americans, 196
natural aristocracy, 181, 188, 190, 191, 193, 194, 195
Nell, Onora, 304
Nietzsche, Friedrich, 319, 336

"nine squares system," 85
Nivison, David, 35, 37, 47, 52, 63, 64
Novak, David, 339
Nussbaum, Martha, 82, 299

Olearius, Johannes, 75, 340
Ouyang Xiu, 152

Paine, Thomas, 167, 179, 184, 185, 189
Pareto efficiency, 299
Parfit, Derek, 264
Parsons, Lynn, 193
Parsons, Lynn Hudson, 197
Paton, H. J., 307
Payson, Edward, 170, 171
Pereira, José, 256
Peters, F.E, 345
Peterson, Claes, 261
Peterson, Willard, 226, 227
Plato, 73, 79
  contrast with al-Ghazali, 342
  contrast with Aristotle, 60
  dialectical argument, 77
  dialogs
    Apology, 27–28
    Charmides, 28
    Euthyphro, 28
    Gorgias, 30, 39–41, 51, 77
    Laches, 28
    Lysis, 28
    Phaedo, 49, 50
    Phaedrus, 50
    Republic, 41–42, 49–50, 77
  Forms, 59
  Forms and later rationalism, 59
  Forms and School of Principle, 59, 209–10, 211
  human nature, 42, 49–51
  inner conflict, 49–51
  neo-Platonism and Islamic philosophy, 347, 350
  property, 91
Pocock, J. G. A., 168–69, 176, 177
Pollock, Sir Frederick, 276, 278, 279
Ponet, John, 135
Portalis, Jean-Étienne-Marie, 275
positivism
  contrast with liberalism, 278–80
  contrast with rationalism, 274–75
  in contemporary philosophy
    Dworkin, Ronald, 285–86
    Hart, H. L. A., 284–85
    Rawls, John, 286
  rejection, 280–84
  rights, 278–80
Posner, Richard, 299, 300, 301
Pothier, Robert, 275

"principle of impartial concern"
  Bentham, Jeremy, 294
  Dworkin, Ronald, 317
  Finnis, John, 72
  George, Robert, 72
  Kant, Immanuel, 302
  Mozi, 35
  Rawls, John, 317
  School of Principle, 218
Protestant writers
  choice, 77
  conscience, 75–76
  right of resistance, 135
Ptolemy da Lucca, 133
Puchta, Georg Friedrich, 278

qi (氣), 5, 48, 49, 63, 64, 203, 209, 213, 257
Qian Dehong, 225, 226
Qin Giuli, 32
Qin law, 105, 106–8
Qin Shi Huang, 105
Qing Code, 106
Qu Tongzu, 109

Radcliffe, Elizabeth, 267, 268
Rakove, Jack, 175
Ranouil, Valérie, 279
"rational intuitionism," 5, 317
rationalism, Western
  contrast with Ibn Sina, 347–48
  contrast with Kant, 303–4
  contrast with legal positivism, 274–75, 276
  contrast with School of Principle, 257
  metaphysics, 255–56, 257
  method, 259–61
  natural law, 253–55, 256, 257–59
  perfection, 261–62
  rights, 262–63
Rau, Charles, 276, 278
Rawls, John
  cognition and volition, 318–19
  conception of the good, 315–16
  contrast with Aristotle, 311, 315–16
  contrast with Hume, 311
  contrast with Kant, 311
  contrast with Mozi, 314–15
  irreconcilable differences, 316–17
  method, 286, 287–88, 289–90, 318–19
  preliberal philosophy, 5–8, 42, 253
  principle of impartial concern, 317
  veil of ignorance, 318–19
Raz, Joseph, 292
  autonomous choice, 326–30
  contrast with Aquinas, 327
  contrast with Aristotle, 327

  contrast with rationalism, 327
  harm principle, 325, 326
reciprocity (shu 恕), 67, 90
Reimann, Matthias, 281
Remonstrance Bureau, 144, 152
Renzong, 228
Republican (Jeffersonian) Party, 181, 186
restitutio, 97
Riker, Stephen, 349
Robinson, David, 238
Roehr, Sabine, 323
Rosemont, Henry, 63
Rosenthal, Alexander, 160
Rush, Benjamin, 171, 182

Sadurski, Wojciech, 326
Samuelson, Paul, 297
Sanderson, Robert, 75, 340
Santayana, George, 291
Sariti, William, 124
Savage, James D., 177
Schiller, Friedrich
  aesthetic sense, 322–23
  aesthetic state, 324–25
  contrast with Kant, 321–22
  freedom, 323–24
Schneider, Hans-Peter, 262
Schnoor, Christian, 302, 303
School of Principle
  contrast with Aristotle, 215
  contrast with Buddhism, 207–8, 212
  contrast with Dai Zhen, 220–21
  contrast with Mencius, 218, 220–21
  contrast with Plato, 210–11
  contrast with Western rationalism, 210
  doctrine, 208
    cognition and volition, 216–19
    desire, 213
    li (理), 208–11
    method, 214–16
    mind, 214
    moral purity, 220
    principle of impartial concern, 218
    qi (氣), 212–13
    Ultimate Principle, 212–13
  Ming dynasty
    autocracy, 238–41
    intolerance, 236
    protest, 242
  Song dynasty
    cult, 230–32
    recognition, 233–34
  Yuan dynasty, 236
School of Universal Mind
  cognition and volition, 223–24

School of Universal Mind (cont.)
  mind, 223
  moral subjectivity, 224–27
  principle (*li* 理), 223
Schwartz, Benjamin, 36
Sedgwick, Sally, 308, 309
Sen, Amartya, 296, 297, 298, 299, 331
Sergeant, John Dickenson, 194
shari'a, 338
Shen-tsung, 142
Shenzong, 125, 151
Shi Meng-li, 226
Shun, Kwong-loi, 36, 47, 63, 81, 89, 90
Sidgwick, Henry, 296
Sidney, Algernon, 156, 157
Sim, Mary, 43
Sima Guang, 124–25, 142, 150, 152
Sinclair, Upton, 313
Skinner, Quentin, 119, 134, 135, 169
slavery, 127, 195–96
Smith, Adam, 296
Smith, Melanchton, 180
Smith, Paul, 144
Socrates
  dialectical argument, 43, 77
  harmony, 43, 49, 272
  human nature, 39–41, 51
  method, 28–29
  mission, 27–28
  self expression, 319
  versus Nietzsche, 319
Song, Jaeyoon, 143, 144
Soto, Domingo de, 82, 96, 97, 118, 134
Stroud, Barry, 267, 268
Su Shi, 112, 150
  opposition to Wang Anshi, 130, 153
  role of the people, 129–30
  rule of law, 114
Suárez, Francisco, 4, 6, 82, 118, 134, 203, 210, 252–56,
    257–59, 338, 347
Sui Code, 111
Sung Lien, 236
Sussman, David, 307
Sweeney, Michael, 351
Sydney, Algernon, 157
synderesis, 75, 76, 162, 253

Taizong, 140, 144, 147
Taizu, 137, 139, 140, 144
Tang Code, 106
  Eight Deliberations, 111–12
  importance, 106
  influence of Confucianism, 109–12
  influence of Qin law, 106–8

origins, 105–6
  Ten Abominations, 112
Taylor, Charles, 119, 155, 162
Tegtmeier, Erwin, 347
Tempier, Stephen, 341, 343
Thompson, Kirill, 210
Tierney, Brian, 98
Tillman, Hoyt, 231
Tiwald, Justin, 219
Trebilcock, Michael, 297
Trenchard, John, 156
Troplong, Raymond-Théodore,
    276
Tu Pen, 235
Tyrrell, James, 156, 157

Unger, Roberto, 288
  critique of liberalism, 283–84
  preliberal philosophy, 8–9, 253
Urvoy, Dominique, 344
utilitarianism
  contrast with Hume, 293, 294
  contrast with Mozi, 295
  contrast with Yang Zhu, 293–95
  pleasure
    Bentham, Jeremy, 292–93
    Mill, John Stuart, 296

Valette, Auguste, 276
van Buren, Martin, 198, 199
van der Meulen, Johann Andreas, 75, 340, 341
Van Norden, Brian W., 52
Vasquez, Gabriel, 254
Vindiciae contra tyrannos, 135
"virtue ethics," 73–74
Vitoria, Francisco de, 82, 97, 98, 118, 119, 122, 127,
    134, 196
Vogel, Ursula, 323
Volksgeist, 274

Walter, J., 75
Wang Anshi, 108, 237
  administration, 151–53
  examination system, 144, 150
  human nature, 48
  New Policies, 150–51
  political theory, 125
Wang Chi, 225
Wang Chong, 46
Wang Tao, 152
Wang Wei, 236
Wang Yung, 141
Wang, Yanping, 106
Washington, George, 155

Watson, Walter, 210
wealth maximization, 299
Webster, Noah, 179
Wei Lü, 105
Weiss, Raymond, 340
Wellmon, Chad, 307
Westerman, Pauline C., 259
Westphal, Kenneth, 302, 303
Whig Party, 198, 199, 200
Wieacker, Karl, 274
Wilkinson, T.M., 313
Wilson, Woodrow, 189
Windscheid, Bernhard, 278
Wolff, Christian, 9, 203, 204, 210, 252–53, 257, 260–63,
    274, 302
Wolff, Robert, 304
Wong, David, 37, 62, 64
Wood, Allan, 302, 308
Wood, Gordon, 172, 335
    "radical Whigs," 179
    Adams-Jefferson controversy, 182, 184, 185
    common good, 167, 168, 170–72
    Constitution of the United States, 175, 176–78
    democratic ideal, 193–94
    mixed constitution, 173, 174–75
    natural aristocracy, 191–92
Wright, R. George, 72
Wu, 140

Xiao He, 105
xin (心), 47, 48, 63
Xin Lü, 105
Xu Yuan, 236
Xunzi
    attack on Mozi, 35–36
    contrast with Aristotle, 60
    contrast with Hume, 272
    good and evil, 51–52
    li (禮), 53
    music, 53

Yang Jian, 106
Yang Xiong, 48
Yang Zhu
    contrast with Bentham, 293–95
    pleasure and pain, 32
    selfishness, 32–33
Ye Shi, 147
Yen Ch'ün, 226
Yi Yin, 65
Yolton, John, 162
Yongle Emperor, 236
Yovel, Yirmiyahu, 307
Yu Zhi, 235
Yuan Hong, 105

Zanchi, Girolamo, 341
Zepper, William, 341
Zhang Juzheng, 227
Zhao Kuangyin, 139
Zhao Pu, 144
Zheng Yu, 230
Zhenzong, 140, 143, 148
zhi (志), 47, 48, 49, 64
Zhu Jiyou, 236
Zhu Xi, 139
Zhu Yuanzhang, 236, 238
Zi Gong, 31
Zisi, 31, 48
Zuchert, Michael, 162, 166

CPSIA information can be obtained
at www.ICGtesting.com
Printed in the USA
LVHW051752080323
741174LV00006B/281